BURT FRANKLIN: RESEARCH & SOURCE WORKS SERIES 369
Selected Papers in Literature & Criticism 28

DANIEL DEFOE

HIS LIFE

AND HITHERTO UNKNOWN WRITINGS

———

VOL. I.

Laudatur et Alget
Juven. Sat. I.

DANIEL DEFOE.

From Vander Gucht's frontispiece to "Jure Divino," fol., 1706.

DANIEL DEFOE

HIS LIFE

AND RECENTLY DISCOVERED WRITINGS:

EXTENDING FROM 1716 TO 1729.

BY

WILLIAM LEE

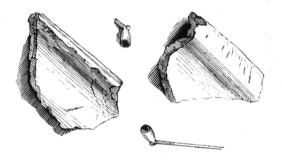

PANTILES AND PIPES RECENTLY FOUND ON SITE OF DEFOE'S TILE WORKS
AT TILBURY.

IN THREE VOLUMES.

Vol. I.— The Life of Daniel Defoe.

**BURT FRANKLIN
NEW YORK**

Published by BURT FRANKLIN
235 East 44th St., New York, N.Y. 10017
Originally Published: 1869
Reprinted: 1969
Printed in the U.S.A.

Library of Congress Card Catalog No.: 78-82017
Burt Franklin: Research and Source Works Series 369
Selected Papers in Literature and Criticism 28

INTRODUCTION.

A CENTURY and a half have elapsed since the time when, according to the belief of all his biographers, Daniel Defoe retired from the political world. He had, for a whole generation previously, stood in the foremost rank of controversial writers; but the remainder of his life was supposed to have been spent in peaceful literary seclusion. Such statements have been heretofore received as unquestionable truth; and, but for a recent accidental discovery, the large collection of his Journalistic Works now to be first published as his, would in all probability have been lost to the world for ever.

The Key to this discovery consists of certain Letters, in his own handwriting, found in 1864, in the State Paper Office, directly naming several political Journals upon which he was engaged during some years after his supposed retirement. External evidence of such a character must preclude incredulity as to the existence of writings by him, hitherto unknown; and a long and laborious investigation of old Newspapers, in the directions thus indicated, has resulted in the Collectanea forming two of the present Volumes.

The internal evidence comprises the coincidence of these newly-discovered writings with the principles and opinions contained in the undisputed works of Defoe,—their strict conformity with the manner in which he would have treated any given subject; and their containing all the peculiar phrases and words in which he was accustomed to express his thoughts. Long and critical study of a great author may result in so full an acquaintance, that his writings will be recognised by the student in a moment, as the voice of a familiar friend. I might presume to prove such acquaintance with Defoe by filling a page of this Introduction with characteristic modes of expression, abounding in his works, but scarcely any of them similarly used by any other writer of that age.* These specialities, therefore, added to his generally plain, homely, colloquial, matter of fact stile, facilitate the task of discriminating, in the absence of other evidence.

It may be admitted, without invalidating such evidence, that the religious and political opinions held by Defoe were similar to those of several authors of his time; and also, that his numerous works published during the last twenty-five years of his life are, with about three exceptions, either anonymous or pseudonymous. An obstacle to identification arises from the fact that he rarely alludes to his previous works or to his private affairs. Occasionally in his *Review,* and more extensively in his *Appeal to Honour and Justice,* may be found fragments of his personal history; but in general, we learn more about him and his works from the slanderous attacks of opponents, than directly from his own pen; and he often left his assailants unanswered, rather than descend from the discussion of important principles to the defence of his own character.

In the numerous Works hitherto attributed to him, from the termination of *Mercator,* in 1714, to his death, in 1731, there is not a word, I believe, leading to the supposition that

---

* The following are a few only of such favourite expressions:—" let the World know"—" I say"—" of which in its place"—" When it came to the Push"—" on that Foot"—" by the Way"—" in few Words"—" it must be confess'd"—" in short"—" to which he answers and says—nothing"—" upon the whole"—" says he"—" Be that as it will"—" in plain English"—" the hands of Justice"—" to that Part"—" But of this by and by"—" at Home and Abroad"—" 'tis true"—" and the like"—" breaking in upon them"— " all Sorts"—" to come into their Measures"—" so nice a Juncture"—" the Shortest Way"—" One of Solomon's Fools"—" To talk Gospel to a Kettle Drum"—" Take this with you as you go."

he had been connected with any Newspaper or Journal during that period. The same may be said as to the absence of any indication, subsequent to 1714, of his having composed any of the numerous pamphlets now for the first time included in the Catalogue of his Works. These are, undoubtedly, weighty considerations; but with the guidance of his own manuscript letters, all difficulties gradually vanished. Without such aid, they would have been insuperable, and the investigation never undertaken, or even thought of.

The earliest "Life of Defoe" was written by Mr. George Chalmers, in 1785. After quoting from the *Appeal to Honour and Justice,* Mr. Chalmers says :—

"Such was the political testament of De Foe. . . . . The " year 1715 may be regarded as the period of our author's " political life. Faction henceforth found other advocates, " and parties procured other writers to propagate their false-" hoods. . . . . But the persecutions of party did not cease " when De Foe ceased to be a party-writer. . . . . . The death " of Anne, and the accession of George I., seems to have con-" vinced De Foe of the vanity of party-writing."

Mr. Walter Wilson, in the absence of all evidence to the contrary, takes the same view, in his *Memoirs of the Life and Times of Daniel Defoe,* (1830,) as follows :—

" De Foe's political life was now drawing to a close. He " had now arrived at a period of life when the mind takes " repose from the turbulence of faction; and the course of " political events having thrown him in the background, he " was destined to beat out a new path to fame, which will " render his name respected, when temporary politics are for-" gotten."*

Ten years afterward Mr. Hazlitt repeats the same words from Mr. Wilson, and adds :—

" The close of De Foe's political life was in truth the begin-

---

* Vol. iii. pp. 386—7.

" ning of his greatness; in the retirement which he now
" quitted no more, the leisure of his active spirit was occupied
" in the creation of a Series of Works, which raised his name
" immeasurably higher than it had ever been before in the
" opinion of his contemporaries, and which will preserve that
" name in freshness and honour so long as the language in
" which they were written endures; so long as penetration,
" wit, genius, and eloquence, preserve their place in the esti-
" mation of mankind."*

And still later, in 1855, Mr. John Forster, in his brilliant
" Essay on Daniel De Foe," reiterates the same conclusion, in
plain though guarded language. His fifth chapter is headed,
" George the First and George the Second. 1714—1731." It
opens with an account of the retirement of Defoe, in 1714, from
the field of political conflict, after thirty-two years of incessant
contention for the principles which were at last securely
established. Before proceeding to quote from the *Appeal to
Honour and Justice,* Mr. Forster says—" This was his language,
" when withdrawn finally and for ever from the struggle, he
" calmly reviewed the part he had taken in it." The next
paragraph commences, " His last political Essay was written
" in 1715."

Having already stated that there was nothing in the heretofore known Works of Defoe, indicating any subsequent interference in politics, it must not be supposed that in the
above quotations any reproach is intended against his numerous
biographers. Mr. Wilson notices that Toland accused Defoe
of writing the Monthly Journal *Mercurius Politicus,* which was
not commenced until 1716; but he was charged with the
authorship of so many publications in which he had no hand,
that the accusation appears to have been discredited. His retirement from politics at that period having been positively
stated by Mr. Chalmers, the supposed fact seems to have been

---

* Life of Defoe, p. ciii.

adopted without question by all subsequent writers; and no one thought of looking into *Mercurius Politicus* to ascertain the correctness or otherwise of Toland's statement. I am bound in candour to confess that, as a matter of private opinion, I held the same error, and when political pamphlets of later date than 1715 were offered to me by booksellers as Defoe's, I rejected them, in the belief that he wrote nothing on political subjects after that year.

The Letters, as already stated, are entirely in the handwriting of Defoe, and were all apparently addressed to Charles De la Fay, Esq.,* of the Secretary of State's Office. There can be no possible doubt of their genuineness. The originals are preserved in the archives of the Government. They are as follows :—

I.

"Sir,—I could not read without Pain to Day in the Public Prints something of an Account of that Traitorous Pamphlet being printed; I mean that which I shewed you, and which I sent to my Lord Sunderland.

---

* This gentleman was probably son of Dr. De la Faye, an eminent Physician of London, who died suddenly of apoplexy, at the Buffler's Head Tavern, on the 19th March, 1720. Charles De la Faye must have been a man of considerable talent. The first notice I find of him in the newspapers is his appointment as Private Secretary to the Lords Justices of Ireland, in the beginning of Sept. 1715. In 1718, as above, he appears to have occupied a highly confidential position in the Secretary of State's office. In May, 1719, he was appointed Secretary to the Lords Justices of the Regency during the King's absence in Hanover. Shortly afterward he was appointed to the sinecure office of one of the King's Tasters of Wine in Ireland; and when Mr. Flurnoe, the other " Taster," died, at the end of the same year, the place was wholly given to Mr. De la Faye. In June, 1720, the King having again gone to Hanover, Mr. De la Faye was re-appointed Secretary to the Regency. In this capacity I find him frequently examining and committing political offenders. In January, 1728, he was promoted to be one of the Gentlemen Sewers to King George II. I do not know the date of his death, but he was probably for half a century a Public Servant. His Library was sold in 1764.

"I beg you will please to assure his Lordship from me, that the Original, which I shewed you, is still in my Hand; and has never been out of my keeping; nor has an Eye seen it, or any Copy been taken of it, that one excepted which I sent to his Lordship.

"I here enclose a Letter, which I have stopt, which I think is worth his Lordship's Notice. I dare not yet come Abroad, but hope to see you in three or four Days if the cold Weather abates. "I am, Sir,

"Your Most Humble Servant,

"DE FOE.

"Newington, April 12, 1718."

II.

"SIR,—Though I doubt not but you have acquainted my Lord Stanhope with what humble Sense of his Lordship's Goodness I received the Account you were pleased to give me, that my little Services are accepted, and that his Lordship is satisfied to go on upon the Foot of former Capitulations, &c.; yet I confess, Sir, I have been anxious on many Accounts, with respect as well to the Service itself, as my own Safety, lest my Lord may think himself ill served by me, even when I may have best performed my Duty.

"I thought it therefore not only a Debt to myself, but a Duty to his Lordship, that I should give his Lordship a short Account, as clear as I can, how far my former Instructions empowered me to Act, and, in a word, what this little Piece of secret Service is, for which I am so much a Subject of his Lordship's present Favour and Bounty.

"It was in the Ministry of my Lord Townshend, when my Lord Chief Justice Parker, to whom I stand obliged for the Favour, was pleased so far to state my Case, that notwithstanding the Misrepresentations under which I had suffered, and notwithstanding some Mistakes which I was the first to acknowledge; I was so happy as to be believed in the Professions I made of a sincere Attachment to the Interest of the present Government, and, speaking with all possible Humility, I hope I have not dishonoured my Lord Parker's Recommendation.

" In considering, after this, which Way I might be rendered most useful to the Government; it was proposed by my Lord Townshend that I should still appear as if I were, as before, under the displeasure of the Government, and separated from the Whigs ; and that I might be more serviceable in a kind of Disguise, than if I appeared openly ; and upon this Foot a weekly Paper, which I was at first directed to write, in opposition to a scandalous Paper called the *Shift Shifted*, was laid aside, and the first Thing I engaged in, was a monthly Book called *Mercurius Politicus*, of which presently. In the interval of this, Dyer, the *News-Letter*-writer, having been dead, and Dormer his successor, being unable by his Troubles to carry on that Work ; I had an offer of a Share in the Property, as well as in the Management of that Work.

" I immediately acquainted my Lord Townshend of it, who, by Mr. Buckley, let me know it would be a very acceptable Piece of Service ; for that Letter was really very prejudicial to the Public, and the most difficult to come at in a judicial Way in Case of Offence given. My Lord was pleased to add, by Mr. Buckley, that he would consider my Service in that Case, as he afterwards did.

" Upon this I engaged in it ; and that so far, that though the Property was not wholly my own, yet the Conduct and Government of the Style and News was so entirely in me, that I ventured to assure his Lordship the Sting of that mischievous Paper should be entirely taken out, though it was granted that the Style should continue Tory, as it was, that the Party might be amused, and not set up another, which would have destroyed the Design : And this Part I therefore take entirely on myself still.

" This went on for a Year, before my Lord Townshend went out of the Office ; and his Lordship, in Consideration of this Service, made me the Appointment which Mr. Buckley knows of, with promise of a further Allowance as Service presented.

" My Lord Sunderland, to whose Goodness I had many Years ago been obliged, when I was in a secret Commission sent to Scotland, was pleased to approve and continue this Service, and the Appointment annexed ; and, with his Lordship's Approbation, I introduced myself, in the Disguise of a Translator of the Foreign News, to be so far concerned in this weekly Paper of *Mist's*, as to be able to keep it within the Circle of a secret Management, also prevent the mischievous Part of it ; and yet neither Mist, or any of those concerned with him, have the least Guess or Suspicion by whose Direction I do it.

" But here it becomes necessary to acquaint my Lord (as I hinted to you, Sir), that this Paper, called the *Journal*, is not in myself in Property, as the other, only in Management ; with this express difference, that if anything happens to be put in without my Knowledge, which may give Offence, or if anything slips my Observation which may be ill taken, his Lordship shall be sure always to know whether he has a Servant to reprove, or a Stranger to correct.

" Upon the whole, however, this is the Consequence, that by this Management, the Weekly *Journal*, and *Dormer's Letter*, as also the *Mercurius Politicus*, which is in the same Nature of Management as the *Journal*, will be always kept (Mistakes excepted) to pass as Tory Papers, and yet be disabled and enervated, so as to do no Mischief, or give any Offence to the Government.

" I beg leave to observe, Sir, one Thing more to his Lordship in my own behalf, and without which, indeed, I may, one Time or other, run the Risk of fatal Misconstructions. I am, Sir, for this Service, posted among Papists, Jacobites, and enraged High Tories—a Generation who, I profess, my very Soul Abhors ; I am obliged to hear traitorous Expressions and outrageous Words against his Majesty's Person and Government, and his most faithful Servants, and smile at it all, as if I approved it ; I am obliged to take all the scandalous and, indeed, villainous Papers that come, and keep them by me as if I would gather Materials from them to put them into the News; nay, I often venture to let Things pass which are a little Shocking, that I may not render myself suspected.

" Thus I bow in the House of *Rimmon,* and must humbly recommend myself to his Lordship's Protection, or I may be undone the sooner, by how much the more faithfully I execute the Commands I am under.

" I forbear to enlarge. I beg you, Sir, to represent these Circumstances to his Lordship, in behalf of a faithful Servant, that shall always endeavour to approve his Fidelity by Actions rather than Words.

" I am, Sir, your most humble Servant,

" De Foe.

" Newington, April 26, 1718.

" P.S.—I send you here one of the Letters stopt at the Press, as I mentioned to you; as to the Manuscript of Sultan Galga, another villainous Paper, I sent the Copy to my Lord Sunderland. If the Original be of any Service, it is ready at your first Orders."

III.

" Sir,—I am extremely concerned that the *Journal* of this Day has copied from the *Post Boy* that ridiculous Paragraph of the Pretender's being in the List of the Queen Dowager's legitimate Children, and I have spoken my Mind very freely to him of it.

" But Sir, I think, in consequence of what I wrote last to you, it is my Duty to assure my Lord, that I have no Part in this Slip, but that Mr. Mist did it, after I had looked over what he had gotten together, which it seems was not sufficient; and though I would, if I may presume so far, intercede for him, yet my Lord may be assured I have no Concern in it, directly or indirectly. This, Sir, I say, I thought myself obliged to Notice to you, to make good what I said in my last, (viz.) that if any Mistake happened, my Lord should always know whether he had a Servant to reprove, or a Stranger to punish.

> "I am, Sir, Your most humble Servant,
>
> "DE FOE.

"May 10, 1718.

"P.S.—He has renewed his Promise to me, that he will be more Wary, and I do think, verily, it was not done Maliciously. But that I leave as I find it.

"Address to—— De la Faye, Esq., Present."

IV.

"SIR,—When I had the Favour of seeing you last, you were pleased to mention to me my particular Concern, and that you would interest yourself in that Part for me. The exceeding Kindness of that offer, Sir, encourages me to give you this Trouble, and to observe to you that the half Year expired the 17th inst.

"I need say no more, but to ask you Pardon for this Freedom, and leave the rest to your own Time and Methods, and shall attend at what Time you please to appoint.

"I hope I have kept the difficult People I have to do with, within the Bounds of Duty; and am in Hopes to draw them gradually into yet narrower Limits of respect. It is a hard Matter to please the Tory Party, as their present Temper operates, without abusing, not only the Government, but the Persons of our Governors, in every Thing they write; but to the best of my Skill, I cause all Letters and Paragraphs, which look that Way, to be intercepted, and stopped at the Press.

"I am a little alarmed at a Prosecution against Morphew, in the King's Bench Court, for a Passage in the *Mercurius Politicus;* which began in a private Person sueing Morphew, on pretence of Damages on a Paragraph, printed from another printed Paper, of a Person hanged, at York, for three Half-pence. But it seems the Court, resenting a Line or two in it as a Reflection on the Judges, have made it a public Cause, and have committed Morphew till Sentence, which it is feared will be severe.

" But, Sir, I think myself obliged to lay before my Lord Stanhope the following Particulars, in Case they should offer to concern me in it. First, that it is two Year or more, since this was done; and, consequently, before the Capitulation made in my Lord Townshend's Time, when all former Mistakes of mine were forgiven. Secondly, that the Thing itself was not mine, neither can any one pretend to charge it on me, otherwise than it might be said I saw, or overlooked the Book; nor, indeed, can they prove so much as that. So that I can in no wise be said to have failed in my Duty on Account of this latent Affair, which indeed seems to me to be but trifling in itself.

" I have an entire dependency on my Lord's Justice, and Goodness; that no Offence, formerly committed (were this really so) shall be remembered to my Prejudice. However I thought it my Duty to give his Lordship this Account, that my Enemies may not anticipate me, by giving wrong and injurious Accounts of it before me.

" I am, Sir, Your most humble Servant,

" DE FOE.

" May 23, 1718.

" P.S.—The Words, as I hear them, which the Judges take Offence at, are the introducing the Story of the Fellow that was executed, saying,—*it was a piece of Justice unmixed with Mercy.*"

V.

" SIR,—Since our last Conference I have entered into a new Treaty with Mr. Mist. I need not trouble you with the Particulars, but in a Word, he professes himself convinced that he has been wrong, that the Government has treated him with Lenity and Forbearance; and he solemnly engages to me to give no more Offence.

" The liberties Mr. Buckley mentioned, viz., to seem on the same Side as before, *to rally the Flying Post*, the Whig writers, and even the Word ' Whig,' &c., and to admit foolish and trifling Things in favour of the Tories. This, as I represented it to him, he agrees is Liberty enough, and resolves his Paper shall, for the future, amuse the Tories, but not affront the Government.

" I have freely told him that this is the only Way to preserve his Paper, to keep himself from a Jail, and to secure the Advantages which now rise to him from it, for that he might be assured the Complaint against him was so general that the Government could bear it no longer.

" I said, Sir, all that could be said on that Head, only reserving the Secret of who I spoke from ; and concluded, that unless he would keep Measures with me, and be punctual in these Things, I could not serve him any farther, or be concerned any more.

" Thus far, Sir, I have acted, I hope in a right Method, in pursuance of which, in his next Paper, he is to make a kind of Declaration in answer to two Letters printed in his last, wherein he shall publish his Resolution not to meddle with, or write anything offensive to the Government.

" In prosecution also of this Reformation, he brought me, this Morning, the enclosed Letter ; which, indeed, I was glad to see, because, though it seems couched in terms which might have been made Public, yet has a secret Gall in it, and a manifest tendency to reproach the Government with Partiality and Injustice, and (as it acknowledges expressly) was written to serve a present Turn. As this is an earnest of his just Intention, I hope he will go on to your Satisfaction.

" Give me leave, Sir, to mention here a Circumstance which concerns myself, and which, indeed is a little Hardship upon me, viz., that I seem to merit less, when I intercept a Piece of barefaced flagrant Treason at the Press, than when I stop such a Letter as this enclosed ; because one seems to be of a kind which no Man would dare to meddle with. But I would perswade myself, Sir, that stopping such notorious Things is not without its good effect, particularly because as it is true that some People are generally found who do venture to print any Thing that offers, so stopping them here, is some Discouragement and Disappointment to them, and they often die in our Hands.

" I speak this, Sir, as well on Occasion of what you were pleased to say upon that Letter which I sent you formerly about *Killing no Murder*, as upon another with Verses in it, which Mr. Mist gave me Yesterday; which, upon my Word, is so villainous and scandalous, that I scarce dare to send it without your Order, and an assurance that my doing so shall be taken well. For I confess, it has a peculiar Insolence in it against his Majesty's Person, which (as blasphemous Words against God), are scarce fit to be repeated.

" I am the more concerned you shall know this also, because if I guess right, and Mr. Mist is of that Opinion too, it is the same Hand that the Manuscript which I shewed Mr. Buckley, of *Sultan Galga*, was written in, and, I suppose comes from the same Quarter.

" If you please to order my sending it, I shall obey; and, in the meantime, assure you no Eye shall see it.

" Here has been a very barbarous Attempt made by Curl, the Bookseller, upon Mr. Mist, (viz.) to trepann him into Words against the Government, with a Design to inform against him. I think Mist has escaped him; but if he brings it into your Office, I shall lay a clear state of the Matter before you. I know the Government is sufficient to itself for punishing Offenders, and is above employing trepanns to draw Men into Offences on purpose to resent them.

" I am, Sir, your most humble and obedient Servant,

" DE FOE.

"Newington, June 4, 1718."

VI.

" SIR,—I gave you the Trouble of a Letter a few Days ago. The Account I gave you there of the Conditions I had engaged Mr. M[ist] to, will I hope be satisfactory, and particularly in his performance of those Conditions.

" I suppose you will remember I hinted when I had last the favour of waiting on you, that there was a Book printing at his House scandalously reflecting on my Lord Sund[erland] ; that M[ist] was willing, as a Testimony of his Sincerity, to consent to a Method how to put it into his Lordship's Hands.

" I have gotten the Sheets into my Hands, in performance of this Promise; and would gladly receive your Commands about them.

" I believe the Time is come when the Journal, instead of affronting and offending the Government, may many Ways be made serviceable to the Government; and I have Mr. M[ist] so absolutely resigned to proper Measures for it, that I am perswaded I may answer for it.

" I am, Sir, your most humble and obedient Servant,

" June 13, 1718."   DE FOE.

These Letters appeared, shortly after their discovery, first in the *London Review ;* accompanied by some disparaging reflections on the character and conduct of Defoe. They were afterward printed in *Notes and Queries ;* and were followed, in that publication, by several articles, in which I endeavoured to consider :—1. The history contained in the Letters. 2. The Criticism of the Reviewer. 3. What Defoe did under his engagement with the Government, as above. And 4. The Morality or otherwise of his conduct.

In this Introduction it is unnecessary to say more than that the above Letters to Mr. De la Faye, were all written within the space of two months in 1718 ; and they demonstrate that the political Life of Defoe, had not closed at that date.

To estimate how much is involved in such an error, it is necessary to consider the versatility of Defoe's mind, the fertility of his genius, the marvellous industry of his pen; and that this veil of obscurity overlaid and probably concealed a great part of his labours, during all the last sixteen years of his life. It will not excite surprise, that opening out the consideration of the Subject, in the articles above referred to, I predicated that these Letters pointed " to the materials for an entirely new chapter of the *History of Defoe's Life and Times.*" With such conviction I immediately searched for the publications upon which he had avowedly so engaged himself, namely *Mercurius Politicus, Dormer's News Letter,* and *Mist's Weekly Journal.* My primary object was to ascertain whether or not he deserved the animadversion of the *London Reviewer ;* but I was soon led to extend my investigation generally to his hitherto unknown Journalistic writings; and to transcribe such portions as might be interesting to readers of the present age. The result is now placed before the world.

I must say, at this preliminary stage, that I have omitted very much that would have illustrated the political history of the period ; believing that party-contention would not necessarily be acceptable, merely because it had been written by Daniel Defoe. My extracts therefore are more historical than political ; but they also include more than three hundred and fifty Essays and Letters, moral and religious—imaginative,—humourous,—amatory,—ironical, and miscellaneous. Writing, as he did, on topics of popular interest, as they daily arose, there is a peculiar freshness in his relations of incidents, and his comments thereon ; and I have been able to extract much in his charming style, on the Rebellion of 1715, and the subsequent proceedings of the Pretender and his adherents ;—on Commerce and Trade ;—the South Sea Scheme and Bubbles,—and other epidemic popular delusions ;—on the Plague in France ; and on offences, political and criminal, and their punishment. The whole is interspersed with a multitude of anecdotes, answers to correspondents, and scraps of news, characteristic of the writer's remarkable faculty of humour.

In his Letters to Mr. De la Faye, Defoe recapitulates the nature of his engagement under Government during the two preceding years. I first commenced my investigation, therefore, with the year 1716, but discovering, as I proceeded, that a new Memoir of the remainder of his life would be necessary,—as an accompaniment to his writings,—and, that the beginning of his engagement with the Government would afford but an indifferent starting point,—I was driven backward, first to the appearance of his *Appeal to Honour and Justice,* in 1715, when it had been believed his non-political life commenced. That pamphlet took me necessarily still farther back to the more remote causes of this supposed entire change in his life; and I became convinced that those causes had been in operation from 1712, culminating at the death of Queen Anne, and the accession of George I. My investigation was therefore extended over the twenty years, from 1712 to the end of Defoe's life, in 1731, and I thus found that he had been, before and afterward, the writer of other Journals, besides those specified in his Letters to Mr. De la Faye.

The party Journals of the last century differed, as in our days, from each other very widely in their views on all subjects of public interest; but there was then, from the lower state of educational refinement, a greater tendency to descend, in controversy, from logical argument to the practice of personal abuse. An actual examination of such newspapers would be necessary to an adequate conception of the coarse, indecent brutality of invective, too often resorted to by rival journalists. No controversial writer of that age was more perfectly free from this great fault than Defoe; yet none was more vilified by his opponents. I must confess, however, that when I have commenced, with some hesitation, to follow his pen on a new track, all doubt has been frequently removed by following, at the same time, the cue of slander against him, published in rival papers; and that, amidst such abuse, there frequently came out valuable facts of personal history, that would otherwise have remained unknown. I was thus induced again to extend my researches by a cursory examination of all the accessible Newspapers and Journals, published during the whole of Defoe's literary life, extending over about fifty years; so that nothing published therein, and relating to him, might be omitted. The labour was great, but it contributed to the accuracy of my Memoir, and especially to the chronological order of events.

The notices and advertisements of new books, &c., in these newspapers, furnished me with the exact dates when the greater part of his known works were published,—led me to the discovery of other works written by, but not heretofore attributed to him,—and compelled me to reject many that had been placed to his authorship, without sufficient, or indeed, any reason. A revision of the entire Catalogue of his Works was an obvious and necessary consequence. In many instances, the arrangement according to their respective proper dates involved much more than an inversion of their previous order; in fact, a corresponding alteration in the sequence of portions of his life.

The contemporary comments in other Journals, as to his character and writings,—the differing versions of passing occurrences,—the facts and statements,—contradictory or confirmatory,—illustrating the topics upon which he was engaged from time to time,—often necessary to the full understanding of the subject,—could only with difficulty, if at all, have been interwoven with his Journalistic Writings, but could all find their proper places in a new Memoir of his Life. Without this, my transcripts might have had interest arising from the genius of their author, but would have wanted that cohesion and unity which a Memoir only could supply.

I cannot speak in too high terms of commendation on the patient industry of Mr. Walter Wilson, in his *Memoirs of the Life and Times of Daniel Defoe*. A Catalogue of the books and tracts, examined and referred to, in his two thousand pages, would alone constitute a considerable pamphlet. His work will always be of value as a reference to the polemical literature of the age in which Defoe lived. But I am bound to add that his volumes furnish abundant proof that his conception of the true character of Defoe was very imperfect and superficial. Himself a democratic reformer, and an advocate for the separation of Church and State,—he has not only freely expressed his own views, but has, perhaps unconsciously, yet persistently, disguised his Conservative hero in the clothes of anti-church radicalism.

Some misgiving, or suspicion that he had herein done Defoe injustice, must have entered Mr. Wilson's mind, while writing his preface, when, at page xiv., after urging that the utility of the machinery that encircles religion must be promoted by divesting it of its political connections, Mr. Wilson adds as a foot-note:—" The reader will bear in mind, that the whole of the present work was composed before the late repeal of the Corporation and Test Acts; and written under the influence of the state of things as they previously existed."

The historical biographer should not only avoid attributing to the person whose life he writes sentiments that his hero would, alive, have indignantly repudiated; but should also be careful not to express his own opinions on such points, so as to mislead even superficial readers to the erroneous conviction that the same principles were held and maintained by the man, whose life is thus brought before the world. The whole of the multitudinous works of Defoe, were written " before the Repeal of the Corporation and Test Acts,"—while numerous other obnoxious disabilities, still weighed heavily on the Dissenters; many of such works were written while the Toleration itself was reduced to a mere exemption from prosecution; but there is not to be found in all his works a sentence that can be construed into a desire to separate Church and State. I am bound to go further, and state, that from first to last Defoe was a sincere, consistent upholder of the Church of England, its Establishment and its Doctrines, though a Dissenter from its forms of worship. Declarations of his moderate principles in this respect are neither few, nor far between ; they extend over the whole of his literary life. One of his favourite positions, for which he was always ready to contend, was, " The Church " of England, as by law established, is the Great Bulwark of " the Protestant Faith ;" and to the question, What is your religion ? his answer is, " A Catholic Christian." If the numerous passages in support of the Church of England were unjustly isolated from his general works, the world might conclude that he was a Churchman, and no Dissenter.

Mr. Wilson has quoted extensively from Defoe's works, but the large-hearted Catholicity of his religious character and principles is not made apparent ; and I regret to add that the systematic suppression of Defoe's real opinions on such topics, is even more to be regretted than the active efforts to make him appear a Sectarian bigot.

To recapitulate briefly :—The unanimous concurrence of all his previous biographers in the dictum that his political life terminated in 1715 ;—the accidental reappearance of his six letters in the State Paper Office, and the Investigation to which they led ;—the exhumation of this large collection of his Journalistic writings, between the years 1716 and 1731 ;— the discovery (guided by the fact of his continued political life), that he was the author of many pamphlets and works not heretofore known to be his ; and that he was not the author of many works, that have been attributed to him ;— the rectification of the chronology of his works ; the consequent alteration, in sequence, of the events of his life ;—the impossibility of interweaving all these circumstances, with the Extracts forming the body of this Work ;—the previous misconception as to the moderate and conservative part of Defoe's character ; and moreover, the fact, that his writings contained in this publication, will be entirely new to the public ;—all conducted to the necessity of re-writing the Memoirs of his Life.

In executing this additional labour, I have studied conciseness, especially in that part extending from his birth, to the

death of Queen Anne; and have afterward taken a more en-
arged view of the public occurrences of the times, so far as
he was concerned therein.

It is necessary to prolong this Introduction by a few remarks on the revised Chronological List of the Works of
Defoe. I am constrained to say, that the Lives of Defoe, by
Chalmers, Wilson, and Hazlitt, each containing a List of his
Works, are,—as to such Lists,—" conspicuous for the absence"
of all critical acumen, and even ordinary knowledge of Defoe's
stile. I desire not to be invidious in this; nor when I add
that the List placed under the name of Defoe, in the recent
edition of *Lowndes' Bibliographer's Manual*, seems to have accumulated all the errors of such Lists, and to have added
those of the Grenville Catalogue, with others of less note;
until a large proportion of his alleged Books, could they move,
would immediately arrange themselves into two politically
hostile armies. Literary justice was therefore a debt still
owing to one of the greatest and most truly consistent of
English Authors.

My reasons for the retention or rejection of each individual
Book, would have occupied too much space to be stated specifically. As to those rejected, I have acted on the simple legal
principle that they have no *locus standi*, and therefore no right
to appear. In no instance, however, have I made any alteration
without an amply sufficient personal investigation, generally consisting of careful reading; and, in case of doubt, repeated
readings, until all doubt was removed. From the List in
Lowndes, I have, in this manner, rejected more than sixty;—
from that prefixed by Mr. Wilson, thirty, including three dupli-
cates, with altered Titles, entered by him as distinct works;—
from Mr. Hazlitt's List of those believed by him to be genuine,
I have rejected twelve; and have retained seven of those he
had rejected. Considering the responsibility of these changes,
I have endeavoured, by patient labour, to show proper deference to the judgment, even when erroneous, of those who had
preceded me.

In addition to a considerable collection of books an pamphlets in my own possession, belonging to the period when Defoe lived, I have examined many thousands in the British Museum, and the Bodleian Library ; and have been enabled to add sixty-four distinct Works to the Catalogue of Defoe's productions. With the exception of six such additions, I have admitted no Book or Tract (not previously attributed to him), until after most careful perusal, both general and verbal, had convinced me that he was the author.

The Catalogue, thus revised and corrected, contains two hundred and fifty-four Works ; all of which, except twelve, (of whose genuineness I have otherwise most satisfactory proof,) I have studiously read. I do not believe that the List now contains all that Defoe wrote ; but that continued research might result in further discoveries. Two things, however, I desire to affirm,—modestly, but with a strong assurance :—That Daniel Defoe was the Author of all the Works I have ascribed to him ; and, that he was not the Author of any of the Works heretofore attributed to him, but which I have omitted. If therefore, in the course of the following Life, no specific mention be found of any Work previously assigned to him, and if such piece be omitted from the following Chronological Catalogue, my readers will please to conclude that I have very carefully examined and rejected the same.

The literary and bibliographical importance of this rectification must be my apology, for any apparent egotism in the above explanation. The World has a right to know that great alterations have not been made without great care.

One further Introductory remark may be useful. Many slanderous attacks on Defoe were published in the form of pamphlets. I have, in most instances, not even quoted the titles of miserable productions which my Author considered unworthy of notice. Many controversies, political and religious, in which Defoe took part, brought before the public numerous other writers of that pamphleteering age. My own collection of these, and Mr. Wilson's volumes, would have enabled me to refer to them in long array, but I have aimed to avoid any display of erudition obtained at the price of being diffuse; and have therefore seldom done more than relate what concerned Defoe in such controversies. Whenever he attacked others or defended himself, I have endeavoured to state the matter justly, but as concisely as the circumstances admitted; remembering, that the controversial part has already been dilated on by others, and may probably form the least interesting portion of my Memoir of Defoe's Life.

WILLIAM LEE.

A CHRONOLOGICAL CATALOGUE

OF

DANIEL DEFOE'S WORKS;

WITH THE DATES OF PUBLICATION.

NOTE.—Those marked with an Asterisk (*) are not in the List attached to any previous Biography.

1.* *A Letter* containing some *Reflections* on His *Majesty's Declaration* for *Liberty* of *Conscience.* Dated the 4th April, 1687 (One Sheet 4to., in double columns.)   .   .   .   About June, **1687**

2. A *New Discovery* of an *Old Intreague.* A Satyr level'd at *Treachery*, and *Ambition :* Calculated to the Nativity of the Rapparee Plott, and the Modesty of the Jacobite Clergy. Designed by Way of Conviction to the 117 Petitioners, and for the Benefit of those that Study the Mathematicks &c. Printed in the Year 1691. (4to. pp. 36.) **1691**

3.* The *Englishman's Choice*, and *True Interest :* In a Vigorous *Prosecution* of the *War* against *France* and Serving *K. William* and *Q. Mary*, and acknowledging their Right. London. Printed in the Year 1694. (4to. pp. 32.) **1694**

4. The *Character* of the late *Dr. Samuel Annesley*, by Way of Elegy. (Folio.) **1697**

5. Some *Reflections* on a Pamphlet lately Published, entitled, "An Argument shewing that a Standing Army is Inconsistent with a Free Government, and absolutely Destructive to the Constitution of the English Monarchy." London. Printed for *E. Whitlock*, 1697. (4to. pp. 28.)   .   .   .   .   1st Edition, **1697**
    (4to. pp. 28.)   .   .   .   .   .   2nd Edition, **1697**

6. An *Enquiry* into the *Occasional Conformity* of *Dissenters* in Cases of Preferment. With a *Preface* to the *Lord Mayor*, Occasioned by his carrying the *Sword* to a *Conventicle.* London. Printed Anno Dom. 1697. (4to. 4 leaves & 28 pages.)   .   . 25 Jan. **1698**

7. An *Essay* upon *Projects.* London. Printed by *R. R.* for *Tho. Cockerill*, at the Corner of Warwick Lane, 1697. (8vo. Title. pp. xiv & 336)   .   .   .   .   1st Edition, 29 May, **1698**
    With a New Title   .   .   .   . 2nd Edition, 23 May, **1702**

8. The *Poor Man's Plea*, in Relation to all the *Proclamations, Declarations, Acts* of *Parliament*, &c. which have been or shall be made or published for a Reformation of Manners, and suppressing Immorality in the Nation. London. Printed in the Year 1698. (4to. 2 leaves, pp. 31.)   .   .   .   . 1st Edition, 31 Mar. **1698**
    2nd Edition, 24 May, **1698**
    3rd Edition, 26 Mar. **1700**

9. An *Argument* shewing that a *Standing Army*, with *Consent* of *Parliament*, is not *Inconsistent* with a *Free Government.* London. E. Whitlock. (4to. 2 leaves & pp. 26.) 1698

10. The *Pacificator*, a Poem. London. Sold by J. Nutt near Stationers' Hall. (Folio. Title & pp. 14.) . . 20 Feb. 1700

11. *The Two Great Questions Consider'd.* I. What the French King will do, with respect to the Spanish Monarchy. II. What Measures the English ought to Take. London. Printed in the Year 1700. (4to. 2 leaves & pp. 28.) . . . . . 15 Nov. 1700

12. An Enquiry into the Occasional Conformity of Dissenters in Cases of Preferment. With a Preface to Mr. How. London. Printed, Anno. Dom. 1701. . . . . . . 20 Nov. 1700

13. The *Two Great Questions further Consider'd.* With some Reply to the Remarks. *Non licet hominem Muliebriter Rixari.* London. (4to.) . . . . 2 Dec. 1700

14. The *Six* distinguishing *Characters* of a *Parliament Man ;* address'd to the good People of England. London. Printed in the Year 1700. (4to. 2 leaves & pp. 22) . . . . . 4 Jan. 1701

15. The *Danger* of the *Protestant Religion* Considered, from the present *Prospect* of a *Religious War in Europe.* Printed in the Year 1701. (4to.) . . . . 9 Jan. 1701

16. The *True-Born Englishman.* A Satyr. Printed in the Year 1700. (4to. 2 leaves & pp. 71.) . . . . 1st Edition, Jan. 1701
   With an Explanatory Preface. (4to. 5 leaves & pp. 60.)
   9th Edition, 1701
   "A *New Edition* Neatly Printed on a Superfine Paper with an Elzevir Letter *very much enlarged* of the *True-born Englishman.* Just Published. London. J. Roberts. (8vo. pp. .) With a New Preface." . . . . 22 March, 1716
   "A *Neat* and *Correct Edition* (on an Elzevir Letter) of the True-born Englishman. A Satyr. To which is prefixed a *New Preface* by the Author, adapted to the Present Reign. Price 6d." . 9 Oct. 1719
   "A *Neat Pocket Edition* (Corrected and *Enlarged* by the Author) of the *True-born Englishman.* A Satyr. Price 6d." . . 2 Nov. 1721

17.* *Considerations* upon *Corrupt Elections of Members* to serve in *Parliament.* London. Printed in the Year 1701. (4to. 2 leaves & pp. 24.) . . . . Jan. 1701

18. The *Freeholders Plea* against *Stock-Jobbing Elections* of *Parliament-Men.* London. Printed in the Year 1701. (4to. 2 leaves & pp. 27.) . . . . . . 1st Edition, 23 Jan. 1701
   2nd Edition, 4 Feb. 1701

19. A *Letter* to Mr. *How* by Way of Reply to his Observations on the *Preface* to the Enquiry into the *Occasional Conformity* of *Dissenters* in Case of *Preferment.* By the *Author of the Preface* and the *Enquiry.* Printed 1701. By *A. Baldwin* in Warwick Lane.
   24 Jan. 1701

20. The *Villainy* of *Stock-Jobbers* detected, and the Causes of the late Run upon the Bank and Bankers Discovered and Considered. London. Printed in the Year 1701 . 1st Edition, 11 Feb. 1701
   (4to Title, & pp. 26.) . . . 2nd Edition, 17 Feb. 1701

21. The *Succession* to the *Crown of England Considered.* London. Printed in the Year 1701 (4to. pp. 38.) . About 1 March, 1701

22. Legion's Memorial to the House of Commons (2 leaves quarto.)
   presented. 14 May, 1701

23. The *History* of the *Kentish Petition.* London. *Printed* in the Year 1701. (4to. Title & Preface 3 leaves & pp. 25.) . August, 1701

24. The *Present State* of *Jacobitism* Considered, in two *Queries*. I. What Measures the *French King* will take with respect to the *Person* and *Title* of the *P. P. of Wales?* II. What the *Jacobites* in *England* ought to do on the same *Account?* London. *A. Baldwin.* (4to. Title & Preface 3 leaves pp. 22.)   . Before Oct. 1701

25. *Reasons* against a *War* with *France;* or, an Argument shewing that the *French King's* Owning the *Prince* of *Wales* as King of *England, Scotland,* and *Ireland,* is no Sufficient Ground of a *War.* London. Printed in the Year 1701. (4to. Title & pp. 30) October, 1701

26. The *Original Power* of the *Collective Body* of the *People* of *England, Examined* and *Asserted.* With a double Dedication to the King, and to the Parliament. *London.* (Folio-Title and Dedications 4 leaves, & pp. 24.) Printed in the year 1702.   27 Dec. 1701

27. Legion's New Paper : Being a Second Memorial to the Gentlemen of a late House of Commons. With Legion's Humble Address to His Majesty. London, Printed and are to be Sold by the Booksellers of London and Westminster. (4to. pp. 18)   1 Jan. 1702

28. The *Mock Mourners,* a Satyr, by way of Elegy on *King William.* By the Author of the True-born Englishman. London. W. Gunne .   .   .   .   .   . 1st Edition, About May, 1702
Corrected. (4to. 2 leaves & pp. 20.) Price 6*d*.   . 2nd Edition, 1702
———— (4to. 2 leaves & pp. 32.)   .   .   . 3rd Edition, 1702
———— (8vo. pp. 16. Corrected by the Author. London. Printed 1702) .   .   .   .   . 7th Edition, 23 Feb. 1703

29. *Reformation* of *Manners.* A Satyr. *Væ Vobis Hypocritè.* Printed in the year 1702. (4to. 2 leaves & pp. 64.)   1702

30. A *New Test* of the *Church* of *England's Loyalty:* or, Whiggish Loyalty and Church Loyalty Compared. *Printed* in the year 1702. (4to. Title & pp. 34.) .   .   .   .   .   . June, 1702

31.* *Good Advice* to the *Ladies:* shewing, that, as the World goes, and is like to go, the best way for them is to keep Unmarried. By the Author of the True-Born Englishman. Printed in the year 1702. (4to. Title & Preface 4 leaves pp. 16.) 1st Edition, 3 Sept. 1702
(The Second Edition corrected.) with the Character of a Beau. London: Printed for R. Smith, without Temple Bar, and are sold by J. Nutt, near Stationers' Hall. (4to. Title and Preface 3 leaves & pp. 16.) .   .   .   .   .   . 2nd Edition, 1705

32. The *Spanish Descent.* A Poem. By the Author of the True-Born Englishman. London. Printed in the year 1702. (4to. pp. 27.)
Nov. 1702

33. An *Enquiry* into *Occasional Conformity.* Shewing that the Dissenters are no Way Concerned in it. By the Author of the Preface to Mr. How. London. (4to. pp. 31) . 1st Edition, Nov. 1702
In his collected Writings, 2nd Edition, 1703
(The same with the following Title) an Enquiry into the Occasional Conformity Bill. By the Author of the True Born Englishman. London. (4to. pp. 14.)   .   .   . 3rd Edition, 1704

34. The *Shortest Way* with the *Dissenters:* or, *Proposals* for the *Establishment* of the *Church.* London. Printed in the year 1702. (4to. Title & pp. 29.) .   .   .   .   .   . 1 Dec. 1702

35. A *Brief Explanation* of a late *Pamphlet,* entitled The *Shortest Way* with the *Dissenters* 1703

36. *King William's Affection* to the *Church* of *England,* Examined. London. (4to. pp. 26.) .   .   .   . 1st Edition, 25 March, 1703
2nd Edition,   1703
(4to. Title & pp. 26.) .   .   . 3rd Edition, 3 April, 1703
(4to. Title & pp. 36.)   .   . 4th Edition, 13 April, 1703

78. An Answer to Lord Haversham's Speech. By Daniel De Foe. (Reprinted from the Review of 24 Nov. 1705.) (4to. pp. 4.) At the end is "London. Printed 1705." . . About 1 Dec. 1705

79. A Hymn to Peace. Occasioned by the two Houses joining in one Address to the Queen. By the Author of the True-born Englishman. London. Printed in the Year 1706. (4to. pp. 60.) 10 Jan. 1706

80. A Reply to a Pamphlet, entitled the L—d Haversham's Vindication of his Speech, &c. By the Author of the Review. London. (4to. pp. 32.) . . . . 15 Jan. 1706

81. A *Review* of the *Affairs of France*; with *Observations* on Transactions at Home. (4to. 4 leaves & pp. 508.) Vol. II. (including the "Little Review," from 6 June, to 21 August, 1705) 1 Jan. 1706

82.* The *Case* of *Protestant Dissenters* in CAROLINA; shewing how a LAW to prevent *Occasional Conformity* there, has ended in the *Total Subversion* of the Constitution in *Church* and *State*. Recommended to the serious Consideration of all that are true Friends of our present Government. *Mutato nomine de te Fabula narratur.* London. Printed in the Year 1706. (4to. pp. 42.) Early in 1706

83. *Remarks* on the *Bill* to prevent *Frauds* committed by *Bankrupts.* With *Observations* on the *Effect* it may have upon TRADE. *London* (4to. Title & pp. 29.) . . . . . 18 April, 1706

84. An *Essay* at *Removing National Prejudices* against a *Union* with SCOTLAND. To be continued during the Treaty here. LONDON. Printed for *B. Bragg.* (4to. Title & pp. 30.) PART I.
1st Edition, 4 May, 1706

85. PART II. (The Title as before.) . . 1st Edition, 28 May, 1706
Edinburgh, Parts I. & II. reprinted in one. (4to. pp. 51.)
2nd Edition, 1706

86. An *Essay* at *Removing National Prejudices* against a *Union* with ENGLAND. By the Author of the two First. [Edinburgh.] Printed in the Year 1706. (4to. pp. 35.) PART III. . . Nov. 1706.

87. A Fourth Essay at Removing National Prejudices; with some Reply to Mr. *H—dges,* and some other Authors, who have Printed their Objections against a Union with England. [Edinburgh.] Printed in the Year 1706. (4to. pp. 44.) PART IV. Dec. 1706

88. A FIFTH *Essay* at *Removing National Prejudices;* with a *Reply* to some *Authors,* who have Printed their Objections against a *Union* with ENGLAND. [Edinburgh.] Printed in the Year 1707. (4to. Title and Preface 4 leaves, pp. 35.) PART V. . . Jany. 1707

89. Two Great Questions Considered—I. What is the Obligation of Parliaments to the Addresses or Petitions of the People, and What the Duty of Addressers? II. Whether the Obligation of the Covenant, or other National Engagements, is concerned in the Treaty of Union? Being a SIXTH Essay at Removing National Prejudices against the Union. [Edinburgh.] Printed in the Year 1707. (4to. pp. 31.) PART VI. . . . Jan. 1707

90. A *Plea* for the *Non Conformists:* Shewing the true State of their Case: &c. &c. By *Thomas de Laune.* With a *Preface* by the *Author* of the *Review.* London. Printed and Sold by W. & J. Marshall, at the Bible in Newgate Street. (4to. Title. [Preface by Defoe, pp. xi.] pp. 66.) . . 1st Edition, 6 June, 1706
Another Edition (8vo. Title, [Preface by Defoe, pp. xvi,] Witness & Contents 3 leaves. Plea pp. 144.) 1712

91. A *Sermon* preached by *Mr. Daniel De Foe,* on the Fitting up of *Dr. Burgess's Meeting House.* (Taken from his *Review* of the 20th June, 1706.) (4to.) . . . . June, 1706

92. A *True Relation* of the *Apparition* of one Mrs. *Veal*, the next *Day* after her *Death*, to one Mrs. *Bargrave* at *Canterbury*, the 8th of September, 1705. Which *Apparition* recommends the *Perusal* of *Drelincourt's* Book of *Consolations against the Fears of Death*. London. Printed for B. Bragg, at the Black Raven.

1st Edition, 5 July, 1706
(8vo. Title and Preface 2 leaves & pp. 12.) 11th Edition.

93. *Jure Divino:* a *Satyr*. In Twelve Books. By the *Author* of the *True-Born Englishman*. London. Printed in the Year 1706. [8vo. SPURIOUS EDITION. Port. Title and Dedication 2 leaves. Preface, pp. xlii. Contents 1 leaf. Poem to the Author, pp. 2. Introduction, pp. 5. Book I. pp. 25. Book II. pp. 24. Book III. pp. 19. Book IV. pp. (68 to 93). Book V. pp. 26. Book VI. pp. 15. Book VII. to the end pp. (135 to 278.) . 20 July, 1706
Jure Divino: a *Satyr*. In Twelve Books. By the *Author* of the *True-Born Englishman*. London. Printed in the Year 1706. (Folio. GENUINE EDITION. Portrait. Title & Dedication 2 leaves. Preface, pp. xxviii. Contents & Poem to Author 2 leaves. Introduction, pp. vii. The 12 Books separately paged. Together, pp. 346 . . . . 20 July, 1706

94. A *Letter* to a *Friend*, giving an *Account* how the *Treaty of Union* has been received here. With remarks on what has been written by Mr. H(odges) and Mr. R(idpath). Edinburgh. (4to.) . 1706

95. The *Dissenters* in *England Vindicated* from *some Reflections* in a late *Pamphlet*, called "Lawful Prejudices," &c. &c. *Edinburgh*. 1706. (4to. pp. 8.) . . . . . 1st Edition, Jan. 1707
Reprinted, *London* . . . . 2nd Edition, 1707

96. *Caledonia*, &c. *A Poem*, in Honour of *Scotland*, and the *Scots Nation*. In three parts. EDINBURGH, Printed by the Heirs and Successors of Andrew Anderson, Printer to the Queen's Most Excellent Majesty. (Folio. Title, Dedication, and Preface 5 leaves. Poem pp. 60.) . . . . . . 1st Edition, 1706
———————— *London* : Printed by J. Matthews, and Sold by John Morphew, near Stationers' Hall. (8vo. Title, Dedication, and List of Subscribers, 4 leaves. Poem, pp. 55.) 2nd Edition, 28 Jan. 1707

97. A *Review* of the state of the *English Nation*. London. (4to. Title and Preface 4 leaves & pp. 688.) . . VOL. III., 6 Feb. 1707

98. A *Short View* of the Present *State* of the *Protestant Religion* in *Britain*, as it is now profest in the Episcopal Church in *England*, the Presbyterian *Church* in Scotland, and the Dissenters in Both. EDINBURGH. Printed in the Year 1707. (8vo. pp. 48.)

1st Edition, March, 1707
The *Dissenters Vindicated :* or, a *Short View* of the Present *State* of the *Protestant Religion* in *Britain*, as it is now professed in the *Episcopal Church* of England, the *Presbyterian Church* in Scotland, and the *Dissenters* in both. In Answer to some Reflections in *Mr. Webster's* two Books published in Scotland. London. J. Morphew. (8vo. pp. 48.) . . . . 2nd Edition, 1 April, 1707

99. A *Voice* from the *South :* or, an *Address* from some *Protestant Dissenters* in *England* to the *Kirk in Scotland*. (From his Reviews of May 10 & 15, 1707.) (4to. pp. 8.) . . . May, 1707

100. *A *Modest Vindication* of the *Present Ministry :* From the *Reflections* published against them in a late *Printed Paper*, Entitled, The *Lord Haversham's Speech*, &c. With a *Review* and *Balance* of the *Present War*. Evincing, That we are not in such a Desperate Condition as that Paper Insinuates. Humbly submitted

to the Consideration of all, but especially to the Right *Honourable* and the *Honourable*, the *North British Lords and Commoners.* By a Well-wisher to the *Peace* of *Britain.* London. Printed in the Year 1707. (4to. Title & pp. 14) **1707**

101.*An Historical Account of the Bitter Sufferings, and Melancholy Circumstances of the Episcopal Church in Scotland, Under the Barbarous Usage and Bloody Persecution of the Presbyterian Church Government. With an Essay on the Nature and Necessity of a Toleration in the North of Britain. Edinburgh. Printed in the Year 1707. (8vo. pp. 40.) **1707**

102.*De Foe's Answer, to Dyer's Scandalous Newsletter. [Edinburgh.] (4to. pp. 3.) . . . . **August, 1707**

103. The *Union Proverb*, viz. "If *Skiddaw* has a *cap*, *Scruffell* wots full well of that." Setting forth, I. The necessity of Uniting, II. The good consequences of Uniting, III. The happy Union of England and Scotland, in case of a Foreign Invasion. *Felix quem faciunt aliena Pericula cautum.* London. G. Sawbridge. (8vo.)
13 March, 1708

104. A *Review* of the *State* of the *British Nation.* London. (4to. Title, Preface 2 leaves & pp. 700.) . VOL. IV., 25 March, **1708**

105. The *Scots Narrative* Examined; or, the *Case* of the *Episcopal Ministers* in *Scotland* stated; and the late *Treatment* of them in the *City* of *Edinburgh*, enquired into. With a brief *Examination* into the *Reasonableness* of the *Grievous Complaint* of *Persecution* in *Scotland*, and a *Defence* of the *Magistrates* of *Edinburgh*, in their *Proceedings* there. Being some *Remarks* on a late *Pamphlet*, entitled *A Narrative of the late Treatment of the Episcopal Ministers, within the City of Edinburgh*, &c. London. Sold by A. Baldwin, in Warwick Lane. (4to. pp. 41. Postscript x.)
19 Feb. 1709

106. A *Review* of the *State* of the *British Nation.* London. (4to. Title and Preface 4 leaves & pp. 632.) . VOL. V., 31 March, **1709**

107. The *History of the Union of Great Britain.* Edinburgh. Printed by the Heirs and Successors of Andrew Anderson, Printer to the Queen's Most Excellent Majesty. (Folio, Portrait, Title, and Dedications 8 leaves. Preface, pp. xxxii., and total pp. 694.) **1709**

108. An *Answer* to a *Paper* concerning *Mr. De Foe*, against the *History* of the *Union.* Edinburgh. (4to. pp 8.) **1709**

109. A *Reproof* to *Mr. Clark*, and a *Brief Vindication* of *Mr. De Foe.* Edinburgh. John Moncur. (4to. pp. 8.) A.D. 1710 . . **1709**

110.*A *Commendatory Sermon*, Preached November 4th, 1709. Being the Birth Day of *King William* of *Glorious Memory.* By *Daniel Defoe.* London. Printed by *J. Dutton*, near Fleet Street. (8vo. pp. 8.) From the Review. . . . . . **Nov. 1709**

111. A *Review* of the *State of the British Nation.* London. (4to. Title and Preface 4 leaves & pp. 600.) . VOL. VI., 23 March, **1710**

112. A *Letter* from *Captain Tom* to the *Mob*, now Raised for *Dr. Sacheverell.* London, Printed for J. Baker at the Black Boy in Paternoster Row. (8vo. pp. 8.) . . . . **11 March, 1710**

113*A *Speech* without *Doors.* London, Printed for A. Baldwin, near the Oxford Arms in Warwick Lane. Price Two Pence. (8vo. pp. 20.) . . . . **19 April, 1710**

114. *Instructions* from *Rome* in Favour of the *Pretender*: Inscribed to the most Elevated *Don Sacheverillio*, and his Brother *Don Higginsco.* And which all *Perkinites, Non-Jurors, High flyers, Popish Desirers, Wooden-shoe Admirers*, and *Absolute Non-resistance Drivers*, are obliged to pursue and maintain (under pain of his

Unholinesses Damnation,) in order to carry on their intended subversion of a *Government,* fixed upon *Revolution Principles.* London.
Sold by J. Baker, at the Black Boy in Paternoster Row. Price 2d.
(8vo. pp. 16.)   .   .   .   .   11 May, 1710

115. An *Essay* upon *Publick Credit:* Being an Enquiry; How the
Publick Credit comes to depend upon the Change of the *Ministry*
or the Dissolutions of *Parliaments;* and whether it does so
or no.   With an Argument, Proving that the *Publick Credit*
may be upheld and maintained in this Nation; and perhaps
brought to a greater Height than it ever yet arriv'd at; Tho'
all the Changes and Dissolutions already made, pretended to,
and now Discoursed of, should come to pass in the world.   London. Printed and Sold by the Booksellers. Price 3d. (8vo.
pp. 28.)   .   .   .   .   23 Aug. 1710

116. A *Word* against a *New Election ;* that the *People* of *England* may
see the *Happy difference* between English *Liberty* and French
Slavery : and may consider well before they make the Exchange.
(8vo. pp. 23.)   .   .   .   .   .   .   Oct. 1710

117. A *New Test* of the *Sense* of the *Nation :* Being a *Modest Comparison* between the ADDRESSES to the late *King James,* and those
to her present *Majesty.*   In order to observe how far the *Sense* of
the *Nation* may be judged of by either of them. *London.* (8vo.
Title & pp. 91.)   .   .   .   .   .   : 12 Oct. 1710

118. An *Essay* upon *Loans :* or, An *Argument* proving That Substantial
FUNDS, settled by Parliament, with the Encouragements of *Interests,* and the Advances of *Prompt Payment* usually allowed, will
bring in *Loans* of *Money* to the *Exchequer,* in spite of all the *Conspiracies* of *Parties* to the Contrary; while a *Just, Honourable,*
and *Punctual Performance* on the Part of the *Government,* supports the *Credit* of the *Nation.* By the Author of the *Essay upon
Credit. London.* Printed and Sold by the Booksellers. (8vo.
pp. 27.)   .   .   .   .   .   .   21 Oct. 1710

119. The *Edinburgh Courant*   .   .   .   .   .   1 Feb. 1711

120.**Atalantis Major.*   Printed in *Olreeky,* the Chief City of the Northern part of Atalantis Major. Anno Mundi 1711. (8vo. Title
& pp. 46.)   .   .   .   .   .   .   early in 1711

121. A *Review* of the *State* of the *British Nation.* London. (4to. Title
and Preface, 4 leaves & pp.   .)   .   .   Vol. VII. 22 Mar. 1711

122. *Eleven Opinions* about *Mr. H(arle)y ;* with *Observations.* London.
J. Baker. (8vo. pp. 89.)   .   .   .   .   14 May, 1711

123.*The Secret History of the October Club : From its Original to
this Time. By a Member. London. Printed in the Year 1711.
Price 1s. (8vo. Title & pp. 86.)   .   1st Edition, 21 April, 1711
                                          2nd Edition, 10 May, 1711

124.*The Secret History of the October Club. From its Original to
this Time. By a Member. Part II. London. Printed for J.
Baker, at the Blackboy in Paternoster Row, (Price 1s.) where may
be had the first Part. (8vo. Title, pp. 93.)   .   About Aug. 1711

125. An *Essay* on the *South Sea Trade :* With an *Enquiry* into the
Grounds and *Reasons* of the present *Dislike* and *Complaint* against
the *Settlement* of a *South Sea Company.* By the *Author of the
Review.* London. J. Baker. (8vo. pp. 47.)   1st Edition, 6 Sept. 1711
     (8vo. pp. 47.) Printed on Title 1712.   2nd Edition, 29 Nov. 1711

126. *Reasons* why *this Nation* ought to put a *Speedy End* to this *Expensive War.* With a *Brief Essay* at the probable *Conditions* on
which the *Peace* now *Negociating* may be *Founded.* Also an *Enquiry* into the *Obligations Britain* lies under to the *Allies,* and

how far she is obliged not to make *Peace* without them. *London.*
J. Baker. (8vo.) . . . . 1st Edition, 6 Oct. 1711
 (8vo. pp. 47.) . . . 2nd Edition, 11 Oct. 1711
 3rd Edition, 13 Oct. 1711

127. *Armageddon :* or, the *Necessity of Carrying on the War* if *such* a
 Peace cannot be obtained, as may render *Europe safe* and *Trade
 secure.* London. J. Baker. Price 6d. (8vo. pp. 47.) . 30 Oct. 1711

128. The *Balance of Europe ;* or, an *Enquiry* into the respective *Dangers*
 of giving the *Spanish Monarchy* to the *Emperor*, as well as to *King
 Philip.* With the *Consequences* that may be expected from either.
 Printed for John Baker. (8vo. pp. 48.) . . . 1 Nov. 1711

129. An *Essay* at a *Plain Exposition* of that *difficult Phrase a Good
 Peace.* By the Author of the *Review.* London. J. Baker.
 Price 6d. (8vo. pp. 52.) . . . . About 27 Nov. 1711

130.*Reasons* why a *Party* among us, and also among the *Confederates*, are obstinately bent against a *Treaty of Peace* with the
 French at this *Time.* By the Author of *Reasons for putting an
 End to this Expensive War.* J. Baker. Price 6d. (8vo.)
 1st Edition, 29 Nov. 1711
 2nd Edition, 8 Dec. 1711

131. The *Felonious Treaty :* or, an *Enquiry* into the *Reasons* which
 Moved his late Majesty *King William* of *Glorious Memory*, to
 enter into a *Treaty* at two Several *Times*, with the *King of France*,
 for the *Partition* of the *Spanish Monarchy.* With an Essay
 proving that it was always the sense of *King William*, and of all
 the *Confederates*, and even of the *Grand Alliance* itself, that the
 Spanish Monarchy should never be united in the] *Person* of the
 Emperor. By the *Author of the Review.* London. J. Baker.
 Price 6d. (8vo. pp. 48.) . . . . . Dec. 1711

132. An *Essay* on the *History* of *Parties* and *Persecution* in *Britain*, beginning with a brief *Account* of the *Test Act* and an *Historical
 Enquiry* into the *Reasons*, the *Original*, and the *Consequences* of
 the *Occasional Conformity* of the *Dissenters ;* with some *Remarks*
 on the several *Attempts*, already made and now making, for an
 Occasional Bill. Enquiring how far the same may be esteemed
 a *Preservation* to the *Church*, or an *Injury to the Dissenters.*
 London. Printed for J. Baker, at the Black Boy, in Paternoster
 Row. Price 6d. (8vo. pp. 48.) . . . . 22 Dec. 1711

133. The *Conduct* of *Parties in England*, more especially of those Whigs,
 who now appear against the new Ministry and a Treaty of Peace.
 (8vo. pp. 42.) . . . . 24 Jan. 1712

134. The *Present State* of *Parties* in *Great Britain :* Particularly an
 Enquiry into the *State* of the *Dissenters* in *England*, and the
 Presbyterians in *Scotland*, their *Religious* and *Public Interests*
 considered as it respects their *Circumstances* before and since the
 late *Acts* against *Occasional Conformity in England*, and for
 Toleration of *Common Prayer* in *Scotland.* London. Printed and
 Sold by J. Baker. Price Five Shillings. (8vo. Title and Pre-
 face 4 leaves & pp. 352.) . . . . 17 May, 1712

135. *Reasons* against *Fighting ;* Being an *Enquiry* into this *Debate*,
 whether it is *Safe* for her *Majesty*, or her *Ministry*, to *Adventure*
 an *Engagement* with the *French*, considering the present *Behaviour*
 of the *Allies.* Printed in the year 1712. Price 6d. (8vo.
 Title & pp. 38.) . . . . 7 June, 1712

136. A *Review* of the *State of the British Nation.* London. (4to.
 pp. 848.) . . . . . . VOL. VIII., 29 July, 1712

137.*An *Enquiry* into the *Real Interest* of *Princes* in the *Persons* of
their *Ambassadors;* and how far the Petty Quarrels of Ambassadors, or the *Servants* and *Dependants* of *Ambassadors*, one
among another, ought to be Resented by their *Principals*. With
an Essay on what *Satisfaction* it is Necessary to Give or Take in
such *Cases*. Impartially applied to the affair of *Monsieur Mesnager*, and the *Count de Rechteren, Plenipotentiaries* at *Utrecht*.
London. J. Baker. (8vo. pp. 23.) .   .   .   . 18 Sept. 1712

138. A Seasonable Warning and Caution against the Insinuations of
Papists and Jacobites in favour of the Pretender. Being a
Letter from an Englishman at the Court of Hanover. Printed
by J. Baker, at the Black Boy. (8vo. pp. 24.)   .   .   .   1712

139. *Hannibal* at the *Gates;* or, the *Progress of Jacobitism* and the
Danger of the *Pretender*. London. J. Baker. (12mo. pp. 40.)
1st Edition, 30 Dec. 1712
With Remarks on a Pamphlet now Published Intituled Hannibal
not at our Gates, &c. (8vo. pp. 48.).   .   . 2nd Edition, 1714

140. *A Strict Enquiry* into the *Circumstances* of a *late Duel*, with some
Account of the *Persons* concern'd on both *Sides*. Being a *Modest
Attempt* to do *Justice* to a Noble *Person* DEAD, and to the *Injured
Honour* of an *Absent Person* LIVING. To which is added the
substance of a *Letter* from *General McCartney* to his *Friend*.
London. (8vo. pp. 30.)   1713

141. *Reasons* against the *Succession* of the *House* of *Hanover*, with an
Enquiry how far the *Abdication* of *King James*, supposing it to
be *legal*, ought to affect the *Person* of the *Pretender*. London.
J. Baker. Price 6d. (8vo. Title & pp. 45.) 1st Edition, 21 Feb. 1713
4th Edition, April, 1713

142. And *What* if the *Pretender* should *Come?* or some *Considerations*
of the *Advantages* and real *Consequences* of the *Pretender's* possessing the *Crown* of *Great Britain*. London. J. Baker. (8vo.
pp. 44.)   .   .   .   .   .   . 1st Edition, 26 March, 1713
2nd Edition, April, 1713

143. An *Answer* to a *Question* that *nobody* thinks of, viz. *What if the
Queen should die?* London. J. Baker. (8vo. pp. 44.) April, 1713

144. An *Essay* on the *Treaty of Commerce with France*, with *Necessary
Expositions*.   .   .   .   .   .   .   1st Edition, May, 1713
London. J. Baker. (8vo. pp. 44.) 2nd Edition, 1713

145.*Considerations upon the Eighth and Ninth Articles of the Treaty
of Commerce and Navigation. Now published by Authority.
With some Enquiries into the DAMAGES that may accrue to the
English Trade from them. London. J. Baker. (8vo. pp. 40.)
2 June, 1713

146. The Review (each Number a single leaf) (4to. pp. 212.) 2 Aug.
1712 to 11 June, 1713.   .   .   .   . Vol. IX., 11 June, 1713

147. *Some Thoughts* upon the *Subject* of *Commerce* with *France*. By
the *Author of the Review*. London. J. Baker. (8vo. ——), June, 1713

148. A General History of Trade, and especially considered as it respects British Commerce, &c. Four fortnightly Numbers.
London. J. Baker. (8vo. each No. about pp. 40), Aug. & Sept. 1713

149. *Whigs* turned *Tories* and *Hanoverian Tories* from their avowed
Principles proved *Whigs;* or each side in the other Mistaken.
Being a plain proof that each party deny that *Charge* which the
others bring against them; and that neither side will disown
those which the other profess. With an *Earnest Exhortation*
to all *Whigs*, as well as *Hanoverian Tories*, to lay aside those
uncharitable heats among such *Protestants*, and seriously to con-

sider, and effectually to provide, against those *Jacobite, Popish,* and *Conforming Tories,* whose principal *Ground* of *Hope* to ruin all *sincere Protestants* is from those *Unchristian* and violent *Feuds* among ourselves. London. J. Baker. (8vo.) . . . 1713

150.* *Union* and no *Union.* Being an Enquiry into the Grievances of the Scots and how far they are right or wrong, who alledge that the Union is dissolved. J. Baker. (8vo. p>. 24.) . . . 1713

151. A *Letter* to the *Dissenters.* London. *Printed* for *J. Morphew* near Stationers' Hall. Price 6d. (8vo. pp. 48.) . 3 Dec. 1713

152.* The *Scots Nation* and *Union Vindicated* from the *Reflections* cast on them in an *Infamous libel* entitled the *Public Spirit of the Whigs,* &c. In wh.ch, the most *Scandalous Paragraphs* contained therein are fairly *quoted* and fully *answered.* London. Printed for A. Bell. (4to. pp. 28.) . . . March, 1714

153. A *View of* the *Real Danger* of the *Protestant Succession.* London. J. Baker. Price 6d. (8vo. pp. 44.) . . . April, 1714

154.* *Reasons* for Im(peaching) the L(or)d H(ig)h Treasurer, and some others of the P(resen) M(inistr)y. Printed and Sold by J. Moore, near St. Paul's. Price 6d. (8vo. pp. 39.) End of April, 1714

155. The Remedy worse than the Disease; or, Reasons against passing the Bill for preventing the Growth of Schism. To which is added a brief Discourse of Toleration and Persecution, shewing their Unavoidable Effects Good or Bad; and Proving that neither Diversity of Religions, nor Diversity in the Same Religion are Dangerous, much less Inconsistent with good Government. In a Letter to a Noble Earl. London. J. Baker. (8vo. pp. 48.) . . . . . . 9 June, 1714

156. *Mercator:* or, *Commerce* Retrieved, Being Considerations on the Subject of British Trade; particularly as it respects Holland, Flanders and the Dutch Barrier; the Trade to and from France, the Trade to Portugal, Spain and the West Indies, and the Fisheries of Newfoundland and Nova Scotia: With other Matters and Advantages accruing to Great Britain, by the Treaties of Peace and Commerce lately Concluded at Utrecht. The whole being founded upon just Authorities, faithfully Collected from Authentick Papers, and now made Publick for General Information . . . 26 May, 1713 to 20 July, 1714

157.* The *Flying* Post and *Medley* (Hurt's). [Written by Daniel Defoe, a small leaf folio published thrice a week, continued to the 21st of Aug. 1714, if not later.] . . 27 July 1714 to 21 Aug. 1714

158. Advice to the People of Great Britain, as to what they ought to expect from the King, and how they ought to behave to him. London. J. Baker . . . . 1st Edition, 7 Oct. 1714
Reprinted in Dublin for G. Risk, Bookseller. (8vo. pp. 30.)
2nd Edition, 1714

159.* A Secret History of One Year. London. J. Baker. (8vo. Title & pp. 40.) 1714

160. The Secret History of the White Staff. Being an Account of Affairs under the Conduct of Some late Ministers; and of what might probably have happened if her Majesty had not died.
J. Baker. (8vo. pp. 71.) . . . . 1st Edition, Oct. 1714
(8vo. pp. 71.) . . . . 2nd Edition, 7 Oct. 1714
,, ... 3rd Edition, Oct. 1714
(8vo. pp. 71.) . . . . 4th Edition, 27 Oct. 1714

161. (8vo. pp. 71.) Part II. . . . . 1st Edition, 27 Oct. 1714
2nd Edition, 1714
(8vo. pp. 71.) . . . . . 3rd Edition, 1714

162. (8vo. pp. 80.) Part III. . . . 1st Edition, 29 Jan. 1715

163. An *Appeal* to *Honour* and *Justice*, tho' it be of his *Worst Enemies*,
by *Daniel Defoe*. *Being a True Account of his Conduct* in Publick Affairs. London. Printed for J. Baker. (8vo. Title &
pp. 58.) . . . . January, 1715
164. A *Reply* to a *Traitorous Libel* entitled, *English Advice* to *the*
Freeholders of England. J. Baker. (8vo. pp. 40.) 29 January, 1715
165. A *Friendly Epistle* by Way of *Reproof*, from one of the People
called *Quakers* to *Thos. Bradbury*, a Dealer in many Words.
London. Printed and Sold by S. Keimer, Paternoster Row.
Price 6d. (8vo. pp. 39.) . . . . . . 19 Feb. 1715
166. The *Family Instructor :* in three Parts. I. Relating to Fathers
and Children. II. To Masters and Servants. III. To Husbands & Wives. By Way of Dialogue, With a Recommendatory Letter by the Rev. Mr. S. Wright. London. E. Matthews.
(12mo. 3 leaves & pp. 444.) . . . . 31 Mar. 1715
————— Corrected by the Author. (Title and Preface 3 leaves,
& pp. 414.) . . . . . 2nd Edition, 17 Sept. 1715
Corrected by the Author. (12mo. Title and Preface 3 leaves, &
pp. 385.) . . . . 8th Edition, 1720
(12mo. pp. 384.) . . . . . . 16th Edition, 1766
167. A *Sharp Rebuke* from one of the *People* called *Quakers* to *Henry*
Sacheverell, the High Priest of Andrews, Holbourn. By the Same
Friend that wrote to Thos. Bradbury. London. Printed and
Sold by S. Keimer, Paternoster Row. Price 6d. (8vo. pp. 35.) 1715
168. A *Seasonable Expostulation*, and *Friendly Reproof* unto *James*
Butler, who by the Men of this *World* is styled the Duke of
O——d, relating to the *Tumults* of the *People*. By the same
Friend that wrote to *Thos. Bradbury*, the Dealer in many *Words*,
and *Henry Sacheverell* the *High Priest of Andrews, Holbourn*.
London. S. Keimer. (8vo. pp. 31.) . 1st Edition, 31 May, 1715
(8vo. pp. 24.) Reprinted in Dublin by Thos. Humes,
2nd Edition, 1715
169.* *History* of the *Wars* of his present Majesty *Charles XII. King of*
Sweden ; from his first Landing in Denmark, to his Return from
Turkey to Pomerania. By a Scots Gentleman, in the Swedish
Service. London. A. Bell. (8vo. 2 leaves & pp. 400.)
1st Edition, 6 July, 1715
With a continuation to his Death. (Portrait. Title and
Preface 2 leaves. Hist. pp. 1 to 248. Continuation, pp. 249
to 402.) . . . . . . 2nd Edition, 21 May, 1720
170. A *Hymn* to *the Mob*. London. Printed and Sold by S. Popping, &c.
Price 6d. (8vo. Title and Preface 3 leaves, & pp. 40.) 14 July, 1715
171.* A *View* of the *Scots Rebellion*. With some Enquiry into what
we have to fear, from the Rebels ? and what is the properest
method to take with them ? London. R. Burleigh, in Amen
Corner. Price 6d. (8vo. pp. 40.) . . . . 15 Oct. 1715
172.* A *Trumpet, Blown* in the *North*, and sounded in the Ears of
JOHN ERESKINE, called by the Men of the World, DUKE of MAR.
By a Ministering Friend of the People called Quakers. With a
word of Advice and Direction to the said JOHN ERESKINE and
his followers. Sold by S. Keimer, at the Cheshire Coffee House
in King's Arms Court, on Ludgate Hill. Price 6d. (8vo. pp. 38.)
10 Nov. 1715
173.* An *Account* of the *Great* and *Generous Actions* of *James Butler*,
(late Duke of Ormond). Dedicated to the Famous University
of Oxford. London. Printed for J. *Moore*. Price 6d. (8vo.
pp. 48.) . . . . Dec. 1715

174. Some *Account* of the *Two Nights Court* at *Greenwich ;* wherein may be seen the Reason, Rise, and Progress of the late Un-natural Rebellion, against his Sacred Majesty, King George and his *Government.* London. J. Baker. (8vo. Title, & pp. 72.) 1716

175.* *Some Considerations* on a *Law* for *Triennial Parliaments ;* with an *Enquiry.* I. Whether there may not be a Time, when it is necessary to suspend the Execution of Such Laws as are most essential to the Liberties of the People? II. Whether this is such a Time or No? London. J. *Baker.* (8vo. pp. 40.) April, 1716

176.* The *Alteration* in the *Triennial Act Considered. London.* R. *Burleigh.* Price 3d. (8vo. pp. 22.) . . . . April, 1716

177.* *Mercurius Politicus :* Being Monthly Observations on the Affairs of Great Britain ; With a Collection of the Most Material Occurrences. [For the Month of May.] By a Lover of Old England. *London.* Printed and Sold by J. *Morphew.* Price one Shilling. (8vo. pp. 96.) [Continued probably later than Sept. 1720). . . . . . May, 1716, to Sept. 1720

178.* *Dormer's News Letter* (conducted by Daniel Defoe for some time. I have found no Copies of this Journal, and, therefore, can give no farther particulars.) *Each Number one Sheet Small Folio.* . . . . June, 1716, to Aug. 1718

179. *Memoirs* of the *Church* of *Scotland,* in 4 Periods. I. The Church in her Infant State, from the Reformation to Queen Mary's Abdication. II. The Church in its Growing State, from the Abdication to the Restoration. III. The Church in its Perse-cuted State, from the Restoration to the Revolution. IV. The Church in its Present State, from the Revolution to the Union. With an Appendix of Some Transactions since the Union. *London. Eman. Matthews.* (8vo. Title and Preface 2 leaves, pp. 232 and 196. Appendix, pp. 9.) . . 26 April, 1717

180.* A Short *Narrative* of the *Life* and *Death* of *John Rhinholdt,* Count *Patkul,* A NOBLEMAN of *Livonia,* who was broke Alive upon the Wheel in *Great Poland,* anno 1707. Together with the manner of his Execution. Written by the Lutheran Minister, who assisted him in his last Hours. Faithfully Trans-lated Out of a High Dutch Manuscript ; and now published for the Information of Count Gyllenborg's English Friends. By L. M. The Second Edition. London. Printed for T. Good-win, Fleet Street. Price 1s. (8vo. 2 leaves, & pp. 59.) April, 1717

181. *Minutes* of the *Negociations* of Mons. *Mesnager,* at the Court of England, Towards the Close of the last Reign. Wherein some of the Most Secret Transactions of that Time, relating to the Interest of the PRETENDER, and a Clandestine Separate Peace are detected and laid open. Written by himself. Done out of French. London. S. Baker. (8vo. pp. 326.)

1st Edition, 17 June, 1717
2nd Edition, 1717
3rd Edition, 8 July, 1731
4th Edition, 1736

182. A *Declaration* of *Truth* to *Benjamin Hoadley,* one of the *High Priests* of the *Land,* and of the Degree whom Men Call *Bishops.* By a Ministering *Friend* who writ to *Tho. Bradbury,* a Dealer in Many Words. London. Printed for E. Moore. Price Six Pence. (8vo. pp. 31.) 1717

183.* The *Weekly Journal ;* or, *Saturday's Post* (Mist's). [*Defoe* first found in it at No. 37, and Continued to No. 101, 15 Nov. 1718. *Defoe* again connected with *Mist's Journal,* 31 January, 1719, and continued its Management, writing Letters Introductory until the beginning of July, 1720; after which he only Watched the Paper, and translated the Articles on Foreign Affairs, and Occasionally Contributed Articles.] (Each Number 1½ Sheets. Small Folio.) 24 August, 1717, to 15 Nov. 1718. 3 Jan. 1719 to July, 1720; and Occasionally afterward, until 24 Oct. 1724

184. A Curious Little Oration, Delivered by Father Andrew, concerning the Great Quarrels that divide the Clergy of France. Translated from the Fourth Edition of the French, by Dan. D. F——e. (8vo. pp. 20.). . . . . 1st Edition, 1717
2nd Edition, 1717

185.*Memoirs of Publick Transactions in the Life and Ministry of his Grace the D. of Shrewsbury. In which will be found much of the History of Parties, and especially of Court Divisions, during the last Four Reigns; which no History has yet given an Account of. *Plus valet occulatus Testis quam Aurite Decem.* London. Printed for Tho. Warner, at the Black Boy, in Paternoster Row, 1718. Price Two Shillings. (8vo. Title and Preface 2 leaves & pp. 139.) . . . . 6th May, 1718

186.*The Case of the War in Italy Stated. Being a Serious Enquiry, how far Great Britain is Engaged to concern itself in the Quarrel between the Emperor and the King of Spain. *Pax Quæritur Bello.* London. T. Warner. Price 6d. (8vo. Title & pp. 34.) 1718

187. Memoirs of the Life and Eminent Conduct of that Learned and Reverend Divine, Daniel Williams, D.D. With some Account of his Scheme, for the Vigorous Propagation of Religion, as well in England as in Scotland, and several other Parts of the World. Address'd to Mr. Peirce. London. Printed for E. Curll. Price 2s. 6d. Bound. (8vo. Title & pp. 86.) 1718

188. The Family Instructor. In Two Parts. I. Relating to Family Breaches, and their obstructing Religious Duties. II. To the Great Mistake of mixing the Passions, in the Managing and Correcting of Children. With a great Variety of Cases of Setting Ill Examples to Children. Vol. II. (12mo. Title & Pref. vi. pp. 404.) . . . . 1st Edition, 1718
(12mo. pp. viii. & 384.) . . . . 8th Edition, 1766

189.*The Whitehall Evening Post. (Commenced and Edited by Defoe. Published every Tuesday, Thursday, and Saturday. He continued to write in it occasionally until June 1720.) (2 leaves small 4to.) . . . . . . 18 Sept. 1718 to June, 1720

190.*A Friendly Rebuke to One Parson Benjamin; Particularly Relating to his Quarrelling with his own Church, and Vindicating Dissenters. By one of the People called Quakers. London. Printed for *E. Moor*, near St. Pauls. Price 6d. (8vo. pp. 32.)
10 Jan. 1719

191. The Life and Strange Surprizing Adventures of Robinson Crusoe, of York, Mariner: Who lived eight and twenty Years all alone, on an uninhabited Island on the Coast of America, near the Mouth of the Great River of Oroonoque; Having been Cast on Shore by Shipwreck, wherein all the Men perished but himself. With an Account how he was at last Strangely delivered by Pyrates. Written by Himself. London. Printed for W. Taylor, at the Ship, in Paternoster Row. (8vo. Frontispiece. Title and Preface 2 leaves & pp. 364.) . 1st Edition, 25 April, 1719
(8vo. Frontispiece. Title and Preface 2 leaves & pp. 364.)
2nd Edition, 12 May, 1719
3rd Edition, 6 June, 1719
4th Edition, 8 Aug. 1719

192. The *Farther Adventures* of *Robinson Crusoe.* Being the *Second* and *Last Part* of his *Life*, and of the *Strange Surprizing Accounts* of his *Travels* Round three *Parts* of the *Globe.* Written by Himself. To which is added a Map of the World, in which is Delineated the *Voyages of Robinson Crusoe. London.* Printed for W. Taylor, at the Ship in *Paternoster Row.* (8vo. Map, Title, Preface and Advertisements 4 leaves & pp. 373.)
1st Edition, 20 Aug. 1719

193. *Serious Reflections* during the Life and Surprizing Adventures of Robinson Crusoe. With his Vision of the *Angelick World.* Written by Himself. *London.* Printed for *W. Taylor* at the Ship in Paternoster Row. (8vo. Frontispiece, Title, Preface, and Introduction 8 leaves & pp. 270, and 84.) . 1st Edition, 6 Aug. 1720
1st and 2nd Vols. Reprinted in the *Original London Post* or Heathcote's Intelligencer . . . 7 Oct. 1719 to 19 Oct. 1720
1st Vol. spuriously abridged, and published by T. Cox at the *Amsterdam Coffee House* in *London* before the . . 7th August, 1719
  5.   First Abridgement in 1 Vol (8vo.) . 5th Edition, 19 Nov. 1720
  6.   In 2 Volumes . . . 6th Edition, 28 Oct. 1721
  7.   An Abridged Edition in 1 Vol. . . . 28 Feb. 1722
  8 Another Edition in 2 Volumes with 14 Copper Plates called 6th Edition . . . . 5 June, 1722
  9.   In 2 Volumes, called 7th Edition 27 Aug. 1726

194. *Some *Account* of the *Life* and most *Remarkable Actions* of *Henry*, *Baron de Goertz, Minister* to the late *King* of *Sweden. London.* Printed for *T. Bickerton.* (8vo. Portrait, Title, & pp. 46.)
About May, 1719

195. *The Daily Post.* [Commenced and Edited by *Daniel Defoe.* Continued connected with it, writing occasionally, until 27 April, 1725.] (Each Number one Leaf small folio.) 4 Oct. 1719 to 27 Ap. 1725

196. A *Letter* to the *Dissenters. London. J. Roberts.* Price 6d. (8vo. pp. 27.) . . . . . . About May, 1719

197. *The *Anatomy* of *Exchange Alley ;* or a System of Stock-Jobbing; proving that Scandalous Trade, as it is now carried on, to be knavish in its private Practice, and Treason in its Publick. Being a Clear Detection. I. Of the private Cheats, used to deceive one another. II. Of their Arts to draw Innocent Families into their Snare, understood by their new Term of Art, viz., being let into the Secret. III. Of their Raising and Spreading false News, to ground the Rise or Fall of Stocks upon. IV. Of the Dangerous Consequences of their Practices, and the necessity there is to Regulate or Suppress them. To which is added some Characters of the most Eminent Persons concern'd now, and for some Years past, in carrying on this pernicious Trade. By a Jobber. Printed for E. Smith near Exchange Alley, and Thomas Warner in Paternoster Row. Price 1s.
(8vo. Title & pp. 64.) . . . 1st Edition, 11 July, 1719
2nd Edition, 26 Mar. 1720

198. The Dumb Philosopher : or, Great Britains Wonder, containing I. A Faithful and very Surprising Account, how Dickory Cronke, a Tinner's Son, in the County of Cornwall, was born Dumb, and continued so for 58 years; and how, some Days before he Died, he came to his Speech. With Memoirs of his Life, and the manner of his Death. II. A Declaration of his Faith and Principles in Religion : With a Collection of Select Meditations composed in his Retirement. III. His Prophetical Observations upon the Affairs of Europe, more particularly of Great

Britain, from 1720 to 1729. The whole extracted from his original Papers, and confirmed by unquestionable authority. To which is annexed, His Elegy, written by a young Cornish Gentleman, of Exeter Coll. in Oxford. With an Epitaph by another Hand. London. Printed for T. Bickerton. Price one Shilling. (8vo. pp. 64.) . . . 1st Edition, 14 Oct. 1719
2nd Edition, 27 May, 1720

199.*Charity still a Christian Virtue : or, an Impartial Account of the Tryal and Conviction of the Reverend Mr. Hendley, for Preaching a Charity Sermon at Chisselhurst. And of Mr. Campman, and Mr. Harding, for Collecting at the same Time the Alms of the Congregation. At the Assizes held at Rochester, on Wednesday, July 15, 1719. Offer'd to the Consideration of the Clergy of the Church of England. London. Printed for T. Bickerton, at the Crown in Pater-Noster Row, 1719. (Price One Shilling.) (8vo. *Frontispiece*. Title and Preface 2 leaves & pp. 72.) . 16 Oct. 1719

200.*The King of Pirates : Being an Account of the Famous Enterprizes of Captain Avery, the Mock King of Madagascar ; with his Rambles and Piracies, wherein all the Sham Accounts formerly published of him are detected. In two Letters from himself, one during his Stay at Madagascar, and one since his Escape from thence. London. A. Bettesworth. Price 1s. 6d. (8vo. Title and Preface pp. vi. and 93.) . 1st Edition, 10 Dec. 1719
(Collation the same) . . . 2nd Edition, 1720

201.*The Chimera : or, The French Way of Paying National Debts Laid Open. Being an Impartial Account of the Proceedings in France for Raising a Paper Credit, and Settling the Mississippi Stock. London, T. Warner. Price One Shilling. (8vo. Title & pp. 76.) . . . . About Jan. 1720

202. The History of the Life and Adventures of Mr. Duncan Campbell. A Gentleman, who though born Deaf and Dumb, writes down any Stranger's Name at First Sight ; and their Future Contingencies of Fortune. Now living in Exeter Court, over against the Savoy in the Strand. London, E. Curll. (8vo. Portrait, Title, Dedication, and Contents xxiv. & pp. 320. 4 Plates.)
1st Edition, 30 April, 1720

203.*Mr. Campbell's Pacquet, for the Entertainment of Gentlemen and Ladies, Containing, I. Verses to Mr. Campbell, Occasioned by the History of his Life and Adventures. By Mrs. Fowke, Mr. Philips, &c. II. The Parallel, a Poem comparing the Poetical Productions of Mr. Pope, with the Prophetical Predictions of Mr. Campbell. By Capt. Stanhope. III. An Account of a Most Surprising Apparition ; sent from Launceston in Cornwall. Attested by the Rev. Mr. Ruddle, Minister there. London, Printed for T. Bickerton, at the Crown in Paternoster Row. (8vo. Title, & pp. 33.) [Section III., by Defoe.] 18 June, 1720
The History of the Life and Adventures of Mr. Duncan Campbell, (with the Pacquet included.) London. E. Curll. (8vo. Portrait & Plates. Title &c. xxiv. Pacquet pp. 33. Life pp. 320.)
2nd Edition, 4 Aug. 1720
2nd Edition reissued 14 Mar. 1721

The Supernatural Philosopher : or, the Mysteries of Magick, in all its Branches clearly unfolded, Containing, I. An Argument proving the Perception, which Mankind have by all the senses, of Demons, Genii, or Familiar Spirits ; and of the Several species of them, both Good and Bad. II. A Philosophical Discourse, concerning the Second Sight, demonstrating it to be Hereditary

to some Families. III. A full Answer to all Objections that
can be brought against the existence of Spirits, Witches, &c.
IV. Of Divination by Dreams, Omens, Spectres, Apparitions
after Death, Predictions, &c. V. Of Enchantment, Necromancy,
Geomancy, Hydromancy, Æromancy, Pyromancy, Chiromancy,
Augury, and Aruspicy. All Exemplified in the History of the
Life and Surprizing Adventures of Mr. Duncan Campbell, a
Scots Gentleman, who though Deaf and Dumb writes down any
Stranger's Name at first Sight, with their Future Contingencies
of Fortune. Collected and Compiled from the most approved
Authorities, wherein is inserted that most celebrated Tract
written by Dr. Wallis, The Method of Teaching Deaf and
Dumb Persons to read, write, and understand a Language. By
William Bond, of Bury St. Edmond's, Suffolk. London. E. Curll.
(8vo. Collation as 2nd Edition, except New Title and the
Portrait omitted) . . . . 3rd Edition, 1728
(This was again reissued as a 2nd Edition) 4th Edition, 21 Dec. 1728

204. *Memoirs* of a *Cavalier :* or a Military Journal of the Wars in Ger-
many, and the Wars in England. From the Year 1632, to the
Year 1648. Written threescore years ago, by an *English* Gen-
tleman, who served first in the Army of *Gustavus Adolphus*, the
Glorious King of *Sweden*, till his Death, and after that in the
Royal Army of King Charles the First, from the Beginning of
the Rebellion to the End of the War. London. Printed for
A. Bell, at the *Cross Keys* in *Cornhill, J. Osborn*, at the *Oxford
Arms* in *Lombard Street, W. Taylor* at the *Ship and Swan*, and
T. Warner, at the *Black Boy* in *Paternoster Row.*
1st Edition, 21 May, 1720
(Leeds, James Lister). (8vo. Title, and Preface, 6 leaves, & pp.
338.) . . . . 2nd Edit

205. The Life, Adventures, and Piracies of the Famous *Captain Singleton :* Containing an Account of his being set on Shore in the
Island of *Madagascar*, his Settlement there, with a Description
of the Place and Inhabitants : Of his Passage from thence in a
Paraguay, to the Main Land of Africa, with an Account of the
Customs and Manners of the People : His great Deliverances
from the Barbarous Natives and Wild Beasts : Of his meeting
with an *Englishman*, a citizen of *London*, amongst the *Indians.*
The great Riches he Acquired, and his Voyage Home to *England.* As also Captain *Singleton's* Return to Sea, with an
Account of his many Adventures, and Pyracies with the famous
Captain *Avery*, and others. London. Printed for *J. Brotherton*,
at the *Black Bull*, in *Cornhill, J. Graves*, in *St. James's Street,
A. Dodd*, at the *Peacock*, without *Temple-bar*, and *T. Warner*, at
the *Black Boy* in *Paternoster Row.* (8vo. Title & pp. 344.)
1st Edition, 4 June, 1720
Reissued in the Post Master or Loyal Mercury, Exeter,
4 Nov. 1720, and following weeks.
Printed and Sold by Nath. Mist, in Great Carter *Lane.*
2nd Edition, 9 Sept. 1721

206. *Applebee's Original Weekly* Journal. [Established in 1714. *Daniel
Defoe* began to write weekly articles, and to assist in the management, and continued to do so nearly six years. The Journal
continued long afterward.] . . 25 June, 1720, to 12 Mar. 1726

207. *The Director. [Defoe wrote Leading Articles in it, but whether
he was the responsible Editor or not I cannot say.] No. I.
published 5 Oct. 1720 . . . . 5 Oct. 1720

208. The Compleat Art of Painting. A Poem. Translated from the
French of M. Du Fresnoy. By D. F., Gent. London. T. Warner. Price One Shilling. (8vo. Title & pp. 53.) . . . 1720

209.*A Vindication of the Honour and Justice of Parliament against
a most Scandalous Libel, Entituled the Speech of John A—— Esq.
London. Printed for A. More, near St. Paul's, and Sold by the
Booksellers of London and Westminster. Price Six Pence. *n. d.*
(Title and Preface 2 leaves & pp. 36.) . . . . Feb. 1721

210.*A Collection of Miscellany Letters, selected out of Mist's Weekly
Journal [12mo, (Vol. I. Title and Dedication 4 leaves, Preface
xiv., Contents 4 leaves & pp. 310.) (Vol. II. Title, &c., xii. pp.
332, Contents 4 leaves.)]
        * Contains many Letters written by Defoe . 9 Jan. 1722

211. The Fortunes and Misfortunes of the Famous Moll Flanders, &c.,
who was born in Newgate, and during a Life of continued Variety, for Threescore Years, beside her Childhood, was Twelve
Years a Whore, Five Times a Wife (whereof once to her own
Brother,) Twelve Years a Thief, Eight Years a Transported Felon
in Virginia, at last grew Rich, liv'd Honest, and died a Penitent.
Written from her own Memorandums. London. W. Chetwood,
1721. (8vo. pp. xiii. & 424.) . . 1st Edition, 27 Jan. 1722
London. J. Brotherton. (8vo. 4 leaves &
pp. 366.) . . . . . . 2nd Edition, 23 July, 1722
London. W. Chetwood. (8vo. 4 leaves &
pp. 366.) . . . . . . 3rd Edition, 21 Dec. 1722
An Abridged Edition (for the Pocket). Lon-
don, J. Read . . . . 4th Edition, 13 July, 1723
A Reissue of the 3rd Edition . . . . 2 Nov. 1723

212. Religious Courtship : Being Historical Discourses on the Necessity of Marrying Religious Husbands and Wives only. As also
of Husbands and Wives being of the same Opinions in Religion
with one Another. With an Appendix of the Necessity of taking
none but Religious Servants, and a Proposal for the better Managing of Servants. London. E. Matthews. (8vo. 4 leaves &
pp. 358.) . . . . 20 Feb. 1722

213. A Journal of the Plague Year : Being Observations or Memorials
of the most Remarkable Occurrences, as well Publick as Private,
which happened in London during the last Great Visitation in
1665. Written by a Citizen, who continued all the while in
London. Never made publick before. London. Printed for E.
Nutt, &c. (8vo. 3 leaves & pp. 287.) . 1st Edition, 17 Mar. 1722
The History of the Great Plague in London, in the Year 1665.
Containing Observations and Memorials of the most Remarkable
Occurrences, both Publick and Private, that happened during that
dreadful Period. By a Citizen who lived the Whole Time in
London. To which is added a Journal of the Plague at Mar-
seilles, in the Year 1720. London. T. and J. Noble. (8vo. Title
& pp. 376.) . . . . 2nd Edition, 1754

214.*The *Life* and *Actions* of *Lewis Dominique Cartouche,* who was broke
alive upon the wheel at Paris, Nov. 28, 1721, *N.S.,* Relating at
large his remarkable *Adventures, Desperate Enterprises,* and Various *Escapes.* With an Account of his Behaviour under Sentence, and upon the Scaffold, and the Manner of his Execution.
Translated from the French. *London. J. Roberts.* Price 1s. 6d.
(8vo. pp. 88.) . . . . 27 April, 1722

215. The *History* and *Remarkable Life* of the truly Honourable *Colonel Jacque,* vulgarly called *Col. Jack,* who was born a *Gentleman ;*

put 'Prentice to a *Pickpocket;* was six and twenty years a *Thief*, and then kidnapped to *Virginia;* came back a *Merchant;* was five times married to four *Whores;* went into the Wars, behaved bravely, got Preferment, was made Colonel of a *Regiment;* came over, and fled with the *Chevalier,* is still abroad Completing a Life of *Wonders*, and resolves to die a *General.* London. *J. Brotherton*, &c. &c.) 8vo. Title and Preface, pp. vii. & pp. 399.)

             1st Edition, 20 Dec. 1722
 (8vo. Title and Preface 4 leaves & pp.
  399.) . . . . 2nd Edition 19 Jan. 1723
 (8vo. Title and Preface 4 leaves & pp.
  399.) . . . . . 3rd Edition, 1724

216.* An *Impartial History* of the *Life* and *Actions* of *Peter Alexowitz* the present *Czar* of *Muscovy:* From his *Birth* down to this present *Time.* Giving an Account of his *Travels* and *Transactions* in the *Several Courts* of *Europe.* With his *Attempts* and *Successes* in the *Northern* and *Eastern Parts* of the World. In which is intermixed the *History* of *Muscovy.* Written by a *British Officer* in the Service of the *Czar.* London. Printed for *W. Chetwood*, at *Cato's Head* in *Russel-Street*, Covent Garden; *J. Stagg* in Westminster Hall; *J. Brotherton* at the Bible, near the Royal Exchange; and *T. Edlin*, at the Princes Arms, over against Exeter Exchange in the Strand. Price bound 5s. (8vo. Title & pp. 420.) 1723

217.* The *Highland Rogue*, or the Memorable *Actions* of the celebrated *Robert Macgregor;* commonly called *Rob Roy.* Containing a Genuine *Account* of his Education, *Grandeur*, and sudden *Misfortune;* his commencing *Robber*, and being elected *Captain* of a formidable Gang; his exploits on the Highway, breaking open *Houses*, taking *Prisoners;* commencing Judge, and Levying Taxes; his Defence of his Manner of Living: his Dispute with a Scotch Parson upon Predestination; his joining with the *Earl of Mar* in the *Rebellion;* his being decoy'd, and imprison'd by the Duke of ——, with the Manner of his Escape, &c. Introduced with the Relation of the Unequall'd Villainies of the Clan of the Mac Gregors several Years past. The whole impartially digested from the Memorandums of an Authentick Scotch MS. London. *J. Billingsby*, &c. &c. Price 1s. (8vo. pp. 63.) 5 Oct. 1723

218. The *Fortunate Mistress:* or, a *History of the Life and Vast Variety of Fortunes of Mademoiselle de' Belau;* afterwards called the Countess of Wintselsheim, in Germany. Being the Person known by the name of the *Lady Roxana*, in the Time of King Charles II. London. *T. Warner*, &c. (8vo. Frontispiece, Title, and Preface 3 leaves, & pp. 407.) 1st Edition, 14 March, 1724

219. The *Great Law* of *Subordination* Consider'd; or, The Insolence, and Unsufferable Behaviour of Servants in England, duly enquired into. Illustrated with a great Variety of Examples, Historical Cases and Remarkable Stories of the Behaviour of some particular Servants, Suited to all the Several Arguments made use of as they go on. In Ten Familiar Letters. Together with a Conclusion, being an Earnest and Moving Remonstrance, to the Housekeepers and Heads of Families in Great Britain, pressing them not to cease using their Utmost Interest, (especially at this Juncture,) to obtain sufficient Laws, for the effectual Regulation of the Manners and Behaviour of their Servants. As also a Proposal, containing such Heads, or Constitutions, as would effectually answer this great End, and bring Servants of

every Class to a just (and yet not a Grievous,) Regulation. *London.* *S. Harding,* and other Booksellers. *Price Three Shillings and Six Pence.* (8vo. Title and Preface 2 leaves & pp. 302.) . . . . 1st Edition, 4 April, 1724

The *Behaviour* of *Servants* in *England,* Inquired into. With a Proposal containing Such Heads or Constitutions as would effectually answer this Great End, and Bring Servants of every Class to a Just Regulation. *London.* H. Whittridge, under the Royal Exchange. Price, *2s.* Stitcht, or *3s.* Bound. (8vo. Title & pp. 302. In fact the sheets of the previous Edition, with suppression of Preface, and Change of Title.) . 2nd Edition, no date.

220. A *Tour* thro' the *whole Island* of *Great Britain;* divided into Circuits or Journies. Giving a Particular and Diverting Account of whatever is Curious and worth Observation, viz. :—I. A Description of the Principal Cities and Towns, their Situation, Magnitude, Government, and Commerce. II. The Customs, Manners, Speech; as also the Exercises, Diversions, and Employment of the People. III. The Produce and Improvements of the Land, the Trade and Manufactures. IV. The Seaports and Fortifications, with the Course of Rivers, and the Inland Navigation. V. The Publick Edifices, Seats and Palaces, of the Gentry and Nobility. With useful Observations on the whole. Particularly fitted for the Reading of Such, as desire to Travel over the Island. By a Gentleman. *London.* *G. Strahan.* (8vo. Plate of the Siege of Colchester in 1648. Title and Preface, vii. & pp. 140, 121, and 127.) . . Vol. I., 1st Edition, 22 May, 1724

221. —— With a Map of England and Wales, by Mr. Moll. (8vo. Map, Title, and Preface, viii. & pp. 192 and 200. Index to Vols 1 and 2, pp. xxxvi.) . . Vol. II., 1st Edition, 8 June, 1725

222. —— Which completes this Work, and contains a Tour thro' Scotland, &c. With a Map of Scotland, by Mr. Moll. (8vo. Map, Title, and Preface 3 leaves & pp. 239 and 230. Index 2 leaves.) . . . Vol. III., 1st Edition, 13 Aug. 1726
Complete . . . 3 Vols., 2nd Edition, 15 June, 1727

223.*A *Narrative* of the *Proceedings* in *France,* for Discovering and Detecting the Murderers of the English Gentlemen, September 21, 1723, Near Calais. With an Account of the Condemnation and Sentence of Joseph Bizeau and Peter Le Febvre, Two Notorious Robbers, who were the principal Actors in the said Murder; particularly in the Killing Mr. Lock. Together with their Discovery and manner of perpetrating that execrable Murder; and also large Memoirs of their Behaviour during their Torture, and upon the Scaffold; their impeaching Several other Criminals, and a brief History of their Past Crimes, as well in Company with their former Captain, the famous Cartouche, as Since his Execution. In which is a great Variety of Remarkable Incidents, and Surprizing Circumstances, never yet made Publick. Translated from the French. *London:* Printed for *J. Roberts,* in Warwick Lane. Price 2s. (8vo. pp. 108.) . . 17 Aug. 1724

224.*The *History* of the *Remarkable Life of John Sheppard.* Containing a Particular Account of his Many Robberies and Escapes, &c., &c. Including his last Escape from the Castle, at Newgate. Printed and Published by John Applebee, in Black Friars. Price one Shilling. (8vo.pp. .) . . . 1st Edition, 19 Oct. 1724
2nd Edition, 26 Oct. 1724
3rd Edition, 12 Nov. 1724

225.* A *Narrative* of all the *Robberies, Escapes,* &c. of *John Sheppard,*
Giving an Exact Description of the Manner of his Wonderful
Escape from the Castle in Newgate, and of the Methods he
took afterward for his Security. Written by *himself* during his
Confinement in the *Middle Stone Room,* after his being retaken
in Drury Lane. To which is Prefix'd a true Representation of
his Escape, from the condemned Hold, Curiously Engraven on a
Copper Plate. The whole Published at the particular request
of the Prisoner. London. Printed and Sold by *John Applebee,*
&c. in Black Friars. Price 6d. (8vo. front. pp. 31.)

1st Edition,	17 Nov. 1724
2nd Edition,	18 Nov. 1724
3rd Edition,	19 Nov. 1724
4th Edition,	20 Nov. 1724
5th Edition,	21 Nov. 1724
6th Edition,	28 Nov. 1724
7th Edition,	12 Dec. 1724

226. A *New Voyage Round* the *World,* By a *Course* never Sailed *before.*
Being a Voyage undertaken by some Merchants, who afterwards
proposed the setting up of an East India Company in Flanders.
Illustrated with Copper Plates. *London.* A. *Bettesworth.* (8vo.
Plates. Title & pp. 208 and 205.) . . . . 8 May, 1725

227. *Everybody's Business* is *Nobody's Business;* or, Private *Abuses,
Publick Grievances.* Exemplified in the Pride, Insolence, and
Exorbitant Wages of our Women Servants, Footmen, &c. By
Andrew Moreton, Esq. . . . .

	1st Edition,	5 June, 1725
	2nd Edition,	9 June, 1725
(8vo. pp. 34) . . .	3rd Edition,	14 June, 1725
	4th Edition,	19 June, 1725
(With the addition of a Preface)	5th Edition,	24 July, 1725
Reprinted		1767

228.* The *True, Genuine,* and *Perfect Account* of the *Life* and *Actions*
of *Jonathan Wild.* Taken from good Authority, and from his
own Writings. Printed and Published by J. Applebee, in Black
Friars. (8vo.) . . . . .

1st Edition,	8 June, 1725
2nd Edition,	10 June, 1725
3rd Edition,	12 June, 1725

229.* An *Account* of the *Conduct* and *Proceedings* of the late *John Gow,*
alias Smith, Captain of the late *Pirates,* executed for Murther
and Piracy, committed on Board the *George Galley,* afterwards
called the *Revenge;* with a Relation of all the horrid Murthers
they committed in Cold Blood. As also of their being taken at
the Islands of Orkney, and sent up prisoners to London.
London. Printed and Sold by J. *Applebee,* in *Black Fryers.*
Price 1s. (8vo. Title, &c. viii. pp. 62.) . . . 11 June, 1725

230. The *Complete English Tradesman,* In Familiar Letters, Directing
him in all the several Parts and Progressions of Trade—viz. I.
His acquainting himself with Business during his Apprenticeship. II. His Writing to his Correspondents, and obtaining a
general Knowledge of Trade, as well what he is not as what he
is employ'd in. III. Of Diligence, and Application, as the Life
of all Business. IV. Cautions against Over-Trading. V. Of
the ordinary Occasions of a Tradesman's Ruin; such as Expensive Living,—Too early Marrying,—Innocent Diversions,—
Giving and Taking too much Credit,—Leaving Business to
Servants,—Being above Business,—Entering into Dangerous
Partnerships, &c. VI. Directions in the several Distresses of

a Tradesman, when he comes to fail. VII. Of Tradesmen Compounding with their Debtors, and why they are so particularly severe. VIII. Of Tradesmen ruining one another, by Rumour and Scandal. IX. Of the Customary Frauds of Trade, which even honest Men allow themselves to practise. X. Of Credit, and how it is only supported by Honesty. XI. Directions for Book-keeping, punctual paying Bills, and thereby maintaining Credit. XII. Of the Dignity and Honour of Trade, in *England*, more than in other Countries; and how the Trading Families in *England* are mingled with the Nobility and Gentry, so as not to be separated, or distinguished. Calculated for the Instruction of Our Inland Tradesmen, and especially of Young Beginners. London. Charles Rivington. (Title & Preface xv, Contents 1 leaf & pp. 447.)   1st Edition, 11 Sept. 1725
Reissued, 1726

(Title as before to Section XII.) The Second Edition. To which is added a Supplement, Containing—I. A Warning against Tradesmen's Borrowing Money upon Interest. II. A Caution against that Destructive Practice, of drawing and Remitting, as also discounting Promissory Bills, meerly for a supply of Cash. III. Directions for the Tradesman's accounts, with brief but plain Examples, and Specimens for Book-keeping. IV. Of keeping a Duplicate, or Pocket Ledger, in Case of Fire. London. Printed for Charles Rivington, at the Bible and Crown in St. Paul's Churchyard. (Title, Preface, and Contents, xx, & pp. 368. Supplement, 148.)
2nd Edition, 10 Sept. 1726
(*Supplement may be had alone. Price 1s.)
Reissued, 1727

231. The *Compleat English Tradesman*. VOLUME II. In two Parts. Part I. Directed chiefly to the more Experienc'd Tradesmen; with Cautions and Advices to them after they are thriven, and suppos'd to be grown rich, viz. I. Against Running out of their Business into needless Projects, and Dangerous Adventures, no Tradesman being above Disaster. II. Against Oppressing one another by Engrossing, Underselling, Combinations in Trade, &c. III. Advices, that when he leaves off his Business, he should part Friends with the World; the great Advantages of it; with a Word of the Scandalous Character of a Purse-proud Tradesman. IV. Against being litigious and Vexatious, and apt to go to Law for Trifles; with some Reasons why Tradesmen's Differences should if possible all be ended by Arbitration. Part II. Being useful Generals in Trade, describing the Principles and Foundation of the Home Trade of Great Britain, with Large Tables of our Manufactures, Calculations of the Product, Shipping, Carriage of Goods by Land, Importation from Abroad, Consumption at Home, &c. by all which the infinite number of our Tradesmen are employ'd, and the General Wealth of the Nation rais'd and increas'd. The whole calculated for the use of our Inland Tradesmen, as well in the City, as in the Country. London. Printed for *Charles Rivington* at the Bible and Crown in St. Paul's Churchyard. (Title, Preface and Contents xiv. & pp. 298 and 176.) . . . . . 1st Edition, 13 May, 1727
Compleat. In 2 Volumes . . 2nd Edition, 10 Aug. 1728

232. The *Friendly Dæmon;* or, the Generous Apparition. Being a True Narrative of a Miraculous Cure newly performed upon that famous Deaf and Dumb Gentleman, Dr. Duncan Campbell,

By a familiar Spirit, that appeared to him in a white surplice, like a Cathedral Singing Boy. *London. J. Roberts.* (8vo. pp. 39. Pp. 13 to 38, by Defoe.) 1726

233. The *Political History* of the *Devil, As* well *Ancient* as Modern. In two Parts. I. Containing a State of the Devil's Circumstances, and the Various Turns in his affairs, from his Expulsion out of Heaven, to the Creation of Man. With remarks on the Several Mistakes concerning the Reason and Manner of his Fall. Also his Proceedings with Mankind, ever since Adam, to the first planting of the Christian Religion in the World. Part II. Containing his more Private Conduct down to the present Times; His Government, his Appearances, his Manner of Working, and the Tools he Works with. *London. T. Warner.* (8vo. Frontispiece, Title, Dedication and Contents 4 leaves, & pp. 408.) . . . . 1st Edition, 7 May, 1726
(8vo. Frontispiece, Title, Preface and Contents 4 leaves pp. 408.)
2nd Edition, 20 April, 1727
Westminster. J. Brindley (8vo. Front. Title, Ded. & Preface 4 leaves & pp. 408.). . . . . 3rd Edition, 1734

234. *Mere Nature Delineated ;* or, a *Body* without a *Soul.* Being Observations upon the young Forester lately brought to Town from Germany. With Suitable Applications. Also a Brief Dissertation upon the Usefulness and necessity of Fools, whether Political or Natural. Price 1s. 6d. *London. T. Warner.* (8vo. 2 leaves & pp. 123.) . . . . 23 July, 1726

235. An *Essay* upon *Literature ;* or, an Enquiry into the Antiquity and Original of Letters. Proving that the two Tables, written by the Finger of God in Mount Sinai, was the first Writing in the World; and that all other Alphabets derive from the Hebrew. With a short view of the methods made use of by the Ancients to supply the want of Letters before, and improve the use of them, after they were known. *London. Thos. Bowles.* (8vo. Title & pp. 127.) 1726

236. A *General History* of the *Principal Discoveries* and *Improvements* in *Useful Arts.* Particularly in the Great Branches of Commerce, Navigation, and Plantation in all Parts of the known World, &c. *London. J. Roberts.* (Complete in Four Monthly Parts. 8vo. Title and Preface viii., pp. 307, and General Index & pp. 5.) . . . . Oct. 1726 to Jan. 1727

237. The *Protestant Monastery,* or, a Complaint against the Brutality of the Present Age. Particularly the Pertness, and Insolence of our Youth to Aged Persons. With a Caution to People in Years how they give the Staff out of their own Hands, and leave themselves to the Mercy of others. Concluding with a Proposal for Erecting a Protestant Monastery, where Persons of small Fortune may End their Days in Plenty, Ease and Credit, without Burthening their Relations, or accepting Publick Charities. By *Andrew Moreton,* Esq., Author of Everybody's Business is Nobody's Business. London. W. Meadows, 1727. Price 6d. (8vo. Title and Preface viii, & pp. 31.) . . . 19 Nov. 1726
Reissued, 1727

238. A *System* of *Magick ;* or, a History of the *Black Art.* Being an Historical Account of Mankind's most early Dealings with the Devil, and how the Acquaintance on both Sides first began. *London. J. Roberts.* (8vo. Front. Title, Preface & Contents 5 leaves & pp. 403.) . . . . 1st Edition, 19 Dec. 1726
With additions . . . 2nd Edition, 16 Jan. 1731

239. *The *Evident Approach* of *a War :* and Something of the Necessity
of it, in order to Establish Peace and Preserve Trade. *Pax
Quæritur Bello.* To which is added an Exact Plan and Descrip-
tion of the Bay and City of Gibraltar. *London,* J. Roberts.
Price 1s. 6d. (8vo. Plan. 2 leaves & pp. 59.)   .   . Jan. 1727
240. *Conjugal Lewdness :* or, *Matrimonial Whoredom,* &c. &c. *London.
T. Warner.* (8vo. Title, Preface, & Contents 4 leaves & pp. 406.)
                                                        30 Jan. 1727
[Reissued with the following Title, but collation as before.]
A Treatise concerning the Use and Abuse of the Marriage Bed.
Shewing—I. The Nature of Matrimony, its Sacred Original, and
the True Meaning of its Institution. II. The gross abuse of
Matrimonial Chastity from the wrong Notions which have pos-
sessed the World, degenerating even to Whoredom. III. The
Diabolical practice of attempting to prevent Childbearing by
Physical Preparations. IV. The Fatal Consequences of Clan-
destine, or forced Marriages, thro' the Persuasion, Interest, or
Influence of Parents and Relations, to wed the Person they have
no love for, but oftentimes an Aversion to. V. Of Unequal
Matches as to the Disproportion of Age; and how such many
Ways occasion a Matrimonial Whoredom. VI. How married
Persons may be guilty of *Conjugal Lewdness,* and that a Man may
in *effect,* make a Whore of his own Wife. Also many other
Particulars of Family Concern. *London. T. Warner.* (8vo.
Title, Preface, & Contents 4 leaves & pp. 4c6.) .   . 10 June, 1727
241. An *Essay* on the *History* and *Reality of Apparitions.* Being an
Account of What they are, and What they are not; Whence
they Come, and Whence they Come not; As also how we may
distinguish the Apparitions of Good and Evil Spirits, and how we
ought to behave to them. With a great Variety of Surprising
and Diverting Examples, never published before. London.
J. Roberts. (8vo. Front. and Plates. Title, Preface, and Contents 6 leaves, & pp. 395.)   .   .   . 1st Edition, 18 March, 1727
The *Secrets* of the *Invisible World Disclos'd :* or, An *Universal History* of *Apparitions, Sacred and Profane,* under all *Denominations;*
whether *Angelical, Diabolical,* or *Human Souls Departed.* Shewing—I. Their Various Returns to this World; with sure Rules
to know, by their *Manner* of *Appearing,* if they are *Good* or *Evil
Ones.* The *Differences* of the *Apparitions* of *Ancient* and *Modern*
Times; and an Enquiry into the *Scriptural Doctrine* of *Spirits.*
III. The many Species of Apparitions; their real Existence and
Operations by Divine Appointment. IV. The *Nature* of Seeing
Ghosts before, and after Death, and how we should behave
towards them. V. The *effects* of Fancy, Vapours, Dreams,
Hyppo, and of real or imaginary Appearances. VI. A Collec-
tion of the most Authentic Relations of Apparitions, particu-
larly that surprizing One attested by the learned Dr. *Scott.* By
Andrew Moreton, Esq. Adorned with Cuts. *London.* Printed
for *J. Peele.* (8vo. Plates, Title, Preface and Contents 6 leaves,
& pp. 395. Only the Title altered.)   .   .   . 23 Nov. 1728
(Printed for John Clarke & A. Millar, &c.)
            Reissued   .   . 2nd Edition, 13 Feb. 1729
242. A *New Family Instructor;* in *Familiar Discourses* between a
Father and his *Children,* on the most Essential *Points* of the
Christian Religion. In Two Parts. Part I. containing a *Father's*
INSTRUCTIONS to his *Son* upon his going to *Travel* into *Popish
Countries;* and to the rest of his Children, on his Son's turning

Papist ; confirming them in the *Protestant Religion*, against the
Absurdities of *Popery.* Part II. Instructions against the *Three
Grand Errors* of the *Times ;* VIZ. 1. Asserting the *Divine Authority* of the *Scriptures ;* against the *Deists.* 2. *Proofs*, that the
Messias is already come, &c.; against the *Atheists* and *Jews.*
3. Asserting, the *Divinity* of *Jesus Christ*, that he was really the
same with the *Messias*, and that the *Messias* was to be really
GOD; against our *Modern Hereticks.* With a *Poem* upon the
Divine Nature of JESUS CHRIST, in *Blank Verse.* By the Author
of the *Family Instructor. London, T. Warner.* (8vo. Title
and Pref. xv. & pp. 384.) . . . . . . 1st Edition, 1727
  With an altered Title . . . . . 2nd Edition, 1732

243. *Parochial Tyranny :* or, the *Housekeeper's Complaint*, against the
insupportable *Exactions* and partial *Assessments* of *Select Vestries.*
With a plain *Detection* of many Abuses committed in the *Distribution* of *Public Charities.* Together with a *Practical Proposal*
for *Amending* the *same :* which will not only take off great *Part*
of the *Parish Taxes* now subsisting, but ease *Parishioners* from
Serving troublesome *Offices*, or paying exorbitant Fines. By
Andrew Moreton, Esq. *London. W. Meadows.* (8vo. Title &
pp. 36.) . . . . 9 Dec. 1727

244. *Augusta Triumphans :* or, the Way to make *London* the most
Flourishing *City* in the *Universe.* I. By Establishing a *University* where Gentlemen may have Academical Education under
the Eyes of their Friends. II. By an *Hospital* for *Foundlings.*
III. By forming an Academy of Sciences at *Christ's Hospital.*
IV. By Suppressing pretended *Mad-Houses*, where many of the
fair Sex are unjustly confined, while their Husbands keep Mistresses, &c. and many Widows are locked up for the sake of their
Jointure. V. To Save our Youth from *Destruction*, by Clearing
the Streets of impudent *Strumpets*, suppressing *Gaming Tables,*
and *Sunday Debauches.* VI. To Save our lower Class of People
from utter *Ruin*, and render them useful, by preventing the immoderate use of Geneva. With a frank Exposition of many
other Common Abuses, and incontestable Rules for Amendment.
Concluding with an Effectual Method to prevent *Street Robberies,*
and a Letter to Col: Robinson, on Account of the Orphan's
Tax. By *Andrew Moreton, Esq. London. J. Roberts.* (8vo.
pp. 63.) . . . . 1st Edition, 16 Mar. 1728
  (Collation the same) . . . . . 2nd Edition, 1729

245. A *Plan* of the *English Commerce.* Being a Compleat *Prospect* of
the *Trade* of this *Nation*, As well the *Home Trade* as the *Foreign.*
In three Parts. Part I. Containing a view of the present *Magnitude* of the *English Trade*, as it respects, 1. The *Exportation* of
our own Growth and Manufacture; 2. The *Importation* of Merchant Goods from Abroad; 3. The *Prodigious Consumption* of
Both at Home. Part II. Containing an Answer to that Great
and Important Question now depending, whether our Trade, and
especially our Manufactures, are in a declining Condition, or
No? Part III. Containing several *Proposals* entirely new, for
Extending and *Improving* our *Trade*, and *Promoting* the *Consumption* of our *Manufactures* in *Countries*, wherewith we have
hitherto had no *Commerce.* Humbly offered to the Consideration
of the *King* and *Parliament : London. C. Rivington* (8vo. pp.
368.) . . . . 1st Edition, 23 March, 1728
A *Plan* of the *English Commerce*, Being a *Compleat Prospect* of the
Trade of this *Nation*, as well the *Home Trade* as the *Foreign.*

Humbly offered to the Consideration of the King and Parliament. The Second Edition. *To which is added*, an APPENDIX, containing A View of the *Increase of Commerce*, not only of *England*, but of all the Trading *Nations* of *Europe*, since the Peace with *Spain*. The whole Containing several *Proposals*, entirely new, for *Extending*, and *Improving* Our *Trade;* and *Promoting* the CONSUMPTION *of our Manufactures* in *Countries*, wherewith we have *hitherto* had no *Commerce. London.* Printed for *C. Rivington*, 1730. (8vo. Title and Pref. xvi. Contents, &c., 4 leaves & pp. 368, and Append. pp. 40.) 2nd Edition, 13 Jan. **1731**

246.*The *Universal Spectator.* No. I. (Impl. 4to. one sheet.)   12 Oct. **1728**

247. *Second Thoughts* are *Best:* or, a Further Improvement of a late *Scheme* to Prevent Street Robberies. By which our Streets will be so strongly Guarded, and so gloriously Illuminated, that any part of London will be as safe and pleasant at Midnight, as at Noonday, and Burglary totally impracticable. With some Thoughts for Suppressing Robberies in all the Publick Roads of England, &c. Humbly offered for the good of his Country, Submitted to the Consideration of the Parliament, and Dedicated to his Sacred Majesty George II. By Andrew Moreton, Esq. London. W. Meadows. Price 6d. (8vo. pp. 24.)   . 12 Oct. **1728**

248.* *Street Robberies* considered. The reason of their being so frequent, with probable means to prevent 'em. To which is added, three short Treatises:—1. A Warning for Travellers: with Rules to Know a Highwayman, and Instructions how to behave upon the occasion. 2. Observations on Housebreakers. How to prevent a Tenement from being broke open. With a Word of Advice concerning Servants. 3. A Caveat for Shopkeepers: with a Description of Shoplifts, how to know 'em, and how to prevent 'em; also a Caution of Delivering Goods: With the Relation of several Cheats, practised lately upon the Publick. Written by a Converted Thief. To which is prefix'd some Memoirs of his Life. *Set a Thief to Catch a Thief. London.* Printed for J. Roberts, in Warwick Lane. Price 1s. (8vo. pp. 72.) 12 Nov. **1728**

249.* *Fog's Weekly Journal.* (An Article by Defoe.)   .   . 11 Jan. **1729**

250. *An Humble Proposal*, to the People of *England*, for the Encrease of their Trade and Encouragement of their Manufactures; whether the present Uncertainty of Affairs issues in Peace or War. By the *Author of* the *Compleat English Tradesman.* London. C. Rivington. (8vo. Title and Preface 2 leaves, & pp. 59.) .   .   .   . 15 March, **1729**

251.* *Reasons* for a *War*, in Order to Establish the Tranquillity and Commerce of Europe. *Pax Quæritur Bello.* London. Printed for A. Dodd, and R. Walker, without Temple Bar; E. Nutt and F. Smith, at the Royal Exchange, and Sold by the Booksellers, and Pamphlet Shops, Mercuries and Hawkers of London and Westminster. Price 6d. (8vo. pp. 32.)   .   . Mar. **1729**

252.* *Servitude:* a Poem. To which is prefix'd an Introduction, humbly submitted to the Consideration of all Noblemen, Gentlemen, and Ladies, who keep many Servants. Also, a Postscript, occasioned by a late trifling Pamphlet, entitled, *Every Body's Business is Nobody's.* Written by a Footman. In Behalf of Good Servants, and to excite the Bad to their Duty. London. *T. Worrall. Price* 6d. [The Prose, comprising the larger part, written by *Defoe;* the Verse by Robert *Dodsley*] (8vo. pp. 32.)   .   .   .   . 20 Sept. **1729**

THE LIFE

OF

DANIEL DEFOE.

CHAPTER I.

Robinson Crusoe an allegory of Defoe's life — His reasons for not writing an autobiography—General silence as to his ancestry, and connexions by marriage — His father — His birth — How his name was changed from Foe to De Foe—Early life and education—Declines to become a dissenting minister—His scholastic attainments—Vindicates his learning—Initiation into business and politics—Character and occasion of his first composition—Death of Charles II.—Accession of James II.—Young Defoe joins the Duke of Monmouth's insurrection—Escapes, and enters into business—Arbitrary proceedings of the King, who dispenses with the penal laws—Defoe's first publication, a letter against the King's declaration, offends his friends—Downfall of the King—Defoe a liveryman of London.

1661—1688.

ON approaching my subject, the first and most obvious feeling is regret, that an author whose powers of narration, —whose skill in word painting from nature, and in delineation of character,—whose simple naturalness in his relations of human intercourse, and in the charm of reality which he imperceptibly spread over the commonest incidents, have all combined to fascinate all readers,—should not have employed his masterly pen in telling the story of his own life to posterity.

When about sixty years of age, Defoe professes to have intended this, in the first and second volumes of " Robinson Crusoe," at least so far as would enable himself to deduce therefrom the *Serious Reflections* on Morals and *Religion* comprised in the third and comparatively unknown volume of the same work; but what he intended to be only veiled, time has rendered obscure.

In the Preface to this third volume he affirms that "the story, though Allegorical, is also Historical. Farther, that there is a man alive, and well known too, the Actions of whose Life are the just subject of these Volumes, and to whom all or most Part of the Story most directly alludes; this may be depended upon for Truth. Without letting the Reader into a nearer Explication of the Matter, I proceed to let him know, that the happy deductions I have employed myself to make from all the circumstances of my Story, will abundantly make him amends for his not having the Emblem explained by the Original. In a Word, there's not a Circumstance in the imaginary Story, but has its just allusion to a real Story, and Chimes Part for Part, and Step for Step with the inimitable ' Life of Robinson Crusoe.' " With respect to the fictitious representation of Crusoe's forced confinement in an island, he says " 'tis as reasonable to represent one kind of Imprisonment by another, as it is to represent any Thing that really exists by that which exists not. Had the common Way of Writing a Man's private History been taken, and I had given you the conduct or Life of a Man you Knew, and whose Misfortunes and Infirmities perhaps you had sometimes unjustly triumphed over; all I could have said would have yielded no Diversion, and perhaps scarce have obtained a Reading, or at best no attention. The Teacher, *like a greater*, having no Honour in his own Country."

From the above it is quite clear that Defoe had seriously considered the propriety or otherwise of writing his autobiography; but having in his surprising adventures " suffered all manner of Violences and Oppressions, injurious Reproaches, contempt of Men, attacks of Devils, corrections from Heaven, and oppositions on Earth; and had innumerable ups and downs in matters of Fortune," he was convinced that the clearing up of his own character and conduct in plain terms would be an indictment against the age in which he had lived. That his contemporaries would either refuse to read, or would resent it.*

There were other reasons of an opposite character, equally

---

* *Vide* " Serious Reflections during the Life and Surprising Adventures of Robinson Crusoe," *Preface,* 1720.

forcible, but which the noble reticence of a true patriot forbade to be divulged, even in vindication of his own honour. Defoe enjoyed the private confidence of King William III., and of the official advisers of three successive monarchs. He was necessarily the depository of many secrets of State, and must have possessed, in the shape of private instructions, and a large correspondence with successive ministers, a mass of documents of the utmost importance.* These were possessions of which an honourable man might have been proud, as heirlooms to posterity, showing that though he had now " no honour in his own country," he had been the honoured instrument in effecting great national good. But nothing of their contents was ever disclosed during his life, nor is there evidence that any vestige of the kind was discovered among his papers after his death. He was frequently employed by Government on secret missions, but the research of his biographers has failed to ascertain anything as to the nature or direction of such services. Noblemen and Ministers of State have thought letters written by him worth preservation, and some of those letters are now carefully preserved among the national treasures; but even the memory of all State secrets was inviolable with Defoe, and he finally buried them in his grave.

Undoubtedly the above reasons weighed upon his mind when he ultimately decided against writing an autobiography, and concluded, as in the Preface from which I have quoted above, that the lessons contained in his own eventful life might be conveyed more profitably to the world under the " Emblem " of " Robinson Crusoe," " without letting the Reader into a nearer Explication of the matter."

It would be a pleasant occupation for those who have leisure

---

* That his loyal heart must have induced him to retain some of these papers to a late period of life, before destroying them, is evident from his anonymous pamphlet, " Mere Nature Delineated," &c. (1726), in which he cautiously says, at p. 85 :—" It is true my Acquaintance does not lead me to examine into the Writing of our *British* Princes, though I have the Honour to have seen the Handwriting of Five Sovereigns, and to have in my possession the Handwriting of most of them, as of King *James* II., of King *William*, of Queen *Anne*, and of King *George*; and I can witness they all wrote very well; though I think the Queen wrote the best of them all, and particularly her Majesty spelt very good English."

and research, to lay open "The Life and Strange Surprizing Adventures of Robinson Crusoe," side by side with "Memoirs of the Life of Daniel Defoe," and to trace throughout the parallels between what he calls the *Emblem* and the *Original.* Possibly by such process fragments of his private history might be eliminated not otherwise ascertainable; but, after the lapse of more than a century and a half, the writer of his Life must be content with such materials as are of evident historical value. The existence, however, of an almost complete parallelism is declared by Defoe to be a fact; and to those inclined for such an excursion I would say, in his own words, "take this with you as you go."

With due respect to ancestry, I shall not attempt to prove that the name of Foe is of Norman origin.* The True-born Englishman, Daniel Defoe, would neither be a greater nor less man, whether his ancestors came in with the Conqueror or not. So far as celebrity is concerned, he may be considered the first and last of his family. He had so much to tell the world in order to make men wiser and better, that he did not even take time to write down anything as to the genealogy of his excellent mother; whether he ever had a sister or brother; or, to tell us whose daughters himself successively married. In a letter to Lord Halifax, dated 1705, he speaks of a brother, without mentioning his name; but as such brother was stated to be incapable of carrying a message, he was, perhaps, only a brother-in-law. His grandfather, DANIEL FOE was in good circumstances in Northamptonshire during the Civil Wars, and kept a pack of hounds; but we only learn that accidentally, in 1711, when, as an apt illustration of party animosity, he states, that "all the generals of both armies were hounds in the pack."† The concluding sentiment of his "True-born Englishman" shows that I have not in this misrepresented him :—

> "Then let us boast of Ancestors no more,
>   Or Deeds of Heroes done in Days of Yore,
>   For Fame of Families is all a cheat:
>   'Tis Personal Virtue only makes us great."

Our author's father was JAMES FOE, citizen and butcher, in

---

* Wilson, i. 4.   † Review VII., *Preface.*

JAMES DUKE OF MONMOUTH,

Under whom young Defoe served in the Rebellion, 1685.

CRIPPLEGATE CHURCH,

Near to which Defoe was born and died.

the City of London. Little is known of him; but that little
is to his advantage. That he was an excellent father may be
concluded from the affectionate reverence with which his son
alludes to him;—that he was prosperous is evident from his
ability to give that son the best education then open to Dissenters. No doubt can be entertained that he was a good
man, and a sincere Christian. He had, in all probability, been
a constant attendant at his parish church, during the ministry
of the pious and Reverend *Samuel Annesley, LL.D.*, and when
that divine was ejected, under the Act of Uniformity, *James
Foe* accompanied his beloved pastor, and became a Nonconformist. He died about 1706-7, full of years; and the last
act recorded of him, (though not by his son,) is his giving a
testimonial to the character of a female domestic, who had
formerly lived two years in his service. He says he should
not have recommended her to Mr. Cave, " that Godly minister,
had not her conversation been becoming the Gospel."

DANIEL FOE, or DE FOE, as he chose afterward to call himself, was born in the parish of St. Giles, Cripplegate, in the
year 1661. The exact date of his birth is not known, there
being no entry of his baptism in the parish register. It is not
improbable that he was baptized by Dr. Annesley, shortly after
that gentleman had been ejected from the Church of England.

The assertions of Oldmixon and Browne, and the conjectures of biographers, as to Defoe's reasons for altering his
name, appear to be without foundation. He was called
DE FOE several years before the death of his venerated father,
who never used any other name but that of FOE. The son
was not a man to be ashamed of the surname of his living
parent; nor the True-born Englishman likely to have been actuated by the vanity of assuming a Norman prefix. His practice disproves the assertion, and shows rather that the form of
his signature was a matter of personal indifference, which continued to the end of his life. It is true that he used the
surname of De Foe, but I am inclined to think it began accidentally, or was adopted for convenience, about 1703, to distinguish him from his father. The latter, from his age and experience, and the former from his commanding ability, were both
then influential members of the Dissenting interest in the city.

They would respectively be spoken of and addressed, orally, as
Mr. Foe, and Mr. D. Foe. The name as spoken, would in
writing become Mr. De Foe, and thus what originated in accident, might be used for convenience, and become more or less
fixed and settled by time. This simple explanation is favoured
by the following proofs of Defoe's indifference in the matter.
His initials and name appear in various forms in his works,
subscribed to dedications, prefaces, &c., and this may be pre-
sumed to have been done by himself. Before 1703 I find only
D. F. In that year Mr. De Foe, and Daniel De Foe. In
the following year D. D. F.; De FOE; and Daniel de Foe.
In 1705, D. F., and three autograph letters, all addressed
within a few months to the Earl of Halifax, are successively
signed D. Foe, De Foe, and Daniel De Foe. In 1706, D. F.;
D. Foe; De Foe; Daniel De Foe. In 1709, D. F.; De
Foe; and Daniel Defoe. In 1710, a letter to Dyer is
signed De Foe. Two autograph signatures by himself, in
1723 and 1727, and two of the same dates by his daughter
Hannah, are Daniel De Foe, and Hannah De Foe. Yet in
1729 a letter to his printer is signed, De Foe; and one to his
son-in-law, in 1730, D. F.

Of the childhood and early youth of Defoe little can, or
need be said. His afterlife and occasional remarks show that
his mind was formed to a love of religion, and that "from a
child he had known the Scriptures." Although sincerely
attached to the cause of Nonconformity, his parents must have
been more than usually free from the asceticism and austerity
of Puritanism; and their son, not being restrained from innocent amusements, displayed, as he grew up, those light and
buoyant spirits, that vivacity of humour, and cheerfulness of
disposition which rendered him a favourite with his companions. There is evidence in his writings that he early discovered the spirit of independence and self-reliance, which
afterward made him so conspicuous as a champion of civil and
religious liberty. He seems also to have been a boy of great
courage; a quality which strongly marked his future character.
This led him no doubt into disputes and contests with boys of
similar age; but no useful lesson was lost to one who had an
inherent sense of justice and moderation. In one of his

Reviews he observes—"From a boxing young English boy, I learnt this early piece of generosity, not to strike my enemy when he is down;"* a disposition which he cherished through the whole of his controversial life. It was not an uncommon practice then, among the Dissenters, to make written copies of the Bible, and it seems that young Defoe applied himself to the task. He says he worked like a horse, till he had written out the whole of the Pentateuch, when he grew so tired that he was willing to risk the rest. This undertaking would no doubt be with the knowledge and permission, probably with the encouragement, of his pious father and mother; but it can scarcely be doubted that the task was self-imposed, or it would not have been abandoned at his own will. He was not capable of being a Puritan, though no man could have had a greater love for the Bible, which was through life his ultimate test and supreme authority, as will be manifest to even a cursory reader of almost any of his works. He deviated in some things from the line of life his parents had marked out for him in his youth, and to this many subsequent misfortunes may perhaps be attributed; but, for the useful direction of his genius, and the manly integrity of his character, he was mainly indebted to the good principles and habits thus instilled into him in his youth.

Mr. Walter Wilson, who is an authority on the former government of Dissenters' academies, says that students remained there *five* years; and that Defoe was about fourteen years of age when placed in one at Newington Green, under the direction of "that polite and profound scholar,"† the Reverend Charles Morton, where he had great advantages for learning and a very agreeable society. The object of his parents, in sending the young student there, was to prepare him for the ministry. To this he alludes many years after, in one of his Reviews:—"It is not often that I trouble you with any of my divinity; the pulpit is none of my office. It was my disaster first to be set apart for, and then to be set apart from, the honour of that sacred employ."‡

I do not enter into the several speculations of Mr. Wilson

---

* Review VI., 573.   † Tong's " Life of Shower," p. 9.
          ‡ Review VI., 341.

as to the causes, which he says are now unknown, that led to
the diversion of Defoe's talents into other channels.   Mr.
Wilson might have made out a correct catalogue of such
causes from a work afterward written by his author, and from
which he has himself quoted.*   Young Defoe the student, removed from home influences, and the guidance which from
infancy had disposed of his welfare, had now opening out
before him the perspective of a future in which he must find
his own place, and do his own work.   Designated by his
parents, his pastor, and friends, for the office of the ministry,
it was natural that such a youth should begin to consider well
the advantages and disadvantages, secular and religious, of
the course upon which he had entered;—the circumstances
of the times, and the prospects of the Dissenting ministry in
which his lot was proposed to be cast.   Defoe was a deep
thinker, an acute observer, and at this early period of his life,
had resolution to act decisively upon sound conviction.   He
was then too young to publish those reasons and convictions
to the world; but he did it many years afterward, in the work
to which I have referred, when the influence of his position
was such as to insure a consideration of his views.

He found that many students were sent to the Academies
more from charity than fitness, intellectually or physi-
cally, for the ministry;—that for want of libraries and polite
conversation, during the short space of *three* years, (when they
were removed to make room for others,) too many of them
became merely pedants, rather than Christian gentlemen of
high learning;—that afterward, many of the young ministers,
" *Fund Bred,*" as he calls them, were consequently unable to get
bread, and had to submit to shameful and degrading practices
in their efforts to obtain congregations and subsistence;—that
parallel with this state of things, eminent ministers were *called*
from all parts of the kingdom to congregations in London,
and induced to come for mercenary considerations, often to
the spiritual ruin and dispersion of the people they left behind;—
that the behaviour of the congregations to their ministers,
who were dependent, was often objectionable and unchristian;—
and, that while so many young London ministers were desti-

---

* *Vide* " The Present State of Parties in Great Britain," pp. 293 to 333.

tute and useless, others even from Scotland found acceptance
in the metropolis, before having received any formal ordi-
nation.

At the end of what I have thus summarized, he makes several
important exceptions in favour of the academy of Mr. Morton,
and never afterward omitted an occasion to do honour to the
memory of his beloved tutor. At Newington, he says, " the
master or tutor read all his lectures, gave all his systems,
whether of philosophy or divinity, in English, and had all his
declaimings and dissertations in the same tongue. And
though the scholars from that place were not destitute in
the languages, yet it is observed of them, they were by this
made masters of the English tongue, and more of them excelled in that particular than of any school at that time.
Here were produced of ministers, Mr. Timothy Cruso, Mr.
Hannot of Yarmouth, Mr. Nathaniel Taylor, Mr. Owen, and
several others; and of another kind, poets, Samuel Wesley,
Daniel De Foe, and two or three of your Western Martyrs,
that, had they lived, would have been extraordinary men of
their kind—viz., Kitt, Battersby, young Jenkyns, Hewling,
and many more."* But it must be remembered that he adduces this as an exception to the general character of Dissenting academies.

This was one turning point of Defoe's life. He had begun
to think for himself, and dearly as he loved the religion of his
parents, and the communion to which he adhered, had made
the discovery that perfection was not to be found in the discipline and government of that part of Christ's Church mili-
tant; nay more, that the imperfections were so many, and of
such magnitude, that painful as the decision was to himself
and his dearest friends, their intention as to his future life
must be abandoned. This explains his somewhat enigmatic
sentence, that it was his disaster, " first to be set apart for, and
then to be set apart from, the honour of that sacred employ."

The open candour of Defoe in admitting and expatiating
upon the defective educational arrangements among the Dissenters, and the sad condition of a great part of their young
ministers, was too truthful to be agreeable to the politicians

---

* " Present State of Parties, &c.," p. 319.

of the party; but the correction was administered with sorrow by a faithful friend, and followed by remedial suggestions. This conduct of our author presents a broad contrast to that of one of his fellow-students, Samuel Wesley, who, after having received an academical education under Mr. Morton at New- ington, entirely at the cost of the Dissenting interest, showed the basest ingratitude, after he had become a clergyman of the Established Church, not only in forgetting those great obligations, but in attacking the loyalty and morality of the Dissenting academies, and particularly that in which he had himself been educated.*

Defoe alludes to the secession of Wesley, and names seven more students and young ministers, adding that there were others, who all went over to the Church from having " been bred—anglice, starved—among the Dissenters."† His own denominational principles were too firmly fixed to be shaken, but in other writings he assigns as grounds of his firm and consistent support of the Church of England, and of its con- nection with the State, the unsettled, imperfect, and divided condition of Dissenters. It is no presumption to conclude that one of the results of this mental conflict, which altered his future destiny, was his catholic charity towards all reli- gious denominations holding the fundamental doctrines of the Gospel; and his life-continued efforts to induce them to forget all party spirit on non-essentials, and to " Study Peace."

As to the scholastic attainments of Defoe we are not left in ignorance. He was able to read the Greek classics, and had not only mastered the most difficult Latin authors, but himself produced Latin compositions for the press; he trans- lated and spoke Spanish, Italian, and French, the latter fluently, and had some knowledge of Dutch. Probably no man ever

---

* "A Letter from a Country Divine to his Friend in London, con- cerning the Education of the Dissenters in their Private Academies, &c.," 1704; "A Defence of a Letter concerning the Education of the Dissenters, &c.," by Samuel Wesley, 1704; "A Reply to Mr. Palmer's Vindication of the Learning, Loyalty, Morals, and most Christian Behaviour of the Dis- senters towards the Church of England," by Samuel Wesley, 1707. Two of these pamphlets were replied to by Samuel Palmer, who afterwards conformed to the Church.

† Defoe's " Present State of Parties," p. 331.

better understood how to use a plain, racy, thorough English style of language. His writings evince his great logical proficiency. Under the direction of his tutors, he went through a complete course of theology, in which he acquired a proficiency that enabled him to cope with the most acute writers of that disputatious age. He had sufficient knowledge of mathematics for the acquirement of astronomy; and as to geography he appears to have been acquainted with every known spot of the earth, its physical character, natural and artificial productions, and the whole trade and commerce of the world. History, ancient and modern, ecclesiastical and civil, appears to have been at his fingers' ends. No man of his time better understood the Constitution of his country, and he was very far in advance of his age in many branches of political and social science. So wide a range of learning has probably been attained by few, under the disadvantages he has himself pointed out; but it must be remembered that Defoe was no common student.

Nor was his learning of a superficial kind. He was a controversialist, and frequently the aggressor; wielding at pleasure not merely logical argument, but also an incomparable delicate irony, that often maddened his antagonists. Though rarely betrayed into any personality except in self-defence— seldom indeed even then—his enraged opponents, when worsted and unable to reply, would frequently taunt him with misfortunes of early life, and even venture to insinuate that he was no scholar. Most generally he was satisfied by holding his own ground, and completing their discomfiture; but occasionally suffered himself to be drawn into a good-natured vindication of his early education, invoking the candour of his readers for saying so much of himself. Conscious of his own genius, and that his fame would survive to future ages, he notices the matter " for their sakes who may see the calumnies when the author is on the other side of time, and can say nothing' for himself."

In reply to attacks of this kind in 1705, he wrote—" Those gentlemen who reproach my learning to applaud their own, shall have it proved that I have more learning than either of them—because I have more manners. I have no concern to tell Dr. Browne I can read English; nor to tell Mr. Tutchin

I understand Latin : *Non ita Latinus sum ut Latine loqui.*   I easily acknowledge myself blockhead enough to have lost the fluency of expression in the Latin, and so far trade has been a prejudice to me; and yet I think I owe this justice to my ancient father, still living, and in whose behalf I freely testify, that if I am a blockhead it was nobody's fault but my own, he having spared nothing in my education that might qualify me to match the accurate Dr. Browne, or the learned ' Observator.'

"As to Mr. Tutchin, I never gave him the least affront ; I have even after base usage in vain invited him to peace, in answer to which he returns unmannerly insults, calumnies, and reproaches.   As to my little learning, and his great capacity, I fairly challenge him to translate with me any Latin, French, or Italian author, and after that, to re-translate them cross-ways for twenty pounds each book ; and by this he shall have an opportunity to show the world how much De Foe, the hosier, is inferior to Mr. Tutchin, the gentleman."*

One of the arts employed by Swift in the *Examiner* against other periodical writers, was an affectation of contempt for their persons and characters.   This was done to supplant them in the estimation of persons not qualified to judge, by an arrogant assumption of superiority.   The *Review* and the *Observator* came in for a share of this coarse abuse, in which he called the writers stupid, illiterate scribblers, idiots, &c.

At first Defoe resolved to remain silent, remarking, " as I have all along practised, with many other scurrilous, angry sons of emptiness, so I shall still, *answer, and say nothing.*" Being goaded, however, by the rudeness of his unprovoked assailant, he afterward taught the *Examiner* that, without using coarse personalities, the author of the *Review* could wound with a sharper edge and a finer point than was possessed by the more pretentious Dean of St. Patrick's.   I quote only a portion of his retort as follows :—

"I have been in my time pretty well master of five languages, and have not lost them yet, though I write no bill over my door, nor set Latin quotations on the front of the *Review*.   But, to my irreparable loss, I was bred only by

* Review II., 149, 150.

halves; for my father, forgetting Juno's Royal Academy, left the language of Billingsgate quite out of my education. Hence, I am perfectly illiterate in the polite style of the street, and am not fit to converse with the porters and carmen of quality, who grace their diction with the beauties of calling names, and cursing their neighbour with a *bonne grace*. I have had the honour to fight a *rascal*, but never could master the eloquence of calling a man so; nor am I yet arrived at the dignity of being laureated at her Majesty's bear-garden. I have also, *illiterate* as I am, made a little progress in science. I read Euclid's Elements, and yet never found the mathematical description of a *scurrilous gentleman*. I have read logic, but could never see a syllogism formed upon the notion of it. I went some length in physics, or natural philosophy, and could never find between the two ends of nature, generation and corruption, one species out of which such a creature could be formed. I thought myself master of geography, and to possess sufficient skill in astronomy to have set up for a country almanac-maker, yet, could in neither of the globes find either in what part of the world such a heterogeneous creature lives, nor under the influence of what heavenly body he can be produced. From whence I conclude very frankly, that either there is no such creature in the world, or that, according to Mr. *Examiner*, I am a stupid idiot, and a very *illiterate fellow*."*

I have dwelt longer upon the scholastic and other attainments of Defoe to show, generally, that the course of training to which he was subjected in early life was the best adapted to produce real greatness in such a mind and genius; in fact, that he was a most learned man for the station to which he was designed by Providence. Specially, I have extended this view of his varied studies and knowledge, as a fit introduction to two interesting essays by him on Learning, in my collection of his newly discovered writings, under dates 30th October and 6 November, 1725; in which it will be found that at the age of *sixty-four* he re-opens the whole subject in a more detailed manner than he had ever previously done, but modestly conceals himself by speaking in the third person of his own great acquirements.

---

* Review VII., 454, 455.

There is an apparent discrepancy between the statements
of Defoe and his biographer Wilson, as to the number
of years during which students remained at the Dissenting
academies.   Defoe says that those who were maintained
and educated out of the general subscription fund remained
only three years, being intended for the ministry, and were
then removed to make room for others.   But these circumstances were not applicable to Defoe, whose father was in
affluent circumstances, and spared no expense in his education.
There were others like himself, who might be called gentlemen
students, independent of all charitable funds, and intended for
other professions or callings, who probably remained the full
term of five years, and contributed indirectly by their pay-
ments towards the support of the establishment.   This would
be in accordance with Mr. Wilson's statement, and would
complete the education of young Defoe at the age of nineteen
years.

Such a mind could not long remain idle; nor would his excellent father fail to obtain for him suitable employment as
soon as possible.   We may also conclude that a father who
had himself prospered in business, would not have set up his
son in a mercantile business when twenty-four years of age,
without some previous term of preparation in a subordinate
position.   Later in life, when sneeringly told that he was an
apprentice to a hosier, Defoe replied that he had been a trader
in hosiery, but denied, with an over-sensitive testiness, that he
had ever been either an apprentice or a hosier.   The solution
of this seems to be, that shortly after finishing his education,
he was placed in the office of a hose-factor, or merchant, having a wholesale warehouse in the City, and probably exporting
abroad, as well as supplying retail dealers at home.   We must
believe that young Defoe was not under articles or in any
menial capacity, but was instructed in book-keeping, management, and such other duties as would fit him to conduct a
similar business on his own account.

From what we find scattered in his works, there can be no
doubt that his leisure hours were spent among young and
ardent spirits like his own; and that he thus early engaged
himself on the popular side in politics, where his ability and

activity raised him to some distinction as an advocate of civil and religious liberty. Even before the accession of James II. the nation was alarmed at the encroachments of Popery; the Court, Government, and the High Church seemed to favour such encroachments; and among the educated young men, in the City, of Defoe's class and party, Protestant feeling was kept in a state of ebullition. Private meetings were held, at which "Popish innovations" "Arbitrary power," and other momentous questions of national policy, were discussed. Defoe attended some of these meetings, and took an active part in the agitation. We have now no means of knowing how such meetings were conducted; but if the business of each began by a short written paper, followed by an oral discussion, we have all the circumstances and machinery exactly fitting what we know of his first appearance as an author.*

The year 1683 was fraught with danger to the Protestant religion and liberty of England. Parliaments were abolished,— the charters of corporations were wrested from them by the King,—patriots were put to death,—and, to meet for the consideration of national grievances was to plot against what was called "the just prerogatives of the Crown." Nor was it in England alone that tyranny threatened the extermination of Protestant liberty. The Hungarian reformers, having been persecuted and proscribed by the Austrian Monarch, had risen in arms; and the Turks, availing themselves of the opportunity, marched professedly to their assistance, and laid siege to Vienna. Considering how much the fate of their Hungarian brethren might forecast their own, it can be no wonder that the English Protestant friends of Defoe looked with great interest on these proceedings; or, that they were inclined to rejoice at the possible downfall of a Popish despot. Defoe took a higher and different view; and, adverting afterwards to this disagreement, he says :—"The first time I had the misfortune to differ from my Friends was about the year 1683, when the Turks were besieging Vienna, and the Whigs in England, generally speaking, were for the Turks taking it;

---

* I am aware that Mr. Wilson has ascribed to Defoe two earlier pamphlets, entitled "Speculum Crape-gownorum, &c.," Parts I. and II., 1682. Defoe had nothing whatever to do with them.

which I, having read the History of the cruelty and perfidious dealings of the Turks in their Wars, and how they had rooted out the name of the Christian Religion in above three score and ten Kingdoms, could by no means agree with ; and, though then but a young man and a younger Author, I opposed it, and wrote against it, which was taken very unkindly indeed."*

From the above it is certain that Defoe wrote something on the subject, at the time it was being publicly debated among his friends ; and that he did something more, he "opposed it ;" which, as distinct from writing, may have been in oral discussion with such friends. This view is borne out by the next paragraph, in which he reiterates the basis of his arguments, prefaced with the words, "*I used to say.*" There is not a word to the effect that what he wrote was published, or even printed.

Upon this slender foundation, Mr. Wilson states that Defoe composed " a Treatise against the Turks, which appeared in 1683 ; but being anonymous, the exact title has never been identified. When De Foe collected his tracts into volumes, he omitted this treatise, perhaps from his inability to procure it."†

Candour obliges me to add, that all the other biographers of Defoe have made similar statements, and yet none of them ever saw, or otherwise heard of any such " Treatise ; " none of the book-hunters who have made collections of the works of Defoe have ever succeeded in finding one copy; and Mr. Wilson is compelled, in support of his hypothesis, to suppose that Defoe himself searched in vain for his own treatise.

It is again remarkable that Defoe reviewed at large, in 1704, (the year intervening between the publication of the first and second volumes of his " Collected Works,") the whole subject of the Turkish invasion of the Empire, and shows that the opinions he held in 1683 were still unchanged; but he makes no allusion to having published anything previously thereon.

The whole difficulty, however, may be set at rest, in accordance with what I have already stated, as gathered from Defoe ; and without going beyond his own words. His views on the siege of Vienna by the Turks differed from those of his friends.

---

* " Appeal to Honour and Justice," p. 51.   † Wilson, i. 90.

He put those views into writing, and they were discussed. He then, in such discussion, maintained his own opinions and opposed theirs; by so doing he offended his friends. And so I leave it.

In the absence of evidence to the contrary, we must believe that a young man, religiously educated, and so dutiful a son, would not recklessly cast off all authority, abandon his business engagements, and quit his home, to throw himself into the midst of an agitation that ultimately ended in rebellion. It may therefore be fairly supposed that the mercantile pupilage of Defoe terminated early in 1685, when the death of Charles II., and the accession of his Roman Catholic brother to the throne, portended the beginning of a great struggle which ended in the Revolution. Subsequent events show that it was the intention of his father that Daniel should commence business on his own account, as soon as arrangements could be made; but such intention was for a little time frustrated.

The first declaration of James II. to his people was answered by addresses, many of which promised him unlimited passive obedience. Encouraged by these, he seized upon the Customs and Excise, though contrary to law, and went publicly to Mass the first Sunday after his accession. The Parliament which soon afterward met, showed its subserviency to the king by settling upon him a large revenue for life, without remonstrance, declaration of grievance, or reservation, even as to the most sacred rights of the nation. Discontent among the people led naturally to agitation, and that to disaffection. JAMES, Duke of MONMOUTH, the son of Charles II. by Lucy Walters, possessed all those qualities of person, disposition, and manners, which were calculated to make him a favourite. Moreover he was a Protestant; a large section of the people of England believed him to be legitimate; and they offered him their allegiance as the representative and protector of all they held dear, against the rapid encroachments of Popery and tyranny. Hence followed the ill-fated expedition from Holland, which landing at Lyme, in Dorsetshire, in June, 1685, ended with the execution of the Duke upon Tower-hill on the 15th of the following month.

Having no business engagements to occupy his time when

this movement began, it was not in the nature of young Defoe to remain an idle spectator. The Religion and the Liberties of his country,—and especially of the Dissenters,—were at stake; the agitation among his friends in the city of London was great; his ardent love of freedom led him to join with them; and, carried away with the tide of popular excitement, he armed and followed the Duke of Monmouth's standard.

Later in life, when personal consequences were no longer to be feared, Defoe alludes to his concern therein, and declares that the king's cause was within a trifle of ruin. For had not the Duke's army been deceived by the darkness of the night, and led to a large ditch of water which they could not pass over, they had certainly surprised and overthrown the King's army, and cut them in pieces, before it was known who had hurt them.* Several other notices of this insurrection occur in the second volume of his " Tour through Great Britain ;" but it does not plainly appear that Defoe was himself engaged in them.

On the failure of the enterprise, and dispersion of the duke's followers, Defoe had the good fortune to escape, facilitated no doubt by the circumstance of his being a native of London, and his person not being known in that part of the kingdom where the insurrection took place. He returned in safety to the metropolis, and thus avoided becoming one of the many victims of Jeffries and Kirk. Three of his friends, Battersby, Jenkyns, and Hewling—all of whom had been students in Mr. Morton's academy—lost their lives on the scaffold. Shortly afterward, in the same year, Defoe entered upon the business for which he had been prepared, the wholesale trade in hosiery, and carried on the same in Freeman's-court, Cornhill, until 1694.

The success of the royal troops, in suppressing the rebellion, so elated the king as to precipitate his arbitrary proceedings. He gave commissions in the army to Papists, dispensing with the tests, and deprived Protestant officers of their commissions. Catholic priests were imported from foreign countries, mass-houses were erected, and the Earl of Castlemaine was sent ambassador to the Pope to solicit the reunion of England with

---

* " Consolidator," pp. 135–6.

the Holy See.   Nor were there wanting in the Church of
England eminent divines to teach and preach the duty of absolute submission, obedience without reserve, subjection to
princes as God's vicegerents, accountable to none, and not to
be withstood.   Defoe says—" I have heard it publicly preached,
that if the King commanded my head, and sent his messengers
to fetch it, I was bound to submit, and stand still while it was
cut off."*   Such doctrines, and his own bigotry, soon infatuated the king; and when the House of Commons objected to
his proposals of increasing the standing army and dispensing
with the tests in favour of Catholic officers, he dismissed his
Parliament, and determined to make his own will the future
rule of his government.   Orders under the royal seal were
soon issued for the admission of Catholics into the Charter-
house and the two Universities.   Finding the Church of England was beginning to resist these encroachments, the king
projected a general toleration, in the hope that by favouring
the Dissenters he would silence their opposition against Popery,
and thus, further his grand design for the subversion of the
Established religion.   The Royal declaration, dispensing with
and suspending all penal and sanguinary laws in matters of
religion, was promulgated in April, 1687.   Defoe well understood the design ; and I cannot better express it than in his
own words—" Was ever anything more absurd than this
conduct of King James and his party, in wheedling the Dissenters ; giving them liberty of conscience by his own arbitrary
dispensing authority, and his expecting they should be content
with their religious liberty at the price of the Constitution ?
A thing, though a few were deluded with, yet the body of
Dissenters soon saw through.   The train indeed was deep laid
and subtilly ; but this was plain to everybody, that it was
wholly inconsistent with the Popish interest to protect the
Dissenters, any otherwise than as it was made a project to
create a feud between them and the Church, and in the end to
destroy both."†

    Mr. Wilson's " conjecture," that Defoe wrote more than
one Tract upon these proceedings, is based upon a passage in
the *Review,* and is a mistake.‡   Our author says, he had the

---

* Review VII., 304.   † Review V., 75.   ‡ Review VIII., 442.

reproaches of his friends when " he blamed their credulity," when he " protested openly" against the addresses ; and " I had their anger again when, in print, I opposed at the utmost hazard the taking off the penal laws and test." No man was more capable of expressing clearly what he intended than Defoe and he has placed the words " in print," as it were in contrast with his previous *open protest,* and so gives force to the greater hazard incurred in his last effort to convince his " honest blinded" friends.

As I believe this to have been the first printed production from Defoe's pen, and none of his biographers succeeded in finding a copy, I may be excused in describing it more fully than will be needful generally. It consists of a single sheet quarto, printed in double columns, and without title-page. In proof of the danger incurred by all concerned in its publica-tion, it is without date, name of printer, or place of publication. The first page is headed " A LETTER, containing some Reflec-tions on His Majesty's *Declaration* for LIBERTY of CONSCIENCE. Dated the 4th April, 1687."* I was agreeably surprised to find that a Tract, written when he was only twenty-six years of age, contained almost as large a proportion of peculiar and characteristic expressions as any of his subsequent works. From the third page I extract the following :—

" We can see no reason to induce us to believe that a *Toleration* of *Religion* is proposed with any other design but either to divide us, or to lay us asleep till it is time to give the alarm for destroying us. . . . . . . It is not so very long since that nothing was to be heard at *Court* but the supporting the *Church of England,* and the Extirpating all the *Nonconformists* . . . . but now all is turned round again."

He then shows that the Declaration is so cautiously worded that, when time and conjuncture present themselves, all the offers of favour can be easily broken through. On the next page : " I will take the boldness to add one thing, that the *King's suspending of Laws* strikes at the root of this whole Government, and subverts it quite. The *Lords* and *Commons* have such a share in it, that no Law can be either *made, re-pealed,* or, which is all one, *suspended,* but by their consent."

---

* Brit. Mus.: " King's Pamphlets," 116, c. 35. (James II. King.)

At page 5 : " When a *Coronation Oath* is so little remembered, other *Promises* must have a proportioned degree of Credit given to them.   One of the Effects of this *Declaration* will be the setting on foot a new run of Addresses over the Nation ; for there is nothing, how Impudent and Base soever, of which the abject flattery of a Slavish spirit is not capable." This is constitutional, yet bold language ; and, had the author been discovered, his death would probably have been the penalty.

The Tract concludes with a Postscript, as follows :—

" These *Reflections* were writ soon after the *Declaration* came to my hands, but the matter of them was so tender, and the conveyance of them to the Press was so uneasy, that they appear now too late to have one Effect that was Designed by them, which was the diverting Men from making *Addresses* upon it ; yet, if what is here proposed makes Men become so far wise as to be ashamed of what they have done, and is a means to keep them from carrying their Courtship further than good words, this Paper will not come too late."

A year later the King renewed his famous Declaration, but this time required the Bishops to cause it to be read in the churches of their respective dioceses.   The refusal of seven, their committal to the Tower, and subsequent acquittal, brought to a crisis the alienation of the King and his subjects. The bigoted claimant of irresistible prerogative and passive obedience,—now scorned and repudiated by the nation,—was betrayed by his own servants, deserted by his friends and family ; and, descending ignominiously the steps of a throne that crumbled beneath him, fled from his capital a fugitive, and sought shelter in a foreign country.

After the danger Defoe had incurred in writing and publishing his Tract against the King's Declaration, he must have felt chagrined that his efforts to serve the Dissenters had only given great offence to many of his friends.   He appears, upon this, to have turned his attention more fully to his commercial duties ; and thinking it expedient to unite himself closely with his fellow citizens, was admitted a liveryman of the City of London, on the 26th of January, 1688, having claimed his freedom by birth.   In the chamberlain's book his name was written *Daniel Foe.*

CHAPTER II.

Defoe joins the Prince of Orange—Resides at Tooting—One of the city guard of honour to the King and Queen—His first publication in verse—Extends his business, and becomes insolvent—His honourable conduct afterward—Declines an offer to reside at Cadiz—Writes " The Englishman's Choice"—Appointed accountant to the Commissioners of the Glass Duty—Connected with Pantile works near Tilbury Fort—Writes an ode to the Athenian Society, and an elegy on Dr. Annesley—Controversy on standing armies—Defoe replies to Trenchard—The Lord Mayor takes the sword to a Dissenters' meeting-house—Defoe publishes " An Inquiry into Occasional Conformity ;"—his " Essay upon Projects"—Publishes the " Poor Man's Plea ;" also, " The Pacificator, a Poem ;" " The Two Great Questions Considered;" and " The Two Great Questions Further Considered"—Publishes " The Danger of the Protestant Religion Considered"—Re-issues his " Inquiry into Occasional Conformity," but now " With a Preface to the Rev. John Howe"—Mr. Howe's reply, and Defoe's rejoinder—Tutchin publishes his poem " The Foreigners," and Defoe replies in " The True-born Englishman."

1688—1701.

IT augured but ill for the success of Defoe's commercial enterprise that his own interest found place only after the general welfare of his native country, the preservation of the Protestant religion, and the freedom of divine worship among all classes of Nonconformists. No sooner did the news arrive of the successful landing and advance of the Dutch, than Defoe, armed and on horseback, left the city, and at Henley-on-Thames joined the second line of the army of the Prince of Orange. On the 18th December, the Prince made his public entry into London ; and we may fairly conclude that Defoe was one of his followers. During the debates of the Convention Defoe was also present, and says it was " with inexpressible joy I heard delivered at the bar of the Lords' House, in a Message from the Commons, by Mr. Hampden, of Buckinghamshire, in 1688—viz., ' That it is inconsistent with the constitution of this Protestant Kingdom to be governed by a Popish Prince.' "

OLD FURNITURE IN VESTRY OF CHAPEL FOUNDED AT TOOTING BY DEFOE.

HOUSE IN WHICH DEFOE RESIDED AT TOOTING.

As an ardent friend of the Revolution, and no less an admirer of King William, Defoe afterward annually commemorated the 4th of November, in token of the National Deliverance, to the end of his life.   During the years he wrote the *Review* this was made the subject of his paper on each returning anniversary.   " A day," says he, " famous on various accounts, and every one of them dear to Britons who love their country, value the Protestant interest, or have an aversion to tyranny and oppression.   On this day he was born ; on this day he married the Daughter of England ; and on this day he rescued the nation from a bondage worse than that of Egypt— a bondage of soul, as well as bodily servitude—a slavery to the ambition and raging lust of a generation set on fire by pride, avarice, cruelty, and blood."*

When the Revolution took place, and probably some little time before, Defoe was a resident at Tooting, in Surrey, where he was the first person who attempted to form the Dissenters of the neighbourhood into a regular congregation.   It appears from a passage in his " Tour through Great Britain," that he also resided several years near the River Thames, in the neighbourhood of Mickleham, in the same county.†

On the 29th of October, 1689, the King and Queen went in state to a banquet given them by the Lord Mayor and Corporation of London, in the Guildhall.   Oldmixon, gives an account of the procession ; " which," he says, " for the great number of liverymen, the full appearance of the militia and artillery company, the rich adornments of the pageants, and the splendour and good order of the whole proceeding, outdid all that had been seen before upon that occasion.   And what deserved to be particularly mentioned, says a reverend historian, was a royal regiment of volunteer horse, made up of the chief citizens, who being gallantly mounted and richly accoutred, were led by the Earl of Monmouth, now Earl of Peterborough, and attended their Majesties from Whitehall. Among these troopers—who were, for the most part, Dis-

---

* Review IV., 453.
† " Tour through Great Britain," vol. i. lett. 2, p. 95.

senters—was *Daniel Foe,* at that time a hosier in Freeman's-yard, Cornhill."*

During the next two years we learn nothing of Defoe, except that he had extended his commercial transactions beyond the home trade of a wholesale house in hosiery, and was engaged in the Spanish and Portuguese trade. There is, however, reason to fear that his mind was too much distracted by politics to ensure success in mercantile pursuits. The *Review,* afterward written by himself, contains ample proof that at this early period of Defoe's life he was no idle spectator, but entered heartily into all that concerned the Revolution. In 1691 was published his first effort in verse, with the following title : — " A New Discovery of an Old Intrigue : a Satyr level'd at Treachery and Ambition ; Calculated to the Nativity of the Rapparee Plott, and the Modesty of the Jacobite Clergy. Designed by way of Conviction to the CXVII Petitioners, and for the Benefit of those that Study the Mathematicks. *Unus Nobis Cunctando Restituit.*—Ennius. Printed in the year 1691."

The first edition of this pamphlet is so rare that none of Defoe's biographers appear to have seen it, except as reprinted fourteen years afterward, in the second volume of his collected writings, or to have known of this early edition. It is a satire upon the Jacobite Plot, in which Lord Preston was concerned, and upon the proceedings in the City thereupon. As a satirist, the author says at the end of his preface, " I never drew my pen before." I cannot agree with Mr. Wilson, that it is greatly inferior to his subsequent poems. Like its successors, it is somewhat rugged, and has frequent occurrences of defective rhymes ; but it contains an average of vigorous passages worthy of quotation.

To return to Defoe's business operations. There is no possibility of fixing accurate dates to the incidental notices scattered through the works of an author, who avoided as much as possible obtruding his private affairs upon the public. It may, however, serve as a guide that the pecuniary

---

* Oldmixon's " Hist. of Eng.," iii. 36.

difficulties, which ended in his becoming insolvent, began about the year 1692. He had before that time become a merchant-adventurer; for speaking of the high rate of insurance he says: "If it has been a Trading Voyage, perhaps the Adventurer has paid three or four premio's, which sometimes make the Ensurer clear more by a Voyage than the Merchant. I myself have paid £100 Ensurances in those small premio's on a Voyage I have not gotten £50 by."* His connection with the trade of Spain appears also to have rendered it expedient for him to go there. He remained some time, and became familiar with the language. In one of his Reviews he gives an account of the loss, in the Bay of Biscay, of a vessel in which he was a shareholder, and records that the crew was inhospitably treated.† A writer in the reign of Queen Anne, who styles himself "A well-wisher to trade and credit," refers opprobriously to Defoe's career in trade, and says, "he has run through the three degrees of comparison: *Pos.*, as a hosier; *Compar.*, as a civet-cat merchant; and *Super.*, as a Pantile merchant."‡

An examination of Defoe's "Compleat Tradesman," one of the most valuable practical books ever published, written in the latter part of his life, shows an inward consciousness of the errors of his early life as a tradesman, and his desire to warn others of the rocks upon which he was wrecked. He says— "An old Sailor that has split upon a rock, and has lost his ship, is not the worst man to make a pilot of for that coast; on the contrary, he is in particular able to guide those that come after him to shun the dangers of that unhappy place."§ Truth requires it to be added that many features of his character were unsuitable to the close application and drudgery of the counting-house. He became aware of it, but not until too late. The following extract shows his estimate of the character of a successful tradesman :—

"The *English* Carriage, which we use in drawing the greatest Burdens or Loads, I mean such as draw Timber, and are, in our Modern Usage, call'd a Wain or Carriage, are in *Kent* and

---

* "Essay upon Projects," p. 115.   † Review VI., 223.
‡ "Observations on the Bankrupts' Bill," 1706, p. 35.
§ "Compleat Tradesman," ii. 105.

Sussex called a *Tug*, from the old Saxon Language, signifying hard Labour ; and the *Waggon* has its derivation from the same Language, wherein the Words are usually expressive of the Manner or Thing which they are used for ; as the Waggon is a Carriage which, being heavily loaden, does but just WAG ON ; but still 'tis observed, it Keeps wagging, and it always goes on, and as softly as it goes, we see some of our carriers come as far as from *Exeter*, a hundred and fifty miles to *London*, with forty to fifty Hundred Weight, and make their journeys constantly, wet or dry, dark or light, blow high blow low, still, according to their true original Name and the meaning of it, they WAG ON.   Thus the prudent Tradesman that goes on carefully and gently lets no Irons burn, and yet lets no Irons cool ; he truly drives his Trade, but does not push it ; keeps it going, but does not overrun it ; keeps within his own Orbit, and within the Circle of his own diurnal Revolution.   This is, in a Word, the Compleat Tradesman."*

On the next page he draws an opposite character, showing the incompatibility of genius with trade, and it looks a little like his own portrait :—

" A Wit turned Tradesman ! What an incongruous Part of Nature is there brought together, consisting of direct contraries !   No Apron Strings will hold him ; 'tis in vain to lock him in behind the Compter, he's gone in a Moment ; instead of Journal and Ledger, he runs away to his *Virgil* and *Horace* ; his Journal Entries are all Pindaricks, and his Ledger all Heroicks ; he is truly dramatic from one End to the other, through the whole Scene of his Trade ; and as the first Part is all Comedy, so the two last Acts are all made up with Tragedy ; a Statute of Bankrupt is his *Exeunt omnes*, and he generally speaks the Epilogue in the *Fleet Prison* or the *Mint*."†

No doubt Defoe suffered as he states in one of his *Reviews*,‡ and also in his *Essay on Projects*,§ from the frauds of systematic swindlers, but these would not have ruined a well-established business.   Inattention to duty and over-trading were, no doubt the causes of his failure.   He was a most

---

* " The Compleat Tradesman," ii. 56-7.
† " Compleat Tradesman," ii. p. 58.   ‡ Review III., 70.
§ " Essay on Projects," p. 225.

abstemious liver, and not given to any of the vicious indul-
gences too often the bane of youth ; but with the usual im-
prudence of superior genius, he was carried by his vivacity
into companies who were delighted by his wit.   Mr. Chalmers
says, " he spent those hours with a small society for the cultivation of polite learning which he ought to have employed
in the calculations of the counting-house ; and being obliged
to abscond from his creditors in 1692, he naturally attributed
those misfortunes to the war, which were probably owing to
his own misconduct.   An angry creditor took out a commission of bankruptcy, which was soon superseded on the petition
of those to whom he was most indebted, who accepted a composition on his single bond.   This he punctually paid by the
efforts of unwearied diligence.   But some of those creditors,
who had been thus satisfied, falling afterwards into distress
themselves, Defoe voluntarily paid them the whole of their
claims, being then in rising circumstances from King William's
favour.   This is such an example of honesty as it would be
unjust to Defoe and to the world to conceal."*

Perhaps a more valuable testimony was never paid to the
honour and integrity of an opponent, for whom he had no
feeling of friendship, than that paid by John Tutchin to
Daniel Defoe, in " a Dialogue between a Dissenter and the
Observator," published in 1702.   I must premise that the
Dissenters were then furious against Defoe for writing his tract,
" The Shortest Way," &c., which they misunderstood.   The
writer of the Dialogue says :—" I must do one piece of justice
to the man, though I love him no better than you do : it is
this—that, meeting a gentleman in a coffeehouse, when I and
every body else were railing at him, the gentleman took us up
with this short speech, ' Gentlemen,' said he, ' I know this
De Foe as well as any of you, for I was one of his creditors,
compounded with him, and discharged him fully.   Several
years afterwards he sent for me, and though he was clearly
discharged, he paid me all the remainder of his debt, voluntarily and of his own accord ; and he told me that, as far as
God should enable him, he intended to do so with every body.
When he had done, he desired me to set my hand to a paper

---

* Chalmers' " Life of Defoe," p. 8, 9.

to acknowledge it, which I readily did, and found a great many names to the paper before me; and I think myself bound to own it, though I am no friend to the book he wrote no more than you.'"

Being reproached by Lord Haversham for mercenariness, he tells him, in 1705, that, "with a numerous family, and no help but his own industry, he had forced his way with undiscouraged diligence through a sea of misfortunes, and reduced his debts, exclusive of composition, from seventeen thousand to less than five thousand pounds."*

The foregoing extracts will serve to shelter the character of Defoe from any dishonourable imputation in temporarily absconding from his creditors, a step which he thought himself justified in taking, during the negotiation for an amicable settlement, in order that he might escape the horrors of a debtors' prison. The result showed that he had acted wisely in so doing; his bankruptcy was immediately superseded, and a composition accepted, as already stated. The evil consequences of this failure in business, as will be seen, pursued him for many years afterwards; but as it is in the wisdom of Providence to overrule partial evil to general good, so these sufferings of Defoe caused him for more than thirty years to wage an incessant warfare against the monstrous cruelties then existing in connection with the laws of bankruptcy, recovery of debts, and the imprisonment of debtors. He lived to see the beginnings of a reformation of these evils, and posterity has completed the work. Mr. Wilson conjectures that when Defoe retired to avoid the fangs of the law, it was to Bristol. I do not doubt that he was, at some period, in that city, but he would certainly not have needed to remain there so long as Mr. Wilson supposes, had his object been only to avoid arrest until he could offer a composition to his creditors.

During this period, from 1692 to 1694, we learn very little about him, but it appears from the third page of the preface to his " Essay on Projects," that he wrote the greater part of that work after his failure in business, and certainly

---

* " Reply to Lord Haversham's ' Vindication.' "

RUDE WOODCUT PORTRAIT OF DEFOE.
From a Penny Edition of " Jure Divino," 1706.

OLD HOUSE IN CASTLE STREET, BRISTOL,
FORMERLY THE RED LION INN, AND THE RESIDENCE OF DEFOE.
From a recent Sketch.

before he became " engaged (in 1694) in proposing ways and
means to the Government."   It was probably during the same
period, also, that he became known to Queen Mary, who died
in the latter year.   The first laying out of Kensington Gardens
was the design of her Majesty, and he says, " The author of
this account having had the honour to attend her Majesty
when she first viewed the ground, and directed the doing it,
speaks this with the more satisfaction."*   Defoe's acquaintance with foreign trade, particularly with that to Spain and
Portugal, in which he had been engaged, joined with the high
opinion his friends had of his honour and integrity, induced
some of them to wish to settle him as a factor at Cadiz.   I
regret that Mr. Wilson should have conjectured any inferior
considerations as inducing Defoe to decline this offer, especially
when about to quote the one lofty motive assigned by Defoe
himself.   Willing to work, and trusting in God, the following
statement shows the simplicity of his religious faith, and the
consciousness of his own great powers, even under most adverse circumstances :—

" Misfortunes in Business having unhing'd me from Matters
of Trade, it was about the year 1694, when I was invited
by some Merchants with whom I had corresponded abroad,
and some also at home, to settle at *Cadiz* in *Spain*, and that
with Offers of very good Commissions ; but Providence, which
had other Work for me to do, placed a secret Aversion in my
Mind to quitting *England* upon any account, and made me
refuse the best Offers of that Kind, to be concern'd with some
eminent Persons at home, in proposing *Ways* and *Means* to
the Government for raising Money to supply the Occasions of
the War then newly begun."†

The chief objects of this War were to support the title of
King William and Queen Mary to the Crown, and to arrest
the conquests of the French Monarch.   While the Revolution
was being enacted, the adherents of the late King sought safety
in silence ; and the distinctions of Whig and Tory, Church and
Dissent, were almost forgotten in the general enthusiasm.

---

* " Tour through Great Britain," vol. ii. lett. 3, p. 14.
† " Appeal to Honour and Justice," p. 5, 6.

This, however, soon passed away,—party spirit was again rampant,—King William had been compelled to change some of his Ministers,—the Jacobites were numerous and active,yet taxation must be increased to carry on the War; it will be obvious, therefore, that, to facilitate increased taxation, one of the most valuable services that could be rendered was to engage the body of the people on the side of the King and Queen, and thus to make the war against France popular. To this labour Defoe set himself in the following Tract, which, being unknown to all his biographers, merits more than a passing notice.— " The ENGLISHMAN'S CHOICE, and true Interest : In the Vigorous Prosecution of the WAR against FRANCE ; and Serving K. WILLIAM and Q. MARY, and Acknowledging their Right. London. Printed in the year 1694."

He begins by stating that those who had sacrificed the religious and civil rights of the nation to the pleasure of the late king had now set up for patriots, in opposing one of the best princes that ever sat on the English throne, and asks,— " Who, says the Wise Satyrist, could endure the Gracchi talking against Sedition? And what true Englishman can with patience hear these Declaim against Taxes for carrying on the War against France, who were eager to give what the Court could ask, in a War against Protestants ?"

The above will show the wisdom of the writer. By reviving, to the recollection of the great mass of the people, the former despotic conduct of those who now sought public favour,—on pretence of opposing increased taxation, but really from disaffection to the existing Government,—he would at the same time neutralize the opposition, and arouse a feeling of loyal devotion to the King and Queen.

The following, from pages 31–2, shows not only his patriotism, but incidentally something of the indomitable spirit which then supported him under a load of private misfortunes :—

" Hannibal at the Gates, as it was used to frighten the Children of Rome ; to the Men was a Call and Incitement, to take care of the Publick Safety. Not to have despaired of the Commonwealth, when its Fortune seem'd most desperate, was as happy to them as it was glorious. And should the issue of opposing France be as dismal, as the most timorous or the most designing pretend to foretell ; it were better that the last

day of our being a free People should overtake us doing our
duty, and struggling against our chains, than helping to put
them on.   And in truth, hardly anything in this life can be a
real affliction, till men begin to sink under the sense of having
brought it upon themselves.   It is doubtless in our Power to
remove the moral and judicial Cause of our Fears ; nor can we
think that all those Ravages, Persecutions, Perfidies, and Con-
tempts of God and Man, shall long go without some remarkable Punishment.   However, Human Greatness has its Limits
and Periods ; and France seems to have seen its best days.   If
we use the means to humble it, by uniting and exerting our
strength, when once we come to grapple with it, and give it
one powerful shock ; like a great Machine screw'd up to the
height, it will never leave turning till it comes to the bottom."

The services thus rendered, no doubt, recommended Defoe
to the Government as a powerful writer, who ought to be employed.   He says—" Some time after this, I was, without the
least application of mine, and being then seventy miles from
London, sent for to be Accountant to the Commissioners of
the Glass Duty, in which service I continued to the determination of their Commission."*   This office closed with the
suppression of the tax, by act of Parliament, on the 1st of
August, 1699.

Subsequently to his misfortunes in business, and probably
about this time, Defoe became secretary to, and ultimately
owner of works at Tilbury, in Essex, for the manufacture
of bricks and pantiles.   The latter had hitherto been a Dutch
manufacture, and were brought in large quantities to London.
These works were erected to supersede the necessity of such
importation, and to provide a new source of employment.
They appear to have prospered until 1703, when Defoe was
deprived of his liberty, by process of law, for writing " The
Shortest Way with the Dissenters," and the undertaking
came to an end.   The capital embarked in the concern must
have been considerable, for he informs us that his own loss by
its failure was three thousand pounds—all of which loss, however, he paid off before March, 1705.   He also laments that a

---

* " Appeal to Honour and Justice," p. 6.

hundred poor labourers were thrown out of work, and they and their families reduced to beg elsewhere for employment. During the whole or part of the time these works were in existence, Defoe had a house in the same neighbourhood, and appears to have kept a pleasure-boat.

In the year 1860, when the London, Tilbury, and Southend Railway was completed, thinking that the excavations might discover some remains of Defoe's tile-works, I made a day's excursion to the locality. The following was written at the time. Immediately on the west side of the Tilbury station a large plot of land was being dug over to form potato-ground for the railway servants; and a deep trench had been previously cut through the same to the river, to drain the Company's estate. In this way the whole of Defoe's brick and pantile works had been laid open, including the claypits, drying-floors, foundations of kilns, and other buildings. Large quantities of bricks and tiles had been excavated, and thrown into heaps, to clear the land for its intended purpose. The pantiles appeared to have attracted very little notice; but the narrowness of the bricks, and the peculiar forms of certain tobacco-pipes, found mixed with both, had excited some little wonderment among the labourers. I asked several how they thought these things came there, and was answered by an ignorant shake of the head. But when I said, "These bricks and tiles were made 160 years since by the same man that made 'Robinson Crusoe'!" I touched a chord that connected these railway "navvies" with the shipwrecked mariner, and that bounded over the intervening period in a single moment. Every eye brightened, every tongue was ready to ask or give information, and every fragment became interesting. Porters, inspector, and stationmaster soon gathered round me, wondering at what was deemed an important historical revelation. The pantiles made at Tilbury were of excellent manufacture, and still retain a fine red colour, close texture, and are quite sonorous. Neither the Dutch nor any other tiles could have driven them out of the market, and the maker would have been able, from proximity to London and facilities of conveyance, either to undersell the foreign dealer or to realize a proportionately larger profit.

DANIEL · DE · FOE ·

A RUDE PORTRAIT OF DEFOE.

From a Penny Chap Book, dated 1706.

TILBURY FORT,

FROM THE SITE OF DEFOE'S TILE YARD.

To return from this digression. The connection of Defoe with the eminent persons engaged under the Government " in raising money to supply the occasions of the War," is not further explained by himself; but it must have been one of considerable pecuniary profit, as it partly induced him to refuse the agency at Cadiz. It must also have brought him into immediate contact with members of the Government, able to appreciate his rising talent. The accountantship of the Glass Duties further improved his circumstances and position, as also did the income from the Tile-works at Tilbury. He was now rapidly paying off his old debts, and had reached that comparatively prosperous condition which continued until the death of the King. In his printed "Letter to Mr. Howe," in January, 1701, he says, " As to Personal Miscarriages and Misfortunes, God in His merciful Providence has healed the Last, and, I hope, has Pardoned the First." His strictly honourable conduct in business had raised him up numerous friends during the season of adversity; and his connections at Court, combined with his high intellectual powers, now procured him the notice of persons of rank and wealth. Among these was Dalby Thomas, Esq., one of the Commissioners of the Glass Duty, afterward knighted; and Sir John Fagg, Bart., M.P. for Steyning in Sussex, where he had a noble ancient seat, and hospitably entertained Defoe in the summer of 1697.

Though a little out of its proper place, I may state here that Defoe wrote some Pindaric Verses, at the request of John Dunton, in honour of the Athenian Society, whose labours were communicated to the world in 1691, and some following years. These verses were prefixed to Charles Gildon's History of the Society, and reprinted in the second volume of " The Athenian Oracle." Dunton was married to a daughter of the Rev. Dr. Annesley, and Mr. Wilson inclines to the opinion that Defoe married another daughter, and that thus he and Dunton were brothers-in-law. Many minute circumstances—which, however, would occupy too much space, and still leave the matter doubtful—induce me to agree with Mr. Wilson, as to the probability that Defoe's first wife was the daughter of

Dr. Annesley.* Early in 1697 Defoe composed for Dunton "The Character of the late Dr. Samuel Annesley, by way of Elegy." The poem is in heroic verse, and shows the writer's great love and reverence of his deceased pastor. It is reprinted in the first volume of his " Collected Works."

The subject that next employed the pen of Defoe was one of very considerable importance in a political point of view. The war between France and England had exhausted the resources of both, and made them anxious for peace. As King William's object had been in some measure attained, he listened to the proposals of the French King; who having consented to relinquish the cause of James, and to acknowledge William as King, a treaty of peace was concluded between them, and signed at Ryswick the 20th of September, 1697. The military habits of the King, and the station to which his character and talents had raised him, as the protector of the liberties of Europe, inclined him to retain, if possible, the veteran army who had contributed so much to his personal glory, and the security of his throne. With feelings of deep pain, therefore, he found classes and parties, usually opposed to each other, united in opposition to the existence of any standing army in time of peace. It is needless now to enter into the various motives urged by the opponents in Parliament, and through the press. One of the earliest pamphlets in the debate was written by John Trenchard, entitled, "An Argument, shewing that a Standing Army is inconsistent with a Free Government, and absolutely destructive to the Constitution of the English Monarchy. London. Printed in the Year 1697." This was an able pamphlet, but anonymous; and the dedication, "to all those whom it may concern," was subscribed A. B. C. D. E. F. G. Although this was the month of December, the year did not end before at least four pamphlets had appeared on one side and the other, followed by at least eight in 1698. Among the writers drawn into the controversy, one of the first was Defoe, who replied very

---

* Another daughter of Dr. Annesley married Samuel Wesley, and became the mother of John and Charles Wesley, the founders of the Wesleyan Methodists.

warmly against Trenchard, directly attacking his reasoning, and impeaching his motives. The pamphlet is entitled, " Some Reflections on a Pamphlet lately published, entituled an Argument shewing that a Standing Army is inconsistent with a Free Government, and Absolutely Destructive to the Constitution of the English Monarchy. London. Printed for E. Whitlock, near Stationers' Hall. 1697." In this production Defoe proved himself a match for his opponent, and a powerful advocate for the King. Some asperity, however, is perceptible in his sarcasms ; and probably his publisher had persuaded him to soften down the title-page, as the running title is, " Reflections on a late Scandalous Pamphlet, Entitled An Argument against a Standing Army." The first edition must have been sold off immediately, as the second also bears the date 1697. Seeking by all honourable means the favour of the court, there were now many reasons why Defoe should not conceal his authorship. The preface was, therefore, intended to be subscribed D. F., and so it stands in the second edition ; but in the first it is misprinted D. T., and the T. afterwards altered, with a pen, to an F. The following year Defoe produced a second pamphlet on the same controversy, entitled, " An Argument shewing that a Standing Army, with consent of Parliament, is not inconsistent with a Free Government. 2 Chron. ix. 25. London. Printed for E. Whitlock, near Stationers' Hall, 1698." This is a most valuable constitutional Tract, of permanent interest, in which is calmly considered all that could be said upon the subject. He reprinted it, on this account probably, in the first volume of his works collected in 1703, at the same time omitting his previous pamphlet on the same subject, because, being a severe and direct controversial answer to Trenchard, its interest was but momentary.

It would be quite beyond the scope of this memoir to consider at large the disadvantages under which the Dissenters suffered by the Test Act and other oppressive and disqualifying laws. In no other part of the Kingdom were these grievances so evident as in London, where a large proportion of the merchant princes were Nonconformists. Several of these had been ennobled, and others attained the highest civic

dignities. The election of such men to the government of the
City proves that Dissenting influence must also have been
strong among the liverymen.   The Romanising tendencies of
James II. had induced him to raise many Dissenters to honour,
in order that he might seem impartial in his favours to the
Catholics, and thus doubly mortify those of the Church who
dared to thwart his encroachments.   The fall of the king revived the action of the Statutes he had illegally suspended ;
and thus, any person serving a public office, without first receiving the sacrament at church, was liable to a penalty of five
hundred pounds.   In the year of the Revolution, Sir John
Shorter, a Nonconformist, filled the office of chief magistrate,
but dying during his mayoralty, his place was supplied by Sir
John Eyles, who was of the same religious persuasion.   The
practice of Occasional Conformity by Dissenters, on accepting
official employments, began about that time, and continued,
without giving much offence to either party, until the 29th September, 1697, when Sir Humphrey Edwin, a Presbyterian, was
elected Lord Mayor. He was an Occasional Conformist, attending one part of the Sunday at church, and the other part at his
usual place of worship among the Dissenters.   This would
probably have excited as little disapprobation as the conduct
of his predecessors, had he not gone in procession to Pinner's
Hall meeting-house, preceded by the City regalia.   Considering that the existing laws merely tolerated dissent, the act was
imprudent, and regretted by the more judicious of his own
party, as tending to create further jealousy, when Dissenters
were already obnoxious to religious bigotry.   The consequences
thus deprecated were soon apparent in a discussion of the
whole practice of Occasional Conformity, which, after many years,
and much agitation, was made illegal by Act of Parliament.

When religious principle was concerned Defoe could not
tolerate expediency.   The offence was one peculiar to that
section of Christ's Church of which he had always been a sincere member.   It was tacitly defended by many whom he
loved and esteemed,—was practised chiefly by the most influential and honourable Dissenters,—and had not yet been openly
discountenanced by ministers or people.   As far as can be
ascertained, Defoe was the first to protest against it publicly,
and he did so in a pamphlet entitled, " An Enquiry into the

Occasional Conformity of Dissenters in Cases of Preferment. With a Preface to the Lord Mayor, occasioned by his carrying the Sword to a Conventicle. *If the Lord be God, follow him ; but if Baal, then follow him.* London. Printed Anno Dom. 1697."*

The genius of Defoe, as a controversialist, was now becoming fully developed ; and his pen was that of a " ready writer." The work is a grave and clear piece of casuistry, the result of deep thought and strong conviction. The writer evidently feels that his arguments are unanswerable, and he urges them with a wise abnegation of all personal self-importance. Although he claimed the pamphlet three years later, when republishing it, yet in this, the first opening of the discussion, he would not that his effort should fail in consequence of the " meanness and imperfections of the author." He therefore withholds his name, and appends as a signature to the Preface, the words, " *One, Two, Three, Four.*" I shall have again briefly to refer to this Tract ; and, as the controversy would now have little interest for the general reader, make only one quotation to show, that thus early in his polemical career, and on so nice a topic, Defoe exhibits that charity which he always entertained toward the Church of England :—

" The Name of Protestant is now the common Title of an Englishman, and the Church of England extends her Protection to the Tender Consciences of her Weaker Brethren, knowing that all may be Christians, tho' not alike informed ; and the Dissenter extends his Charity to the Church of England, believing that in his due time God shall reveal even this unto them. If this is not, I wish this were the Temper of both Parties ; and I am sure it is already the Temper of some of each Side, and those few are of the Wisest, most Pious, and most Judicious." pp. 9—10.

I have now to notice the first work of Defoe that attained

---

* To avoid an apparent anachronism, as to this and some others of Defoe's Works, I may advert to the fact that the year was *then* most generally computed from the latter end of March. The first quarter of the eighteenth century might be called a transition period, some printers beginning the year at Lady-Day, and some on the first of January. The above pamphlet by Defoe was published on the 25th January, 1698.

to the dignity of a volume.   " An Essay upon Projects.
London.   Printed by R. R. for Thomas Cockerill, at the
corner of Warwick Lane, near Paternoster Row.   1697."
Mr. Wilson and others have made a mistake in stating that it
was published towards the close of the War in January
1696–7.   Although dated in the latter year, it was not published until the 29th of March, 1698.   It consists of 350
pages, and might rather be called a series of Essays upon important public improvements suggested by the author.   After
an Introduction, and a short History of Projects and Projectors, the first scheme he recommends is a Royal or National
Bank, with affiliated Provincial Establishments.   The next
relates to Public Highways, and their improvement in construction, repair, and management.   Then follows a proposal
of Assurances, under which he includes Insurance against
Shipwreck, Fires, Titles of Lands, &c., but singularly says, he
cannot admire insuring of Life.   In recommending Friendly
Societies, which he says, " is in short a number of People
entering into a Mutual Compact to help one another, in Case
any Disaster or Distress fall upon them," he has many excellent suggestions, showing that the principle admits of great
extension ; instancing assistance of seamen, and support of
destitute widows.   He then proposes a Pension Office in every
County, for the reception of deposits from the poor for their
relief in sickness and old age ; this was an anticipation of the
modern institution of Savings Banks, combined with the still
more recent provision for conversion into annuities.   Under
the head " Of Fools," he urges the erection of an Institution
for the care and maintenance of Idiots ; whom he calls " a
particular Rentcharge on the great Family of Mankind."
For the benefit of Trade, and honest but unfortunate Traders,
he next projects a Commission of Enquiry into bankruptcy.
In the true spirit of improvement, our author suggests the
formation of Academies to supply some neglected branches of
education.   One of these was the Refinement and Correction
of the English Language, and suppression of profane swearing
and vulgarisms.   Another important recommendation, that he
esteemed the most noble and useful in his book, was an
Academy for Military Studies.   Supplementary thereto, he
proposes an Academy for Military Exercises.   Under this

Head he has also a project for an Academy for Women. The last scheme in the series is one for the Registration of all the Seamen of the United Kingdom.

Thus I have enumerated the topics of this remarkable embodiment of Defoe's benevolence, sagacity, and foresight. He truly remarks of the period when this book was written, that it was a "Projecting Age." Lotteries, Wagering, and schemes of a swindling description abounded. The journals contained numerous advertisements, such as "A House worth 500*l.* for ten shillings," "A service of Plate for a shilling ;" and, even of the more reputable proposals, the general intention was the pecuniary advantage of the projectors, at the expense of their dupes. Defoe's object in all his Projects was the greatest possible good to his fellow-creatures, without any private advantage to himself. That he was at least a century in advance of his age is apparent from the fact that nearly all the national and philanthropic measures he propounded have since been practically effected, though some of them only within the present generation. The book is comparatively little known, but it appeared so important to Mr. Walter Wilson that he has devoted to its contents a whole chapter of his "Life and Times of Defoe."* It is related of Benjamin Franklin that, when young, he found a copy of this book in his father's library, and declared afterward that he had received impressions from it that had influenced the principal events of his life.† A second edition was published in 1702, or rather the bookseller placed a new title-page before the remaining copies of the same impression.

. Another philanthropic work on which Defoe had engaged himself was the reformation of manners. His Essay on the subject had been written before the publication of the volume last noticed, but not being in the nature of a project, was issued separately two days afterward, under the title of "The Poor Man's Plea, in Relation to all the Proclamations, Declarations, Acts of Parliament, &c., which have been, or shall be made, or published, for a Reformation of Manners, and suppressing Immorality in the Nation. London : Printed in the

---

* Vol. i. pp. 256 to 268.   † Dodsley's " Ann. Reg.," xxxvi. 242.

year 1698." He sketches the gradual depravation of morals
from the Reformation to the reign of Charles II., and in the
character of a poor man seconds the laudable efforts of William
III. to prevent and punish profaneness and immorality, by
appealing to the Nobility, Gentry, Justices of the Peace, and
Clergy, to stop the flood of Vice and profanity by good
example; and urges, by forcible declamation against the great
influence of bad example, that the " whole weight of this
blessed work of Reformation lies on the shoulders of the
Gentry." He says—" Laws are *in Terrorem* Punishments;
and Magistrates compel and put a force on Men's minds; but
Example is persuasive and gentle, and draws by a secret, invisible, and almost involuntary power." Years afterward,
Defoe looked back with satisfaction to his having written this
Tract, and took frequent occasion, in his Reviews, to insist
upon the impartial enforcement of the law on the subject.
The pamphlet was popular, having passed through three edi-
tions before it was included in the first volume of his " Collected
Writings."

An interregnum of nearly two years occurred before the
appearance of Defoe's next publication, " The Pacificator. A
Poem. London : Printed and are to be sold by J. Nutt, near
Stationers'-Hall. 1700." It was published on the 20th of February in that year; it consists of four sheets folio, and the first
edition is of great rarity. This is Defoe's second Satire, and,
so far from being " not distinguished by any merit that would
render it popular beyond the fleeting occasion," I consider it
one of Defoe's best productions in verse. The plan consists of
an imaginary war among all the living authors of eminence,
the author ranging them into two adverse parties, " the Men
of Sense against the Men of Wit."

The following couplets from page 12 show that the poem
has antithetic force and point :—

> " *Wit*, like a hasty Flood, may over-run us,
> And too much *Sense* has oftentimes undone us.
> *Wit* is a Flux, a Looseness of the Brain,
> And *Sense-abstract* has too much Pride to reign.

> " *Wit* is a King without a Parliament,
> And *Sense* a Democratick Government.

> *Wit* without *Sense* is like the Laughing-Evil,
> And *Sense* unmix'd with *Fancy* is the Devil."

He shows great skill in weaving into his verse the names of living authors. I have only room for one instance, where, after urging the cessation of personal contention and abuse, he recommends;—

> " That each may choose the Part he can do well,
> And let the Strife be only to Excel;
> To their own Province let them all confine,
> Doctors to Heal, to Preaching the Divine;
> *Dryden* to Tragedy,—let *Creech* Translate,—
> *Durfey* make Ballads,—Psalms and Hymns for *Tate:*
> Let *Prior* Flatter Kings in Panegyrick,—
> *Ratcliff* Burlesque,—and *Wycherly* be Lyrick:
> Let *Congreve* write the Comick,—*Foe* Lampoon,—
> *Wessley* the Banter,—*Milbourn* the Buffoon;
> And the Transgressing Muse receive the Fate
> Of Contumacy, Excommunicate."

The death of Charles II. of Spain brought to a crisis the disputed succession to the crown of that monarchy. The treaty of Partition between the Kings of France and England and the States of Holland was unpopular in Spain and England. It had, however, been made in good faith by King William, and should the French monarch break through it, and acknowledge the Duke of Anjou as the future King of Spain, it appeared to many that a War between England and France would be inevitable. Although an important point in the history of Europe, I must say little more than that, before the decision of the French King was known, Defoe wrote, and on the 15th of November published, a pamphlet with the following title:—"The Two Great Questions Considered—I. What the French King will Do, with respect to the Spanish Monarchy? II. What Measures the English ought to take? London: Printed in the year 1700." A short preface announces that since the sheets were in the Press, " Letters from France advise that the King of France has saluted his Grandson, the Duke D'Anjou, as King of Spain."* On the 23rd of the same

---

* Defoe had already begun to be pirated. The *English Post*, 21 Nov., 1700, advertises " That there is a Sham Edition of the same Book, without the Preface, printed upon a very bad Paper: wherein are very great Omissions and Mistakes."

month appeared " Remarks upon a late Pamphlet, intituled
' The Two Great Questions Considered,' &c.   London : 1700."
It has been said that this anonymous writer " rudely assailed "
Defoe; but I cannot perceive anything of the kind, unless at
page 15, where he says, " If ever man petitioned in print for
a Place, surely our Author does in this Book."   On the 2nd of
December, Defoe rejoined with, "The Two Great Questions
further Considered. With some Reply to the Remarks. London:
1700." I think this able and exhaustive political Tract betrays
more warmth of personal feeling than the occasion called for ;
but it was the first time Defoe had been publicly criticised, and
he evidently could not bear the lash.   He little thought that
in a few years he would endure the most cruel scourgings, and
be able to work on, as if impenetrable.

There was a religious aspect of the question which had not
been considered.   Defoe saw that Protestantism in England
and Holland was in danger, by the French King's breach of
the Partition Treaty ; that the disbanding of King William's
army had weakened the nation ; that another source of weakness existed in the great number of Jacobites at home ; that
there was no confederacy with other nations, by which the
Protestant Religion could be protected ; while the accession of
a French prince to the throne of Spain consolidated the Popish
Power in France, Spain, Italy, and the Netherlands.   Believing that Protestantism was thus menaced, he urged an alliance
with the Austrian Emperor, who was the natural rival of the
French King ; and also, a defensive Union of all Protestant
States.   Such is a brief abstract of the substance of a well-
written pamphlet which Defoe gave to the world on the 9th of
January, intituled " The Danger of the Protestant Religion Considered, from the present Prospect of a Religious War in Europe.
Printed in the year 1701."   It was dedicated to the King ;
and, from the plain freedom of the address, there can be little
doubt the writer already knew that his Majesty approved the
contents.   His former opponent returned to the charge on the
21st of January with a *Second Part* of " Remarks on the Two
Great Questions, wherein the Grand Question of all is considered, viz., What the Dutch ought to do at this Juncture ?
London : 1701."

I must now return to the 20th November, 1700, when
Defoe reissued from the Press his "Enquiry into the Occasional
Conformity of Dissenters in cases of Preferment," &c.   He
now cancelled the former Preface, and substituted one to the
Rev. John Howe, an eminently pious and learned Nonconformist divine, whose name still ranks among Christians with
those of Annesley, Owen, and Baxter.   The occasion of this
Preface was, that Sir Thomas Abney, Lord Mayor of London,
and one of Mr. Howe's church members, had, upon his
recent induction to office, attended and received the sacrament
according to the Church of England.   During three years, no
substantial answer had been given to Defoe's former publication, and he was anxious to elicit from so influential a minister,
under the circumstances already stated, some expression of
approval or disapproval of the practice.   The preface is short,
and in the most respectful terms that could be used ; but concluding, " If none of these Requests shall be granted, the
World must believe, *That Dissenters do allow themselves to
Practise what they cannot Defend.*   Your very humble
servant, D. F."

In these few words there was felt to be a sting ; and it is
to be regretted that so excellent a man as Howe should have
lost his temper, and written a reply not creditable to his
Christian character, in a Tract entitled " Some Consideration of
a Preface to an Enquiry concerning the Occasional Conformity
of Dissenters, &c. By John Howe, Minister of the Gospel.
To whom that Preface (as he conceives) is addressed. London.
Printed for Thomas Parkhurst, 1700."   Mr. Howe's pamphlet
was published on the 28th of December ; and on the 24th of
the following month appeared a very carefully written and
calm rejoinder from Defoe ; who, knowing that his own principles were impregnable, but the "unhappy writer" open to
personal animadversion, seems throughout to have studied how
to express the strongest arguments in the most modest and
unexceptionable terms, as to charity and good manners.   His
pamphlet is entitled, " A Letter to Mr. Howe, by way of
Reply to his Observations on the Preface to the Enquiry into
the Occasional Conformity of Dissenters in cases of Preferment.   By the Author of the Preface and the Enquiry.
London.   Printed 1701.   A. Baldwin, in Warwick Lane."

After this, it is said that no efforts could persuade Mr. Howe to continue the debate. In the absence of provocation Defoe addressed himself to other subject, and the matter rested again for a year.

On the 1st of August, 1700, there appeared what Defoe calls, " a vile abhorred Pamphlet, in very ill verse, written by one Mr. Tutchin, and called *The Foreigners ;* in which the author, who he was I then knew not, fell personally upon the King himself, and then upon the Dutch Nation. And after having reproached his Majesty with Crimes that his worst Enemies could not think of without horror, he sums up all in the odious name of a *Foreigner.* This filled me with a kind of Rage against the Book, and gave birth to a trifle which I never could hope should have met with so general an acceptance as it did ; I mean The True-Born Englishman."* As our author declares that he was " filled with a kind of Rage," it is observable that " The True-Born Englishman" was not published until the beginning of January, 1701, five months after the offending pamphlet ; and that, between the two, Defoe gave to the world at least three distinct productions of his pen. Possibly he might not see *The Foreigners* immediately on its first appearance ; or he might have written part of his " Satyr" in reply, and be compelled to lay it aside by considerations more immediately pressing. Several answers to Tutchin quickly appeared ;† but they, and the poem itself, were soon extinguished and forgotten in the fame of Defoe's admirable pamphlet. This, in its turn, was followed by many productions in prose and verse, called answers, but none of them possessed any vitality.‡ In the collections of the curious,

---

* " Appeal to Honour and Justice," p. 6.

† On the 24th of August, 1700, was published " The Reverse ; or the Tables Turn'd. A Poem. Written in Answer, Paragraph by Paragraph, to a late Scurrilous and Malicious Medley of Rhimes call'd *The Foreigners.*" On the 11th of September " The Natives : An Answer to *The Foreigners.*"

‡ Jan. 31.—" An Answer to a late abusive Pamphlet entituled *The True-Born Englishman,* &c. Together with the True Character of a True Englishman." Feb. 1.—" The True-Born Englishman. A Satyr. Answered Paragraph by Paragraph." (This antagonist had so little knowledge or discernment as to believe he was answering John Toland.) Feb. 27. —" The English Gentleman Justified. A Poem. Written on the Occasion

copies of some of them may be found, but, only as appendages to " The True-Born Englishman. A Satyr." This work, which was printed without any name of author or bookseller, instantly took possession of all readers, from the King on his throne to the humble buyers of penny piracies hawked in the streets. It is very probable, that from the invention of printing to the end of 1701, an equal number of copies had never been sold of any book within the space of one year. In the Preface to the second volume of his collected writings he complained of the pecuniary loss he had sustained by spurious editions of the work ; and, speaking only from recollection of four years, shows that even he had a very inadequate notion of its large circulation. He says, " the True-born Englishman is a remarkable Example, by which the Author, tho' in it he eyed no Profit, had he been to enjoy the Profit of his own Labour, had gain'd above £1000. A Book that besides Nine Editions of the Author, has been Twelve Times printed by other Hands ; some of which have been sold for one penny, others twopence, and others sixpence, the Author's Editions being fairly printed, and on good Paper, and could not be sold under a shilling. Eighty thousand of the small ones have been sold in the Streets for twopence, or at a penny : and the author thus abused and discouraged had no remedy but Patience."

In 1705, when Defoe wrote the above paragraph, new editions of The True-Born Englishman were still being issued, yet there were at least nine genuine editions published before the end of 1701, and I have seen more than twelve spurious editions not later than 1704. The popularity of this satire has been as permanent as it was at first sudden, and it is still frequently reprinted as a separate pamphlet. The " True-Born Englishman" was always a favourite with our author, who associated himself with it on the title-pages of many of his subsequent writings. It had a favourable effect upon his circumstances

---

of a late Scurrilous Satyr, Intitled, *The True-Born Englishman*." March 1. —" The Fable of the Cuckoo: or the Sentence on the Ill Bird that defiled his own Nest. Shewing in a Dissenter's Dream, some Satyrical Reflections on a late Infamous Libel, call'd *The True-Born Englishman*." March 25.— " The Female Critick, &c. With a Letter in Answer to *The True-Born Englishman*."

in recommending him to the personal friendship of King William. Many years afterward he alluded to the fact as follows :—" How this Poem was the occasion of my being known to his Majesty; how I was afterwards received by him; how employed; and how, above my capacity of deserving, rewarded, is no part of the present Case; and is only mentioned here, as I take all Occasions to do, for the expressing the honour I ever preserved for the immortal and glorious memory of that greatest and best of Princes, whom it was my honour and advantage to call Master as well as Sovereign."*

The object of the Satire was to reproach his countrymen with ingratitude for abusing King William as a Foreigner; and in doing this he traces the origin of the English Nation, and describes it as made up from the admixture of the overflowings and offscourings of other races; all leading to the conclusion, that—

> " A True-Born Englishman's a contradiction,
>   In speech an irony, in fact a fiction.
>   A metaphor, invented to express
>   A Man *akin* to all the Universe."

More than a quarter of a century later he speaks of the effect produced upon the nation by this performance. " None of our Countrymen have been known to boast of being *True-Born Englishmen,* or so much as to use the word as a title or appellation, ever since a late satire upon that national folly was published. Nothing was more frequent in our mouths *before* that, nothing so universally blushed for and laughed at since."†

---

* " Appeal to Honour and Justice," p. 7.
† " Use and Abuse of the Marriage Bed," p. 400-1.

CHAPTER III.

Dissolution of Parliament—Defoe publishes " Six Distinguishing Cha-
racters of a Parliament Man" — " Considerations upon Corrupt
Elections "—" The Freeholder's Plea"—" The Villainy of Stock-
jobbers Detected"—" The Succession of the Crown of England Con-
sidered"—Presents " Legion's Memorial" to the Speaker—Publishes
" History of the Kentish Petition"—" The present State of Jacobitism
Considered"—" Reasons against a War with France"—" Original
Power of the Collective Body of the People Asserted"—Death of
King William—Defoe publishes " The Mock Mourners"—" A New
Test of the Church of England's Loyalty"—" Reformation of Man-
ners"—" Good Advice to the Ladies"—" The Spanish Descent"—
Bill to prevent occasional conformity — Defoe publishes another
pamphlet thereon ; also, " The Shortest Way with the Dissenters"—
Proclamation for his discovery—His pamphlet burnt—He surrenders
—Publishes an explanation—Is committed to prison—Writes " King
William's Affection to the Church of England"—First volume of
his collected writings published—" More Reformation"—His trial
and sentence.

1701—3.

THE position of the king in 1700 was one of great uneasiness : the dispersion of his tried troops, followed by a
gross breach of faith in the King of France, and accompanied
by continuous struggles of enraged political parties in England, who in their heat did not refrain from assailing the
private character of their great deliverer :—all these induced
him to spend great part of the summer on the continent. He
had been compelled to part with his Whig ministers, and his
absence from the kingdom afforded the new ministry opportunities of concerting measures for strengthening their own
power, and weakening that of their rivals. The first step of
ministers after his Majesty's return, was to procure a dissolution
of Parliament, which took place on the 19th of December ; and a
new Parliament, in which they hoped to obtain an addition to
their numbers, was appointed to assemble on the 6th of the following February. Meantime the press was actively employed
by both parties, and many able pamphlets were produced, which

have yet a value to all who love the constitution of the English
Government.

Defoe now stood high in the private confidence of the King,
who must have fully appreciated his political wisdom, and
found in him an able exponent of views identical with his own
on great national questions.   Reverting a few years later to
the injurious treatment of the King at this time, Defoe says,
" I am not at all vain in saying, I had the honour to know
more of his Majesty than some of those who have thus insulted
him knew of his horse; and I think, if my testimony was
able to add to his bright reputation, I could give such particulars of his being not a man of morals only, but of serious
piety and religion, as few kings in the world, in these latter
ages of time, can come up to."*

Defoe's pen was most active at this juncture, and it may be
fairly inferred that the king coincided with the opinions and
recommendations contained in three Tracts rapidly given to
the public by our author. On the 4th of January, 1701, was published, " The Six Distinguishing Characters of a Parliament
Man.   Addressed to the good People of England.   London.
Printed in the year 1700."   Its contents may be summed up
by saying that Parliament men should be Loyal,—Religious,—
Men of Sense,—of Years,—Honesty,—and Morals.   A few
days later appeared, " Considerations upon Corrupt Elections
of Members to serve in Parliament.   London.   Printed in the
year 1701."   This is, of course, directed against bribery, in all
its forms, of eating and drinking, buying and selling of individual votes, and the then newly-commenced practice of wholesale buying and selling seats.   In this he alludes to joint-
stocks and funds, used for procuring the election of persons in
the interest of the new East India Company.   Both the above
pamphlets, having been addressed to constituencies, as from
without, on the characters of candidates, and the conduct of
elections, Defoe now assumed his right as a freeholder, and
his third Tract, published on the 23rd of January, seems designed
to influence the new Parliament in dealing with disputed elections.   It is entitled, " The Freeholder's Plea against Stock-
Jobbing Elections of Parliament Men.   London.   Printed in

---

* Review IV. 67.

the year 1701." It exposes the jobbing and selling of seats
in Parliament, upon the Stock Exchange in London, by
brokers; as the prices rose or fell, like East India, or any
other stock.

Having taken in hand the unconstitutional proceedings of
Stock-Jobbers with reference to the Elections, he thought it
right, before quitting them, to expose the vile practices by
which they succeeded in raising or lowering at pleasure the
value of all property and securities; and, the disastrous consequences of these proceedings to all persons connected with
the trade and commerce of the country.   This he did in a
pamphlet published on the 11th of February, entitled, " The
Villainy of Stock-Jobbers Detected, and the Causes of the Late
Run upon the Bank and Bankers, Discovered and Considered.
London.   Printed in the year 1701." It will be observed
that his title is written in strong language; and correspond-
ingly, the tract is an unsparing denunciation of what was most
abominable to the mind of Defoe,—villainy practised without
breaking any law.   Years afterward he returned to the subject
frequently in his *Reviews*, and memorably again in 1720, in
his " Anatomy of Exchange Alley." It is deeply to be regretted that no·effectual remedy has ever been found for the
evils so long ago denounced; and that gambling on the Exchange has been, so recently as 1866, successful in over-
throwing large financial undertakings, otherwise solvent;
and reducing to poverty thousands of families previously in
affluence.

The fifth Parliament of King William, in the composition
of which Defoe had taken so much interest, assembled on the
6th of February, 1701, when Robert Harley, Esq., who made so
distinguished a figure in the next reign, was chosen Speaker.
The Duke of Gloucester, son of the Princess Anne, had died
in the preceding July, and the King had consequently, during
his absence on the continent, concerted measures, with the
Princess Sophia, for the future succession of the House of
Hanover, and the security of the Protestant religion.   Defoe
refers afterward, in his " History of the Union," to his Majesty's
deep anxiety and disinterestedness at this time for the future

VOL. I.

welfare of the kingdom.*   In his speech at the opening of the
new Parliament, the king urged the subject upon the immediate
consideration of both Houses ; but the intended Bill was not
brought forward until the third of March, and our author had,
about two days before, published, " The Succession to the Crown
of England Considered.   London.   Printed in the year 1701."
In this pamphlet he examines the claims of all those who were
supposed to be heirs to the Crown.   He holds that all the
Roman Catholics are excluded on the ground of religion ; and
after admitting that the Duke of Monmouth's legitimacy was
never proved, concludes that the House of Hanover has the
only indisputable title.   He retains, however, an affectionate
regard for the memory of the Duke of Monmouth, who was
valued and beloved by the nation ; and, acknowledging that
the point was tender, craves leave to suggest an inquiry,
" Whether the Legitimacy of his Birth could be made out or
no ? or, That, if his Posterity have any Argument to prove it,
they shall be heard."   He continues on this to the end of the
Tract ; but no investigation was made, and the Bill for settling
the Succession became an Act of Parliament.

The factiousness of a majority of the House of Commons
with reference to the Partition Treaty, (brought under consideration in consequence of the French recognition of the
Duke of Anjou, and the fortifying of Flanders, so as to
threaten the Dutch,) was such as to bring them speedily into
conflict with the House of Lords, and with the King.   A
Committee of the Commons was appointed to prepare Articles
of Impeachment against the Earls of Portland and Orford, and
Lords Somers and Halifax,—who were esteemed friends of his
Majesty,—and the King was daily mortified by the personal
affronts heaped upon him ; while the opposition, and mutual
recriminations between the two Houses, greatly hindered
public business.   This antagonism of the Commons against
the Lords, and against a King so much beloved by his people,
produced its natural results ; petitions and remonstrances
began to appear, until by one fatal act the unpopularity of the

---

* " Hist. of the Union," p. 41-2.

House of Commons became so great that the members were paralysed by fear of the popular rage.

Too much space would be required to enter into a full account of the Kentish Petition, which concluded by calling upon the House to give his Majesty such Supplies as would enable him to provide for the interests of the Kingdom, and assist his allies, before it was too late. The document was signed by the Deputy Lieutenants, Justices, Grand Jury, &c., and presented in person by five of their number, who were, after an angry discussion, ordered to be taken into custody by the Serjeant-at-Arms. They continued in his charge from the 8th May until the 13th, when they were, by further order of the House, under the Speaker's Warrant, committed to the Gate-House prison, where they remained until the end of the Session.

The day following their commitment, Defoe, with patriotic courage rarely equalled, went to the House of Commons, guarded by about sixteen gentlemen of quality, (who, if necessary, were prepared to carry him off by force,) and boldly delivered to the Speaker his celebrated "Legion's Memorial." In a Letter enclosed with it, the Speaker is "Commanded by 200,000 Englishmen to deliver it to the House of Commons, and to inform them that it is no banter, but serious truth; and a serious regard to it is expected." Of the Memorial itself it is difficult to decide whether is most admirable,—the terseness of composition;—the plain but full assertion of the rights of the people, and the duty of Parliament;—or, the magisterial tone which throughout treats the assembled House as servants, who must obey their superiors. In the original, the document occupies four pages quarto, closely printed, and concludes as follows—

"Thus, *Gentlemen*, you have your Duty laid before you, which 'tis hoped you will think of; but if you continue to neglect it, you may expect to be treated according to the Resentments of an *injur'd Nation; for Englishmen* are no more to be Slaves to *Parliaments*, than to a King.

"*Our Name is Legion, and we are Many.*"

The Paper seems to have struck such a terror into the dominant party of the House that not another word was said

about proceeding against the Kentish Petitioners. No real
effort was made to discover the author of the Memorial,—the
Members began to drop off and get into the country, the
necessary supplies were voted as quickly as possible, Parliament
rose on the 24th of June, when the Petitioners were liberated ;
and, to celebrate their triumph, a noble entertainment was
given at Mercers' Hall ; where, next to the Kentish Worthies,
sat the Author of the Legion Letter.

The press teemed with publications upon the subject ; and,
as some evidence of the inclination of the Court, one of the
first was, " The Kentish Worthies, a Poem, by Mr. Tate, Poet-
Laureate to his Majesty. Printed for A. Baldwin. London.
1701." This panegyric, which was published on the 30th of
July, was reflected upon by an opponent, but met with no dis-
favour from the King ; and, a few days afterward Defoe published, " The History of the Kentish Petition. London.
Printed in the year 1701." I may add that, at the same time
Lord Somers, another confidential friend of the King, issued
his " *Jura Populi Anglicani :* or, the Subject's Right of Petitioning set forth. Occasioned by the Case of the Kentish
Petitioners," &c. &c. 1701. A conclusion may be fairly
drawn from the above facts as to the King's love of liberty,
and his care, through the instrumentality of able men, closely
attached to him, to hand down to posterity these accounts of
one of the most remarkable occurrences in the history of Parliaments ; and, to record the firm establishment of the constitutional right of petitioning.

On the sixteenth of September, in the same year, an event
occurred, that in its consequences, increased the antipathy of
England towards France. This was the death of James II.,
and the immediate fulfilment by the French King of a promise made to him, by causing the Son of the deceased to be
proclaimed King of England, Scotland, and Ireland ; he also
prevailed upon the King of Spain, the Pope, and the Duke of
Savoy, to follow his example. The intelligence of this, occasioned a national outburst of indignation, that a foreign power
should prescribe them a King without their consent ; and
addresses to King William, re-echoing the patriotic sentiments
of the Kentish Petition, poured in upon him from every

quarter.   The death of James weakened the attachment of the
Jacobites to his family, and the Protestants of the party (being
disposed to join the Whigs against the encroachments of
France,) everything seemed to predicate a war between the two
countries.   Defoe, thinking this a suitable opportunity, invited
all such to transfer their allegiance; addressing them in a
pamphlet entitled, " The Present State of Jacobitism considered, in Two Queries :—1. What Measures the French King
will take with respect to the Person and Title of the Pretended
Prince of Wales ? 2. What the Jacobites in England ought
to do on the Same Account ? London.   Printed in the year
1701."   Our author seems to have seen the extreme tendencies of party spirit, and in this, and the next following
pamphlet, to have commenced those efforts towards moderation
and peace, which he never after relinquished.   He was
answered by the learned and pious, and I may add, moderate,
Nonjuror, Thomas Wagstaff, who admits the kind language
of the invitation, but puts a construction upon it not intended
by Defoe.

The warlike spirit now rising in the nation was greatly encouraged by pamphlets favourable to the policy of the King,
and perhaps the most powerful of them was one from the pen
of Lord Somers, entitled *" Anguis in Herba :* or, the Fatal
Consequences of a Treaty with France," &c. &c.   London,
1701.   No greater proof could be given of the true independence of Defoe, than that his great admiration of, and devotion to, the King, could not materially influence his thoughts
and actions, on such an occasion.   The cry for war was now
become general, and he had joined in it as to the French
King's breach of the Partition Treaty ; but on this most recent
point of the dispute, he dissented ; and, in order to moderate
the general excitement, or at least to clear the quarrel from
all extraneous considerations, he published, in the same month
of October, " Reasons against a War with France ; or, an
Argument shewing, that the French King's owning the Prince
of Wales as King of England, Scotland and Ireland, is No
Sufficient Ground of a War.   London.   Printed in the year
1701."   The argument of Defoe is that the French King only
bound himself by the Treaty of Ryswick not to afford any
assistance to any person against King William ; but, that it

contains not a word to prevent his continuing to James, or his posterity, the empty title of King of England, &c. He admits this to be a personal affront to King William, and wishes that before he had recalled his Ambassador he had ordered him to demand satisfaction; but he denies it to be a just ground for war. He shows that we are bound by treaty to the Emperor of Austria; and, with him to make war against the Duke of Anjou for the throne of Spain,—and should the King of France support his grandson, we shall then have just ground of war,— but that no sufficient cause yet exists. I have stated that Defoe wrote this Tract against the views of some of the King's most able advisers,—it was equally contrary to the wishes and feelings of an excited nation;—but it is a masterly perform-ance, for clear discernment and temperate discussion, for solid reasoning and conclusions, and it has been pronounced one of the finest political tracts in the English language. Several at-tempts were made to answer it, but they all so signally failed, that our Author did not consider any of them worthy of notice.

During the controversy between the two Houses of Parlia-ment, Sir Humphrey Mackworth published, " A Vindication of the Rights of the Commons of England. By a Member of the Honourable the House of Commons. London. 1701." In this tract he advanced claims on behalf of the House of which he was a member, inconsistent with the rights of the subject, by placing it above the law. The cause of the Lords was taken up in " A Vindication of the Rights and Prerogatives of the Right Honourable the House of Lords : wherein, a late discourse, intitled ' A Vindication of the Rights of the Commons of England,' is considered. London. 1701." This was an able production, and was probably written by Lord Somers.

As a politician Defoe may be said to have now attained the full maturity of his genius and power. Perceiving that the disputants had overlooked, or not properly stated, the rights of the people, he published, on the 27th of December, 1701, his celebrated pamphlet, " The Original Power of the Collective Body of the People of England, Examined and Asserted. With a double Dedication to the King, and to the Parliament. London. Printed in the year 1702."

The paragraphs presenting themselves as worthy of quotation are so numerous, and the work so connected by a chain of powerful arguments, tending to one conclusion, that I must forbear attempting its character in this volume.   Mr. Chalmers says of it, " Every lover of liberty must be pleased with the perusal of a treatise, which vies with Mr. Locke's famous tract in power of reasoning, and is superior to it in the graces of style."*   Mr. Wilson has devoted an entire chapter of his Life and Times of Defoe to this pamphlet.†   Yet it is remarkable that a work of so much merit should have been seldom reprinted, and that a copy is now rarely to be met with.

The first edition is in the inconvenient form of a folio, and those not bound up with other tracts must have soon perished. The second Edition is in Defoe's Collected Writings, published in 1703, but singularly, is omitted from the Table of Contents. During the contest between the House of Commons and Mr. Wilkes, who was refused his seat, though repeatedly elected a member, this work was republished, in octavo, in 1769, with " Some Distinguishing Characters of a Parliament Man, by the same Author;" and was dedicated to the Lord Mayor, Aldermen, and Commons of the City of London.   The editor, after adverting to the struggle between the City and Parliament, and the prevalent ignorance as to constitutional rights, says, " The reprinting, therefore, of this excellent piece of the celebrated Daniel De Foe, who seems to have understood as well as any man, the civil constitution of the Kingdom, wherein the nature of our Constitution is set in the clearest light, upon self-evident principles, and the Original Power of the Collective Body of the People asserted, seemed to be altogether seasonable and fitting."‡

In the summer of 1701 King William visited the continent, and formed an alliance with Holland and the Emperor against the power of France.   During his absence the strife of parties continued; but as Parliament was not sitting, the warfare was carried on through the press, and the nation was inundated with pamphlets.   The ministers were sinking in reputation, the popularity of their opponents revived, and the passions of

---

* " Life of Defoe," p. 20, Oxford edit.   † Vol. i. pp. 416 to 436.
‡ Dedication, p. iii.

the people were heated to excess.   It was the intention of the King to return to England in October, but he was delayed at the Hague until the 4th of November, in consequence of severe indisposition.   Soon after his arrival the Parliament was dissolved, and another called, to meet on the 30th of December.

The general election was hotly contested, and one method of opposition adopted was the publication by the Whigs of the celebrated libel, called the *Black List,* consisting of the names, &c., of one hundred and sixty-seven Tory members who had been most adverse to the measures of the King and the Lords, in the preceding parliament; and who, according to this *Black List,* "ought to be opposed in the ensuing elections, by all that intend to save their native country from being made a province of France."   It was contrary to the high principles of Defoe thus to expose men to the fury of a rabble; and about two years later he wrote, "I am no *Black List* man, and always abhorred that unfair way of charging men by name with facts I could not prove; and which I look upon as ungentlemanlike and unchristian."*   Indeed, there is every reason to believe that the result of his great efforts to guide the electors, twelve months previously, had convinced him that the masses were inaccessible to reason during such occasions of excitement; and, that he took no prominent part in any of the elections.   The success of Legion's Memorial induced him again to aim at the elected, rather than the constituencies; and the King having opened the new Parliament with a speech from the throne, on the last day of the year, our author published, on the following day, a pamphlet, entitled, " Legion's New Paper: Being a Second Memorial to the Gentlemen of a late House of Commons.   With Legion's humble Address to his Majesty.   London: Printed and Sold by the Booksellers of London and Westminster, 1702."   In explanation of the expression "*late* House of Commons," in the above title, it is probable that motives of safety might suggest the insertion of the word "late," as this was a work to be offered for public sale.   Also, that, as only forty-six of the names contained in the *Black List* were left out of the new Parliament, the pamphlet would still apply to those for whom it was designed.

---

* Review I. 337.

The nervous eloquence,—the power of invective,—and the lofty scorn, exhibited by the writer, must remind modern readers of some of the finest passages of Junius, albeit free from the personalities of that writer. The following is the manner in which he commences his address to a branch of the legislature :—" Gentlemen,—The greatest respect which could possibly have been shewn to you by the People of England, had been to have let your Actions have sunk into forgetfulness ; and in Kindness to you, have let neither you nor your Deeds have been nam'd any more in your Native Country." He concludes in a similar spirit, on the twelfth page, and then occupies the remainder of the pamphlet with " Legion's Address to His Majesty," couched in terms of the most devoted loyalty ; in assurance of the affection and fidelity of the people, and of their gratitude for the blessings he has secured to the nation. The contrast between the tone of the two parts of this Tract was undoubtedly designed. A greater transition could scarcely be conceived.

War having been determined upon, it became the duty of every patriot to serve his country ; and it is equally creditable to the King and Defoe that their difference of opinion as to the sufficiency of the grounds for war, did not disturb the confidence of the monarch in the wisdom and fidelity of his servant. Defoe was consulted by the King on various points relating to the impending hostilities, and drew up a scheme of operations against the Spanish West Indies, shewing that thus the enemy would be most crippled, and the war made self-supporting. The plan was fully approved by the King ; and had he lived, Defoe would have had an honourable part in its execution.*

When the King was ill at the Hague, in the preceding October, he directed that his indisposition should be kept secret. He knew the diseased condition of his lungs, and must have been convinced that the attack was a premonition of approaching dissolution. Shortly after his return while walking in his garden at Hampton Court, he was pleased

---

* *Vide* Review VII. 511-13.

to tell the Earl of Portland he found himself so weak that he did not expect to live another summer, but charged him at the same time to say nothing of it until he was dead.*   This affords a striking proof of the heroic fortitude of his majesty, who continued to employ his thoughts and attention assiduously in providing for the public safety ; declining no public business, nor discovering any anxiety as to his approaching end. That end was accelerated by a fall from his horse, on the 21st of February ; and after lingering a fortnight, during which he prepared himself in such a manner as to heighten, if possible, the esteem and veneration of all who were near him, died,— with an even and calm mind, in full possession of all his great faculties,—without the least alteration of countenance, on the 8th of March, 1702, in the fifty-second year of his age.

This is not the place for any character or eulogium of King William III.   The Prince who delivered from jeopardy our religion and liberties,—who secured the rights,—and confirmed the privileges in which every Englishman still glories, needs no commendation from my weak pen ;—his name will be held in sacred remembrance so long as the greatness and power of England shall endure, or its constitutional freedom survive in offspring nations, to remotest ages.

This national bereavement forms an epoch in the life of Daniel Defoe.   The congeniality of principles, and even of temper between him and the King was very great ; the reticence of both, as to private confidences, was unable entirely to conceal it.   The King was naturally cautious and reserved,— of few words,—an observer of distance and decorum.   He was careful not to sully his grandeur with condescensions that were mean and trifling.   His confidential intercourse therefore with a subject, who had no influence but that of his wisdom, genius, and patriotism to recommend him—redounds to their mutual honour.   Had the life of King William been spared to old age, it is most probable that Defoe would have attained a high and noble position, as he had clearly before him a prospect of great national influence, and its usual attendant, substantial rewards.   But it is in vain to speculate whether or not he

---

* " Life of William III.," 8vo, 1703, p. 632.

QUEEN MARY, Wife of William III.

WILLIAM III., Defoe's Friend.

From a Painting by Adrian van der Werff.

would have done more, under the shadow of the King's greatness, to carry down his own name to posterity, than was ultimately effected by his indomitable courage and incessant
labours, when struggling alone against opposition and neglect,
during some parts of the remaining thirty years of his life.

In the latter end of this reign Defoe resided at Hackney,
and continued there until 1707.   There, some of his children
were born.   In the parish register is the following entry :—
" Sophia, daughter to Daniel Defoe, by Mary, his wife, was
baptized December 24th, 1701.   Martha Defoe, a child, was
carried out of the parish to be buried in 1707."

Immediately after the death of King William, the slumber-
ing spirit of Jacobitism and faction awoke to fresh vigour.
The " Life of James II." was published in London, and soon
passed through two editions.   In the pulpit, and on the plat-
form, the people were told to rejoice that the Royal Family was
again come to the throne of their ancestors ; and the departed
hero was made the subject of malignant speeches, toasts, and
lampoons.   The affectionate sorrow of Defoe, at the decease of
his master and kind benefactor, could ill brook these unjust
reflections ; and, to show his sense of conduct so unnatural, as
well as to testify his admiration of departed excellence, he
produced, in the month of May, his poem, " The Mock
Mourners : a Satyr, by way of Elegy on King William.
London : M. Gunne. 1702." It was dedicated to Queen Anne,
and the reception it met with from the public could not fail
to be gratifying to the author, as proving that the silent but
sincere mourners far outnumbered the traducers of the King's
memory.   It passed through six large editions before the end
of the year ; the seventh, corrected by the author, was printed
the same year.   A few months later it was reprinted in the
first volume of his collected writings, and again in " Poems on
Affairs of State."

A very little time was sufficient after the accession of
Queen Anne to convince Defoe that, however great a disaster
the death of King William was to the nation at large, it
would probably be ruinous to all his own immediate worldly

prospects.   Although at her first Council the Queen declared her resolution to adhere to the policy of the late King, and to prosecute his intended war against France and Spain ; yet were the names of Lords Somers and Halifax early erased from the list of Privy Councillors, and some of the bitterest enemies of William were taken into favour.   Cunningham remarks, " The dearer any one had been to the late King, so much the more violently was he attacked with various calumnies."*

The letting loose of Jacobitism and political faction, without doors, has been already adverted to ;—the change in the religious world was equally marked, and speedy.   The Church of England had indeed been divided during the preceding reign, but the moderate or Low church party being in favour, their opponents were held in check.   Now, a spirit of intolerant bigotry began to display itself among the High Churchmen, who not only unchurched their more moderate brethren, the great majority of the clergy and laity, but treated the whole body of Dissenters as heretics, totally out of the pale of Christ's church, and who ought to be suppressed by the civil power.   It was known that the Queen was firmly attached to the interests of the Church of England ; but justice requires it to be stated that she not only disapproved of the fury of the High Church, but occasionally felt it her duty to reprove their persecuting tendencies.   In the speech she delivered to her first parliament at the close of the session, she said, " I shall always wish that no difference of opinion among those that are equally affected to my service, may be the occasion of heats and animosities among themselves.   I shall be very careful to preserve and maintain the Act of Toleration, and to set the minds of all my people at quiet.   My own principles must always keep me entirely firm to the interests and religion of the Church of England, and will incline me to countenance those who have the truest zeal to support it."

Defoe says the Queen did not imagine the evil use that would be made of the latter part of the above ; and during the whole of her reign, he constantly, but vainly reminded the furious party of the former part, in which her Majesty deprecated religious " heats and animosities," and expressed her

* Cunningham's " Great Britain," i. p. 259.

determination to "preserve and maintain the Act of Toleration." He has given a full account how they seized upon the word ZEAL, and used it as the Queen's authority for the extermination of all who differed from them in religion.*

Impelled by popular feeling against France, and all preparations having been made, on the 4th of May, 1702, the Queen declared war against that country and Spain ; and thus opened the way to a successive course of victories which shed the highest glory on a reign that would otherwise have been remembered chiefly for its domestic broils.

Within about two months of the Queen's accession, the whole of the Whig Ministry of King William had been displaced, and a Tory Government appointed. The influence of these changes upon the High Church, and the House of Commons, was very great ; and was exerted adversely to the peace and well-being of the nation. All the old principles of non-resistance and arbitrary government were taught from the pulpit, and a sermon preached by Dr. Binkes before Convocation, gave so much offence as to be censured by parliament. This induced Defoe, in June, to publish, " A New Test of the Church of England's Loyalty : or Whiggish Loyalty and Church Loyalty compared. Printed in the year 1702." Judging merely from the title, it would be supposed that this pamphlet is levelled at the Church as an Establishment, and I regret that Mr. Wilson has so treated it. But the most superficial examination of our author's arguments will show that it is directed only against the same party, now resuscitated, who after preaching non-resistance and all its cognate doctrines, in the reign of James II., turned, as soon as he laid his finger upon them, and aided in driving him from the throne. At page 24 he says, " Nor do I think I am writing a Satyr against the Church of England, nor is it at all intended to be so ;" and the following ten pages are occupied in proving that the reformed Church of England never held or practised the tenets inculcated by Dr. Binkes. Several editions of Defoe's Tract appeared before the end of the year ; and it was

---

* *Vide* " The Present State of Parties," pp. 14-17.

answered by Dr. Drake; and also by the eccentric Mrs. Ellinor James.

Unfortunately Defoe's efforts in the way of moderation and peace were unavailing. In the same month appeared a Sermon preached before the University of Oxford, dated June 2nd, 1702, by Dr. Sacheverell, who now endeavoured to surpass, in furious zeal, all others of the High Church party. It is entitled, " The Political Union : a Discourse shewing the dependence of Government on Religion in general ; and of the English Monarchy on the Church of England in particular." This is the celebrated production in which, under the prostituted word " Union," he *hung out " the bloody flag and banner of defiance,"* against all who dissented from what he called the Church of England. It was ably answered by John Dennis, who published on the 8th of August, " The Danger of Priestcraft to Religion and Government : with some Politick Reasons for Toleration. Occasioned by a Discourse of Mr. Sacheverel's, intitul'd, *The Political Union, &c.,* lately printed at Oxford. In a Letter to a newly elected Member of Parliament. London, Printed in the year 1702." Charles Lesley professed to reply to Dennis, in the first part of his " New Association :" but he returns only railing and abuse against plain temperate argument.

Though a little out of its place in chronological order, I must notice here a rather long poetical production by Defoe during this year, entitled, " Reformation of Manners, a Satyr. Væ Vobis Hypocrite. Printed in the year 1702." This is a general satire in verse upon the vices and follies of the age, many of the characters being Justices of the Peace, and other persons of authority, leading ill-lives, and yet taking active part with the Societies for the Reformation of Manners. He describes their persons and conduct without publicly exposing their names, and urges upon them personal reformation. The publication made him enemies among those who thought themselves, or friends, reflected upon ; and he was compelled afterward to feel bitterly the offence he had given. Many portions of the work afforded evidence of having been written some considerable time previously, when his versification was even less polished than now, and when the individuals satirised would have been too easily recognisable by their fellow-citizens for safe publication.   This is but probable conjecture; yet, the less personal and latter portions, are superior as respects composition.

This he supplemented, on the 3rd of September, with a further poetical Satire intitled, " Good Advice to the Ladies : Shewing that as the World goes, and is like to go, the best way for them is to keep Unmarried.   By the Author of the True-born Englishman.   Printed in the year 1702."   His argument with the Ladies against getting married, is based on the prevalent debauchery of the male sex.   His preface is addressed " to the criticks of all sorts," and concludes, " But you will say, 'tis a great fault to persuade People against Marriage : I answer, That to the utmost of my power I will ever expose those Infamous, Impertinent, Cowardly, Censorious, Sauntering, Idle Wretches, called Wits and Beaux, the Plague of the Nation, and the Scandal of Mankind.   But if Lesbia is sure she has found a Man of Honour, Religion, and Virtue, I will never forbid the Banns ;   let her love him as much as she pleases, and value him as an Angel, and be married to-morrow if she will."   Mr. Wilson rejected this work, on the mistaken notion that Defoe had himself disavowed it ;   which he never did, objecting only to an incorrect and pirated edition.   Mr. Wilson seems not to have known the book, thinking it first appeared in 1705, which was the date of the second genuine edition.*   There is, therefore, nothing to allege against Defoe's title thereto.

The first expedition of the War was under the command of Sir George Rooke and the Duke of Ormond, intended against Cadiz, but unsuccessful ; and, by the voice of public clamour, declared culpably so.   The subsequent taking and destroying the Galleons in the harbour of Vigo, was, however, a timely success, that saved both commanders from resentment, except a formal inquiry, ending in nothing, and a few harmless satirical effusions from the Press.   One of these, published in November, was entitled " The Spanish Descent, a Poem.   By the Author of the True-Born Englishman.   London, Printed in

---

* Wilson's " Life of Defoe," ii. 353.

the year 1702." I regret that I have not room to quote at
length from it, as it contains, in my judgment, some happy
thoughts, very pointedly expressed. Thus, when false news
reached England that the expedition had been successful ; we
have a complete picture in the following four lines :—

> " The Learned *Mob* brought Compasses and Scales,
> And every Barber knew the *Bay* of *Cales* ;
> Show'd us the Army here, and there the Fleet,
> Here the Troops land, and there the Foes retreat."

His philosophical reflections, when it became known that
the forces had left Cadiz without doing anything, are very
characteristic :—

> " Mischances sometimes are a Nation's Good,
> Rightly Improv'd, and nicely Understood."

Again, the premature rejoicings in France on the News that
the English Fleet had sailed from the coast of Spain on their
way homeward ; and that all the Galleons with their cargoes
of Gold and Silver were safe at Vigo ; and consequently how
vigorously they would now prosecute the war :—

> " New Fleets, new Armies, and new Leagues contrive,
> And swallow Men and Nations up alive.
> Prescribe no Bounds to their ambitious Pride,
> But first the Wealth, and then the World divide."

Followed by dismay when the English Forces reappeared
suddenly before Vigo, and saw—

> " The wish'd for Fleets embay'd, in Harbour lye,
> Unfit to fight, and more unfit to fly."

Immediately after the accession of Queen Anne, the controversy as to Occasional Conformity was revived with great acri-
mony ; and on the 4th of November, Mr. Wm. Bromley and Mr.
Arthur Annesley brought into the House of Commons a Bill for
its prevention, which during the month was passed, and carried
to the Lords on the 2nd of December, where it received so many
amendments, that after numerous conferences between the two
Houses, it was lost. While the Bill was pending in Parliament, swarms of pamphlets were issued, and among them
Defoe published, " An Enquiry into Occasional Conformity,
shewing that the Dissenters are in no Ways concerned in it.

By the author of the Preface to Mr. Howe. London. Printed
in the year 1702." He wrote under a consciousness that he
should be considered arrogant, and further displease his
friends ; but he also knew that he was right, and therefore his
only care was to express his views clearly, and with due humility. So far as the Dissenters were concerned, he thought the
measure would rather consolidate their true interests than ac-
complish the ruin intended ; but the injustice and persecution
of its promoters was not the less to be condemned on that
account. The pamphlet was an able one, but quotation would
have little interest now. It was republished, the following
year, in the first volume of his Collected Writings.

This memoir has now arrived at the month of December,
1702. The opening of that year had seen Defoe the honoured
and confidential friend of his King, and apparently on the high
road to fame and fortune. How changed is now his condition, as to all external circumstances ! Unrecognised by the
Court, and courtiers—the popular branch of the legislature
opposed to the political principles of the Revolution ;—a
furious party in church and state anathematizing, and threatening with destruction, the religious denomination to which he
belonged ; and the members of that denomination treating him
adversely because he told them the truth : well might he complain, in the work above noticed, that he was alone, and surrounded by enemies. " To me it is wonderful to find no Body
of my Mind, and yet be Positively assured that I am in the
Right." (p. 4.) We shall have, presently, to see him proscribed,—
brought to what was then called justice,—fined, pilloried, imprisoned,—his business thereby ruined,—and his wife and children
destitute ; but at the same time, we shall witness in him a
remarkable instance of the sustaining power of conscious integrity. " *Positively assured" that he was in the right*, with
indomitable courage he refused to be silenced. He was still
pursuing the high road to fame, though not apparently to
fortune.

As the threatenings of persecution, thundered forth by the
High Church Clergy, denoted in themselves an unchristian
spirit, so the moderate party turned in disgust from such teaching. Bad passions were stirred up among indifferent professors

of religion, and a panic seized the sincere Dissenters, who believed that their toleration was about to be withdrawn, and
public worship of God, according to their consciences, interdicted.   Defoe found that plain argument had little weight
with those who, in the name of the Church, had unfurled the
bloody flag and banner of defiance ; and, being well acquainted
with what they had promulgated from the pulpit and the press,
he embodied such views in suitable language, for the purpose
of exposing their folly.   The result was published, under the
title of " The Shortest Way with the Dissenters : or Proposals
for the Establishment of the Church.   London.   Printed in
the year 1702."

To understand the inimitable irony of this production, it
must be read.   No mere quotations or abstract can convey an
adequate impression of its completeness.   The artfulness with
which the writer gravely concealed his art, under an apparent
simplicity of purpose ; the mental transmutation, by which he
was able to see through the eyes and read the thoughts of these
violent men ; and then, so perfectly to express all their wishes,
exactly in their own style, within less than thirty small pages,
are proofs of the greatness of that genius which was destined
to captivate all readers.   Mr. John Forster has well remarked,
" If a justification of this masterly pamphlet were needed,
would it not be strikingly visible in the existence of a state of
society wherein such arguments as these could be taken to
have grave intention ?"   Such, however, was the state of the
public mind, and the irresistible reality of the book, that timid
and cowardly Dissenters were immediately struck with direful
apprehensions ; while the High-flying bigots embraced it, as
the legitimate offspring of, what they falsely called, the Church.
A Fellow of one of the colleges in Cambridge, to whom his
bookseller had forwarded a copy, wrote to thank him, saying,
" I received yours, and with it that Pamphlet which makes so
much noise, called ' The Shortest Way with the Dissenters,' for
which I thank you : I joyn with that Author in all he says,
and have such a value for the Book, that, next to the Holy
Bible, and the Sacred Comments, I take it for the most
valuable Piece I have.   I pray God put it it into her Majesty's
Heart to put what is there proposed in Execution."   That is,
to exterminate them all.

Defoe gave a full account afterward of the reception of the book, and its consequences, in his work on " The Present State of Parties."*   It must suffice to say here, that the tract was soon discovered to be the work of a dissenter, and a satire upon the High Church party.   Then they saw that they were taken in their own net; and, though determined to destroy the author, if possible, they also perceived that in doing so they must condemn the book; and that act would hamper them in pursuing their rage against the Dissenters.   Thus, from having first applauded the work, they were driven to declare, from the press and the pulpit, that it was a horrible slander upon the Church.   Nor could they clear the Church without condemning religious persecution; and that, again, was a censure of the High Church clergy, who had, in other words, said the same thing in print.   Truly, as Defoe says, in the work above referred to, *The Shortest Way* "cut the throat of the whole party."   As soon as the name of the author became known, his object was apparent; and, blind with madness at their own folly, they determined to immolate all their principles in vengeance.   During the first outburst of fury, Defoe sought concealment, but the Tory Government, moved by his enemies, resolved to crush him by a state prosecution; and a proclamation, offering a reward for his discovery, was advertised in the *London Gazette* of the 10th of January, 1703. I insert it in full, for the description it gives of his person :—

" Whereas, Daniel De Foe, alias De Fooe, is charged with writing a scandalous and seditious pamphlet, intitled ' The Shortest Way with the Dissenters'.   He is a middle-sized spare man, about forty years old, of a brown complexion, and dark-brown coloured hair, but wears a wig; a hooked nose, a sharp chin, grey eyes, and a large mole near his mouth : was born in London, and for many years was a hose-factor, in Freeman's Yard, in Cornhill; and now is owner of the brick and pantile works, near Tilbury Fort, in Essex : whoever shall discover the said Daniel De Foe to one of her Majesty's principal Secretaries of State, or any of her Majesty's justices of the peace, so he may be apprehended, shall have a reward of £50, which her Majesty has ordered immediately to be paid on such discovery."

---

* Pp. 18-24.

The fury of his enemies is not less apparent in the next step of vengeance, which could not injure their victim; the pamphlet was brought under the notice of the House of Commons on the 25th of February, and ordered to be burnt by the hands of the common hangman, on the following day, in New Palace Yard. The printer and bookseller having now been taken into custody, Defoe voluntarily surrendered himself, resolving, as he expresses it, "to throw himself upon the favour of government rather than that others should be ruined by his mistake."

Anxious that his motives should not be misunderstood, even by the most ignorant of friends or enemies;—astonished at the universal delusion effected by this effort of his own genius;—and having a desire to drive home against the High Church the application of his pamphlet; Defoe employed his retirement in composing " A Brief Explanation of a late Pamphlet, intitled, ' The Shortest Way with the Dissenters.' London. Printed in the year 1703." In this explanation there is no retreating; but, after referring to what had been said by the High Church, he adds, " The Author humbly hopes, he shall find no harder treatment for plain English, without design, than those gentlemen for their plain design, in duller and darker English." This explanation must have been published in February, immediately before his surrender, as he was indicted at the Old Bailey on the 24th of that month, and the trial appointed to take place in July. Alluding, many years afterward, to this great and unmerited fall, he says, " I have seen the rough side of the world as well as the smooth; and have, in less than half a year, tasted the difference between the closet of a King, and the dungeon of Newgate."

Between the committal and the trial of Defoe, turn we for a little space from the infuriated howls of the High Church Legion, to the den into which they had hunted him. His occupation there is known by his published labours, the first of which, issued on the 25th of March, was intitled, "King William's Affection to the Church of England Examined. London. Printed in the year 1703." There is something refreshing in the title. Amidst the burning heat of party rage, it fell like gentle rain; and, as we have already noticed the great popu-

larity of " The Mock Mourners," so this second tribute of our
author to the King's memory, proved also that moderation and
true patriotism still pervaded the great mass of the people. It
passed through four editions by the 13th of April. " King William's Affection to the Church of England Examined," begins in
irony, and proceeds in banter; but the author gradually drops
disguise, and concludes with an eloquent denunciation of the
calumniators of the late King, and a vindication of his
memory.

While in the state of suspense preceding his trial, he prepared for publication the first Volume of his Works, under the
title of " A true Collection of the Writings of the Author of
the True-Born Englishman.   Corrected by himself.   London.
1703."   In the Preface he complains of a spurious and incorrect publication of this kind some time previously; and,
that he had resolved to disabuse the world with a corrected
copy.   The Volume contains twenty-two pieces, including
" The Shortest Way with the Dissenters," for which he was
about to be tried; and he takes advantage of the preface to
offer a further explanation of his motives in writing that Tract.
He refers, at the close, to a further work he was about to publish, concerning his own errors, and those of others; " to settle
Matters between Vice and Repentance a little, and that they
may have no Excuse to reject the Admonition because the Re-
prover is not an Angel."   The work thus alluded to is entitled,
" More Reformation.   A Satyr upon himself.   By the Author
of the True-Born Englishman.   London.   Printed in the
year 1703."   This pamphlet was also written while he was in
confinement, and was published on the 16th of July, about ten
days after his trial.   In a preface of six pages, he recurs to " The
Shortest Way," and confesses his grand mistake to have been,
a too favourable opinion of the discernment of the public, as
to the real intention of that work.   He also notices the ill-
feeling displayed toward him on account of his satire, called
" Reformation of Manners," and gives explanations. In " More
Reformation," he is careful to avoid the possibility of personal
application, except to himself.   The following evinces a grim
conviction of his folly, and refers to the description of his
person, in the advertisement for his apprehension :—

> " And wouldst thou now describe a *Modern Tool*,
> To Wit, to Parties, and himself, a Fool,
> Embroil'd with State to do his Friends no good,
> And by his Friends themselves misunderstood ?
> Misconstru'd first in every word he said,
> By these unpitied, and by those unpaid :
> All Men would say the Picture was thy own,
> *No Gazette Marks* were half so quickly known."

During the uncertainty of his fate, he was still upheld by an approving conscience, but he felt keenly the desertion of all those in whose cause he was suffering, and says :—

> " *Unhappy Satyr*, now Review thy Fate,
> And see the *Threatening Anger* of the State !
> But learn thy sinking Fortunes to despise,
> And all thy *Coward Friends,*—turn'd Enemies."

More than any punishment that the law might inflict upon him, was the pain he endured from the conduct of three different Dissenting Ministers of religion, whom he had fed in the days of recent prosperity, and " with constant charity reliev'd their Poor ;" yet, they all now refused his petition to visit and pray with him in his distress.

Having confessed himself the Author of " The Shortest Way with the Dissenters," he was urged, and unwisely consented, to withdraw his defence,—and his justification from the like writings of the High Church,—and to throw himself upon the mercy of the Queen, with a promise of protection, if not of escape. This promise was, on his trial, immediately violated by Sir Simon Harcourt, who aggravated his offence ; and the jury, without further trouble, found him guilty of composing and publishing a seditious libel. The Court, having obtained its object of preventing an exposition of the tenets of the exterminating party, failed him now, by passing an infamous sentence, That he should pay a fine of 200 marks to the Queen ; stand three times in the Pillory ; be imprisoned during the Queen's pleasure ; and find sureties for his good behaviour for seven years.*

---

* In the British Museum, (K.P. 110, f. 27,) is a copy of " The Shortest Way with the Dissenters," with some MS. notes in a contemporary hand. Behind the title-page is the following :— " NOTA.—At the Sessions in the Old Baily 7, 8, & 9 July, 1703 Daniell Deffoe a supposed Dissenter, Sometime a

Hosier in Cornell, pleaded guilty to an indictment for the writing and publishing of this seditious libell and had Judgment to stand thrice in the Pillory
with a Paper of his crime, executed accordingly and to find sureties of his
good behaviour for 7 years and to pay cc Marks and to lye in Prison till all
be performed." At the end of the copy is the following, in the same hand:
—" Nota.—The Author hereof Pilloryed for the same is quite a Good Champion for the Moderate Church of England, by a Review in opposition to
Jacobite and Non-Juror & the High Churchmen of Passive Obedience."

CHAPTER IV.

Defoe in Newgate—Publishes " The Shortest Way to Peace and Union"—
" Hymn to the Pillory"—" The Sincerity of Dissenters Vindicated—
" A Challenge of Peace to the Whole Nation"—Asgill's tract on
Translation without Death, answered by Defoe—Answers also, Dr.
Davenant, on " Appeals to the People"—Publishes " Peace without
Union"—" The Liberty of Episcopal Dissenters in Scotland"—" The
Dissenters' Answer to the High-church Challenge"—" An Essay on the
Regulation of the Press"—" A Serious Inquiry"—" The Parallel"—
Commences the " Review"—" The Layman's Sermon upon the late
Storm"—" Royal Religion"—" Legion's Address to the Lords"—
" More Short Ways with the Dissenters"—" The Dissenters Misrepre-
sented and Represented"—Mr. Harley undertakes Defoe's cause—
" The Storm"—" A New Test of the Church of England's Honesty"—
" An Elegy on the Author of the True-born Englishman, and an
Essay on the Storm"—The Queen gives Defoe money to pay his fine,
and restores him to liberty—Affray between W. Colepeper and Sir
George Rooke—Defoe publishes an account thereof—" A Hymn to
Victory"—" The Protestant Jesuit Unmasked"—Groundless rumours
as to Defoe's retirement—He offers a reward for the discovery of the
authors.

1703–4.

AFTER the passing of sentence, Defoe was confined in
Newgate; and an interval of twenty days was allowed
to elapse before he should be publicly exposed in the Pillory.
During that time he bore up under this load of injustice, and
armed himself with a resolution of mind that enabled him to
convert his punishment into a cutting satire upon its authors.
He also remembered that he was a Christian, having a high
duty to perform in the inculcation of peace between the blind
and distracted parties in religion. Considering his outward
circumstances, there is something of moral grandeur in the
fact that he immediately sat down and completed a work upon
which, he says, he had been engaged some time before, viz.,
" The Shortest Way to Peace and Union. By the Author of
' The Shortest Way with the Dissenters.' London. Printed
in the year 1703." The object of this pamphlet is, to convince
Dissenters that there ought to be an established religion, in con-

nection with the state ; and, that the Church of England is not
only the most fit, but the only capable Institution for that
supremacy.   He therefore exhorts Dissenters to avoid all conflict with the Church, and to be content with the many privileges, civil and religious, which they enjoy.   The High Church
are urged, on the other hand, to cease from all attempts to
deprive their Dissenting brethren of their Toleration ; to act
out the true moderate spirit of the Church ; and, that by these
means mutual Charity, and Peace and Union, may be established.   Thus the noble Christian peacemaker endeavoured to
return good for evil, to the enemies who had laboured to crush
him, and to the friends who had forsaken him.   The second
work I have alluded to, as being composed between his sentence and its execution, is his celebrated Satire, " A Hymn to
the Pillory.   Printed in the year 1703."   This, and " The
Shortest Way to Peace and Union," were both published on the
same day, July the 29th, on which he was made a public spectacle to the people, before the Royal Exchange, in Cornhill.
The next following day he was similarly exhibited near the
conduit in Cheapside, and on the third day at Temple Bar.

The people of England have an innate sense of justice,
and a detestation of oppression.   The multitude formed a
guard to protect him from any injury or insult.   It was
summer time, and they decked the pillory with garlands of
flowers.   They drank his health,—wished those who set him
there were placed in his room,—expressed their affection by
loud shouts and acclamations when he was taken down,—
and they provided refreshments for him, after his exhibition.
The triumph was as great as the moment would admit of, but
he had a more lasting triumph in store ; his High Church
enemies had made him a gazingstock to the world for three
hours, but his satirical Hymn pilloried them for all time.

The " Hymn to the Pillory" became at once popular.   A
large edition was immediately sold, it is said, among the crowd
present ; and it was not until a second issue had been exhausted, that the author could find time to correct the errors
incidental to the peculiar circumstances of its first appearance.*

---

* I am indebted to my friend, Edward Riggall, Esq., for a careful verbal
collation of the *first* and *third* editions of the " Hymn to the Pillory," both
of which appeared in 1703, proving that in the distressing circumstances

Although he had, with a consciousness of moral and intellectual superiority, indignantly bid the Pillory—

> "Tell them the Men that placed him here
> Are Scandals to the Times;
> Are at a loss to find his Guilt,
> And can't commit his Crimes."

yet the Ministry did not venture to prosecute him for this fresh insult; they found that public opinion was against their proceedings, and the people construed such forbearance into an acknowledgment of error. I regret to omit the bibliographical and literary references connected with " The Shortest Way" and the punishment of its author. The titles of the books written on both sides, and the references to comments on this part of our author's history, would fill too much paper.

The long imprisonment Defoe was now to suffer could not but be ruinous to any business with which he was connected; and the Pantile Works, that since the death of King William had been the chief source of his income, were obliged to be given up, in the absence of the principal. By the abandonment of this undertaking he tells us, he lost upwards of three thousand five hundred pounds. For some time he had been able to keep his coach, and a proportionable domestic establishment at Hackney. He was now deprived of his liberty, with a wife and six children dependent upon him, and no other resource but the product of his pen. Now was the time to test his principles; because those who, stung by his satire, were treating him with so much rigour, had yet the highest opinion of his talents. Could he be tempted? Would he, for a consideration, reveal the confidence of the late King? If so, they would release him with a slight punishment, and promise to employ him in the service of the Government. We are told by Oldmixon, who had no favour for Defoe, that the Earl of Nottingham sent, if he did not go to him, in Newgate, and offered him the mercy of the Government, if he would

---

under which the poem was composed, the author was unable to correct his manuscript. The later edition contains no less than *thirty-six* important emendations, and is accurately reprinted in the second volume of Defoe's writings, 1705.

DEFOE IN THE PILLORY AT TEMPLE BAR.

From a painting by Eyre Crowe.

discover who set him on to write "The Shortest Way." The
Jacobite Author of "The True-Born Huguenot, or Daniel De
Foe, a Satyr," says, that two peers visited him in Newgate.
He had no confederates to impeach,—adversity and ruin
afforded no access to his virtue,—and he remained a prisoner.
That a temptation was offered, by those who had the power to
release him, and the baseness to insult him with a disgraceful
condition, is plain from an unpublished Letter, to which I shall
have again to refer, written by Defoe to Lord Halifax about six
months after he had obtained his freedom; in which he says,
he "Scorned to come out of Newgate at the price of betraying a Dead Master, or discovering those Things which nobody
would have been the worse for."

Newgate was a very different place in 1703 from what it is
now; there was then no proper separation of sexes, or sufficient classification of offenders. Political prisoners were occasionally forced, to some extent, into the society of thieves and
murderers. There was no system of regulations for the health
of inmates ; and, as consequences, fever was endemic, with frequent outbursts of the epidemic, emphatically called "Gaol
Distemper." Nor was the general morality of the place
higher than its physical condition. At a time when nearly
every theft was a capital offence, the female prisoners considered it expedient to qualify themselves, if not already so
qualified, for the investigation of a jury of matrons ; hoping
that the necessary respite from death would be ultimately com-
muted to transportation. Defoe had probably a solitary cell
into which he could retire at pleasure to pursue his studies ;
yet it is difficult to conceive more unfavourable circumstances
for the exertions of literary genius. And can we designate as
otherwise than marvellous, the courage and industry which
enabled him to produce many works, still valuable, while so
incarcerated.

We have seen that the Rev. John Howe declined to defend
Occasional Conformity against Defoe; but the controversy being
still continued, the Rev. James Owen, a learned Dissenting
minister, at Shrewsbury, undertook the defence of Occasional
Conformity in a pamphlet which appeared on the day when
Defoe stood in the Pillory for the third time. It was intitled

" Moderation a virtue ; or the Occasional Conformist justified
from the imputation of Hypocrisy, &c., &c., 1703." It has
been said of this pamphlet that it would have come better
from a moderate Churchman than from a Dissenter. I hold
the reproach to be the highest praise to which it was entitled ;
but, as it defended a practice to which Defoe was strongly opposed, he replied on the 18th of September, in " The Sincerity of
the Dissenters Vindicated from the Scandal of Occasional Conformity. With some Considerations on a late Book, entitled
' Moderation a Virtue.' London. Printed in the year 1703."
This is a very vigorous and conclusive pamphlet, written from a
deep religious conviction, and exhibits one of the strong characteristics of its author, namely, the absence of any effort at
controversial skill for the sake of victory, and appealing to
the plain Word of God as the end of all argument.

On the side of the High Church Mr. Owen found many
opponents, to several of whom he replied in a pamphlet intitled " Moderation still a Virtue," &c., but made no reply to
Defoe's publication.

Parliament met on the 9th of November, and the Queen earnestly desired both Houses to cultivate peace and union, and to
avoid heats and divisions, which would give encouragement to
the common enemies of Church and State. Defoe seized the opportunity of enforcing advice so much in unison with the
wishes of his heart, and on the 23rd of the same month dedicated to the Queen, " A Challenge of Peace, addressed to the
whole Nation. With an Enquiry into Ways and Means for
bringing it to pass. London. Printed in the year 1703." The
Dedication consists of four pages carefully written, in which he
assures her Majesty of the deep loyalty of her Dissenting subjects, and their resolve to be the first who shall publicly practise the Peace and Union she has commanded. But there is
no cringing, and he tells her of the High Church, " 'Tis an
unhappy Violence these Men offer to your Majesty's Character,
that they would be content to have your Majesty become a
Tyrant, so they might but be capable to prove the Dissenters disloyal to your Government." The body of the
pamphlet is to the same effect, inculcating peace and moderate
principles, and adding, " The Dissenters were always content,

and ever will be pleased to have the Power rest in the hands
of the Church." So little heed, however, did the House of
Commons pay to the Queen's exhortation, that not many days
elapsed before they revived the Bill for preventing Occasional
Conformity. It passed on the 7th of December, and was sent up
to the House of Lords, where, however, it met with so much
opposition that it was rejected on the second reading. Mortified by their defeat, the Tories made another effort, by tacking the measure to a bill of supply, but public opinion was on
the side of the Lords, and it was not carried.

I must now return a little to notice another of Defoe's
early prison labours upon a question of purely religious controversy. John Asgill, Esq., a Barrister in the Temple, was a
man of piety, and of great learning and intellectual power,
but an enthusiast. During a voluntary seclusion in his
chambers, studying the Bible more than books of Law, he
was deeply arrested by the words of our Saviour in St. John
xi. 25, 26, and his eccentric imaginings ultimately took the
form of a pamphlet, with the following title :—" An Argument
proving, that according to the Covenant of Eternal Life revealed in the Scriptures, Man may be translated from hence
into that Eternal Life, without passing through Death, altho'
the Humane Nature of Christ himself could not be thus
translated till he had passed through Death. Anno Dom.
1700." This was reprinted, and the Author having become a
Member of the Irish Parliament, he was by vote, on the 11th of
October, 1703, expelled for this innocent delusion, and was
declared incapable of being chosen, returned, or sitting again.
On the first appearance of Asgill's book Defoe had written,
and actually printed an answer to it ; but as the excitement
quickly abated, and he would not be guilty of writing to no
purpose, he suppressed the sheets. The expulsion of Mr.
Asgill having revived the discussion, Defoe published, on
the 4th of November, " An Enquiry into the case of Mr. Asgill's
General Translation ; Showing that 'tis not a nearer way
to Heaven than the Grave. By the Author of the True-
Born Englishman. London. 1703." The Dedication, to
the Honourable the Commons of Ireland assembled in Parliament, is signed in full, Daniel de Foe ; but, alluding to his

then condition, he throws himself upon their charity for pre-
suming " to subscribe his most despicable Name." Defoe's
hard and clear head easily took in pieces, and confuted, the
argument of Asgill; but he does this with all the seriousness due
to the sacred character of the subject.   He also deals gently
and respectfully with the man, concluding his preface by saying, " As for the unworthiness of Authors, and Truth suffering
on their account; I have Reason to have more charity for
him and all Men, on that account, than any other Body, having more occasion for it myself."

Dr. Charles Davenant had recently published his " Essays
upon Peace at Home, and War Abroad. London. 1703." The
work was dedicated to the Queen, with the ostensible object
of promoting the peace and union urged in her Majesty's
speech; but its author experienced the difficulty of changing
sides in politics without some appearance of inconsistency;
and in this production, his first in the character of a Whig, he
was so unfortunate as to devote Chapter I. to " The Danger
of Appeals to the People."   It was scarcely to be expected that
Defoe, who had already handled the subject, would remain silent,
and on the 10th of December, 1703, he published " Some Remarks on the First Chapter in Dr. Davenant's Essays. London.
Printed and sold by A. Baldwin. 1704." His arguments
are skilfully wielded, and his powerful antagonist found them
unanswerable. He quotes largely from his previous tract, *The
Original Power of the Collective Body of the People*, and assigns
as a reason for so doing, " because no Man has ever yet
thought fit to confront it, either with Reason or History."
He could not doubt that his doctrine would be unpopular with
the Government and the House of Commons; but while doing
full justice to the subject, his calmness of temper avoided all
ground for further personal oppression.   The above title was
found too general to effect the sale of the book, and shortly
after the commencement of the year it was reissued, with the
title of " Original Right; or the Reasonableness of Appeals to
the People : Being an Answer to the First Chapter in Dr.
Davenant's Essays, entitled ' Peace at Home, and War Abroad.'
London.   Printed and sold by A. Baldwin. 1704."
In the pamphlet just noticed Defoe quietly remarks, " How

easy 'tis for Men of Wit to give any thing a fair Face, and by a
happy turn of Language call things of contrary Subjects by
the same Name ; Dr. Davenant depriving the People of all
Power but what is representative, and giving the Delegated
Power a superiority over the Power Delegating. Sir Humphrey
Mackworth defending an Occasional Bill, and both presented
to the world with the Equi-Vocal Title of Peace at Home, and
dedicated to the Queen with high Strains of Eloquence, of
which both are very good Masters, complimenting her Majesty
on the Head of Peace, proposed in her Speech to the Parliament." The latter part of the above quotation has reference
to the following work :—" Peace at Home : or a Vindication
of the Proceedings of the Honourable the House of Commons,
on the Bill for Preventing Danger from Occasional Conformity.
Showing the Reasonableness and even Necessity of such a
Bill, for the better Security of the Established Government,
for preserving the Public Peace both in Church and State, and
for Quieting the Minds of her Majesty's Subjects. By Sir
Humphrey Mackworth, a Member of the Honourable House
of Commons. London. Printed by Freeman Collins, and
are to be sold by J. Nutt, near Stationers' Hall, 1703." Sir
Humphrey's proposal (however apparently inconsistent the
several parts of his title) was to pass laws which should tie
all Dissenters hand and foot ; deprive them of all places, public
offices, and privileges ; and thus to secure to them and the
Church, " Peace at Home." He assures her Majesty that,
" the Conscientious Dissenter will be thanful for his Toleration." To this insult upon common sense Defoe answered,
from his prison-house, in the same month of December, in
" Peace without Union. By Way of Reply to Sir H——
M——'s Peace at Home. London. Printed in the year
1703." With an admirable mastery over language,—with the
most respectful deference, amounting even to compliment,—and
with an imperturbable coolness,—Defoe denies the premises of
his opponent, disproves his arguments, and scatters his conclusions like withered leaves. I must make room for a short
quotation from page 4. " If this Learned Gentleman can think
to convince us that thus to humble the Dissenters by a Law,
and to offer them the restraint he proposes, is the Way to
Peace at Home, he cannot at the same time but suppose that

the Dissenters are very blind Ignorant People. Nor can he
suppose that this will tend to the Peace which her Majesty
has proposed to us, *Peace join'd with Union.* The French
King has brought about the Destruction of the Protestants in
France with a full Peace, but not with Union. 'Tis *Union* is
the matter, which as it is the Essence of Peace, so 'tis the
only thing can make this Nation happy, and I would be glad
to see how the least Prospect of an Union of Parties can be
seen in the Scheme he hath drawn." He takes occasion, as
in all his works that fairly admit it, to show that so far from
wishing to injure the Established Church, the Dissenters would
support it to their utmost power, as they did against King
James II. He declares that in principle and practice he dis-
approves of Occasional Conformity, but objects that the Bill
would deprive them of a liberty they now possess.

Defoe's pamphlet must have attained a large circulation, as
it passed through three editions in less than as many months,
and to the fourth he added a preface, signed " De Foe." Sir
Humphrey received many other replies, which cannot here be
noticed.

The High Church principles set up in England encouraged
the Episcopalians in Scotland to attempt an invasion of the
legal rights of the Established Presbyterian Church there, and
with the like lamentable results of sectarian bitterness. There
was, however, this important difference in the two countries,
that the domination and persecution attempted in England
was in the name of the Established Church, while the assump-
tions in Scotland had no such shelter, and were contrary to
the written law. In order to place the matter in a clear
light, Defoe published a pamphlet, intitled, " The Liberty of
Episcopal Dissenters in Scotland truly stated. By a Gentleman. London. Printed in the Year 1703." In subsequent
works he gives a history of the proceedings of both parties.*

We return to England, and the beginning of the year 1704.
Notwithstanding the rejection of the Bill against Occasional
Conformity, the High party were so far from abandoning

---

* " Present State of Parties," pp.143-163 ; also, " Memoirs of the Church
of Scotland," pp. 320-1.

their efforts against the Dissenters, that a swarm of pamphlets issued from the press, darkening the truth, as locusts did the land of Egypt, and descending to the most personal attacks and invectives. The Dissenters were not behindhand in defending themselves, but with much more decency and forbearance.

One of the most considerable of the attacks, was that by Lesley, in " The Wolf Stript of his Shepherd's Clothing. An Answer to a celebrated Book, intitled, ' Moderation a Virtue,' &c. &c." This was primarily directed against Mr. Owen's pamphlet, but Defoe was not forgotten ; and after him, the toleration of the whole body of Dissenters was virulently assailed, with that great ability which constituted its author the pamphleteering champion of the High Church party. Having been roused by Defoe's tracts on Peace and Union, Lesley challenges the Dissenters, in his eighth page, to " give in, to the present Convocation, a List of such indifferent Things, which if granted, they will promise to conform, and heal the Schism." The intolerant tone of his book is such as to make it evident that no submission would be followed by any good effect ; yet Defoe knowing that the consideration of any such proposal would show which party was blameable, immediately, on the 5th of January, published " The Dissenter's Answer to the High Church Challenge. London : Printed in the year 1704." His proposals are much similar to those laid before Charles II. after the Restoration, and being then rejected by the High Church party, were followed by the Act of Uniformity, and its deplorable consequences. The contrast between the Christian temper of our author, and the rancorous spirit of Lesley, is very striking. In one paragraph only, he gives vent to an eloquent indignation, that terms should be offered without authority, which the Church had authoritatively refused, and would refuse again. Still he adds, " Get the Convocation to pass it into an Act, that the Church will not quarrel with us about Habits, Ceremonies, Liturgies, and Ordinations,—the Schism be upon us if we do not conform. We are ready to Conform upon your own Terms ; we take you at your own Words ; do but perform what you have voluntarily proposed, we are your own."

Lesley having charged the Dissenters with plots against

governments, Defoe gives him in the above tract, an interesting illustration of their loyalty to the monarchy. " The Dissenters, Sir, have been guilty of more Plots against the Government than you charge them with, and more have been executed
for it than you tell us of; for, I assure you, the Author of this
wears a Mourning Ring on his Finger, given at the Funeral
of Mr. Christopher Love, a Presbyterian Minister, beheaded
Anno 1653, for the horrid Phanatick Plot, contriv'd for the
bringing in, *as they then called him,* CHARLES STUART, and the
restoring of Monarchy."

In the latter end of the reign of King William the comparative freedom of the press had become very obnoxious to
the High Church party; but they were unable to move, as a
body, either in Convocation or Parliament, so as to restrain
this freedom, and silence their opponents.   Pamphlets on both
sides were published in 1698, 9, and 1700 ; but the moderation
of the bishops prevented anything more.   In the reign of
Queen Anne, however, the Lower House of Convocation having
wisely come to the conclusion that anything contrary to their
own views was an attack upon religion, desired the Upper
House to use its influence in Parliament for a Bill to restrain
the licentiousness of the press.   Ever ready to contend for
freedom of thought and discussion, as a mighty agent of progress and safety, Defoe published, on the 7th of January, " An
Essay on the Regulation of the Press.   Sold by the Booksellers
of London and Westminster.   1704."   He was seconded in a
short but able tract by Dr. Tindal, entitled, " Reasons against
Restraining the Press.   London.   Printed in the Year 1704."

While the Bill against Occasional Conformity was before
Parliament, Defoe had written some further thoughts upon
the subject.   Leaving the practice of Occasional Conformity
entirely out of the question, as a matter of conscience to be
settled by the Dissenters themselves, he took his stand upon
the foundation of reason, and challenged the advocates of the
measure to public discussion.   The rejection of the Bill caused
him to suppress, for the time, what he had written ; but the
agitation being kept alive by the High Church party, he
changed his resolution early in this year, and published one of

the most strictly logical and conclusive of his pamphlets, under the title of "A Serious Inquiry into this Grand Question ; whether a Law to prevent the Occasional Conformity of Dissenters would not be Inconsistent with the Act of Toleration, and a Breach of the Queen's Promise. London : Printed in the Year 1704." The half-title calls it "A Serious Inquiry into the Unreasonableness of a Law against Occasional Conformity."

We have seen that the religious epidemic of High Church exclusiveness and intolerance had extended from England to Scotland, and must now take notice that Ireland did not escape the infection. At the accession of Queen Anne, the Protestants did not constitute more than one-fourth of the population of Ireland ; and probably one-half those Protestants were Presbyterians. Down to this period, however, there had been no animosity between the Church and Presbyterians ; they had a common tie of Protestantism, and their mutual energies were directed to defend themselves against the unremitted endeavours of the Papists to Romanize the kingdom. To stop such efforts, the Irish Parliament passed a Bill "to prevent the growth of Popery," and it was presented to the Lord Lieutenant, that he might lay it before the Queen and her ministers for the royal assent. When returned, the Protestants found, to their amazement, that a clause had been inserted, by the English ministers, requiring all Protestant Dissenters holding any office under government, to conform to the Established Church, and receive the Sacrament therein, or be incapacitated from continuing in the public service. The Irish Parliament adopted the alteration, but the persecuting tendency was dishonourable to all the parties concerned ; because, by weakening and dividing the Protestants, the clause strengthened the Papists, whom it was the professed object of the Bill to counteract. Strong, but ineffectual, appeals were made to the English government on the subject; and to forward such representations, Defoe published "The Parallel : or Persecution of Protestants the Shortest Way to prevent the Growth of Popery in Ireland. London. 1704." This tract is written in the name of the Protestant Dissenters of Ireland, and dedicated to the Queen. It concludes with a very moving

address to their brethren, the members of the Established
Church.

I now come to notice the commencement of Defoe's greatest
work—greatest undoubtedly, as to its magnitude, and perhaps,
in value and importance; yet the least known of his multifarious writings.   I allude to the "Review," a periodical paper
in quarto, the first number of which was published on the 19th
of February, 1704.   We have already considered some sixteen
distinct works produced since he was immured in Newgate,
and shall have to mention many more, written ere he was permitted to step forth from his dungeon, a free man; but the
commencement and prosecution of this project is one of the
strongest recorded instances of unsubdued energy, and per-
severing industry, under adverse circumstances.   The "Review"
was intended to treat of news, foreign and domestic; of politics
British and European; of trade, particular and universal.   Our
author saw, however, that such subjects would interest but a
small class of readers, and that his Paper must be diverting
to be successful.   He therefore instituted, in connection with
its pages, a Scandal Club, to exalt virtue, to correct vice
and folly, and to discuss casuistical questions from real or fictitious correspondents, in divinity, morals, language, science,
poetry, love, &c.   Within such a scope, there must be obviously a great proportion of merely temporary matter, and
from this cause, among others, the work did not outlive its
day, and has never been reprinted.   Yet there are to be found
in the "Review" many passages, both of prose and verse,
which, for fineness of wit, delicacy of expression, force of
morality, and historical value, are not to be surpassed in the
whole range of English literature.   A careful selection of
such pieces as are of permanent interest, would produce one
or more valuable volumes acceptable to all readers, and the
writer of this hopes, God willing, to undertake such a task.

The "Review" was published at first as a weekly paper;
but, after the eighth number, it appeared twice each week; and,
after the eighth number of the second volume, thrice each week,
on Tuesday, Thursday, and Saturday, until the 29th of July,
1712.   Each number, excepting the first four, consisted of two
leaves, and the whole was comprised in eight yearly volumes.

In the latter part of the first year, 1704, the press of matter was so great, that the " Advices of the Scandal Club" were given in five monthly supplements, each containing about twenty-eight pages ; but on the 6th of June, 1705, this part of the scheme was transferred to a separate publication, called "The Little Review," of the same size as the *Review*, but published every Wednesday and Friday, for about half a year ; so that, during that time, there were published five *Reviews* weekly. The imposition of a stamp at the end of July, 1712, induced Defoe to terminate the work, in its original size and form ; but on the 2nd of August he commenced a new series, each number consisting of a single leaf, and published twice a week, until the 11th of June, 1713, the last, ending with the words, " Exit *Review.*"

When it is remembered, that no other pen was ever employed than that of Defoe, upon a work appearing at such frequent intervals, extending over more than nine years, and embracing, in more than five thousand printed pages, essays on almost every branch of human knowledge, the achievement must be pronounced a great one, even had he written nothing else. If we add that, between the dates of the first and last numbers of the *Review*, he wrote and published no less than eighty other distinct works, containing 4727 pages, and perhaps more, not now known, the fertility of his genius must appear as astonishing as the greatness of his capacity for labour.

Nor must it be forgotten that the *Review* was written when his knowledge of the world and its affairs,—of men and manners,—was matured by experience,—his judgment in its full ripeness, but chastened by trial,—his style of composition settled, and his wit refined,—his powers of humour, of satire, and of pathos, in full vigour ;—and that all the faculties of his genius were exerted in one unvaried direction,—the promotion of virtue and religion—in other words, the temporal and eternal welfare of mankind, all these considerations give force to the conclusion, that only those who have read the " Review" can be thoroughly acquainted with Daniel Defoe.

I have already stated that the *Review* was commenced while the author was in Newgate. It was continued, under those circumstances, during the remainder of his imprison-

ment. Afterward, between 1706 and 1711, when his official
duties, in promoting the Union of England and Scotland, compelled him to travel many times each way between London
and Edinburgh, a journey then occupying several weeks,
during all such journeys, his *Reviews* were duly written, and
dispatched for publication in London. While in Edinburgh,
at one time above a year and a half, engaged in his onerous
duties, and cut off from all immediate sources of news, the
composition and postage of his manuscript was unfailing, and
the publication only once or twice interrupted, by delay of a
parcel in transit. His "History of the Union," a folio of
more than seven hundred pages, was written and published in
Edinburgh; but his *Review* meantime went on in London, as
if he had been in his study at home, and no otherwise engaged.
Controversial in politics and religion, the *Review* excited many
opponents; and, throughout its existence, writers of the greatest
talent were arrayed against it; but truth armed its author
against their assaults, and enabled him to triumph over all
opposition.*

I must now return to the solitary monotony of Newgate, that
we may see how little influence confinement had, apparently, in
depressing the energy of the prisoner. On the 27th of November,
1703, occurred the most violent and destructive storm of wind
known in modern times. As Defoe afterward wrote a history
of this catastrophe, which I shall have to notice shortly, it
will suffice to say here that he immediately seized upon the
event as the ground of a very clever piece of serious irony,
partly political. This he published on the 24th of February,
1704, under the title of "The Lay-Man's Sermon upon the
late Storm; Held forth at an Honest Coffee-House-Conventicle.
Not so much a Jest as 'tis thought to be. Printed in the
Year 1704." The pamphlet begins with the text from
Nahum i. 3, and proceeds, with the utmost seriousness, to consider the duty of observing the extraordinary actings of Providence; and that, as in public calamities every circumstance is a

---

* Only one complete copy of the "Review" is known to exist. It is in
the possession of James Crossley, Esq. The British Museum contains
Volumes I. to VII., and some subsequent numbers; and the Bodleian Library has recently acquired several of the earlier volumes.

sermon, the writer, though a layman, may assist in the application.   He notices how capriciously different minds appropriate
its signification, and thinks it a severe animadversion upon
the feuds and storms of parties, kept up with such unaccountable fury in the nation.   Having thus opened the way for
his satire, he deals severely, in the remainder of his work, with
the opponents of moderation, who had seen so recently in the
tempest, how the most immoveable objects may be overturned by Providence, and yet acted as if they believed that a
kingdom might stand, though it were divided against itself.

To turn from the fury of party politics, to any consideration
of the character of the departed King, was always delightful
to Defoe, and the retrospection was especially congenial during
his captivity.   In the beginning of the year, Dr. Moore, bishop
of Norwich, published a small pamphlet, intitled " A Form of
Prayers used by King William.   London, 1704."   This
afforded our Author an opportunity of stating what he knew,
in a Tract called, " Royal Religion : Being some Enquiry after
the Piety of Princes.   With Remarks on a Book entituled ' A
Form of Prayers, us'd by King William.'   London.   Printed
in the year 1704."   After speaking satirically as to the religion of some princes ; and saying he has heard Archbishop
Tillotson give the highest testimony respecting King William's
observance of religious duties,—both public and private,—he
adds,—" I take the freedom to affirm, from unquestionable
authority, and some little positive knowledge, he was a Prince
of the greatest piety, sincerity, and unfeigned religion, either
history relates, or memory informs of, in the world."   Thus
again Defoe struck the chords of the people's affection for the
deceased Monarch, and two editions of his pamphlet were immediately sold off.

The loss of the Bill against Occasional Conformity,—and
other proceedings of the House of Lords to secure the Protestant Succession of the Crown, and the rights and liberties of
the people,—had excited so much hostility in a majority of the
House of Commons, that they addressed her Majesty to extend
her prerogative against the Upper House.
This desertion of their trust by the Commons, and constitu-

tional conduct of the Lords, induced Defoe to appear again in the
character of Legion ; and a paper, consisting of one leaf folio,
without date or printer's name, was dispersed, under the heading, " Legion's Humble Address to the Lords." The Address
is full of loyalty to the Queen, and applauds the House of
Lords, as a bulwark of English liberty ; but it denounces, in the
plainest language, the despotic and illegal conduct of the
Commons. It concludes by urging the Lords to persevere,
and adds, " We Resolve as One Man, to Live and Die with
You. Our Name is Million, and we are More."

It was presented while the House was " assembled in Parliament," and therefore before the 3rd of April, 1704, on which
day the Queen closed the Session with a speech, in which she
regretted that her former recommendation to unanimity had
been so little regarded. The Tories were greatly exasperated
at the Address of Legion ; and, to humour them, the Queen
issued a proclamation, offering a reward of one hundred pounds
for the apprehension of the author, and fifty pounds for the
printer, but no real effort was made to discover them, and
nothing was brought to light. Defoe was pointed at as the
author ; and, in order to divert suspicion, he inserted in the
" Review" of June 3rd, a very clever jeering account of his appealing to the Scandal Club, " against a very scandalous letter
sent them, charging a certain person with saying, he would
inform against the author of the ' Review,' as the author of
' Legion's Address to the Lords.' " Nothing could be more
natural than that, being already in prison, he should willingly
avoid anything that was calculated to aggravate his sufferings ;
and his object seems to have been completely effected by
throwing up a cloud of dust ; enveloped in which, he does not
utter one word denying the authorship, but merely challenges
any one to prove it. He would have denied it, could he have
truly done so ; and, as it contains even more marked internal
evidence of his pen than either of the preceding Legion papers,
I have never entertained a doubt upon the subject.

From what has been above stated, it will be evident that
some decision, on the part of the Queen, had become absolutely
necessary. The Constitution of the country was upon its
trial ; the House of Commons and the Tory Ministry did not
represent public opinion ; the nation was distracted by

parties;—the two houses of parliament directly hostile to each other; and, that which should have been the popular branch, driving, as to religion, in the direction of Popery, and open persecution of the Dissenters; and in civil matters, preparing the way for the Pretender and absolute Monarchy. The Duke of Marlborough and Lord Godolphin found it impossible to carry on the war in concert with Ministers who fostered dissensions, and they were seconded in their representations to the Queen, by her husband, Prince George of Denmark. Mr. Harley, Speaker of the House of Commons, also called to her service, urged moderate and healing counsels; and convinced her Majesty that the bitter and furious spirit of persecution, exhibited by the High party against the Dissenters, was contrary to the true interests of her Kingdom. The Queen was at length convinced how greatly she had been imposed upon; and, before the end of April a revolution at Court was effected, by the displacement of Sir Edward Seymour's party, and the formation of a Whig Government. This change gave general satisfaction to the nation, by placing the Queen, her Ministers, the House of Lords, and her subjects, in harmony with each other.

The last noticed work of Defoe indicates that he considered a crisis imminent; and therefore, parallel to the efforts of Mr. Harley, he published on the 28th April, "More Short-Ways with the Dissenters. London: Printed in the Year 1704." After reverting to his proofs that the author of "The Shortest Way" was punished for repeating the same story which the High Church preached, printed, and said; he turns to the recent attacks by the Rev. Samuel Wesley,—against the Dissenting Academies, as nurseries of rebellious principles,—and declares this a "Short Way", by suppressing the Dissenters' schools, to prevent their posterity from being Dissenters. As I have adverted to Mr. Wesley's conduct, when considering the early education of Defoe, it is unnecessary to say more here than that our Author warmly defends the character of his old tutor the Rev. Charles Morton, and shows much indignation against the ingratitude of his quondam fellow-student, of whom he says, "If I should say, that a Mercenary Renegado was hired to expose the private Academies of the Dissenters, as Nurseries of Rebellious Principles, I should say nothing but what was in too many mouths to remain a secret." He concludes his very able but warmly written pamphlet, by dissecting Sacheverell's recent Assize Sermon at Oxford. In the last paragraph he states, " I design once a month to give a particular account of the Misrepresentations, and base treatment the Dissenters receive from this party, till I have gone through the whole history."

When Defoe wrote the above words he had no doubt prepared the materials for his next publication, " The Dissenters Misrepresented and Represented. London, 1704." This was published in May, and as will be inferred, shows how the Dissenters had been calumniated by the High Church zealots, and defends them against such aspersions.

It does not appear that Defoe proceeded any farther at that time with his intention of publishing " once a month" the history of the Dissenters' wrongs. The reason for abandoning his design was that a ray of light entered into his dungeon, and brought with it hopes of liberty. We have had abundant proof that the terrors of a prison were powerless to subdue his spirit; but his bodily health was shattered, by close confinement, and sedentary employment. Thoughts and hopes of personal freedom involved, in his mind, better days for the people he loved, and the great cause for which he had suffered. Should those hopes be realized, he would be the first to lay aside even defensive controversy ; and, in pursuance of the royal injunction, promote by example that Peace and Union he had so often invited. We have noticed that, after the prorogation of Parliament, during the preliminaries for a change of the administration, Mr. Harley, being called to the office of Secretary of State, had laid before her Majesty generally, the injustice done and designed toward the Dissenters ; and the inexpediency of oppressing so considerable a body of her subjects. We have no direct statement on record that, in the same interviews, Harley illustrated his arguments by a recital of the cruel sufferings, imprisonment, and ruin of her loyal and talented subject, Daniel Defoe ; but the latter tells us that " when her Majesty came to be rightly informed of these things, it filled her with a just indignation at the instruments." Inferentially the conclusion is irresistible, that Harley at the same time laid the whole case of Defoe before the Queen; and, that this practical example had much to do with her immediate determination.

I must for a moment anticipate, by stating that Defoe obtained his liberty early in August 1704, but not, as he tells us, until "four months after" the following occurrences took place. We are therefore brought back to the month of April, for Harley's intervention on his behalf; and this was when the Parliament was prorogued, and the new Ministry appointed. I make no apology for a long quotation from Defoe's " Appeal to Honour and Justice," because the relation explains the reasons for his subsequent gratitude to Harley, and is alike honourable to both parties.

" While I lay friendless and distressed in the Prison of Newgate, my Family ruin'd, and myself, without Hope of Deliverance, a Message was brought me from a Person of Honour, who, till that time, I had never had the least Acquaintance with, or Knowledge of, other than by Fame, or by Sight, as we know Men of Quality by seeing them on Publick Occasions. I gave no present Answer to the Person who brought it, having not duly weighed the Import of the Message. The Message was by Word of Mouth thus : *Pray ask that Gentleman, what I can do for him ?* But in return to this kind and generous Message, I immediately took my Pen and Ink, and writ the Story of the blind Man in the Gospel, who followed our Saviour, and to whom our Blessed Lord put the Question, *What wilt thou that I should do unto thee ?* Who, as if he had made it strange that such a Question should be asked, or as if he had said, *Lord, doest thou see that I am blind, and yet ask me what thou shalt do for me ?* My Answer is plain in my Misery, *Lord, that I may receive my sight !*

" I needed not to make the Application; and from this time, altho' I lay four Months in Prison after this, and heard no more of it, yet from this time, as I learn'd afterwards, this noble Person made it his Business to have my Case represented to her Majesty, and Methods taken for my Deliverance."*

---

* " Appeal to Honour and Justice," pp. 11, 12.

The momentary light that had thus shone upon him, would seem illusory, during the following months of ignorance as to any movement towards his release.   To dispel the gloom, he endeavoured to divert his thoughts from the wrongs of himself and his people, and to find solace in collecting and compiling a history of the great Tempest of the preceding November, with conclusions and reflections on so terrible a Providence. This he published on the 17th of July, with the title of, " The Storm ; or, a Collection of the Most Remarkable Casualties and Disasters, which happened in the late Dreadful Tempest, both by Sea and Land.   London. 1704."   This is an octavo volume of nearly three hundred pages ; and, though scores of other publications on the same subject appeared, Defoe's book remains to this time as the one genuine and authentic history of the event.   In addition to the numerous letters he has in- serted from clergymen and others, he must have received the verbal relations of many eye-witnesses ; and these are told with the peculiar circumstantiality of his genius, so that no doubt can exist of their reality.   The only difficulty felt arises from our knowledge of the fact that the writer was all the time shut up in a prison.   Religion was with him a present reality, and on this, as on all fitting occasions, he urges the necessity of living as under the eye, and at the disposal of, an Almighty Providence.

While his history of the storm was in the hands of the printer, he returned to the feud between the High Church and the Dissenters, and wrote " A New Test of the Church of England's Honesty.   London : Printed in the year 1704."   This pamphlet consists of only twenty-four pages, and was published on the 16th of July.   He first takes care not to be mistaken as if speaking generally against the Church of England : " By the Church, now, I must be allowed to understand those who *call themselves the Church ;* those Bishops and Clergy of the Church, who have so carefully distinguish'd themselves, as to condemn all the *Low Churchmen,* as they call them, for Traitors to the Church, and Betrayers of her Doctrine and Discipline."   Having made this distinction, he charges the High Church with dishonesty, in having broken the compact of peace and union made between the Church and Dissenters, when they united to dethrone a Popish King, and to invite the Prince of Orange. He illustrates this breach, by a personal reference and apostrophe to himself:—" What then is the Meaning of all this Clamour at the Dissenters? What is to be done with us, Gentlemen, if we must neither Conform nor Dissent, and your *Bloody Flag* and *Banner of Defiance* is spread against us? What is to be done? Truly, there is nothing we can see before us but *the Shortest Way*. Alas, *Poor Defoe!* what hast thou been doing, and for what hast thou suffered? When all things are examined, either these Gentlemen are guilty of the Vilest Dishonesty, are all Cheats and Hypocrites, or else *the Shortest Way* is at the Bottom, and Mr. *Defoe* has done them no wrong; and if he has done them none, somebody has done him a great deal."

During several of the latter months of his confinement, Defoe occupied his occasional leisure in composing an Elegy on himself. Part of his sentence being a bond for his good behaviour during seven years, he considers himself metaphorically dead; and takes it hard that he should still be insulted by the scribblers of the town, when they know that he cannot appear in his own defence. He quotes from this poem in his *Review* of the 25th of July, but it was not published until the 15th of August. A poem on the Storm, also written before his release, was appended, and the pamphlet is entitled, " An Elegy on the Author of the True-Born Englishman. With an Essay on the late Storm. By the Author of the Hymn to the Pillory. London, Printed in the year, 1704." Behind the title is a Latin poem of twenty-two lines, omitted the following year when the poem was reprinted in his " Collected Writings." The Preface to the Elegy was written after his liberation. Both the poems contain powerful passages; that on the Storm being, to a considerable extent, a poetic version of the sentiments of his " Layman's Sermon" on the same subject. I cannot forbear one quotation, as to the Supreme Being who had directed the Storm :—

> " Ancient as Time, and Elder than the Light,
> Ere the First Day, or Antecedent Night;
> Ere Matter into settl'd Form became,
> And long before Existence had a Name;

Before th' Expanse of indigested Space,
While the vast *No-where* fill'd the Room of Place,
Liv'd *the First Cause*, The First Great *Where* and *Why*,
Existing *to and from* Eternity,
Of His Great Self,—and of Necessity.
This I call God, that One great Word of Fear,
    At whose great sound,
When from his Mighty Breath 'tis echoed round,
Nature pays Homage with a trembling bow,
And conscious Men would faintly disallow ;
The Secret Trepidation racks the Soul,
And while he says, No God, replies, Thou Fool !"

Thus wrote the man who had now been in Newgate more than a year and a half,—thrice pilloried,—punished without crime,—to the lasting infamy of those who placed him there. We have seen how he had been sustained by his high religious principles ;—he was now to be restored to liberty, and having honoured God, in deep affliction, be raised himself again to honour.   His own words will best describe what took place.

" When Her Majesty came to have the Truth of the Case laid before her, I soon felt the Effects of her Royal Goodness and Compassion.   And first, Her Majesty declar'd, That she left all that Matter to a certain Person, and did not think he would have used me in such a Manner.   Perhaps these Words may seem imaginary to some, and the speaking them to be of no Value, and so they would have been if they had not been followed with farther and more convincing Proofs of what they imported, which were these, That Her Majesty was pleased particularly to enquire into my Circumstances and Family, and by my Lord Treasurer Godolphin, to send a considerable Supply to my Wife and Family, and to send me to the Prison Money to pay my Fine, and the Expenses of my Discharge. Whether this be a just Foundation, let my Enemies judge.

" Here is the Foundation on which I built my first Sense of Duty to Her Majesty's Person, and the indelible Bond of Gratitude to my first Benefactor.   Gratitude and Fidelity are inseparable from an honest Man.   But to be thus obliged by a Stranger, by a Man of Quality and Honour, and after that by the Sovereign, under whose Administration I was suffering, let any one put himself in my stead, and examine upon what principles I could ever act against either such a Queen, or

such a Benefactor; and what must my own Heart reproach
me with, what blushes must have cover'd my Face when I had
look'd in, and call'd myself ungrateful to him that sav'd me
thus from distress?   Or Her that fetch'd me out of the Dungeon, and gave my Family Relief?   Let any Man, who knows
what Principles are, what Engagements of Honour and Gratitude are, make this Case his own, and say what I could have
done less or more than I have done."*

Mr. Wilson has very properly remarked, that these grateful
sentiments came warm from the heart of Defoe, long afterward, when he could have no expectation of preferment from
either of the parties; for Queen Anne was then lifeless in the
grave, and Harley was in the Tower, with an impeachment
hanging over his head.   The "certain Person" referred to by
the queen as having used Defoe "in such a Manner," was the
Earl of Nottingham.   He was a Tory, one of the High Church
party; and, at the instigation of others, used his official power
to inflict vengeance upon our author.

To avoid the town-talk, and the public gaze,—and also to
repair his shattered health,—Defoe retired immediately to St.
Edmund's Bury, where he continued some time, but did not
allow his pen to rest, giving to the public no less than four
pamphlets within a month, besides his stated quantity of two
Reviews each week.

William Colepeper, Esq., an influential magistrate, in the
county of Kent, was one of the celebrated Kentish Petitioners,
whose illegal imprisonment by the House of Commons, led to
Legion's Memorial.   From that time a friendship existed
between him and Defoe; and, when the latter was sentenced
for writing "The Shortest Way," Mr. Colepeper endeavoured
vainly to procure a mitigation of his punishment.   Just before
Defoe's release from Newgate, a political quarrel took place
between Mr. Colepeper and Admiral Sir George Rooke, which
ended in a trial for assault and conspiracy, Sir George and
several of his friends being defendants.   Lesley, in his *Rehearsals*, took the side of Sir George Rooke; and the cause
of Mr. Colepeper was warmly advocated by Defoe in several

---

* "Appeal to Honour and Justice," pp. 13, 14.

Reviews. The quarrel gave rise to a publication on the 22nd of August, written no doubt by Defoe, though perhaps compiled from Mr. Colepeper's papers. I abbreviate the long title here, because the subject would now possess little general interest, and it is stated in full in my catalogue of Defoe's works. It is called " A True State of the Difference between Sir George Rooke, Knt., and William Colepeper, Esq. ; together with an Account of the Trial, &c. &c. 1704."

As I may not have again to mention Mr. Colepeper, I cannot forbear noticing the estimation in which he held the genius of our author. When it is borne in mind, that in 1704, Defoe had done little to immortalize his name, compared with his subsequent more numerous and remarkable works, there seems something akin to prophetic discernment in the following words of Mr. Colepeper :—" W. C. is not afraid of having his judgment called in question by affirming, that the world has not, in any age, produced a man beyond Mr. De Foe, for his miraculous fancy, and lively invention, in all his writings, both verse and prose."

With more of union in the administration of government at home, the war against France was conducted vigorously, and the successes of the army under the Duke of Marlborough, became the theme of many poets, among whom Defoe published, on the 29th of August, " A Hymn to Victory. London. Printed for J. Nutt, near Stationers' Hall. 1704." It is prefaced by a poetical dedication of six pages, addressed to the queen, and signed " De Foe." The poem, as might be expected, warmly praises the Queen and the duke, but without being fulsome ; and, as he attributes the recent successes, humanly speaking, to the change of government, he does not hesitate to lash with severe satire the leading members of the late ministry,—Seymour, Nottingham, and Rochester,—to whom he owed his deep suffering. In the moment of poetic and patriotic exultation, at the great victories achieved through the instrumentality of British prowess, he ascribes the success to the hand of God. This pious ascription was not intended for public effect, as plainly appears in a private Letter, written 31st August, to his friend Mr. Samuel Elisha, of Shrewsbury. He had sent a parcel containing fifty copies of the " Hymn to Victory" for distri-

bution there, and though he states, " 'Tis midnight, and I hope
you will excuse me more," yet he must write, " you will see by
the enclosed what wonderful Things God is doing in the
World." The " Hymn to Victory" was pirated as soon as
published, and within a week the author complained that there
were three sham editions being sold, " full of faults, the sense
mangled, and several lines altered—in some, near to blas-
phemy." On the 9th of September he published a second edition, which has a page of Latin verse behind the title, not in
the first edition, nor reprinted in his " Collected Writings."

In the month of June, Lesley, the High Church champion,
published a thick pamphlet, with the obscure title, " Cassandra.
(But I hope not.) Telling what will come of it. Num. I.
In answer to the Occasional Letter, Num. I., wherein the
New Associations, &c., are considered. London. 1704."
This was quickly followed by a second part. The title was
derived from Cassandra's predictions of evil to the Trojans ;
and Lesley's object was to frighten the people of England with
the fatal consequences of moderation in church and state.
These coarse but powerful productions were quickly answered
by Defoe, who advertised, in his *Review* of the 12th of September, his work entitled, " The Protestant Jesuit Unmasked. In
Answer to the two Parts of Cassandra. Wherein the Author
and his Libels are laid open ; with the True Reasons why he
would have the Dissenters Humbled. With my service to Mr.
Lesley. London. Printed in the year 1704." This is one of our
author's most carefully finished productions,—in which, the fineness and temper of his satire is comparable to the edge of the
blade, that, in the hand of a master, equally cuts through the
gossamer or a bar of steel. Lesley made a few acrimonious
remarks on the " Protestant Jesuit," in his *Rehearsal* dated
the 20th of January following ; but did not attempt to answer
it. This is one of the scarcest of Defoe's works. The only
copy I have seen is in the Bodleian Library.

The liberation of Defoe from prison, was a fact immediately
known to the public, and caused deep mortification to those
who had been offended by his writings. His being taken into
favour by the Queen and her Ministers, and the reasons of his

temporary absence from the Metropolis, in search of health,
were known only to the parties concerned, not being of a
nature to be communicated to the public.   In consequence of
this ignorance, the most unfounded reports and surmises were
immediately circulated, as to the causes of his retreat.   Writing
within a fortnight of his release, he says, in the Preface to the
Elegy on himself, " I tried Retirement, and banish'd myself
from the town.   I thought, as the Boys us'd to say, 'twas but
fair they should let me alone, while I did not meddle with
them.   But neither a Country Recess, any more than a Stone
Doublet, can secure a Man from the clamour of the Pen."
The annoyance being continued, with the aggravation that he
had absconded and fled from justice, he felt called upon to notice
the slander in his *Review* for the 7th of October, and to say that
the government knew where he was, and that he should always
be ready to shew himself to the faces of his enemies.   In a
second unpublished Letter to a friend in Shrewsbury, dated
the 11th of October 1704, after stating that he had been out of
Town for above three weeks, he adds, " What Treatment I
have had since I have been Abroad you will see in yᵉ Review,
where I have been oblig'd to vindicate my self by an Advertisement, and had not yᵉ Malice of People reported me fled from
Justice, wᶜʰ made me think it necessary to come up and sho'
my self, I don't kno' but I might have given you a short visit."
Dyer, the proprietor of the Tory " News Letter," and Fox, a
Bookseller in Westminster Hall, were the circulators and
probably the fabricators of the malicious reports.   Defoe's
public notice of the falsity of such statements proved that he
was annoyed ; and that was a sufficient incentive to repeat the
offence,—with the further aggravation, that he had been searched
for by Messengers, but could not be found.   Having returned
to London, he inserted an advertisement in the *Review* of the
4th of November, offering a reward of 20*l.* for the discovery
of the author or publisher of these calumnious reports.

CHAPTER V.

Defoe publishes " Giving Alms no Charity"—His sickness—Publishes " The Double Welcome"—The second volume of his " Collected Writings" —" Persecution Anatomized"—" The Consolidator," and " Supplemental tracts"— " The Experiment"— Letter of Defoe to Lord Halifax —" Advice to all Parties"—" The Dyet of Poland"—Ruinous consequences of his imprisonment—" The High-Church Legion"—Two Letters to Lord Halifax—" Declaration without Doors"—" Party Tyranny" " The Case of Protestant Dissenters in Carolina"—Answers Lord Haversham's speech—" A Hymn to Peace"—" Remarks on the Bill to prevent Frauds by Bankrupts"—" Preface to De Laune's Plea for the Nonconformists"—" Sermon on the fitting up of Dr. Burgess's late Meeting-house"—" Apparition of Mrs. Veal"—" Jure Divino: a Satyr"—" An Essay at Removing National Prejudices against a Union with Scotland" Part I. and Part II.—Appointed to promote the Union—Publishes four additional " Essays at Removing National Prejudices"—" The Dissenters in England Vindicated"—" A Short Review of the Present State of the Protestant Religion"—" Caledonia: a Poem."

1704—7.

HER Majesty opened parliament on the 24th of October, and shortly afterward Sir Humphrey Mackworth introduced a Bill into the House of Commons for the employment of the poor, by establishing in every parish a parochial manufactory, and to provide a fund for the support thereof. This Bill, being printed and circulated, Defoe judged, that though it was still under the consideration of parliament, no apology was necessary for freely discussing its contents. Convinced that the framer of the Bill was in error, as to the proposed remedy for the grievance, our author came forward in his capacity of an English Freeholder, and respectfully addressed, " To the Knights, Citizens and Burgesses in Parliament assembled," a pamphlet distinguished by its practical sagacity. It is difficult to say whether comprehensive knowledge, acuteness of penetration, or soundness of judgment, is most apparent in this masterpiece of political economy. It was published on the 18th of November and is entitled, " Giving Alms no Charity, and

Employing the Poor a Grievance to the Nation ; Being an Essay upon this Great Question, Whether Work-houses, Corporations, and Houses of Correction for Employing the Poor, as now practis'd in England; or Parish-Stocks, as propos'd in a late Pamphlet, entitled, *A Bill for the better Relief, Imployment and Settlement of the Poor, &c.*, are not mischievous to the Nation, tending to the Destruction of our Trade, and to Encrease the Number and Misery of the Poor. London, &c., 1704." Sir Humphrey Mackworth succeeded in passing his Bill through the Commons ; but the Lords proceeded with more circumspection, and ultimately rejected it, as incompatible with the interests of the Nation.

Although the speech of her Majesty in parliament deprecated contention, and expressed a spirit of conciliation, the Tories soon introduced the Occasional Conformity Bill, for the third time, into the House of Commons. The influence of the new Ministry succeeded in preventing the Bill from being tacked to the Land-Tax Bill, so as to secure its passage in the Lords ; but as the Tories were still a majority, the Ministers could not prevent the Bill passing the house as a separate measure. It was rejected by the House of Lords on the second reading.

The unconstitutional effort to deprive the Lords of their legislative authority, by tacking an obnoxious measure to a Money Bill, brought great unpopularity upon the " One Hundred and Thirty-four," as the Tackers were called. They were ridiculed, and held up to public contempt, in pamphlets, satires, lampoons, ballads, and black lists, so as to become " a bye-word and hissing to the whole nation." Defoe complains, that many such things were cried in the streets in his name, but that he had written nothing on the subject except what appeared in the *Review*. While the Bill was before Parliament, however, he reprinted his pamphlet of 1702, on Occasional Conformity, with the following new title, " An Enquiry into the Occasional Conformity Bill. By the Author of the True-Born Englishman. Printed, and are to be sold by most Booksellers in London and Westminster. 1704."

There is reason to think that long confinement had seriously injured Defoe's health ; but whatever might be the cause, or

the nature of his indisposition, he returned to London before
the end of October, unable to prepare the November supplement of the *Review ;* and he continued very ill until beyond
the middle of January.   There was no interruption in the
current numbers of the *Review ;* nor could sickness prevent
his loyal muse from contributing to the general acclamations
that greeted the Duke of Marlborough's return to England.
On the 9th of January, Defoe published, " The Double Welcome.
A Poem to the Duke of Marlbro'. London, Printed in the year
1705."   I have not observed in any of his poems so many
terse and forcible expressions within the same compass, as in
these thirty pages, and regret that I have not space for many
that are worth repetition.

He speaks of his own condition as—

> " Abject and low, and *scorched by Party-Fire.*"

His muse had sung the Truth in Satire, and

> " For this they've damn'd the Poet and his Rimes,
> And slain the Unhappy Muse *for want of Crimes.*"

He enumerates the victories the Duke had achieved, and
then sums them in the following couplet :—

> " From Deeds too mighty to be spoke by Words,
> Printed in Death, engrav'd *with English Swords.*"

Probably from ill-health, combined with the absence of
pecuniary profit, our author announced his intention to
terminate the *Review* at the end of the first yearly volume.
He had miscalculated the public estimate of its value, and he
yielded to the earnest request of many influential persons that
it might be continued.   An anonymous admirer of the work
also sent him a large sum of money to distribute at his discretion among the poor.   His *Review* of February 20, 1705,
describes his mode of distribution, and relates with the most
Christian feeling, in his own admirable manner, some of the
cases of severe distress he had been thus enabled to relieve.
This munificence was repeated, and though Defoe advertised
that a strict account of all the disbursements was at the service
of the donor, it does not appear that he was ever discovered.

The beginning of the year 1705, saw the second edition of

the first volume of his " Collected Writings," and the publication
of another volume, containing eighteen pieces, with the title,
" A Second Volume of the Writings of the Author of the
True-Born Englishman. Some whereof never before printed.
Corrected and enlarged by the Author. London. Printed and
sold by the Booksellers. 1705." These must have been prepared for the press while he was at St. Edmunds-Bury, and
during sickness which incapacitated him for more original composition than was necessary. From the circumstance that the
volumes were not advertised in his *Review*, it is probable that
pecuniary considerations had induced him to sell the right of
publishing this edition to one or more booksellers. This
supposition is strengthened by the fact that the third edition,
published in December, 1710, was advertised in the *Review*
immediately preceding. The two volumes came to a fourth
edition, on the 1st of July, 1713. The preface to the second
volume shows that he was still smarting under a sense of the
cruel injuries that had been inflicted on him.

The rankling of the same feeling is apparent in the next
tract he gave to the press ; which he appears to have been
prevented by illness from completing, until after the rejection
of the Occasional Bill. It was published on the 22nd of
February, and is entitled, " Persecution Anatomized : or, An
Answer to the following Questions. viz. I. What Persecution
for Conscience Sake is ? II. Whether any High Church that
promote the Occasional Bill, may not properly be called Persecutors ?   III. Whether any Church whatever, whilst it
savours of a Persecuting Spirit, is a true Church ? IV. Who
are the greatest Promoters of a Nation's Welfare, the High
Church, or Dissenters ? London. Printed in the year 1705."
The copious title-page explains, generally, the scope of this
valuable and characteristic pamphlet ; but, as it was unknown
to Defoe's biographers, I add one or two brief quotations.
After guarding himself, as usual, against the imputation of any
opposition against the Church of England, he says, " I would
not be thought to conclude that all the Members of the *Church
of England* are for Persecution, for we have great reason to
believe that many, nay, most of them, are of a quite contrary
Opinion ; but only, that there is a Design carried on by the

High Church, as they call themselves, to extirpate the *Dis-senters* if possible : which, if they cannot effect otherwise, then they are for *Fire* and *Faggot,* or any thing else, to Destroy 'em *the Shortest Way."* (p. 3.) " There can be no greater Enemies to the Established Church than those who violently promote so untimely a Bill to prevent Occasional Conformity. For 'tis a great Chance, if the Posterity of them that Occasion-ally conform now, will not Totally conform at last ;—But to prevent their Conforming at all, is to drive them from the Church ; and so consequently the highest Persecution imagin-able." (p. 9.)   " The Doctrine of the Gospel has the Face of a *Lamb,*—the Innocence and Simplicity of the *Dove ;* but the Doctrine of Persecution has the Face of a *Lion,* and the Revenge and Subtilty of the *Tyger.*   I hope, if we bring the Head of the Church for your Example, Gentlemen, you won't take it amiss, because you are so forward to profess yourselves Members of that Head : And, therefore, I say, If you take Ex-ample by our Saviour, and his Apostles, as you ought to do, you will find, by perusing the Transactions of those Times, That they Erected no *Bloody Flags,* and *Banners* of *Defiance,* against those that would not come in." (p. 13.)   Speaking of Sacheverell's Oxford Sermon, he says,—" I shall only give my Opinion of the whole, in a Word, or two, and that is this, *That the Morose Author deserves a Pillory, as much, if not more, than the Unhappy Rehearser of the* Shortest Way." (p. 22.)

From the peculiar machinery upon which our author's next work is constructed, it must have occupied him at intervals for some considerable time previously.   It is an octavo volume of 360 pages, without preface, explanation, division, or index ; and is entitled, " The Consolidator ; or, Memoirs of Sundry Transactions from the World in the Moon.   Translated from the Lunar Language, By the Author of the True-born Englishman.   London, &c., 1705."   The book is a prose satire on national and European politics, on the follies of the times ; and also, includes criticisms and animadversions upon the poets, men of literature, metaphysicians, and freethinkers of the age.   The work is valuable for its reference to the per-sonal circumstances of the author ; and, though wanting the elements of a popular book, in consequence of the enigmatic

travestie of proper names, into the assumed Lunar language,—
it abounds with passages of well-pointed satire, such as no other
living man,—Swift alone excepted,—could have approached;
and displays an exuberance of imagination, and adaptive
fancy, not surpassed in any other of Defoe's productions.

Shortly after the appearance of the "Consolidator" there were
published several Papers which might be considered appendices thereto. The first was entitled, " A Journey to the
World in the Moon, &c. By the Author of the True-born
Englishman." It consists of two leaves, small quarto, printed
in double columns. This was followed by " A Letter from
the Man in the Moon, to the Author of the True-born
Englishman." It was succeeded by " A Second and more
Strange Journey to the World in the Moon; containing a
comical Description of that remarkable country, with the
Characters and Humours of the Inhabitants, &c. By the
Author of the True-born Englishman." All the three Tracts
were of the same size, and first printed in London, after which
they were " Reprinted at Edinburgh by James Watson in
Craigs-close, 1705." Mr. Wilson says, " All these were
piracies from the author's book, and cried about the street at
a low price, for the benefit of some needy printer." It is
true that some parts of these pamphlets were taken from the
" Consolidator;" but they also contain original matter from
Defoe's pen, not found in the first edition of that work, and
are therefore not piracies.

A second edition of the Consolidator, " with additions,"
was published on the 17th of November, 1705. The form and
cast of this satire must have been an agreeable amusement to
the Author, as he returned to it in his *Review* of the 29th of
April and 6th of May, 1710, giving an amusing story of a
Lunar Tailor who made a coat that fitted many persons.
These may be considered as further Appendices to the " Consolidator."

Defoe's next production is a careful compilation of a case
that excited much attention in the religious world at the time,
and brought him into a controversy that lasted some years. It
is entitled " The Experiment : or, the Shortest Way with the
Dissenters exemplified. Being the Case of Mr. Abraham

Gill, a Dissenting Minister in the Isle of Ely, and a Full
Account of his being sent for a Soldier, by Mr. Fern (an
Ecclesiastical Justice of Peace,) and other Conspirators. To
the Eternal Honour of the Temper and Moderation of High
Church Principles. Humbly Dedicated to the Queen.
London. 1705."

This Gill had been a clergyman of the Church of England,
and incumbent of an episcopal chapel, but ceased to use the
liturgy, and in fact became a Dissenter, yet refused to retire
from the living. He was thus involved in litigation with the
Rector of the parish; and much ill-blood on one side, was
met by great obstinacy on the other. There can be no doubt
he was barbarously used, by a clerical magistrate treating
him, under colour of an Act of Parliament then existing, as
" an idle vagabond," and forcibly impressing him as a soldier.
Some of the London Dissenters took the matter up, obtained many affidavits and other papers, which they placed in
the hands of our author for the purpose of this pamphlet; and
Defoe did not in the least strain the facts to make out a case.
The High Church party endeavoured to justify their proceedings by charges against Gill's private character, and he culpably neglected to vindicate himself in a court of justice, when
he had an opportunity of doing so. Upon this, his London
friends declined his further defence; and Defoe concluded his
part in the affair by offering to produce publicly in a court of
justice all the attested affidavits, certificates, with their proper
vouchers, and also the parties to the *Experiment,* " in order
that the case may be legally sifted, and the man punished, if
they can justify their proceedings against him." The enemies
of Gill allege that the Dissenters stopped the circulation of the
pamphlet; but this is untrue. It was undoubtedly stopped,
because Defoe declined any further connection with the case.
He had no interest in the copyright; and a quarrel happening
shortly afterward, between him and Bragg the publisher, of
which I shall speak hereafter, the latter issued the remaining copies of this pamphlet with a new title, on the 19th of
October, 1706. The last reply to it was not published until 1710.

The House of Commons continuing their factious hostility
to the liberal and enlightened proceedings of the House of

Lords, her Majesty put an end to the session on the 14th of March, 1705, and the parliament was soon afterward dissolved. Her speech, on dismissing them, indirectly censured their proceedings, and recommended prudence and moderation for the future.

In the month of March, Defoe seems to have regained his usual health; but, whatever good intentions her Majesty had towards him, and however he might be indebted to her bounty, I think it will be seen that no active service was imposed upon him by the government, after his liberation, until his health was re-established. It is true that ten years afterward he wrote from recollection, " Being deliver'd from the Distress I was in, Her Majesty, who was not satisfy'd to do me good by a single Act of her Bounty, had the Goodness to think of taking me into her Service, and I had the Honour to be employ'd in several honourable, tho' secret Services, by the Interposition of my first Benefactor."* It does not necessarily follow that the Queen took him into her service immediately after his release; and it may be concluded from the following extract of a letter written by Defoe to Lord Halifax, dated the 5th April, 1705, that he had not yet been actually employed by the Ministry.†

" MY LORD

" I most humbly Thank y^r Lordship for Expressions of yor favour and Goodness w^h I had as little Reason to Expect from y^r L^{d}ship as I have Capacity to Merit. My Ld Treasurer has frequently Express^d himself w^h concern on my behalf, and Mr Secretary Harley The like. But I my L^d am like ye Cripple at ye Pool, when ye Moment happen'd No Man was at hand to put ye Wretch into ye Water; and my Talent of Sollicitation is absolutely a Cripple, and Unquallified to help it Self.

" I wish yor Lordship could Understand by my Imperfect Expressions ye Sence I have of yor Unexpected Goodness, in menconing me to my Ld Treasurer. I could be very well

---

* " Appeal to Honour and Justice," p. 14.

† Unpublished, and hitherto unnoticed, except by Mr. Forster. In Brit. Mus. Addit. MS., 7121, f. 23.

pleas'd to wait till yor Merit and ye Nacon's want of you, shall place yor Lordship in ye Path of ye Publick Affaires where I might owe any Benefitt I shall receiv from it to yor Goodness; and might be able to act something for your Service, as well as that of ye Publick. My L^d, The Proposall yor Lordship was pleas'd to make by my Brother, ye bearer, is Exceeding Pleasant to me to Perform, as well as usefull to be done, agreeable to Every Thing ye Masterly Genius of yor Lordship has Produc'd in this Age. But my Missfortune is, ye bearer whose head is not that way, has given me so Imperfect an Acco^t that makes me yor Lordship's most humble Peticoner for some hints to Ground my Observations upon. I was wholly Ignorant of ye Design of that act, not Knowing it had such a Noble Originall. Pardon my Importunate Application to yor L^{d}ship, for some hints of the Substance and Design of that Act, and, if yor L^{d}ship please, ye Name again of some book wch my Dull Messeng^r forgott, and wch yor Lordship was Pleas'd to say had spoke to this Head. I the rather press yor L^{d}ship on this head, because the very next Article wch of Course I proposed to enter upon in y^e *Review* being that of Paper Credit, I shall at once do my Self ye honour to Obey your Lordship's Dictate, and Observe ye Stated order of The Discourse I am upon.

"I shall not Presume to offer it against yor Lordships opinion, and would be farthest of all from Exposing yor Lordship to any Tongues, but if ever yor Lordship shall Think this Despicable Thing, who Scorn'd to come out of Newgate at ye Price of betraying a Dead Master, or Discovering those Things wch No body would ha' been ye Worse for, fitt to be Trusted in yor Presence, tho' never so much Incognito, he will certainly, Exclusive of what he may comunicate to yor Lordship for ye Publick Service, receive from you such Instrucions as are suitable to y^r known Genius, and the Benefitt of this Nacon.

. . . . . "I am, May it Please yor L^{d}ship
        "Yo^r Most Humble and Obed^t Ser^t
                                  "D. FOE."
"April 5, 1705.
   "To The Right Honble The Ld Hallifax
      "Humbly Present."

Besides the principal object for which I have copied this Letter, it is interesting as being the only existing reference to any brother of Defoe's. According however to the then custom of using the term with reference to brothers by affinity, I am, as already stated, inclined to think the "Dull Messenger" was only a "Brother" by marriage. In an earlier part of this Memoir I have quoted a remarkable expression from the concluding paragraph.

The approach of a general election set before Defoe the prospect of violent conflicts between the contending parties in the state; and, on the 17th of April, he published a *Review* containing an eloquent exhortation on the words STUDY PEACE. He says, " For this, I freely expose myself to Fines, Gaols, Pillories, and Exorbitant and unjust Sentences. If the worst Enemy to me, or my writing, will calmly prove I ever wrote any thing that did not tend to this Peace, I'll explode it, and own myself in an Error; if any thing I am yet upon has any other End, I'll freely decline it; and if my Silence would farther it, I'd never write more. The End of Debate should be a right understanding; and, no War can be just, but what is made for Peace. This is my ultimate End,—ought to be every Christian's wish,—and, if an Angel from Heaven preach'd any other Doctrine to us, to me he shall be accursed." (p.73.) "The Church can be in no Danger from *Men of Peace*; nor can the Church have any safety but in Men of Peace. From Men of Peace, Dissenters can have nothing to fear, tho' they are Churchmen; 'tis our desire the Government should be in the Hands of Churchmen,—'tis our free choice, that we should have a Church Parliament, only let them be *Men of Peace*; other qualifications may be requisite, but this is absolutely necessary." (p. 75.)*

In furtherance of the same object, he published, on the 30th of the month, a tract entitled, "Advice to all Parties. By the Author of the True-born Englishman. London.

---

* In the *Review* Nov. 25, 1708, he states that he had written three years before, urging all classes to *Study Peace*, and adds, " Some People gave me publick Thanks for my sincere Endeavours that way, and told me, I had done a great service by it. They did me the Honour in a Body to compliment me on that Performance; and made me Print five Thousand of that *Review*, to be sent all over the Nation, to move us to Peace, and paid me very frankly for them."

1705." The Preface reveals to us a portion of the Earl of Nottingham's descreditable conduct towards Defoe, from which we may judge, whether or not he would leave undone anything in his power to complete the destruction of a hapless victim, whom he had beguiled into submission, by an empty promise of Royal grace :—

" These Sheets having, with their unhappy Author, fall'n into the barbarous and unjust Hands of the late Ministry, had never seen the Light, had not Providence seem'd to reserve them for two Ends : 1. As a standing Monument of the dex'-trous Management of a certain most exquisite Statesman, whose strictest Scrutiny all these Papers pass'd, and yet came home, as Things relating to the Author's private concerns ; and with them, several other Manuscripts, which no body but such an over-vigilant Minister would ha' parted with. 2. As a Subject for which there was yet a more proper Juncture coming, when it would be more than ordinarily useful. They were wrote three Years ago, just at the Election of the last Parliament ; but, with very few Alterations, seem so exactly calculated to the present Occasion, that the Author thought he could do no less than let the World see them."

The different Parties to whom our Author successively offers his advice in this pamphlet, are—1. The High Church Tories. 2. The Pretender's or Hereditary-Right party. 3. The late Ministry. 4. The Church of England. 5. The Dissenters.

The Catholic spirit of Defoe, and his veneration for and support of the Established Church, have been several times already adverted to, and it seemed needful, in the early part of this Memoir, in consequence of the disingenuous suppression of the fact by several of his most eminent biographers. When, however, I declare generally that his sentiments on this point are to be found in almost every work he wrote,—within the scope of which such avowal could fairly be made,—it will be less necessary in future to make special reference thereto. I conclude my notice of this Tract, with part of his Advice to the Dissenters :—

" We are all Christians, all Protestants, all Englishmen ;—let us be all Brethren, and act like such on all Occasions. The Church of England, and the Dissenters, have but one Interest, one Foundation, and but one End. The moderate Church-

men, and the charitable Dissenters, are the same Denomination
of Christians, and all the Difference which, now look'd at near
the Eye, shows large, if view'd at the Distance of Heaven,
shows not itself. Neither will Catholick Christianity, in that
Realm of Light, appear in any Party-colour'd Garment."

In his *Review* of the 2nd of June, he reiterates similar
advice to that given to the Dissenters in the above pamphlet :
—" I observe, the most approv'd way of Destroying the Pro-
testant Interest in England, is to begin with the Church of
England. Consequently, the only way the Dissenters in
England can take, Effectually to support themselves and the
Protestant Religion, is to stand by, Defend, and Maintain the
Church of England, and its legal Power and Establishment.
That if the Church of England was either divided, broken, or
suppressed, the Dissenters could not be able to defend them-
selves against Popery and Jacobitism."

In the month of June, Defoe had, in his *Review*, accused Mr.
Buckley of giving, without design, erroneous French news in
the *Daily Courant*. Immediately afterward, the *Courant* fell
under the displeasure of the Government, on which Defoe
voluntarily and publicly expressed regret, saying, " if he had
known the fact, he would have taken no notice of the error,
even had Mr. Buckley been the worst enemy he had." The
whole of the *Courant* of July 6, is occupied with the controversy ; and, considering the too common violence of Journalistic
disputes at that period, the contrast furnished by this case of
difference between two Christian men, is as refreshing as unusual. Mr. Buckley says that the incoherence of his own
article was intended as a disguise ; and though, in the soreness
of the moment, he cannot fully acquit the Author of the
Review from some malice ; yet he designates him " an accom-
plish'd Writer," and says " he is usually very fortunate in his
choice of Epithets." He adds that his opponent is a man of
great reading, and sagacious observation.

We have now to notice a severe political Satire, in verse,
by Defoe, on the late House of Commons, and the late Ministry. It is entitled, " The Dyet of Poland ; a Satyr. Printed
at Dantzick in the year 1705." At the end of the preface
he signs himself " Anglipoloski of Lithuania." The names of

persons are throughout the poem obscured under Polish forms
and terminations, but the characters are easily distinguishable.
Lords Halifax, Russell, and Somers are warmly praised ; while
he censures with much asperity Lords Nottingham, Rochester,
Seymour, and other distinguished Tories.   Harley and Godolphin, the leading members of the new administration, are ex-
tolled for their ability and integrity, and their elevation partly
attributed to the folly of their predecessors.

The ruinous consequences of Defoe's imprisonment to his
business at Tilbury, and to his private affairs generally, have
been already glanced at.   These consequences he began to
feel, almost immediately after his release, in the form of debts
he was unable to pay, followed by writs and other legal proceedings.   So furious was the determination of his enemies,
that sham actions were raised against him for monies about
which he declares he knew nothing, but that the object was
" to harrass him with suits and charges."   Of this extreme
and diabolical persecution he complains in his *Reviews,* as an
unspeakable burden to a man of integrity, who had been deprived of all resources, except flight, for the preservation of his
personal liberty.   Under these circumstances he resolved to
leave London, and conceal himself beyond " the reach of implacable and unreasonable men."   He was now on terms of
respectful confidence with Harley, visiting and corresponding
with him, apparently without reserve.   It is in the highest
degree honourable to the character and discernment of this
great statesman that he should have interested himself so
thoroughly on behalf of oppressed genius. The British Museum
contains a long autograph letter from Defoe to his friend and
benefactor, written the day after one of their evening conversations, which I must now summarise in correction of an error
into which his several biographers, Wilson, Hazlitt, and Forster,
have all successively fallen.*   The letter encloses some promised papers, seemingly reasons why Sir George Rooke should
be removed from the command of the fleet ; and then, the
writer says he is preparing horses, &c., with joy to execute the
Minister's   command.   He requests a letter, giving Mr.

---

* Brit. Mus., Birch's MSS., 4291.   Wilson's " Life of Defoe," ii. 357-60.

Christopher Hurt (a name assumed by him for the occasion) leave to be absent on his private affairs for two months or more ;—asks for instructions for his special conduct ;—and also, for a certificate, or pass, to prevent being questioned, searched, or detained, by the impertinence of a country justice. He desires time, before going away, to complete and publish his Satire, " The Dyet of Poland," that he may carry it into the country with him, as he is sure of its being very useful, and he expects strange effects from it as to the future House of Commons. He promises to send Harley some papers " per post" when ready, especially " as to an office for secret intelligence at home and abroad." On the last point he says " I shall take time while I am *abroad* to finish a perfect scheme." Such is a brief abstract of Defoe's autograph letter, from one word in which,— " abroad,"—only used there by the writer as the equivalent of *from home*, Mr. Walter Wilson has stated that our author " was appointed by Harley to execute some mission, of a secret nature, which required his presence upon the continent," and that such mission was attended with some danger.

Now, " The Dyet of Poland" was written and published in May, when the Parliament, lashed by the severe satire of our author, had been dissolved. The general election began in May, and Defoe thought the carrying this pamphlet, and dispersing it freely in the country, would promote the Whig interest, and affect the character of the new Parliament. His *Reviews* during his absence were frequently devoted to the progress of the Elections. On the 25th of August he tells a ludicrous story of the dangers he had incurred while in Devonshire, &c., among foolish justices, when travelling with only a friend, and that friend's servant. On the 11th of October he seems almost ready to despair, stating that his life was threatened, and merciless creditors pursuing him still. " I have been," he says, " a long journey into the country, chiefly indeed to be out of the reach of implacable and unreasonable Men ; which may serve for an answer to an impertinent Vilifier, who in print, had the Impudence to demand, what Business I had in Devonshire ?" In his *Reviews* of this period he gives a very full account of his journey, mentioning many of the towns visited, " in near 1100 miles riding ;" and plainly proving that his mission was the removal of prejudice against the Government, and the inculcation of peace and union.

That Defoe could not possibly have been on the continent will be obvious from the above, and also from other facts. England was at war with France and Spain; only the States of Holland were open to him. He was able to *post* Papers during his absence, and to send Letters of the most secret character to Sir Robert Harley, Secretary of State, in London. His *Reviews*, written with his own hand, were published, without any intermission, every Tuesday, Thursday, and Saturday, during his absence; and, from the 6th of June, the *Little Review*, of the same size, was published every Wednesday and Friday. "At home," and "abroad," were constantly used by him as merely opposite terms; and, if my readers will revert to the extract I have given from a Letter dated the preceding October, to his friend in Shrewsbury, they will find him speaking of the interval that had then elapsed since his release from Newgate, as the time "since I have been *abroad*," meaning at liberty.

I must apologize for the space occupied with this rectification; and conclude, that· pecuniary difficulties, compelling Defoe to leave London *incognito*, his friend Harley commissioned him to visit the south-western counties, containing a multitude of small Boroughs, and to promote, by all honourable means, the election of such candidates as would support the Ministry in the new House of Commons.

The successes of the war, and the more liberal influence of the new Ministry, had their due effect in quieting the minds of the reasonable, and making the Government popular. This was soon felt by the furious party, and their mortification vented itself in language more indecent than ever, against the Queen, her Ministers, the House of Lords, the bishops, and all moderation. Intoxicated by a pretended zeal for religion, they adopted a new motto, and again unfurling the bloody flag, inscribed upon it the much-abused words, THE CHURCH IS IN DANGER. Books were written, and dispersed over the nation, with great industry, to possess the people with apprehensions that the Church was about to be given over to the hands of the Dissenters; and, that nothing but the political extinction

VOL. I.

of both Whigs and Dissenters could save her.   In aid of this insanity, and to influence the Elections, Dr. Drake was secretly employed to write his celebrated pamphlet, " The Memorial of the Church of England, humbly offered to the Consideration of all the True Lovers of our Church and Constitution. London. 1705." I shall only need quote one sentence of the writer's treasonable threatenings against the Queen's Government :— " The principles of the Church of England will dispose men to bear a great deal; but he's a Madman who tries how much : for when men are very much provoked, nature is very apt to rebel against principle, and then the odds are vast on nature's side.   Whether the provocation given to the Church of England may not, if continued, be strong enough to rouse nature, some of our statesmen would do well to consider in time." The pamphlet was burnt by the common hangman, and a royal proclamation issued for the discovery of the author and printer. The latter was apprehended and imprisoned, but though Dr. Drake was suspected of being the author, no further proceedings were taken, for want of legal evidence.

As the " Memorial" had just been published before Defoe set out on his long journey into the south-western counties, he took a copy with him, and says, in the *Review*, " On all Occasions I have shewn it as a Thing which carries its own Evidence along with it ; requiring nothing to move the people of England to a suitable abhorrence of it, but to have it seen."   He considered the " Memorial" in several other numbers ; and suggested, that the Government should order a hundred thousand to be printed, and sent into all the counties of England, that her Majesty's subjects might see the temper and disloyalty of the party.   As, however, the public indignation could not by such means be sufficiently stirred up, he wrote a direct reply, which was published on the 17th of July, and entitled, " The High-Church Legion : or, The Memorial Examin'd.   Being, a New Test of Moderation.   As 'tis recommended to all that love the Church of England, and the Constitution.   London. Printed in the year 1705."   This pamphlet was published anonymously, though dedicated to Lord Godolphin, the Lord High Treasurer.   Defoe was not in official connection with his Lordship ; but this admirable defence of the Queen and Ministry must have highly recommended him, and shortly after his return from the west, our author was introduced by Harley,— became an attendant at his Lordship's levées,—was honoured by his confidence,—and retained his friendship many years.

The following Letter has not been noticed by any of Defoe's biographers, nor, I believe, published.*   It was addressed to Lord Halifax with copies of the above pamphlet, and is chiefly valuable for the opinion of Defoe, that the Duke of Buckingham was concerned in *The Memorial of the Church of England :—*

" MY LORD
        " I had gone on Farther to reply to this most Insolent Memoriall, But y^t the Subject of the *Review,* being before This book came out, Enter'd upon ye same Article, viz. The Danger of ye Church, I shall handle it apart.   I think it my Duty to Lay it before yor L^{d}ship as it is, and have sent Six of them ; Not That I Think it worth yor L^{d}ship's recommend- ing, but That if yor L^{d}ship Please to concern yor Self for me so far, yor own hand may make This Empty Returne to the (to me unknown) Benefactors, of whose Goodness to me yor Lordship was Pleas'd to be a Medium, and wch I have no other Way to Acknowledge.
        " If I knew how to ask my Ld Treasurer Pardon, either for the Weakness of my Defence in his Case, or ye Rudeness of a Dedicacon without a Name, I should be glad to do it, But I am too Obscure and Remote to do it Personally, and ye same Reason That Obliges me not to sign ye Dedicacon, Obliges me Not to do it Publickly.   The Writing this Book I hear is charg'd upon Dr. Drake.   I can not forbear Assuring yor L^{d}ship That however he might be the Drudge or rather Amanuensis in ye Work—his Master The Duke of Bucks is as plainly Pictured to me wth his Pen in his hand Correcting, Dic- tating and Instructing, as if I had been of ye Club wth Them.
        " I ask yor L^{d}ship's Pardon for This freedome and am
                " Yo^r L^{d}ship's Most Humble and Obed^t Ser^t.
                                " DE FOE."

" To the Right Honble
        " Charles Ld Hallifax
                " Humbly Pres^t."

---

* Brit. Mus. Addit. MS. 7121, f. 25.

It may be gathered from the above, that Lord Halifax had been found a convenient medium for remitting a sum of money from the Queen or Lord Godolphin to Defoe, while the latter was absent from London on his secret Election Commission ; and that, having written and published his " High-Church Legion," he forwarded copies and Thanks to his Lordship.

Riding the whole of his journey,—which continued much longer than was originally intended,—on horseback, and in company,—so as to be unable to write or compose while travelling,—attending meetings, public and social,—making speeches, consulting, advising, and thus, when not upon the road, in continual intercourse with men of all classes and opinions,— severed from all the surroundings that dispose the studious author to his work,—and immersed instead, in circumstances most calculated to dissipate thought,— our wonder is excited that he could grasp, from necessary repose, sufficient time to dash from his pen, on each of five days out of every six, a manuscript number of his *Review ;* so written as, on all occasions, to defy the criticism of rival journalists and implacable enemies.

In the same Volume of Manuscripts, in the British Museum, is a third Letter from Defoe to the same Nobleman. It is without date, and unpublished, except as to a quotation by Mr. Forster ; but seems to be connected, to some extent, with the preceding. We have it from other sources that Defoe's services on this occasion were successful and very satisfactory to the Government ; and, if this letter was written shortly after his return, it follows, that the ministry, with the wariness that became them in so delicate a matter, had placed a further considerable sum of money in the hands of Lord Halifax, who after an agreeable interview with Defoe, presented the amount to him with very kind assurances of esteem, but without informing him specifically from whom he was receiving so munificent a reward.

" PARDON ME MY LORD
  " If to a Man that has seen Nothing for some yeares but the Rough face of Things, the Exceeding goodness of yor Lords$^{p's}$ discourse Softnd me Even to a weakness, I could not

Conceal. I am a Plain and Unpolish'd Man, and Perfectly Unquallified to make formal Acknowledgements ;—and a Temper
     by a Series of Affliccons, rendre me still y^e more Awk-
ward in y^e rec^d method of common Gratitude, I mean y^e
Ceremony of Thanks.---But, my L^d, if to be Encourag'd in
giving my Self up to That Service yor Lordship is pleas'd So
much to Overvallue, if goeing on wth ye more Cheerfullness, in
being usefull to, and promoting the General Peace and Interest
of this Nacon ; if to ye Last Vigorously Opposing a Stupid
Distracted Party, that are for ruining themselves rather than
not Destroy their Neighbours,—If this be to Merit so much
Regard, yor Lordship binds me in The Most Durable, and to
me the Most pleasant Engagement in y^e World, because 'tis
a Service that wth my Gratitude to yor Lordship, keeps an
exact Unison with my Reason, my Principle, my Inclination, and The Duty Every Man Owes to his Country and his
Posterity. — — — — — — — — — — — — — — —
   " As to the Exceeding Bounty I have now Rec^d, and w^{ch}
yo$_r$ Lordship obliges me to reserv my Acknowledgm^{ts} of, for a
yet Unknown Benefactor, yor Lordship's favour to me has at
Least so much Share in y^e conduct of it, if not in y^e Sub-
stance, that I am Perswaded I can not be more Obliged to y^e
Donor, than to your Lordship's Singular goodness ; which tho'
I can Not Deserve, yet I shall allways Sencibly reflect on &
Improve.   And I should be Doubly blest, if Providence would
put it into my hands, to render yor Lordship some Service,
Suited to ye Sence I have of yor Lordship's Extraordinary
Favour.   And yet I am yor Lordship's most Humble Peticoner
That if Possible I may Kno' the Originalls of this Munificence.
Sure That Hand That Can Suppose me to Merit so much
Regard, must believ me Fitt to be Trusted wth The Knowledge
of my Benefactor, and Uncapable of Discovering any Part of
it that should be conceal'd ; But I submitt This to yor Lordship
and the Persons concern'd.
   " I Frankly Acknowledge to yor Lordship and to ye Unknown Rewarders of my Mean Performances, That I do not
see ye Merit They are Thus Pleas'd to Vallue.   The most I
wish and wch I hope I can answer for is That I shall Allways
Preserv the Homely Despicable Title of *an Honest Man*.   If
this will recomend me, yor Lordship shall never be Asham'd of

giveing me that Title.   Nor my Enemys be able by Fear or
Reward to make me otherwise.— — — — — — — — — —
 " I am, May it Please yor Lordship,
   " Yo^r L^dship's Highly Oblig'd
    " Most Humble and Most Obed^t Sert^t
      " DANIEL DE FOE."
" To The Right Honble
 " Charles Lord Hallifax
  " Humbly Present."

From July to October Defoe published nothing known
except his *Reviews*.   In several numbers of that paper, between
the 13th and the 24th of the latter month, he addressed himself
to the members of the new Parliament,—on the importance of
their duties ;—the peculiar circumstances of the times,—the
plots of the high party,—the exuberance of the press,—and the
desirableness of an Act of Parliament, under which every book
ought to be required to show the name of the author, or responsible publisher.   He urged on them punctual and constant
attention to the interests of the country, and moderation in all
their proceedings.   The substance of these addresses he reprinted in a pamphlet published on the 24th of October, with
the title of " A Declaration without Doors.   By the Author of
the True-Born Englishman.   Sold by the Booksellers of
London and Westminster, 1705."   The Parliament assembled
the following day, and was opened by a pacific speech from
the throne ; which was re-echoed in the addresses adopted by
both Houses, and thus, for the time, was harmony restored,
between all the branches of the Legislature.

The province of Carolina, in North America, was granted by
Charles II., in 1663, to certain English noblemen and gentlemen ; and, by the terms of the charter, express provision was
made for a toleration and indulgence, to all Christians, in the
free exercise of their religion.   In consequence of this, there
were among the English settlers many families of Dissenters,
who lived in harmony with their Episcopalian brethren ; and
the colony increased in numbers and prosperity, until the death
of King William.   Lord Granville, whose bitterness against.
the Dissenters was displayed both in and out of Parliament, was

Palatine, or president of the proprietary, shortly after the accession of Queen Anne; and, through his influence, a bill was passed, in a packed House of the colonial legislature, enacting that each member, on taking his seat, should produce to the Speaker a certificate of his receiving the Sacrament in conformity with the rites of the Church of England, signed by the minister, or by two creditable witnesses on oath. By virtue of this Act every Dissenter was at once turned out of the House of Assembly. The High Church party having thus seized the government, and rendered the Dissenters infamous by law, it will be unnecessary to pursue the persecution that followed, except to say that they were doomed to destruction by the hands of an armed mob. Various unsuccessful representations were made to the Lords Proprietors in England, until the oppression having become intolerable, an Address, representing their Grievances, was adopted on the 26th of June, 1705,—signed by one hundred and fifty of the inhabitants,—and brought to England by Mr. John Ash, a former member of the Assembly. He unfortunately died soon after his arrival. A further representation, still more numerously signed, was brought by Mr. Jos^h Boon; and, after many delays, a meeting of the Proprietors was convened, at which Mr. Archdale, one of that body, and previously Governor of Carolina, advocated the cause of the petitioners, but was put down by the arbitrary and imperious Palatine, who concluded, " I'll do as I see fit; I see no Harm at all in the Bill, and am resolved to pass it."

On this failure to obtain justice, some Dissenting merchants in the City of London, trading to Carolina, took up the matter, towards the end of the year, and Defoe having been called to their councils, the documents brought by Mr. Boon were placed in his hands, and the first result was a speedy publication of an able and convincing pamphlet, entitled, " Party-Tyranny: or, An Occasional Bill in Miniature; as now Practised in Carolina. Humbly offered to the Consideration of both Houses of Parliament. London: Printed in the year 1705." Copies of this were sent to the members of both Houses; and was followed, in the beginning of 1706, by a petition to the House of Lords. Having deferred the matter, on the request of Lord Granville, and having heard counsel on his behalf against the petition, their Lordships, on the 12th of

March, adopted an Address to the Queen, in favour of the petitioners, condemning in the strongest language the arbitrary oppression of the province, and beseeching her to order the persons guilty thereof to be prosecuted according to law. Our author was not idle, but having obtained additional information from Mr. Archdale and Mr. Boone, he took a more general view of the subject; and about the same date as the condemnation by the Lords, he published a second pamphlet, entitled, " The Case of Protestant Dissenters in Carolina: Shewing how a Law to prevent Occasional Conformity there, has ended in the Total Subversion of the Constitution in Church and State. Recommended to the serious Consideration of all that are true Friends of our present Government. London. Printed in the year 1706." The Queen returned a favourable answer to the address; and, on the advice of her ministers, referred the matter to the Lords of the Committee of Trade, who reported on the 24th of May, that the Act was altogether illegal;—an abuse of the Charter, and a Forfeiture thereof. This was followed by a Declaration of her Majesty, dated the 10th of June, 1706, that such Law was Null and Void. Thus the Proprietors, and the Colonial Assembly, were compelled to retrace their steps; peace was restored to the province, and the efforts of Daniel Defoe crowned with complete success.

I am unwilling to occupy so much space in correcting material errors, as to matters of so little present interest. In this affair of Carolina, Mr. Wilson forgot that the year had not then entirely ceased to be reckoned from Ladyday. One document, belonging to the year 1706, he found to be dated March 1705, and, to prevent confusion, he unfortunately suppressed, or altered, all the other dates to correspond; thus placing the whole proceedings a year too early, and under a different Parliament. Again, " The Case of the Protestant Dissenters in Carolina, 1706," contains as indubitable evidence of Defoe's hand, as its predecessor on the same subject; and furnishes one peculiar scriptural illustration, repeated probably twenty times in his other various works, but never seen by me in the writings of any other author. Mr. W. has attributed this pamphlet to Mr. Archdale, probably in mistake for a publication, bearing the name of that gentleman, in 1707, and

entitled " A New Description of that Fertile and Pleasant
Province of Carolina," &c.   The two are as unlike, in stile
and thought, as could well be conceived.

Since the change of Ministry, Lord Haversham had united
with the Tories, and on the 15th of November, 1705, made a
speech in the House of Lords on the State of the Nation.
This he afterward printed as a pamphlet, and Defoe, having
made some remarks on it in the *Review*, reprinted them as
" An Answer to the Lord Haversham's Speech.   London,
1705."   Our author disclaims meddling with what was transacted in Parliament; but in dealing with a printed pamphlet,
he says, " The anonymous author is nothing to me, be he a
Lord or a Tinker."   His Lordship was highly incensed at this
freedom; and, finding himself unable to bring the author to
the bar of the House, lost his temper, and in the most undig-
nified personal abuse, wrote and published, " The Lord
Haversham's Vindication of his Speech in Parliament, November 15, 1705," &c.   He calls the author of the *Review* " a
mean and mercenary prostitute;" and considers Defoe as
fighting the battles of the Ministers, from whom he received
" both his encouragement and instructions."   The former
pamphlets, of four, and eight pages, had been but skirmishing.
By branding Defoe with the abject condition to which party
oppression alone had reduced him, his Lordship aroused an antagonist far too powerful for him to contend against.   In a
pamphlet of thirty-two pages, published on the 15th of January,
1706, our author at once strips off his Lordship's panoply as a
peer,—vindicates his own character, as a wounded but uncon-
quered patriot; and quietly exposes his blundering, frenzied
adversary to public contempt.   It is entitled, " A Reply to a
Pamphlet, intitled, ' The Lord Haversham's Vindication of his
Speech,' &c.   By the Author of the *Review*.   London.
Printed in the year 1706."

From the nervous and touching eloquence of this tract, I
quote part of his reply to the charge of meanness, in which the
noble-man, and the mean-fellow are made to change places.
" I had the honour to be trusted, esteemed, and, much more
than I deserved, valued, by the best King England ever saw;
and yet whose Judgment I cannot undervalue, because he gave

his Lordship his honour and his dignity ; which was, some time before, as mean as mine.   But Fate, that makes foot-balls of Men, kicks some Men up stairs, and some down ; some are advanced without Honour, others suppressed without Infamy ; some are raised without Merit, some are crushed without Crime ; and nŏ Man knows, by the beginning of Things, whether his Course shall issue in a Peerage or a Pillory : Time was, that no Man could have determined it between his Lordship and this mean Fellow, except those who knew his Lordship's merit more particularly than outsides could have detected.   In the Grave, we shall come to a second and more exact Equality ; and what difference follows next, will be formed on no foot of advantage from Dignity or Character here ; so that this mean Fellow has less Disparity to struggle with, than the usage of him seems to allow.   But to return to the Days of King William, and to matters of Honour. If I should say I had the Honour to know some Things from his Majesty, and to transact some Things for his Majesty, that he would not have trusted his Lordship with, perhaps there may be more Truth than Modesty in it ; and if I should say, also, these Honours done me, helped to make me that mean Thing some People think fit to represent me, perhaps it should be very true also."*

The next publication of Defoe arose from a movement, in both Houses of Parliament, against the faction cry of the Church being in danger.   Resolutions were embodied in an Address to her Majesty, declaring the Church of England to be in a safe and flourishing condition ; and denouncing those who suggested otherwise as enemies to the Queen, the Church, and the Kingdom.   This effort to assuage the heat of parties, by showing the concord between the several branches of the Legislature, our author commemorates in a long Pindaric Poem, which contains many fine passages.   It was published on the 10th of January, and is entitled, " A Hymn to Peace. Occasion'd, by the two Houses Joining in One Address to the

---

* Mr. Walter Wilson has attributed to the pen of Defoe a pamphlet entitled " The Christianity of the High Church Considered. Dedicated to a Noble Peer. London, 1704." The " Noble Peer" thus flattered was Lord Haversham, and the author the Rev. Dr. White Kennett.   I correct the error, that Defoe may not seem inconsistent.

Queen. By the Author of the True-born Englishman. London : Printed in the Year 1706." In this poem he adverts to his own labours for the promotion of general peace, and speaks of the deprivation of his own. He says—

> " Storms of Men,
> Voracious and Unsatisfied as Death,
> Spoil in their Hands, and Poison in their Breath,
>   With Rage of Devils hunt me down,
> And to abate my Peace, destroy their own."

Many of the couplets concluding his paragraphs, are finely pointed ; as—

> " That bind the Hands from Industry,
>   Pinion the willing Wings, and bid Men fly."

And—

> " So first they rifle me *the Shortest Way*,
>   And when they've stript me Naked, bid me Pay !"

After describing the unjust Magistrate who covers the Bench with fraud and Vice, he adds—

> " Yet when by Law he studies to oppress,
>   He's called a *Justice of the Peace*."

The poem concludes with ten pages in heroic verse addressed to the Queen, in praise of Peace and Union. The loftiness of thought, and vigour of expression in this part, amply compensate for an occasional rugged line ; and probably could not be surpassed, if equalled, by any composition of similar length from the pen of Dryden.

In February this year, Defoe again complained in the *Review*, of the injuries done him by pirate Printers, in abridging, corrupting, and reprinting, every thing he wrote ; and, even of printing his name to any scandalous thing in which he had no concern, and then crying it about the streets as his. He mentions also several other " printer's cheats," such as, " The Quaker's Catechism, to which, as a Shoeing-horn to draw in the people to buy it, is added to the title, *The Shortest Way with Daniel Defoe*." Another method of annoyance, was the collection of disjointed sentences from the *Review*, and forming them into a book to make them look frightful to the world ; and he also states, that the numbers of his *Review* were systematically stolen from coffee-houses, by the high-party, in order that they might not be read.

It was the intention of Defoe, to devote as large a portion of the third volume of his *Review* as possible, to the consideration of Trade, and the laws by which it was governed. His misfortunes had made him acquainted with the evils connected with bankruptcy; and, from the middle of February to the end of March, this subject occupied much of his attention. He relates his own grievous losses from fraudulent debtors; and dilates upon the exorbitant power of angry creditors, to punish a debtor with life-long imprisonment, for claims which can never be paid. It seems very probable that he was consulted by Mr. Harley on the subject; and, that his writings and personal representations had much influence in forwarding " An Act to Prevent Frauds committed by Bankrupts," which passed in March. When serious argument was no longer necessary, Defoe employed one of his *Reviews* in a clever banter, without personal reflections, upon those who had opposed the Bill from interested motives; upon which, one of the citizens concerned, threatened to cane our author for what he had written. A man of Defoe's courage was not likely to be convinced by such an argument, and he replied in the next *Review*, " I take the Liberty to tell him, he talks more with his Tongue than he will attempt with his Hands; and that such impertinence deserves no notice till he has put it in Practice; for which, on the least hint to the Author, he shall never want an opportunity."

On the 18th of April, after the rising of Parliament, Defoe published an able pamphlet on the whole subject, entitled " Remarks on the Bill to Prevent Frauds committed by Bankrupts. With Observations on the Effect it may have upon Trade. London. Printed in the Year 1706." After congratulating himself on the success of his exertions, he enters at length into the imperfections of the old law, and the benefits that will accrue from the new measure. He concludes by jeering the myrmidons who had so long existed upon the miseries of their countrymen; and advises, that ten thousand catchpoles go and serve on board the fleet; and recommends the Attorneys and Solicitors to turn their hands to the more laudable practice of picking pockets, according to the letter of it, and assures them they may thus, in time, meet with the reward of their former merit.

Thomas De Laune, a Baptist schoolmaster, wrote a book in the year 1683, called, " A Plea for the Nonconformists," for which he was committed to Newgate, and in the following January, tried before the notorious Judge Jeffries.   He was sentenced to pay a hundred marks, as a fine, to find security for a year, and his book to be publicly burnt.   Unable to pay the fine, he lingered for fifteen months ; and, after much suffering, died in prison.   No answer had ever appeared, and similarity of suffering, in the same cause, moved Defoe to reprint De Laune's work.   This was published on the 6th of June, 1706, " *With a Preface by the Author of the Review.*" Our author shows the barbarous usage to which De Laune was subjected ; having no subsistence but what was contributed by such friends as came to visit him ; the invincible patience he exhibited under the greatest extremities, when his wife and two small children died in prison with him ; and the heartlessness of the whole body of Dissenters in England, who would not raise him 66*l.* 13*s.* 4*d.* to save his life.   Defoe concludes his Preface, " 'Tis pity, after his death, he has no better hand to recommend him to the world ; but, since no man will build a monument upon his grave, I thought it a debt due to his ill-rewarded merit, to write this as a monument upon his work, and I am sorry it is performed no better."

' From grave to gay.'   The church of St. Martin's in the Fields, being too small for the congregation, and Daniel Burgess, the eccentric Dissenting preacher, leaving his meeting-house, in Russell Court, some of the inhabitants of that end of the parish obtained the building to make a Chapel of Ease.   It was old and incommodious ; so that 600*l.* was required to repair, and fit it up.   A voluntary collection failed to raise the amount ; and, as the Drury-Lane Play-house occupied the adjacent ground, Mr. Rich, one of the patentees and manager, was applied to, and an arrangement was made that the proceeds of one day's acting, in the Theatre, should be given to the fund.   This was advertised in the *Daily Courant* of June 18th, 1706, the performance being, the tragedy of

Hamlet, Prince of Denmark, with singing and an entertainment of Dancing.   Two days afterward Defoe occupied his *Review* with an excellent piece of wit and ridicule, on the incongruity of identifying the interests of the Church and the Play-house.   This afforded so much amusement to the town, that it was immediately reprinted and largely sold in the streets, under the title of " A Sermon preached by Mr. Daniel Defoe, on the fitting up of Dr. Burgess's late Meeting House. Taken from his *Review*, of Thursday, the 20th of June, 1706." Our author was always strongly opposed to all theatrical performances ; and their generally immoral character at that period was fully exposed by Jeremy Collier, the Nonjuror and High Churchman.   Defoe bids him, " Never talk of the Stage any more, for if the Church cannot be repaired or fitted up without the Play-house, to write against the Play-house is to write against the Church. Can our Church be in danger ? How is it possible ? The whole Nation is solicitous, and at work, for her safety and prosperity ! The Parliament address ; the Queen consults ; the Ministry execute ; the Army fights ; and all for the Church ! But at home, we have other Heroes that act for the Church. Peggy Hughes sings ; Monsieur Ramadon plays ; Miss Santlow dances ; Monsieur Cherrier teaches ; and all for the Church ! Here's heavenly doings ! Here's harmony ! Your singing Psalms is hurdy-gurdy to this Music ; and all your preaching Actors are Fools to these."   He concludes by recommending an inscription over the door of the chapel to commemorate the event, as a " Reproach to the Church of England and the Protestant Religion."

As might have been expected, the caustic wit of our author offended some, and a pamphlet was published in reply.   He returned to the subject however in the *Review* of the 25th, assuming a tone of more serious irony, in which he says, " We talk of reforming our Manners, and setting up rules of Government ; but to attempt it this way, seems to me to make a Comedy of the Government, and a Tragedy of the Church. This, I think, is certain, let the Play be what it will ; 'tis a Tragedy to the Church, and one of the ' Shortest Ways ' to pull her down."

Soon afterward he turned, in a still more serious tone of reproval, to the University authorities at Oxford, for having licensed a company to act plays in that city.   He notices in terms of commendation that the Vice-chancellor of Cambridge had refused to allow the players there.   Whether Defoe's salutary admonitions had any effect or not, it is a fact that the players were not permitted to exercise their calling in Oxford the following year.

The biographers of Defoe, since Mr. Chalmers, all relate a pleasant story, very creditable to his genius.   It appears to have been originally based upon an alleged tradition among the booksellers ; but time, which too frequently obscures the past, seems, in this instance, to have gradually removed all doubt from the minds of successive writers of his life.   The following is the relation, in few words :—When Drelincourt's book on the Fear of Death first appeared, in the English language, the publisher was disappointed in the sale ; and, being a heavy work, he is said to have complained to Defoe of the loss he was likely to sustain by it.   Defoe asked him if the author had blended anything marvellous with his pious advice, which the bookseller answered in the negative.   " If you wish to have your book sell," replied he, " I will put you in the way of it ; " and he immediately sat down and composed the story of the Apparition of Mrs. Veal, which was made to recommend Drelincourt's book, and has been appended to every subsequent edition.   After this, there was no complaint for want of a sale, and since then, the work has passed through more than fifty editions.

All this is circumstantial, and we have the dialogue, apparently in the words of the parties ; but it is singular that the title of Drelincourt's book is incorrectly given ; that of Defoe's pamphlet is inaccurate ; the year in which both, or either of them, appeared is misstated ; and the very name of the bookseller is omitted.

The first edition of Defoe's pamphlet was published on the 5th of July, 1706, by B. Bragg, at the Black Raven in Paternoster Row, and was entitled,—" A True Relation of the Apparition of one Mrs. Veal, the next day after her death, to one Mrs. Bargrave at Canterbury, the 8th of September, 1705." The advertisement of its title contains no reference to Drelincourt's book, which was then rapidly running through its *third* English edition ; and was published by J. Robinson, at the

Golden Lyon, in St. Paul's Church Yard. We have strong indirect proof, that the " Apparition " was Bragg's trade property, because he continued to publish the only separate editions, after having fraudulently issued a spurious edition of our author's *Jure Divino* ; for which act of dishonesty, Defoe ceased to have any further dealings with him. However that may be, an arrangement was made that Robinson should be allowed to reprint Defoe's pamphlet in the *fourth* Edition of Drelincourt, which was published on the 30th of September, 1706. " With an Account of an Apparition at Canterbury, which gave a great Character of the aforesaid Book." So far from this 4th Edition going off rapidly, it continued to be advertised until the end of the following January ; and the 5th Edition was not published until the 3rd of May, 1707, by " R. Clavell, J. Robinson, and A. and J. Churchill," who dispensed with Defoe's Tract, and substituted—" To which is added, the great character of the Author in Mr. Boyle's great Historical Dictionary." In the meantime Defoe's Apparition was making its own way, the *third* separate Edition being published by Bragg, on the 9th of April, 1707, but now stating prominently, that it recommends the perusal of Drelincourt's Book. That the latter was a readable and popular work is evident from the 6th Edition being advertised as published, without any reference to the Apparition of Mrs. Veal, on the 20th of September, 1709. I am unable to say when Defoe's " Apparition " became a necessary appendage to the book ; but think, that since the eleventh edition, to the present time, Drelincourt has never been published without it. No one can read this marvellous creation of our author, and study the whole of its details, without concurring in the eulogistic criticism of Sir Walter Scott, and other writers who have considered it. The Apparition of Mrs. Veal could never have happened in reality ; and yet, it is perhaps the most perfect fiction of its kind that ever was written.

During Defoe's long imprisonment in 1703–4, he had laid the groundwork, and made some progress in the composition, of a large poetical work on government. It was advertised as early as September, 1704, to be published by subscription, in near a hundred sheets folio, the price to be ten shillings, one-fourth to be paid down, and no more to be printed than subscribed for. His illness, after his release,—the persuasion of friends, who believed that the then Tory Parliament would suppress both it and the author together,—his enforced absence from town, and other pressing subjects for his pen,—having delayed the publication, some of his subscribers became clamorous; and, it was maliciously reported, by his enemies, that he did not intend to print it. He complained of this, in his *Review*, as "a hard suggestion, absurd in itself, and false." The work was ultimately published on the 20th of July, 1706, with the following title, "Jure Divino: a Satyr. In Twelve Books. By the Author of the True-Born Englishman. London. Printed in the Year 1706." A portrait of the author, varying considerably from that prefixed to his collected works, accompanies the volume. Announcing, in his *Review*, this long-expected book, the grievous mortification was forced upon him of noticing the actual publication of a spurious edition, printed in octavo, and to be sold for five shillings. It was on a bad paper, with an ill-executed portrait; and, as he states, full of mistakes. In several subsequent numbers of the *Review*, he writes bitterly of this "base and villainous transaction." He properly calls the persons concerned, thieves, "picking the pockets of the buyer, as they have done that of the author." He says, "Whoever has a mind to encourage such Robbery of other men's Studies at their own Expence, may be furnished with the said Book at Mr. Benjamin Bragg's, Publisher in ordinary to the Pirates."

The manner in which this gross act of dishonesty had been practised was by bribing a pressman, in the office where the genuine folio was being printed, to steal copies of the sheets as they were successively printed. Though Defoe knew what was threatened, yet the mode of action was concealed sufficiently until all was ready, when the pirate had the shameless audacity to announce, that it was "to be sold for the sole Benefit of the Author." The conduct of Bragg in this matter was greatly aggravated by the circumstance that he had been often employed by our author, and had published his last preceding work. When remonstrated with, he put on a bold face, and told Defoe that an author had no right to publish anything except through a bookseller; and that, *on principle*, he would in future pirate anything so published. Defoe was able

to congratulate himself that he did not find one of his subscribers had gone off; and therefore, as only the number of
copies subscribed for had been printed, he was perhaps saved
from immediate loss.   Still the fraudulent intention of the
spurious edition was not the less to be condemned.   In his
preface, Defoe warned those concerned in the fraud, " Let
them be sure of this, whoever attempts it will lose by it,—
And let them take my Word, or not take it, as they please."
The retribution thus predicted was not slow in its accomplishment; the profits anticipated by the first pirates, were con-
sumed by a still lower class of their own fraternity, who reprinted the twelve books of " Jure Divino" in as many penny
pamphlets, on the coarsest ballad paper, with rude woodcut
" effigies" of the author, for sale by the street-hawkers.   The
only copies I have seen of these, are several in my own possession, all dated 1706.

As an upright and innocent but unfortunate man, Defoe
took the earliest opportunity of surrendering to the Commissioners appointed under the Act of Parliament recently passed
for the relief of debtors.   His *Review* for the 20th of August,
and subsequent numbers, contain painful details of a relentless
persecution,—much of it arising from political animosity,—to
which he was subjected during these proceedings.   Suffice it to
say, that he gave up all he possessed, with full accounts of the
balance of his affairs; beginning at his first business misfortunes, fourteen years previously, and including the completion
of his ruin in prison, when he was—" stripped naked by the
government, and the foundations torn up, on which he had
built the prospect of paying his debts, and raising his family."
After four severe examinations on oath,—in which the bitterness of the lawyer opposed to him was so great, that Defoe
told him it had " in it all the Villainy of abstract Malice,"—
the Commissioners appear to have been fully satisfied with
his conduct, as they refused to listen to a witness who proposed, on payment of his expenses only, to prove that Defoe
was then possessed of an estate of 400*l.* per annum.

The *Review* of May 21, 1706, is occupied by a poem " On
the Fight at Ramellies," the news of which had reached
England only two days previously.   It is in blank verse, and

Defoe trusts the grand national interest of the subject—and
that he had only three hours in which to write it,—will excuse
the lines being " something incorrect." It consists of 128
lines of very unequal merit, but with forcible passages, as will
appear from the following :—

> " When strong Triumphant Death, o're-gorged with Blood,
> Bid France desist th' unequal strife, and fly.
>
> *   *   *   *   *
>
> Where fled the angry Spirits from the Field
> When Wounds dismiss'd them from their Cage of Flesh?
> Were there no Hurries in the crowded Air,
> Where Souls retaining all the feuds of Rage,
> Renew'd the War, and fighting as they pass'd,
> Rais'd Storms and Strong Convulsions in th' Abyss?"

The Union of England and Scotland had always been an
object of desire to William III., but the distraction of the
times forbad any effort towards its accomplishment. The Tory
government in the earlier part of the reign of Queen Anne was,
from its attachment to Episcopalian High Church principles,
looked upon by the Presbyterian Church of Scotland with too
much suspicion to render tolerable any proposition to that
effect. The accession of a Whig administration, and the election of a Liberal House of Commons in England, afforded a
more favourable juncture, than had previously existed. Acts
of Parliament were therefore passed in both countries, empowering the Queen to appoint Commissioners to treat for a
Union. They met for the first time on the 16th of April,
1706, at the Cockpit, Whitehall. There is no reason to think
that, at that time, Defoe had an idea he would be called upon
to take any part in the great work ; but its success lay near to
his heart, as a true patriot, and he did not forget the wishes
of the deceased monarch, whom it was his pride to call master.
On the 4th of May, therefore, he published " An Essay at
Removing National Prejudices against a Union with Scotland.
To be continued during the Treaty here. Part I. London :
Printed in the Year 1706." This was followed on the 28th of
the same month, by another pamphlet having the same title,
and called " Part II." The Lord Treasurer Godolphin, and
Harley, Secretary of State, were two of the Commissioners,
and the sequel proved that the government must have highly

appreciated our author's co-operation.* The Articles of Union were signed in London on the 22nd of July, and remitted, for ratification by the Parliament of Scotland.

By the recommendation of Harley, Defoe had, as already stated, acquired the favour and patronage of Lord Godolphin, who seems ever after to have entertained as high an opinion of his abilities and integrity as his first benefactor. On the nomination of these ministers, he was now openly taken into the service of the Queen; and, he says, " I had the Honour to be employed in several honourable, tho' secret Services." The fact of such services being secret, prevented his ever afterward divulging their nature, or his instructions; but there can be no doubt that one was his Mission to Scotland, to promote the Union. His religious and political principles, no less than his ready talents, his charming manners, his faculty for business, and his extensive knowledge of trade and commerce, all combined to make him acceptable to the Scots people, and to fit him for the appointment. At a later period of his life he says, " I had the happiness to discharge myself in all these Trusts so much to the Satisfaction of those who employed me, tho' often times with Difficulty and Danger, that my Lord Treasurer Godolphin, whose Memory I have always honour'd, was pleased to continue his Favour to me, and to do me all good Offices with Her Majesty, even after an unhappy Breach had separated him from my first benefactor." Before his departure to Scotland, Defoe had the honour of his first introduction to the Queen, and kissed her hand upon his appointment.

The date of this arrangement is not specifically stated. It was probably towards the end of August, but could not have been later than early in September. There were then no stage coaches,—a journey to Scotland by land could only be accomplished by hiring horses from town to town, and occupied some weeks. The Scotch Parliament was appointed to meet on the 3rd of October, and some preliminaries would doubtless require our author's attention. It must also be remembered that during his journey he was obliged to write his *Reviews,* and

---

* Mr. Wilson has attributed to Defoe a tract intitled, " The Advantages of the Act of Security, compared with those of the intended Union, 1706." But he could never have seen a copy. It must have been written by a Jacobite.

dispatch them regularly for publication.   Almost immediately
after his arrival in Edinburgh there appeared a pamphlet, probably intended for circulation in both countries, entitled " A
Letter to a Friend, giving an Account how the Treaty of
Union has been received here.   With Remarks on what has
been written by Mr. Hodges and Mr. Ridpath.   Edinburgh.
1706."   Mr. Wilson attributes this to Defoe, although he does
not appear to have ever seen a copy. Not having myself been more
successful, I adopt a saying of our author, and " leave it as I
find it."   His two " Essays at Removing National Prejudices
against a Union with Scotland," had been written for the
English people ; but he now caused them to be reprinted in
Edinburgh ; and followed them up by four additional Essays
for the same purpose, but addressed to the inhabitants of
Scotland, to remove National Prejudices against a Union with
England.   I need not set out their respective titles here, as
they will be found, at large, in the List of Defoe's works. They
were all published in Edinburgh ; the Third and Fourth probably in November and December,—the Fifth and Sixth in
January, 1707.

Mr. James Webster, Minister of the Tolbooth Church in
Edinburgh, a learned man, and a popular preacher, appeared
vigorously for the Union of the two kingdoms, all the time of
the treaty ; and Defoe says he had often heard him declare, he
believed the Church of Scotland could not be safe without the
Union.   Yet the very week the Treaty was finished, 16th of
January, 1707, the same Mr. Webster published a pamphlet
entitled " Lawful Prejudices against an Incorporating Union
with England ; or, some Modest Considerations on the Sinful-
ness of this Union, and the Danger flowing from it to the
Church of Scotland. Edinburgh : 1707."   In this pamphlet he
fell, in a very unhandsome manner, upon the Dissenters in
England, insinuating that an Act of Comprehension would
deprive the Church of Scotland of all help or assistance from
England.   Defoe was much surprised, and entered with great
reluctance into a controversy against one for whom he had entertained so much respect ; but,—after a vain attempt to procure
a private interview, to discuss the matter,—felt himself compelled
to publish a tract of a single sheet, entitled, " The Dissenters
in England Vindicated, from some Reflections in a late Pam-

phlet called ' *Lawful Prejudices,* ' &c., Edinburgh, 1707."
In this performance, Defoe treated his opponent with the
utmost tenderness and civility; professing that nothing but
his sense of justice and duty, to an absent and injured
people, could have drawn him into such a contest. The
very calmness of the reply, however, seems to have goaded
the reverend gentleman into a passion; in which he published an answer, flying out upon our author in all the
opprobrious language his fury could dictate. It seems that
somebody had sent him an offensive letter, which he erroneously ascribed to Defoe; and, though all his ministerial and
other friends endeavoured to convince him of the wrong, he
continued deaf to reason. In this state of things they
applied to our author, and urged him, for the sake of Mr.
Webster's character, and of religion generally, not to write
again. Defoe had offered to meet him in a friendly manner,
or to refer the whole dispute to six of their ministers, all of
whom should be named by Mr. Webster himself, but the
worthy gentleman continued inexorable; and, for the sake of
peace, Defoe suppressed, at his own cost, a reply that was
actually printed, under the title, " Passion and Prejudice the
Support of one another, and, both destructive to the Happiness of the Nation, &c." Although, however, he had, in compliance with the wishes of their mutual friends, consented to
overlook the personal attack of Mr. Webster, yet he did not
consider himself obliged to desert the defence of his friends in
England, or the cause of the Union he had so much at heart.
He therefore stated the case afresh, in a larger pamphlet,
published in March, with the following title, " A Short View
of the Present State of the Protestant Religion in Britain, as
it is now Profest in the Episcopal Church in England, the
Presbyterian Church in Scotland, and the Dissenters in Both.
Edinburgh: Printed in the year 1707." This was not merely
seasonable, but still remains one of the most valuable historical and argumentative tracts Defoe ever wrote. It was of
great service at the time, by its inculcation of peace; its
interest is lasting, as an epitome of the status of the respective
religious bodies concerned; and also, for its references to a
portion of our author's personal history. He discusses all the
points at issue between Mr. Webster and himself, but does not

mention his name; and manifests throughout, the highest parts of a Christian's character, striving mightily for peace. His opponent must, as a minister of religion, have felt the rebuke implied in the following, " For myself, I shall say little,—I have quitted the just Resentment at unsufferable Insolencies, that I might with the utmost calmness of mind move Scotland to Peace, and practise the thing I exhort to;—the Gentleman that opposes me in this, shall not rally me only in Print, but he shall trample me under his Feet; I am content to be all that is contemptible and vile in his Eyes, and in every man's else, if I can but be instrumental, in the least, to this blessed healing Temper."

Lest his opponents should think that fear of themselves, or subserviency to the government, influenced his conduct, he adds, " I bless God, I was never a slave to any Government in the World; I was never frighted by Power, when I was crush'd by its Fury; and I could never be brib'd by its Gifts, when in the most proper circumstances to want them. I would not write a Word, no, not for the Queen herself, if my Conscience and Principles did not say Amen to the Subject; and I challenge the World to say whenever I acted otherwise.

" The Party therefore in nothing more mistake me, than in thinking, that when, for Peace sake, I avoid Reflecting on their Follies, 'tis for any Value or Fear of their Resentment. They must be little acquainted with the Scenes I have acted in the World, who know me no better than that; and I refer them to the Resentments of Men, much more Capital than their Ambitious Thoughts can pretend to, and let them see the influence Anger has had on me."

This pamphlet was reprinted in London, and published on the first of April, 1707, the title being a little altered, and Mr. Webster's name mentioned thereon, so that English readers might know who was the opponent referred to in the body of the work.

Near the end of the year 1706, and while the treaty of Union was still under debate, Defoe composed his first acknowledged publication in Scotland; and he endeavoured to give it, as much as possible, the character of a State document. The title is, " Caledonia, &c., a Poem, in Honour of Scotland and the Scots Nation. In three Parts. Edinburgh.

Printed by the Heirs and Successors of Andrew Anderson, printer to the Queen's most Excellent Majesty, Anno Dom. 1706." Besides being in folio, and by the Queen's printers, it set forth, at large, the Licence of the Lords of the Privy Council, dated from the Palace at Holy-rood, granting to *Daniel De Foe, Esquire,* the exclusive right of publishing it for seven years. The Dedication, to his Grace the Duke of Queensbury, Her Majesty's High Commissioner, is signed with the author's name in full; and a Preface of six pages, addressed to the Parliament, is also subscribed with his name.

In the preface he says, " I am sorry to see so much differing about uniting; and more, to see so much uniting about differing." To show that he is not biassed by party, he declares that the Union is not concerned in the poem, but he has been surprised to see, that although " the Land, the Sea, the Climate, and the People, of Scotland, are all adapted for Plenty, Riches, and Fruitfulness," yet the Nation is poor, and Improvement is neglected. " With or without an Union the Lands may be improved, the Tenants incouraged, the Fields inclosed, Woods planted, the Moors and Wastes fed, and Scotland recovered from languishing Poverty." After recapitulating other desirable improvements, all irrespective of a Union, he archly adds, " I have been, my Lords, two or three times going to address the Nobility in this Humble manner, that your Lordships would be pleased to condescend to double your Estates." The poem occupies sixty pages, and the notes display extensive reading and much care. On the 28th of January, 1707, an octavo edition of this work was printed in London, the preface being omitted, and a List of the names of subscribers and benefactors added.

The position of Defoe in Scotland, relative to the Union, seems to have been a semi-official one, in which he was under no paity ties, but employed by the Queen, and the Prime Minister of England, to render all the assistance in his power in promoting the Union; yet apparently, in Edinburgh on his own account, and generally unfettered in his discretion. Without this key there would seem an inconsistency between his statements in the " History of the Union," and at a later period, in his " Appeal to Honour and Justice." Considered in this light the connection affords another proof of the discernment of the Queen and her Minister, and was highly honourable to the subject treated with so great confidence. When writing on the subject, he appears to avoid, as much as possible, relating what was merely personal to himself, apologizing that his only reason for doing so is that when Posterity shall read the History of the Union they may know that the author was capable of giving a true account of the matter. He says, "I had the Honour to be frequently sent for into the several Committees· of Parliament, which were appointed to state some difficult Points relating to Equalities, Taxes, Prohibitions, &c. 'Tis for those Gentlemen to say, whether I was useful or not, that's none of my Business here." He states very fully the methods by which, after the printing and circulation of the Articles of Union, the people became excited to opposition, and even to riot, in Edinburgh, Glasgow, Dumfries, and other parts of the Kingdom. Describing the Tumult in Edinburgh, when the Rabble went roving up and down the town, breaking the windows of members of Parliament, and insulting them in the streets, he says, "They put out all the Lights, that they might not be discovered ; and the Author of this had one great Stone thrown at him, but for looking out at a Window ; for they suffered no body to look out, lest they should know Faces, and inform against them afterwards." Again he says, "The Author of this had his share in the Danger of this Tumult, and tho' unknown to him, was watch'd and set by the Mob, in order to know where to find him ;—had his chamber-windows insulted, and the Windows below him broken by mistake.—But by the prudence of his Friends, the shortness of its continuance, and God's Providence, he escaped." The city continued in possession of the mob until one o'clock in the morning, when a battalion of the Guards were marched into the Town, and the riot was soon ended.

Defoe could not fail to observe "one significant *Omen* of the future good success of this Treaty,—and which I must own" (he says) "very much encouraged me to think it would go on, notwithstanding all the vigorous Opposition it met with, was that it was Voted on the most remarkable Day for public Deliverance, that ever happened in this Island." His allusion is that the first Article of the Union, which virtually decided the whole measure, was carried in the Parliament of Scotland by a majority of 116, against 83, on the 4th of November, the anniversary of the birth of King William, and also of the day on which he landed at Torbay.

Defoe's time must have been fully occupied with interviews, consultations, attendance on parliamentary committees,—calculating statistics of excise, taxes, and public finance—controversies with opponents of the Union, writing pamphlets, composing poems, preparing his *Reviews ;* and,—amidst all the scenes of disorder and distraction,—collecting the documents and other materials for his admirable History of the Union afterward published. The scope of this memoir forbids me to say more of the Union than relates to our author, and I therefore only add that, notwithstanding the efforts of a minority, who could agree in nothing else but in opposition to this measure, all the articles were successively passed, and the Act, as a whole, ratified by the Scots Parliament on the 16th of January, 1707. It was similarly ratified without amendment by the English Parliament, and received the royal assent on the 6th of March. Thus was brought to a happy consummation, a Union,—fraught with the greatest national blessings to Great Britain;— a Union, which has been growing closer and stronger from generation to generation ; and which,—whatever features of distinct and differing nationality may still exist,—no Briton would now desire to sever. Well might the clear, penetrating mind of Defoe be unable altogether to conceal, in his " History of this Union," and also in his *Reviews,* a degree of pride, that posterity should know something of his honourable share in so glorious a work, and even wish for no better inscription on his grave.

Defoe pays a just tribute of eulogy to the Duke of Queensbury, her Majesty's High Commissioner, for the wisdom and moderation with which he conducted the proceedings in Scotland ; and in this he seems but to reciprocate the esteem in which he was held by His Grace, who entertained him at Drumlanrig Castle, and consulted him as to the introduction of some English improvements upon the estate. Defoe's residence in Scotland, and his genius, brought him acquainted with many persons of consideration in that kingdom, from some of whom he received tokens of great kindness and friendship ; among them may be mentioned Lord Belhaven, and the Earl of Buchan.

CHAPTER VI.

*Defoe publishes " A Voice from the South"—Entertains thoughts of re-
siding in Scotland—Lord Haversham, having insulted the Queen and
Ministry, Defoe publishes " A Modest Vindication," &c.—Returns to
London—Harley dismissed from office—Defoe's account of the conse-
quences to himself—His second audience with the Queen—Sent again
to Scotland—Publishes " The Union Proverb"—Death of the Queen's
husband—Defoe's eulogy of the Prince's character—Publishes " The
Scots Narrative Examined"—The Review republished in Scotland—
" The History of the Union of Great Britain"—" A Commendatory
Sermon"—Sacheverell's " Perils among False Brethren"—Defoe ridi-
cules him, but with moderation—Is threatened with assassination—" A
Letter from Captain Tom to the Mob"—" A Speech without Doors"—
" Instructions from Rome in favour of the Pretender"—The Addresses
—Change of the Ministry—Harley again in office—The funds de-
cline.*

1707–10.

IMMEDIATELY after the completion of the Union, Defoe
wrote and circulated a pamphlet in Scotland, entitled, " A
Voice from the South : or, an Address from some Protestant
Dissenters in England, to the Kirk of Scotland. 1707." It
was either taken from, or reprinted in, the *Reviews* for May
the 10th and 15th, and urges thankfulness and harmony among
themselves, and the cultivation of mutual confidence " and
brotherly correspondence between all sorts of Protestants in
the whole Island, but especially between the Dissenters in
England, and the Kirk of Scotland."

There was no falling off in the quality of Defoe's *Reviews*
during his harassing engagements in promoting the Union.
Perhaps one of his finest Essays, moral and imaginative, (extending over the Numbers for Nov. 2nd, 5th, and 7th, 1706,) is
in reply to a bantering, jesting correspondent, who asked, " What
is the colour of the Devil ?" He seems also, about the same
time, to have entertained the thought of making Scotland his
permanent residence. In the *Review* of Nov. 16th, he writes
of " being not only at present out of Town, but out of the

Kingdom, pursuing my private, lawful, and known Design of settling my Family abroad, and letting the World know, I do not live by Scribbling, as is suggested." The enemies of our Author, in England, were perplexed at the possibility of his finding time to write, in Scotland, the *Reviews* that were published every other day in London ; and, to lessen the reputation and value of the Paper, they spread a malicious Report, that it was not now written by him. This statement he silenced in the number for the 31st of December, 1706, by declaring, " This is to assure the World, that no Person whatever has, or ever had, any concern in writing the said Paper, entitled the *Review*, than the known Author, D. F. That wherever the Author may be, the Papers are wrote with his own hand, and the Originals may be seen at the Printers." Yet he had experience of the difficulties attending its punctual appearance under the circumstances, and he recurs to this in the preface to the volume for 1707 :—" And after all this I must tell you, it is none of the easiest things in the World to write a Paper to come out three times a Week among you, and perhaps be liable to more Censure, and ill Usage also, than other Papers are, and yet at the same Time reside for 16 months together, at almost 400 Miles distance from London, and sometimes at more."

On the 15th of February, 1707, when the articles of the Union came before the House of Lords for ratification, the Queen being present, Lord Haversham not only spoke warmly against the Union, but insulted her Majesty, by reference to a *She*-FAVOURITE at the palace, to whom Court must be made, for favours belonging only to the Sovereign. With a worse spirit,—that of ingratitude,—he vilely aspersed the memory of King William, who had raised him, from comparative obscurity, to the Peerage. Having as little delicacy as gratitude, his Lordship, as usual, printed his speech, and it was cried about the streets. The Scots were looking, with the utmost anxiety, to the proceedings of the English Parliament, and when the news of this speech reached Scotland, in March, Defoe was urged to answer it ; he notices the matter in a subsequent *Review*, but seems disposed to refrain from a formal reply, to what he calls, " a rhapsody of wayward expressions, calculated for the mal-content genius of a party." What, however, he avoided doing formally in Edinburgh, he thought proper, shortly afterward, to perform anonymously; and, about the beginning of April, published in London, "A Modest Vindication of the Present Ministry; from the Reflections publish'd against them in a late Printed Paper, entitled, *The Lord Haversham's Speech*, &c. &c. Humbly submitted to the consideration of all, but especially to the Right Honourable,· and the Honourable, the North British Lords and Commoners. By a Well-wisher to the Peace of Britain. London. Printed in the year 1707." In this pamphlet, he seriously, and ably, defends the Ministry and the Union; but treats his Lordship, personally, as unworthy of more consideration than polite banter, and scarcely concealed contempt. Of his transformation, our author says, "Last Reign, a certain Lord was look'd upon as a violent Dissenter, and last Session of this Parliament he was Orator and Champion for the Bishops: In the first Session of this Parliament he was for bringing in the Scotch Cattle, and last Session for keeping out the Scotch Men." He rebukes his Lordship's ingratitude to the memory of the deceased King; and, taking up the prophetic words,— "*that what has been, may be*,"—with which his Lordship's speech concluded, says,—" I agree with the Author, *That some things that have been, may be.* And I shall balance that with a North-British Proverb, I don't think improper here, viz. *It's hard to ding out o' the Flesh what's bred i' the Banes.* 'Tis such an uneasy matter to please some People, that I doubt they will be long out of Humour: and perhaps that's the reason, *That what has been, is now, and like to be, as long as somebody is.*"

Defoe still continued in Scotland, and his *Review* of March 29th, 1707, was written while listening to the cannon upon Edinburgh Castle booming forth on the occasion. He was jubilant, and, besides the pardonable self-gratulation already referred to, he recounts how he had been in other ways instrumental to the national benefit during his residence there. He says, "I have told them of improvements in Trade, Wealth, and Shipping, and am like to be one of the first Men that shall give them the pleasure of the experiment." He had told them how to improve their Coal Trade; and of their Salt, "am now contracting for English Merchants for Scots Salt, to the value of above £10,000 per annum." He had also told them

of Linen Manufactures, and had already above a hundred
Families at work on that Trade.   He continued, in his *Re-*
views, to urge the reciprocal advantages that would result to
Trade and Commerce from the Union ; commenting from time
to time upon all occurring topics of British interest; but, as
far as we know, he only permitted himself, during the remainder of 1707, to be drawn away, in one instance, from the
preparation of his great work, " The History of the Union."

Towards the close of that year, Lesley revived, in his *Re-*
hearsals, most serious charges against the Established Church
in Scotland, of cruelly persecuting the Episcopal Ministers
there.   Being in Scotland, Defoe had means of knowing for
himself, and ascertaining from others, that such charges were
without reasonable foundation ; that they were designed to
weaken the Protestant interest, and to prevent the peaceable
fusion of the two Kingdoms, intended by the recent Act of
Union.   He therefore wrote an able pamphlet on the subject,
giving a List in detail, of all the names and localities of 165
Episcopal Ministers, who had been permitted to retain possession of as many parishes in Scotland, although most of them
would not own the national ecclesiastical government, refused
to take the oath of allegiance to the Queen, and instead of
praying for her, many of them publicly prayed for the Pretender, under the name of King James VIII.   Notwithstanding these disloyal and Jacobite practices, the moderation and
forbearance of the Church of Scotland had restrained the dis-
possession of the offenders ; and, instead of persecution, new
Meeting Houses for Presbyterian worship had been erected, in
many parishes, in which the kirks were held by these Episcopal
Dissenters.   There is no word of Satire, or irony, in the body of
this Tract ; it consists of a plain statement of facts, supported
by grave and suitable arguments, fully vindicating the Church
of Scotland.   But it was intended also, to undeceive the people
of England, who had been prejudiced by misrepresentation ;
and Defoe chose, for these, or other reasons, to send it into the
world with a masked Jacobite title, as follows :—" An Historical Account of the Bitter Sufferings, and Melancholy Circumstances of the Episcopal Church in Scotland, Under the
Barbarous Usage and Bloody Persecution of the Presbyterian

Church Government. With an Essay on the Nature and Necessity of a Toleration in North Britain. Edinburgh. Printed
in the year 1707."

There can be no doubt, because he confesses it, that Defoe
unwillingly remained in Scotland that he might be out of the
reach of five or six implacable Creditors, whose pecuniary
claims, only cloaked their political hostility. His motives were
impeached,—his public services undervalued ; he was accused of
writing for the Court,—and of writing for bread,—and then—he
was fled from justice. Rumour and surmise,—clamour and persecution,—continued to assail him in his retreat, both by letter,
and in the public journals opposed to him. To these he frequently replied in his *Reviews ;* sometimes in defence,—at other
times in defiance,—and occasionally in a tone that betrays the
deep anguish of a soul—bent under a load of misfortunes, too
heavy to bear,—and incapable of removal.

Yet nothing is more remarkable than the elasticity with
which his patriotic spirit rebounds from the consideration of
private calamities, whenever the rights and privileges to which
he is entitled as an Englishman, are brought in question. He
had commented, in his *Review,* upon the unaccountable conduct of the King of Sweden,—who remained inactive in Saxony
with an army capable of turning the scale of Europe,—and also
on the treatment of the Livonians by Sweden. This was said,
by his enemies, to have given offence to Count Zober, the
Swedish Ambassador, who had complained to the Government ;
it was added, in Dyer's News Letter, that Queen's Messengers
were in search of him, and that he was to be bound hand and
foot, and surrendered to the Swedes. To this he first replied,
with a tone of defiance and much bitterness, in a small Tract
of half a sheet quarto, written and printed in Edinburgh, but
without date. It is headed, " De Foe's Answer, to Dyer's
Scandalous News Letter." In it he declares his resolve, God
willing, to go away publicly to England in about fourteen days,
to print that he is coming, to print his arrival, and to " invite
all Men to come and charge me with crimes publick or private,
and to offer myself to all kinds of Justice." Probably, only a
few copies of this Tract were privately printed for presentation
to his Scotch friends, and for dispatch to the English Govern-

ment.   However that may be, it is so rare that none of his
biographers was aware of its existence, and I have not seen, or
heard, of any other copy except my own.

He also immediately took up the subject in his *Review,* more
calmly, but in the following patriotic strain :—" The liberty of
Englishmen is in better case; no man can be punished here
at the will of the Prince, a jury of equals must determine the
fact.   An Englishman is born a Freeman ; no Power can insult
him ; no Superior oppress him ; this is the confidence and glory
of our Island.   He that will abandon this liberty, is not a Fool
only, but a Knave ; a Knave to himself, and to his Family ; a
Knave to his Posterity, and to the Constitution of the Nation ;
for he gives up the Right of a Subject, and leaves an example
of wilful Bondage to his Countrymen.   Let none of my Friends
be afraid for me; if I have broken the Law, they ought to
abandon me to the Law, and I ask no Favour.   If I have not,—
no King, no Threatening, no, not all the Powers of Europe, can
make her Majesty break in upon her People's Liberties, or de-
viate from Justice, in the Satisfaction of which all her Subjects
are easy and safe, and I among the rest."

He does not deny the charge of writing for the Court and
Government, but repels what was intended as a calumnious
reflection, in the following manly and eloquent words :—" If I
have espoused a wrong Cause ; if I have acted in a good Cause
in an unfair Manner ; if I have for fear, favour, or by the bias
of any Man in the World, great or small, acted against what I
always professed, or what is the known interest of the Nation ;
if I have in any way abandoned that glorious principle of Truth
and Liberty, which I was ever embarked in, and which I trust,
I shall never through Fear or Hope, step one inch back from ;
if I have done thus, then, as Job says, in another Case, *Let
Thistles grow instead of Wheat, and Cockles instead of Barley.*
Then, and not till then, may I be esteemed a Mercenary, a
Missionary, a Spy, or what you please.   But, if the Cause be
just, if it be the Peace, Security, and Happiness of both Nations ;
if I have done it honestly and effectually, how does it alter the
Case if I have been fairly encouraged, supported, and rewarded
in the Work, as God knows I have not ?   Does the Mission
disable the Messenger, or does it depend upon the merit of the
Message ?   Cease your enquiry then, about my being sent by

this or that person, or party, till you can agree who it is, when I shall be glad of an opportunity to own it, as I see no cause to be ashamed of my errand.

" Oh, but 'tis a scandalous employment to write for bread ! The worse for him, gentlemen, that he should take so much pains, run so many risks, make himself so many enemies, and expose himself to so much scurrilous treatment for bread ; and not get it neither. Assure yourselves, had not Providence found out other, and unlooked for supplies, by mere wonders of goodness, you had long ago had the desire of your hearts, to starve him out of this employment. But, after all, suppose you say true, that all I do is for bread, which I assure you is very false, what are all the employments in the World pursued for, but for bread ? But though it has been quite otherwise in my case, I am easy, and can depend upon that promise, *Thy bread shall be given thee, and thy waters shall be sure.* I have espoused an honest interest, and have steadily adhered to it all my days : I never forsook it when it was oppressed, I never made a gain by it when it was advanced ; and I thank God it is not in the power of all the courts and parties in Christendom to bid a price high enough to buy me off from it, or make me desert it."*

The above long extracts show externally, the great burden of corroding care and unhappiness our author had to endure, amidst incessant intellectual labours ; and, the internal sources of his strength,—unfaltering faith in divine Providence,—conscious personal integrity,—and the conviction that he was working in the interest of truth, justice, and peace ; for the glory of God, the good of his country, and the benefit of mankind. All these sustained him, and enabled him to withstand all opposition, to overcome all obstacles, and to persevere in the noble work of benefiting and instructing his own and future ages.

I have had continually to resist the temptation to extend this Memoir by quoting striking and beautiful passages from his *Reviews,* written on the spur of the moment, upon passing events of national interest, and accompanied with reflections of wit, humour, and imagination, clothed in natural and simple

---

* Review IV., 346-352.

language, and tempered with wisdom, morality and religion. On the 23rd of October, when Parliament was about to meet, he addressed the members as on a former occasion, exhorting them to a regular attendance, to moderation, and to unanimity in their proceedings. He followed this with an Address to the High-party. On the 4th of November he devoted his paper, as usual, to the memory of William III., and the blessings he had under God conferred upon the nation. On the 15th, to the drowning of Sir Cloudesley Shovell and the British Fleet, eloquently rebuking those who fail to see the hand of Providence in National Calamities. In the next number he returns to the subject, deploring the profanity and Vice of our Soldiers and Sailors, with an intensely vivid picture of the *Rumney* Man of War, within a quarter of an hour before she was swallowed up; and, out of a thousand miserables, that "went down quick into the Pit, with hardly Time to cast a Thought towards Him that made them, or a Cry to him for Mercy,—ONE,—and but ONE—Man was saved." In the same number he highly commends our Enemies, the French Government, because they had appointed a National Fast after the battle and defeat at Ramillies. The next following *Review* contains a beautiful exemplification of Christian Charity and forgiveness on Occasion of the Death of his adversary John Tutchin, the author of the "Observator." In a fine eulogium Defoe pronounces him "a Wall of Brass against Persecution, Slavery and Jacobitism." He says, "A small Charity will cover his want of Temper." As to his ill-treatment of our author, "he was moved to it not by Inclination so much as Solicitation." In December he animadverts on the misgovernment of the American Colonies, urging improved management, so as to attach them more firmly to the Mother Country. And so ends the year 1707.

Having completed the collection of all the materials for his "History of the Union," being anxious again to see his wife and children, after an absence of about sixteen months; and hoping to obtain a settlement of his private affairs, which his negociations with his creditors seemed now to favour, Defoe left Scotland early in January, 1708, and returned to London. It is probable that he had a further inducement to this return, in some confidential communication of political intrigues that were beginning to agitate the Court, and to jeopardize the position of his benefactor Harley, the Secretary of State.

This is not the place to enter into even a brief relation of the circumstances, farther than they affect the fortunes of our author, and therefore it must suffice to say that Abigail Hill, afterward Mrs. Masham, was dresser to the Queen, and a lady of the bed-chamber. She was ambitious, insinuating in her manners, assiduous in her attentions, and acquired an ascendancy over her Majesty, by professed zeal for the Church, and the interests of the Stuarts. She was cousin to the Duchess of Marlborough, and stood in the same relation to Mr. Harley. As her influence at Court increased, that of the Duchess, who had been her Majesty's bosom friend for twenty years, declined; and, on investigation, the change was attributed to the counsels and intrigues of the Minister Harley. On this, the Duke of Marlborough consulted his friends; and, with Lord Godolphin, waited upon the Queen, requesting her to remove Mr. Harley from his office and her Court, if she wished them to remain in her service. After a week's delay her Majesty yielded, and full of resentment against them, mixed with tears, dismissed Mr. Harley from his Secretaryship.

I must now permit Defoe to tell his own story, in which it is difficult to say, which is most to be admired, the great delicacy of his conduct, in the apparent sacrifice of his own prospects, to the fidelity he owed his fallen benefactor; the generosity of Harley in immediately releasing him from all obligations of honour; or, the high-minded friendliness of Lord Godolphin, who received him with full confidence, and continued him in the service of the State, without imposing any restriction upon his honest independence.

" When upon that fatal Breach, the Secretary of State was dismissed from the Service, I look'd upon myself as lost, it being a general Rule in such Cases, when a great Officer falls, that they who came in by his Interest fall with him. And resolving never to abandon the Fortunes of the Man to whom I ow'd so much of my own, I quitted the usual Applications I had made to my Lord Treasurer. But my generous Benefactor, when he understood it, frankly told me, that I should by no means do so; for, said he, in the most engaging terms, ' My

Lord Treasurer will employ you in nothing but what is for the public service, and agreeable to your own sentiments of things : And besides, it is the Queen you are serving, who has been very good to you.   Pray apply yourself as you used to do ; I shall not take it ill from you in the least.'

" Upon this I went to wait on my Lord Treasurer, who receiv'd me with great Freedom, and told me smiling, He had not seen me a long while.   I told his Lordship very frankly the Occasion, that the unhappy Breach that had fallen out, had made me doubtful whether I should be acceptable to his Lordship.   That I knew it was usual, when great Persons fall, that all who were in their Interest fell with them.   That his Lordship knew the Obligations I was under, and that I could not but fear my Interest in his Lordship was lessen'd on that account.   ' Not at all Mr. De Foe,' replied his Lordship ; ' I always think a Man honest, till I find to the contrary.'   Upon this I attended his Lordship as usual, and being resolved to remove all possible ground of suspicion that I kept any secret correspondence, I never visited, or wrote to, or any way corresponded with my principal Benefactor for above three years ; which he so well knew the reason of, and so well approved that punctual Behaviour in me, that he never took it ill from me at all.

" In consequence of this reception, my Lord Godolphin had the goodness not only to introduce me for the second time to her Majesty, and to the Honour of Kissing her Hand, but obtained for me the continuance of an Appointment which her Majesty had been pleas'd to make me in consideration of a former special service I had done, and in which I had run as much risk of my Life as a Grenadier upon the Counterscarp ; and which Appointment was first obtain'd for me at the intercession of my first Benefactor, and is all owing to that intercession, and her Majesty's Bounty.   Upon this second Introduction her Majesty was pleased to tell me, with a Goodness peculiar to Herself, that she had such Satisfaction in my former Services, that she had appointed me for another Affair, which was something Nice, and that my Lord Treasurer should tell me the rest ; and so I withdrew. The next day his Lordship having commanded me to attend, told me, that he must send me to Scotland ; and gave me but three days to prepare myself.   Accordingly I went to Scotland, where neither my Business, nor the manner of discharging it is material to this Tract, nor will it ever be any part of my Character that I reveal what should be concealed; and yet my Errand was such as was far from being unfit for a Sovereign to direct, or an honest Man to perform; and the Service I did on that Occasion, as it is not unknown to the greatest Man now in the Nation under the King and the Prince, so I dare say, his Grace was never displeased with the Part I had in it, and I hope will not forget it.

"These things I mention upon this Account, and no other, viz. to state the Obligation I have been in all along to her Majesty personally, and to my first Benefactor principally, by which, I say, I think I was at least obliged not to act against them even in those things which I might not approve. Whether I have acted with them farther than I ought, shall be spoken of by itself. Having said thus much of the Obligations laid upon me, and the Persons by whom, I have this only to add, that I think no Man will say a Subject could be under greater Bonds to his Prince, or a private Person to a Minister of State; and I shall ever preserve this Principle, that an honest Man cannot be ungrateful to his Benefactor."*

The latter part of the above quotation has reference to the motives of Defoe's conduct during the remainder of Queen Anne's reign, when he fell under the censure of the Whig party because he did not oppose the coalition government under Harley. The earlier portion, which relates to his second journey to Scotland, within so short a time after his return, is what now demands consideration. It was an honourable, but secret service; and, there were forcible reasons why the nature of it should not be revealed by him, even after the lapse of years. A glance at the circumstances of the time may, however, make plain what honour forbad him to publish.

The Pretender had a considerable number of adherents in Scotland; and, judging from the recent opposition to the Union, they fancied their party more numerous and powerful than it was in reality. The French King, misled by their representations, and disheartened by his severe losses on the

---

* "Appeal to Honour and Justice," pp. 14-17.

continent, concluded that an invasion of Scotland would serve
the Pretender, and cause a diversion of the war, favourable to
his own affairs.   Early in the year 1708 the Queen's Government received intelligence of hostile preparations; and in the
month of March, Admiral Fourbin appeared off the Frith of
Forth, with a French Fleet and Army.   Finding an English
force ready to receive him, he sailed northward, but was driven
out to sea by a storm; and, after a month's delay, returned to
Dunkirk, with the loss of one ship, and about four thousand men.
Defoe had so strong a conviction of the general loyalty of the
Scots people, that on the first report of the expected invasion,
he recommended that a reward should be issued for the apprehension of the Pretender, and wrote in his *Review,* " Let but
forty or fifty of the chief Heads of Clans, and known Jacobites,
be secured, and he may come when he pleases ; he'll meet with
but cold enteratinment in the North of Britain." This suggestion the Government appears to have acted upon, a considerable number of the Jacobite leaders were arrested on suspicion,
and confined in the Castle at Ediuburgh.   In the midst of the
general alarm, he also published, on the 13th of March, a short
but seasonable pamphlet, entitled, " The Union Proverb," viz :—

> " If Skiddaw has a cap
> Scruffel wots full well of that."

Setting forth, I. The necessity of Uniting.   II. The good
consequences of Uniting.   III. The happy Union of England
and Scotland, in case of a Foreign Invasion.   *Felix quem
faciunt aliena Pericula cautum.*   London. 1708." The explanation of the proverb is, that when the clouds are seen to rest
on Skiddaw, an English mountain in Cumberland, it will not
be long ere the same will happen to the Scotch mountain
Scruffell in Annandale.   The application is obvious, that the
two nations are so united, that any evil that may happen to
one, will be sure to affect the other.   Defoe considers the
proverb as a most politic and prudent caution against foreign
invasions ; he advances strong arguments in favour of unanimity
at this juncture,—warns his readers that nothing but intestine
divisions can invite the French King to set foot upon English
or Scotch ground ; and, that unless we are all of one mind now,
we may be fellow-sufferers upon the upshot of such invasion.

The direction of the intended invasion, no less than the title of the pamphlet, indicate that it was chiefly addressed to the Scotch people; and, it was probably composed immediately before the commencement of Defoe's journey northward, as he appears to have been in Edinburgh when the *Review* of March 25th was written, and it was not then known what had become of the French fleet. From the 9th of March to the end of the month, much of his Paper is taken up with the Pretender's expedition; and on the 13th of May he addresses a *Review* to the Prisoners in Scotland, taken for the late Rebellion. Lord Belhaven was one of these State Prisoners, though innocent, and was confined in the Castle of Edinburgh, where Defoe visited him early in the month of April. They had been previously acquainted, in consequence of his Lordship having strongly, but conscientiously, opposed the Union. This had, for the moment, associated him with the Jacobites, with whom he had no other sympathy, and had led him to be now wrongly suspected of disloyalty. At this long interview, and by letter afterward, Lord Belhaven made Defoe acquainted with his public life, for twenty-seven years, as a loyal Protestant; and requested our author to say what he might think proper and true, for his personal vindication. The prisoners were brought to London on the 14th of June, and Lord Belhaven died one week afterward, of grief and indignation. The *Review* of July 11th contains a complete vindication of his character, equally honourable to the subject and the writer. I have dwelt upon this case because his Lordship's communications with our author would be inexplicable on any other theory than that Defoe's secret commission in Scotland was, to find out the suspected persons, to ascertain the extent of disloyalty; to warn those who might be in danger; to encourage a feeling of patriotism, and duty to the Government; to endeavour to prevent a rebellion, and to clear those who might be innocent. The entire failure of the French Expedition rendered it no longer necessary for him to remain, and we find him soon after actively concerned in the Parliamentary elections in England.

Probably the dissolution of the first parliament of Great Britain, on the 15th of April, and the fears entertained by the Government, that great efforts would be made by the High-

Tory party to recover their ascendancy in the House of Commons, was an inducement to the recal of Defoe from Scotland; and his re-employment, during the elections, in a similar manner to that three years previously. On this occasion he does not appear to have been equally successful in the prevention of intimidation, bribery and corruption. His *Review*, the ready channel for communicating passing events, says, " I have been among a great many of your Electors myself. I have seen the possibility, aye, and too much the practice of men's voting implicitly, here for ale, there for influence, here again for parties, and there by persuasion. And, God knows, I speak it with regret for you all, and for your posterity, it is not an impossible thing to debauch this Nation into a choice of thieves, knaves, devils, or any thing, comparatively, by the power of various intoxications."

Immediately after the elections, in the month of June, Defoe was again dispatched to Scotland. He observes the same secrecy as before respecting the duties with which he was entrusted by the Government; but it may be gathered from the *Review* that he was engaged in dispelling all feeling of dissatisfaction and irritation, that had been stirred up by the Jacobites, against her Majesty's Government and the Union; and in promoting a spirit of loyalty among all classes of the people. He continued, on this occasion, several months in Scotland, where his stores of wisdom and knowledge, on all subjects, and the warm interest he took in promoting the welfare of the country, had made him many friends. The shrewdness of the people, their piety and hospitality, their love of liberty, and the purity of their Church, were all congenial to him; and it is not saying too much, that the Scots never had a more zealous and sincere friend among the English people.

Defoe returned from Scotland in September 1708, and seems to have given full satisfaction to the Government; for proof of which, he was able to appeal long afterward to the Duke of Marlborough. He had, while in the north, inquired into the continued misunderstandings between the Established Presbyterian Church, and the Episcopalians there. Lesley had represented the latter, in his *Rehearsals*, as being the victims of persecution; in reply to which, Defoe shows, in the *Review* of

Oct. 28th, as he had before done in a pamphlet form, that a large proportion of the Episcopalian Clergy in Scotland were Nonjurors, who had not only refused the Oaths to Queen Anne, but also, constantly omitted her name in the Liturgy.

On the 28th of October, in this year, died Prince George of Denmark, consort of the Queen. During twenty-five years he had been as good a husband as he was a man; and their lives had presented a noble example of conjugal attachment. The Queen, and the Nation, mourned their mutual loss, with sincere affection, and deep sorrow.

When eulogising the characters of great and good persons deceased, the peculiar stile of Defoe's composition is always seen to much advantage. Numerous instances prove him to have been aware of the fact; and, to have carefully corrected every expression, into the most simple, but happily chosen language; so that the subject alone might appear to adorn his page. His *Review*, for the 23rd of November, furnishes an instance in point, on the Death of the Prince, the Queen's Husband. I quote from it, at some length, because I cannot doubt, that the heart of every true born Englishman, of this age, will feel the parallelism, between the character of him whose loss is thus recorded by our author; and, the illustrious Prince, whose death, our own beloved Queen, and all her subjects, will never cease to mourn.

" Death has made a very deep incision in the public tranquillity, in the person of the Prince of Denmark. His Royal Highness was a great and good man;—a friend to England and her interest,—and true and hearty in the cause of Liberty." The writer then glances at the noble conduct of the Prince in steadily adhering to the Protestant interest, before and at the Revolution;—alludes to his determination to stand or fall by the laws, religion, and privileges of the nation;—shows that the deceased had pursued the same exalted course during all the reign of King William, and at the battle of the Boyne;—and declares, that he ought ever to be remembered with gratitude, by all who love their country. He adds, " If I had a design to run through the character of the Prince, I would next observe upon the excellency of his temper,— the calmness of his passions,—and the sedateness of his judg-

ment,—which commanded respect from the whole nation, in a
manner peculiar to himself; so that every party,—however
jarring or opposite,—paid him their homage; although nothing
was more averse to his temper, than the divisions which un-
happily agitate the nation.   Nor can it be doubted, that his
Highness derived peculiar satisfaction from his not interfering
in public affairs, more than his exalted station obliged him;
since he saw it was impossible to do so without committing
himself to a Party, which he was always averse to.   He sincerely lamented our divisions, but never encouraged or approved them.   By his steady conduct, joined with a general
courtesy to all sorts of people, he acquired the esteem and love
of all parties; and that, more than any person of his degree
that ever went before him.   I need not note, how next to impossible it is in this divided nation, for the most consummate
prudence to steer through the variety of interests, and gain a
universal good opinion; or, indeed, to avoid universal censure.
How the Prince attained that great point, I shall not attempt
to examine; but this, I think, ought to be recorded to posterity, that one Man in Britain was found, of whom no man
spoke evil: *and this was he!*"

Brief reference has been made to the charge, against the
Presbyterian Church of Scotland, of persecuting the Episcopalians there.   In the latter part of the year the grievance was
published in a pamphlet, entitled, "A Narrative of the late
Treatment of the Episcopal Ministers within the City of
Edinburgh, since March 1708, until their Imprisonment in
July thereafter.   London.   1708."   The writer was a Non-
juror, who charges the Presbyterians with injustice and
cruelty, and loads the Established Church of Scotland with
many unwarrantable terms of reproach.   Defoe would have
had the Episcopalian Dissenters in Scotland to enjoy the fullest
toleration he ever claimed for the Dissenters in England; but
he knew that many of the proceedings of the Scotch Episcopalians were contrary to law; and, that many of their ministers
refused even to recognise the government of the country.   He
therefore published, on the 19th of February following a reply,
entitled, "The Scots Narrative Examined: or, the Case of the
Episcopal Ministers in Scotland Stated; and the late Treat-

ment of them in the City of Edinburgh enquired into.   With
a brief Examination into the Reasonableness of the grievous
Complaint of Persecution in Scotland, and a Defence of the
Magistrates of Edinburgh, in their Proceedings there, &c. &c.
London. 1709." As the subject is now only of slight historical interest, I need say no more than that Defoe temperately
refutes the arguments, and points out the errors in the pamphlet he was opposing, and concludes with an account of the
proceedings before the magistrates, attested by the Town-clerk
of Edinburgh, proving that such proceedings were strictly legal.

In closing the fifth Volume of the *Review* on the 31st of
March 1709, he says, " Some Gentlemen in Scotland, have by
their own voluntary subscription encourag'd the re-printing of
it at Edinburgh, and being to begin at this Quarter, have
desired the Volume, and their Subscription, may go on together." On June 4th in the same year the *Review* contains a
long advertisement that " the Paper is reprinted three times a
week, in Edinburgh, and published in all the principal Towns
and Cities of Scotland," and directs how advertisements may
be forwarded. Then follows a note, that " The counties of
Northumberland and Westmoreland, together with the towns
of Belfast, Carrick-fergus, and the City of Londonderry in Ireland, are supplied with this Paper from Scotland."

Defoe had announced in the *Review,* so early as the 29th of
March, 1707, that he was preparing for the press a work to
which I have already several times alluded; but,—from its magnitude,—the frequent hindrances of travelling,—and attendance to duties that could not be delayed,—he was unable to
complete before the end of two years. It was now published,
as a Folio of more than seven hundred pages, with the title of
" The History of the Union of Great Britain. Edinburgh.
Printed by the Heirs and Successors of Andrew Anderson,
Printers to the Queen's most Excellent Majesty. Anno Dom.
1709." The Royal arms are printed on the title-page, and
there is prefixed a well-executed portrait of the author by
Vander Gucht. Pendant, are the author's arms and crest, surrounded with the motto " Probitas Laudatur et Alget," and
beneath, is inscribed, " Mr. Daniel De Foe, Author of the True-

born Englishman." There are two Dedications to the first
Edition; one to the Queen, and the other to the Duke of
Queensbury, Secretary of State for Scotland. Copies of the
work vary, however, some having only the dedication to the
Queen, and others only that to the Duke.

Mr. Chalmers has well observed, that " the writers who are
permitted to dedicate their Works to royal patrons, ought to
peruse Defoe's dedicatory epistles to King William and Queen
Anne; wherein they will find dignity of sentiment, and delicacy
of praise, conveyed in language at once elegant and instructive." The remark is justified in the Work before us, which is
equally exempt from the fulsomeness of flattery, and servility
of stile too common in Defoe's time. In the dedication to
the Queen he thus alludes to himself:—" The Humble Author
of these Sheets, Madam, having amidst a Throng of Disasters
and Sorrows, been Honoured by your Majesty, in being rendered Serviceable to this great Transaction, and having passed
thro' all the Hazards, Tumults, and Disorders of that Critical
Time, in his humble Endeavours to forward the Glorious Design of your Majesty, for your Subjects' Prosperity; thinks
himself doubly Rewarded, in having the Honour to lay this
Account of these Things at your Majesty's Feet."

What I have already stated, as to the progress of the Union,
was chiefly derived from this work; so that it is the less necessary to occupy space with extracts from so large a book.
The Preface is very valuable, as giving the best account that
has been written of several important events that occurred
during the two years, between the completion of the Union,
and the publication of the " History." The first is an account
of the French Invasion of Scotland in 1708; and the second,
on the distractions which followed, in Religious matters, in
consequence of the proceedings against the Nonjuring Episcopal ministers, and the case of Mr. Greenshields. The body
of the work consists of a general history of Unions; of the
affairs of both Kingdoms, introductory to a treaty of Union;
of the last treaty, properly called the Union, so far as concerns
the proceedings in London; of the carrying on the treaty in
Scotland; minutes of the Scotch Parliament, with Observations; the treaty of Union as finished in Scotland, and as exemplified in England. There are two Appendices, Part I. con-

sisting of Abridgements of the Alterations in Laws, Trade, and Customs, in both Kingdoms by the Union; and II., Proclamations and documents.   As to the manner in which Defoe performed his great task, it may be observed, that the narrative is exceedingly interesting, from the circumstantial way in which he relates what he saw and heard; and, from the natural descriptions it represents of the manners and sentiments of the Scottish people, in an age when a large proportion, even of the gentry, had little intercourse with the English.   It has been said that " The History of the Union" would alone have preserved Defoe's name to posterity; and, that it is a performance of so great value as to place its author among the soundest historians of the day.

A second Edition was printed in London in 1712, and it was reprinted in quarto in 1786, when a memoir of the author, written by Mr. George Chalmers, was prefixed.   This was the first attempt to bring together the scattered incidents of Defoe's life, and to do justice to his merits.

Defoe had now a considerable interest in Scotland.   The printing and publishing of his " History of the Union," and the reprinting, and large circulation of his *Reviews* there, probably required his presence in Edinburgh.   He does not appear, however, to have had any government duties to perform. His *Review* of October 13th is on the price of corn, of which he thinks there is no scarcity; and he gives particulars of his personal observations, during a recent journey to Scotland.   He calls his progress, " Perambulations I have taken thro' Britain since the beginning of August," and says he left London just as the Harvest was commencing in Hertfordshire.   He was in Bedfordshire, Cambridgeshire, and Huntingdonshire about the 17th of August;—passed through St. Neots, to Kimbolton, Thrapston, and Rockingham; thence through Leicestershire, and the south sides of Derby and Nottinghamshire.   He was in Derby about the 22nd of August, and went through Chesterfield and Scarsdale into Yorkshire; thence by Pontefract, Durham, and Newcastle, Morpeth and Alnwick to Woller, entering Scotland by the Cheviot Hills and Kelsoe.

The publication of " The History of the Union" occasioned a controversy between Defoe and the Rev. James Clark, minister of the Tron Church at Glasgow.   An allusion is made in "The History of the Union" to this gentleman, as having uttered some intemperate words in a sermon, wherein he told the people that Addresses against the Union would not do, and prayer alone would be insufficient, "Wherefore up, and be valiant for the City of our God." These words were the more ominous, as a riot commenced within two hours afterward in Glasgow. Defoe says he believes this to have been the hasty expression of a good man, who did not properly think of the deplorable consequences that might follow. Some friend, however, must needs defend Mr. Clark, in a tract called, "A Paper concerning Daniel De Foe. Edin. 1709." To the strictures of this writer our author rejoined in "An Answer to a Paper concerning Mr. De Foe, against the History of the Union. *Edin.* 1709." Mr. Clark, finding that his friend's intervention had not cleared him from blame, published soon afterward, "A Just Reprimand to Daniel De Foe. In a Letter to a Gentleman in South Britain. Edin. 1709." (A single sheet.) In this tract he denies having excited the tumult, or the use of any language than that of peaceable opposition. Defoe again answered him in "A Reproof to Mr. Clark, and a Brief Vindication of Mr. De Foe. Edin. 1709." With this, the dispute ended; but, while Defoe never forgot the respect due to his opponent, Mr. Clark gave way to acrimonious and intemperate language.

On the 5th of November, 1709, the *Review* was filled, as usual on that anniversary, with an essay on King William, which was in a few days afterward separately published; and, as the name of a respectable bookseller appears upon the title-page, without any subsequent complaint in the *Review* of piracy, there can be little doubt that the reprint was by authority. The following is the singular title prefixed, "A Commendatory Sermon, Preached November 4, 1709. Being the Birth Day of King William, of Glorious Memory. By Dan. Defoe. London. 1709." A text is added in the reprint to give it more the character of a Sermon:—2 Samuel, i. 24. A quotation, in the *Review,* from his poem of "The Mock Mourners," is omitted in the pamphlet.

The year 1709 was now drawing towards its close, but was

yet to witness an event that should find much employment for
Defoe's pen,—should justify before the world all that he had
ever written, as to the temper and ultimate intentions of the
High Church party,—and produce one of those wild, ungovern-
able moral epidemics, that enables an unprincipled, and otherwise contemptible individual, to agitate a whole nation.   On
the 5th of November Dr. Sacheverell preached, before the
Lord Mayor and Aldermen, at St. Paul's Cathedral, his famous
Sermon upon *Perils among False Brethren.* This he immediately afterward published, with a dedication to the Lord
Mayor; and the sensation that was produced, has probably,
neither before nor since, had any parallel in English history.

In writing against it, Defoe kept in view two objects : first,
to prevent, (by treating the matter with ridicule,) the serious
consequences that would be sure to follow, if prosecution should
unfortunately elevate the preacher into a hero, and a martyr ;
and secondly, to convince the world, and especially his Dissenting friends, that this sermon contained, in plain words,
the formal propositions of extermination, which himself had
ironically embodied in "The Shortest Way with the Dissenters."

The following, from the *Review,* will show Defoe's manner
of dealing with the Doctor and his Discourse :—" How merry
a tale it is to hear him prove the doctrine of non-resistance,
from the Prince of Orange's Declaration ; and reconcile the
Revolution to the principle of unconditional subjection,
because it was founded on the vacancy of the Throne.   As if
the Prince of Orange had not brought an Army with him to
resist, but came with fourteen thousand Men at his heels, to
stand and look on, while the English Gentry and Clergy, with
prayers and tears, besought King James to run away and
leave the Throne vacant !"   Again, " I assure you, I shall be
none of those that prompt you to resent the Doctor's ill-
usage ; and my reasons are, because the faster he runs, the
sooner he will be out of Breath ; and because by this method
the High flying Gentlemen really expose themselves, not you."
" Upon the whole, I think the roaring of this Beast ought
to give you no manner of disturbance.   You ought to laugh
at it ; he'll vent his gall, and then he'll be quiet."   He returns
to the subject repeatedly,—proving how incapable he was of
harbouring any feeling of revenge towards the party who had

wreaked its vengeance upon him. " For my part," says he, " I really think these Ecclesiastic Faggot-sticks, when they are thus lighted at both ends, do no harm. They awaken the People, and bring them to their Senses; and these Senses are their protection against all the High-flying Lunacies of the Age."

Other counsels, however, prevailed, and after the impeach--ment of Sacheverell had been resolved upon, Defoe wrote thus :—" Let the Parliament-justice end where it will, I have nothing to do with it here ; but calling him to the Bar, and impeaching him before the Lords, together with such a Vote as his Sermon being Scandalous, Seditious and Malicious, is setting him upon a State Machine with a witness. The bar of the House of Commons is the worst Pillory in the Nation. You may bear with me for being warmer in this Case than in another ; my part in it has been very hard. I adore the wonders of retaliating Providence, that has suffered the Wicked to fall thus into their own Net, and has given a Testimony greater than I could ever have hoped for, to the justice and seasonableness of those fatal observations I made on this very Man's preaching, and his party's practice ; for which, and I bless God for standing to the truth of it, I suffered the overthrow of my Fortune and Family, and under the weight of it remain as a banished Man to this Day."

Addressing the Dissenters, he says, " This is the Man that held out the Bloody Flag, in his Sermon at Oxford ; and now to explain himself more effectually, he has indicted you all for Traitors, condemned you as False Brethren, and delivered you up to the Devil and his Angels. Is this the *Shortest Way with the Dissenters,* or is it not ? and was D. F. right before in personating him, or was he not ?" Alluding to their former treatment of himself, he says, " Well, Gentlemen, I know that in your Ignorance you did it ; and as I said, before, I have never, in regret for this, stepped one Foot out of the cause of English liberty, or withheld one Word that I could speak to serve that interest to thisDay ; and I trust shall not. No fear has deterred me, though often threatened, bullied, and insulted ; no favour has withdrawn me, though often caressed and tempted *cum montibus auri.* I am to this day ruffled by your Enemies, insulted by those that hate you, threatened and maltreated for the little endeavours I use to serve you. And by yourselves, I am used—How? Just as you know, and as I expected! And who am I, to repine? Am I better than De Laune, who starved for you, or D——, that hanged for you? No, no! he that will serve you must be hated and neglected by you, must starve and hang for you, and must yet serve you; *and thus I do.*"*

Defoe does not seem to have imagined that Parliament would do more than condemn the doctrines and principles contained in Sacheverell's Sermon; and therefore, while the impeachment was going on, he occupied two of his *Reviews* in urging the two Houses to affix the brand of infamy upon the principles, rather than upon the offender. Considering the depth and height of all Defoe's past suffering, from the malice of Sacheverell's party, it must be confessed that the following, written when our author apprehended that the Doctor would be punished with loss of liberty, breathes the true spirit of the Gospel of Christ :—" For my part, though I have as much reason to desire justice upon him as anybody, yet I am looking another way, and I hope it is the right way. I had rather see the crime punished than the man; I had rather see the wound cured, than the hand that gave it cut off. And in this I am sure I pursue the general good, whether I please private resentment or no."†

It was not long before the government and parliament had sufficient proof of the error committed, in proceeding against Sacheverell by impeachment. True he was only interdicted from preaching for three years; but the rabbles, tumults, plundering of houses, demolishing meeting-houses, insulting and threatening all who were supposed to be unfriendly to the accused; and by the same mob who, as Defoe says, " were encouraged by the Doctor, and his friends, to wait upon him to and from Westminster, in cavalcade, more like an Ambassador of State than a Criminal, going to the bar of Justice;"—all these revived again, in their most aggravated form, the party heats and religious animosities, which for three years had been almost laid asleep.

As to the excited state of public feeling, and the extent to which it entered even into domestic affairs, Defoe gives an amusing account in his *Review* :—" Mobs, rabbles, and

---

* Review VI., 421, 2, 3, 6, 7, 9; 445-6; 455.   † Ibid., p. 469.

tumults, possess the Streets; the dressing, the powdering the
beau-monde is adjourned to the chocolate-houses, and is all among
the men: the Ladies are otherwise engaged; even the little
boys and girls talk politics.   Little Miss has Dr. Sacheverell's
picture put into her prayer-book, that God and the Doctor
may take her up in the morning before breakfast; and all
manner of discourse among the women runs now upon War
and Government.   This new Invasion of the politician's province is an eminent demonstration of the sympathetic influence
of the clergy upon the Sex, and the near affinity between the
gown and the petticoat; since all the errors of our past and
present administrators, and all breaches made upon our politics, could never embark the Ladies till you fell upon the
Clergy.   But as soon as you pinch the Parson, he holds out
his hand to the Ladies for assistance, and they appear as one
Woman in his Defence."

Notwithstanding the moderation Defoe had shown towards
the Doctor personally, the High party felt unable to withstand his denunciation of their principles; and, as they could
not silence him, either by argument or persecution, some of
their adherents (for our author does not charge the crime
upon the party), attempted to do it by threats of assassination,
but with no better success.   He says, " I have by me fifteen
Letters from Gentlemen of more anger than honour, who have
faithfully promised to come and kill me by such and such a
day; nay, some have descended to tell me the very manner;
yet not one of them has been so good as his word.   Once, I
had the misfortune to come into a room where five Gentlemen
had been killing me a quarter of an hour before; yet, to the
reproach of their villanous design, as well as of their courage,
they did not dare to own it to a poor defenceless Man, when he
was too much in their power.   Should I tell the World, the
repeated cautions given me by my Friends not to appear in
the Streets, nor to show myself; letters sent to bid me remember Sir Edmundbury Godfrey, Mr. Tutchin, and the like;
should I let you know how I have been three times beset and
waylaid for the mischief designed, but still I live; you would
wonder what I mean.   Wherefore, my brief resolution is
this:—While I live they may be assured I shall never desist
doing my duty, in exposing the doctrines that oppose God and

the Revolution; such as passive submission to Tyrants, and non-resistance in cases of Oppression. If those who are at a loss for arguments, are resolved to better their Cause by Violence and Blood, I leave the issue to God's Providence; and must do as well with them as I can. As to defence, I have had some thoughts to stay at home by night, and by day to wear a piece of armour on my back; the first, because I am persuaded these murderers will not do their work by day-light; and the second, because I firmly believe they will never attempt it fairly to my Face." He determines to persevere in exposing error, and in opening the eyes of the people, and concludes, " Whether, in this work I meet with punishment or praise, safety or hazard, life or death, *Te Deum laudamus.*"

This Memoir has nothing to do with the bonfires, illuminations, and disturbances that succeeded the trial of Sacheverell, and during his progresses; except to say that while this extravagant conduct of his deluded followers excited alarm and despondency among the Whigs, the effect produced upon Defoe, who had foreseen and deprecated the probable consequences, was to place him still more prominently forward as the dauntless champion of truth and liberty. He encourages the weak, and taunts the fearful among his friends, in the following defiant language :—" I am satisfied that the Cause of Liberty is the cause of Truth ; and it is from this Principle only that I oppose the high-church darling Sacheverell; and do it in the teeth of his Mob, when his cause would be thought to be rising, and when I see Men that pretend to Revolution-principles cowed and afraid. I have nothing to say to the Man ; I owe him neither good nor ill ; it is the temper of insulting the Laws, and preaching up Tyranny, that I oppose ; and this I will oppose, if the Tyrant were an Emperor."

Sacheverell's Sermon induced Defoe to reprint " The Shortest Way with the Dissenters," adding to the titlepage, " Taken from Dr. Sacheverell's Sermon, and others." On the 15th of December he also reissued *De Laune's Plea*, with the following title :—" Dr. Sacheverell's Recantation ; or the Fire of St. Paul's quickly quenched, by a Plea for the Non-conformists. London. 1709." Mr. Wilson has attributed to our author an original pamphlet that appeared shortly afterward, called " The New Wonder ; or, a Trip to St. Paul's. By the Author of

the True-born Englishman. Printed in the year 1710." There
is however good reason to conclude this was only passed off as
Defoe's by the printer, to make it sell. Another pamphlet
entitled, "The High Church Address to Dr. Henry Sacheverell," &c., &c., has also been attributed to Defoe; but without
any reason whatever. It is a very inferior production to anything from his pen.

On the 11th of March 1710, was published a small Tract
of banter and irony, admirably adapted to the capacities and
modes of thinking among the multitude, who were in danger
of being drawn into the rabble then destroying property in
the name of the Church. In its composition Defoe personates
a mythic leader of all tumults at that period, under the title
of, "A letter from Captain Tom to the Mobb now raised for
Dr. Sacheverell. London. Printed for J. Baker at the Black
Boy in Paternoster Row, 1710." This is, I believe, the first
work of our author published by Baker, whose name was soon
to appear upon the *Reviews,* and upon many other publications
of Defoe.

The efforts of the Tories and High Churchmen against the
Review were almost exhausted. Constantly stung and mortified by the author's caustic wit, and pointed arguments, they
had succeeded in procuring its presentment by several Grand
Juries, but without any result; they had in vain solicited the
government to discourage and silence it; they had threatened
to suppress the paper and its author, at one stroke, by assassination; and in return he laughed at them, ridiculed, defied
them to their teeth, and quietly went on galling them with
his plain truth. Their last poor shift was to frighten, and
tamper with, the publisher and distributors of the paper; and
in this they were successful,—but only for a moment. On the
21st of March there began to be published at the end of each
number of the *Review,* an Advertisement stating that great
industry had been used to suppress the paper, but that they
might still be had at certain shops, which were specified.
This continued until the 25th of April, when an explanation
was given in a full number, in which he says, "Alas, poor
Review! The Rage of the Party has reached thee among the
rest; and the World is deprived of this day's Publication."

He does not seem to blame Matthews, whom he calls "the honest Publisher," and upon whom "a party of High Churchmen had fallen;" adding, "when People are frighted, they are not Masters of their usual Resolution, nor indeed of their Understandings." He announces that he has consequently removed the paper from the usual place of publication, and that it will in future be published by Mr. Baker, "who will not be biass'd, terrified, or any way prevail'd upon to keep it back." It seems that every bookseller had been solicited by the Sacheverellites to suppress the *Review*; and, now having completed the new arrangements securing its regular publication for the future, Defoe naïvely remarks—"The Physick really makes the Party Sick; I hope it may work kindly, and do them good."

Further to dispel the infatuation that possessed the more ignorant classes, Defoe published, on the 11th of May, a pamphlet containing twenty closely printed pages octavo, of small type, at the low price of twopence, in order that it might reach those for whose benefit it was designed. It is entitled, "A Speech without Doors. London. 1710." The object of it is stated in a short Advertisement, printed behind the title, as follows:—"They who have read Dr. Sacheverell's Sermons, may easily know who was not the Author of his Speech. The Doctor was not contented to deliver this Speech to the Lords, his Judges, but has also published it in a small print, and by his Party industriously spread it throughout the Kingdom. This is an Appeal from the Lords to a much inferior Order. But since the proceedings of our Legislators will be beyond the reach of such readers, and that it is nevertheless fit that these should not be deluded; this Speech is fitted both to the Pockets and Understandings of the Doctor's *Judges without Doors.*"

This plain, argumentative, and valuable Tract,—in which he shows that the doctrine of absolute Non-resistance, advocated by Sacheverell, cannot stop short of re-establishing Popery and the Pretender,—was followed on the 11th of May, by a most severe satire, intended for the same class of readers, and entitled, "Instructions from Rome, in favour of the Pretender; Inscribed to the most elevated Don *Sacheverellio*, and his Brother Don *Higginisco.* And which all Perkinites, Nonjurors, High-flyers, Popish-Desirers, Wooden-Shoe Admirers, and Absolute Non-Resistance Drivers are obliged to pursue and maintain, (upon pain of his Unholinesses Damnation,) in order to carry on their intended Subversion of a Government, fix'd upon Revolution Principles. London. J. Baker." [1710.] In this publication the writer personates the Pope, and though the sentiments are such as might be inferred from the sermons of Sacheverell and Higgins, the language put into the Pope's mouth is of the most furious character. They are instructed to " Assert that English Fanaticks are greater Monsters than Jews and Mahometans; that there is no difference between True-born Englishmen and Turkey Slaves." They are to " Endeavour to suppress that damned *Review*,—that's a plaguey Fellow; nothing but a miracle wrought by a Power not related to us, has preserv'd that Wretch to be a Scourge to our Faction." And it closes with the following benediction :—" May your Foreheads be as Walls of Corinthian Brass, your Tongues tipt with Syren's Musick, and your *Ignis Fatuus* lead all Europe."

The diffusion of Sacheverell's Sermons, and other High Church publications; the fame of his undergoing a state trial; and his subsequent speeches and other efforts, during his progress in provincial towns; created a spirit of *quasi* loyalty to the Queen and the Church, which took the form of Addresses to her Majesty. Many of these were patterns of servility, exalting the prerogative above the law, and some asserted the doctrine of non-resistance in most unqualified terms. Defoe says, ignorant people were drawn in to set their names to what they did not understand, and others had their names inserted without their consent. " Would any Man that had seen the temper of this People, in the time of the late King James, believe it possible, without a judicial Infatuation, that the same People should reassume their Blindness, and rise up again for Bondage? Never, since the Children of Israel demanded to go back and make Bricks without Straw, and to feed on Onions and Garlick, was any Nation in the World so sordid, and so unaccountably bewitched."

The Queen was flattered to be so approached; there was

much in the Addresses congenial to her natural inclinations; and this hereditary tendency, in a Stuart, was encouraged and strengthened by the new favourite, Mrs. Masham, whose intrigues had not ceased since her kinsman Harley was dismissed from the royal service. His restoration to office was impracticable so long as Godolphin remained Lord Treasurer, or the Ministry consisted exclusively of Whigs; but the expressed devotion of the Tories seemed favourable to a coalition, and to this proposal, instigated by Harley, her Majesty acceded. In June the Earl of Sunderland was removed, and replaced by Lord Dartmouth; shortly afterward Harley was appointed Chancellor of the Exchequer; Mr. St. John, Secretary of State, in the room of Mr. Boyle; the Earl of Rochester, President of the Council; and Sir Simon Harcourt, made Keeper of the Great Seal.

This turn in public affairs gave a shock to credit, that was as embarrassing to the new Ministers as it was injurious to all parties. The public funds declined, many Whigs withdrew their capital, and a national crisis was the result.

Let us now return to Defoe's conduct under these circumstances. I have already shown that in his *Reviews* he publicly reprobated the unconstitutional Addresses instigated by the high party. The changes in the Ministry occasioned melancholy forebodings for his country, and himself; but faithful to the former, he did not for a moment swerve from the first duty of a patriot. He had for three years refrained from all intercourse with Mr. Harley, towards whom his gratitude was undying; and now that benefactor was again in office, and perhaps the most influential member of the Government; but had allied himself with statesmen whom Defoe looked upon as enemies of their country. He could expect no favour from this party; who well knew his talent, and the inflexibility of his principles. Nor could he remain silent, except so far as to avoid any personal attack against the Minister to whom he owed so much. He could no more forsake the friends whom Mr. Harley had displaced, than he could divest himself of gratitude or patriotism. His *Reviews*, therefore, contain eulogies on the dismissed Ministers, collectively and individually; and he quietly tells us, that in these remarks, he shall not be suspected of flattery; for when men flatter, 'tis generally the rising, not the falling party. It was rumoured that the new Ministry would find it necessary to dissolve the Parliament, "Without which," Defoe says, "it is evident Truth will have another Year to breathe in; and Time, the great Friend of Illuminations, may wear off the scales from the Eyes of the deluded People. And, indeed, they have gone so far, that a Dissolution seems to be absolutely necessary to them, like a Pardon to a Thief." Yet the man who, at such a juncture, did not hesitate thus to write and publish his opinions was called a "Mercenary Scribbler," was accused of being patronized and paid by Harley, and was branded as a renegade advocate of Toryism.

The following is Defoe's own account of his conduct under these trying circumstances:—" I come now historically to the point of time when my Lord Godolphin was dismissed from his employment, and the late unhappy division broke out at Court. I waited on my Lord the day he was displaced, and humbly asked his Lordship's direction what course I should take? His Lordship's answer was, ' That he had the same ' good will to assist me, but not the same Power; That I ' was the Queen's Servant, and that all he had done for me, ' was by her Majesty's special and particular direction; and ' that whoever should succeed him, it was not material to me, ' he supposed I should be employed in nothing relating to the ' present Differences: My business was to wait till I saw ' things settled, and then apply myself to the Ministers of ' State to receive her Majesty's commands from them.' It occurred to me immediately, as a Principle for my Conduct, that it was not material to me what Ministers her Majesty was pleased to employ, my Duty was to go along with every Ministry, so far as they did not break in upon the Constitution, and the Laws and Liberties of my country; my part being only the Duty of a subject, viz., to submit to all lawful commands, and to enter into no Service which was not justifiable by the Laws: To all which I have exactly obliged myself.

" By this I was providentially cast back upon my Original Benefactor, who, according to his wonted goodness, was pleased to lay my case before her Majesty, and thereby I preserved

my Interest in her Majesty's favour; but without any engagement of Service.   As for consideration, pension, gratification,
or reward, I declare to all the world I have had none; except
only that old appointment which her Majesty was pleased to
make me in the days of the Ministry of my Lord Godolphin;
of which I have spoken already, and which was for services
done in a foreign Country some years before.   Neither have I
been employed, or directed, or ordered, by my Lord Treasurer
aforesaid, to do, or not to do, anything in the Affairs of the
unhappy Differences which have so long perplex'd us, and for
which I have suffered so many, and such unjust Reproaches."*
Every reader will conclude that the above relation is creditable
to the characters of the Queen, the two rival statesmen concerned, and to Defoe himself.

Briefly to recapitulate;—the national agitation consequent
on Sacheverell's trial, led to an inundation of Tory addresses;
which, being willingly, though mistakenly, accepted by the
Queen, as the voice of the Nation, was followed by the dismissal of part of her Whig Ministry, and the appointment of
Tories in their places.   Immediately public credit was shaken,
the funds were depressed, and a financial panic succeeded;
which added to other anticipated difficulties, forced upon the
new Administration the consideration of dissolving the Parliament.   Defoe fully and fearlessly discussed, in his *Review*,
all these important topics, as they respectively arose; and, on
several of them he also published valuable pamphlets.

---

* "Appeal to Honour and Justice," pp. 21-2.

CHAPTER VII.

Defoe publishes " An Essay upon Public Credit," and " An Essay upon Loans"—Parliament dissolved—Defoe publishes " A Word against a New Election," and " A New Test of the Sense of the Nation"—He goes to Scotland—Becomes publisher of the " Edinburgh Courant"— " Atalantis Major"—Attempt to assassinate Mr. Harley—Defoe publishes " Eleven Opinions about Mr. Harley"—" An Essay on the South Sea Trade"—" The Secret History of the October Club"— Harley created Earl of Oxford—Defoe publishes " Reasons why this Nation ought to put a speedy End to the War"—" Armageddon"— " The Balance of Europe"—" An Essay at a plain Exposition of that difficult phrase, A Good Peace"—" Reasons why a Party, &c., are against a Peace"—" The Felonious Treaty"—" An Essay on the History of Parties and Persecution."

1710—11.

THE financial depression, alluded to at the close of the preceding chapter, greatly affected the Trade and Commerce of the Nation; and required immediate consideration. On the 23rd of August Defoe published, " An Essay upon Public Credit: Being an Enquiry how the Public Credit comes to depend upon the change of the Ministry, or the Dissolutions of Parliaments; and whether it does so or no. With an Argument, proving that the Public Credit may be upheld and maintained in this Nation; and perhaps brought to a greater height than it ever yet arrived at, though all the Changes or Dissolutions already made, pretended to, and now discours'd of, should come to pass in the World. London. 1710." This very seasonable Tract had no reference to party politics; it was well received by all, and greatly aided in restoring confidence in the money market. The argument, in short, is that public credit rests firmly and securely upon the probity of the national government; and does not depend upon any set of Ministers for the time being. It was translated into the French language, and may yet be referred to as an authority. Many of the Whig Capitalists, however, still continued backward to invest their Money in

Government Securities ; and as funds were greatly needed for carrying on the War with France, Defoe published a supplementary pamphlet on the 21st of October, entitled, "An Essay upon Loans : or, an Argument proving that substantial Funds settled by Parliament, with the Encouragement of Interests, and the Advances of Prompt Payment usually allowed, will bring in Loans of Money to the Exchequer, in spite of all the Conspiracies of Parties to the contrary ; while a just, honourable, and punctual Performance on the part of the Government, supports the credit of the Nation.   By the Author of the Essay upon Credit. London. 1710."   In the first paragraph, he refers to the success of his previous pamphlet ; and, having discoursed ably on the nature, origin, advantages, and security of National Loans,—which involves a sketch of the history of the National Debt ;—he concludes by announcing that if he should appear again, it would be on the subject of Funds.   I am not aware of the existence of any such Essay, and therefore suppose that the author was diverted by other pressing duties.   These two pamphlets have been attributed to Mr. Harley ; I know not upon what ground ;— as they contain indubitable evidence of Defoe's authorship.

The Ministry had been much divided on the subject of dissolving the Parliament.   They had little prospect of maintaining their ground with the existing House of Commons, and the Tory Members of the Administration were therefore anxious for a general election ; in the full assurance that the High Church agitation, which was still raging throughout the country, would be of great advantage to their party.   On the other hand, the monied interest was so shaken by the unsettled state of the Nation ; that the Bank Directors are represented, on the authority of Addison, to have declared that they must shut their doors upon the first issuing of the writs.   Monied men brought their stocks to market on the mere rumour,— there were more sellers than buyers,—and it was predicted that financial ruin would inevitably follow upon a dissolution. Mr. Harley's policy was that of moderation, he desired a medium between the parties ; and in the embarrassment caused by his Tory Colleagues, made some overtures toward a junction with the Whigs, but only to find any compromise impossible.

A proclamation for the dissolution of parliament was consequently issued on the 21st of September; and, as soon as it
appeared, all England was in an uproar such as had never before been known on a like occasion.   Defoe was one of the
patriots who courageously stepped in between his country, and
the men who aimed at the destruction of its liberties.   Before
the election began he published a pamphlet entitled, "A Word
against a New Election.   That the People of England may see
the happy Difference between English Liberty, and French
Slavery ; and may consider well before they make the Exchange.
Printed in the year 1710."   While the elections were going
on, he also took a circuit, as on similar occasions previously,
through several counties; and his *Reviews*, for nearly the
whole month of October, are filled with details of the scenes
of drunkenness, corruption, personal violence, and fury, of
which he was a witness.   He concludes one paper, after expressing his amazement, by saying—"Doubtless, God who
governs the World he made, has designed some extraordinary
Event from this strange *phenomenon ;* and Men's minds cannot
bear this Fermentation without some Eruption which, like that
at Etna, must put the whole Country into Confusion."*

The High Church Addresses, being calculated to serve the
interests of the rising party, it was decided to publish them,
and an Advertisement of the Book having appeared in the
Post Boy, Defoe copied it into his *Review,* of July the 4th, as
follows,—" A Collection of the Addresses that have been presented to the Queen since the Impeachment of Dr. Henry
Sacheverell, whereby it most evidently appears, that the sense
of the Nation, whether Nobility, Clergy, Gentry, or Commonalty, is express for the Doctrine of Passive-Obedience and
Non-Resistance, and for her Majesty's Hereditary Title to the
Throne of her Ancestors."   He then adds, immediately below,
that he will publish in a few days, " A Collection of the
several Addresses in King James's time, &c., &c., by which it
may be seen that the Sense of the Nation, &c., was universally
for Arbitrary Power, for Government by a Standing Army,
and for tolerating Popery, as the best Method to preserve the

---

* Review VII., 337.

Monarchy, and support the Church of England : and, that they promised to choose such a Parliament as should concur to those ends." He does not appear to have had any serious intention of publishing such a collection ; but in that, and a succeeding number, continues the discussion, showing the little value of such addresses so far as the people are concerned ; and, that with princes they ought to pass for nothing. He says, " The practice of Addressing was a Jest that was put upon Richard Cromwell, and yet they deprived him three weeks afterwards. It was a second time put upon King James II. and they all flew in his face a year after." He adds, " If these things are the *Sense of the Nation*, we must acknowledge it looks as if the Nation had *lost its Senses ;* and thank God, and our wiser Ancestors, 'tis what *never* was the Sense of the Nation before."*

He appears to have been unable to resume the subject until after the dissolution of Parliament, and then to have chosen the more compact and effective form of a pamphlet, which he published on the 12th of October, entitled, " A New Test of the Sense of the Nation. Being a Modest Comparison between the Addresses to the late King James, and those to her present Majesty. In order to observe how far the Sense of the Nation may be judged by either of them. London. 1710." The question was one of only temporary interest, but his arguments, proving that the addresses to both monarchs meant nothing at all, beyond a compliment or a jest, are full of his characteristic satire.

Defoe's *Review*, during the latter half of the year 1710, affords internal evidence of the difficult and delicate position in which he was placed as a writer on public affairs. When he avoided directly attacking the new ministry, and declared his opinion that their measures would be moderate and constitutional, he pleased neither Whigs nor Tories, and was accused by both of making court for a place. When his enemies strove to embroil him with the government, he warily replied, " The case of the new Ministry, and the case of the author of the *Review*, however opposite, stand exactly on the same footing. While they do nothing in breach of the Laws, or against

---

* Review VII., 173-5.

the Constitution, though I make no court to them, on the one hand, yet I have no business to affront them on the other. *Vice versâ:* While I write or speak nothing but the Truth, and that truth, however plainly, yet with decency and respect, they can have nothing to say to me."*   Attempts were made to entrap him by questions and by letters; and it was hoped that his replies would bring him under the resentment of the government, so that his Paper might be silenced.   Some were goading him to oppose the ministers, while others were industrious in stimulating the Government to fall upon him. To one of the latter class he replies, " He therefore, whoever he was, that published a Paper in the City of Edinburgh, en-titled ' Now or Never,' in which, with a Head as full of Igno-rance, as a Heart full of Malice, he takes upon him to prompt my Lord Dartmouth, to whom he addresses his libel, to fall upon the Author of the *Review,* has most scandalously abused my Lord Dartmouth, as well as betrayed his own Folly,—and were it not that his seeming a stranger to England, may make some excuse for his ridiculous Excursion, I should farther expose him."   It can be no matter of wonder that finding himself surrounded with watchful enemies, Defoe should write with caution, and abstain from giving needless offence to the administration.   This was at once seen, and he now was charged with wavering in his politics.   To this he makes the following manly reply in his Paper of November 2nd.   " The Author of this Paper finding the times perilous, the age cen-sorious, enemies furious, friends cautious, and espousing truth dangerous, and knowing not how long he may be permitted to speak in this manner, humbly desires to state a little the case of the Paper and its Author.   It is now seven years since this Work first began; during which time the Author has had the fate of pleasing and displeasing in their turn, as must be the lot of every Man who writes in an Age when so many parties have alternately governed, and where the Men of the same party have so often been of several opinions about the same thing.   All the World will bear me witness that this is not a Tory paper; as the rage with which I am daily treated will testify.   Yet, because I cannot run the length that some

---

* Review VII., 275.

would have me, new Scandals fill their mouths; and now they
report I am gone over to the new Ministry. These are the
Men who, it seems, are angry that I write for upholding Credit,
without regard to changes in the Administration.* I have had
some conference with these Men, and I thank God I have; for
it has taught me to abhor their temper, pity their folly, and
laugh at their censure. The scandal, therefore, of changing
my principles, because I am not for ruining my Country, is what
I despise. I shall trouble the World with no more apologies.
The method I shall take for the future, in speaking of public
Affairs, will be with the same desire to support and defend
Truth, yet with more caution of embroiling myself with a party
that has no Mercy, and for a party that has no sense of Service."

I have already remarked that Defoe never thought fit to
trouble the world with information as to his family and
domestic affairs. It is certain however that he was at this
time residing at Stoke-Newington in a large house; but although he had probably got rid of the incubus of his old
debts, I think his biographers not justified in concluding that
he was now easy in his pecuniary circumstances. Whether he
received a commission from Harley, or went away in consequence of his own private affairs, either in London or Edinburgh; or was driven by the persecution of his enemies to
absent himself for a season, it is certain that in the month
of November he left his home and his family, on a journey to
Scotland, where he remained several months. His complaints,
shortly afterward, could only relate to what had occurred before
his departure, and it must be admitted that they seem to
point only at the remorseless cruelty of political opponents.
He says that sham writs were served on him by sham officers,
for sham debts, and one of the villains being caught, the Justice refused to punish him, when informed that Daniel Defoe
was the prosecutor. Also, that he was plundered of some goods
he had on board of a ship, the only reason given being that
they belonged to Defoe, the author of the *Review*. He concludes by exclaiming, "Thus, Gentlemen, I am ready to be
Assassinated, Arrested without Warrant, Robb'd and Plunder'd

---

* This sentence almost proves him the Author of the "Essay on Credit."
—W. L.

by all sides,—I can neither Trade nor Live, and what is this for? Only, as I can yet see, because there being 'Faults on both sides,' I tell both sides of it too plainly."*

The *Scots Postman* of August 1, 1710, advertises:—"Such of the Subscribers to Mr. De Foe's *Reviews* as are in the Country please leave a Note at Mrs. Anderson's Shop, informing where the *Reviews* shall be left for them so as to come to their hands." From the Public Records of Edinburgh, 13th December, 1710, it appears that a Contract was on that day entered into "between David Fearn, Advocate, and Daniel De Foe, about printing and publishing a Newspaper called *The Postman.*" And, on the 7th August 1711, is a document in the form of a Power of Attorney, indorsed, "Factory—— Daniel De Foe to Hannah Goodale, empowering her to act for him during his absence from Scotland."

The *Review* gives scarcely any information as to his employment in Scotland at the end of 1710, and the early months of the following year; beyond the obvious fact, that its numbers were regularly written and transmitted to London for publication. During his absence, he continued to write in support of public credit; and eloquently vindicated himself against an attack by Swift, in the *Examiner*. He also discussed the advantages of Trade with France and the West Indies; and congratulated his readers that the new Parliament was taking measures to ameliorate the condition of poor but honest Insolvents, on whose behalf he had so long and so strenuously laboured. In itself the incident is of little import, that on the 1st of February 1711, the Corporation of Edinburgh empowered Defoe to publish the *Edinburgh Courant*, in the room of Adam Booge, deceased. When, however, we take into account how strong the Scots national feeling still was, and the prominent part Defoe had taken in the Union of the two Kingdoms, we may conclude not only that the civic authorities now looked with calmness and satisfaction upon the results of the measure, but also that they highly appreciated our author's labours, and were grateful for the many other services he had

---

* Review VII., p. 491.

subsequently rendered them.   It would now be a useless speculation as to what motives induced Defoe, at that time, to
undertake the publication, and doubtless the writing, of an
Edinburgh newspaper ; whether or not, the kindness and affectionate respect he received from the Scotch, contrasted in his
mind with the ungrateful reward of all his toils in England,
revived a former desire to remove his family, and to spend the
remainder of his days in Scotland.   But whatever might have
been his intentions, affairs of a pressing nature recalled him
to London about the month of March, and in all probability
the *Courant* was then transferred to other hands.

The only pamphlet I have been able to discover as having
been certainly written by Defoe, during this absence from England, is an amusing piece of banter with the following title,
" Atalantis Major.   Printed in *Olreeky*, the chief City of the
North Part of Atalantis Major.   Anno Mundi 1711."   The
occasion of the Tract was the election of the sixteen Scotch
representative Lords, and their rage at the Oaths they had to
take as members of the British Parliament.   With two or
three exceptions, they were well known to be in the interest of
the Pretender, and some of them had appeared in arms for him.

I must not in this Memoir consider at large the dissensions
which soon broke out in a Ministry composed of such heterogeneous materials as that now in office.   Mr. Harley still retained his attachment to Whig principles; he had been the
principal instrument in persuading her Majesty to make the
recent changes, and having been previously the head of the
opposition, he expected to retain the precedence, when in office.
On the removal of Lord Godolphin, the Treasury had been
placed under five Commissioners, of whom Harley was one,
and was also Chancellor of the Exchequer.   The Earl of
Rochester claimed to be head, from his long experience, and
near relationship to the Queen.   Mr. St. John, conscious of
his own superior talents, was too ambitious to be contented
with a subordinate place.   This internal disunion must shortly
have broken up the Ministry, had not the daring attempt of
the Marquis de Guiscard, on the 8th of March, to assassinate
Mr. Harley, interested the Queen more deeply in his favour,
and given him an unrivalled claim to preference and honour.

VOL. I.

The high station to which Harley had raised himself,—the intrigues attributed to him,—the profession of Whig principles, while seeking alliance in office with high Tories,—the moderation of his measures, and the evident efforts to restrain his colleagues,—the secresy he affected in all transactions of a public nature, so as to set conjecture at defiance,—all these constituted him a political enigma. That he was an eloquent speaker and a great Statesman was unquestionable; but as to his political virtue, the most opposite opinions were held during his life, and have continued to the present moment. Defoe was no mean judge of character; he had better opportunities of knowing Harley's mind than those without doors;—they took counsel together, and though our author says he did not, in his judgment "join in many things that were done," yet he always believed Harley to be a true patriot, and an honest Minister. It is probable, that the attempt on Harley's life was the cause of Defoe's sudden departure from Scotland; it is certain, that while the subject was the one topic of conversation, he arrived in London, and actively engaged in directing the popular excitement in favour of his benefactor. With this object he published, on the 14th of May, a thick pamphlet, entitled, " Eleven Opinions about Mr. H——y; with Observations. London. Printed for J. Baker. 1711." After moralizing on the nature of prejudice, and the differing opinions of men upon the same subjects, he recapitulates the most important events in Harley's public life, and proceeds to detail the opinions entertained of him, by,—1. The Queen. 2. The Old Ministry. 3. The Whigs. 4. The Dissenters. 5. The October Club. 6. The Jacobites. 7. The Confederates. 8. Moderate Men on all Sides. Here he stops, concluding as follows:—" I have yet several Opinions behind, according to the Title, and I purposed to have added two Heads in particular, which would have been very diverting, as well as instructing, viz. 1. My own Opinion of Mr. H——y, and 2. Mr. H——y's opinion of himself. But this Tract does not allow me room for it; and perhaps the Subject may deserve a farther Consideration, as the follies and contention of Men increase; for, as Madmen grow sober, Fools wise, and obstinate Men persuadable, the World can never be without Occasion for an observing by-stander, to make such Observations as may be very useful to them all."

The author professes to state all the above opinions, and the reasons some had for supporting, and others for opposing Mr. Harley, " with as much Coldness to his Character as he can, merely to shun the shadow of Partiality." In this endeavour he has avoided any direct eulogium ; but no reader can possibly doubt that the pamphlet was written by a sincere friend of the minister. Several of the heads required to be treated with great care ; and though there is no concealment of truth, Defoe admits that he was obliged to adopt much circumlocution in telling his story. He had been treated with kindness and confidence by both Harley and Lord Godolphin, who had successively displaced each other from office, and were now bitter political adversaries. It therefore required much judgment and delicacy to state the opinion of the " Old Ministry" respecting Mr. Harley, with due regard to personal obligations, and his political connections with both. Upon the whole, the tract is very dexterously written, and must have been of great service. He does not appear to have fulfilled the expectation held out, of writing a supplementary pamphlet.

Public credit still continued in a state of great exhaustion, funds were required for carrying on the War, and for paying off the debts of the Kingdom. The Parliament was in session, and it was the duty of Harley, as Chancellor of the Exchequer, to propose the necessary ways and means. His life was not considered to be out of danger until the end of five weeks, and he would not entrust his colleagues with the secret of his intended measures. After the House of Commons had been compelled to adjourn for several days on account of his absence, he ventured, though still very weak from his wounds, and laid before Parliament his project for retrieving the finances, by a Trade to the South Seas. The proposal was approved, although Lord Rochester, and some other of the ministers, did all in their power to defeat it.

This was no new subject to Defoe. He had laid a scheme before King William for sending an expedition to America to destroy the Spanish trade, and diminish the resources of France. The same had been urged upon the Lord Treasurer

Godolphin, who had laid it aside until a convenient opportunity; and, as we find the same proposition now advocated in
the *Review*, at the time when Harley laid his scheme before
Parliament, it is not presumptuous to conclude that he and
Defoe had conferred together thereon. We may deduce from
thence, that our Author was admitted by the head of the
Ministry to a degree of private confidence that was evidently
refused to her Majesty's uncle, and the other Tory members
of the administration. In consequence of the opposition to
the measure, Defoe embodied the Scheme, and its advantages,
in a separate pamphlet, published on the 6th of September, and
entitled, "An Essay on the South Sea Trade. With an
Enquiry into the Grounds and Reasons of the present Dislike
and Complaint against the Settlement of a South-Sea Company. By the Author of the Review. London. Printed for
J. Baker. 1711." This able exposition was so well received
that a second edition was issued on the 29th of the following
November, and reissued again early in 1712.

Thus we see how important a part our author took in
ushering into the world this great scheme; but, not all the
sagacity and foresight of himself or Harley, could have conceived that what they might now grasp with the hand, would
within ten years thereafter, overspread the whole nation with a
delusive epidemic,—madness of avarice,—and lust of gain,—followed by a delirium of ruin and despair,—that should make the
very history of the South-Sea year a wonder to successive ages.

In this latter half of the nineteenth century, when penny
newspapers, containing yesterday's transactions in nearly every
part of the globe, are to-day circulated to the remotest
corners of the kingdom; it is difficult adequately to appreciate the great services rendered by literary genius to the
Statesman of the reign of Queen Anne. The diffusion of
knowledge on political events was then chiefly by means of
pamphlets; and an able writer was an acquisition to any
government. We admire the discernment and tact of the
Minister who could engage, in support of his policy, the pens of
such men as Addison, Swift, Defoe, Steele, Arbuthnot, Prior,
and Davenant; although some of them were opposed to each
other, personally and politically. Oldmixon couples Defoe

with Swift, as fellow-labourers in the service of Harley, and
says, " that he paid Defoe better than he did Swift; looking
on him as the shrewder head of the two for business."*   That
they did so labour is apparent from their respective pamphlets
in support of the administration, on several great questions
during the latter years of the Queen's reign, but it is scarcely
probable that they ever met face to face; had they done
so, they must have differed in opinion.   The cynical,
abusive wit of the Tory *Examiner* prompted its writer to
speak of " the fellow that was pillored," but whose name he
professed to have forgotten; and to call the Author of the
Review " stupid and illiterate."   We have already seen that
the Doctor found his match in keenness of wit, though not in
scurrility ; and there was little else in their characters common
to both.   The motives that attached them to the Government
of Harley, were as diverse as possible.

In one of his Letters to Stella, Swift speaks with real, or
assumed, indignation of having refused a note for fifty pounds,
which Harley put into his hand as a reward for his advocacy.
But was the " vaulting ambition" less mercenary that, rejecting
this gift, sought, though in vain, the highest office in the
Church, as a recompense for exercising his great talent of political sarcasm, too often tinctured with moral pollution ?   The
connection of Defoe with the same Minister may be best told
in his own words, which show that the grand test with him,
was ever that of right and wrong.   The free Bible and the
Reformation, were the bases of his religion ;—liberty and the
constitutional principles of the Revolution those of his politics.
" No obligation," he says, " could excuse me in calling evil
good, or good evil."   He had been stript of property and of
liberty for speaking truth when men could not bear to hear
it, and he was able to boast that the world could not bribe him
to do anything not justifiable in itself.   Years later, he writes :—

" It is a general Suggestion, and is affirmed with such
assurance, that it is in vain to contradict it; that I have been
employed by the Lord Treasurer in the late Disputes about
public Affairs, to write for him, or to put it into their own
particulars, have written by his direction, taken the materials

---

* " Life of Maynwaring," p. 276.

from him, been dictated to, or instructed by him, or by other
Persons from him, by his order, and the like; and that I have
received a Pension, or Salary, or Payment from his Lordship
for such Services.   One would think it was impossible, but
that since these things have been so confidently affirmed, some
Evidence might be produced, some Facts appear, or some Body
might be found that could speak of certain Knowledge.   To
say things have been carried too closely to be discovered, is
saying nothing; for then they must own, that it is not discovered; and how then can they affirm it, as they do, with
such an Assurance, as nothing ought to be affirmed by honest
Men, unless they were able to prove it?   Were the Reproach
upon me only in this particular, I should not mention it, I
should not think it a Reproach to be directed by a Man to
whom the Queen had entrusted the Administration of the
Government.   But as it is a Reproach upon his Lordship, Justice
requires that I do right in this Case.   The thing is true or false.

"In Answer to the Charge, I bear witness to Posterity,
that every part of it is false and forged.   And I solemnly
protest in the fear and presence of Him that shall Judge
us all, both the Slanderers and the Slandered, that I have
not received any Instructions, Directions, Orders, or let
them call it what they will of that kind, for the writing any
part of what I have written, or any Materials for the putting
together any Book or Pamphlet whatsoever, from the said Earl
of Oxford, or from any person by his Order or direction, since
the time that the late Earl of Godolphin was Lord Treasurer.
Neither did I ever shew, or caused to be shewed to his Lordship,
for his approbation, correction, alteration, or for any other
cause, any Book, Paper, or Pamphlet which I have written,
before the same was Printed and Published.   If any Man
living can detect me of the least Prevarication in this, or in
any part of it, I desire him to do it by all means; and I
Challenge all the World to do it.   And if they cannot, then I
appeal to the Honour and Justice of my worst Enemies, to
know upon what Foundation of Truth or Conscience they can
affirm these things, and for what it is that I bear these Reproaches.   In all my writing, I ever capitulated for Liberty to
speak according to my own Judgment of Things; I ever had
that Liberty allowed me, nor was I ever imposed upon to write

this way or that, against my Judgment, by any Person whatsoever."*

Little comment is needful on the above triumphant vindication of honest independence. It will be observed that our author does not anywhere deny that, being in her Majesty's service, he received remuneration. He avows also his intercourse with the head of the Administration; and it may be admitted that he knew the sentiments of Harley on important matters of state; but he made it an essential condition of his service that he should be left free to write and publish what he thought proper; and the confidence of the Minister accorded him such liberty.

The downfall of the previous Ministry, and the accession of one comprising some of the Tory party, had during the first session raised,—among the highfliers, and most violent partizans,—hopes that were destined never to be realized. The temporising conduct of Harley gave so much offence to these men, that a cabal of more than a hundred, chiefly country members, formed themselves into a Society, meeting at the Bell tavern, in Westminster, under the name of " The October Club;"—the title having reference to the favourite beer brewed in October. Their present objects were, discussion against the Government, organised opposition in Parliament, agitation of the country; and the ascendancy of ultra Toryism. A large proportion of the members were known adherents of the Pretender. For some time the Ministry seemed not to regard this confederacy, but Swift says, " One of them in confidence told me, that there must be something thought on to settle things better." The Minister in question was doubtless Harley, who was so obnoxious to the Club. Swift soon afterward published " Some Advice Humbly Offered to the Members of the October Club," &c. This is the advice of a Tory to his friends,—full of expediency,—representing the Ministry as being disposed, though unable, to do everything the Club could desire; and as having already done all that was possible. He represents that in a little time the Whig party must of necessity fall to pieces; and urges those he addressed to wait

---

* " Appeal to Honour and Justice," pp. 18-21.

with patience. The pamphlet was calculated to serve the turn of the Government, so far as procrastination would avail; but it is scarcely possible that the author was self-deceived, while so palpably deceiving both the Club and the Minister.

Far different was the course adopted by Defoe. Knowing that many of the members of this Club were actual traitors at heart, especially the Jacobites from Scotland;—and, that the whole were hostile to the true interests of his country; he charged them home with all his powers of argument, wit, and raillery,—exposed their principles, and even the transactions of their secret meetings;—and, giving them no quarter, held up all the prominent members, so that they might be identified and execrated. This he did in two pamphlets published during the summer, the title of the first being, " The Secret History of the Octobe: Club : From its Original to this Time. By a Member. London. Printed in the Year 1711. Price 1s." The commencement recites the title, and adds, " With some Friendly Characters of the Illustrious Members of that Honourable Society." This was speedily followed by " Part II. London. Printed for J. Baker, at the Black Boy in Paternoster Row. 1711. (Price 1s.) Where may be had the first Part." I have only space to refer to the effects of his overwhelming attack. He says that certain monsters, whom he called *Cacafogoes*, the offspring of human parents, are occasionally born in Japan; and, that they are like " the October Club, whose whole Life and Actions may be comprised in this short History;—It would open its Eyes,—Eat, Speak, F—t, and Die." This was so far verified, that the more moderate Members of the Society ceased to attend, the meetings became less frequent, and the October Club soon ceased to exist.

On the 2nd of May died suddenly, Laurence Hyde, Earl of Rochester, the Queen's Uncle, and the President of her Council. He was a man of great integrity, and some wisdom, but a high Tory, and a formidable rival of Harley in the administration. The way was now open to some appearance of union, and the other Tories in the Ministry engaged to support Harley, and to acknowledge him as their head. He had acquired great popularity since the late attack upon his life, and the Queen, who thought no reward too great for his services, raised him to the peerage on the 24th of May, by the title of Earl of Oxford and Mortimer; and, on the 29th of the same month, he was made Lord High Treasurer. This promotion was followed by many other changes in the Ministry, all of which gave satisfaction to the Tories.

The war with France, which the victories of Marlborough made popular, had long been distasteful to the Tories; and the great burthen of taxation now began to produce a desire for peace. The French King hailed the accession of the Tories to power; and resolved to profit by the altered tone of the nation. Mons. Mesnager was sent privately to England, empowered to ascertain the views of the English Ministers; and Matthew Prior, the poet, who had been employed in a former negociation, was sent secretly to France to explain the bases upon which a treaty might be negociated. The preliminaries were signed by the English Ministers on the 27th of September. To this point the affair had been kept from the knowledge of the Allies, and as soon as the conditions became known, the Dutch were greatly dissatisfied. They prohibited the French plenipotentiaries from entering their territories, but on the Queen threatening to withdraw the English troops, they gradually gave way, and consented to a Congress, which was to be opened the following January at Utrecht.

One of the objects of the War had been, on the part of the Confederacy, to prevent the King of France from setting his grandson, the Duke of Anjou, upon the throne of Spain. Defoe had always supported his exclusion, and British blood had been shed abundantly in Spain to secure that Kingdom to Charles; but when the latter succeeded his brother in the Empire of Germany, the balance of Europe required reconsideration, and many wise men now thought it as dangerous that Spain should be attached to Germany as to France. Among them was our author, who urged that the safest course would be, to balance the two great Powers, by partitioning between them the Spanish dominions in Europe, and leaving the possessions of Spain in America to England and Holland. It is important to bear in mind that this change, if any, was the result of national circumstances, and not an abandonment of his former views. The English administration were eager for peace; they felt that their stability depended on it, and peace must therefore be had at any price, except the loss of office. The King of France had secret information of all that was transacting, and resolved to secure Spain for his grandson.

While the negociations were pending, the press teemed with pamphlets; and, in several of those adverse to the Government, Defoe was accused of inconsistency; his former statements were quoted against him,—and without allusion to the altered circumstances of the case, his enemies " wondered what Sovereign medicine had been since applied to his eyes, and by how much Gold they had been rubbed."* He was similarly attacked by Maynwaring, and had no difficulty in vindicating himself in his *Review;* but his assailants were not to be convinced, and during the remainder of the Queen's life he continued to be charged with dishonestly supporting a Tory ministry. These explanations will render it unnecessary for me to do more than mention the pamphlets in which he advocated his own views; and, in so far as they coincided, the views of the Ministry. The first is entitled, " Reasons why this Nation ought to put a Speedy End to this Expensive War; with a Brief Essay, at the Probable Conditions on which the Peace now Negociating may be Founded. Also, an Enquiry into the Obligations Britain lies under to the Allies; and how far she is obliged not to make Peace without them. Printed for J. Baker at the Black Boy in Paternoster Row. 1711." The first edition was published on the 6th of October; and it is strong proof that the moderate, peaceful, and Christian views of our author were acceptable to numerous readers, that the third edition was issued on that day week.

In the *Minutes of the Negociations of M. Mesnager,* 1717, pp. 108–9, there is an interesting anecdote of the Frenchman's zeal, and the incorruptibility of Defoe's patriotism. After speaking of the great talent in the English pamphlets and the avidity with which they were read, he says that an author whom he had employed to write in the interest of France having died, he could never get one like him, " except a certain Person, who the Swedish Resident, Monsieur Lyencroon, recommended, and who wrote an excellent Tract in our Interest,

---

* " A Letter to a Member of the October Club," p. 42.

entituled, *Reasons why this Nation* (meaning England) *ought to put an End to this Expensive War,* &c. I was extremely pleased with that Piece, tho' I could not read it distinctly, and for that Reason had it translated into French, and caused it to be printed at St. Omer in Flanders, and dispersed thro' the Low Countries, and at Paris for the publick Information of our own People. Monsieur Lyencroon used his Endeavour to bring this Author into my Measures; and to facilitate the Thing, I caused an hundred Pistoles to be conveyed to him, as a Compliment for that Book, and let him know, it came from a Hand that was as able to treat him honourably, as he was sensible of his Service. But I missed my Aim in the Person, tho' perhaps the Money was not wholly lost; for I afterwards understood that the Man was in the Service of the State, and that he had let the Queen know of the hundred Pistoles he had received; so I was obliged to sit still, and be very well satisfied that I had not discovered my self to him, for it was not our Season yet."

To return. On the 30th of the same month Defoe published a pamphlet entitled, " Armageddon : or, the Necessity of Carrying on the War, if such a Peace cannot be obtained, as may render Europe Safe, and Trade Secure. London. J. Baker." The title of this production did not appeal so directly to the popular understanding. It was not reprinted, and is now very scarce. Defoe deprecates any failure in the negociations, but looks the consequences in the face, and speaking for the Ministry says, " *Pax Quæritur Bello* is the motto of their present opinion relating to the War." Only two days were allowed to elapse before our Author was again in print with an excellent Tract, entitled " The Ballance of Europe : or, an Enquiry into the respective Dangers of giving the Spanish Monarchy to the Emperor, as well as to King Philip; with the Consequences that may be expected from Either. Printed for J. Baker, at the Black Boy in Paternoster Row. 1711." In this, after a full consideration of both sides of the question, he comes to the conclusion, that if France can give Securities against undue encroachments, either commercial or civil, upon Spain and its Colonies, and everything be left to its native channel, it will be safer to give Spain to King Philip, than to the Emperor of Germany; that this will prevent the protrac-

tion of an expensive and bloody War; " and, that King Philip
and his Posterity will be as much Spaniards in a very short
time as ever Philip II. was, or any of his other Predecessors."

The prolific pen of our author was, at the same time, engaged
on this blessed work of Peace in his tri-weekly *Reviews;* but this
was not sufficient, and about the 27th of November he published,
" An Essay at a Plain Exposition of that Difficult Phrase, a
Good Peace. By the Author of the Review. J. Baker, 1711."
In the introduction, he complains of a hardship that affects
him, as he says, "more than any other Author, in that, others
are wary in what they write for fear of displeasing the Government, and irritating Men in Power, my difficulty is a Clamour
raised by those, who, without Arrogance I may say, cannot
confute me, pretending that I am too careful to please Men in
Power, in which I have the Reproach without the Profit of the
Charge. I only introduce this with a brief Challenge to them,
to find any change of Principle in all I have written, if they
can; and if what I wrote under the late Ministry, and under
this Ministry agrees, it must be some Body else that has changed
Principle, not me : Let the issue determine it."   He then goes
on to complain, as he had frequent occasion to do, of books on
this subject being called his, as well of one side as the other;
in order to make them sell, or to bring scandal on his name.
Then follows a sentence which I am bound to notice, because,
for want of a little critical examination, Mr. Wilson has so far
misunderstood its meaning as to reject all the other pamphlets
written by Defoe on the same subject, although in a foot-note
he gives the titles of two, and says, " They not only breathe
his sentiments, but participate of his stile and phraseology."*
The error consists only in a misplaced comma after the word
" subject," instead of being after " anything." Thus corrected
it reads—" Hitherto I have said nothing on the Subject nor
do I purpose to say anything,—but what I will fairly own and
defend; and that I hope may Answer the People who call
everything they don't like by my Name."   I think his meaning very obvious, viz., that he is ready to own and defend all
that he has written, or may yet write, upon the subject of

---

* " Life of Defoe," iii. 233.

Peace. The body of the pamphlet is strictly in accordance with its predecessors. On the 29th of the same month appeared a fifth pamphlet from our student of Peace, entitled, " Reasons why a Party among us, and also among the Confederates, are obstinately bent against a Treaty of Peace with the French at this Time. By the Author of *Reasons for Putting an End to this Expensive War*. London. J. Baker. 1711." A second edition was published on the 8th of December. The versatility of Defoe is as remarkably exhibited in this series of pamphlets, as his great industry. Although the text of them all is contained in the word PEACE, and they harmonize with each other, I have not found that in any instance he has repeated himself.

During the progress of this literary warfare, there was much party spirit among those opposed to the ministry; but the mind of Defoe appears to have been as peaceful as his subject. One form of bitterness, was a revival of the reproaches cast upon the memory of King William on account of the Treaty of Partition; and in a debate in the House of Commons, John Howe, Esq., member for Gloucestershire, had called it *the Felonious Treaty*.* Defoe could not remain silent when his royal master was aspersed, and he therefore published in the beginning of December a pamphlet entitled, "The Felonious Treaty: or, an Enquiry into the Reasons which moved his late Majesty King William, of Glorious Memory, to enter into a Treaty at two several Times with the King of France for the partition of the Spanish Monarchy. With an Essay proving that it was always the Sense both of King William, and of all

---

* After Howe had been made joint Paymaster of the Forces with Sir Stephen Fox, our author was considering, in his Review, the different classes of men who always rail at Government, and he took occasion to lash Mr. Howe with the following satire:—" We have a third sort of People, who always go with their mouths open, in order to have them stopped; like a sort of Dogs I have met with, that when they attend under your Table, bark that they may be fed. I remember a man of some note who practised this with great success, and canted a long while in the House of Commons about abuses in the management, misapplying the public treasure, making *Felonious Treaties*, and the like; but a wise old Fox no sooner halved his Den to this Badger, but he put a stop to the clamour; and the Nation's Treasure was never misapplied since, because a good share of it ran his way."—*Review* VIII., 525.

the Confederates, and even of the Grand Alliance itself, That the Spanish Monarchy should never be united in the Person of the Emperor.   By the Author of the *Review*.   London. J. Baker.   1711." In the early part of the tract he thus alludes to an event in his own history not before noticed.   " I am the freer in entering upon the Subject at this critical Juncture, because, as I had the Honour, *from his Majesty's own mouth*, to hear many of his Reasons for making that Treaty, and some of the Views he had in it for the future Good and Peace of Europe, so I have on all Occasions, long before this, declared, and once in particular, when under examination before some Men of the greatest Power in this Kingdom, and the greatest Enemies of that Treaty, who will remember, if they see these Sheets, that it was then my Opinion, that after seven Years' War, we should be glad to make Peace on the foot of a Partition." He says this will answer the suggestions of his enemies that he had adopted such opinion in compliance with the times, and that he had expressed his opinion in *his Majesty's own Words.*

In answer to the increasing personal reproaches with which he was assailed towards the end of the year, he says in his *Review*, " I am one of those unhappy few, who, guided as I hope by Truth, and unconcerned at Reproach, which Men blindly throw out on every side, stand fast in defence of that true Interest of my Country which I bless God from the bottom of my Soul, I espoused in my Youth, and never could be frighted by parties, nor bribed by persuasions, no, not of the greatest in the Nation, to forsake.   I confess I defend it now under very unhappy Circumstances, viz., that they say the French and I argue for the same thing ; the Tory interest is wrapped up in my Argument ; and, rash Men ! some will have it that I am turned Highflier." In reply to these assertions he coolly assures them, " After I have first turned Papist, and then Mahometan, I may list for the Pretender ; but take my Word for it, I must do both the other first."*

Notwithstanding the professions of the Earl of Oxford that he adhered to moderate principles, it will have been observed that he was unable to control the increasing power of the

---

* Review VIII., 414.

Tories in the ministry. The High Church party were a majority of the House of Commons, and the Dissenters were again menaced with persecution. To prepare the minds of the people for what was to follow,—the proceedings of both Houses of Parliament, upon the former Occasional Conformity Bill, were reprinted,—with " Reasons for bringing in such a useful Bill as this must be to the Church and Kingdom, this present Session of Parliament." The anticipated difficulty was with the House of Lords, who had always rejected such a measure; but as that House had offended the ministry, by an Address to her Majesty against a concession of Spanish Dominions to any of the Bourbons, the Government in December took the bold step of strengthening themselves by creating twelve new Peers in one day. In addition to this, a temporary coalition was effected, by which the ministerial party should concur in placing this new bond upon the Dissenters, in return for the support of the Earl of Nottingham and his party, to a speedy treaty of peace with France. Other arrangements having secured the silence of the Whigs, the Earl of Nottingham brought forward his measure, for the prevention of Occasional Conformity, on the 15th of December; and, meeting with no opposition, the Bill went through its several stages in three days. It passed the Commons in an equally short time; and such was the eagerness displayed, that a petition from foreign Protestants, residing in London, praying to be exempted from its provisions, was rejected with contempt. The Earl of Oxford, had been a Presbyterian nearly all his life, and many of his relatives so continued; but now, all applications to him on the part of the alarmed Dissenters, were unavailing; and the Bill received the royal Assent on the 22nd of December, being one week after its first introduction.

Little time was allowed for any efforts that Defoe, or others, might make to prevent the passing of this Bill; and there is no reason to think that any such efforts would have been successful. His *Reviews* were full of despondency. He says, the measure " will infallibly ruin many hundreds of Dissenting Families, or cause them to act against their Consciences for Bread; which I think is one of the worst kinds of Persecution."*

---

* Review VIII., 470.

Bearing in mind the successful resistance of himself and others against the previous attempts to pass such Bill, he says,"The Dissenters in England,as they stood united in Interest with the Low-Churchmen, could have received no fatal Blow but from themselves.   Three times the united Power of their Enemies had attacked them, and could never prevail; but given up by their Friends, they fall of course."*

The freedom with which he expresses his opinion, arguing that the toleration of the Dissenters was a legal establishment, stipulated for, and granted at the Revolution; and that its inviolability had been repeatedly promised by the Queen and her Government, is the strongest possible proof that no power could control his pen, or change his principles.   Whatever appointment he might hold under her Majesty, and however employed by the head of her Government, he was not deterred from publicly charging both, by implication, with breach of faith, and of the Constitution.   Nor did he do this without consideration of consequences, but adds, " If persecuting Laws are set up, and the Liberty of Dissenters, established at the Revolution is attempted, God forbid that I should cease, though humbly, to complain of the Injury, let what human Authority soever prohibit it.   If they make it Criminal, I am ready to suffer; but I will never lose my little share in the Liberties of my Country, without crying out against both the Mischief and the contrivers of it, let them be who they will."†

As a last effort against the Bill, our author published a pamphlet on the 22nd of December, in which he besought the Queen in pathetic terms to interpose in favour of her subjects, whose interests were in jeopardy.   It is entitled, " An Essay on the History of Parties and Persecution in Britain.   Beginning with a brief Account of the Test Act, and an Historical Enquiry into the Reasons, the Original, and the Consequences of the Occasional Conformity of the Dissenters.   With some Remarks on the several Attempts already made, and now making for an Occasional Bill.   Enquiring how far the same may be esteemed a Preservation to the Church, or an Injury to the Dissenters.   London.   Printed for J. Baker.   1711."

---

* Review VIII., 473.   † Ibid. 468.

Part of the pamphlet is addressed to the Dissenters, whom he assures, that these Acts passed against them are not so much with any view of bringing them over to the Church, as to shut them out of all civil Employments; and he tells the Whigs that they can never resist Popery and Slavery, which the projects of the Tories are tending to, without the assistance of the Dissenters. The appeal to the Queen was in vain, her assent to the Bill being given, as already stated, on the same day that this tract was published. Thus ended the strivings of Defoe for truth and liberty in the year 1711.

CHAPTER VIII.

Defoe publishes " The Conduct of Parties in England"—" The Present
State of Parties in Great Britain."—" An Enquiry into the real In-
terest of Princes in the Persons of their Ambassadors"—" Reasons
against Fighting"—Defoe's opinions on restraints of the Press—Re-
trospection of his Review—Commences and terminates a new series—
Writes against the Pretender—Publishes " A Seasonable Warning
and Caution"—" Hannibal at the Gates"—" Reasons against the
Succession of the House of Hanover"—" And What if the Pretender
should Come ?"—" A Question that Nobody thinks of, What if the
Queen should die ?"—Defoe apprehended, insulted, imprisoned, and
pardoned—The Treaty of Peace signed at Utrecht—Defoe publishes
" An Essay on the Treaty of Commerce with France"—Establishes
" Mercator, or Commerce Retrieved"—Publishes " Considerations on
the Eighth and Ninth Articles of the Treaty of Commerce"—" Some
Thoughts upon the Subject of Commerce with France ;"—and " A
General History of Trade."

1712—13.

THE state of parties in Parliament, and throughout the
kingdom, at the opening of the year 1712, was that of
distraction, confusion, and distrust. The Queen's Ministry
comprised a Whig chief, with some few followers of the same
party, acting with several sorts of Tories. Some of these were
petty leaders of small cliques ; others supporters of doctrines
which placed the Church above the State, but which unchris-
tianised the Church of Scotland, and the whole of the Dissenters in England. And, it must be admitted, that in the
same Administration were members who scarcely attempted to
conceal their intrigues for placing the Pretender upon the
throne. In the two Houses of the Legislature the same condition of demoralization was manifest. Peace was necessary
to the existence of the Ministry, and therefore Whigs opposed
it,—abandoned the Dissenters,—joined with Highfliers,—the
members of the October Club,—or any one else. The Earl of
Nottingham, and his friends, were found supporting his political adversary the Earl of Oxford ;—and Bishop Burnet sate

silent while the civil and religious liberties of the Revolution
were trampled upon by his peers. It is needless to add
that the same elements of disorganization existed out of doors,
and that the characteristic tendency of the times was national
retrogression. Lamenting this, Defoe says, " Our divisions
are now come to a formidable height, and every good Man
trembles at the event. He alone, that can bring meat out of
the eater, and good out of evil, can bring safety out of
the threatened destruction, and order out of this confusion."
One phase of the confusion he freely canvassed, in a
pamphlet entitled, " The Conduct of Parties in England,
more especially of those Whigs, who now appear against
the New Ministry, and a Treaty of Peace. Printed in the
year 1712."

Having proved their strength, in putting fetters upon the
Dissenters in England, the Tories turned their attention towards Scotland, with the view of taking off similar fetters
from the Episcopalians there. For such purpose, a bill was
brought into the House of Commons on the 21st of January,
to repeal an Act of the Scotch Parliament, which subjected
episcopalian Dissenters to the discipline of the Kirk-courts,
and to legalise the use of the liturgy in Scotland. This was
a subject that had been well considered at the time of the
Union, and the then existing laws remained undisturbed. The
present proposal spread a general alarm throughout Scotland,
and Defoe, who was thoroughly acquainted with the public
feeling, devoted his *Review* of the 29th of January to an exposition of the whole question, deprecating the measure in
cautious but very plain language. Neither petitions nor
remonstrances, however, were heeded; the bill quickly passed,
and the church politics of its framers and supporters were
involved in the absurdity of obliging all public officers in
England to be members of the national Church; while a
month afterward, they passed a law by which public officers
in Scotland were allowed to dissent from the national Church.
Defoe's great discernment was not required to foresee that
party spirit would soon become too hot to allow further public
discussion of legislative politics; and, fearing that he might be
prevented from speaking his mind in print, by the suppression

of his *Review,* he turned his attention to the completion of a large work, upon which he had been occasionally engaged above eight years, on the State of Parties.   In the meantime he expresses himself thus :—" I know not but I may speak at the hazard of my Life, and believe I do, for some reasons that I have heard; yet I will discharge my Conscience and Duty to the Church of Scotland, whose Ruin I see is aimed at.   It shall not fall for want of the Case being truly stated, and the frauds and treacherous dealings of her Enemies being exposed and detected. If my Liberty of Speech be taken away, I cannot help it; I shall still have the Satisfaction of having applied it right while I had it."*

The arbitrary suppression of individual journals that might be obnoxious to the government, but did not transgress the law, was too impolitic a course to be adopted; and it was therefore resolved to impose a general stamp of one halfpenny for every half sheet, upon all periodical publications.   The intention became known to the public in April, but the tax was not to come into operation until the 2nd of August.   A consciousness of restraint upon the freedom of our Author's pen at this period is apparent.   During the whole month of April his *Reviews* had been occupied with the negociations for Peace, and he did not cease to lament the punctilios, ceremonies, niceties, and delays attending the establishment of Peace between nations who make War without ceremony to God, or civility to men.   But he knew that his views were far in advance of the age, when he ventured also to lament, that we had not continued to trade with France during the whole of the War; and, that in expressing ·such opinion he laid himself open to the reproach of writing for the French interest. After continuing the same subject, he concludes,—" I am now drawing this Volume to a close; I have, indeed, continued it longer than usual, expecting some Period should have been put to the general Liberty of the Press, and to this Work among the rest. And very glad I should have been to lay down the ungrateful Task of Informing those who think they know, and Reproving those who think they cannot Mistake."

---

* Review VIII., 678, and *ante.*

The work to which passing reference has been already made was published on the 17th of May, with the following title, " The Present State of Parties in Great Britain : Particularly an Enquiry into the State of the Dissenters in England, and the Presbyterians in Scotland; their Religious and Politick Interest Considered, as it respects their Circumstances before and since the late Acts against Occasional Conformity in England; and for Toleration of Common Prayer in Scotland. London.   Printed and sold by J. Baker in Paternoster Row. 1712.   Price five Shillings."

I have already quoted from this valuable work, which embodies much of the political history of the Dissenters from the Revolution to the time when it was written; and also of the ecclesiastical affairs of Scotland.   It is divided into seven chapters, the last of which is devoted to—a friendly but faithful review of the state of Dissenters in England,—the causes which impede their progress,—and advice as to the best course to be adopted in their present depressed condition.   It might be supposed, from the title, that this book would be a dry detail of facts; but there is thrown over it the same charm of interesting narration and anecdote, found in his History of the Union,—and it abounds with lessons of wisdom that ought to be learnt, and practised, in the present day.

The negociations for Peace were conducted so slowly as to produce great murmuring and dissatisfaction.   A year had been occupied since the first secret and indirect proceedings of the French government, and several months had elapsed since the meeting of the plenipotentiaries at Utrecht.   The public uneasiness was aggravated by the profound secrecy with which the proceedings were managed,—giving rise to unfavourable rumours,—and settling into a vague apprehension, that the conditions insisted upon, and likely to be submitted to, would sully the triumphs and glories the English had obtained, during the war.   The little authentic information obtained, related to suspension of sittings for further instructions, and to misunderstandings between the Ambassadors.   The feeling between the French and the Dutch was far from being friendly, and a trifling event, beginning in what would now be called " flunkeyism," came very near to throw back all Europe into

the horrors of war.   A full account of the affair is contained
in a pamphlet by Defoe, entitled, " An Enquiry into the Real
Interest of Princes in the Persons of their Ambassadors; and
how far the Petty Quarrels of Ambassadors, or the Servants
and Dependants of Ambassadors, one among another, ought to
be resented by their Principals.   With an Essay on what
Satisfaction it is necessary to Give and Take in such Cases.
Impartially applied to the Affair of Monsieur Mesnager, and
the Count de Rechteren, Plenipotentiaries at Utrecht.   London.
J. Baker.   1712."   The origin of the matter seems to have
been, that as the Count de Rechteren, in his coach, was passing
by Monsieur Mesnager's door, the Footmen at the latter made
grimaces at the Footmen behind the coach.   This disrespect,
instead of being passed over as unworthy of notice, was highly
resented by the Count, who demanded a degree of reparation
which M. Mesnager felt himself unable to comply with.   From
this the quarrel rose, step by step, until the King of France and
the Dutch government became involved, and the negociations
were temporarily suspended.   Defoe holds very high the sacred
character of an Ambassador, but he concludes that the Dutch
were wrong, and that an apology was due to France.

The Dutch were much less anxious for Peace than the
English Government.   They had unpleasantly interfered with
the conduct of the war, but the commanding influence of the
Duke of Marlborough had sufficed to restrain them on all
emergent occasions.   They were offended that the English
Ministry had listened to any proposals of Peace from France
until they, and the other Confederates, had been consulted.
The insult, as they called it, of Count de Rechteren, chafed
and irritated them; they protracted the negociations by their
altercations, and desired that the allied army should attack the
French.   The Duke of Ormond, who had succeeded Marlborough, asked for instructions from the English government;
and it was alleged, at home, that he was directed not to fight.
This report caused much debate among the ignorant, who
thought it a national disgrace, that an English General with a
powerful army at his back, should refuse to fight the French.
To remove these misapprehensions, Defoe did not hesitate to
take the unpopular side of the question, and on the 7th of June

he published a pamphlet with the following title, " Reasons
against Fighting. Being an Enquiry into this Great Debate,
whether it is Safe for her Majesty, or her Ministry, to Adventure an Engagement with the French, considering the present
Behaviour of the Allies. Printed in the year 1712." Our
author first declines to admit that the Duke had orders not to
fight ;—and then assuming that the rumour was correct, claims
the right of the Queen to give such orders as would influence
the Allies, because the Dutch had exercised the same authority,
through their Field Deputies, in every Council of War, during
the whole career of the Duke of Marlborough ; and, because
the Plenipotentiaries were acting as if they wished to prolong
the war ;—thus justifying the Queen in saying, " If ye will not
treat of Peace, neither will I carry on the War." He remarks
that the discontented parties at home wished for another battle ;
because, on the one hand, defeat would ruin the Ministry ; and
on the other, victory would put an end to the negociations.
This conduct of the English government brought the Allies
suddenly to their senses ; and the preliminaries, being adjusted,
were presented to the British Parliament on the 6th of June.
As soon as the terms of peace became known, they created so
much dissatisfaction throughout the nation, that the Ministers
adjourned the Parliament on the 21st, to avoid the outburst of
opprobrium with which they were threatened.

Defoe had written much on the regulation of the press, and
deplored the licentious and irreligious publications of the
age. He would have removed the abuses, by making authors
and publishers more directly responsible to the law, and have
given them an equivalent for increased responsibility, by suppressing piracy ; yet he could neither approve of any revival
of a censorship of the press, nor of the recent act for a stamp
duty on all pamphlets and journals. His objections are freely
stated in his *Reviews*, in which he shows, that " to tax any
Trade so that it cannot subsist under the payment, is not a
means to raise the Money, but to destroy the Trade." After
showing that, as a source of revenue, the Act would be
futile, he says, there can be no doubt that the intention is to
suppress the newspapers : and he calculates that three thousand
families would be immediately thrown out of employment.

He also earnestly calls upon Parliament to make exceptions in favour of such publications as are intended " for the propagation of Christian knowledge, the fear of God, and the instruction of the Children of the Poor." It was a satisfaction to him that this recommendation was at once complied with. Referring to the manner in which Dyer's and other written News-letters were conducted and circulated, he shows the folly of all attempts to stifle public opinion, and also threatens the Ministry in the following bantering strain :—" Written Scandal shall revive, and the Nation shall swarm with lampoons, pasquinades, satires, and an inconceivable flood of written New's-Letters. For my part, I am already preparing a scheme for a written *Review*, which I design to invite all my Correspondents in Britain to subscribe for. I purpose also to hire some large Hall, or great Room, in the City, to propagate the other purposes of a new Undertaking, that the Poor may not want Employment. One Manufacture being suppressed, we must erect others. I doubt not to employ thirty or forty Clerks to write news, lampoons, ballads, any thing in the World besides, that may keep up the paper Trade. Two or three dozen Emissaries may be useful to gather in lies, scandal, rumour, and all the Excrements of that lying jade Fame ; another Class to digest, hatch, and lick into shape, every Whelp of Fancy which it may be found useful to bring into the World, to croak Treason, snarl at Government, and debauch the principles of the People. No Tax can reach us here. Printed Scandal may be punished ; written Treason can never be traced. Faction, strife, reproach, and discontented humours will spread ten thousand times faster among the People by Writing than by Printing; and innumerable Crowds of News-writers are already preparing for the War, drawing their Forces together, and forming suitable Correspondences for the Work. News must be written, if it cannot be Printed."*

Defoe protracted the eighth volume of his *Review* four months beyond the usual time, until the new stamp duty came into operation, when it was closed on the 29th of July 1712, with a double paper, containing a Preface, and the following

---

* Review VIII., 708.

Title: " A Review of the State of the British Nation. Vol. VIII. London. Printed in the Year 1712." The Preface is an important document, in which he gives a retrospect of the whole work,—the treatment it has received during its progress of more than eight years,—including many affecting particulars of his past life,—and the existing state of his circumstances. The following is an epitome of the topics introduced : He declares that, from the beginning of the undertaking, he has always " calculated it for the support and defence of truth and liberty." He expected to make enemies by speaking plain, and in that expectation he had not been deceived ; but he had thought, that an uninterrupted fidelity, and steady adhering to an honest principle, for nearly forty years, would have been some plea in his behalf; and that the shipwreck of his fortunes, and the ruin which an enraged party had inflicted on him, might have lodged a little in the breasts of his Dissenting friends. He had also thought, when he had given such proof, that he could neither be bribed from the truth, nor Threatened nor Terrified from his principles, it might have been a ground for honest impartial men to examine, before censuring him. He then complains, that he is still " condemned by common Clamour as writing for Money, for particular Persons, by great Men's directions, and the like." He declares this abominably false, and that his accusers know they have no evidence. This ingratitude, from a people for whom he had run so many risks, had given him a great deal of disturbance. " But," he says, " I thank God that operation is over, and I endeavour to make other uses of it, than perhaps the People themselves think I do.

" First, I look in, and upon the narrowest Search I can make of my own thoughts, desires, and designs, I find a clear untainted Principle, and consequently, an entire calm of Conscience, founded upon the satisfying Sense, that I neither am touched with Bribes, guided or influenced by Fear, Favour, Hope, Dependence, or Reward, from any Person or Party under Heaven ; and that I have Written, and do write nothing but what is my native, free, undirected Opinion and Judgment; and, which was so many Years ago, as I think I made unanswerably appear by the very last *Review* in this Volume.

" Next, I look up, and without examining into His Ways, the

Sovereignty of whose Providence I adore, I submit with an entire Resignation to whatever happens to me, as being by the immediate direction of that Goodness, and for such wise and glorious Ends as, however I may not yet see through, will at last issue in good, even to me; fully depending, that I shall yet be delivered from the power of Slander and Reproach, and the Sincerity of my Conduct be yet cleared up to the World: and if not, *Te Deum Laudamus.*"

He then goes on to hope that the Dissenters will yet see the wrong they have done him; but whether or not, he will stand by their cause to the last, because it is just and righteous—the cause of Truth and Liberty. He is thus able to see them revile and reproach him, and use him in the worst manner imaginable; without being moved, either to return them ill, or refrain from doing them good. He adds, " And this is the true meaning of that Command which I thank God I cheerfully obey, viz., to Pray for *them* that despitefully use me." Two authors of Journals had asserted so positively that he wrote under the direction of others, and for reward, that he had openly challenged them, and offered a hundred guineas upon proof of it; but they were unable to do so, and thus " gave the Lie and Rascal to themselves." He says, " What I approve, I defend; what I dislike, I censure, without any respect of Persons; only endeavouring to give my reasons, and to make it appear that I approve and dislike upon good and sufficient Grounds; which being first well assured of, the time is yet to come, that I ever refrain to speak my Mind for fear of the face of Man." Immediately afterward he gives the best possible proof that his pen was unfettered, by denouncing the recent Act against Occasional Conformity, saying " their Interest fills me with Resentment at the Barbarity of the treatment which the Dissenters have received;" but he warns them not to expect that the Act would be repealed if the Low-Churchmen should come to the Administration.

Returning to his own case, and his unconcern at mere human opinion, he advises his enemies to consider of some better improvement to make of their passions, than to waste them on a man, that is both above and below the reach of them; and sums up his experience in the following eloquent words :—" I know too much of the World to expect good in

it, and have learnt to value it too little to be concerned at the
evil.   I have gone through a life of Wonders, and am the
subject of a vast variety of Providences; I have been fed
more by Miracle than Elijah, when the Ravens were his Pur-
veyors.   I sometime ago summed up the scenes of my Life in
this distich :—

> No man has tasted differing fortunes more,
> And thirteen times I have been rich and poor.

In the School of Affliction I have learnt more Philosophy than
at the Academy, and more Divinity than from the Pulpit; in
Prison I have learnt to know that Liberty does not consist
in open Doors, and the free ingress and regress of Locomotion.
I have seen the rough side of the World as well as the smooth ;
and in less than half a Year, tasted the difference between the
closet of a King, and the dungeon of Newgate.   I have suffered deeply for cleaving to Principles, of which Integrity I have
lived to say, none but those I suffered for, ever Reproached me
with it.   The immediate causes of my Suffering have been the
being betrayed by those I have trusted, and scorning to betray
those who trusted me."

He states that he has even been reproached for his courage,
and replies, " Truth inspires Nature,—he that is Honest must
be Brave ;" and in defence of truth he thinks,—repeating the
word,—" I say, I *think* I could dare to Die ; but a Child may
beat me if I am in the wrong."   He concludes by an affecting
allusion to his private calamities,—the debts he had been
unable wholly to pay by stripping himself naked,—the conduct
of creditors, by which most of the debts he had been able to
discharge had cost him forty shillings in the pound.   Yet he
rejoices that his wife and six children have never wanted what
they should enjoy, nor spent what they ought to save ; and,
that, " by a constant serious Application to the great, solemn,
and weighty Work of Resignation to the will of Heaven," he
had always been kept cheerful, easy, and quiet, enjoying a
perfect calm of mind, clearness of thought ; and, a satisfaction not to be broken in upon by whatever might happen to
him.   Even this inadequate sketch of his Address on the termination of his untaxed *Review*, will, I trust, assist the reader
in forming a just character of this bold, uncompromising,

honest patriot;—and yet sincere and humble Christian,—
Daniel Defoe.

Notwithstanding the tax upon Papers, and his resolution to
end the *Review*, he found the railing spirit of the times, and of
the people; would not only triumph over him as slain in the
battle,—but that the cause in which he had so long struggled
would be endangered,—if he should hold his peace. In consequence of this conviction, he commenced the first volume of
a new series, in the beginning of August, each number consisting of a single leaf, quarto, headed " *Review;*" it was published twice weekly, and part of the time thrice weekly, until
the 11th of June 1713, when it had reached the 106th
Number, and terminated with the words " Exit Review."
Until within the last few years, no complete set of this new
Series, improperly called the Ninth Volume of the *Review*, was
known to exist. Mr. Crossley, of Manchester, is now the
happy possessor of the whole; and to him I am indebted for
the particulars of its extent and termination. I shall have to
advert, in its proper place, to the circumstances under which
Defoe finally laid it down.

When noticing the numerous pamphlets written by Defoe on
the conditions of Peace, I stated that he thought the Spanish
Dominions should not be given, altogether, either to the House
of Bourbon or to the House of Austria, but that, pursuant to the
design of King William, in the Treaty of Partition, the bone
of contention should be broken in pieces, and the Protestant
interest strengthened by the conquest of the Spanish West
Indies. In the honest expression of such opinions, both in his
pamphlets and *Reviews*, he must have greatly risked the displeasure of Lord Oxford; and yet, as we have seen, he was
subjected to calumny and reproach, as being hired and bribed
to defend a bad peace, and was also accused of writing in the
French interest. He says, " Whenever any Piece comes out
which is not liked, I am immediately charged with being the
Author, and very often the first Knowledge I have had of a
Book being published, has been from seeing myself abused for
being the Author of it, in some other Pamphlet published in
answer to it." Finding himself treated in this manner, without

any means of redress, he says he declined writing anything except the *Review*. To be out of the reach of clamour, he afterward was long absent in the north of England. The time during which he appears to have been thus silent, was from the beginning of June 1712, to nearly the end of December. Defoe probably left London immediately after the completion of the eighth volume of his Review; and, from some statements in Watson's " History of Halifax," Mr. Wilson conjectures that he resided in that town, during his retirement.

The following is important, as showing in his own words the motives that induced him, while in the north of England, to begin writing the series of pamphlets against the Pretender, for several of which he was again unjustly prosecuted. " Observing the Insolence of the Jacobite party, and how they insinuated fine Things into the heads of the common People, of the right and claim of the Pretender, and of the great things he would do for us if he was to come in; of his being to turn a Protestant, of his being resolved to maintain our Liberties, support our Funds, give Liberty to the Dissenters, and the like; and finding the People began to be deluded, and that the Jacobites gained ground among them by these Insinuations, I thought it the best Service I could do the Protestant Interest, and the best way to open the People's eyes to the Advantages of the Protestant Succession, if I took some course effectually to alarm the People with what they really ought to expect if the Pretender should come to be King. And this made me set Pen to Paper again." He goes on to say, " In order to detect the influence of Jacobite Emissaries, as above, the first thing I wrote, was a small Tract called, *A Seasonable Caution;* a Book sincerely written to open the Eyes of the poor ignorant Country People, and to warn them against the subtle insinuations of the Emissaries of the Pretender; and that it might be effectual to that purpose, I prevail'd with several of my Friends to give them away among the poor People all over England, especially in the North; and several thousands were actually given away, the Price being reduced so low, that the bare expence of Paper and Press was only preserv'd, that every one might be convinced, that nothing of Gain was design'd, but a sincere endeavour to do a Publick Good, and assist to keep the

People entirely in the Interest of the Protestant Succession."* The following is the full title of the work, " A Seasonable Warning and Caution against the Insinuations of Papists and Jacobites in favour of the Pretender. Being a Letter from an Englishman at the Court of Hanover. Printed for J. Baker at the Black Boy. 1712." The object of the above pamphlet having been sufficiently explained by its author, I need not further allude to its contents.

In order to keep alive the suspicions of the people, Defoe published a further tract upon the same subject, on the 30th of December, with the following title :—" Hannibal at the Gates : or, the Progress of Jacobitism. With the present Danger of the Pretender. London. Printed for J. Baker, 1712." Mr. Wilson was mistaken in doubting that Defoe wrote this pamphlet. In 1714, there appeared a Tory tract with the title, " Hannibal not at our Gates : or, an Enquiry into the Grounds of our present Fears of Popery and the Pretender, &c." This has been considered a reply to the preceding pamphlet ; but beyond the title it makes no direct reference to Defoe's tract. It induced our author, however, to issue a second edition, with title as before, but adding, " With some Remarks on a Pamphlet now Published, Intituled, *Hannibal not at our Gates.* London J. Baker, 1714." The " remarks " are contained in eight additional pages.

Having thus, with much success, written two pamphlets in plain language adapted to the popular understanding of the country ; and, finding the leaven of Jacobitism still at work, our unfortunate author was tempted, early in the year 1713, to exercise his inimitable vein of irony on the same subject ; and a second time became the victim of his own wit. Unlike the *Shortest Way,* however, he did not now attempt an entire personification of one of the extreme party ; but dexterously constructed the title pages of three consecutive pamphlets so as to throw over their contents a thin veil of apparent Jacobitism, sufficient only to attract purchasers, and to engage readers in the perusal of what was really designed to promote the Protestant Succession of the House of Hanover. It seems highly incredible that an honest and loyal intention, so little

---

* " Appeal to Honour and Justice," pp. 25, 26.

concealed, should have been unperceived by the dullest mental capacity; more, that the great Whig party were so blinded, as to concentrate their rage against the Ministry, upon the head of our hapless, but innocent author.

The first of these three Tracts was published on the 21st of February, with the title, " Reasons against the Succession of the House of Hanover; with an Enquiry How far the Abdication of King James, supposing it to be Legal, ought to affect the Pretender. *Si Populus vult Decipi, Decipiatur.* London : Printed for J. Baker at the Black Boy in Pater-noster Row. 1713." This ran through four editions within two months. The second Tract was published on the 26th of March, with the title, " And What if the Pretender should come ? or, Some Considerations of the Advantages and Real Consequences of the Pretender's Possessing the Crown of Great Britain. London. J. Baker, &c., 1713." This reached a second Edition in little more than a week. The third appeared early in April, entitled, " An Answer to a Question that No body thinks of, viz. But what if the Queen should die ? London. J. Baker, &c., 1713."

I shall be unable to quote at length from these able tracts, in which Defoe throws out on all sides his characteristic ridicule. I must, however, by a short reference to each, show how plainly his loyal intentions are manifested. He begins the first with a curious picture of national broils, disturbing the peace of a family. The despicable scullions in the kitchen learn to cry *High-Church, No Dutch Kings, No Hanover,*—that they may do it dexterously when they come into the next Mob; and their Antagonists of the dripping-pan practise the other side clamour, *No French Peace, No Pretender, No Popery.* In the Shops and Warehouses the Prentices throw *High-Church* and *Low-Church* at one another's heads, like battledore and shuttlecock, instead of posting their books. A Story higher, the Ladies, instead of their innocent sports and diversions, are all falling out with each other, the mother and daughters, the children and servants, and the very little sisters, one among another. If the chamber-maid is a slattern, " hang her, she is a High-flier;" or, " I warrant she is a Whig. Nay, go up to your very Bed-chambers, and even in Bed, the Man and his Wife shall quarrel about it. People ! People ! "

he exclaims, " What will become of you at this Rate ?" and
after showing that such a condition of things must end in
ruin, he draws his first conclusion, as follows :—" This is one
sufficient Reason why we should say Nothing and do Nothing,
about the Succession, but just let it rest where it is, and endeavour to be quiet."

The second Tract sets out with a profession of impartially
stating the advantages or disadvantages of the crown being
possessed by the Pretender, or by the House of Hanover.
" 1. As they are offered to us by the respective Parties who
are for or against. 2. As they really appear by an impartial
deduction from them both." Although the *Review* was still
being published, he speaks of its writer as, " the author of the
Review, one of the most Furious Opposers of the Name and
Interest of the Pretender ;" and says, he has been making
people " believe strange and terrible Things of what shall be-
fal the Nation in case of the Pretender's Coming in, such as
Popery, Slavery, French Power, destroying of our Credit, and
devouring our Funds." He then professes to consider and
answer these allegations *seriatim ;* and in so doing, really proves
that Great Britain would become subject to French Greatness,
the Slaves of Arbitrary power and Non-resistance, and be all
reunited to the Church of Rome.

In the third Tract there is even less concealment than in
the others. The author does not so much profess to answer
the question, *What if the Queen should die ?* as to show that
it is the pivot upon which all the distraction of the nation at
present turns. The book concludes with the following words :—
" The People of Britain want only to be shewn what imminent
Danger they are in, in case of the Queen's Decease. How
much their Safety and Felicity depend upon the Life of her
Majesty, and what a State of Confusion, Distress, and all sorts
of dreadful Calamities they will fall into at her Majesty's
Death, if something be not done to Settle them before her
Death ; and if they are not, during Her Majesty's Life secured
from the Power of France, and the Danger of the Pretender."
The most devoted adherents of the Pretender must have been
startled at the contents of these three pamphlets, and convinced
that they were calculated to damage his cause to the utmost ;
and I repeat, that only party fury could have made any Whigs

so mad as to attempt to construe them into the productions of
a Jacobite.   It is still more difficult to realize the fact, that
their author could have been arraigned, insulted, condemned,
and sent to prison by the highest criminal tribunal, of learned
and professedly impartial English judges.

Defoe has himself given an account of the circumstances
and consequences of these publications, to which I can do little
more than refer.*   He says they met with so much approbation among persons sincere for the Protestant Succession, that
they were sent all over the Kingdom; about seven editions of
them were printed, and they were reprinted in other places.
He protests that if the Elector of Hanover had given him a
thousand pounds to promote his Interest, and to make that of
the Pretender odious and ridiculous, he could have done
nothing more effectual to those purposes than writing these
books.   He adds that, according to his design, the Jacobites
were deluded by the titles, and when they came to read the
books they cursed the author.   Had the Pretender ever come
to the throne, the author could have expected nothing but
Death.   He goes on, "I leave it to any considering Man to
judge, what a Surprize it must be to me, to meet with all the
publick Clamour that Informers could invent, as being Guilty
of writing against the Hanover Succession, and as having
written several Pamphlets *in favour of the* Pretender."   He
recounts his opposition, for twenty years, at all hazards, to
King James, his pretended son, and all the Highfliers and
Jacobites.   He adds, "For these Books I was prosecuted,
taken into Custody, and oblig'd to give Eight hundred Pound
bail."   His friends expostulated with some of the men who
appeared in it, who answered with more Truth than Honesty,
that Defoe had disobliged them, and they were resolved both
to punish and expose him.   "Upon the several Days appointed, I appear'd at the Queen's Bench Bar to discharge
my Bail; and at last had an Indictment for High Crimes and
Misdemeanors exhibited against me by Her Majesty's Attorney
General, which, as I was informed, contained two hundred
Sheets of Paper."   He never saw the particulars, but was told

---

* *Vide* "Appeal to Honour and Justice," pp. 27-36.

that he would be brought to Trial the very next Term. Knowing the motives of his enemies, he petitioned the Queen, laying before her the design of the books, and the malice of his persecutors. This was considered in the Privy Council, and the books looked into, when her Majesty said, " *She saw nothing but private Pique in the first Prosecution,*" and a full Pardon was immediately issued. In Defoe's tract, from which this Abstract has been taken, the Preamble for the Royal Patent of such Pardon is set out in full.

Oldmixon has given an account of these proceedings against Defoe,* in which he shows his usual bitterness toward our author. Yet even from his statements no other conclusions can be drawn than that the accused was prejudged, treated with indecent harshness; and, though innocent, only saved from severe punishment by the interposition of the Queen.

The *Flying Post* was a Whig publication, owned and written by George Ridpath, who had always entertained a personal dislike towards Defoe. From this hostile paper, and from the *Post-Boy* of the 16th of April, I take the following partial account. It appears that an influential Whig member of the House of Commons† made complaint to my Lord Chief Justice Parker, of " several Treasonable Libels against the Protestant Succession of the House of Hanover." The titles of Defoe's three tracts, and of one by Pettis, are then set forth, and the account goes on—" Information was given upon Oath, that Mr. John Baker, of the Black Boy, in Paternoster Row, Publisher, and Mr. Richard Janeway, in White Friars, Printer, were the Persons concerned in the Printing and Publishing the said Libels. His Lordship issued his Warrant to bring them before him, that the authors might be discovered. Mr. Baker and Mr. Janeway being brought before his Lordship, they readily depos'd upon Oath, and also prov'd by their Servants, and by Part of the Copies and Proof Sheets, that Daniel de Foe, *Author of the Review,* was the Author of the three first-mentioned Libels; and that one Pettis, who has also formerly stood in the Pillory, was author of the *Jus Sacrum,* &c. Upon which his Lordship issued his warrant for apprehending the said Defoe and Pettis. Mr. De Foe

---

* " Oldmixon," iii. 509, 510.   † William Benson, Esq.

having taken Precautions to make his House at Newington
as secure to him as was necessary for a Man in his Circumstances, his Lordship's Officers were forced to take Constables,
and a great many other Persons to their Assistance; and with
much Difficulty and Hazard got into the House, and secur'd
him, and brought him from thence to Town; which gave
Occasion to a Report, that he was committed to Newgate for
High Treason. Whereas he only remained in Custody of the
Tipstaff, for want of sufficient Bail, as appeared by enquiry
(made) to the Gentleman that complained. But Mr. Borrett,
Solicitor to the Treasury, unexpectedly appearing on Tuesday
in the Afternoon, and declaring that he was satisfied in the
Bail that Mr. De Foe offered, he was admitted to Bail, himself
in £800, and one John Grantham, at the Stationers' Arms in
Aldersgate Street, a Stationer or Printer; and Thomas
Warner, in Ave Mary Lane, Stationer, in £400 apiece."
The partiality and unfairness of Ridpath is apparent in this
statement. He conceals the name of his patron Benson, the
complainant in these disgraceful proceedings. He also omits
to notice that Benson endeavoured, by offering a retaining fee
of ten guineas, to induce Sir Edward Northey, the Attorney
General, to plead against Defoe; and being indignantly refused, he immediately endeavoured to procure Defoe's deten-
tion in custody, by personally objecting against two of the
wealthiest members of the Stationers' Company (whom Defoe
offered as his Bail), that "they were Persons of small substance." This malicious conduct roused the Government to
take the matter out of Benson's hands, in the manner which
Ridpath goes on to relate.

A week was to elapse ere Defoe would have to appear again
before the Court; and, conscious of his own innocence, stung
by gross injustice, his outraged feelings found vent by a statement of the case in the intervening numbers of the *Review*,
in which he indiscreetly,—but under the circumstances par-
donably,—referred to the conduct of the Lord Chief Justice.
It became whispered, too, that the Ministry intended to save
him,—that the first step would be to indict him merely for a
misdemeanour,—and then to pardon him; a course that filled
his Whig enemies with rage and chagrin.

Their oracle, the *Flying Post* of the 23rd of April, resumes

the narrative as follows :—" Yesterday, being the first day of
the Term, Daniel de Foe, amongst others, appeared at the
Court of Queen's Bench; and her Majesty's Attorney General,
acquainting the Court that he was order'd to Prosecute him for
the three Libels mentioned in my former, he was continued on
his Recognizance; but before he went out of Court my Lord
Chief Justice caused the two *Reviews* of Thursday and Saturday last to be shewn to him, and asked him whether he was
the author of them, which, after some Hesitation he confess'd;
whereupon his Lordship declar'd that those two Papers were
very insolent Libels against him in particular, and also against
the Laws of England; but that his Lordship being personally
concern'd, he would leave it to the other Judges, to do what
they thought fitting in that matter; and the two *Reviews*
being then distinctly read, their Lordships concurred in
opinion, that they were highly insolent to the Lord Chief
Justice, and a notorious Contempt of that Court, and the Laws
of the Nation, and that the said Daniel De Foe should be committed Prisoner to the Queen's Bench for his said Offence.
The Court was Unanimous, That the Books for which he was
bound over, were *Scandalous, Wicked, and Treasonable Libels;*
but Mr. De Foe, endeavouring to excuse himself, by saying
the Books were writ Ironically, he was told by one of the
Judges, after several Learned Arguments to prove the Absurdity of that Pretence, that ' he might come to be hang'd,
drawn, and quarter'd for those Books.' "

The justice of committing the culprit to prison, for unwisely
alluding in the *Review* to his own case, was paralleled by that
of the unanimous Bench in pronouncing condemnation upon
his books as *Treasonable,* before even the Indictment had been
drawn, for the trial which they were never to be permitted to
hold.   Sir Thomas Powis was the worthy Judge whose
" learned arguments" twisted and tortured Defoe's words into
most uncommon sense,—so as, if possible, to convince the author
of the pamphlets that he had not written them ironically,—and
who then considerately assisted him in realising,—by anticipation,—what to himself, his wife, and his six children, might be
included in his being " hang'd, drawn, and quarter'd."

It was fortunate for Defoe that his first benefactor was still

in power, and had the disposition to befriend him.   Lord
Oxford was thoroughly acquainted with Defoe's loyalty to the
Queen, and the Protestant Succession; and determined that
he should not be crushed by the malice of the Whigs, for an
offence that was purely imaginary.   So inveterate, however,
was become the enmity of the Whigs, that Defoe's pardon
under the Great Seal,—confuting the charges brought against
him, and exempting him from any consequences thereafter on
account of those publications,—was adduced by the party writers
of the time, as a convincing proof of Lord Oxford's attachment
to the Pretender; it was insinuated that the Queen herself
was inclined in the same direction; and, that Defoe, notwithstanding his disavowal, was a Jacobite at heart.

The treaty of peace, after a protracted negociation, was at
length signed at Utrecht, on the 11th of April, 1713.   The
address of the French plenipotentiaries had enabled them to
take advantage of the dissensions among the Allies, by advancing new demands, until the English Ministry became
wearied with suspense, and made concessions unwarranted by
the glorious successes of a long and expensive war.   Only
France was satisfied with the treaty.   The object of the war
had been abandoned,—the fruits of many victories thrown
away; and, instead of the expected consolidation of party
power at home, the Ministry was internally disturbed by a
factious spirit, which in a short time effected its overthrow.

At the commencement of the treaty, Defoe had declared
himself a friend to peace, if it could be obtained upon honourable terms; and, as we have seen, he wrote much upon the
subject, without appearing as the advocate of the Ministry.
His attachment to the Earl of Oxford was a snare, so far as
his gratitude for past favours imposed silence on those points
of policy which he could not approve; and this forbearance
brought upon him all the odium of being retained to expound
the views of Ministers.   He served them, by smoothing the
way to peace; but he disapproved of the terms upon which it
was concluded, and expressed his disapprobation in the *Review*,
even at the risk of displeasing Lord Oxford.   He acquiesced,
however, in the peace, when it was accomplished, as a good
subject bound by a national obligation; and the treaty having

imposed upon the Ministry the arduous duty of fixing, with the other Powers concerned, the future commercial relations of the countiy, Defoe was ready to assist with his great knowledge of the subject.

The principles of Trade and Commerce had formed an important part of the design of Defoe in the conduct of his *Review;* and he frequently regretted, in its columns, that the political " fury of the times," prevented all his efforts to continue the discussion in a connected form. In an advertisement appended to the Review of the 8th July, 1710, he says he had received many importunate Letters, pressing him to go on with his so often promised Discourses upon Trade; and adds, " Some Gentlemen, who desired that Work to be carried on, have made a Proposal for the writing a *Review,* to be entirely taken up upon the Subject of Trade." Nearly three years had elapsed since that proposal; and now, peace being restored to the maritime nations, came a favourable opportunity for effecting such a design.

On the 9th of May her Majesty communicated to the House of Commons the several Treaties of Peace and Commerce between Great Britain and France. Very shortly afterward Defoe published an able Tract, entitled " An Essay on the Treaty·of Commerce with France : with Necessary Expositions. London. Printed for J. Baker, at the Black-Boy in Paternoster Row, 1713." Our author was nearly a century and a half in advance of general public opinion on these topics. He believed that international reduction and abolition of duties, would increase trade, cheapen commodities, promote national and individual prosperity, and become the most powerful guarantee of a lasting peace. To use the modern phrase, Defoe was the first and foremost advocate of " Free Trade."

In conjunction with some others, who had become enlightened by the essays in his *Review,*—and certainly with the approbation of the Earl of Oxford,—it was determined to commence a new periodical paper, to be confined entirely to this subject. In pursuance of such resolution, while the Bill on Commerce was before Parliament, on the 26th of May, 1713, appeared the

first number of " Mercator, or Commerce Retrieved.   Being
Considerations on the State of the British Trade, particularly
as it respects Holland, France, and the Dutch Barrier; the Trade
to and from France; the Trade to Portugal, Spain, and the West
Indies, and the Fisheries of Newfoundland and Nova Scotia.
With other Matters and Advantages accruing to Great Britain by
the Treaty of Peace and Commerce, lately concluded at Utrecht."
Each number of *Mercator* consisted of one leaf small folio, and
it was continued every Tuesday, Thursday, and Saturday, until
the 20th of July, 1714, the last number being 181.   The
Ministry not only sanctioned but assisted the Managers of the
Paper, by placing at their service the Customs Returns of
Imports and Exports, and other national sources of commercial
revenue, for statistical purposes.   It is a significant fact, that
Mercator ceased to exist only seven days before the discord
which had long reigned in the Cabinet was brought to a climax,
by the dismissal of the Earl of Oxford from his office of Lord
Treasurer.

I shall have to consider presently the writers of *Mercator*;
and would observe here, that the supporters of the Paper,—of
the Treaty of Commerce,—and the doctrines of Free Trade,
were chiefly Tories; the Whigs espousing the principles of
protection and prohibition.   To promote the latter, a Paper
was established in opposition to *Mercator*, with the title of
the " British Merchant, or Commerce Preserved."   This was
published twice weekly, and was written by Henry Martin,
afterward Inspector-General of Exports and Imports, assisted
by several eminent Whig merchants, and patronised by the
Earls of Halifax and Stanhope.   The *British Merchant* was
but too successful in exciting the alarm of the ignorant multitude; and in convincing them that the continuance of prohibi-
tory duties, and restrictions on imports from abroad, were
necessary to prevent the threatened destruction of home manufactures.   Beneath this popular agitation, however, there was
concealed, an object far more important to the political partizan than the Trade of the Kingdom, namely, the defeat of the
Government; and this was accomplished when the House of
Commons, by a majority of nine votes, rejected the Treaty of
Commerce, and deprived the Nation of the only substantial
Advantage it could have derived from the negociations at

Utrecht.   The superficial and narrow doctrines of the *British Merchant* long retained their hold, not only upon the unthinking, but on the esteem of merchants, economists, and statesmen.   The work was several times reprinted, and is even now commonly met with.

When the political strife ended with its occasion, the teachings of *Mercator* were forgotten.   Few understood, and fewer cared for, the far-sighted views, and the peaceful and happy consequences of a free interchange, among all nations, of the peculiar productions of each.   The work was never reprinted ; it soon sank into oblivion ; and, within the present century a perfect copy was not known to exist.   Now, that the world has grown wiser, and adopted Free Trade, it may be interesting to state that a complete set is to be found in the British Museum, another in the Bodleian Library, and that several other copies are known.

I must notice, as briefly as possible, the controverted opinions that have been expressed as to the authorship of *Mercator*.   That Defoe was concerned in its origin, and wrote for it to some extent, has never, I believe, been disputed. Contemporary authors, inimical to him, including Boyer, Oldmixon, Tindal, and the writers of the British Merchant, reviled him as being in the same sense the Author of *Mercator*, as he had been for many years of the *Review*.   Within six months after the termination of *Mercator*, Defoe vindicated himself, in his " Appeal to Honour and Justice," against these reproaches, in words which I shall presently consider.   From a misunderstanding of such vindication, Mr. Chalmers, Defoe's first biographer, rejected Mercator, stating as his reason, that Defoe had himself repudiated it, and that it was " written by William Brown and his assistants ;" and he consistently, though in error, omitted it from his List of Defoe's Works. Mr. Wilson, however, has inserted *Mercator* in his Catalogue of Defoe's Writings, though he states that Defoe had little to do with it, and adds, " Mr. Chalmers, whose judgment will be most approved, gives the true history and character of these papers."   It is but justice to Mr. Wilson to say that he does not appear to have ever seen *Mercator;* and that, while forbearing to express any decisive opinion, he has supplied all

the evidence he could obtain.*   Mr. Hazlitt, whose Life of
Defoe is, in most respects, a mere abstract from Wilson, omits
any reference to *Mercator ;* and appends a " chronological
catalogue of the Works of Daniel Defoe," from which it is
also excluded.   But he adds a List of " Works which have
been attributed" to him ; and in such List, *Mercator* is included, with the statements quoted by Mr. Wilson.   Mr.
Forster, with far greater discernment, though less research,
says Defoe argued " the question of Free Trade, which he
dealt with in a spirit greatly in advance of his time, chiefly in
a Government Paper, called the *Mercator,* set on foot by
Harley, in which he had no personal or pecuniary interest,
and over which he exercised no control, but to whose pages
he contributed a series of most remarkable papers on commercial subjects."†

At the time when *Mercator* was commenced, in May
1713, our author was in the anomalous position of awaiting
his trial on a government Indictment, for the publication of his
three Tracts in favour of the Protestant Succession.   It is
easy to suppose him assured that such trial should never take
place, that the Queen would issue a pardon and indemnity ;
yet that Pardon did not receive the Great Seal until the 20th
of November following.   It must be remembered, also, that
on the 22nd of April, he had been committed to the Queen's
Bench prison for an inadvertent reflection, in his *Review,* on
the Lord Chief Justice ; and whether or not he had been
liberated, before the commencement of *Mercator,* of which
we have no evidence, he could not but feel that his future
freedom of action was uncertain, and beset with difficulty.
Further, his *Review* was still in existence ; and peremptorily
required the preparation of two numbers weekly.   We may
believe therefore that, with the concurrence of Lords Oxford
and Bolingbroke, Defoe was the active originator of *Mercator ;*
but, that there were satisfactory reasons for his declining the
official responsibility of conducting the Paper ; and, that it was
accordingly placed in the hands of William Brown, Defoe undertaking gratuitous assistance and advice.   The *Mercator* was

---

* Wilson's " Life of Defoe," iii. pp. 331-8.
† " Daniel Defoe," by John Forster, 1855, p. 126.

but fairly launched, however, when it became known that it would soon have to contend with a rival, powerfully supported by the opponents of the government; and, it seems probable that, under the circumstances, Defoe was induced to lay down the *Review*, on the 11th of June, in order that the whole strength of the advocates of Free Trade might be consolidated against the projected *British Merchant*.

I must make one further remark before quoting Defoe's own explanation; because, from the misunderstanding of a single word, has resulted all the confusion already noticed, as to the authorship of *Mercator*. The word "Author," had a much wider signification in literature, during the early part of the last century, than now; and when applied to a Journal, or periodical publication, meant neither more nor less than the modern term "editor." A man might be the responsible author of a Paper, and yet, any proportion of its numbers, not the product of his own pen. Inversely, a gratuitous writer, of any number of Essays, might not be the author of the Paper. Defoe says—"There is a mighty charge against me for being Author and Publisher of a Paper call'd The MERCATOR. I'll state the Fact first, and then speak to the Subject. It is true, that being desir'd to give my Opinion in the Affair of the Commerce with France, I did, as I often had done in Print many Years before, declare, That it was my Opinion we ought to have an open Trade with France, because I did believe we might have the Advantage by such a Trade; and of this opinion I am still. What Part I had in the *Mercator* is well known; and would Men answer with Argument, and not with personal Abuses, I would, at any Time, defend every Part of the *Mercator* which was of my doing. But to say the Mercator was mine, is false; I was neither the Author of it, had the Property of it, the Printing of it, or the Profit by it. I never had any Payment or Reward for writing any Part of it; nor had I the Power to put what I would into it : Yet the whole Clamour fell upon me, because they knew not who else to load with it. And when they came to Answer, the method was, instead of Argument, to threaten, and reflect upon me; reproach me with private Circumstances and Misfortunes, and give Language which no Christian ought to give, and which no Gentleman ought to take. I thought any Englishman had the Liberty to speak his Opinion in such Things ; for this had nothing to do with the Publick.   The Press was open to me as well as to others ; and how, or when I lost my English Liberty of speaking my Mind, I know not ; neither how my speaking my Opinion without Fee or Reward could authorize them to call me Villain, Rascal, Traytor, and such opprobrious Names."*

It is scarcely necessary to recapitulate.   Defoe was charged, under the words " Author and Publisher," with being the proprietor, editor, manager, and writer of *Mercator*.   He admits having had a part in it, and having written for it ; but denies that it was entirely his writing, or that he was the conductor, or had the control over it, or received payment for what he wrote. All this is true ; and is yet quite consistent with the fact,— obvious to any critical student of the *Review* and the *Mercator*, —that the same principles of Trade and Commerce,—the same mind and genius,—the same happy turns of thought, and power of illustration,—the same clearness, even to redundancy, of expression,—and the same decorum and calmness of temper under extreme provocation, animates both these Works.   The *Mercator* is the sequel to the *Review ;* it had been conceived years before in Defoe's mind ; and though some parts of it were not actually written with his pen, any List of his Works, from which *Mercator* was excluded, would certainly be incomplete.

So much time has been occupied in clearing up the authorship of *Mercator*, that I must only refer briefly to other Works of Defoe on the same subject.   On the 2nd of June he published a pamphlet, entitled " Considerations upon the Eighth and Ninth Articles of the Treaty of Commerce and Navigation.   Now publish'd by Authority.   With some Enquiries into the Damages that may accrue to the English Trade from them.   London.   J. Baker.   1713."   This was immediately followed by another, entitled " Some Thoughts upon the Subject of Commerce with France.   By the Author of the Review. London.   J. Baker.   1713."   In the beginning of August he commenced a further work, which he published in four fort-

---

* " Appeal to Honour and Justice," pp. 47-8.

nightly parts, during that and the following month, with the title of " A General History of Trade ; and Especially considered as it respects British Commerce, &c. &c. London. J. Baker. 1713." In Part I., published August 1st, he considered " the Improvement of our Trade in particular." Part II. contains " a Discourse of the Use of Harbours and Roads for Shipping, and particularly to the filling up the Harbour of Dunkirk." Part III. contains " An Attempt to State and Moderate the present Disputes about settling a Commerce between Great Britain and France." I have not been able to see the fourth and last Part.

CHAPTER IX.

Defoe publishes " Whigs turned Tories, and Hanoverian Tories proved Whigs"—" A Strict Enquiry into the Circumstance of a late Duel"— " Union and no Union"—" A Letter to the Dissenters"—" The Scots Nation and Union Vindicated"—"A View of the real Danger of the Protestant Succession"—" Reasons for Impeaching the Lord High Treasurer"—An Act passed to prevent the growth of Schism—Defoe publishes " The Remedy worse than the Disease" — Dissension in the Ministry—Lord Oxford dismissed — The Queen dies — Defoe writes " The Flying Post and Medley"—Defoe committed for trial on a charge of reflecting on the Lords Regents — Writes his " Appeal to Honour and Justice"—Publishes " Advice to the People of Great Britain"—" The Secret History of the White Staff," Part I. and Part II.—Defoe struck with apoplexy—Publishes Part III. of " The Secret History of the White Staff"—" A Reply to a Traitorous Libel"—" A Friendly Reproof to Thomas Bradbury."

1713–15.

THE disorganized condition of parties in Church and State has been already noticed. The Tories were divided and subdivided; the same·might be said of the Whigs. In Convocation, and among the clergy generally, the differences were as numerous, and animosity equally violent. Repulsion rather than cohesion, and faction instead of party, had become so much the character of the time, that while the extremes continued to diverge, some Tories acted as Whigs, and some Whigs appeared as Tories. Moderate men still existed, but in Church and in State, there were open advocates of the Pretender. Clergymen were to be found teaching all the errors of Popery, while some of their brethren inculcated a Sceptical latitudinarianism. Defoe had long persevered in unthankful efforts to promote peace and union, and foreseeing that the increasing estrangement and exasperation tended to a national crisis, he now published a pamphlet, entitled " Whigs turned Tories ; and Hanoverian Tories, from their avowed Principles, proved Whigs ; or, each in the other mistaken. Being a plain proof that each Party deny that Charge which the others bring against them ; and that neither Side will disown those which the other profess. With an earnest Exhortation to all Whigs as well as Hanoverian Tories to lay aside those uncharitable heats among such Protestants, and seriously to consider, and effectually to provide against those Jacobite, Popish, and conforming Tories, whose principal Ground of Hope to ruin all sincere Protestants, is from those unchristian and violent Feuds among ourselves. London. Printed for J. Baker. 1713."

An unhappy illustration of the spirit of the times, in suggesting the commission of the very highest crimes as the result of party rage, is afforded by the doubly fatal duel between the Duke of Hamilton and Lord Mohun, which occurred on the 15th of November, 1712. Col. Macartney, the Second of Lord Mohun, fled to the Continent, but Col. Hamilton, who had attended the Duke, surrendered ; and, in his examination before a Committee of Council, insinuated that, after both the noble Lords had fallen, his Grace received his death-blow from Macartney. The Duke was a high Tory, and attempts were immediately made, on the part of the Jacobites, to show that a foul murder had been committed ; and, that Whig politics were concerned in the matter. Boyer gives currency to so base a rumour by saying, " My Lord Mohun and Macartney were incited to undertake this Quarrel, by a certain Party of Men, who were no great Friends to the Government."* Ill as the Whigs had used Defoe, he could not suffer the party to be falsely branded with this horrid deed ; and early in the following year he wrote and published, " A Strict Enquiry Into the Circumstance of a late Duel, with some Account of the Persons concern'd on both Sides. Being a Modest Attempt to do Justice to the Injur'd Memory of a Noble Person DEAD, and to the Injur'd Honour of an Absent Person LIVING. To which is added the Substance of a Letter from General Macartney to his Friend. London. J. Baker. 1713." In this tract our author shows, that the quarrel between the two Lords was entirely about their respective property rights, and that they were engaged in a Chancery Suit against each other. To clear Macartney's honour in the matter, he shows the almost certainty that the Duke, being the insulted person, was the challenger. He is properly severe on the *Post-Boy* and the

---

* Boyer's " Life of Queen Anne," 1721. ii. 503-4.

Examiner, and also refers to Dyer, the Tory *News-writer*, but neither the severity of his facts or arguments prevented the repetition of so grave a political charge.

During the session of Parliament which ended on the 6th of July in this year, the people of Scotland showed much uneasiness on account of several alleged violations of the Treaty of Union; and particularly as to the great burden of the Malt Tax. After four of their Members had ineffectually attended upon her Majesty to seek for redress, it was resolved to bring their grievances before the House of Lords, which was done by the Earl of Finlater on the 28th of May, in a representation under four heads; and concluding with a motion for leave to bring in a bill " for dissolving the Union, and securing the Protestant succession in the House of Hanover, securing the Queen's Prerogative in both Kingdoms, and preserving an entire Amity and good Correspondence between the two Nations." The English Peers manifested so much indifference, that when the question was put, it was rejected by a majority of but four voices.   Defoe's interest in the welfare of Scotland, and the maintenance of the Union, was too great to admit of silence on such an occasion, and he published a pamphlet entitled, " Union and No Union. Being an Enquiry into the Grievances of the Scots.   And how far they are right or wrong, who allege that the Union is dissolved.   London, J. Baker, 1713."   The pamphlet is written with much tenderness to the Scotch People, but with equal faithfulness.   He admits that the imposition of the Malt Duty will be a great burden; but that the Articles of the Union only exempted Scotland during the War, leaving the future to the British Parliament.   He denies that those who are moving in the matter with so much resentment, speak the language of Scotland ; and shows that there is no ground for the assertion that the Union is dissolved.

The factious subdivisions into which the great national parties had now split, precluded all efficient legislative action. Each was so weak individually, as to require support, which could only be purchased by subservience; and each became exposed to the oppression of any two or more factions who

might temporarily unite for any common object. The disunion also gave a degree of prominence to individuals of each
clique, that could never have been attained so long as the term
Whig or Tory comprised the general policy of the legislature.
Every class had now its leaders, pushing with blind fury at
others, and apparently regardless of all consequences. The
Dissenters, in and out of Parliament, forgot how unable they
were to withstand any assault made by the High Church Tories
upon the Toleration, and joined themselves with the adherents
of the " old Ministry," in the most violent opposition to the
existing Government. Should they succeed, the Dissenters
would be immediately cast aside by their present allies, who
had recently assisted in passing, against them, the Occasional
Conformity Act. In case of failure, they would be abandoned
to the rage of an exasperated administration. · Defoe saw the
jeopardy of the people whom he had all his life endeavoured
to serve; and, notwithstanding their ingratitude, he was still
anxious to save them. On the 3rd of December, therefore,
he published a Tract, entitled, " A Letter to the Dissenters.
London. J. Morphew. 1713." The proceedings of the
Dissenters had already incensed the ministry, and this Tract
seems to convey that its writer had in some manner become
acquainted with the fact that a severe measure of repression
was contemplated. I allude to the Bill shortly afterward
brought into the House of Commons, by the Chancellor of
the Exchequer, to prevent the growth of Schism. This will
be considered presently, and is only mentioned now, as furnish-
ing a key to the otherwise inexplicable tone of threatening
with which Defoe supplements his arguments and advice to
the Dissenters. The opposition to the government had proceeded so far, that Defoe says it was made the Test of the faction, to which the political Dissenters had joined themselves,
" to drink an Unchristian, Bloody, and Treasonable Health,
viz., *To send the House of* HANOVER *speedily to the Throne.*"
And he says that some Dissenters had been drawn in to drink
it. He advises the whole body, that so long as the Queen and
her Ministry, (to whom they owe the continuance of their
Toleration,) do not break in upon the Constitution of the
Country, their measures should be supported ; but that, at
least, the Dissenters would serve their own interests by neu-
trality, much better than by their present conduct. His secret

information of what was contemplated against the Dissenters; and also, the disrepute in which he was now held by the Whigs, in consequence of the partial support, which his gratitude constrained him still to give to the general policy of Lord Oxford, rendered concealment necessary, in order that this pamphlet should obtain due attention. His stile appears somewhat disguised, and the publisher was changed, to avoid suspicion. The Tract was twice reprinted in 1714.

The last parliament of Queen Anne assembled, after several prorogations in consequence of her Majesty's illness, on the 16th of February, 1714, and soon gave promise of exceeding in faction, if possible, its predecessor. The Pretender and the Protestant Succession were the subjects of stormy debates in the early part of the Session, and the same topics agitated the whole country. Private friendships had been long giving way to the animosity of party spirit, and everything seemed to portend the near approach of a terrible Revolution. Something of the feverish state of the nation may be gathered from the severities inflicted at this time upon authors on both sides. On the day before the meeting of parliament Hilkiah Bedford was tried before Lord Chief Justice Parker, for writing a book which the Queen is said to have graciously accepted, entitled "The Hereditary Right of the Crown of England Asserted." He was sentenced to pay a fine of a thousand marks, to be imprisoned three years, and to find sureties in 5000*l.*, for his good behaviour during Life. To counteract the threatening aspect of the times Steele had in December preceding published his celebrated pamphlet "The Crisis," in support of the succession of the House of Hanover. He was a member of the new parliament, but for writing this tract, was in March, expelled from the House of Commons. Swift replied to Steele in a pamphlet entitled "The Publick Spirit of the Whigs," and for some scandalous reflections upon the Scottish peers, the House of Lords apprehended the printer and publisher,— Lord Oxford sent Swift, the author, 100*l.*, for the service of such printer and publisher,—and the Queen offered a reward of 300*l.* for the apprehension of the author,—who was pretended to be unknown. Swift's pamphlet was reprinted, and in the third edition he expunged the obnoxious paragraphs against the Scots,

yet Defoe again manifested his regard in a tract of unusual
warmth, entitled "The Scots Nation and Union Vindicated;
from the Reflections cast on them in an Infamous Libel, entitled *The Publick Spirit of the Whigs,* &c.   In which the most
Scandalous Paragraphs contained therein are fairly Quoted, and
fully Answered.   London.   A. Bell and J. Baker.   1714."

A considerable part of the month of April was taken up
with debates, in both Houses of parliament, on the question
whether or not the Protestant Succession was in danger under
her Majesty's Administration; and, in the midst of this agitation, Defoe prepared a very timely and assuring tract, the
title of which was intentionally designed to attract, but
does not fully agree with the contents.   It is called "A View
of the Real Danger of the Protestant Succession.   London.
J. Baker, 1714."   The object is to shew that the Government,
in their stipulations for peace, and the French King, in his
concessions under treaty, have done all that was possible to
secure the Protestant Succession; and that the suspicious
fears of those who lay so much stress upon our Treaty with
France, and upon the French influence, not only dishonour our
own Nation, but really weaken the Succession itself.   And this,
because the People of Britain are able to support the Succession,
and the Laws and Constitution, against the whole World.

While these discussions were going on, Baron Schutz, the
Minister from Hanover, was advised to apply for a writ calling
the Elector to the House of Lords, by the title of Duke
of Cambridge; in the hope that his presence would counteract
the intrigues of the Jacobites.   This gave offence to the Queen,
who, acting on the unwise counsel of some of her Ministers,
forbade the Count to appear again at Court.   Smarting under
this indignity he returned to Hanover, where the insult was
not suffered to be forgotten, until afterward avenged on the
offenders, and all connected with them.

The dissensions among the Ministers, especially between
Lords Oxford and Bolingbroke, had degenerated into intense
hatred, and many of the more moderate Supporters of the
Government deserted them; but they were still able to com-
mand majorities affirming, in both Houses, that the Protestant
Succession was not in danger under her Majesty's Administra-

tion.   Dark hints, and rumours of impeachments, against one
or more of the Ministry began to be whispered; and, in closing
the debate of the House of Commons, Sir Thomas Hanmer,
the Speaker, said "that a great deal of pains had been taken
to screen some Persons."   He also noticed that Sir Patrick
Lawless, an outlawed adherent of King James II., had been "suffered to come over, and admitted to an Audience of the Queen."

We have recently seen Defoe answering with some bitterness a book written by Swift, whom Lord Oxford rewarded
for the same.   Other, and abundant proof might be given of
our author's continued independence; and, that his heart still
beat true to the same principles that had guided him through
life.   But his sagacious mind foresaw that love of power had
connected Lord Oxford with associates who would effect his
destruction.   Defoe believed, and he was probably right, that
his Lordship was still warmly attached to the Protestant
interest; but he did not share his Lordship's belief that he
still could over-rule, or circumvent, those with whom he was
acting.   About a week after the close of the remarkable
debate above mentioned, Defoe published,—with the hope of
saving his first benefactor from what he perceived was impending,—a pamphlet bearing the following remarkable title,
"Reasons for Im——— the L——d H——— T——-r, And
some others of the P——— M———.   Printed and Sold
by J. Moore near St. Pauls."*   The tract is written with
great profession of impartiality, and much skill.   He urges
that the authors of every evil thing should be brought to
Justice, "however great they may be, or whatever Protection
they may seek shelter under;" but innocent persons should be
defended and cleared from "Slander and unjust Reproach
which the great Men now so much complain of."   He thinks
that in the debates on the danger of the Protestant Succession,

---

* Notwithstanding the secresy observed in the publication of this pam-
phlet, its authorship was quickly known.   In a tract called "The
Impeachment, &c., &c.   By the unknown Author of Neck or Nothing,"
(John Dunton,) published a few days afterward, six columns are devoted to
"An Answer to D——— F———'s daring the P———t to impeach the P———
M———, as I find it inserted in his Ironical Treatise, intituled, *Reasons
for Im——— the L——— H——— T———r, and some others of the P———
M———.*"

the words *under the Queen's Administration* were ill brought
in; and says, that the Queen's name is alleged to be used as
" a screen under which the People pointed at are sheltered
from the Prosecution which would otherwise be brought against
them." He adds, the first thing that ought to have been
settled was whether the Succession was in danger, or not. Few
men could, under such a title, have so dexterously managed a
constitutional argument in support of the Ministry; yet
assuming throughout, that to endanger the Protestant Succession would deserve impeachment.

It would be but a probable speculation that when Defoe
wrote his " Letter to the Dissenters," cautioning them to
moderation in political conduct, and warning them of threatened
evil, he had received an intimation from Lord Oxford of the
measure then being concocted by Lord Bolingbroke, and his
section of the Ministry. However that might be, on the 12th
of May, a bill was brought into the Commons by Sir William
Wyndham, Chancellor of the Exchequer, " To prevent the
Growth of Schism, and for the further Security of the Church
of England, as by law Established." By this Bill no person
was to act as a Schoolmaster, without a license from the
bishop, and a certificate of conformity, from the clergyman of
his parish; and no catechism was to be taught except that in
the Book of Common Prayer. By such means it was intended
to shut up all the schools of Dissenters throughout the
Kingdom; and to take out of their hands the education of
their own children. The measure was strongly opposed in
both Houses, but it passed the Commons on the 1st of June,
the Lords on the 15th, and received the royal assent ten days
afterward. This unjust Act, which even the Earl of Nottingham designated " a barbarous invasion of the natural rights
of parents," was to have come into operation on the very day
the Queen died. Soon after the accession of George I. it was
repealed. Justice to Lord Treasurer Oxford requires me to
say, that he endeavoured to prevent this crushing blow at the
Dissenters; he then made an effort to modify it,—but his influence in the Government, of which he was still the nominal
head,—was rapidly declining, and he absented himself from the
House upon the final decision.

Defoe could not remain silent on a subject involving the very existence of those for whose rights he had earnestly contended, during more than a quarter of a century. On the 9th of June he therefore published a pamphlet entitled, "The Remedy worse than the Disease : or, Reasons against passing the Bill for preventing the Growth of Schism. To which is added, a brief Discourse of Toleration and Persecution, Shewing their unavoidable Effects, Good or Bad ; and Proving that neither Diversity of Religions, nor Diversity in the same Religion, are dangerous, much less Inconsistent with good Government. In a Letter to a Noble Earl. *Hæc sunt enim Fundamenta firmissima nostræ Libertatis, sui quemque juris et retinendi et dimittendi esse dominum.* Cic. in Orat. pro Balbo. London. Printed for J. Baker, 1714." Valuable as this pamphlet was designed to be, its voice fell upon the ears of those who were deaf to conviction. But the boldness and faithfulness of his arguments and denunciations,—at a period when it was dangerous to speak plainly against Government,— and by a writer under the false imputation of being the paid hireling of the same Government, invest this publication with peculiar importance, as a permanent refutation of the calumnies with which Defoe was at that time assailed.

Except so far as he was an Englishman, who had taken an active part in public affairs, the few remaining events of the Queen's reign little concern the personal history of Defoe. Her Majesty could no longer bear the load of distracting care that weighed upon her, and the Parliament was hastily prorogued on the 9th of July. The Ministry were now not merely in open hostility among themselves, but in their struggles for superiority they dealt out the bitterest reproaches and personal recriminations, even in the royal presence. The intrigues of Bolingbroke at length succeeded, and on the evening of the 27th of July, her Majesty reluctantly dismissed Lord Oxford from her service. After this, the Cabinet became a scene of anarchy. The Queen was upon the borders of the grave ; Lord Bolingbroke aspired to the chief direction of affairs, and this occasioned a fresh outburst of fury, which was carried into the chamber of the Queen, and was there prolonged, with noise and fierceness, until past mid-

night.   As a consequence of this cruel disturbance, she was
thrown into dreadful agitation; followed by alarming symptoms,
that continued to increase, and indicated a speedy dissolution.
In this emergency the Privy Council met, and agreed to
recommend the Duke of Shrewsbury for the Office of Lord
Treasurer, so that there might be a responsible head of the
Ministry.   This being intimated to the dying Queen, during a
lucid interval, she readily placed the Staff in the Duke's hands;
and, by so doing, added despair to the already overflowing rage
of Lord Bolingbroke and his friends.   The Queen relapsed
soon afterward into insensibility; and, upon the following day,
being the first of August, she expired, at Kensington, in the
fiftieth year of her age, and the thirteenth of her reign.

I have already stated that the *Mercator* was discontinued on
the 20th of July, 1714, when the fall of the Earl of Oxford was
imminent, and the Customs returns, upon which the statistics
of the Paper were based, would probably be no longer accessible.   Its adversary, the *British Merchant,* also retired from
the field on the 31st of the same month.   I have also noticed
that Ridpath, the owner and writer of the *Flying Post,* was
bitterly hostile to Defoe.   At the time when the *Mercator*
ceased, Ridpath " was out of the country," (probably in Scotland, his native place,) and had left his Paper in charge of
several Whig friends, with full powers.   William Hurt had
been for a long time the printer and publisher of Ridpath's
Paper; but, it having reached the ears of the temporary
managers, that he had some intercourse or audience with the
obnoxious writer of the late *Mercator,* the *Flying Post* was so
instantly taken out of Hurt's hands, that the next number,
July 24th, appeared as printed and published by R. Tookey.
This act of petty tyranny was practically resented, by Defoe
undertaking to write for Hurt; and, on the 27th, was published
the first number of a Paper, of the same size and form as
Ridpath's, but bearing the title of " The Flying Post and
Medley."   The word " Medley" was dropped after the first few
numbers, and thus there were two Papers having the same
title, and each published thrice a week.   Ridpath, in derision,
distinguished his opponent by the name of " The *Sham Flying
Post.*"   In the opening number of the new Paper, Hurt is

made to address his readers in the third person, " Hoping, without any invidious competitions, that the Person he employs may answer the publick Expectation, whether on the score of a News or a Political Writer, as well as any of those Gentlemen who are set up against him, as he thinks, without any just reason." In this undertaking Defoe no doubt calculated upon the hostility of Ridpath and his friends, who would carefully watch for any opportunity of silencing him ; but he knew that in so doing they would only pursue the same course they had done for years ; and, when resisting oppression, or advocating the truth, he was too fearless to regard the utmost malice of men.

It is not my intention to occupy unnecessary space with the labours of Defoe upon this Paper, but as this episode of his life and writings, will be new to the world, I cannot forbear transcribing the following eloquently drawn character of King George I., published the 14th of August, 1714, in the *Flying Post*, Number IX., before the King had left Hanover, and written by Defoe in the form of a Letter from abroad :—" You write to me to give you my Thoughts of his Majesty, and tell me, the People of England long to Know something of the King that is to govern them. I am very uncapable to give a just Character of his Person, or of his personal Accomplishments, tho' I have resided at his Court for Twelve Years ; but I am very free to tell you, in few Words, he will fully answer the Expectations, nay, the very Wishes, of the People of England ; and has a Temper so suited to the Majesty of his Office as King, and to the Genius of the Nation he is to govern, as will abundantly testify, that Providence has determin'd him from his Infancy to fill that Throne.

" In few Words then, his Person is Comely and Grave, his Countenance has Majesty and Sweetness so mixt, that nothing can be better suited to the Throne of a King ;—He speaks readily rather than fluently, apt and proper, without long Premeditation, or Affectation of being quick. His Temper is Goodness itself; inexpressible Obliging,—to the last degree Courteous and Kind, yet not lowered beneath the Dignity of his Birth. He is steady in Council,—Sedate in Resolving,— Vigorous in Executing,—Brave and Gallant in the Field,—

Wise and Politick in the Camp,—Enterprizing in the matter of
Action,—and yet of so calm a Courage, that he who dares do
any thing that is fit to do, can never be in danger of precipi-
tating into what is impracticable to be done.   In short, if it
may be said of any Man in Europe, it may be said of his
Majesty, that he is born for Council, and fitted to command
the World.

·   " It has been suggested by the sworn Enemies of your Religion and Liberties, that his Majesty was of arbitrary Principles, positive and reserv'd, that having been an absolute
Prince in his own Dominions, he would be impatient of the
Restraint which our Laws and Constitution in Britain seem to
lay upon the Crown,—and the like slanderous Jacobite Notions;
but assure yourselves in England, that these are very unjust
and groundless Suggestions, his Majesty being by his Native
Inclinations, Generous and Compassionate, far from any Arbitrary and Tyrannical Principles, full of Clemency and Goodness: And tho' in his own Dominions the Nature of his
Government differs from ours in England, and puts it more in
the Power of the Prince to oppress his People, yet he is far
from exercising his Sovereignty in an Arbitrary and Tyrannical
Manner; and seeing this Prince is universally beloved of his
own Subjects, and that there is not the least Complaint of
Oppression or Severity among them, even where it is so much
in his Power to do it, this methinks, should convince an un-
prejudiced Person, that it is not in his Nature to Oppress, and
that his Majesty has not any Taint of Arbitrary or Tyrannical
Principles in him.

" It is a Work not to be prescribed by the short compass of
a Letter, to give a full Character of this Prince.   I conclude
with assuring you, that you will have great Reason to believe
yourselves happy under his Government, and that you may
expect from him all that Sweetness of Disposition, that
Clemency of Government, that unperverted Justice to the
Constitution, and that Affection to the People of Britain, that
can be desired, and that are requisite to the constituting a
Prince the true Father of his Country.   God send his Majesty
safe among you, and that when you have him, you may lay
aside your Parties, your private Feuds and Animosities, that you
may make his Days happy, and his Reign Glorious.   Amen."

In the Regency appointed to govern the country until the arrival of the King, was included the name of the Earl of Anglesey, who had been dispatched in the latter part of July to Ireland, by the Bolingbroke faction of the Ministry, to assist the Jacobite Lord Chancellor, Sir Constantine Phipps, in arbitrarily putting down the Whig Corporation of Dublin. His Lordship had however only arrived 14 or 15 hours, before an Express came with news of the Queen's death; upon which their evil intentions were frustrated, and Lord Anglesey immediately reimbarked for England, to take his seat among the Lords Regents. This remarkable journey,—one way to strengthen the Pretender's interest, and back again to support King George,—was but an unit among numerous strange metamorphoses consequent upon the distraction of parties, and the Queen's unexpected decease. The circumstances having been variously reported, Defoe wrote the following Letter, and inserted it in Hurt's *Flying Post* of the 19th August :—

" Sir, You cannot be ignorant of the late Journey of a No : Pe–r to Ireland, being dispatched thither by the new modelled Juncto of the last Ministry ; part of the Design of which we are assur'd was, to new model the Forces there, and particularly to break no less than 70 of the Honest Officers of the Army, and to fill up their Places with the Tools and Creatures of Con. Phi—s, and such a Rabble of Cut-throats as were fit for the Work that they had for them to do. Among these, I am assur'd Capt. Tho. Hales was to be one to be disbanded,—the same who commanded at the Tolsey in Dublin, at the Time of the Election for that City, and at the late Tumult there, when the honest Recorder, and a great many Protestant Gentlemen, had been made a Sacrifice to a Popish Rabble, if the said Captain Hales had not sent his Guard to their Relief. But Heaven has defeated this wicked Contrivance, and now the Wretches who had swallowed up the Protestant Interest in Ireland in the Hopes of their Party, and who were resolved in a short time to have betray'd that Kingdom into the Hands of Popery and the Pretender, are in the greatest Confusion imaginable, and have little to expect but the Punishment they have deserved.

" The said Capt. Hales, with Col. Windervis, Col. Fane, Capt. Walker, and several other Protestant Officers, are now going to their Post; and, no question it will be a Satisfaction to the City of Dublin to see that worthy Officer,—who so timely rescued that City from the Fury of a Popish Tumult,— be again at the Head of the same brave Troops with which he perform'd it; and this, notwithstanding the arbitrary Scheme of some People lately in Power.   Your Humble Servant."

In any general history of the times, the above document would scarcely find a place; but as part of the history of Daniel Defoe, it may be doubted whether he ever penned a more important political paper.   It was indeed the axis upon which all his future life was made to turn; as will be shortly apparent.   Nor was it, in its results, of small importance to the high state officials in Ireland, whose maladministration it dragged before the public.

I must observe that though the Letter indicates the Earl of Anglesey, it neither names him, nor alludes to the Lords Regents, nor to the fact that the Earl was one of that illustrious body;—which consisted of twenty-six members,—about three-fourths of whom were Whigs.   His Lordship must therefore have been highly enraged before he was induced, on the 21st, to complain to their Excellencies of this Letter, as a reflection calling for their interference.

The *Post-Boy*, (a Tory Paper,) of the 24th, says, " By particular Directions of the Lords Justices, the Printer and Publisher of the Flying Post, were order'd to be taken up last Saturday, for scandalous Reflections, lately printed in that Paper, upon several of his Majesty's Loyal Subjects, particularly their Excellencies."   After an examination they were liberated on bail; and Defoe, to release them from the charge, avowed himself the author of the Letter; and was committed for trial, but similarly liberated.   These circumstances, however, induced the Lords Regents to inquire into the allegations of the Letter; and, in the beginning of September, notwithstanding all the efforts of the Earl of Anglesey, and two or three other members, Sir Constantine Phipps and the Archbishop of Armagh, were both removed from being Lords Justices of Ireland, and immediately after the King's arrival, Sir Constantine was also dismissed from his office of Lord Chancellor.

Little more than a year had elapsed since Defoe had stood arraigned of writing three Tracts in favour of the Pretender; and, when he affirmed that they were ironical, and in favour of the House of Hanover, he was reviled, by a Judge on the Bench, with the horrors of a traitor's death.   Now, the cause in which he had so long and so patriotically struggled was triumphant; — the Protestant religion was no longer in danger,—and the House of Hanover had succeeded to the throne of Great Britain; but Defoe, who in the loyalty of his heart had written and published that character of the new King which I have transcribed into these pages, was within a week thereafter, in the grasp, not of the law,—nor of justice,— but of his enemies, for writing in the same Journal openly and unmistakeably against the Pretender, and his adherents. True, he was not in prison; but, taking all the circumstances into account, could his future be more full of gloomy apprehensions ?   Under heavy bail to appear and take his trial, as a criminal to the state,—should he continue to write in the Flying Post, or otherwise in favour of the government, he would be reproached with fawning and cringing to obtain mercy;—and, if he should remain silent under this new misfortune, his enemies would rejoice, that at length they had crushed him.   Add to this the sense of desolation; he was unhinged,—cast off,—separated from all parties,—and apparently shut out from any further service of his country,—or benefit to himself and family.   The reaction of his hitherto indomitable spirit was now clearly failing him, or he would have seen that the speedy dismissal of Sir Constantine Phipps and others, against all the efforts of his accuser Lord Anglesey, was a virtual justification of himself, and an assurance that he need not fear the result of his impending trial.

I cannot doubt it was in this state of mind and circumstance, bending under the weight of calumny and injustice, and stung by the ingratitude of his friends, that he sat down and wrote one of the most manly yet deeply pathetic utterances of a human heart,—his " Appeal to Honour and Justice. Tho' it be of his Worst Enemies.   By Daniel De Foe.   Being a True Account of his Conduct in Publick Affairs.   London. Printed for J. Baker, 1715."   This was not published until

the first week in January, but had been written some time
before he was struck down with apoplexy, about the middle
of the preceding November. The biographers of Defoe, not
knowing at what time in 1715, this book was published, have
experienced great difficulty in explaining some parts of its
contents consistently with the periods at which other works by
him were evidently composed, between the death of the Queen
and the publication of this "Appeal." Speaking of works
being attributed to him that he had no hand in writing, he
says, "I have now resolved, for some time, to write nothing
at all; and yet I find it the same thing."*

These specific words include all forms of writing for publication, and prove that the "Appeal" was not begun on the
19th of August, when we last find him in the *Flying Post*.
He must have finished writing this "Appeal" not later than
about the 1st of October, because within two pages from the
end he says, "I have meddled neither one way or other, nor
written one Book since the Queen's Death."† Yet his pamphlet entitled, "Advice to the People of Great Britain," was
published on the 7th of October. That Defoe was carefully
accurate in these statements is evident, in that he does not
here disclaim having written in Journals on ordinary topics
since the Queen's death, but only books. This rectification
removes all difficulty as to the chronology of his Works during
the latter part of 1714, and the early part of the following
year; and, I trust will be considered of some importance. A
natural shrinking from a public "Appeal" as to his own
conduct, and that of his friends and foes,—the desire to carefully revise a manuscript that challenged "even his worst
Enemies;" and, moreover, the expressed intention of extending
it, sufficiently account for its non-publication during October
and the early part of November.

Defoe had not forgotten the offence, taken the year preceding by the Lord Chief Justice, at his then allusion in the
Review to proceedings *sub judice*, and, therefore, he does not
refer, in his "Appeal," to the Indictment now hanging over
his head; but, in order to show the circumstances in which he

---

* "Appeal to Honour and Justice," p. 47.   † Ibid. p. 55.

was placed, he says, "No sooner was the Queen Dead, and the King, as Right required, proclaim'd, but the Rage of Men Encreased upon me to that Degree, that the Threats and Insults I receiv'd were such as I am not able to express. If I offered to say a word in favour of the Present Settlement, it was called fawning and turning round again; on the other hand, tho' I have meddled neither one way or other, nor written one Book since the Queen's Death, yet a great many things are call'd by my Name, and I bear every Day the Reproaches which all the Answerers of those Books cast as well upon the Subject as the Authors. I have not seen or spoken to my Lord of Oxford but once since the King's Landing, nor received the least Message, Order, or Writing from his Lordship, or any other way Corresponded with him, yet he bears the Reproach of my Writing in his Defence, and I the Rage of Men for doing it. I cannot say it is no Affliction to me to be thus used, tho' my being entirely clear of the Facts is a true support to me. I am unconcerned at the Rage and Clamour of Party-Men; but I cannot be unconcerned to hear Men, who I think are good Men and good Christians, prepossessed and mistaken about me: However, I cannot doubt but some time or other it will please God to open such Men's Eyes. A Constant, steady adhering to personal Virtue, and to publick Peace, which, I thank God I can appeal to him, has always been my Practice; will at last restore me to the Opinion of sober and impartial Men, and that is all I desire."

I have already referred to the time of writing Defoe's pamphlet entitled, "Advice to the People of Great Britain, With respect to Two Important Points of their Future Conduct. I. What they ought to expect from the King. II. How they ought to behave to him. London. J. Baker, 1714." It must suffice here to say that it is a loyal and earnest exhortation to all Britons to consider their present happy circumstances, and to lay aside all faction and feuds of parties, to cultivate a Spirit of Moderation and Union,—to study to be quiet, like good subjects, faithfully, loyally, with obedience and affection;—and, like good Christians, living under the King in all godliness and honesty. Part of the Tract seems to have been composed before the King arrived in England, on the

18th of September, though it was not published until the following month.

The accession of the new King, and the fall of the late
Government accused of desiring to restore popery and arbitrary power, conducted Defoe's mind back to the period
immediately following the Revolution.   There is nothing more
to connect his next publication with the time of its appearance,
which was shortly after the Queen's death ; and probably, the
substance of the Tract had been long previously written.   It
is entitled, " A Secret History of One Year.   London.   Sold
by J. Baker at the Black Boy in Pater-Noster Row.   Pr. 6d.
1714." 8vo. pp. 40.   The year, of which the pamphlet forms
the secret history, is the first after the Revolution, and the
author vindicates King William's memory, 1st, from the charge
of self-interest and ambition in seeking and obtaining the
Crown ; and 2nd, from criminal clemency in not punishing
the abettors of King James's arbitrary Government.   The
" secret" part consists of what " a certain grave Gentleman,
well-known, if it were convenient to publish his Name" relates
" from the Mouth of his late Majesty K. William ;" and
though there is some little effort to mistify the reader, yet
there can be very little doubt that the supposed " Relator" was
Defoe himself.   He shews that the King first advanced and
employed men who had been prominently concerned in forwarding the Revolution ; but that the rapacity of too many of.
them, for places and pensions, became so insatiable that his
Majesty was at length compelled, for his own sake, and by his
duty to the Nation, to dismiss them from the Court and
Government ; and, as a consequence, to employ men belonging
to the other great party in the state, but who had abandoned
the cause of the late King.   I think this one of the most
valuable of Defoe's historical tracts.

The storm of calumny and reproach that fell upon Defoe
immediately after the Queen's death, was but a sprinkling of
the general execration which on every side assailed her
Ministers, and especially the Earl of Oxford.   The Tower,
impeachment, and the scaffold, began to be topics of discourse
in the streets and coffee-houses, and were soon after the subjects
of a swarm of pamphlets, openly published.   At such a time,

and under such circumstances, personal and relative, we are constrained to admire the courage, the faithfulness and gratitude of Defoe. He could not have been blamed had he remained silent,—the late Lord Treasurer's recent policy was such as he could by no means approve; but he could never forget the benefactor who had taken him out of a dungeon, and procured him the royal favour,—nor hold his peace while that benefactor was threatened with destruction. To vindicate his Lordship, therefore, he published in the beginning of October a shilling pamphlet entitled, "The Secret History of the White Staff, Being an Account of Affairs under the Conduct of some late Ministers, and of what might have happened if Her Majesty had not Died. London. J. Baker. 1714." The agitated condition of public opinion may be judged of, to some extent, by the fact that the first edition was instantly sold; the *second* was issued on the 7th, and on the 27th of the same month the *fourth* edition was published. Taking advantage of the avidity with which it had been received, "Part II." having the same title, appeared on the last-mentioned day. This was almost equally successful, three editions having been sold off before the end of the year. There is good reason to believe that the manuscript of a third part was in a forward state when our Author was attacked with Apoplexy about the middle of November, and it was necessarily laid aside, until after his recovery, being published, as "Part III." on the 29th of January, 1715, with the same title, as before. The three parts were republished as a complete work of more than two hundred pages on the 25th of February. These pamphlets gave rise to so much controversy that I must forbear quoting even the titles of those written on one side or the other. I cannot, however, omit to notice one point, upon which there rests an obscurity that I think can never be entirely removed. A long list of contemporary works might be given, every one of which, without hesitation, ascribes "The History of the White Staff" to Defoe; while I know of but one that expresses a doubt; upon mere hearsay, of the third or fourth remove, and casts the work among the herd of booksellers' pamphleteers, to find a parent for itself.* But it has been said that Defoe disclaims

---

* "The Secret History of the Secret History of the White Staff, Purse and Mitre," pp. 16, 17.

the Authorship, in his "Appeal to Honour and Justice ;" and, therefore, the statement must be considered.*

Part of this objection has been already answered indirectly. There is no question that the *Advice to the People of Great Britain* was written by Defoe, and published on the 7th of October, 1714. On, and after that day, he could not truly say that he had not "written one Book since the Queen's Death." The conclusion is inevitable that these words were written before that day. The argument, as to the several parts of *The Secret History of the White Staff*, is conclusive for the same reason,—they were composed, if by him, after the writing of that portion of his "Appeal," which has been supposed to disavow them. I might apply the same argument to an earlier part of the same "Appeal," in which he says more specifically, but with intentional ambiguity :—" Two Books lately published being called mine, for no other reason that I know of, than that, at the Request of the Printer, I revised two Sheets of them at the Press, and that they seemed to be written in favour of a certain Person." It may be granted that the Earl of Oxford is the person referred to ; and, that the first and Second Parts of the " Secret History," were the most considerable books that appeared in his Lordship's favour in 1714, but, amidst so many pamphlets as were then published on both sides, it by no means follows that these were the " two Books " intended by Defoe; and if not, he has nowhere disowned them. They were written by a friend to the Earl of Oxford, and with the intention of serving him ; by one who was entirely in his confidence, and had been made acquainted not only with cabinet secrets, but also with the reasons and motives of his Lordship's conduct. They contain statements of what was probably unknown to any but himself and Defoe, thus preclud-

---

* Mr. George Chalmers says, " there can be no doubt that Defoe was not the author ; for he solemnly asserts by his Appeal, in 1715, That he had written nothing since the Queen's death," (" Life of Defoe," Oxford edition, 1841, p. 65.) Yet the editors have, in the same volume, included *The Secret History of the White Staff*, in the List of Defoe's works. It is also contained in Mr. Walter Wilson's List, although he avoids expressing any opinion of his own as to the authorship. He says, " It is certain that Defoe had the credit of it at the time, and the most prevailing tradition has continued to appropriate it to him ever since." (" Life and Times of Defoe," iii. 381.) Mr. Hazlitt imitates Wilson.

ing all others on the ground of competency. The interregnum between the second and third Parts, exactly corresponding with the period of Defoe's illness and recovery, favours the conclusion that he was the author; and it may be fairly asked, who else,—when Swift, Arbuthnot, and other able writers, (who had long fed upon his Lordship's bounty,) forsook his fallen fortunes, and derisively called him *the dragon*,—who else could be named, with the manly courage and faithfulness to perform such a task, but Daniel Defoe? Setting aside all that I have stated, the books afford internal evidence, in the principles enunciated, the manner of thought, and stile of expression, sufficient in themselves to justify the decision that he was the author.*

I have quoted so frequently from Defoe's " Appeal to Honour and Justice," that, though it is far from being exhausted as to valuable materials of his personal history, I must further transcribe only two short paragraphs,—the former containing one of his reasons for writing the book ; and, the melancholy sequel, printed upon its last page. He says. " By the Hints of Mortality, and by the Infirmities of a Life of Sorrow and Fatigue, I have Reason to think that I am not a great way off from, if not very near to, the great Ocean of Eternity, and the time may not be long ere I embark on the last Voyage : Wherefore, I think I should *even Accounts* with this World before I go, that no Actions (Slanders) may lie against my Heirs, Executors, Administrators, and Assigns, to disturb them in the peaceable Possession of their Father's (Character) Inheritance." The pamphlet abruptly terminates as follows :

---

* While the Earl of Oxford was a prisoner in the Tower, awaiting his trial, he was informed that certain pamphlets in circulation were attributed to him, and that it would be prudent to disavow them publicly; which he did by Advertisement in the *London Gazette* of the 19th of July, as follows :—
" Whereas some months since a Pamphlet, Entituled, *The Secret History of the White Staff*, and lately another Pamphlet entituled, *An Account of the Conduct of Robert Earl of Oxford*, have been printed and published ; these are to inform the Publick, that neither of the said Pamphlets have been written by the said Earl, or with his Knowledge, or by his Directioneral Encouragement; but on the contrary he has reason to believe from sev or Passages therein contained, that it was the intention of the Author, or Authors, to do him a Prejudice, and that the last of the said Pamphlets is Published at this Juncture to that end.   " OXFORD."

" CONCLUSION *by the Publisher*.   While this was in the Press,
and the Copy was thus far finish'd, the Author was seiz'd with
a violent Fit of Apoplexy, whereby he was disabled finishing
what he design'd in his farther Defence ; and continuing now
for above Six Weeks in a Weak and Languishing Condition,
neither able to go on, or likely to recover, at least in any short
time, his Friends thought it not fit to delay the Publication of
this any longer.   If he recovers, he may be able to finish
what he began ; if not, it is the Opinion of most that know
him, that the Treatment which he here complains of, and some
others that he would have spoken of, have been the apparent
Cause of his Disaster."

The suddenness of the Queen's death had paralyzed the
Jacobite interest, as well as the Tories and the High-Church.
Lord Bolingbroke and his faction had been dismissed, with
marks of disgrace, before the King's arrival ; and replaced by
ministers better affected to the Protestant interest.   The
government being now restored to a state more agreeable to
the known wishes of his Majesty and the Nation, the coronation took place with great magnificence upon the 20th of
October ; but, there was no amnesty of political offences on the
joyful occasion.   The triumph of the Whigs was as complete
as it was unexpected ; and their accession to power was immediately followed by injudicious resentment against their late
opponents, whose real and imaginary misdeeds were dragged
to light, and threatened with exemplary punishment.   No
feeling of clemency was permitted towards any, from the
peerage down to the lowest officials of the late ministry ; a
clean sweeping out of all government departments was effected,
and the displacement descended even to messengers, con-
tractors, tradesmen, tide-waiters, and the printers of the
London Gazette.   These severities were most unwise ; multitudes of innocent persons were ruined, and the really
disaffected, who might have been won over by kindness
and moderation, went forth desperate, and employed themselves in sowing the seeds which ripened into the Rebellion of
1715.   Defoe owed everything to the favour of the Queen and
the Earl of Oxford ; and the death of the former, accompanied
by the fall of the latter, appeared to him the signals of his

own ruin. No writer had pleaded the Succession of the House of Hanover with greater zeal, yet, instead of being rewarded for his great services, he was now discountenanced, maligned, and prosecuted. There can be no doubt that he now lost the appointment under the crown which he had enjoyed for many years ; and that, while he was patriotically giving *Advice to the People of Great Britain, what they ought to expect from the King, and how they ought to behave to him,* the national triumph of Protestant freedom was to himself productive only of loss and affliction. Even now, had his " Advice " been listened to, and those in power had wisdom to follow it, the Rebellion would never have existed. His prospects were dark, his bodily frame was shattered, and death stared him in the face ; but his loyalty and his patriotism were unmoved, in this great extremity: he continued to labour for his country until he fell prostrate ; yet, when consciousness and ability returned, he resumed his pen with the same earnestness and loyalty as he would have done if rewarded with the highest honours.

The Parliament, which had been prorogued by the Lords Regents before the King's arrival, was dissolved by Proclamation, on the 5th of January 1715, and a new election ordered to take place. In anticipation of this, Bishop Atterbury had, a few days previously, published a pamphlet intitled " English Advice to the Freeholders of England." This first embryo of the Rebellion was powerfully written, but treasonable against the King, libellous upon the new Ministers, and branded the whole body of the Whigs as enemies to the Church, and the true interests of the Nation. A Proclamation was immediately issued offering a thousand pounds for the apprehension of the author, and five hundred pounds for the printer. The latter, Isaac Dalton, was taken and convicted, but the Author, for want of evidence, escaped with impunity. Among numerous Answers to Atterbury's pamphlet was one by Defoe, written probably in his sick chamber, and published on the 29th of January, entitled " A Reply to a traitorous Libel, intitled ' English Advice to the People of England.' London. J. Baker. 1715." Our author deals very summarily with his opponent, affirming, of fifteen or sixteen paragraphs, that nothing more need be written than this : " *The Freeholders of*

England know this to be false."   Against as many more
" might be writ, *Not a word of this can be made out ;"* and, in
many places, " this marginal note would be more than sufficient : *Billingsgate proves Nothing."*   He adds truly, " The
whole Composure is a Mixture of party Fury, with notorious
Slander and Forgery."

During these political commotions, when a prelate of the
Church of England was found capable of writing and publishing treason, and Dissenting teachers called from the pulpit for
vengeance against all connected with the late government ; the
only people who remained undisturbed, and endeavoured, individually, and as a body, to calm the general rage, were the
Quakers.   One of them obtained an interview with the Earl
of Oxford in the Tower, that he might be able authoritatively
to confute the slanders with which his Lordship was assailed.
Another visited Defoe, at a time when he says, " he found the
poor Man in a very dangerous condition, having had a Fit of
an Apoplexy, and being very Weak, insomuch, that his Life
was despair'd of." *   This act of Christian kindness, and the
peaceful spirit of the Quakers, at such a time, appear to have
made a deep impression on the mind of our author, as a practical exemplification of his own earnest entreaties for many
years, that people would study Peace.   Among others infected
with the prevalent spirit of railing was an eminent Dissenting
Minister, whom Defoe wished publicly to reprove, without
giving personal offence ; and in order to this he adopted the
stile and manner of a Quaker, in a pamphlet published on the
19th of February, entitled, " A Friendly Epistle By Way of
Reproof From one of the People called Quakers, To Thomas
Bradbury, a Dealer in many Words.   London.   S. Keimer.
1715."   The admirable manner in which the impersonation is
sustained will be evident from one or two sentences :—" Men,
especially Thomas, Preaching Men, as thou art, ought much
rather to move their People and their Brethren to forbear and
forgive one another, than to move and excite them to Severi-

---

* *Vide* "The Secret History of the Secret History of the White Staff,
Purse, and Mitre. London, 1715," p. 16.   This pamphlet was published on
the 6th d y of January, and is important in fixing the time of Defoe's
illness, and thereby determining the chronological order of several of his works.

ties, and to executing Revenge upon one another, lest the Day
come, when that which they call Justice, may be deemed Injustice. . . . I counsel thee therefore, that thou forbear to
excite thy Sons of Belial to do wickedly; but rather that thou
preach to them that they Repent, for the Kingdom of Heaven
is at Hand; which I meekly advertise thee is the proper Duty
of thy Employment, whereas the other is the Work of Darkness, and tendeth to Blood." He points out the great revival
of theatrical representations, and the growing immoralities of
the times, as proper subjects of pulpit animadversion, and pays
a dutiful tribute to the virtue and piety of the late Queen.
The general tone of the Tract is that of plain and solemn faithfulness, but he occasionally descends to grave irony, and here
and there a faint smile is perceptible, as when speaking of the
new administration, which included the Duke of Marlborough,
and several others not free from the imputation of covetousness,
—he says, " I must lead thee by the Hand, not by the Nose,
Thomas,—Others have done thee that Office already,—that
thou may'st be Convinced, yea even Confounded, for those whom
thou hast, with so great Confidence, taken on thee to recommend
as good Men, and *Men fearing God*. I do thee Justice, Thomas,
—and therefore observe in thy behalf, that thy Modesty would
not permit thee to say, *They were Men hating Covetousness.*"

It is a proof of the sensitive and excited state of the nation,
that the above, and one or two similar remarks, alarmed the
Quakers, and produced the following Advertisement, which
appeared in the *London Gazette* of the 5th of March, and the
Daily Courant of the 7th March 1715. The necessity of dis-
owning it is a testimony to the author's genius.

" Whereas there hath been a pamphlet lately published, intituled, ' A Friendly Epistle by way of Reproof, (pretended to
be) from one of the People called Quakers, To Thomas
Bradbury, a Dealer in many Words;' wherein are sundry
irreverent Expressions Reflecting upon the King, Princes, and
Rulers : We the People called Quakers do hereby Advertise all
concerned, That we had no Hand in the said Pamphlet, but do
utterly disown it, believing it to have been a Contrivance of
some Adversary of Ours, whereby to vent his own Invectives
against the Government in our Name, and to expose us to the
Displeasure thereof, and the Censure of Sober People."

CHAPTER X.

Defoe writes " The Family Instructor"—Publishes " A sharp rebuke to Henry Sacheverell" — " A Seasonable Expostulation unto James Butler"—" The History of the Wars of Charles XII., King of Sweden"—Defoe brought to trial, found guilty, and sentence deferred —State of the country before the Rebellion—Defoe publishes " A Hymn to the Mob"—"A View of the Scots Rebellion"—"A Trumpet blown in the North"—Lord Chief Justice Parker intercedes with the Government for Defoe—His explanation—Released without sentence, and employed by the Ministry—Publishes "An Account of the Great and Generous Actions of the Duke of Ormond" " Two Nights Court at Greenwich"—" Considerations on a Law for Triennial Parliaments," and " The Alteration in the Triennial Act considered."

1715—16.

THE next published work of Defoe was heretofore believed to have been the first fruit of a new life of literary seclusion, and written after he had withdrawn finally from the political world. It appeared on the 31st of March, and is entitled, " The Family Instructor. In Three Parts. I. Relating to Fathers and Children. II. To Masters and Servants. III. To Husbands and Wives. By Way of Dialogue. With a Recommendatory Letter, by the Rev. Mr. S. Wright. London. Eman. Matthews. 1715." It is now certain that no such retirement from the world occurred ; and I must add, that this work was evidently written long before publication ; probably at intervals between pressing engagements, during the two preceding years. In January, Defoe was so dangerously ill that he was not expected to recover. When he afterward became convalescent he would continue, for some time, incapable of severe mental or physical labour ; yet I have shown that in that weak condition he produced two important pamphlets. It cannot be thought possible, under the circumstances, that he could have added to those labours, the composition and correction of a book containing about 450 pages ; and, that it should be disposed of, put into type, revised, the sheets

submitted to, and read by, the reverend gentleman whose name
is prefixed, and the whole printed off and published by the end
of March.   There it not a tittle of evidence in support of any
such supposition.

The few facts, when gathered together, lead to the conclusion
that, having the manuscript by him in a finished state during
his fit of apoplexy, he sold it absolutely, when consciousness
was restored, to Matthews the publisher, and was probably induced to do so by pecuniary reasons.   The arrangement was
made when a load of obloquy rested on his name ; and he tells
us afterward, that " The unworthy Author earnestly desired, and
to his utmost endeavoured, to be for ever Concealed, lest some
Men, suffering their prejudices to prevail even over their Zeal for
public Good, might be tempted to lay the Imperfections of the
Author of this Book as a stumbling Block in the way of those
who might otherwise receive Benefit by it."*   He was incapable of writing any preface or introduction, and there is
reason to believe he never saw a single proof sheet of the work.
It will be observed in the following, that the desire of concealment prevented him from specifying the reason of his incapacity :—" The first Edition of this Work was so ill Printed, and by
Reason of the Author's absence from the Press was so uncorrect,
that it stood more than ordinarily in need of the help of a
good Introduction."†   The dangerous illness of the author
compelled the publisher to seek the aid of an eminent Presbyterian Divine to write an Introduction, which was addressed to
the publisher, and it does not appear that the writer of such
Introduction knew who was the author of the book.   I infer
that Mr. Matthews forbore to trouble Defoe with anything
relating to the first edition ; because, although the author
afterward expressed his obligation to " the Reverend Person
who did it the favour to give it the first Recommendation,"
yet Mr. Wright's introduction was omitted from all subsequent
editions.   No other explanation would account for the author's
Preface and corrections being added to the second edition, as the
final completion of the volume.

I should waste the reader's time by commenting upon the

* Preface to the Second Edition, published the 17th September, 1715, p. 2.
† Ibid. p. 1.

contents of this admirable, unsectarian, though religious, Manual. Few, if any, seriously disposed persons are unacquainted with its value. It has found its way into the libraries of kings, and into the cottages of peasants : it has passed through innumerable editions, and is still popular ; it has been made a blessing, under God, to thousands of souls, and will continue to be the same, wherever the English language is known, and so long as that which is pure and peaceable, shall continue to be lovely, and of good report.

Our author followed the disguise he had recently assumed, by writing other Tracts in the character of a Quaker; and it is to be remarked,—as their general characteristic,—that they were all consistent with the principles of that people, in reproving extreme conduct whether in politics or religion; and in the inculcation of peace. The next in order of such Tracts is entitled " A sharp Rebuke from one of the People called Quakers to Henry Sacheverell, the High Priest of Andrew's Holbourn. By the same Friend that wrote to Thomas Bradbury. London. S. Keimer. 1715." This rebuke is not for the doctor's private sins ; but, that he had done more than any man living to stir up wrath and strife among men. With much plainness and faithfulness, there is the same quaintness and grave irony as in the previous pamphlet. To remind the doctor that he has ground for thankful reflection, the writer says " neither hath any brought the Execution of Justice upon themselves with more just Demerit, than thou hast, albeit they have pass'd out of the Body therefor, and thou remainest for a while." Defoe foresaw the approaching Rebellion, and endeavoured by rebukes, exhortations, exposure of disloyalty, and every other means in his power to prevent the spread of disaffection, and to alarm the patriotism of the nation. He says, there is a person of good name in Canterbury, " who affirmeth, and offereth thee, by me, Henry, to affirm it to thy Face, saying, That he hath seen thee kneel upon thy knees, and drink to the Health, as thou callest it, of the STRANGER, calling him by the Title and name of King James III." He charges the doctor with adding hypocrisy and perjury to his treason, in that he had solemnly abjured the Pretender, whom his soul loved ; and had sworn fidelity to the King, whom he

DR. SACHEVERELL, Defoe's "High Priest of Andrews Holbourn."

From the Original Portrait by T. Gibson.

THE THREE FALSE BRETHREN—SACHEVERELL, THE POPE, AND THE DEVIL.

From a rare Caricature published in 1710.

now cursed with his lips.   In the following severe terms, the
writer anticipates the verdict of posterity :—" For these Things
hath the Lord made thee a Hissing and a By Word among
the People of the Land, and thy name will be a Curse unto
all Generations :—And it shall be, hereafter, that when one
man shall curse another, he shall say,—*The Lord make thee as
Sacheverell, whom the People of the Land abhorr'd.*"* I remark
here the great contrast between the warmth of Defoe's language when speaking of treason against God or the King ;
and the meekness of his replies to the most unjust personal
treatment against himself.

The third of this series of pamphlets was published on the
31st of May, and is entitled, " A Seasonable Expostulation
with, and Friendly Reproof unto James Butler, who, by the
men of this world, is stil'd the Duke of O———d, Relating
to the Tumults of the People.   By the same Friend that
wrote to Thomas Bradbury, the Dealer in many Words, and
Henry Sacheverell, the High Priest of Andrew's Holbourn.
London. S. Keimer. 1715."   This pamphlet is of a much
gentler character than its predecessor.   The writer does not
accuse the Duke of disloyalty, but rather of being seduced by
his vanity into an encouragement of the tumultuous mobs of
the Jacobite and High-Church party.   He kindly expostulates
with his Grace upon the danger of this course, at a time when
he is under the frowns of the Government ; and warns him
that he may permit his name to be used for factious purposes
until his destruction shall become necessary to the state.
Although so kindly disposed, the writer seems to have had as
low an estimate of the Duke's wisdom and prudence, as of his
honour.   When his Grace of Ormond succeeded to the command of the Confederate army in Flanders, as successor to
Marlborough, it was with instructions not to fight ; a condition, which at the time was considered a disgrace to a soldier.
Defoe reminds him that he was publicly caricatured for this,—
" and therefore was it, that certain vile Persons made open

---

* At the end of the pamphlet is a long publisher's advertisement, osten-
sibly in answer to the Quakers disavowal of the " Epistle to Thomas Bradbury ;" but really to announce the publication of the *fifth* edition of that
pamphlet.

representations of thee in Pictures, wherein thy Sword had,
plac'd thereon, a certain machine, commonly called Padlock,
which was shewn among the People of the Land, to thy great
Shame and Reproach." Then adroitly withdrawing the
stigma, on the ground that the Quakers oppose all wars, he
says, " We count not the same as an Offence,—desiring that
the Swords of all the Mighty Men of Valour may be, in like
manner, fastened in their Places; nay rather that they should
be beaten into Plough-Shares." Well would it have been for the
Duke had he listened to the well-meant expostulations of a man
much wiser than himself. Only by self-banishment did he ultimately escape the punishment of which Defoe here warned him.

Defoe's *Review*, extending from 1704 to 1713,—and, containing not only the transactions of the times, but also frequent
references to anterior events within the writer's memory, is a
store-house of history; from which he probably gathered part
of the materials for his next publication. This is a volume of
four hundred pages, worthy of standing by the side of the
most fascinating productions of his great genius, yet hitherto
unnoticed by any of his biographers, and almost unknown to
the world. It was published on the 6th of July, and is entitled " The History of the Wars of his Present Majesty Charles
XII., King of Sweden; From his first Landing in Denmark,
to his Return from Turkey to Pomerania. By a Scots Gentleman in the Swedish Service. London. A. Bell, &c. 1715."
In the preface he says that it contains " a Relation of Things
transacted within the View, and perhaps in the Memory of
most that shall now read them, and need no better Appeal
for their Authority and Truth, than to the General Knowledge
of Mankind; the Assent of which in this Age, must needs pass
for Approbation in the next. The Subject is as fruitful of
Great Events, as any real History can pretend to, and is
Grac'd with as many Glorious Actions, Battles, Sieges, and
Gallant Enterprizes,—Things which make a History Pleasant as
well as Profitable,—as can be met with in any History of so
few years that is now extant in the World." He goes on to
say that his Hero " has done Actions that Posterity will have
room to Fable upon, till they make his History Incredible,
and turn it into Romance."

As to the new War, just commenced at the time when this work was completed, in which Prussia had entered into a League, offensive and defensive, with the Danes, Poles and Muscovites, against the King of Sweden, our author says, " the farther Account of it must be referred to a Time when they shall be more properly spoken to, when also the History of all the Transactions and Proceedings on every side shall, if the Author of these Memoirs Survives them, be fully and Impartially related."

In pursuance of this promise, a second edition of the work was published on the 21st of May 1720, with a continuation to the death of the Swedish monarch. This being printed in a much smaller type, the matter contained in its predecessor occupies only 248 pages, and the Appendix begins with a sub-title,—" A Continuation of the History of the Reign, and of the Wars, of his late Majesty Charles the XII., King of Sweden : From his Return into his Dominions, after his long Residence in Turkey, to his Death in Norway. By the same Author." The addition occupies 154 closely printed pages, and would have well sufficed for a second volume. He refers to the general acceptance and good reception of the first volume, and says the approbation it had received " not only from many of the Gentlemen who were present in the most remarkable Actions, but even from the King of Sweden himself, has been such as the Author has too much Modesty to enter upon : But the Bounty and Goodness of his Swedish Majesty to an Author unknown and remote, &c., has been such as he cannot but acknowledge." He also states that the first volume had already been published abroad in several languages. A well executed portrait of the King faces the title-page of this second edition.

It will be remembered that Defoe had been at large upon his recognizances, since the previous August, for an article relating to the Earl of Anglesey, published in *Hurt's Flying Post*. On the 12th of July 1715, he and some others were brought to trial at the Court of King's Bench; and, as he had acknowledged the authorship, the only question for the Court seems to have been to decide whether or not he had broken the law, and what punishment should be inflicted for the offence. The proceedings were noticed in most of the

Papers, but I extract the following from the *Weekly Journal* of Saturday the 16th :—

" On Tuesday last came on the Trials of Mr. Daniel Defoe, late Author of the Review; Mr. James Watson, Printer; and Mr. William Wind, Perfumer; the first for a Paragraph inserted in a Paper call'd the *Flying Post*, Printed for Wm. Hurt, &c., soon after the Death of the Queen, which contained a Reflection on the Earl of Anglesey, (one of the Lords of the Regency,) in relation to a Journey, that 'tis inferred therein, his Lordship design'd to make to Ireland ; the second for dispersing a Libel, call'd *A Defence of his Majesty's Speech, &c.* ; and the latter, for writing a Book entituled, *Reasons for abrogating the Observation of the 30th of January, &c.* They were all found guilty, and their sentences deferr'd till next Term."

The repressive and vindictive conduct of the new government against the Jacobites and the High-church party, already alluded to, extended to all who were, or had been, conspicuous against the Whigs. Many of the malcontents, however, now openly avowed their principles; and severity was daily increasing their numbers. The allegiance of multitudes was but a slender thread, in danger of being snapt at both extremes. On the birthday of the Duke of Ormond, riotous mobs had compelled an illumination of houses ; breaking the windows of those who refused. In the middle of July, crowds of Men and Boys ran about the streets of London crying, *Down with the Rump !* Some Members of the legislature fled to the Continent, while others began to organize resistance, and riot was being rapidly transformed into Rebellion. The Earl of Oxford lay ill in the Tower, unable to prepare for the trial his enemies had already commenced ; and their indecent haste compelled him to petition that his presence might be dispensed with. Great part of the domestic News of this and the following month relates to the apprehension of suspected Jacobites ; searches for horses and arms ; arrests of persons concerned in writing, printing and selling treasonable pamphlets and ballads ; proclamations of the government against treasonable practices ; the compulsory application of tests in the forms of oaths of allegiance, supremacy, and adjuration; recruiting and movements of soldiers; impressing for, and equipment of the Navy ; committals of

persons for cursing the King, or for drinking the health of the
Pretender; and, accounts of Sacheverellite mobs, burning and
destroying Meeting-Houses; and engaged in other outrages
against all who were on the side of the King and his government.

Under these circumstances, on the 14th of July, Defoe published, "A Hymn to the Mob. London. Printed and sold
by S. Popping, &c. 1715." It is a satire in Pindaric Verse,
and like nearly all Defoe's poetic compositions, is rugged, and
abounds in defective rhymes; but it is equally full of good
sense, and many of the sections contain great truths happily
expressed. He sketches the history of mobs from the creation,
and approves their action in defence of natural right, and the
liberties of Nations. Of the concentrated and disciplined
force of a mob in legitimate warfare, he finely says,—

> " Thy Valour storm'd the Leaguer of *Turine*,
> Tho' all the Glory's giv'n to Great *Eugene*.
> *Blenheim* and *Ramillies* were fought by thee,
> Whoever claims the Crown of Victory;
> And, all the Ancient Temples built to Fame,
> Should have been consecrated to thy Name."

But of the blind passion of a factious mob, seeking to over-
awe the Magistrates and Rulers of a Nation, and to trample
on its laws and liberties, he says,—

> " But as the wild Possession first took Place
> In spite of Sense, in spite of Grace,
> Headlong with strong impetuous haste they go,
> Merely by their own Weight, as Waters flow.
> It must not be,—this is too coarse a Jest!
> The Rabble must be dispossest!
> The Devil's got in!—why then that Devil must out
> Nor is the Manner how, a Doubt.
> Persuasion must *attempt* to make them still,
> But if Persuasion w'on't, the Gallows will."

The rebellion quickly followed the disorganized condition of
society I have already briefly sketched, and was not entirely
suppressed until the end of the year. Although Defoe remained silent during several months after writing his *Hymn to
the Mob*, yet he was far from being an unconcerned spectator.
Much as he loved Scotland, he loved Great Britain more; and
as he had once taken arms in defence of law and order against

a Popish King, so he now took up his pen once more against the Pretender and his adherents. On the 15th October, he published, " A View of the Scots Rebellion. With some Enquiry into what we have to fear from the Rebels ? And what is the properest Method to take with them. London. R. Burleigh. 1715." Devoted as our author was to the inculcation of peace, this pamphlet proves that his great sagacity extended also to the art of War. Knowing well the character of the country, he urges that the King's forces should hedge in the Highlanders between Stirling and the Clyde, thus preventing their march southward, and cutting them off from all resources. He confidently affirms, "this would soon put an end to this Rebellion, without much Blood." I do not presume that this recommendation was known to the Duke of Argyle, but it is certain that the movements indicated by Defoe were those adopted; and resulted in the decisive victory obtained over the Earl of Mar on the 13th of the following month.

In addition to the above, our author put on his Quaker habiliments for the fourth time, and on the 10th of November published a pamphlet entitled, " A Trumpet blown in the North, and sounded in the Ears of John Ereskine, call'd by the Men of the World, Duke of Mar. By a Ministring Friend of the People called Quakers; with a Word of Advice and Direction to the said John Ereskine and his Followers. Sold by S. Keimer, at the Cheshire Coffee House in King's Arms Court on Ludgate Hill. 1715."

The address begins, " Obadiah a Friend to Truth and Peace, to thee John Ereskine, Lord Mar, a Master of Sedition, and a Leader of the Wicked among the People, Leteth to Wot." He makes no special reference to any of his other Quaker Tracts, but says generally, " I signify to thee, Lord Mar, that this person who now writeth unto thee, hath been accustomed to speak even to the Princes and Great Men of the Earth, words of Reproof, as oft as they do evil." It is an able Tract, of clear, calm and loyal reasoning against this " Son of Vanity," as the author calls him, and is less severe than the circumstances would have warranted.

About the day on which the above was published, Defoe should have appeared in Court, with the persons convicted during the previous term, but Ridpath says, in the *Flying Post* of the 15th November, " Mr. Daniel Defoe, having forfeited his Recognizance, by not appearing last week at the Court of King's Bench, a Process is order'd against him and his Bail." The *Weekly Packet* says they were ordered to receive sentence on Monday the 21st, but adds, " Mr. Defoe is said to have withdrawn himself." Sentence was duly passed upon the other delinquents, but Defoe was not present,—his name was not mentioned in Court, nor did any of the Journals again allude to him in connection with this charge. Ridpath would gladly have seen Defoe imprisoned for contempt of Court, and his Bail forfeited ; but the statement he had made was incorrect. The true reason of Defoe's absence was, that Lord Chief Justice Parker had become convinced that he had done him grievous injustice in the year 1713, in refusing, with the other Judges, to believe that the three Tracts for which our author was then arraigned, —at the same Bar as now,—were ironical, and against the Pretender. The Queen's pardon was a direct reflection upon such conduct of the Judges. The Chief Justice had no sympathy for the Earl of Anglesey, or the Jacobites ; and the offence with which Defoe was now charged was indisputably that of writing against the cause of the Pretender. The stricture upon Lord Anglesey- could not be construed into an offence against the Lords Regents, merely because his Lordship was a member of that body ; but even if it could, the Regency was necessarily superseded when the King landed in England, more than a year ago. This was not a time to punish an able writer, for having plainly opposed the first incipient acts of a Rebellion, that had since spread over the face of the land.

Many of the above considerations were no doubt urged upon Lord Chief Justice Parker, in a Letter written to him by Defoe, which has not come down to us ; though all the circumstances are related by himself in a work published five years afterward. He says " I know a Man who had a particular Case befallen him, wherein he was under the Displeasure of the Government, and was prosecuted for a Misdemeanour, and brought to a Tryal in the King's Bench Court, where a Verdict was brought against him, and he was Cast. The Times running very hard at that Time against the Party he was of, he was afraid to stand the Hazard of a Sentence, and absconded, taking care to make due Provision for his Bail, and to pay them whatever they might suffer.   In this Circumstance he was in great Distress, and no Way presented to him but to fly out of the Kingdom, which being to leave his Family, Children, and Employment, was very bitter to him, and he knew not what to do; all his Friends advising him not to put himself into the Hands of the Law, which tho' the Offence was not Capital, yet in his Circumstances seemed to threaten his utter Ruin.   In this extremity he felt one Morning, (just as he had awaked, and the Thoughts of his Misfortune began to return upon him ;) I say, he felt a strong Impulse darting into his Mind thus, *Write a Letter to them !*   It spoke so distinctly to him, and as it were forcibly, that as he has often said since, he can scarcely persuade himself not to believe but that he heard it ; but he grants that he did not really hear it, too.   However, it repeated the Words daily and hourly to him, till at length, walking about in his Chamber where he was hidden, very pensive and sad, it Jogg'd him again, and he answered aloud to it, as if it had been a Voice, *Who shall I write to ?*   It returned immediately, *Write to the Judge !* This pursued him again for several Days, till at length he took his Pen, Ink and Paper, and sat down to write, but knew not one Word of what he should say, but *Dabitur in hac hora,* he wanted not Words. It was immediately impressed on his Mind, and the Words flowed upon his Pen in a manner that even charmed himself, and filled him with Expectations of Success.   The Letter was so strenuous in Argument, so pathe-tick in its Eloquence, and so moving and persuasive, that as soon as the Judge had read it, he sent him Word he should be easie, for he would endeavour to make that Matter light to him ; and, in a Word, never left till he had obtained to stop Prosecution, and restore him to his Liberty and to his Family."*

This part of the life of Defoe was wholly unknown to his biographers ; although all his future course turns upon it.   It is remarkable that his own statement, as above, should not have led to any investigation, as to its meaning and application. Mr. Wilson quotes the whole passage, and says, " Perhaps it has an immediate reference to himself."†   Defoe's declaration,

---

* " Vision of the Angelick World," pp. 48-50.
† " Life of Defoe," III., pp. 556-8.

that the actions of his own life were contained in *The Adventures of Robinson Crusoe*, was forgotten by his biographers.

It was under these singular circumstances that Lord Chief Justice Parker not only prevented any further proceedings against Defoe, but also, to atone for past injuries, sought an interview with Lord Townshend, the Secretary of State, and represented the case of our author so favourably as to remove the calumnies under which he had suffered, and to convince the minister that Defoe was sincerely attached to the King and the present Government. Upon this happy reconciliation between our author and the great Whig party of the nation, Lord Townshend, who well knew the great value of Defoe's literary genius, began to consider in what way he might be rendered most useful to the Government. This was towards the end of November 1715, when the Rebellion had scarcely ended, and most seditious and treasonable articles continued to be published in Tory and Jacobite Journals. These virulent attacks were not confined to members of the administration, but reached also the person of the King ; and greatly harassed the Government. Prosecutions seemed of litle avail, and a bill for restraining the press could not be seriously entertained. Under these considerations Lord Townshend proposed that Defoe should be taken into the service of the Government, but that the world should not be informed of the fact, and still consider him under displeasure, and separated from the Whigs.

In this way it was thought he would be better able to counteract the designs of disaffected journalists, and be more serviceable, than by appearing openly in support of the government. The object was, to prevent treasonable publications, by intercepting them before they reached the press, and by deleting that which was contrary to law ; rather than (after the poison had been diffused throughout the nation,) punishing the miserable printers and publishers, without being able to take hold of the writers. The whole of the arrangements in question are stated by Defoe in the six autograph letters discovered in the State Paper Office in the year 1864, and which I have transcribed into the Introduction prefixed to this Memoir. Neither in those Letters, nor in anything I have been able to discover, is there any condition or stipulation, direct or implied, that he should ever write a word contrary to his conscience, or to the principles which had directed his whole life :—nor have I found that he ever did so. On these conditions Defoe engaged himself with the Government; and, in his consequent services, he neither " dishonoured Lord Parker's recommendation,"—the King's Government,—or his own character.

It does not appear that any fixed remuneration was proposed in the first instance ; but at the end of a year, before the 11th of December, 1716, when Lord Townshend went out of office, our author's services had been so satisfactory, that he received an appointment, " with promise of further Allowance as service presented." There is reason to believe that Defoe continued to hold this appointment until March, 1726, when the dynasty of the House of Hanover had become so consolidated in the hearts of the British people, as to exclude all fear of any rival pretension to the throne. To that security, his faithful services had greatly contributed :—how much, can only be inadequately conceived, even· by those who have patiently searched through the Journals of the time, inasmuch as treason, suppressed and prevented, died in silence. His written and published labours, under such engagement, will, by the present publication, be more capable of appreciation, and entitle him, irrespective of his many other claims, to the gratitude and admiration of posterity. It is to the honour of Defoe, that he alone, of all the eminent political writers who supported the last Ministry of Queen Anne,—(including Prior, Swift, Arbuthnot, Gay, and many others),—was ever employed again in the service of his country.

The Duke of Ormond having refused to listen to the counsel of friends, whether Quakers or otherwise, became more entangled with the disaffected; until, fearing the consequences, he fled to France in August, 1715, and was attainted shortly afterwards. The Oxford Riots, of which he was the occasion, had occurred in May, but they gave rise to disputes and proceedings that lasted until 1717, when Dr. Gardiner, the Vice-Chancellor, published an anonymous vindication of himself and the University. About the end of the year 1715, however, Defoe wrote and published a respectful but severe prose satire on the subject, entitled, " An Account of the Great and

Generous Actions of James Butler (Late Duke of Ormond.)
Dedicated to the Famous University of Oxford. London.
Printed for J. Moore, near St. Pauls, and sold by the Booksellers." The dedication is intended to be the more important,
and occupies the greater part of the pamphlet. The writer
exalts the dignity, learning, and piety of the University; and
affects to disbelieve the rumours that its members had joined
in the late riots and tumults there; in which the name of their
Chancellor, the Duke of Ormond, had been mixed up with
breaking of windows, demolishing the Dissenters Chapel, and
other outrages committed by a Mob, under the cry of "*An
Ormond;—an Ormond! No Hanover;—no King George! High-
Church;—High-Church!* He denounces the accusation as
calumnious, and calls upon the Vice-Chancellor, and other
authorities, to vindicate the University by publicly declaring
that its members were in no respect implicated in such disgraceful and disloyal proceedings. The latter part of the pamphlet is
designed to shew that vanity, ambition, and the prodigal
squandering of a princely fortune, constituted the only claims
of the Duke to the popularity he had sought and obtained.

The Rebellion being suppressed, Defoe thought it important
that some memorial should exist as to the secret causes of its
origin, and with this view he prepared and published, early in
the year 1716, a thick pamphlet, entitled " Some Account of the
Two Nights Court at Greenwich; Wherein may be seen the
Reason, Rise, and Progress of the late Unnatural Rebellion,
against His Sacred Majesty King George, and his Government.
London. J. Baker, 1716." The author shows, that the unexpected death of Queen Anne so disconcerted the measures of
the Jacobite faction of her ministry that they were first compelled to proclaim King George for their own safety, and then
to cabal in order to persuade him, if possible, that they were
devoted to his interest. The King was to land at Greenwich,
and thither the faction went to meet him, and present their
pretended loyal obedience. The Lords of the Regency, and
the leaders of the Whig party, were also there, and graciously
received, while the Tories were not even informed of the King's
arrival, until he had actually landed. They soon found that
all their past proceedings were known to his Majesty, and that

there was. no hope for them; on which, they determined to raise a rebellion in favour of the Pretender. The people were to be divided, and stirred up, by all means, the High-Church was to preach up the cause, and they made sure of co-operation from abroad. The manner in which their design was to have been effected is clearly stated, and many of the conspirators distinctly alluded to. In the events that followed however, all this was happily frustrated.

The pusillanimous inactivity of the Pretender, from the death of Queen Anne to the latter end of 1715, ill deserved the undaunted pertinacity of his adherents in England and Scotland. While he kept himself in safety, and spent his time alternating between frivolity and bigotry; many of them sacrificed their fortunes, and some their lives in his service. The disastrous conclusion of the Rebellion only damped the ardour of their misplaced loyalty. The agitation was still continued, and the hopeful Jacobites were already making preparations for the next General election, when they trusted to carry many of their friends into the House of Commons; and perhaps take advantage of the mobs and riots, which had become almost universal on such occasions, to bring about a general rising of the country.

The experience of twenty years had convinced all moderate men, that the Act limiting the duration of each parliament to three years, kept the nation in a state of chronic agitation, which, at this juncture, would be highly favourable to the schemes of the disloyal. To counteract this,—to quench the yet smouldering embers of the rebellion,—and to procure time for peaceable consolidation of the new government, a short bill was brought into the House of Lords on the 10th of April, 1716, to extend the duration of that, and future parliaments, to seven years; and it had passed both Houses on the 26th of the same month. Defoe wrote two pamphlets in support of this measure, the former of which was entitled, " Some Considerations on a Law for Triennial Parliaments, with an Enquiry, I. Whether there may not be a time when it is necessary to suspend the Execution of such Laws as are most essential to the Liberties of the People? II. Whether this is such a time or no? London. J. Baker. 1 16." The second Tract was written after the

Bill had passed the House of Lords, and was before the Commons. It is entitled, " The Alteration in the Triennial Act considered. London. R. Burleigh. 1716." This is a very clear, able, and convincing pamphlet, in which the author balances the respective powers of King, Lords, Commons, and Administration. He shows that the measure will only add to the weight of the lower House of Parliament sufficiently to establish an equipoise between the several branches of the constitution; and, that the Septennial Bill was highly necessary to the Security of the Government.

A series of remarkable blunders have been committed respecting these two Tracts. In the *Political State* for April, 1716, Boyer recites the titles of seven pamphlets in favour of the Government measure; including both the above. He then goes on to say that only one pamphlet was published on the other side; that it was adjudged " to be written by that prostituted Tool of the Ministry, D—D—F. ;" but he adds, that whatever was offered against the Bill " was fully answered and confuted" by a pamphlet which he attributes to Addison, and reprints verbatim. In this, Boyer exhibits at once his malignity against Defoe, and his incapacity as a critic. He first approvingly classes, on his own side, the pamphlets Defoe actually wrote ; then ignorantly and maliciously charges him with writing one on the opposite side,—not knowing that our author was then in the service of the Government ;—and he concludes with designating the one he attributes to Addison, a specific answer and confutation ; whereas it is written in the most general terms possible, and contains no reference to any other publication. The next blunder was by Defoe himself. Writing about a year afterward in *Mercurius Politicus,* he refers to this attack of Boyer, but instead of turning to the *Political State* to refresh his memory, he speaks from mere recollection, and says " the Book which he praised so impertinently, I was the Author of, and that Book he let fly his Dirt upon, I had no concern in." As to the latter, Defoe was undoubtedly correct, but he had clearly forgotten which one, of all the Tracts in favour of the measure, Boyer had praised. Our author could not, and would not, have written the Tract Boyer attributed to Addison ; and had he referred to Boyer's book, his words would assuredly have been " what I did write he referred to approvingly, and the book he let fly his dirt upon, I had no concern in." The next error relates to Mr. Chalmers, who, when writing the Life of Defoe, seems to have met with this passage in Boyer, and calls it an insult; but does not appear to have taken the least pains to ascertain whether or not Defoe wrote on one side or the other. Mr. Wilson adds to the confusion, by mistaking Chalmers, Boyer, and Defoe, and entering upon no research. The stumbling-block of both biographers was of their own making, viz., That the year 1715 was the termination of Defoe's political life.*

---

* On the above blunders, *vide* an able article signed *James Crossley,* (*Notes and Queries,* 1st series, vol. 5, p. 577.)

CHAPTER XI.

Retrospect of Defoe's literary career—"Mercurius Politicus"—"Dormer's News Letter"—Publishes "Memoirs of the Church of Scotland"— "The Life and Death of Count Patkul"—"Minutes of the Negociations of Mons. Mesnager"—"Declaration of Truth to Benjamin Hoadley"—Defoe engages himself on "Mist's Journal"—Originates editorial "Letters Introductory" in Journals—Translates "Curious Oration of Father Andrews"—Publishes "Memoirs of the Duke of Shrewsbury"—"The Case of the War in Italy Stated"—Writes his Six Letters to Mr. C. De la Faye—"Memoirs of the Life of Daniel Williams, D.D."—Second volume of "The Family Instructor"— Establishes "The Whitehall Evening Post"—Mist apprehended— His untruthful statement as to Defoe—Poems against Defoe in "Read's Journal"—Defoe leaves Mist—Publishes "A Friendly Rebuke to one Parson Benjamin."

1716—1719.

WE have now to consider Defoe under a new character; and it will be well first to look backward. Until the year 1700, his works had either been published anonymously, or with only his initials to any dedication or preface. He was humble, and knew that his name, if given in full, would not increase the circulation of his books. The production of *The True-born Englishman* was the commencement of a new epoch in his life. He had become famous. His poem was quoted in the pulpit, and in the senate; it was sold by ten thousands in the streets, and it procured him the favour and friendship of the king. Many of his succeeding works, and the collected editions, were announced as being written by the *Author of the True-born Englishman.* It was his proudest title, and he associated it with his proper name for many years. When oppression attempted to crush him, he rebounded in scorn, as the *Author of the Hymn to the Pillory;* but after a few publications, calmly returned to the designation upon which his then literary reputation was based. The great popularity of his *Review,* induced him afterward occasionally to issue pamphlets, especially on Trade and Commerce, as being *by the Author of the Review*. But, under any of these expressions, every reader knew who was indicated as well as if Daniel Defoe had been printed on the title-pages. During the same period he had undoubtedly published many anonymous pieces ; but pamphlets were then generally without the names of the writers, and there were often strong reasons for such concealment. It is probable that, to the time when his "first benefactor," the Earl of Oxford, admitted some of the Tories into the Ministry, there was no equally voluminous political writer whose authorship was less open to doubt.

From that period nearly all his works, excepting the *Review*, were anonymous, until the publication of his *Appeal to Honour and Justice*, on the front of which his name was printed in full. Gratitude,—that made him keep silence,—as to many acts of which he could not approve,—and urged him to support the government when he could conscientiously do so ; brought him under the unmerited obloquy of writing many things his soul abhorred. The weight of these reproaches seems to have settled into a morbid conviction that his name alone would suffice to blast the success of anything depending upon public approbation. Such conviction continued, during the production of a long series of subsequent works that have made his fame undying ; and, it ended only with his life. He had previously shown a commendable pride in his literary reputation ; but after 1715, his works were apparently authorless, or issued under fictitious and assumed names ; and, with the exceptions of his initials to two translations, and a newspaper, Daniel Defoe never appeared again before the world, as an Author, in his proper person, nor laid any public claim to productions of his own pen that were so popular as to have passed through half-a-dozen editions within less than a month.

These preliminary remarks seemed to be especially called for here, when we are to witness so entire an abnegation of himself in the service of his country, as the writing for, and taking part in the management of, periodical publications, under the essential condition that his connection with them should be carefully concealed. The nature of his engagement with the government has been already stated generally ; but the object would obviously be frustrated should the fact of his engagement be disclosed to the owners of such Journals, or the

public.   Some of those Journals were known only by the
names of their proprietors, as *Dormer's News Letter ; Mist's
Journal; Applebee's Original Weekly Journal, &c. ;* and in
them it was necessary not only to conceal the connection, but
to avoid his own individuality, and to speak in the name of the
ostensible proprietor.

The first of such periodicals that he began to write, was entitled, " Mercurius Politicus : Being Monthly Observations on
the Affairs of Great Britain.   With a Collection of the Most
Material Occurrences.   By a Lover of Old England.   London.
J. Morphew.   No. I.   May, 1716."   Each number constitutes
an octavo pamphlet of nearly a hundred pages.   The first
number contains some introductory remarks, of which the
following is an abstract :—After a brief reference to the Rebellion, then just terminated, and to the trials of the rebels,
still going on, he alludes to the violent party spirit exhibited
by writers in the public prints, and says, they have " noto-
riously deviated from the duty of Historians,—so deficient in
fact,—so partial in relation."   He undertakes that *Mercurius
Politicus* shall do " what we cannot find any Writer has yet
done, viz.—to speak *freely, plainly,* and with the utmost *impartiality,* without respect to Party, or byas to Persons."   He
says it is not a mistake, but a most scandalous crime, and " must
fill the minds of honest Men with horror, to see Atheists,
Deists, Heretics, profane and irreligious Persons, and others
who call themselves Churchmen, falling upon the Church,"
and defaming the Clergy and Religion.   He concludes " Our
business is to mend these scandalous parts in this Work ;—to
write Truth,—and to make our Account as full and as perfect
as we can ; by this we hope we shall serve and oblige Posterity ;
and, in the meantime displease no Body."

Starting with such views and intentions, which accord with
the profession and practice of his whole life, this monthly
record of national events was continued by him until September,
1720, and probably much longer ; but I do not know whether
or not a complete set exists.   I am possessed of four Numbers,
but have only found three others in the British Museum, and
two in the Bodleian Library.   A few extracts from these are
in my collection of Defoe's recently discovered writings.

Defoe informs us that Dormer, the proprietor of the *News Letter*, being unable to carry it on, in consequence of some trouble, made him an offer of a share in the property, and the management of the Work. Defoe did not accept the offer without the approbation of Lord Townshend, who thought " it would be a very acceptable piece of service, for that Letter was really very prejudicial to the Public, and the most difficult to come at in a judicial way in case of Offence given." The difficulty alluded to, arose from the fact that what were called " News Letters," were not printed, nor published in the usual way and openly sold, but were only transcribed by hand, and sent by post to all the subscribers. The *News* " Letter" in question had been for a long time of Tory and High-Church principles ; in Defoe's hands the sting was taken out, and the mischief prevented. It still seemed to be Tory, so as to amuse the party, and prevent their setting up another violent paper, which would have destroyed the design. Defoe became part proprietor and manager in June, 1716, and Mr. Dormer died in March, 1718, but was succeeded by his brother. Defoe continued connected with the Paper until August following, but I cannot state whether it then terminated or not, as I have been unable to find a fragment even of the work, during such period, in any public or private collection.

With the exception of the two periodical publications just noticed, we have no record of any product of Defoe's pen during the year 1716, later than the month of April.

No doubt the establishment and conduct of *Mercurius Politicus* would occupy much of his attention, but I have generally found, in my researches into the chronological order of his writings, that any blank period predicates the appearance of some work or works of proportionate magnitude. The present is a case in point. On the 26th of April following, he published a volume of near 450 pages, entitled, " Memoirs of the Church of Scotland. In Four Periods. I. The Church in her Infant State, from the Reformation to the Queen Mary's Abdication. II. The Church in its Growing State, from the Abdication to the Restoration. III. The Church in its Persecuted State, from the Restoration to the Revolution. IV. The Church in its Present State, from the Revolution to the

Union. With an Appendix of some Transactions since the Union. London. E. Matthews. 1717." The author speaks modestly of his work, as in itself but a Preface or Introduction to some larger and fuller History, by better hands, some time or other. He says, " It is a moving Reflection, that these larger and fuller Accounts have been so often promised, and so long ago undertaken by several able and worthy Hands, and that yet Nothing has been finished, in a Cause wherein History is so much in debt to Truth. This Consideration has made an officious Stranger concern himself in the Work ; he could not bear to think that the Memory of the most glorious Scene of *Action*, and the most dismal Scene of *Suffering*, which the Church of Scotland has passed through, should lie buried in their own Ashes, and not a Man to be found who would effectually employ himself, and set seriously about the Work of ransoming things of such Consequence from the Grave of Forgetfulness." The Work is a testimony of Defoe's disinterested zeal to do justice and service to the people of Scotland ; it contains many fine passages of eloquent pathos ; and his account of the troubles during the times of the Covenanters and the battles of Claverhouse, are crowded with interesting details, related in his happiest stile of descriptive writing. The existence of the later works of Woodrow and Dr. M'Crie, does not altogether satisfactorily account for the fact that this most interesting volume has never been reprinted ; its contents are consequently almost unknown.

In his *Review* of August the 20th, 1709, Defoe had given an Account of the murder of Count Patkul ; and had also briefly noticed the same in his *History of the Wars* of Charles XII.* Early in the year 1717, the Government had reason to suspect that a conspiracy was in progress for another rebellion, to be aided by an invasion in favour of the Pretender. In consequence of secret information, the residence of Count Gyllenborg, the Swedish Ambassador, in London, was surrounded, all his Papers seized, and the whole plot was discovered. Under cover of the sacred character he bore, it was found that the Count was the active agent of the English

---

* Pp. 275-6.

Jacobites, and that the correspondence relative to such plot was carried on between him and Baron Goertz, another Swedish Ambassador abroad.   As soon as the facts became generally known, a strong feeling of resentment against the King of Sweden was created throughout the country ; and, as the reflex of such feeling would manifest itself in loyalty to King George and his Government, Defoe revived the account of the King of Sweden's cruelty to Count Patkul, in a pamphlet published in April, with the following title :—" A Short Narrative of the Life and Death of John Rhinholdt, Count Patkul, a Nobleman of Livonia, who was broke alive upon the Wheel, in Great Poland, anno 1707.   Together with the Manner of his Execution : Written by the Lutheran Minister who assisted him in his last Hours.   Faithfully Translated out of a High Dutch Manuscript ; and now Publish'd for the Information of Count Gyllenborg's English Friends.   By L. M. Regibus, *Boni quam Mali suspectiores sunt, Gratia oneri, Ultio in quæstis habetur.* Tacitus.   London.   T. Goodwin.   1717." It is impossible to say with certainty whether this is a translation or an original composition ; but I am inclined to think the latter, because he quotes nearly four pages from his own book published within two years, and speaks of it as " a late Book call'd *The History of the Wars of Charles XII., King of Sweden,* written, as 'tis pretended, by a Scotch Gentleman in that King's Army." This account of Patkul is a well-written and valuable historical Tract, calculated to excite deep pity for the noble victim, and to arouse strong indignation against the barbarity of the King of Sweden.

The Earl of Oxford still continued a prisoner in the Tower ; and there is a remarkable coincidence between the date of the next publication by Defoe, and that of his Lordship's trial. The lasting gratitude which originated when our Author was himself delivered out of a prison, through the instrumentality of his Lordship, would naturally impel him to offer to his " first benefactor" all possible assistance in preparing for the impending trial.   Could we suppose such assistance actually, but privately, offered and accepted, Defoe would undoubtedly have access to all available sources of private information bearing upon his Lordship's justification.   This can only be a specula-

tion ; yet, as the articles of impeachment were almost confined
to the negociations for peace with France, during the last years
of Queen Anne's life, so the book I am about to notice related
to the same, and was directly calculated to exonerate his Lordship from the charge of treason. After lying in the Tower two
years, the Earl's trial was fixed to take place, in the House of
Lords, on the 13th of June, 1717, but adjourned to the 24th ;
and on the 1st of July he was discharged.   On the 17th of
June, the book in question was published, entitled, " Minutes
of the Negociations of Monsr. Mesnager at the Court of
England, towards the close of the last Reign.   Wherein some
of the most Secret Transactions of that Time, relating to the
Interest of the Pretender, and a Clandestine separate Peace,
are detected and laid open.   Written by Himself.   Done out
of French.   London.   S. Baker.   1717."   The publication
was timed, so as to admit of being read before and during
Lord Oxford's trial, but without affording any opportunity of
neutralizing the favourable impression, until after the proceedings should have terminated.   The volume undoubtedly
produced a great sensation ; so that a second edition, and
also a reprint in Antwerp, were published during the same
year.   There were several later editions.   All contemporary
writers attributed the work to Defoe, and Oldmixon says that
he composed it " by direction of the quondam Treasurer,
Harley, who could not but be well acquainted with the subject described."   Savage and Boyer declared it a forgery ;
and the latter poured out his vial of abuse upon our Author
in the *Political State* for the month of June, in the same
year.   Defoe immediately replied, in the form of a Letter published in the next number of *Mercurius Politicus* ; but I regret
being unable to quote such reply in his own words.   Boyer,
however, notices the matter again in his *Political State* for July,
saying, " One D. F., thinking himself the Person meant by me,
has lately in Print, deny'd himself to be the Author of the
said Forgery."   Boyer had a great aptitude for misrepresent-
ing Defoe ; but supposing him not to have done so in this instance, the words may either be taken as a denial that the
book was a Forgery ; or, a repudiation of Original Authorship.
There is nothing inconsistent with Defoe having translated,
either the manuscript or book, out of the French, and this

would be strictly in accordance with his title page. Mr. Wilson having erroneously closed the political life of our Author two years before, endeavours to be consistent, by saying,—" There is nothing but traditional authority for ascribing this work to Defoe, and its internal character affords just reason for suspecting that it has no solid foundation."* Yet he must have felt strong misgivings, as to the accuracy of his own judgment, for he has inserted it in his List of Defoe's Works. I leave undecided the question, whether it is wholly, or partially fictitious; or, merely a translation from the French. But I must pronounce, in addition to all concurrent traditional authority, that the book contains, in my judgment, indisputable internal evidence that it came from Defoe's hand.

On the 31st of March, 1717, the Lord Bishop of Bangor preached before the King, his celebrated Sermon on *The Nature of the Kingdom or Church of Christ*. This being calculated to prepare the way for the repeal of the Occasional Conformity Act, and the Schism Act, gave the greatest possible offence to the High-Church clergy. It brought upon the Bishop a host of antagonists, and gave rise to what has ever since been known as the Bangorian Controversy. From the divine words,—" *My Kingdom is not of this World*,"—his Lordship deduced the unscriptural character of assumed Church authority in temporal and secular affairs, and struck at the root of all imposition of civil disabilities on grounds of religious belief and practice. As might be expected, the various denominations of Dissenters highly approved the Bishop's doctrine; and in order to enforce it practically, Defoe again assumed the disguise of a Quaker, and published,—" A Declaration of Truth to Benjamin Hoadly, one of the High Priests of the Land, and of the Degree whom Men call Bishops. By a Ministering Friend, who writ to Tho. Bradbury, a Dealer in many Words. London. E. More. 1717." In this work, the Bishop is commended for his manly avowal of Scriptural truth, which the writer assures him Friends have always tenaciously held. They do not doubt that the King, in whose hearing the Truth has been spoken, will be the Bishop's strong helper, and they hope that his Majesty may

---

* "Life of Defoe," iii. pp. 417-18.

be so enlightened that his Heart may be brought over to the
Friends.   There is an almost indescribable fineness of satire
running through the apparent grave sincerity of many parts of
this admirable pamphlet.   The reader will perceive this by endeavouring to imagine the Bishop's compliance with the following earnest exhortation :—" Wherefore, Friend Benjamin,
as I know that the Truth hath been spoken by thee, I warn
thee, for thy good, that thou come out speedily from among
them; lay down thy painted Vestments, and prophane
Trinkets, the Ensigns of that Usurpation upon thy Lord and
Master's Kingdom, which thou hast so faithfully born thy
Testimony against; I say, I exhort thee to lay them down
speedily, and come out from among them forthwith, *joyning thyself unto us*, whose Principles thou hast acknowledged.   So
shall thy Life and Doctrine be Uniform, and thou shalt be
sure to deserve that Blessing, which attends those who are not
ashamed to Practice the things which they Profess."

The first of Defoe's Letters which I have inserted in the
Introduction hereto, refers to the fact of his having been employed in Scotland by Lord Sunderland during the reign of
Queen Anne; and, that when his Lordship again came into
office under King George, he was pleased to approve and continue the service and appointment conferred on the writer by
Lord Townshend.   Defoe goes on to say, that with his Lordship's
approbation, he introduced himself, first as a translator of the
foreign news, to be concerned in *Mist's Journal,* and to keep
it in the circle of a secret management, so that it might pass
as a Tory paper, and yet be disabled and enervated of its treasonable character, " so as to do no mischief, or give any offence
to the Government."   Defoe had no share in the property of
this Paper, and had therefore no absolute power to reject improper communications; but he trusted to the moral influence
he should be able to acquire and maintain over *Mist*, the proprietor, who had no suspicion that the government was indirectly concerned in the matter.   This *Journal* was the organ
of the Pretender's interest; and its correspondents and supporters were, he tells us, " Papists, Jacobites, and enraged
High Tories, a generation who, I profess, my very soul
abhors."   In the performance of his duty he was compelled to

hear traitorous expressions against his Majesty's person and government, and to take scandalous and villainous papers, and keep them by him, as if he would gather materials from them to put into the news, but really with a determination to suppress them.   This was no system of espionage ;—here was no incitement to, or permission of treason, for the purpose of entangling the offenders, and bringing them within the grasp of the law.   The rebellion was yet smouldering, though subdued ; and the laws, liberties, and religion of the country were threatened.   This weekly Journal, inspired from the Court of the Pretender, and supported by the money and intelligence of attainted nobles abroad, and their adherents at home ; had laboured to keep alive the spirit of treason, until circumstances should be favourable for again spreading the flames of rebellion through the land.   If therefore moral persuasion is more effectual than legal repression, and prevention better than cure ; then no stigma, beyond that of concealment, attaches to the character of Defoe on account of his connection with *Mist's Journal.*   Rather should we admire the intellectual power capable of holding in check, without extraneous influence known to *Mist,* such men as Ormond, Atterbury, Bolingbroke, Mar, Wharton, and their satellites, among the Jacobite and nonjuring writers.   It required a large amount of patriotic courage to place himself as an impassable barrier between the invectives of such men and the reading public; and no less reservation and tact in exercising this influence in such a manner as to avoid suspicion.   He closes the letter with a favourite expression from Scripture, frequently cited in his writings, showing the sensitiveness of his mind, even as to the concealment necessary to the efficient service of his country. His words evince that he was conscious of the danger and difficulty of his duties ; and also, that his position was a questionable one ;—but there is no invidious self-reflection involved, when he says,—" Thus I bow myself in the house of Rimmon, and most humbly recommend myself to his Lordship's protection, or I may be undone the sooner, by how much the more faithfully I execute the commands I am under."

Mist's Journal was first published on the 15th of December, 1716, with the title of, " The Weekly Journal ; or Saturday's Post ;" but I do not find Defoe's hand in it until No. 37,

published on the 24th of August 1717.   The Paper continued,
from that time, under his management until the 15th of November 1718, when Mr. *Mist* becoming refractory, Defoe
abandoned him, but was induced to resume his connection on
the 31st of January 1719, and retained its direction until the
beginning of July 1720, when a second rupture occurred and
Defoe refused to be further responsible for the general character of the Paper.   For some time afterward, however, he translated and prepared the articles on foreign affairs, and occasionally contributed as a correspondent until the latter part of
1724.   The particulars of these changes will be noticed in
their proper places ;   and selections from his writings in the
Journal will be found in my collection of his newly-discovered
works.

The *Journal* consisted of six pages small folio, and for some
time each number began with " Foreign Affairs," arranged
under separate headings for the several countries.   After that
followed Letters from correspondents ;   then paragraphs of
Home news ; and finally, advertisements.   In Number 68, published on the 29th of March 1718, an important change was
made ; so that, in addition to the Letters from outside correspondents, each number contained an Essay or communication
on some subject of public interest, written in the form of a
letter,—generally by Defoe himself, so long as he continued in
the management,—and addressed to Mr. *Mist,* but signed with
any letter or name that might, for the appearance of variety,
occur at the moment.   This new practice, stamping upon the
Journal an individuality and consistency not previously existing, was presently adopted by the other weekly papers.   These
articles were placed at the commencement of each number,
and shortly became distinguished, whenever subsequently referred to, by the title of " Letter Introductory" of such a date.
The writer of such letters also, in each Journal, respectively,
became dignified with the title of Author, as for example,
" Mist's Author ;" or " the Author of Applebee's Journal."
Thus, I claim for Daniel Defoe, that he first originated, and
exemplified in his own person, those mighty agencies, in the
formation and direction of public opinion, now comprehended
in the words " Editor," and " Leading Article."

On the 28th of December 1717, when Defoe wrote the fine

article on the Bankruptcy laws, (which will be found in its place in my collection of his writings, and is subscribed with his initials, D. D. F.) he was clearly in the general management of *Mist's Journal.*

He states that though he had some need of the clemency he pleaded for, yet to take away the possible objection that he pleaded for himself, he was willing to be specially exempted from the benefits of the Act, if he could but assist in procuring a Law that would, like the Jubilee, once in every fifty years, deliver honest-minded Debtors from the hands of merciless Creditors. He adds, " I am the Man, who having had the Honour of drawing up the late Act for giving Bankrupts a Discharge, by Certificate, upon their surrendering all their Effects to their Creditors, voluntarily added the Clause which deliver'd all those who made fraudulent surrenders to be hang'd." And, as it is through their iniquity that honest but unfortunate Men suffer, he says, he would leave them to the same fate still.

The bitter controversy going on in France, during the early part of the century, between the Jesuits and the Jansenists, occasioned the publication of many pamphlets, one of which Defoe thought would promote the cause of Protestantism in England, and he therefore published a translation, with the following title, " A Curious Little Oration, Delivered by Father Andrews, concerning the Great Quarrels that divide the Clergy of France. Translated from the Fourth Edition of the French, by Dan. De F—e. London. J. Roberts, &c. 1717." This Tract passed through two editions the same year. Mr. Wilson quotes the title incorrectly, and dates it 1719.

There was undoubtedly some connection between Daniel Defoe, and John Dunton, the eccentric bookseller, author, and literary projector ; but it is very improbable that the nature of such connection will ever be discovered, and speculation would therefore be useless. There was no congeniality between the two, they differed in profession of religion ; Defoe never employed Dunton as his publisher, and at times the latter appears to have had a strong animosity towards the former, although he often mentions him, and is constrained to pay tribute to the

great genius, wit, integrity, and high courage, of the man he
dislikes.   I do not remember that Defoe more than once, in
all his writings, alludes to Dunton; and that was indirectly,
in scorn, that the latter had challenged him publicly to fight a
duel.   Defoe had been brought up under the ministry of Dr.
Annesley, and as we have seen, had the highest veneration for
the character of his pastor.   Dunton, though a churchman,
married the daughter of Dr. Annesley; and it is possible that
Defoe's first wife was another daughter, but of this we have no
proof.   Their friendship, such as it was, might have commenced at the discussion meetings of Whig apprentices and
young politicians, during the reign of James II.; it continued
until about 1702, when an entire estrangement took place,
which lasted for fifteen years.   I do not think their intercourse
was then, or ever afterward, renewed; although Mr. J. B.
Nichols,* and after him Mr. Walter Wilson,† have stated that
on the 28th October 1717, an Agreement was entered into
between Defoe and Dunton for writing a weekly Paper, to be
entitled "The Hanover Spy."   The foundation of such statement is contained in a volume of miscellaneous manuscript in
the handwriting of Dunton, now in the Bodleian Library.‡
On examination of this document, I saw reason to believe that
it was only one of the multifarious projects of Dunton's fertile
brain; and probably Defoe never knew of its existence.   I
have been since favoured by my friend, the Rev. W. D.
Macray, of the Bodleian Library, with a copy of the manuscript, and am confirmed in my previous opinion.   At that
time Defoe was composing numerous pamphlets and voluminous works for the press; and, unknown to Dunton, he was
also writing and conducting three periodical publications.   He
had little leisure, and probably no inclination, toward such a
proposal; and as I think he never entered into any agreement
of the kind, I refrain from inserting a copy of the document.
My conclusion is strengthened by the fact that, shortly afterward, Dunton published the materials he had prepared for such
Paper, in a thick pamphlet, entitled, "The Hanover Spy; or,
Secret History of St. James's, &c.   1718."

---

* " Life and Errors of John Dunton," 1818, vol. I. p. xxviii.
† " Life and Times of Daniel Defoe," 1830, vol. III. p. 417.
‡ Rawlinson MS. Miscell. 72 f. 49 b.

In the dawn of 1718, departed this life a statesman, the most remarkable for his personal idiosyncrasies, in that or perhaps any other age.   It was the good fortune of the Duke of Shrewsbury to serve his country during four reigns; and, without genius or enterprise, without even an effort, to save the Constitution from threatened destruction.   Amidst the political factions that raged during the last years of Queen Anne, to which I have sufficiently alluded, when deadly hatred divided her responsible ministers, the Duke stood between the parties, unmoveably neutral.   Cold and cautious, he would run no hazards, and retreated from all extremity.   Personal safety, was his ambition; and ease, more precious than wealth.   His inactivity disqualified him from leading in any policy; and his indifference compelled the factions to keep him out of their councils.   He was little depended on, by any of the parties in the State, yet had influence with all.   On the dismissal of the Earl of Oxford, the Pretender's party, with Lord Bolingbroke at their head, were jubilant; but, when the dying Queen placed the Lord Treasurer's Staff in the hands of the Duke of Shrewsbury, amazement succeeded; and her Majesty's immediate decease,—leaving the power of the government in his hands,—paralysed the disloyal, and gave a death-blow to the cause of the Pretender.   The Duke quietly directed the proclamation of King George, but did little else that he could avoid; and, as he could not resign his office until the King's arrival, he did so shortly afterward, and retired altogether from public affairs during the remainder of his life.

Within a few months after the Duke's death, three different memoirs of him were published, the most considerable of which was written by Defoe, and is entitled " Memoirs of publick Transactions in the Life and Ministry of his Grace the D. of Shrewsbury.   In which will be found much of the History of Parties, and especially of Court-Divisions during the last Four Reigns, which no History has yet given an Account of.   *Plus valet occulatis Testis, quam auriti decem.*   London. Printed for Thos. Warner, at the Black Boy in Paternoster Row, 1718.   Price two shillings."   This large pamphlet must be considered as more than a memoir of the Duke, viz., the complement of our author's political history of the period comprised in his previous works, the *Secret History of the*

*White Staff;—Two Nights Court at Greenwich;—*and, *Minutes of the Negociations of M. Mesnager.*   Defoe must have been greatly pressed for time when composing this memoir.   It is historically correct, and valuable on that account ; but contains more than usual of his characteristic repetition of matter, and redundancy of verbal expression ; and it appears to have been printed without any correction of the manuscript.

Early in the same year it became evident to France and England that an attack was about to be made by Spain upon the Austrian provinces in Italy ; and steps were taken, in the month of May, to induce Holland to join in a triple-alliance against Spain, with the hope that the latter would desist, on finding a strong confederacy against her.   To forward the design of Government, Defoe published a pamphlet entitled, " The Case of the War in Italy Stated : Being a Serious Enquiry how far Great Britain is Engaged to concern itself in the Quarrel between the Emperor and the King of Spain. *Pax Quæritur Bello.*   London.   T. Warner, 1718."   The author urges that Great Britain is bound not to let Spain dis-' member the Italian Provinces of Austria ;—that therefore we ought to side with the Emperor ; and if needful, to send a Fleet against the Spanish West Indies.

Between April and June, the Six Letters, recently discovered in the State Paper Office, and which occasioned my investigations herein, were written by Defoe, and addressed to Charles De la Faye, Esq., one of the Secretaries under the Earl of Sunderland.   Copies of the Letters are in the Introduction hereto.

It was a redeeming feature in the character of the infamous publisher Curll, that though he pandered to vice so indecently as to bring himself several-times under severe correction of the law, he yet procured to be written and published, in the form of thick pamphlets, many valuable memoirs of eminent persons then recently deceased.   Among these, Defoe wrote for him, " Memoirs of the Life and Eminent Conduct of that Learned and Reverend Divine, Daniel Williams, D.D.   With some Account of his Scheme for the vigorous Propagation of Religion,

as well in England as in Scotland, and several other Parts of
the World. Addressed to Mr. Pierce. London. E. Curll.
1718." Dr. Williams was the most influential Presbyterian
Divine in London, from the time of William III., (with whom
he was on terms of intimate friendship,) to his own death in
1716. He was a man of great piety, of catholic spirit, and
of large acquaintance with the true interests of the nation.
He was a liberal benefactor to the Dissenters, and besides
founding, for their use, the public library, still known by his
name, he bequeathed a very considerable property to charitable
and educational purposes. The memoir of such a man was a
congenial subject for our author's pen, and the book is valuable and interesting.

Encouraged by the success of his former volume of
The Family Instructor, which had reached the fourth edition,
Defoe now added a second volume, entitled, " The Family
Instructor. In Two Parts. I. Relating to Family Breaches,
and their Obstructing Religious Duties. II. To the great
Mistake of Mixing the Passions in the Managing and Correcting of Children. With a great Variety of Cases relating
to setting Ill Examples to Children and Servants. Vol. II.
London. Eman. Matthews. 1718." He says in his preface,
" The modern Readers of Books have a general Opinion,
which they entertain like a Fundamental Principle in Reading,
that Second Parts never come up to the Spirit of the First;
tho' perhaps here they may find an Exception to that Rule."
He admits, therefore, that it is a bold adventure to write a
second volume of anything; and cites " Mr. Milton," whose
Paradise Regained " could never obtain to be named with
Paradise Lost," and who believed the reason of the common
dislike to be, " That the People had a general sense of the
Loss of Paradise, but not an equal Gust for the Regaining of
it." Of this Second Volume he says, " the whole Scene now
presented, is so entirely differing from all that went before,
and so eminently directed to another Species of Readers, that
it seems to be as perfectly new, as if no other Part had been
published before it." Referring to books written merely to
divert the world, reaching to the seventh and eighth volume,
he says, if this subject is less pleasing than those looser works,

" it must be because we have less Pleasure in Things instructing, than in Things merely humouring and diverting; less
Patience in bearing a just Reproof, and less Humility in
applying it, than we ought to have." After speaking of the
onerous duties of Parents and Masters, and the great discretion requisite in the necessary obligation of Correction, he
adds, "The same Desire of doing Good, which moved the
First Part, has been sincerely the Occasion of a Second. With
all possible Humility and Thankfulness, I acknowledge and
believe I have had the same Presence and Assistance, and I
cannot but hope for the same Blessings and Success; and
with the Comfort and Confidence of this, I cheerfully send it
into the World, not concerned at all at the Opposition it shall
meet with from the Infirmities and Unworthiness of its
Author." The volume is in no sense inferior to its predecessor. It is equally unsectarian, catholic, and evangelical.
It abounds in excellent maxims of piety and wisdom, calculated
to arouse the attention, to enlighten the understanding, and
kindle the best affections of the heart. The young have been
attracted by the incidental narratives in this, and the companion volume;—to the old, they constitute a manual of
social duty;—the sweet simplicity of the dialogue commends
the work to the meanest capacity,—while the accurate delineation of human nature must extort praise, from the most refined and critical student. There are few books better adapted
for the perusal of all to whom the education of the young is
committed; the clergy of every denomination,—teachers of
National and Sunday Schools, parents, children, and servants.
And as Mr. Wilson truly observes, "if the author had written
nothing else, these volumes alone possess a sufficient merit to
give him a high place amongst English moralists."

I must now return to Defoe as a news-writer, and observe
generally, that, as in his *Reviews,* so in *Mercurius Politicus,*
Mist's Journal, and the other Papers with which he afterward
became connected, a very considerable part of his hitherto unknown writings consists of Foreign and other news that have
ceased to be interesting, except as the materials of History. To
have copied all that was written by his hand, merely because
it was his, would have greatly extended my manuscript; and

therefore, I have aimed only at a resuscitation of what may be
of permanent interest.

The change produced by Defoe's influence in the character
of *Mist's* Journal was so surprising, that it soon began to be
commented upon by contemporary Journals; but it was a considerable time before our author was named as the cause of
such change. In June 1718, an exaggerated account reached
England that the Island of St. Vincent had been destroyed by
an Earthquake, upon which Defoe wrote a long and wonderfully circumstantial narrative of the catastrophe, and inserted
it in Mist's paper, for which Mr. Mist was rallied the following week in *Read's* (Whig) *Journal,* for printing an imaginary
story, instead of the racy, political, and violent article he was
wont to give the public. The taunt concluded, " his Wings
are clipped, and he only flutters about like a wounded Bird."

The position of Defoe with respect to *Mist's Journal* was an
irksome one. He had not only to meet continually persons
very uncongenial to him, as already stated, but also to contend
against the prejudice, bigotry, disloyalty, and immediate pecuniary interest of the printer and publisher, who was doubtless
in the pay of the Jacobites. The consciousness that he was
serving the best interests of his country sustained him for a
time; but he painfully felt that his influence, however successful, was of a negative kind, and that he was restrained
from writing, in Mist's paper, anything directly in favour of his
honest political views. Besides his own great secret, of employment by the government, a certain degree of concealment
from the public also, as to their connection, was thought by
himself and Mr. Mist essential to the efficiency of his services;
and, when the latter secret could be no longer kept, Defoe had to
bear in silence, the most virulent personal attacks from two of
the Whig Journals. Under these circumstances, it cannot be
surprising that he desired to have the means of directly advocating his sincere and honest principles, in a Journal free
from such unsatisfactory associations. With such view he set
on foot, " The Whitehall Evening Post," a paper consisting of
two leaves small quarto, published on Tuesday, Thursday, and
Saturday. The first number appeared on the 18th of September 1718, and Defoe continued to be connected with it
until June 1720. The paper existed many years afterward.

In the *Weekly Journal and British Gazetteer*, (which for the sake of brevity I shall in future call *Read's Journal*,) of October 4th, 1718, there was a Letter, in which the connection between Mist and Defoe is first publicly spoken of, and that in the following opprobrious terms :—" That notorious, insignificant animal *Mist* permits his scandalous Author, *Daniel Foe*, to take the Liberty at all times insipidly to ridicule and insult his Majesty's Friends and Allies with foolish comparisons and dull reflections." In the following week the same Journal speaks of them, in a matter of fact way, as " *Daniel Foe* and his Printer." No remark can be necessary here in vindication of Defoe against the charge of insulting the friends and allies of the King.

On the 25th October, Mist insisted upon inserting a Letter, from a correspondent, signed *Sir Andrew Politick;* taking a somewhat anti-English view of the war with Spain. It was certainly an objectionable Jacobite article, but contained no direct reflections on either the King or the Administration. Defoe strongly objected to its publication, and the dispute was compromised by his being allowed to revise the Letter, and add an Editorial note of dissent by way of antidote, as follows :—

" *Mist's* answer to all this is, that he believes Sir Andrew desires no other reply than to have his doubts recommended to the World ; for he could not expect that they should be answer'd in his way ; but he says now, and without turning Whig too, that he cannot be so much of Sir Andrew's mind in the Naval part as perhaps he expects ; and he thinks, tho' he has nothing to say about the beginning of the War ; yet as to the end of it, he thinks Jack Spaniard may be made to pay for the Supper, whoever pays for the Breakfast ; and besides, Sir Andrew mistakes his Man a little in these Enquiries ; for that *Mist*, as much a Party Man as Sir Andrew takes him for, yet having served in a Station in the Royal Navy, and in those Seas in particular, he is not so out of love with a War at Sea as Sir Andrew thinks he is ; and especially with the Spaniards, who he must acknowledge he believes can never be brought by any new Measures, or new Management in the World to be a Match at Sea for the British Nation. As for the rest of the Queries *he answers* and *saith Nothing*."

Defoe was, however, still unsatisfied, and in the next number inserted a long and full answer to Sir Andrew's Letter. I have quoted the above, because it proves that a crisis was approaching between the two men. The Jacobite supporters of Mist began to be furious at the emasculated character of the publication; and Defoe had insisted that, beyond " rallying the *Flying Post* and the Whig writers, and the admission of any foolish and trifling Things in favour of the Tories," he could have no part with him. He says, " I have freely told him that this is the only Way to preserve his Paper, and keep himself from a Jail, and concluded that unless he would keep measures with me, and be punctual in these Things, I could not serve him any farther, or be concerned any more." All warnings, however, were now useless, the rallying of the Whigs became personal bitterness, the foreign news was contrary to the policy of the government, and the *Journal* became, notwithstanding all Defoe's efforts, much more violent than it had been for some time before.

In the *Whitehall Evening Post* of the 1st of November 1718, Defoe had the unpleasant duty of announcing that the premises of *Mist* had been searched for the Letter of Sir Andrew Politick, under a warrant from government; that a seditious libel was found hid in the ceiling,—that all the persons on the premises were seized,—and that *Mist*, on this surrendered, and was committed into the custody of a messenger. The account is long, and thus much only concerns our author; except that through his influence the delinquent was discharged almost immediately afterward.

On the same day, *Read's Journal* contains a Letter congratulating the Editor on having discovered that *Mist's Journal*, and the *Whitehall Evening Post* are written by the same hand, and that D. Foe was the man. The writer goes on to state, that Defoe has a security of 500*l.* from Mist, not to discover him, so that he may write with the greater insolence against the government; and hopes the persons concerned with the other Paper will not similarly screen him, but let him stand or fall by his own works. The writer continues, " But Sir, there needs no other proof of his binomical Performance, than the agreeableness of the Style and Manner; the little Art he is truly master of, of forging a Story, and imposing it on the World for Truth. Witness that of the Gentleman and his

Horse, which he murder'd in Shropshire, with all the little embellishments of Lies that are contriv'd to set it off, are not more Miraculous than False."* The whole of the communication, though unwillingly evincing an appreciation of Defoe's genius, was written under the erroneous impression that he was now a Tory and a Jacobite, opposing the government. The only truth being that he was concerned in the two papers named.

On the 8th of November, Mist came forth in his own person, and occupied a column of his *Journal* in explaining the circumstances of his arrest, and answering the charges made against Defoe and himself, in *Read's Journal*. Except in denying that Defoe was the "Author" of his Journal, in the technical sense of the word, and his denial that he had given Defoe a bond for 500*l.*, I am obliged to say that this statement of *Mist* is contrary to the truth, in matters about which he could not possibly be mistaken. He is contradicted not only by the Letters Defoe had written to the government a few months previously; but by the internal evidence of the Journal itself, down to the date of his attempted vindication. As to Defoe's concern in his Journal, Mist states,—" That whereas the same *Read* has likewise published, that the Author of the *Whitehall Post*, is the Author of the *Saturday's Post*, this is also a *Lye*; and Mr. *Mist* affirms that person neither is, or ever was the Author of the *Weekly Journal, or Saturday's Post*; nor has he any concern at all in it, or ever had, except that formerly he has sometimes translated some Foreign Letters, in the absence of the Person who was more constantly employed for that part; and this also he defies him to contradict, and wonders men that pretend to other things, can publish such audacious untruths. Another of the Forgeries of these Writers is this, viz. that Mr. *Mist* has given a bond to Mr. *Daniel Defoe* for 500*l.* obliging himself in the penalty of 500*l.*, not to dis-

---

* The same journal contains the following vile paragraph:—" Last Tuesday some Hawkers roar'd about the Streets very dismal News, contain'd in an Elegy upon Daniel Foe, Author of *Mist's* Scandalous *Journal*, and the *Whitehall Evening Post*, who hang'd himself at Newington the day before: but we have been since inform'd, that tho' that scurrilous Fellow has no superfluity of Grace, Loyalty, and common Honesty, yet has he just Wit enough not to befriend the Hangman, by becoming a *Felo de se*, which he knows would be the *Shortest Way* to the *D——l.*"

cover his being the writer of his Paper. This Mr. *Mist* declares to be false, and that he never gave any Bond, or Writing, or Obligation of any kind whatsoever to Mr. Defoe, or to any other else on his account," &c.

Although no direct provocation had been given, yet *Read's Journal*, of the same date, contains a whole column of most scandalous and libellous verse, in the form of an Elegy on Defoe. It adds nothing to our knowledge, and is unworthy of quotation. I cannot but notice his *apparent* indifference to these atrocious and unfounded libels ; and his self-command, in never being betrayed, even under the greatest aggravation, into " railing against railing." The circumstances related above, determined him to abandon *Mist* and his Journal ; which he did after the next issue, with a playful challenge of his opponents to a kind of literary duel, in which he proposed that each party should produce as many instances as he could find, in which the foreign news published by the other had been contradicted by later advices, " and those who have told most Lies in print, shall be obliged to submit, and lay down their Paper, and print no more."

The only response to this meekness and Christian spirit, was a most obscene and blasphemous attack upon Defoe, Mist, and Mawson the publisher, in *Read's Journal* of the following Saturday (Nov. 22nd). It occupies about a column and a half of octo-syllabic rhyme, and represents the three as being taken by Charon to Hell. The following is all that can be quoted with regard to decency. The poem contains nothing new of Defoe, unless it be a fact that, at some time, he had traded in civet-cats, which had been asserted against him as an offence many years before. Charon is here made to address him as to the voyage across the Styx, thus :—

> " I'll bring thee o're the *Shortest Way*,
> I'll set thee up a *Ragged Hose*,
> Worn out at Heels and eke at Toes.
> *Mist's Journals*, they shall be thy Sails,
> And *Samon's Canvase* Hoop'd with *Whales*.
> *Mercators*, they shall be thy Streamers,
> With *Keimer's* Visions and his Dreamers.
> For Jack and Pendants I will chuse,
> Your *Mercurys* and your *Reviews*.
> And that no Ornament be lost,
> I'll hoist up *Whitehall Evening Post*,

> *Jure Divino, Polish Dyet,*
> And *Pillory Hymn* to make you quiet.
> Or, if you please, I'll hang the Vane
> With your own *True-born Englishman.*
> And since I must be your Conductor
> I'll add your *Family Instructor.*
> Thus Rigg'd and Trimm'd like Paper Kite,
> I'll bring thee to the D——l's sight
> And show him *who all these did write.*"

The same number contains a Letter, flatly contradicting Mist's denial of Defoe's share in the composition of that worthy's Journal, and citing the evidence of his own workmen against him. Defoe had now emancipated himself from a position that had been painful to him, without the compensation of having been able to control the treasonable tendencies of Mist and his supporters. The consequence was immediately apparent to the public. A writer in *Read's Journal* of the 29th Nov. observed of Mist, " and furthermore I declare, he can no more write, *tho' he pretends to do it in his last Week's Paper,* than he durst to fight." The first effect upon Defoe, of this release from unmerited odium, was the publication of an admirable article, in which the penitential parts could only have emanated from one of the noblest of minds. It was inserted in the form of a Letter to the Undertakers of the *Whitehall Evening Post,* Dec. 2nd, 1718, and will be found in this collection of his writings.

The separation of Defoe from Mist was commemorated in *Read's Journal* of the 6th of December, in a poem, from which it is evident that the act was that of Defoe. Though unfriendly, it is much less bitter than the preceding strictures in the same Paper, yet it is evidently from the same hand. The following extract must suffice :—

> " What strange Adventures could untwist
> Such True-born Knaves as *Foe* and *Mist ?*
> They quarrel'd sure about the Pelf,
> For Dan's a needy, greedy Elf,
> And *Mist* has not much Coin to spare
> If Colonel *Hebburn* had his share.
> As Rats do run from falling Houses,
> So *Dan* another Cause espouses;
> Leaves poor *Nat* sinking in the Mire,
> Writes *Whitehall Evening Post* for hire."

On the 13th of December, the Government introduced a Bill into Parliament for repealing the two Acts, passed near the end of the preceding reign, against Occasional Conformity, and against Schism. These persecuting laws had deprived the Dissenters of their legal Toleration, on the ground of *greater Security to the Church of England*. The Bill for their repeal was entitled, *An Act for Strengthening the Protestant Interest in these Kingdoms*. We have no direct evidence of Defoe's influence in this removal of unjust fetters from the Dissenters; but the Bill was brought in by Lord Stanhope, with whom our author was in official intercourse; and he seizes the opportunity of closing his editorial year, with an excellent article on the subject, in the *Whitehall Evening Post* of the 30th December, in which he says :—" And first of all, how can you avoid taking Notice, how Generous a part the *Church* act in this, and how they adhere to that happy Declaration so often made by her Clergy, that *Persecution is contrary to the Church of England*." He also alludes to his own past exertions on behalf of the Dissenters, and concludes by a declaration of their loyal obedience to the Government, and to the laws and institutions of the country. He states that, " so far from being desirous to pull down or overthrow the Church, *as has been suggested*, they must be, on all Occasions, even by the nature of Things always ready to uphold it."

In the discussion upon the above Bill, the Bishop of Bangor spoke ably in favour of the Dissenters, whom he said he had endeavoured to bring over to the Church; but he was ever of opinion that gentle means were the most effectual for that purpose; and he proved that the Occasional and Schism Acts were persecuting Laws. Defoe had a high regard for the Bishop, but thought him generally too fond of controversy; and he therefore took occasion to commend, and yet at the same time reprove him, in a Quaker Tract, which was published on the 10th of January 1719, under the title of, "A Friendly Rebuke to one Parson Benjamin ; Particularly relating to his Quarrelling with his Own Church, and Vindicating Dissenters. By one of the People called Quakers. London. E. Moore. 1719." After showing him that the heat of controversy had drawn him into inconsistencies, and had raised him up a host of opponents, without advancing the cause of true religion; the writer urges that all the Bishop can admit of erroneous practice of his own Church; and all the advocacy he can give to the cause of the Dissenters, is neutralized by his continuing in the communion of that Church. He says:—" We have the Testimony of thy Practice against thy Insincerity; that whereas thou hast declared thyself persuaded of Error in the constitution of thy Hierarchy, yet thou dost not separate from the same. Fie, Fie, Benjamin! Either separate from them thy self, or thou wilt very ill justify our Separation; it will be a most desperate Piece of Service for thee to engage in, at once to justify us that separate, and thy self who conformest." The pamphlet is sustained throughout by a spirit of quiet ironical argument, and is such a faithful but friendly rebuke, as perhaps no man but Defoe could have written.

CHAPTER XII.

"Whitehall Evening Post" enlarged—Defoe again undertakes "Mist's Journal"—Alexander Selkirk—Defoe publishes the first and second volumes of "Robinson Crusoe"—Gildon's strictures on "Robinson Crusoe"—Defoe publishes "Serious Reflections of Robinson Crusoe"— "An Account of the Baron de Goertz"—Defection of Dissenters from the doctrine of the Trinity—Defoe publishes "A Letter to the Dissenters"—"Anatomy of Exchange Alley"—Beneficial influence of Defoe on Tory journals—Compelled to coerce Mr. Mist—Establishes "The Daily Post"—Cessation of personal hostilities between Read and Defoe—Publishes "A Faithful Account of 'Dickory Cronke'"— "Charity still a Christian Virtue"—"The King of the Pirates, Captain Avery."

1719.

WITH the beginning of the year 1719, the *Whitehall Evening Post* ceased to be printed by Boreham, of Paternoster Row; and began to be issued by J. Roberts, at the Oxford Arms, in Warwick Lane. It was also printed upon considerably larger paper. In the number dated the 15th of January, Defoe relates an interesting story told him in 1674, by a relative, who served in Flanders, in an English Regiment commanded by the brave Earl of Ossory. The article containing the account will be found in my collection of his writings; but nothing further is said of the relation in question.

I have now to notice Defoe's second engagement on *Mist's Journal*. In this, he was doubtless directed by the Government; with the same laudable object as before, namely, the suppression of treason at its source, before it could be printed and dispersed abroad to taint the minds of the people. The apprehension of Mr. Mist, already noticed, must have convinced that wrong-headed politician of his error, in spurning the advice and guidance of Defoe. After their separation, Mist speedily discovered further, by its rapidly declining circulation, that the good genius of his Journal had departed. Self-interest, therefore, compelled him to seek and put himself again into the hands of Defoe, who resumed the control, on his own absolute terms, in the beginning of January 1719. We have seen on former occasions the man, whose keen satire could rouse great parties in the state to political madness ; yet always refusing to reciprocate personal rancour, under the grossest provocation. Here we have another feature of Defoe's Christian character, in the placability that blotted out, on confession, the injustice of Mr. Mist, without apparent scrutiny as to the purity of his motives. The following, which appeared in Read's Journal, soon afterward, shows that, though the personal engagements of our author were soon known, the nature of his censorship was perfectly concealed :—" Mr. Read, you are often telling us of Treaties that are carrying on ; I can acquaint you now with one that they say is finish'd : It is betwixt Mr. Mist, and the famous Daniel, who is now again to undertake the Dirty Work of penning his Journal. The reason I hear is, that Mr. Mist, having found the Sale of his Paper decline, for want of a little of the old Scandal, it occasion'd this Accommodation ; of which I doubt not you will soon hear the confirmation ; it being fit the World shou'd be appriz'd of an Affair of so much conse-quence." Defoe's hand and mind, are evident in the number of Mist's Journal, dated the 3rd January 1719. During several months following, all personalities were carefully avoided,—even the Whigs were scarcely rallied,—the proceed-ings of the Government were not called in question ; and Mr. Mist and his politics, are scarcely more palpable than would be designated by his name. I mark, from the same date, a falling off in the quality of the Whitehall Evening Post, which contains nothing characteristic from the pen of Defoe, though I think it continued in his general management, and that he occasionally translated for it the news from Amsterdam.

Under the Quadruple Alliance, England had joined in the War against Spain, yet the Jacobites and High Tories favoured the cause of Spain. In April of this year, the Pretender was at the Spanish Court, and the expatriated Duke of Ormond was not only with him, but engaged in command of a Naval and Military force to invade England or Ireland. The war news, concocted on both sides in party spirit, was of the most contradictory character ; and that from Spain, for Mist's

Journal, evidently written by an enemy to England. The labour Defoe bestowed on these missives, in order to separate truth from treason and falsehood, must have been very great, and the process perplexing. He appears to have been unable to entrust any part of this work to other hands, and yet frequently adds such sentences as the following, " We must, as Times go, caution the Readers of News, as well Ours as other Men's, always to make Allowance for Men telling their own Tale." His wisdom and impartiality, in this difficult part of his duty, is as admirable as his caution. Thus, he frequently states, at length, the war news according to the reports of both Whigs and Tories, and having set before the public these conflicting accounts, concludes gravely,—" We must therefore leave People to judge of the Probability of these things as they shall think fit."

Defoe appears to have been possessed of One Hundred and Twenty-seven Pounds ten Shillings in South Sea Stock, and on the 22nd of March 1719, he authorised Mordecai Jenkins of London, who was probably a stockbroker, to sell the same for him. The original deed or memorandum of this appointment was in the possession of the late Mr. Upcott, and Mr. Wilson has copied it at length into his Life of Defoe.*

Our Author was now in the fifty-eighth year of his age, and had already given to the world a greater number of distinct Works than any other living writer ; yet his past labours, whether considered with respect to their number,—the marvellous capacity of his genius,—the astonishing rapidity of his composition,—or his title thereby to undying fame,—appear to sink into comparative insignificance, when we contemplate his productions during the twelve remaining years of his life. The inexhaustible fertility of his invention,—stimulating a hand and frame inured by long habit to the toil of composition,—has called forth the wonder and astonishment of many of the greatest writers and critics of modern times. But they were all unaware that in addition to the Herculean labours claiming their admiration, there were also, a monthly publication of

---

* Vol. III. p. 425.

Clark & Pine Sc.

[FRONTISPIECE TO THE 1ST EDITION OF
ROBINSON CRUSOE, 1719.]

nearly a hundred pages; a Paper published weekly; another
appearing thrice a week; and, a great part of the time, a fourth,
issued daily; besides about twenty biographical, historical, and
political pamphlets, and several considerable volumes, then
unknown to be his. So great an amount of intellectual toil
would be incredible were not the facts before us, in the works
themselves. Much of the time for recruiting exhausted Nature
with necessary food and sleep,—all his goings and returnings—
his seasons of social intercourse, if any,—in fact, during every
waking moment, must that calm and clear head have been
able to concentrate his faculties upon whatever subject engaged
his pen at the time. Let the eye glance at the List of his
works from the beginning of 1719 to 1724,—let the attention
be directed to the short periods between the publication of
successive volumes,—and adding thereto, his Journalistic
labours, it may fairly be asked if the history of the world contains proof that an equally prolific literary genius has existed?

This is not the place in which to dilate upon the wide grasp
of Defoe's mind, as exhibited in his later writings,—which included almost every branch of literature; nor to enlarge upon
his peculiar and happy manner of treating every subject, so as
to interest all ranks and classes of readers. Such considerations belong rather to retrospection than anticipation; and I
must therefore apologize for desiring that the readers of this
Memoir should,—while hearing of the production of his successive works,—be enabled to carry along with them a general
impression of his multifarious and daily engagements as a
journalist, admitting of no postponement or delay; and his
untiring indomitable industry, which enabled him to achieve
the results we have further to consider.

Alexander Selkirk, born at Largs, in the County of Fife, in
1676, became a sailor on board Captain Stradling's ship in the
cruising expedition of Captain Dampier to the South Seas.
Having quarrelled with his captain, he deserted the ship at the
island of Juan Fernandez, in September 1704, and lived alone
there four years and four months, until he was released by
Captain Woodes Rogers, in the month of February, 1709,
when he became mate during the remainder of Rogers's expedition, and returned to England in the month of October, 1711,

with a booty of 800*l*., after an absence of rather more than eight years.   In 1712, Captain Rogers published an Account of his Voyage, which contains a brief relation of Selkirk's residence on the Island.·   Several other meagre accounts were published; and Selkirk being in London, was seen by Steele, who, on the 3rd of December 1713, occupied the 26th number of the " Englishman" with a short narrative of the information Selkirk gave him about his adventures.

Such is the ground-work upon which Defoe built his most celebrated romance; the first volume of which was published on the 25th of April 1719, with the following title, " The Life and Strange Surprising Adventures of Robinson Crusoe, of York, Mariner: who lived Eight and Twenty Years all alone in an Uninhabited Island on the Coast of America, near the Mouth of the Great River Oroonoque; Having been cast on Shore by Shipwreck, wherein All the Men perished but himself.   With an Account how he was at last as strangely deliver'd by Pyrates.   Written by himself.   London.   Printed for W. Taylor at the Ship in Paternoster Row.   1719."

Defoe must have felt that, in writing a preface, his task was needless, as a recommendation.   His brief and simple address is therefore intended to aid the little artifice that he had merely edited Crusoe's own narrative.   " If ever the Story of any private Man's Adventures in the World were worth making Publick, and were acceptable when Publish'd, the Editor of this Account thinks this will be so.   The Wonders of this Man's Life exceed all that (he thinks) is to be found extant; the Life of one Man being scarce capable of a greater Variety. The Story is told with so much Modesty, with Seriousness, and with a religious Application of Events to the Uses to which wise Men always apply them, (viz.), to the Instruction of others by this Example, and to justify and honour the Wisdom of Providence in all the Variety of our Circumstances, let them happen how they will. The Editor believes the thing to be a just History of Fact; neither is there any appearance of Fiction in it: and however thinks, because all such things are dispatch'd, that the Improvement of it, as well to the Diversion as to the Instruction of the Reader, will be the same , and as such, he thinks, without further Compliment to the World, he does them a great Service in the Publication."

THE
LIFE
AND
STRANGE SURPRIZING
ADVENTURES
OF
ROBINSON CRUSOE,
Of *YORK*, MARINER:

Who lived Eight and Twenty Years,
all alone in an un-inhabited Ifland on the
Coaft of AMERICA, near the Mouth of
the Great River of OROONOQUE;

Having been caft on Shore by Shipwreck, wherein all the Men perifhed but himfelf.

WITH
An Account how he was at laft as ftrangely deliver'd by PYRATES.

Written by Himfelf.

LONDON:
Printed for W. TAYLOR at the *Ship* in *Pater-Nofter-
Row.* MDCCXIX.

1ST EDITION OF ROBINSON CRUSOE]

Mr. Chalmers says that the manuscript of " Robinson Crusoe" passed through the whole circle of the publishing trade before it could find a purchaser.   He gives no evidence upon this point, and I think the statement very improbable, as the talents of the author were too well known and appreciated for anything from his pen to go begging.'   It is certain, however, that he sold all property in it, and probably for a very inadequate sum.   William Taylor, the publisher, gained a very large amount by the whole of the volumes, besides the indirect advantage of its bringing him into great note, and extending his general business; so that he rapidly amassed a considerable fortune.*   So instantaneous was the demand, that the second edition was published only seventeen days after the first; the third edition followed twenty-five days later, and the fourth edition on the 8th of August.

This favourable reception, notwithstanding some insidious attempts to prejudice the public against it, encouraged Defoe to pursue the subject.   A second Volume, which must have occupied him very little time in its composition, was published on the 20th August, with the following title, " The Farther Adventures of Robinson Crusoe; Being the Second and Last Part of his Life, and of the Strange Surprising Accounts of his Travels round three Parts of the Globe.   Written by Himself. To which is added a Map of the World, in which is Delineated the Voyages of Robinson Crusoe.   London.   Printed for William Taylor at the Ship in Paternoster Row.   1719." 1 have said that this volume must have occupied very little time in its composition.   From the four months intervening between the appearance of the first and second volumes, must be deducted a considerable part during which the latter was in the press; and also that taken up with the composition of

---

* Mr. Taylor died a young man, only five years after he had published the first volume of Robinson Crusoe.

Read's Journal, 9 May, 1724. — " On Tuesday last (5th) died of a violent Fever, Mr. William Taylor, at his House in Paternoster Row, an eminent Bookseller, reputed to be worth between forty and fifty thousand pounds."

London Journal, 16 January, 1725.—" On Tuesday last (14th) Mr. Innys, an eminent Bookseller, in St. Paul's Churchyard, was marry'd to the Relict of Mr. Taylor, late of Paternoster Row, worth thirty thousand Pounds."

several other works published between the two parts of
Robinson Crusoe, and which I shall have to notice shortly.

The respect due to everything sanctioned by so great an
authority as Sir Henry Ellis, compels me to notice a strange,
surprizing account of the authorship of the first volume of
" Robinson Crusoe."   In 1843, Sir Henry edited, for the
Camden Society, a handsome quarto volume, entitled " Original
Letters of Eminent Literary Men."   At p. 320, is a Letter
by *T. Warton*, dated 1774, stating that the Rev. *Benjamin
Holloway* told him, that Lord *Sunderland* told him, that the
first volume of " Robinson Crusoe" was written by Lord Oxford,
while a Prisoner in the Tower, " as an amusement under confinement," and was given to Defoe, who frequently visited him
there; and, that Defoe printed it as his own, with his Lordship's approbation, and added the second volume, " the in-
feriority of which is generally acknowledged."   Not a word is
said as to who told Lord Sunderland.   The Earl of Oxford was
committed to the Tower in July 1715, and discharged from his
Impeachment, by the House of Lords, on the 1st July, 1717.
During the whole proceedings against Lord Oxford, Lord
Sunderland spoke and voted against him, on every occasion.
There could be no intercourse, much less private confidence,
between the prisoner, and the man who believed him a traitor,
and sought to bring his head to the block.   Defoe would not
have breathed to any man, especially to the Earl of Sunderland, that a confidential intercourse existed between himself
and Lord Oxford, the prisoner.   The latter was " his first
benefactor," and gratitude would have forbidden it.   Duty did
not require him to sacrifice his position under Government by
such a piece of gratuitous information; and therefore, had it
been true, self-interest would have made him reticent.   His
appointment continued years afterward, which alone demon-
strates that he never told such a thing.   If true, the fact
could only have been known to Lord Oxford and Defoe, and
there is not a tittle of evidence that either ever said a word on
the subject.

Those who related so unfounded a story ought to have
known that Lord Oxford was so seriously ill during the greater
part of his incarceration, that it was matter of speculation
whether or not he would live to be tried; that his illness in-

capacitated him from preparing his defence; and that on this account the House of Lords, from time to time, granted his petitions for postponement of his trial.   I will not ask whether it can be thought possible that this great statesman, prostrated by disease, knowing that his enemies were crying out for that life he had not strength to defend, could yet find time and inclination to write a romance—"as an amusement under confinement."   Lord Oxford was not excelled by any man of his age in accurate knowledge of human character, and no man better appreciated the genius of Daniel Defoe.   The absurdity, therefore, is magnified if we suppose his Lordship first to have neglected the defence of his life and honour, by writing *Robinson Crusoe*, and then making a present of the manuscript to one whom he knew more capable than any other to compose such a work.   Finally, the smallest share of critical acumen is sufficient to decide that the first and second volumes of " Robinson Crusoe" are equally the offspring of the same parent.

About the beginning of August a mutilated abridgment of the first volume of " Crusoe" was clandestinely printed for T. Cox, at the Amsterdam Coffee-House, on which Taylor warned the public against being imposed on, and stated his intention, as proprietor, of prosecuting the vendors according to law.* To this Cox replied in a long rambling statement, which is only valuable for one sentence of gross abuse and insult against Defoe, proving that although the work was published anonymously, there was no doubt, from the first, as to the authorship.†

To these circumstances Defoe alludes in the preface to the second volume, in which he adheres to the artifice of being only the editor; and, in that capacity, at liberty to whet the public appetite by praising the performance.   There is no apparent elation at success, but only the calm admiration of a third party, who is prepared to admit that the first volume contains portions that may be called invention.   It is worth transcribing, as illustrating the history of the work:—

" The Success the former Part of this Work has met with in the World, has yet been no other than is acknowledged to

---

* Advertisement in " The St. James's Post," 7th August, 1719.
† Advertisement in " The Flying Post," 29th October, 1719.

be due to the Surprizing Variety of the Subject, and to the
agreeable Manner of the Performance. All the Endeavours of
envious People to reproach it with being a Romance, to search
it for Errors in Geography, Inconsistency in the Relation, and
Contradictions in the Fact, have proved abortive, and as im-
potent as malicious. The just Application of every Incident,
the religious and useful Inferences drawn from every Part, are
so many Testimonies to the good Design of making it publick;
and must legitimate all the Part that may be call'd Invention,
or Parable, in the Story. The Second Part, if the Editor's
Opinion may pass, is (contrary to the Usage of Second Parts,)
every Way as entertaining as the First, contains as strange and
surprizing Incidents, and as great a Variety of them; nor is
the Application less serious, or suitable; and doubtless will, to
the sober, as well as ingenious Reader, be every way as profitable and diverting; and this makes the abridging this Work,
as scandalous, as it is knavish and ridiculous, seeing, while to
shorten the Book, that they may seem to reduce the Value,
they strip it of all those Reflections, as well religious as moral,
which are not only the greatest Beauties of the Work, but are
calculated for the infinite Advantage of the Reader. By this
they leave the Work naked of its brightest Ornaments; and if
they would, at the same Time pretend, that the Author has supply'd the Story out of his Invention, they take from it the
Improvement, which alone recommends that Invention to
wise and good Men. The Injury these Men do the Proprietor
of this Work, is a Practice all honest Men abhor; and he
believes he may challenge them to shew the Difference between
that and Robbing on the Highway, or Breaking open a House.
If they can't shew any Difference in the Crime, they will find
it hard to shew any Difference in the Punishment. And he
will answer for it, that nothing shall be wanting on his Part,
to do them Justice."

In whatever character Defoe appeared before the world,
whether as a politician, a moralist, or a writer of fiction,—
whether provoking resentment by his satire on the public and
private vices of the age, or exhorting to peace and union,—the
malice of party still assailed him, and his name was a signal
of reproach. Considering his high moral and religious prin-

THE FARTHER
ADVENTURES
OF
ROBINSON CRUSOE;

Being the Second and Laſt Part

OF HIS
LIFE,

And of the Strange Surprizing

Accounts of his Travels

Round three Parts of the Globe.

Written by Himſelf.

To which is added a Map of the World, in which is
Delineated the Voyages of *ROBINSON CRUSOE.*

LONDON: Printed for W. Taylor at the
Ship in *Pater-Noſter-Row.* MDCCXIX.

ciples, this conduct, continued towards him many years after
his biographers believed him to have retired from political life,
has been an enigma hitherto unexplained.   Without abating
from one of the highest characters in literary history—for
integrity, consistency, and independence,—we shall find some
grounds of extenuation in favour of his enemies, by endeavouring to appreciate the light in which he appeared to their eyes,
assuming them to be acquainted with his *Appeal to Honour
and Justice,* and disposed to accept his assertion that gratitude
to the Earl of Oxford had kept him silent respecting measures
of the late Ministry that could not be approved.   They knew
he had in that pamphlet avowed that his political principles
were unchanged; but what must they think after such
avowal, of the man whom they believed to be afterward
the writer of *Mist's Journal,* the organ of Jacobites and
traitors, and a strenuous opponent of the present Whig
Government?   They could not know, and Defoe could not
tell them, the nature of his connection with Mist; or of the
Sultan Galga, the *Killing no Murder,* the numerous other treasonable essays and letters that he quietly consigned to the flames
every week, thereby saving the authors from the gallows, and
his country from the danger of another rebellion.   They
could not be informed that he did all this with the knowledge
and approbation of the Ministry; nor, that he was in the confidential service of the Government, and had been so for
several years.   This is the key to the reproaches and calumnies that continued to be heaped upon him,—to the silence
with which he bore insult and scandal without deserving it,—
and to the anonymous publication, and non-recognition by
himself subsequently, of even his most celebrated works.

The first public attack made upon " Robinson Crusoe" and
its author, was by Charles Gildon,—a clever writer, but a
sorry wit,—who published, on the 28th September, a pamphlet
which had nothing to recommend it but the following title,
" The Life and Strange Surprizing Adventures of Mr. D—
De F—, of London, Hosier, who has lived above fifty years
by himself, in the Kingdoms of North and South Britain.
The various Shapes he has appear'd in, and the Discoveries he
has made for the Benefit of his Country.   In a Dialogue
between *Him, Robinson Crusoe,* and his Man *Friday.*   With

Remarks Serious and Comical upon the Life of Crusoe. *Qui vult decipi, decipiatur.* London. Printed for J. Roberts in Warwick Lane. 1719. Price 1*s.*" The title and Dialogue occupy eighteen pages, then follows—" An Epistle to D— D' F—e, the reputed Author of Robinson Crusoe,"—occupying twenty-nine pages; and, a Postscript of nineteen pages, having reference to the second volume. I shall say little of this production, but that it is indecent and scurrilous; that it sneers at the author's religion, and at those parts of his work which treat of Divine Providence, and the vindication of the ways of God to man. " Robinson Crusoe" was, even thus early, above the reach of such criticism as Gildon's; who is obliged to confess that " Crusoe" was already " fam'd from Tuttle Street to Limehouse-hole. There is not an old Woman," says he, " that can go to the Price of it, but buys thy ' Life and Adventures,' and leaves it as a Legacy, with the ' Pilgrim's Progress,' the ' Practice of Piety,' and ' God's Revenge against Murther,' to her Posterity." So that on the testimony, even of this acrimonious slandering infidel,—" Robinson Crusoe" had,—before it was completed,—taken its place as one of the household books of England, to be considered as a treasure, and to be handed down, as such, from generation to generation. Crusoe had already made his way to the hearts of men, and women, and boys, as the detractor admits, from one end of London to the other; and, in a few months, had outsped the footsteps of envy. The work was translated immediately into French and German, and shortly, into all European tongues; it has from that time to this received the applause of the enlightened of all nations; it has been printed in every language spoken by civilized man,—and, in innumerable editions, has become the common property of the world.

The narrative of Robinson Crusoe was completed in the two volumes already noticed; but whether it was from a reluctance to lay down a title that had been received with so much favour by the public; or, that the acceptability of occasional moral reflections in the story of Crusoe, had inspired him with a hope that a volume of instruction and morality would be equally well received, under a similar title, can only be matter of conjecture. He was undoubtedly studious to please, but he was still more desirous of being useful; and he believed that the

highest aim of a writer should be, to communicate such knowledge as would make men better citizens and Christians, and fitter
candidates for heaven. We have also his own authority, as I
have already pointed out, at the commencement of this memoir,
that the vicissitudes of his own life, being parabolically enclosed
in the narrative of Crusoe, it was fitting that the moral and
religious reflections which had guided and sustained him through
all his afflictions, should also be enveloped under the same
covering, in order to avoid any pharisaic appearance of vain-
glory. With such motives he composed the sequel to his
celebrated work, and it was published on the 6th of August
1720, with the title—" Serious Reflections during the Life
and Surprising Adventures of Robinson Crusoe : With his
Vision of the Angelick World. Written by himself. London.
Printed for W. Taylor, at the Ship and Black Swan in Paternoster Row. 1720." The Preface to this volume is much
longer than that of its predecessors, and is subscribed " Robinson
Crusoe." It is followed by the Publisher's Introduction, consisting of three pages, in which sanguine expectations are
indulged, that the success will be equal to that of the former
volumes. Mr. Taylor says, " while the parable has been so
diverting, the moral must certainly be equally agreeable." He
remarks that the Envy that has been expressed has been from
the Men of Trade, at their having no share in the profits ; and
adds, exultingly, " I must do the Author the Justice to say,
that not a Dog has wagg'd his Tongue at the work itself,
nor has a Word been said to lessen the Value of it, but
which has been the visible Effect of that Envy at the good
Fortune of the Bookseller." The title page affords evidence
of this good fortune, Since the publication of the second
volume, Taylor had added the adjoining building, called the
Black Swan, to his business premises. He was deceived, however, in his hopes that the third volume would be equally
popular with the others. It contains profound thought, great
wisdom, morality of the highest character, an extensive acquaintance with metaphysical subtleties, and is pervaded with
a solemn tone of religious instruction, doctrinal and practical.
Multitudes, however, who had read the previous volumes with
avidity would have no relish for this ; and, both author and publisher were destined to learn, that the popular inculcation of im-

portant truths can only be attained by mingling diversion with instruction.   To those, however, who are capable of appreciating the volume, it contains a mine of intellectual, moral, and religious thoughts, surpassed by very few books in the English language.   Occasionally his discourse is enlivened by examples and dialogues, but generally he speaks with deep earnestness ; and it is impossible to read his admonitions and reflections without being convinced that he was a sincerely pious man.   I scarcely need add that the " Serious Reflections" were not reprinted with the narrative volumes, for many years afterward ; and that, of the myriads of those who have read " Robinson Crusoe," very few are aware of the existence of his " Serious Reflections."

The great reputation of " Robinson Crusoe" has attached a degree of interest to every fact connected with its history. Even so minute a circumstance as the place where it was written has not escaped controversy, and the claims of different localities have been numerous.   Most of these claims rest upon an erroneous assertion, that he was, at that time, under the frowns of government, and obliged to conceal himself.   A house in Halifax is pointed out in the history of that town.   Gateshead in Durham has claimed the honour.   A house in Harrow Alley, Whitechapel Market, has been said to be the birthplace of both " Robinson Crusoe," and the " Journal of the Plague," although three years intervened between their publication.   A correspondent assured Mr. Wilson that it was written in the back chamber over the wash-house of a cottage in the little village of Hartley in Kent.   It might be deemed conclusive that Gildon, *writing at the time*, lays the scene of his libellous dialogue in a field at Stoke Newington, where Defoe would be near his home. We now know, however, additionally, that he was in London, where his duties under the government imperatively required his presence,—that he was under no necessity of concealment ;—and, that " Robinson Crusoe" could only have been written in his own house at Stoke Newington.*

---

* Among the numerous imitations of " Robinson Crusoe," Mr. Wilson classes " Philip Quarll," published in 1727, as the first.   I have a List, in chronological order, with the days of publication, in which *Quarll* is No. 10. One of them was published at Boston, in New England.

Serious Reflections

DURING THE

LIFE

And Surprising

ADVENTURES

OF

ROBINSON CRUSOE:

WITH HIS

VISION

OF THE

Angelick WORLD.

Written by Himself.

LONDON: Printed for W. TAYLOR, at the *Ship* and *Black-Swan* in *Pater-noster-Row.* 1720.

I have already stated that Defoe composed and published several independent works during the interval that elapsed between the appearance of the first and second volumes of " Robinson Crusoe."   On the 21st of March 1719, doubtless when the first volume of Crusoe was preparing for the press, and its author perhaps did not contemplate a second, he opened the article on " Foreign Affairs," in *Mist's Journal* with the following characteristic words :—" Our Letters from abroad come very well stored with News this week, and some Incidents have happened, which are very particular.   From Sweden (N.B., We begin at the farther end, that we may talk our way home.) they have surprized us with the sudden Dispatch of their Judicial Proceedings in the case of Baron Goertz and Count Vandernath, whom, since our last Accounts, they have try'd, and condemn'd ; and have executed the former; when we were expecting that those Gentlemen, who insisted that they had done nothing without the King of Sweden's express order, would have been released."   He then proceeds to give an account of the last moments of the Baron, but being pressed for time and space, he probably took home the papers from Mist's office, to wait for a more favourable opportunity. Thus enabling me, after the lapse of a century and a half, to prefix the above, as his own preface, to an interesting pamphlet he shortly afterward published with the following title, " Some Account of the Life and Most Remarkable Actions of George Henry, Baron De Goertz, Privy Counsellor, and Chief Minister of State, to the late King of Sweden.   London. Printed for T. Bickerton, at the Crown, in Paternoster Row. 1719."   It is almost needless to say that Defoe extols the wisdom and courage of this great statesman, and reprobates the popular rage and resentment to which the Baron had been sacrificed, as being a contempt against the memory of their late king.

In the early part of the year the Nonconformists throughout England, but especially in the South-western counties, were much agitated by the spread of Unitarian doctrines among both ministers and members.   *Mist's Journal* of the 4th of April contained a list of the names of no less than 53 ministers, who had, acting in concert, formally rejected the doctrine of the Trinity. The infection had also reached the City of London, and in the Journal of the following week Defoe notices it in the following terms :—" We have a War, begun and carried on as religious Controversies always are, with Rage, Fury, Wrath and Strife, and all Uncharitableness. The Parties have had one pitched Battle in a place very proper for such an Engagement, called Salters' Hall, where the majority made no conscience of dethroning our Saviour, and turned the conquer'd Party out of Doors. We hear the next Battle will beat the Bear Garden." On the 30th of May he also published on this subject in *Mist's Journal*, one of the finest of his short essays. It will be found among his appended writings of that date. But though our author thus satirized the disgraceful and violent proceedings which brought so much obloquy upon the Dissenters, and exposed them to the derision and contempt of the irreligious, he was not the less pained at the defection from the orthodox faith of many for whom he had entertained the highest regard. Numerous pamphlets were published, on both sides, abounding in censures and recriminations. This induced him to appear once more as a peacemaker, and to conjure both sides to lay aside their quarrels, so that, if they could not agree, on so momentous a subject, they might at least study the things that make for peace. His Tract is entitled, "A Letter to the Dissenters. London. Printed for J. Roberts, in Warwick Lane. 1719." Defoe had had too much sad experience in the character of a peacemaker to hope for success on this occasion, and says, "The passions of Men are none of their best Friends ; and though, when Passions are most violent, they stand at that time in most need of Advice, it seems, of all times, the most unseasonable to offer it." Nevertheless he gave them much judicious counsel for allaying their animosities, though without apparent advantage. This pamphlet, like that preceding, and also the following, seem to have been written and published between the composition of the first and second volumes of " Robinson Crusoe."

It will be remembered that in the reign of King William, Defoe had powerfully exposed the wicked practices of Stock-Jobbers. During nearly twenty years following he had, in the

Review, and other writings, omitted no suitableo ccasion for adverting to the subject.. In July 1719, the schemes of Mr. Law
were beginning to develope themselves in Paris, and it seems probable that Defoe's sagacity enabled him to foresee some general
disturbance of the finance of other nations, affording an opportunity for villainous practices.   I do not presume to say
that he anticipated the national madness of the following year,
but he certainly thought it necessary to caution and warn the
public of possible danger.   With such view he published on
the 11th of that month a thick pamphlet entitled, " The
Anatomy of Exchange Alley : or, a System of Stock-Jobbing :
Proving that Scandalous Trade, as it is now carried on, to be
Knavish in its private Practice, and Treason in its Publick,
&c., &c.   By a Jobber.   Printed for E. Smith, near Exchange
Alley, and T. Warner in Paternoster Row. 1719.   Price 1*s.*"

This pamphlet points to the probability that a late false report, of the Pretender's being taken and confined in the Castle
at Milan, was concerted between the attainted Earl of Mar,
and certain Stock-brokers in London, for the purpose of Jobbing
the Stocks. The Author gives instances in which he has known
credulous fools to be robbed ; relating the dialogues between
them and their dupes.   The following shows the character of
this withering denunciation of the Projectors and Jobbers :—
" What Tricking, what Fraud, what laying Plots as deep as
Hell, and as far as the ends of the Earth, is here !   What
cheating of Fathers, and Mothers, and Brothers, gulling
Widows and Orphans, couzening the most Wary, and plundering the Unwary !   And how much meaner Robberies than
these bring the Friendless even to the Gallows every Sessions !"
The old fire of outspoken independence still burnt within him
when falsehood and dishonesty were to be denounced, and he
was not to be silenced by considerations of self-interest,—
because men in power were among the criminals, and were
patronised and honoured by Royalty itself. He had been
cautioned that, as many of the principal leaders were Whigs,
Members of Parliament, and Friends of the Government, he
had best have a care what he said of them.   He replies, " My
first Answer is, *So I will.*   I will have a care of them ; and,
in the next Place, let them have a Care of me ; for if I should
tpeak the whole Truth of some of them, they might still be

Whigs, but I dare say they would be neither Parliament Men,
nor Friends to the Government very long ; and it is very hard
his Majesty should not be told what kind of Friends to him
such Men are." He immediately proceeds to prove that Stock-
Jobbing as now practised, is High Treason, in its nature and
consequences ; and that Stock-Jobbers, who are guilty of such
practices as he will detect, are eventually Traitors to King
George. Having described the characters of several of the
principal Jobbers, he boldly says,—" But to see Statesmen turn
Dealers, and Men of Honour stoop to the Chicanery of Jobbing ;
to see Men at the Offices in the Morning, at the Parliament
House about Noon, at the Cabinet at Night, and at Exchange
Alley in the proper Intervals, What new Phenomena are these?
What fatal things may these shining Planets (like the late
great Light), foretel to the State, and to the Publick, for when
Statesmen turn Jobbers, the State may be Jobbed."

I cannot avoid noticing here, the remarkable sequel, exhibited in several of his ' Letters Introductory' for March and
April 1721. They will be found in his annexed writings, and
exhibit some of the highest qualities of his genius and independence. In the endeavour to serve the ruined thousands
of South-Sea victims, he stands out boldly as a Journalist,
known to, and employed by the Government, and indicates as
among the plunderers some of its most prominent members,
and even Lord Sunderland, to whose influence partly, he owed
his appointment. It is true he does not name them specifically, but he points to them so plainly as not to be mistaken.

At page 35, Defoe gives us the following geographical description of a locality since greatly changed, and destined soon
to disappear :—" The centre of the Jobbing is in the Kingdom
of Exchange Alley, and its Adjacencies ; the Limits are easily
surrounded in about a minute and a half, viz. Stepping out of
Jonathan's into the Alley, you turn your face full South,
moving on a few Paces, and then turning due East, you advance
to Garraway's ; from thence going out at the other Door, you
go on still East into Birchin Lane ; and then halting a little
at the Sword-Blade Bank, to do much mischief in fewest words ;
you immediately face to the North, enter Cornhill, visit two or
three petty Provinces there, in your way West : And thus,
having Box'd Your Compass, and sail'd round the whole

Stock-Jobbing Globe, you turn into Jonathan's again; and so, as most of the great Follies of Life oblige us to do, you end just where you began."

The pamphlet was of course published anonymously, but there was no further effort to conceal its authorship. He openly quotes about seven pages from his work printed in 1701, called *The Freeholder's Plea against Stock-Jobbing Elections of Parliament Men;* which he says was laid first before King William, and afterward before the Parliament, adding the following remarkable admission of his own political influence at that time, " and it was his Majesty's Sense of the Consequence, that made him resolve to bring the two East India Companies to unite their Stocks; for, in a Word, the Stock-Jobbers embroil'd the whole Nation." He also refers to his early pamphlet, entitled, *The Villainy of Stock-Jobbers Detected.*

In addition to what has been already said, as to the impossibility of Defoe's absence from London in 1719, I may state that scarcely a week elapsed in which he did not complain of the contradictory and unreliable character of the pretended foreign News Letters, with which he was compelled to deal. Thus, on the 6th of June, he says, " We must confess these People's Way of Writing is a Keen Satyr upon the credulity of the Age; and they take care to let the World know, that the English Nation are all BELIEVERS; for did they not think we were credulous to a Degree beyond all the POPERY that ever we pretended to quarrel with, they could never impose such Trumpery for News, and such Forgeries for Intelligence." The exaggerations were equally indulged in by both sides, and our author, as representing *Mist,* is occasionally very severe in his banter of the Whigs; who, when the Germans had only 13,000 men in Sicily, put them down at 20,000, and one paper at 50,000; while they stated the Spanish forces as only 4000, when they were about 15,000. Yet the influence of Defoe in moderating party rancour was so generally appreciated at this time by the public press, that all personal attacks upon him and Mr. Mist appear to have temporarily ceased. A hotheaded correspondent of *Read's Journal* finds great fault with the proprietor of that Paper on this account, and accuses him of having entered into a treaty of peace with Mr. Mist, after having been his most bitter antagonist.

At the risk of appearing tedious, I think that no possible doubt should be suffered to remain on the mind of any reader as to the manner in which Defoe's influence was exercised in *Mist's Journal*. The two following sentences, dated 14th July, show that when he could not wholly suppress objectionable foreign news, he would counteract exaggeration, and inculcate moderation and peace. Alluding to a report that the Czar intended entirely to subdue Sweden, he says,—" Three of his Men of War, two of 60 guns each, and one of 40, have, after a Bloody Fight, taken a Swedish Man of War of 50 guns, and two Frigates. Memorandum, *Two Troopers and a Dragoon beat a little Boy, &c.*" Then, turning to the conflicting accounts given by the Whigs and Tories, as to the War in Sicily, where a battle was expected, he says,— " What will follow we must all wait for. It were to be wished.we could all wait for it with as much Indifferency as might consist with Quietness and Peaceableness among ourselves,—that we might treat one another, about these Things, with more good Neighbourhood and good Manners, till the weighty Affair is decided by the Sword."

The same number of *Read's Journal* that advertised the second volume of " Robinson Crusoe," as being published two days previously, contains a communication, showing that it was then publicly known that Defoe was the author of the book, and was also connected with *Mist's Journal*. The writer, severely criticising the latter Journal, professes to have discovered a geographical mistake, committed by our author in the foreign News, and exultingly exclaims, " Certainly the infallible *Robinson Crusoe*, that great Traveller and Geographer, could not be guilty of so Monstrous a Blunder."

Conscious of the rectitude of his own conduct, Defoe did not attempt to conceal, that *Mist's Journal* received letters from Spain ; and even from the camp of the Spanish General in Sicily, at a time when England was at war with the Spaniards. No doubt he did this designedly, to show the anti-English source of such communications ; but the facts were calculated to excite suspicion against him in the minds of those who were truly loyal, yet necessarily ignorant of his real position. At times he departed from the mere routine of translating the advices of foreign news; and being roused, expressed freely his own natural sentiments, even in *Mist's Journal*. Such an occasion occurred on the 12th of September 1719, when he denounced at great length, with indignant eloquence, the cruelties and oppressions inflicted upon the poor Swedes by a barbarous army of invading Russians. This powerful article will be found appended in its proper place.

Another similar outburst of loyal patriotism occurred immediately afterward, when a young man named Matthews was apprehended for printing a pamphlet entitled *Vox Populi Vox Dei*, in which was plainly asserted the Pretender's right to the Crown of England. Mr. Mist, or some one in his office, inserted in his Journal a paragraph which seemed to sympathize with the prisoner, and stated, " He's reported to be betrayed by his own Servants." This incited our author to inflict a most powerful and unmerciful castigation upon *Mist* in the form of a long letter, which he insisted should be published, and which accordingly appeared in *Mist's Journal* of the 26th September. I only forbear quoting from it here, because it may be read at length in my Collection of Defoe's hitherto uncollected writings; but I would confidently leave the bitterest enemy he ever had, or can have, to decide, upon due consideration of all the circumstances, as to his incorruptible integrity, and the perfect consistency of his political conduct. Even the Editorial Note at the end, in which Mr. Mist is made to speak in his own person, is dictated in Defoe's words.

It can scarcely be supposed that any cordial feeling existed, at this time, between Mist and Defoe. The former submitted, because he knew that the talent, the judgment, and moderating influence of the latter, were necessary to the continued existence of his Paper; the latter continued his irksome labours, from a loyal sense of duty to the government of his country. But he was weary of the extravagance of party spirit; of witnessing statements, diametrically opposite to each other, put before the world as truth; and, of the odium incurred by his supposed participation in these things. That these and other similar motives actuated him, is obvious from the Introductory Address of a new daily Paper established by him, called " The Daily Post," the first number of which was published on the 4th October 1719. Like its older daily contemporary, the *Courant*, it consisted of a single leaf small folio, the first side of which contained the foreign and home news, and the second chiefly announcements and advertisements. The small size of the Paper did not admit of Essays and Letters from outside Contributors, as part of its general arrangements; but Defoe seems to have used it, during the whole period of his management, for such occasional Letters and communications, from his own pen, as he was desirous of placing before the public without any delay. For such purpose it was suited, by its diurnal issue. Nothing in the *Daily Post* shows whether he was interested in it as a proprietor, or only as chief manager; but the style and manner proves that he had a competent assistant for the ordinary routine, himself retaining the oversight and control. As nearly as I can judge, he continued his connection with this Paper until the 27th April 1725, during all which time, and until years after his death, it maintained its place, and had a large circulation.

The Introductory Address to which I have already alluded is so characteristic of its Author's love of peace and truth; and so briefly, but clearly, exhibits a model of what a newspaper ought to be, that I make no apology for transcribing it, as follows :—

" Though we shall not set out this Undertaking with large Promises, and great Boasts of our Performances, yet as our Circumstances, at the first Appearance in the World, are something uncommon, it seems absolutely necessary to say something, as well of our Design, as of the Manner of our pursuing it, and the Reason of our undertaking it.

" The Multitude of Papers already publish'd, is no Discouragement to us at all; it will be no Arrogance in us to say, 'Tis the Misfortune of the Town to have much News, but little Intelligence; Truth ill told,—Lies ill cover'd, Parties ill serv'd,—and, in a Word, the Readers vilely impos'd upon on all Sides.

" Even the Government itself suffers Indignities, and is oblig'd to bear with daily Impertinencies from their Friends as well as Enemies ; and may be said sometimes to be at a Loss, whether to Reward or Resent, when sordid Men simply flatter them, and sometimes grossly affront their Superiors in the very Things which they say with Design to please them.

" If an indifferent way of Writing, neither courting Friends, or making Enemies,—giving just Accounts of Facts, in plain Words,—neither lessening one Side, or magnifying the other, with clear and Unbyass'd Reasonings, to explain doubtful Cases ; we say, if ever this were useful, we think 'tis so now, when almost every Transaction is set in a false Light, when Misrepresentation is, as it were, the Business of every Writer, and whether they speak of private Persons or of publick, the character of no Man seems to be safe, but Scandal and Slander make Havock of Men's Reputation without Mercy.

" We shall, in the Prosecution of this Work, do all the Justice we can to any Person, but Injury to no Man ; we resolve to be of no Party, and to meddle with no Quarrels, publick or private, Civil or Religious : Our Business is to give an Account of the News, Foreign and Domestick, in the best and clearest Manner we can, and this we shall endeavour to do, in such a Manner, and from such Intelligence, as we cannot doubt will give our Readers satisfaction.

" If any Writers or Proprietors of Papers may think themselves concerned in our setting up this *Daily Post*, we hope, however, they can charge us with no Injury to them ; the Press is open and the Stage clear ; we have nothing to say to them but this, Let them *Forbear* to ENVY, and *Strive* to EXCEL."

The *Daily Post* seems to have aimed at becoming the Advertising organ of the Booksellers. In No. 6, thirteen out of fifteen advertisements are of books just published.

I have before noticed the comparative cessation of abuse towards Defoe in other Journals, especially *Read's*. It seems however that *Mist* afterward inadvertently admitted a Letter in which *Read* was termed a " Wretch." In his Journal, of the 10th October, *Read* complains of this mark of distinction, and attempts to fasten it upon Defoe, under the designation of

" Mr. Mist's Author." The following conclusion of such complaint is interesting :—

" N.B. Foe is desired to declare whether he did not authorise a certain Publisher, not long ago, to come to Mr. Read, to desire a Cessation of all Personal Hostilities? If so, why he treacherously breaks the Articles, which Mr. Read has endeavoured to keep, by razing out many Scandalous Epithets, usually tacked to his Name, by his weekly Correspondents?"

Defoe made no reply to these questions. No doubt he had sent a friend to remonstrate with Mr. Read, and to " desire a cessation of all personal hostilities;" but there had been no treaty, because Defoe had never used an abusive word, nor made any reply to the grossest calumnies published in *Read's Journal.* Nor had such treaty, supposing it to exist, been now broken by Defoe, inasmuch as the offensive word had not been used by him, nor with his sanction. The mistake arose from Mr. Read not knowing the peculiar nature of Defoe's connection with Mist : and the incident exhibits a bitter opponent, in the character of an unintentional witness, testifying that our author had, when vilely slandered, endeavoured to practise the injunction, *As much as lieth in you, live peaceably with all Men.*

We must now turn away from politics and newspapers,—in which we might suppose our author to have been wholly occupied,—and we shall find that he must notwithstanding have had some hours of relaxation ; if that term may be applied to the production of another singular work of his fertile imagination. On the 14th of October was published a thick pamphlet, with the following circumstantial title, " The Dumb Philosopher ; or, Great Britain's Wonder. Containing I. A Faithful and very Surprizing Account how Dickory Cronke, a Tinner's Son in the County of Cornwall, was born Dumb, and continued so for 58 Years ; and how some Days before he died, he came to his Speech ; With Memoirs of his Life, and the Manner of his Death. II. A Declaration of his Faith and Principles in Religion : With a Collection of Select Meditations, Composed in his Retirement. III. His Prophetical Observations upon the Affairs of Europe, more particularly of Great Britain, from 1720 to 1729. The whole

extracted from his Original Papers, and confirmed by unquestionable Authority.   To which is annexed, His Elegy, written
by a Young Cornish Gentleman, of Exeter Coll. in Oxford ;
with an Epitaph by another Hand.   *Non quis, sed quid.*
London.   Printed for Tho. Bickerton, at the Crown in Paternoster Row.   1719."

It is worthy of observation in the outset, though I lay no
stress upon it, that there are some points of resemblance
between " Dickory Cronke," and " Robinson Crusoe ;" so far as
relates to circumstances influencing moral character.   Cronke
was, in a certain sense, like Crusoe, isolated, and shut out
from intercourse with mankind, for a great portion of his life.
Both were afterward enabled to enjoy the blessing of human
intercourse.   Both were reflective and religious men, and
wrote meditations worthy of being published to the world.
The accounts of both were " surprizing,"—the first and second
volumes of Crusoe were written in the same year as Dickory
Cronke, and the latter is interposed, in point of time, between
the second and third volumes of Crusoe.   There is the same
atmosphere of truth surrounding all the details of both, so that
the reader lives in the reality of each story, and scepticism
itself is set at defiance.   In Crusoe, the Author has declared
that the history of his own life is allegorically enclosed ; and,
though I will not positively affirm, that portions of his inner
life are contained in Dickory Cronke, yet I believe so.   It is
noticeable that Cronke's life is made to begin about the same
time as Defoe's,—to terminate at the author's age when
writing this book ; and that, like himself, Cronke had a fit of
apoplexy.

I have had frequent occasion to speak of the Catholick
spirit of Defoe, of his frequently expressed veneration of, and
regard for, the Church of England ; and, of the unfortunate
suppression of this by his biographers.   I might have extracted
a multitude of passages from his various works breathing the
same spirit as the following, from Dickory Cronke :—" The
Church of England is doubtless the great Bulwark of the
ancient Catholick and Apostolick Faith all over the World.
A Church that has all the Advantages that the Nature of a
Church is capable of.   From the Doctrine and Principles of
the Church of England we are taught Loyalty to our Prince,

Fidelity to our Country, and Justice to all Mankind; and therefore, I look upon this to be one of the most excellent Branches of the Church Universal. It stands, as 'twere, in a Parenthesis, between Superstition and Hypocrisy."

After the publication of the above work, only two days elapsed ere Defoe again appeared before the world as an Author. The occasion was briefly as follows:—The Congregation of St. Anne's, Aldersgate, had a Charity School for clothing and educating 50 poor children. Their maintenance depending on voluntary contributions, Mr. Prat, the Incumbent of Orpington and St. Mary Craye, in the County of Kent, agreed that two Charity Sermons should be preached there for the benefit of the Institution; and, on the 27th July 1718, some of the Managers took the poor children down, but the design was frustrated, by the arbitrary interference of a local justice of the peace, who threatened to treat both committee and children as vagrants. Defoe gave an indignant account of these proceedings in the next number of *Mist's Journal* (2nd August 1718,) which will be found among his appended writings. This unchristian behaviour caused a feeling of resentment, and an offer being made of the Church at Chisselhurst, the children were taken there and the Sermon preached on the 24th of August, a license for that purpose having been previously granted by the Bishop of Rochester. Undeterred, even by this, the Justices proceeded against the Clergyman and those of the Committee who collected in Church,—as beggars and vagrants, rogues and vagabonds,—and committed them for trial at the next Assizes, at Rochester; where, on the 15th of July 1719, by a mockery of Justice they were fined, and left to seek a remedy by Writ of Error. At this point Defoe again took up the matter, and on the 16th October published a thick pamphlet, entitled, " Charity still a Christian Virtue: or, an Account of the Tryal and Conviction of the Reverend Mr. Hendley, for Preaching a Charity Sermon at Chisselhurst. And of Mr. Campman, Mr. Prat, and Mr. Harding, for Collecting at the same Time the Alms of the Congregation. At the Assizes held at Rochester, on Wednesday, July 15, 1719. Offer'd to the Consideration of the Clergy of the Church of England. London: Printed for T. Bickerton, at the Crown in Paternoster Row. 1719. Price One Shilling."

This is, in many respects, one of Defoe's ablest minor productions. After a short preface, an Introduction contains—" the Occasion of the Trial,"—then follow—" Reflections upon the Matters of Fact above mentioned." He shows himself thoroughly conversant with the statute law relating to Beggars, Vagrants, and Rogues, from the earliest times; and his expositions are clear, and pointed with the keenest irony, when he states specifically how enactments, made to punish the lowest offenders, have been applied in this case, to the prosecution of a Christian clergyman, and the charitable patrons of innocent children. His polished sarcasms are plentifully bestowed upon the prosecutors, and their paid counsel; but the Judge and jury are not permitted to escape, and the names of all concerned are recorded in full, " for the admiration of posterity." After pointing out the various classes of Rogues and Cheats comprehended in the 39 *Eliz. c.* 4, *s.* 2. He says :—
" If the above mention'd Act was calculated for the Extinction of all charitable Collections for the Poor, to destroy even Charity Schools, and the Foundations of Virtue, the Act carries a lying Preamble in its Front. It is no Act to punish Vagabonds; and rather, if it punishes one, it makes twenty, and even eats into its own Bowels. Nay, it must declare, that these poor Children, rescu'd by the Piety of others from Infidelity and perfect Barbarianism, are *Rogues*. That those who, in the Pulpit, incite others by the Duty of their Office, and by the Bowels of Christianity, to contribute, are *Rogues*; and that those who give their Money, are *Rogues* likewise. This is the plain and unavoidable Consequence, if those Children are Vagrants in the Eye of the Law. O my God! In what an Age do we live! Are the Precepts of Christianity repeal'd by the Act against Vagabonds and Rogues? Are Six Thousand Children bred up in the Principles of the *Church of England*, and of Virtue, only collected out to be turn'd into Rogues?"

Conscious of the severity and even personality of his strictures, he says further on :—" The Reader may, perhaps, be offended at my Interesting myself in this dispute, even to a transport, which is owing to the natural Temper of my Mind that feels a secret Pleasure at the sight of those Children; and indeed it is the only pleasant Spectacle I ever delighted in, though I have been present at many publick Entries and fine Shows. However, if they must be destroy'd; if the Protestant Religion is not secure, till an Universal Ignorance and Barbarity prevails; I desire Mr. *Justice* to desist till he has more Law on his Side. Let him stay for some new Act of Parliament, for as we are Englishmen we insist upon our Laws, our Contracts, and our Coronation-Oaths, the Barriers of our Liberties, and surely no Whig has anything to say against these Topicks. But alas! Power is an Asylum both to the Just and Unjust." He concludes with an earnest appeal, on the rights and privileges of the Church of England, assailed in the person of Mr. Hendley:—" I have seen ancient Buildings venerable in their Ruins, but to see an Ancient and Apostolical Church fall ignominiously and contemptibly into nothing, by the Supineness of its Pastors, is a lamentable Prospect. Will future Generations believe, that History, eight hundred years before their time, has had any Truth? That Magna Charta was anything more than the Fiction of Sick-brain'd Writers,—if it should be their Fate to see their Clergy Tried, in common with Thieves and Felons,—if they shall see their Pastors expos'd to the Power of Justices of the Peace,—and the Canons and Rubrics explain'd at the Sessions?" Proceedings were commenced in the Bishop's Court against the two prosecuting justices, for disturbing and interrupting Divine Service in the Church of the Parish of Chisselhurst, on the 24th of August 1718, but in the meantime Mr. Hendley the clergyman died, and they escaped the punishment their conduct merited.

Readers of Defoe's imaginary voyages and travels have wondered how he obtained his great knowledge of geography; and not less, how he became so minutely acquainted with the peculiarities and habits of sailors, and all the technicalities of a sea-faring life. When personating a sailor, and describing the working of a ship, in any part of the world, he appears as much in his proper element, as when discoursing on inland trade, or discussing the home politics of the day. No material inaccuracy, in these respects, has ever been detected in his writings. He confessed to having all the world at his fingers' ends, but how he became so learned is left to conjecture. At

that time, the gradations were practically almost imperceptible
between the privateer, the buccaneer, and the pirate, however
clearly defined by the law.   The wars connected with the
Spanish Succession encouraged a race of bold adventurers, such
as no other age of the world has produced.   Defoe must have
learnt much of their surprising encounters and hair-breadth
escapes, from personal narrations ; and we know, by the catalogue of his own Library, that it was well stored with Voyages
and Travels.   His actual experience of the sea was small ; and
it must have been from books and men that he gathered the
professionalities so skilfully converted by his genius into a series
of imaginary voyages.   Among the class of sea-rovers, none
had attained so great a name, become the hero of such marvellous stories, or the reputed possessor of so much wealth, as the
subject of Defoe's next publication, which appeared on the 10th
December 1719, entitled, " The King of the Pirates ; Being
an Account of the famous Enterprizes of Captain Avery, the
Mock King of Madagascar.   With his Rambles and Piracies ;
wherein all the Sham Accounts formerly publish'd of him, are
detected.   In two Letters from himself ; one during his Stay
at Madagascar, and one since his Escape from thence.   London.
Printed for A. Bettesworth in Paternoster Row ; C. King, in
Westminster Hall ; J. Brotherton, and W. Meadows in Cornhill ; W. Chetwood in Covent Garden ; and sold by W. Boreham in Paternoster Row.   1720."* This work, like Crusoe,
has the advantage of addressing the reader directly, as an autobiography.   Speaking of one of his Prizes, Avery says, " the
Commander was a Quaker, but yet had he been equal to us in
Force, it appear'd by his countenance he would not have been
afraid of his Flesh, or have baulk'd using the carnal Weapon
of offence, viz., the Cannon-Ball."   In one of our author's
works of the following year he introduces a Quaker Pirate.
Captain Avery relates an account of a visit paid by his expedition to the island of St. Juan Fernandez, where his men
hunted goats, took in water, and remained twenty-two days ;
but he makes no mention of Alexander Selkirk.   At page 16,

---

* I have copied this long array of Booksellers, for the purpose of illustrating the fact, that the Trade were so chagrined at Taylor having secured
the enormous profits of " Robinson Crusoe" to himself, that they formed a
confederacy to publish future works of our author's imaginative genius.

he gives a description of the astonishment of the pirates on
first seeing a heap of 160,000 pieces of gold, " as good as any
in the World. We began to Embrace one another in Congratulation of our good Fortune." There is something admirable
in the verisimilitude of honesty, and even honour towards each
other, among these lawless men ; and an open candour in
their nefarious dealings with others, is generally professed, as
when Avery replies to a question, asking who they were, " I
told them jestingly, we were good, honest Christian Pirates."
Much of the pamphlet, however, illustrates the great incumbrance of wealth dishonestly obtained ; the trepidation, the
sense of personal insecurity, the jealousy of others, and the
general misery, it causes to its possessors.

CHAPTER XIII.

*French Finance under John Law—Defoe publishes " The Chimera"—
Writes against English projects—The " Halfpenny Post" rallies
Defoe—Writes " The Life of Duncan Campbell"—Writes " A Re-
markable Passage of an Apparition, 1665;" and part of " The
Friendly Dæmon, 1726"—" Memoirs of a Cavalier"—" The Life, &c.,
of Captain Singleton"—Rupture between Mist and Defoe—Mist com-
mitted to prison—Defoe undertakes to write the Letters Introductory
for "Applebee's Original Weekly Journal"—Defoe's reasons for writing
Romances of Criminal Life—Translates " The Complete Art of
Painting"—South-Sea Panic—Defoe commences a journal called
" The Director."*

1720.

ALTHOUGH the financial schemes of John Law had been
in operation in France during considerable part of the
past year, I have refrained from referring generally to the progress of this more than national mania, until England should
appear likely to be affected. From early in September 1719,
however, the Journals, in which Defoe took special charge of
" Foreign Affairs," had regularly marked the progress of the distemper in Paris. In the beginning of 1720, there were
symptoms in London, foreboding the general distraction that
followed : a period—the most irrational in the world's precedent
history,—fitly designated—" The Bubble year." Many accounts
of these events have been published, but all that I have seen
are meagre and unsatisfactory. Contemporary statements were
almost entirely those of persons interested, one way or other ;
and were limited to the narrow observation of individual writers.
Of the more recent accounts, it may be affirmed, that none have
been derived from the original daily records of the occurrences ;
and therefore, that they lack the freshness and living interest
of events, passing, at the moment, before the eye of the reader.
This is my apology, if any be needed, for the introduction of
so much from our author's pen, on the South Sea and other
Bubbles. He was not, until now, known to have written anything on the subject.

Defoe never joined in any of the speculative projects, nor
even in any of the apparently substantial investments of the
time.   He was only concerned as a spectator of what was
going on; but his connection with no less than four Journals
laid open, immediately to his view, every incident that occurred;
from the gigantic swindle, involving millions of pounds, to the
ostler or bar-maid who subscribed eighteen pence to become a
holder of Stock.   These he recorded, with his opinions,
advice, and arguments,—clothing a multitude of anecdotes
with his happy humour,—sympathizing with the unfortunate;
but denouncing and exposing, with keenest satire, the legion of
successful plunderers.   In separate pamphlets,—in Essays and
Letters Introductory,—in communications as from outside
correspondents,—in translations of French and Dutch Letters
of advice,—in the proceedings of Quincampoix Street and Exchange Alley,—in scraps and paragraphs of strange expedients, and wonderful gains and losses,—in accounts of the
extravagance and delirium of the successful,—and the despair
and suicide of the ruined,—and, in comments upon the degradation and punishment of some of the greatest offenders;—he
has left all the materials for a more complete history of the
madness of the times than has yet been printed, except as thus
recorded by his own pen.   These I have gathered together,
and prefer to place such portions thereof as seem desirable,
among his hitherto unknown works, in their chronological
order, without further arrangement, or remarks of my own,
except what may be absolutely necessary by way of explanation.

Apart from what had appeared in the Journals, near the end
of 1719, the first separate publication of Defoe, on the projects
of the period, was a thick pamphlet, with the following title,
" The Chimera: or, the French Way of Paying National
Debts Laid Open.   Being an Impartial Account of the Proceedings in France, for Raising a Paper Credit, and Settling
the Mississippi Stock.   London.   Printed for T. Warner, at
the Black Boy in Paternoster Row.   1720.   (Price One
Shilling.)"   The title of this tract partially explains its character, as an honest, unsparing exposition of the tyranny
exercised by the Government of the Regency in France, in
disposing arbitrarily of the fortunes and property of the
people; and contrasting such tyranny with the comparative

safety of the public creditor in England.   The great knowledge
our author possessed of all matters connected with Trade and
Finance, combined with his remarkable foresight, induced him,
in addition to the pamphlet on Exchange Alley, to set up this
further warning against the danger and ruin that followed.
It was published about the month of January, when the mania
had not really begun in England, and the apparent prosperity
at Paris was almost at its zenith ; yet Defoe was impelled to
conclude his pamphlet with the following portentous words :—

" When I begun this Work, it was not possible to imagine,
but I might have given some Account of the Ebb, as I have
of the Flood of this *Phantasme,* for I can call it yet no more.
Its fate, without question, must come ere long ; since there is
no Foundation equal to the Structure that now Stands upon
it.   But the time is not yet ; the little decrease, or fall, which
happened a few days ago, is not of the kind of that which must
blow up the Machine ; but it stopt as above, by the appearance of an approaching Dividend of Profits.*   But this cannot
support it long,—it must fall at last,—and all I can say of it
at present can be only this, that when it comes—*Great will be
the Fall of it.*"   In the early part of this able and characteristic
pamphlet he gives a sketch of the prior state of finance in
France, in order that the influence of Mr. Law's operations
may be more clearly perceived.

In *Mist's Journal* of the 2nd January 1720, Defoe follows
up the warning to his own country, in a highly satirical Letter,
professedly written from Paris, in which he relates a ludicrous account of one of the new gentry, a quondam footman, who nimbly, but inadvertently, stept up behind his
own coach, " which made us all in the Coffee-House very
Merry."

Among the writings of Defoe now collected together, will
be found many notices of the persecutions of the Palatines.   It
is needless to say that the religious views of our author were
ultra-Protestant ;—or, that he lived in an age when the Inqui-
sition was still in existence, and when severe persecution of
Protestants was still practised.   As he began in January of

---

* From the 19th to the 26th of December, 1719.

this year to direct attention to the subject, and continued to
do so for some time afterward, it will not be out of place
briefly to explain, that the Palatinate had been a Protestant
state since the Reformation, but that recently the Elector had
become a convert to the Roman Catholic faith. He soon
showed himself a great zealot, and was surrounded with none
but Catholics, from his most responsible advisers, down to the
meanest domestic servants. He also determined to force his
religion on his unwilling subjects ; and, for such purpose, seized
the great church at Heidelberg, called the Church of the
Holy Ghost,—stopped the Protestant worship there, and instituted the Romish service in its place ; he turned a deaf ear to
all the entreaties and petitions of the people, and drove them
to the verge of rebellion. He paid no regard to threats from
Prussia and other Protestant German states, that if he proceeded in such oppression they would prohibit the exercise of
the Roman Catholic religion in their dominions ; and, at the
time when Defoe engaged his pen in their behalf, the matter
was before the Emperor, to whom the miserable Palatines had
appealed, against their own Prince.

The madness of the English people, in running after financial bubbles, had now commenced, and was becoming every
day greater. The supply of projects was, in the beginning of
February, endeavouring to keep pace with the demand.
Although Defoe had little hope of arresting so general an infatuation, yet he inserted in Mist's Journal, of the 13th
February, an excellent letter on the evils of the Stock Exchange ; and, in the latter part, directs common sense, in a few
words, to the very pith of the whole matter, thus—" If new Shares
are at Market, vendable at double their intrinsick Value, where
must it fall when the Price abates, and when what is bought for
200, may sell but at par ?" The two following weeks, he directed
his great power of ridicule against the Bubblers, by issuing a
Mock Project of two Millions sterling, for a company for
emptying Necessary-Houses throughout England. Another of a
million and a half, for making planks and boards out of chips
and shavings ; and a third with a capital of half a million, for
" cleaning your Honour's Shoes." On the 19th of March he
inserted a mock proclamation against swindlers ; and on the

26th of the same month republished his able pamphlet entitled " The Anatomy of Exchange Alley."

Among the numerous Journals existing in London, under the title of " Post," there was one called the *The Half-penny Post,* which on the 16th of April 1720, addressed a Letter to the Author of *The Daily Post,* showing that it was known among the writers of these Papers that Defoe was the Author or Editor of the one addressed. It accuses him of inserting silly and false news, and says, " I'll never take thy Word again, so long as thy Name is Daniel. But that which Scandalizes me more than anything else, is this, That thou dost write Letters to thyself, saying that thy Paper is the best and most sensible of all the Newspapers; just like the fulsome Stuff that we have in *Mist's Journal,* which is supposed to come from the same Mint." The writer hoped to provoke a reply from Defoe, but was destined to disappointment. The peace had not been again broken between our author and *Read's Journal;* and on the 23rd of April the latter quoted from Defoe with approbation, as an authority.

We have now arrived at the end of April 1720, when the " Ebb-tide" which Defoe predicted in the *Chimera,* had taken place at Paris. Credit had declined there; and, while the government was resorting to the most tyrannical and cruel expedients to prevent universal ruin, the people, so lately maddened by prosperity, were being carried along by the frantic fury of despair. Riotous mobs of the Parisians had come into conflict with an armed police called Archers, many lives had already been lost in the streets; and our author says that multitudes who had come from the Provinces to get Fortunes, could not now get Bread. In London the wild enthusiasm of speculation had not yet nearly reached its height; and Defoe was still vainly striving to convince by ridicule, a people blind to all ordinary common sense. On the 30th, he inserted in *Mist's Journal* a clever article, under the disguise of a Projector, who could not procure a Dinner, describing his Scheme for a Great Brewhouse to be erected in the City, to supply London with Beer and other Liquors, through pipes under the streets, with taps in the Houses. This he affirmed must pay, as the business of *The Salt-Fish Company* would create a general thirst, that must be assuaged. The capital was fixed at ten millions. The scheme will be found in its proper place among his writings. No exertions could save a people acting as if bent on destruction; yet it may fairly be hoped that Defoe's incessant efforts were not altogether in vain.

There had resided in London, for many years, a celebrated fortune-teller named Duncan Campbell, who professed to be, and I believe was, deaf and dumb. He also claimed the faculty of second-sight, and in this was probably an impostor. Even in those credulous days, however, he could not have acquired the fame he undoubtedly possessed, among the polite and well-educated, without rare natural powers, improved by habit and practice, to a degree of refined discernment almost incredible. The reputation of Campbell secured him the notice of the *Tatler;* and the *Spectator* (No. 560), says of him, " The blind Tiresias was not more famous in Greece, than this dumb artist has been for some years last past in the Cities of London and Westminster." His gains must have been large, but he was a wit, a social companion, a frequenter of taverns, and was extravagant in his expenditure; moreover, he was subject to fits which frequently incapacitated him from following his profession, and so far from having amassed a fortune, as stated by Mr. Wilson, there is every reason to believe that his poverty often drove him to seek charity in the polite forms of fees, presents, loans, and the sale of books giving accounts of his truly wonderful genius. He was full of expedients for keeping his name before the public, but his death seems to have left his family unprovided for.

Defoe's love of the marvellous and supernatural, would doubtless incline him to take an interest in such a character; but whether friendship to Campbell, or a proposal of remuneration from Curll, the publisher, induced our author to write the following work, published on the 30th of April, can only be matter of conjecture. It is entitled, " The History of the Life and Adventures of Mr. Duncan Campbell, a Gentleman, who tho' Deaf and Dumb, writes down any Stranger's Name at first Sight; with their future Contingencies of Fortune.

Now living in Exeter Court, over against the Savoy in the Strand. London: Printed for E. Curll; and sold by W. Mears, &c. 1720."* There is prefixed to the book an Epistle Dedicatory, " To the Ladies and Gentlemen of Great Britain ;" in which he says, " The good old Gentleman who wrote the Adventures of my Life, has made it his Business to treat them with a great variety of entertaining passages, which always terminate in Morals, that tend to the Edification of all Readers, of whatsoever Sex, Age, or Profession." It would occupy too much space here to say more of this volume than that it is amusing and instructive.

On the 18th of June, in the same year, there was published a pamphlet of two and a half sheets, entitled, " Mr. Campbell's Pacquet, for the Entertainment of Gentlemen and Ladies. Containing I. Verses to Mr. Campbell, Occasioned by the History of his Life and Adventures. By Mrs. Fowke, Mr. Philips, &c. II. The Parallel, a Poem. Comparing the Poetical Productions of Mr. Pope, with the Prophetical Predictions of Mr. Campbell. By Capt. Stanhope. III. An Account of a most surprizing Apparition ; sent from Launceston in Cornwall. Attested by the Rev. Mr. Ruddle, Minister there. London. Printed for T. Bickerton, at the Crown in Paternoster Row. 1720."

I have only now to do with the *third* section of this pamphlet, which occupies from pages 20 to 33 inclusive, and is headed, " A Remarkable Passage of an Apparition. 1665." There can be no more doubt that this was written by Defoe, than that he wrote the *Apparition of Mrs. Veal;* and although it has no reference to Campbell, yet I believe that having solicited the poems, forming the first and second parts, in order to puff the sale of his " Life," Campbell found them in-

---

* *Daily Post,* Wednesday, 4 May, 1720.—" Last Monday, Mr. Campbell, the Deaf and Dumb Gentleman (introduced by Colonel Carr) Kiss'd the King's Hand, and presented to his Majesty *The History of his Life and Adventures,* which was by his Majesty most graciously receiv'd." The *Daily Post* of the 9th May, contains a Letter from the Oxford Club, in commendation of the book, signed W. Langley, Secretary. And the same Paper of the 12th of May states that *Campbell* had been introduced by Lord Stanhope to the Prince and Princess, and had presented his Book, " which their Royal Highnesses very favourably receiv'd."

sufficient to make a sixpenny pamphlet, and begged the manuscript of this Apparition from Defoe to supply the deficiency.

Nothing that has been said in praise of the *Apparition of Mrs. Veal,* by the greatest critics, can be misapplied to the "Apparition" we are now considering. Let those who are willing to be carried away by the illusion, into the belief of a Ghost, read it; I fear to destroy the charm by attempting an abstract. The professed relator, Mr. Ruddle, a young clergyman, kept a school in Launceston, and some of his Scholars died of a Disease that happened in the town. Among them was *John Elliott,* the eldest son of *Edward Elliott, of Treberse,* Esq. At the youth's request, Mr. Ruddle preached a Sermon at the Funeral, "which happened on the 20th Day of June 1665." An Ancient Gentleman in the Church was much affected by the Discourse, having a son who, a few months before, had a character like that given of young Elliott; but had changed greatly to the affliction of his parents. The old man afterward addressed Mr. Ruddle, and importuned him to visit him at his House. There seems to have been considerable difficulty in fixing a day convenient to all parties; but at last, on arriving, he found there a Brother of the Coat, a neighbouring Minister; and, as soon as an opportunity occurred after Dinner, the two clergymen went into the Garden, when Mr. Ruddle learnt that this poor Boy had grown melancholy from being, as he stated, haunted with a Ghost. After several conferences with the parents, it was agreed that Mr. Ruddle should talk with the Boy alone, before giving his advice. "He told me," Mr. Ruddle says, "with all naked Freedom, and a Flood of Tears, that his Friends were unkind and unjust to him, neither to believe nor pity him; and that if any Man (making a bow to me) would but goe with him to the Place, he might be convinc'd that the Thing was real," &c. "This Woman which appears to me (saith he) lived a Neighbour here to my Father; and dyed about eight Years since, her name *Dorothy Dingley,* of such a Stature, such Age, and such a Complexion." She met him on his way to and from School, morning and evening, "in a Field called the *Higher-Broom Quartils.*" He began to be much alarmed and says, "Then I changed my Way, and went to School the under Horse-Road,

and then she always met me in the Narrow Lane, between the
Quarry Parke and the Nursery, which was worse." He goes
on to describe his growing horrors ; "Night and Day, Sleeping
and Waking, the Shape was ever running in my Mind ; and I
often did repeat these Places of Scripture, (with that he takes
a small Bible out of his Pocket,) Job. 7. 14.—*Thou scarest me
with Dreams, and terrifiest me through Visions ;*—and Deut. 28.
67.—*In the morning thou shalt say, would God it were Evening,*"
—&c. &c.   At last his misery became insupportable,. and he
told his Brother William, who acquainted their Parents.
Mr. Ruddle, by arrangement, went next morning with
Master *Sam.* to see the Spectrum.   He says, " The Field he
led me to, I guessed to be about twenty Acres, in an open
Country, and about three Furlongs from any House."   Both
saw the Ghost, but had no communication with it then, and
Mr. Ruddle was compelled to return to Launceston the same
evening.   He could not go again, in consequence of his
wife being taken ill, until three weeks afterward, but he
says, " I studied the Case, resolving by the help of God
to see the utmost."   After several visits to the Field, generally alone, all of which are described in the most circumstantial manner, he persisted on Thursday, the 28th of
July 1665, in speaking to it, " until it spake again, and
gave me Satisfaction.   But the Work could not be finish'd
at this time ; wherefore the same Evening, an Hour after
Sun-set, it met me again near the same Place, and after a
few Words on each side it quietly vanished, and neither doth
appear since, nor ever will more, to any Man's disturbance.
The Discourse in the Morning lasted about a quarter of an
Hour."

He then solemnly affirms the truth of his narrative, answers
the arguments urged by the incredulous, and fortifies himself
in a Postscript, by referring to the ancient Fathers of the
Church, and quoting from *St. Cyprian,* and Pamelius's Notes
on *Tertullian.*   It is observable that he artfully conceals every
word of his discourse with the Ghost, intending no doubt to
leave that to the individual imagination of the reader, but
assigning as his reason, " I being a Clergyman, and young,
and a stranger in these Parts, do apprehend silence and
secrecy to be my best security.   *In rebus abstrussimus abundans*

cautela non nocet." The Account is subscribed with the date, " September 4th, 1665."

It must have been near the time when the *Apparition* was published, that some worthy, who was collecting literary matter relating to *Launceston,* transcribed the whole account into his common-place book or Notes; and the Papers of such Collector coming many years afterward, into the hands of a reverend gentleman, were thought to be in Mr. *Ruddle's* (as Defoe called him, or Dr. *Ruddell's,* as the transcriber called him,) own hand-writing. As such, the manuscript was lent to Mr. *C. S. Gilbert,* and by him inserted in his *History of Cornwall,* as an original and inedited document. On this " Remarkable Passage of an Apparition, 1665," as she saw it in *Gilbert's* work, Mrs. *Bray* founded a considerable part of her very graphic and interesting romance of *Trelawney of Trelawney.* Afterward she was surprised to find the story, in the Appendix to the *Life of Duncan Campbell* (Talboy's Edition, Oxford, 1840), and, in her perplexity says, that if she had not previously known the circumstances, she " should have fancied it a fiction of Defoe himself, like *the story of the Ghost of Mrs. Veal, prefixed to Drelincourt on Death.*"*

On the 4th of August 1720, was published, " The Second Edition Corrected, of the *History of the Life and Adventures of Duncan Campbell ;* in which the only alterations I have observed, are a better and more highly finished portrait of Campbell, a new titlepage, and the insertion (between the Contents and page 1,) of the pamphlet—" Mr. Campbell's Pacquet." The title of the Pacquet is cancelled, but the sheets are evidently the first impression, and have no connection with the volume in which they are bound. This second Edition was re-issued on the 14th March 1721; and in the year 1728, the same Book appeared, entitled, " The Supernatural Philosopher : or, the Mysteries of Magick, in all its Branches, clearly Un-folded," &c. &c. &c. " All Exemplified in the History of the Life and Surprizing Adventures of Mr. Duncan Campbell, a Scots Gentleman ; who, though Deaf and Dumb, writes down any Stranger's name at first Sight, with their future Con-

---

* *Vide* her account of the matter in her General Preface to the first volume of the reprint, in series, of her Novels and Romances.

tingencies of Fortune, &c. &c." By *William Bond*, Esq.; of Bury St. Edmund's, Suffolk. The Second Edition. London. Printed for E. Curll, over against Catherine Street in the Strand. 1728." I have abridged this very long title-page, but it will be found at length in the list of Defoe's Works, prefixed hereto.

There was a practice among disreputable booksellers of that period, of inventing new title-pages for unsold books, and thus getting rid of old stock by deceiving the public. Mr. Curll was an adept at this, and the technical verb for the process was—*to fub*. The book with the above title, stating the work to be By " William Bond, Esq.," is no other than Defoe's Life of Duncan Campbell, with a " fubbed" titlepage, and the omission of the portrait. All the remainder of the Volume consists of the first impressions of the work; and even the pamphlet called " Campbell's Pacquet" is again bound up in the same place as before. Defoe had no interest in the copyright of his work; nor could he be concerned in the act as derogatory to his fame in the eyes of posterity.

I have no concern with either of the Works relating to Duncan Campbell, entitled, " A Spy on the Conjuror," or " The Dumb Projector," simply because Defoe had nothing to do with them; but I entertain no doubt he had a hand in the following, which I notice here, that I may not have to revert to the subject again :—" The Friendly Dæmon, or the Generous Apparition; Being a True Narrative of a Miraculous Cure, newly perform'd upon that famous Deaf and Dumb Gentleman, Dr. Duncan Campbell, by a familiar Spirit that appear'd to him in a White Surplice, like a Cathedral Singing Boy. London; Printed and Sold by J. Roberts in Warwick Lane. 1726." The first twelve pages of this pamphlet consist of a Letter pretendedly written by Duncan Campbell himself, addressed, " To my anonymous worthy Friend, Physician and Philosopher, whose Name, for certain Reasons, I forbear to mention." The reply, which occupies pages 13 to 38, I have little doubt is by Defoe. It is addressed as follows :—" To my Deaf and Dumb Friend, Mr. Duncan Campbell, in answer to his Letter to an anonymous worthy Friend, Physician and Philosopher." Though not actually stated, it is plainly to be inferred, that a

long illness had incapacitated Campbell from his practice of
fortune telling ; and, that being now recovered, necessity induced him to assume the title of "Doctor" and resort to
Quackery. He set up therefore to cure all kinds of Fits, by
means of the Loadstone, and by a miraculous Powder, secretly
communicated to him by a good Genius ; and, he wished his
pretensions to be strengthened, by the public sanction of a
Physician. It is useless to conceal that there is in this, many
of the marks of an Imposture, and hence it is important to
consider Defoe's reply. He was evidently desirous of assisting the
unfortunate applicant, if possible ; but conscience was always pa-
ramount, and he could not benefit a friend in distress by sanction-
ing untruth, even in a communication necessarily anonymous.
In the first paragraph he says, " I therefore think not the
Means to which you ascribe your Cure, or the Manner of the
Recipe's being communicated to you, a proper Subject for a
Physical Enquiry, unless you had sent me the Prescription of
your *Genius*, which I understand by your Letter, you are
obliged to conceal ; also, how far your Guardian Angel is a
Regular Proficient in the modern Practice of Physick." So
much respecting the Powder. As to the Loadstone he says,
" in any other Case excepting your own, I never heard of a
Cure so much as facilitated or attempted to be perform'd
thereby, as the Use of it in any Disease is quite Foreign to
the common Practice of Physick." Yet he ingeniously and
felicitously enfolds these remarks in a learned dissertation on
Genii, Dæmons, Apparitions, and the alleged virtues of the *Loadstone*, and *Sympathetic Powder* ; in which he introduces the
opinions and experience of all who have believed therein, from
Socrates downward, to Sir Kenelm Digby and Mr. Greatrex.
Mr. Campbell was probably greatly served ; but Defoe had not
to any extent approved of the medicines proposed.*

I have now to consider a work, admitted by all who have

---

* Duncan Campbell died about the year 1730, after a long and severe
illness, which baffled the Loadstone, and the powder of his good *Genius*.
In 1732, was published a volume entitled, " Secret Memoirs of the late Mr.
Duncan Campbell, the Famous Deaf and Dumb Gentleman. Written by Him-
self, who ordered they should be published after his Decease." The *Friendly
Dæmon* is reprinted in this work.

read it, and were capable of forming a correct judgment, to be
one of the finest military memoirs extant, in any language.
It was published on the 21st of May 1720, and is entitled—
" Memoirs of a Cavalier : Or, a Military Journal of the Wars
in Germany, and the Wars in England ; from the year 1632
to the year 1648.   Written Three score Years ago by an
English Gentleman, who served first in the Army of Gustavus
Adolphus, the glorious King of Sweden, till his death ; and
after that, in the Royal Army of King Charles the First, from
the Beginning of the Rebellion, to the End of that War.
London.   Printed for A. Bell at the Crosskeys in Cornhill,
&c."   This book has passed through many editions, and has
been more than once published as a purely historical account,
by a real person, who took part in the events related.   The
simple truthfulness of its narrations is so convincing, that all
notion of its being a work of imagination is lost sight of ; and
thus it has been read and believed, by thousands of all classes,
including even such men as the great Earl of Chatham.   On
the other hand, the biographers of Defoe have, as far as I know,
without exception, believed the " Cavalier " to be an imaginary
hero, and the book a fictitious romance.   The controversy, if
such it may be called, is nearly as old as the book.   The
Leeds publisher of the second edition says, in an address to
the Reader, that " the republication of these Memoirs will
renew the Enquiry which has been oft made, *Who wrote them ?*
Some have imagin'd the whole to be a Romance ; if it be, 'tis
a Romance the likest to Truth that I ever read."   Having no
idea of Defoe being connected with the work, this publisher
adds, " He says he was the second Son of a Shropshire Gentleman, who was made a Peer in the Reign of King Charles I.,
whose Seat lay eight Miles from Shrewsbury.   This Account
suits no one so well as Andrew Newport, Esq. ; second Son to
Richard Newport, of High Ercoll, Esq., which Richard was
created Lord Newport, October 14th, 1642. This Andrew Newport, Esq. ; whom we suppose our Author to be, was after the
Restoration made a Commissioner of the Customs, probably in
Reward of his Zeal and good Services for the Royal Cause."

We now turn to the Preface of the first edition, which was
undoubtedly written by Defoe, who gives the following account
of these Memoirs, " The Persons now concerned in the Publi-

cation, assure the Reader, that they have been in their Possession finished, as they now appear, above twenty Years : That they were so long ago found, by great Accident, among other valuable Papers, in the Closet of an eminent publick Minister, of no less figure than one of King William's Secretaries of State."* Somewhat ambiguously he adduces the above " as an Evidence that *'tis very probable* these Memorials were written many years ago." He immediately adds, " it is not proper to trace them any farther," but assigns no reason why; except, that the actions mentioned therein " have a sufficient Sanction from all the Histories of the Times to which they relate ;" which is only equivalent to asserting, that historical authenticity renders improper any enquiry as to the genuineness of the book. He goes on to state, however, that " no small Labour has been thrown away upon the Enquiry, and all we have been able to arrive to of Discovery in this Affair is, that a Memorandum was found with this Manuscript, in these Words, but not signed by any Name, only the two Letters of a Name, which gives us no Light into the Matter, which was as follows :—

' Memorandum,
  ' I found this Manuscript among my Father's Writings, and
  ' I understand that he got them as Plunder, at, or after, the
  ' Fight at Worcester, where he serv'd as Major of ————'s
  ' Regiment of Horse on the side of the Parliament.
                                    ' I. K.' "

Making due allowance for an author's licence to enhance the reputation of any fictitious work by representations as to its truth ; still it must be admitted that whatever weight the above is entitled to, if any, is on the side of the existence of a manuscript, many years before the publication of the book.

---

* It is singular that I find the following paragraph in the *Post-Boy* of the 30th of *September* 1699. " Some Days since, the Honourable *Andrew Newport*, Esq., Brother to the Right Honourable the Earl of *Bradford*, died at *Eyton* upon *Seavern*, in *Shropshire*, and is much lamented, he being extraordinary well beloved." If we can suppose Defoe—speaking from the recollection of twenty years,—to have written " Secretaries of State," instead of " Commissioners of Customs," the time of its discovery would be exactly accounted for, by supposing it found in the closet of his office, after his decease. But the memorandum relating to its capture at Worcester previously, would be still a difficulty.

In the latter part of the Preface he has a hypothesis that the
author may have written another Part of this work, which
may have fallen into other hands, and may yet be discovered ;
or, he may have gone abroad, as most of the Gentlemen of
Quality did ; or, that he might not have lived " to the end
of that time."   I can only suppose our author intended by
this to hold out the probability that his readers might be
gratified with a continuation of the work.   But as the Preface was probably the last written part of the book, he seems
to have forgotten that the " Cavalier's " Military Life terminated with the end of the Civil Wars in 1646,—that there was
no further fighting to do,—that his military career is all professedly related in the present volume,—and, not a word suggests
that he ever again took sword in hand.   It appears also to
have escaped Defoe, that the titlepage extends the period to
two years later than the actual end of the war.   The memorandum says the manuscript fell into the hands of a Major in
the Parliamentary Army at Worcester, which was in 1651 ;
after that event, it is needless to say, the " Cavalier " could
make no additions ; yet it is clear from the latter part of the
Memoirs themselves, that they were not completed until after
the Restoration.   So again, if the manuscript was captured in
1651, it must have been written seventy years, and not sixty,
as stated in the titlepage.   There is nothing in the Memoirs
themselves to show that they had been written so long as
" threescore years ago."   I infer, that from lapse of time, or
other cause, the chronology of these Memoirs was not fresh in
the memory of Defoe, when he wrote the preface.   It cannot
be denied that he evinces a great desire that the public should
believe the " Cavalier " to be a real personage.   In this, he
was justified by many considerations,—it would increase the
interest of the reader in the book, and it enabled him to speak
in terms of unreserved praise of the hero and his Work.   Yet,
while effecting his object by the relation of specific circumstances, there is obviously much concealment, not to be found
combined in any other of his works ; viz., the omission of the
name of the " Cavalier" himself, and consequently, of his family
and connections ; the same as to the place of his birth, and name
of his college at Oxford ; the same again, as to the name of the
officer who captured the manuscript at Worcester, and the desig-

nation of the Regiment in which that officer was Major; and also the name of the Secretary of State in whose closet the manuscript was said to be afterward found.   Should it be objected, that to have furnished these particulars would have afforded proof that the whole was a fiction; I answer that Defoe was too wise to create needless or gratuitous difficulties, and then to say " it is not proper to trace them any farther." His object was to obtain implicit credence for the book, and not to excite suspicion; and therefore, I am more inclined to believe, that the concealment of these important particulars was intentional; and a proof, as far as it goes, that some such manuscript really was found, in the manner stated.   But there are numerous expressions used in the Memoirs, which, if Defoe had any hand in them, would not have been used until within twenty years of their publication.   I would not lay great stress upon a note quoting Ludlow's Memoirs (published in 1698-9), but I may mention, " Jure Divino," " Obser-vator," " Tale of a Tub," &c., as showing that any manuscript of these Memoirs, existing in the reign of King William, was subsequently altered.

To claim for Defoe the authorship of the " Cavalier," as a work of pure fiction, would be equivalent to a claim of almost superhuman genius.   It is entirely based upon historical facts, otherwise history would have confuted it.   Parts of the book are undoubtedly fictitious, as the verbal dialogues, at which the author was not present.   But it may be said the history can be correct, and the hero imaginary !   This is granted,—as a hypo-thesis,—but Defoe says he was a real person, and the author of a manuscript; and if this be corroborated, I may fairly ask what evidence is there to the contrary?   The answer is, that not a tittle has ever been produced.   If it should be replied, that he has said the same of the heroes of his other fictions, I answer, that in no case has he done so in like circumstances as in this, nor in any other, can his statement be corroborated by evidence.

There are passages in these Memoirs that could not have been consistently written by any person, of himself; as, that he never designed to write a book, and kept no journal; yet, in another place, he speaks of his Memoirs of Italy.   He was in that country at least half a year, but turns entirely away from its material grandeur, and simply says,—" I had no gust for Antiquities." Yet soon afterward, in Germany, he appears to have had a fine taste for what was ancient and beautiful in art ; and at Munich, regrets that he could not take " a very exact account" of the Duke's great chamber of rarities.   Of the same class is his being distinguished as " The Cavalier," while only a young officer, among many other English and Scots gentlemen, in the army of Gustavus Adolphus ;—the designation belonging in common, and not distinctively, only to those on the King's side, during the subsequent Civil Wars in England.   With equal truth it may be affirmed, that there are many passages in these Memoirs, which Defoe neither could, nor would, have written.   It will be sufficient to allude only to the great hatred expressed toward the Scotch nation in various parts of the work.   They are branded with infamy, for having sold their honesty, and rebelled for money against the King, to whom they had sworn allegiance.   In another place he calls them " these cursed Scots,"—and towards the end of the Memoirs, declares bitterly, that they sold the King for money, into the hands of his murderous enemies.   I may also remark, that while there is nothing in the " Cavalier," or his Story, unbecoming the high character of an English gentleman, yet is there little to be seen of the moral and religious spirit of dependence upon Providence, and appeal to the Scriptures, so characteristic of Defoe, even in his works of fiction.

In stile and diction, I may say that there are occasionally whole paragraphs that scarcely afford a trace of Defoe's pen ; although, generally, he appears to have revised, and often rewritten and extended the manuscript.   His mind as well as his hand is much more perceptible in the latter part of the book than in the former ; and, as he was better acquainted with the geography and physical character of his own country than that of Germany, this part of the narrative is often very characteristic of his genius.

From what has been already stated, I am of opinion that a manuscript came into Defoe's possession, according to his own statement, many years before its publication ; that he then filled out and extended it into the form in which we now have the book ; and, that the wonderful success of Robinson Crusoe, induced him to write the Preface and publish the work he had long before completed, as " The Memoirs of a

Cavalier." I am further confirmed in this conclusion by another pamphlet of Defoe's, published six years earlier,* in which he defends the honour of the nobility and gentry of Scotland, against an attack from Dean Swift, by referring to the great numbers who had served with distinction under the same Gustavus Adolphus, King of Sweden ; and he speaks of a Manuscript, as his authority, thus :—" The Manuscript I have had in my Hands many Years, neither is it to be contradicted, the Histories of those Times making frequent mention of all their Names." The conclusion that the " Cavalier" had been laid by, as a completed work, and now, only needed the printer's services, is also strengthened by the fact, that it was published on the twenty-first day after the " Life of Duncan Campbell ;" and was followed, in fourteen days, by another volume of equal size from our author's pen. I need not extend this long notice by quotation, or by any further commendation of the " Memoirs of a Cavalier." It contains the best, the most impartial, and most interesting account of the Civil Wars that has been written ; and, though less strictly original than a work of fiction, it gains the importance of being ranked henceforth as truly historical ; and is not the less entitled to be placed among the writings of Defoe, because based upon one acknowledged authority ; than it would have been if collected from the published histories of the times.

The facile pen of Defoe, equally ready upon all subjects of interest, whether on land or sea, was now turned again to a description of the lawless but enterprizing career of an English Pirate. The idea was probably formed while he was engaged upon the pamphlet respecting Captain Avery ; but as that worthy had a real history, and the design of the author was restricted to two supposed letters from him, it may be that much of perilous adventure presented itself to his imagination that could not well be brought within the scope of such pamphlet ; and, that the present production, in which Captain Avery again appears, was the result. The volume was published on the 4th of June, and is entitled, " The Life, Adventures, and Pyracies of the famous Captain Singleton : Contain-

---

* " The Scots Nation and Union Vindicated," p. 24.

ing an Account of his being set on Shore in the Island of Madagascar, his Settlement there, with a Description of the Place and Inhabitants : Of his Passage from thence in a Paraguay, to the main Land of Africa, with an Account of the Customs and Manners of the People : His great Deliverances from the barbarous Natives and wild Beasts : Of his Meeting with an Englishman, a Citizen of London, among the Indians, the great Riches he acquired, and his Voyage Home to England : As also Captain Singleton's Return to Sea, with an Account of his many Adventures and Pyracies with the famous Captain Avery and others. London. J. Brotherton, &c. 1720." This work has been spoken of in comparatively disparaging terms by several of the biographers of Defoe. I take leave entirely to dissent from such judgment, and to say, that making allowance for the absence of that charm which, in some of his works, is due to the isolation of his hero, and the concentrated interest arising therefrom, Singleton comes in no sense behind the other literary creations of our author. It is true that the pirate is not an honest man, because that would be a contradiction of terms, but natural conscience is always at work, and the book itself abounds in moral reflections. Only the latter portion contains the piratical adventures of Singleton ; and they are full of striking incidents, and of appropriate dialogue ; each part, however, contributes to the unity of the whole, as a true representation of the times. The Quaker pirate is the moralist of the work, and was not introduced by Defoe, as an important character, without due consideration. Few men had better studied, or more highly respected, the body of Friends, called Quakers, whose religious and moral principles were closely allied to his own ; but there were undoubtedly, in the reigns of Queen Anne and George I., professed Quakers, such as we know nothing of now. London had several who kept taverns,—one, who was an owner of race-horses, that ran for wagers on Banstead Downs ; and several Quakers were transported, for burglaries and highway robberies. There is therefore no moral or literary improbability in Singleton's connection with one of that body, whose sister he afterward married. The titlepage of the book however, shows that Defoe considered the former part as the more important, containing the escape of the mutineers from Madagascar to Mozambique, and their

subsequent marvellous journey by land across the most deso-
late and unknown part of the continent of Africa, to its western
coast. I hold the conception and execution of this part of his
work, considered in all the detail of its circumstances, to be
one of the highest and most successful efforts of Defoe's
genius. I have traced this route on the map of Africa, in
Wyld's great Atlas of 1849 ; and where I find on the map
carte blanche for more than a thousand miles, Defoe's Captain
Singleton, of 1720, has guided me along the shores of the
mighty Lakes,—which he declared to be the true sources of the
Nile,—through dreary deserts, and across primeval mountains,—
inhabited by many races of savage men, and more savage
beasts ; and the whole journey, to use his own words,—" full of
Adventures that were never heard or read of before." This
knowledge of the interior of Africa appears the more amazing
since the recent researches of Livingstone, Baker, Grant, and
other explorers, have confirmed what our author had so long
before stated.* On the wonderful geographical knowledge
possessed by Defoe, and exemplified in this journey, Dr. Bird-
wood read a most interesting Paper before the Bombay Branch
of the Royal Asiatic Society, on the 11th of June 1863. It is
entitled, " On Recent Discovery in Eastern Africa, and the
Adventures of Captain Singleton (Defoe)."†

In the beginning of June 1720, the loyal Protestant sympathy of the country was gladdened by news from Heidelberg
that the Elector Palatine had restored to his Protestant subjects most of their invaded rights, and especially the use of
their Catechism for the instruction of their children. It was
well known that this relaxation of persecution had, to a great
extent, been effected through the interposition of the King of
England ; but *Mist's* German correspondents were papists, and
in their letters of advice they resented and reflected upon such
interference. As if bent on his own destruction, Mist refused
to suppress these reflections, and thus caused a rupture between

---

* In Purchas's "Pilgrims," (vol. ii. fol. 1544,) is an Abridgment of
Father Dos Santo's *Ethiopia Oriental*, in which some hints are given of the
Great Lake, (Nyassi, *i e.* Sea,) Naravi. It is possible Defoe may have read
the account, but it would only help him to the single fact.

† Printed in the Society's Journal, No. 22, vol vii. pp. 49-65.

him and Defoe, who seems to have been so incensed as to have left him to the consequences of his own obstinacy. In the *Daily Post* of the 8th June, our author makes no allusion to the article in *Mist's Journal,* but concludes a long paragraph upon the same subject, as follows :—" In a word, the Figure the Protestant Interest makes at this time in the World, is such, that the Roman Catholick Interest, were it more united than it is, has but little Encouragement to make a general Breach with them. How much of this is owing to the happy Union of the Protestant Princes, at this Time, and particularly to the Influence of the British Court in all Parts of Europe, the World is not ignorant of."

The gratuitous exhibition of *Mist's* subserviency to foreign and anti-English influence was quickly resented. Dr. Richard Willis, the Bishop of Gloucester, brought the matter before the House of Lords, who ordered the offender to be prosecuted by the Attorney-General ; and *Mist* was accordingly apprehended, and committed to the King's Bench prison to await his trial. It must be confessed that he met with as little public sympathy as he deserved ; the following, from *Read's Journal* of June 11th, is the sneering notice of his incarceration :—" In return to our Brother *Mist's* kindness, in wishing us well off when we were in Tribulation, we cannot but condole him in the present Situation of his Affairs ; and wish him a safe Delivery from an Information now laid against him, and from the Resentment of all true Protestants." Defoe must have been thoroughly convinced that Mr. *Mist* was not merely unmanageable but incorrigible ; yet being in prison, and unable at once to make arrangements for the continuance of the *Journal,* our author appears to have generously offered his temporary assistance in its conduct, but only on condition that he should not be interfered with, until some permanent arrangement could be effected. He was also probably moved to this by his duty to the Government, inasmuch as the Paper might have otherwise been mismanaged, by Mist's servants, as offensively as if its proprietor had been at large. Yet he showed his settled determination to change his position, by entering into an arrangement with the owner of " Applebee's Original Weekly Journal," to write the Letters Introductory, and take some part in the general management of that paper.

The Original Weekly Journal had been established on the 2nd October 1714. It was published on Saturdays, and consisted, like the other weekly papers, of three leaves, small folio. It professed Tory principles, and occasionally rallied the Whigs; but this appeared to be rather to secure its circulation among the Tories, than from any hostility to the Whig Ministry. The same consideration precluded any active or avowed support of the Whig party; but its principles were thoroughly English,—it was truly loyal to the House of Hanover, and in our own day it would have been correctly designated a *Liberal-Conservative* Paper. As Defoe might be properly termed a *Conservative-Liberal*, he had no sacrifice of principle or conduct to make in this new engagement; but was perfectly free to advocate, in his own way, the political, social, and religious interests of his country, with the additional advantage that his views would influence the moderate and patriotic Tories, and thus aid in strengthening the administration. His first article in *Applebee's Journal* was published on the 25th June 1720, which was the day following that on which the Act of Parliament and Royal Proclamation, for the instant suppression of all further Bubbling Schemes, had come into operation. The subject he adopted was the strange and sudden alterations produced by the Act, in Exchange Alley, and the streets, taverns, and coffee-houses, near that centre of recent "Whimsical Transactions." He describes these changes in his happiest and most playful manner, signing his communication "OLIVER OLDWAY." It will be found in its place among his writings; and, in addition to the amusement it will afford, has a permanent interest as part of the history of the national delusion. Defoe continued to write weekly articles in *Applebee's Journal* until the 12th of March 1726, and the largest portion of his hitherto uncollected writings discovered in my research, have been transcribed from its pages. The *Journal* continued in existence until many years after Defoe's death.

I have now to explain briefly an important point, that has hitherto perplexed not only all biographers of Defoe, but also many of his readers; namely, the motives and circumstances that induced him, at sixty years of age, to commence writing a series of volumes professedly recording the lives of notorious criminals, whose many offences and immoralities had subjected them to the penalties of the laws they had broken. His personal honesty and integrity, the purity of his life, nay even his high religious character, has never been called in question by any well-informed writer, and is attested by the excellence of his numerous moral works ;—composed, not only previously, but interposed between, and continued after, the publication of those which are felt to be offensive to modern notions of delicacy. It has also excited inquiry how he became acquainted with the class of persons from whom alone he could have obtained such an intimate knowledge of their habits, manners, and associations ; not only at home,—but in the Plantations to which they were transported,—as was requisite for the production of these works. As to the latter of these inquiries, the only answer has been based on the horrible manner in which prisoners were confined together in Newgate, almost without discrimination of offence, or of sex. It has been supposed that when Defoe was imprisoned for writing *The Shortest Way*,—in the beginning of the reign of Queen Anne,—he was compelled to associate ordinarily with the most abandoned of both sexes; and then acquired the knowledge that enabled him, nearly twenty years afterward, to write the books in question. I must state that there is not the slightest foundation for believing that he was ever subjected, against his will, to so barbarous an indignity. In the eyes even of those who condemned him, he had only written and published a libel; and the numerous works he composed while in prison, not only show upon what subjects his mind and attention were then engaged, but also that he was able to pursue his studies, without great disturbance. There is not a word to be found in any of his prison writings, or later productions, giving countenance to any assertion that he had been exposed, for more than a year, to degrading associations, which, with his sense of morality and religion, would have been worse than a thousand deaths.

Pecuniary motives, arising from straitened circumstances, have been assigned, as having induced him to write what his conscience might not approve. I must also strongly dissent from this, as a libel upon his moral character. Such

humiliation of their hero, by his biographers, has arisen from
their belief, that during the last fifteen years of his life, he was
in poverty ; and entirely dependent, for the support of himself
and family, upon the sale of the books heretofore known as his
writings.   But when it is considered that all his children were
now grown up, and some of them no longer a burden ; that
he appears to have been no longer harassed by his former
pecuniary misfortunes ; that he had an adequate income from
the Government ; that he was paid for his services in connection with three or four Journals, and periodical publications ;
and that, in addition,—his other works were a large and increasing source of revenue,—it will be readily believed that he
had never been in such prosperity as now, since the death of
King William III.   It is undeniable that he composed these
works ; and as he had not treasured up any degrading ex-
periences of an imprisonment twenty years previously, nor was
urged by necessity, we must conclude that he wrote them
under circumstances not heretofore known, voluntarily, and
from motives justified by his own enlightened conscience.

A glance at the moral, or immoral, condition of large classes
of the people, during the latter part of the reign of Queen
Anne, and the whole reign of George I., is requisite to a right
judgment of this matter.   To narrow the question as much as
possible, we may leave out of consideration the leaven of de-
pravity, which, commencing with the Court after the Restoration, had now leavened the mass of society.   Nor need we do
more than name, that somewhat similar influences in France
culminated, at the period with which we have now to do, in
the Cartouchian organization of robbers and murderers.   It
will be sufficient to say of England, that her pirates, the offspring of the buccaneers, infested every sea in the known
world ; that the *Owlers* were leagued with justices and landed
gentry in defrauding the Customs of the country, to an extent
that would now be thought incredible ; that the *Blacks*, who were
organized in many of the western counties for burglaries, comprised substantial yeomen and well-to-do farmers in their numbers ; that among the army of highwaymen, in and about London,
was a barrister, several attornies, a graduate of the University
of Cambridge, a stockbroker, and many keepers of apparently
respectable taverns.   These are but the salient points, below

which, there existed an undistinguished mass of ignorance,
dishonesty, lewdness, and brutality; which there was no
police to prevent, and the sanguinary laws of the period
were totally unable to repress. One or two annually
appointed constables in each parish, and a few decrepid night
watchmen, constituted the only police of the metropolis. All
the coaches plying between Hampstead and the city would be
stopped, and the passengers robbed in the open daylight; and,
by the same mounted desperadoes,—day after day,—for a week
together. The same on the roads from Islington, and from
Hackney, and other suburban towns and villages. The apprehension of any of these villains was of no avail; their places
were immediately filled by others, and the supply of highwaymen seemed inexhaustible. No private carriage could travel
safely without an escort of armed servants; the mails were
constantly robbed of their valuable contents,—that between
Bristol and London being plundered about five times in as
many weeks. In hopes of safety, plate and jewels were frequently
sent in stage-waggons, and several of these were stopped successively between Notting-hill and Tyburn-gate, the harness cut, the
waggons unloaded, and the boxes and packages opened and rifled,
on the public road, during the space of several hours; after
which, the thieves rode off unmolested with their spoil. Foot-
pads plied their profitable trades on pedestrians, and the occu-
pants of chairs, in such places as Charing Cross, Holborn, Fleet
Street, and St. Paul's Churchyard, not unfrequently, if resisted,
adding murder to robbery. The weekly hanging-day at Tyburn
was the market of all the lower class of male pickpockets; the
fallen of the other sex infesting the streets, taverns, and places
of amusement; while the more aristocratic of both sexes filched
pocket-books, papers, and purses, in the city, and on the Exchange. Truly, the period between 1720 and 1730 may be
called, by way of climax, the Age of Crime, and Jonathan
Wild, the creature of circumstances. The newspapers from
1721 to 1725 frequently contained a string of paragraphs more
than a column in length, of robberies committed, without any
of the thieves having been apprehended; and another column
of short advertisements, in small type, as to pocket-books, bills,
notes, and securities, &c., all of which were said to be—" Lost."
Rewards were offered to those who would bring the property

to Mr. Jonathan Wild, at the King's Head in the Old Bailey, "and no questions asked." I counted fifty-seven acts of criminality related in one journal of that period; and, in another, thirty-three cases of pockets picked, of an aggregate sum of more than 22,000*l*. What was there to counteract this flood of iniquity? The Societies for the Reformation of Manners attempted it, and I have before me a printed List containing the Christian and surnames of about one hundred and twenty keepers of "Bawdy Houses" *fined ;*—of forty who were *carted ;* and of one hundred and sixty prostitutes who were whipped in Bridewell, within a short period, through the exertions of these Societies. All the culprits, doubtless, immediately returned to their vile avocations. The Gallows could not contain all that were condemned to die, although sometimes from ten to twenty were hung together ; and therefore, the greater number of the condemned were offered the alternative,—which they always accepted,—of being transported to the Plantations in America, with the certainty that, if they should ever return to England, identification would be the only step between them and death. Ships were continually dispatched to the American Colonies, with cargoes of these condemned wretches, varying from one hundred to three hundred, according to the size of the vessels ; and on their arrival the prisoners were sold as Slaves to the Planters. They had no religious instruction ; and, with such servants, the strong hand of the planter contained the power of life and death. Many committed additional crimes in the colonies, and perished miserably, others found their way back to England, hoping by disguise to conceal themselves; in this some succeeded, but many were executed, either "for returning from transportation," or for the crimes into which they again relapsed. What could be done with such an army of tens of thousands of men and women, whose "hands were against every man, and every man's hands against them ?" The moral efforts of the Reformation Societies were as futile, to use the language of Defoe, "as preaching the Gospel to a Kettle-Drum." The punitive exertions of the same Society added no shame to the shameless, fining and exposure no remorse, and whipping no amendment. The Gallows at Tyburn, certainly rid the world of those who were actually suspended there ; but it had lost its terrors for the masses who

crowded the long line of march from Newgate, and swelled the
procession of sympathising admirers of the condemned. As a
specific deterrent against crime, it was an utter failure ;—in an
age when every serious offence was punishable with death. The
multitude of criminals at large who attended these *levées,* to
see their friends and companions " turned off," looked upon
the gallows as their own final destination, and determined that
" their lives, if short, should be merry."

Mr. *John Applebee,* the proprietor of *The Original Journal,*
carried on the general business of a printer in Water Lane,
Whitefriars.   He might also with propriety be designated the
official printer of Newgate, and from his office were issued the
printed Papers of the Ordinary,—as to the conduct of the condemned felons under his spiritual care,—and their confessions,
if any.   The last dying speeches of criminals were known to
be correct, if Mr. Applebee's name was printed on the papers ;
and, in any extraordinary case, with the consent of the condemned, the narrative of his life was taken from his own lips,
or any paper he had written was given to Mr. Applebee, and
embodied in a pamphlet, often printed before, but published
immediately after, the execution.   For these purposes, Mr.
Applebee, or any one authorised to represent him, had access
to the prisoners in Newgate, during all the six years that
Daniel Defoe was connected with the management of *The
Original Journal.*

A short experience would suffice to convince our author
that the largest proportion of these papers and books circulated among the criminal population, and were read with great
avidity.   An examination of the lowest class of thieves' literature of the time printed in other offices, shows that successful
highwaymen and burglars were exalted into heroes, whose great
deeds were more held up as examples for imitation, than as
warnings to be avoided ; and even those who had expiated their
crimes upon the scaffold were objects of highest admiration when
they " died game."*   If any such became penitents, they were

---

* *Vide* " Tyburn's Worthies."   " Compleat Account of Robberies committed by James Carrick and others."   " Account of Robberies committed
by William Hawkins and others."   " Account of Robberies committed by
Wilson."   " History of the Robberies of all the celebrated Highwaymen to
the year 1722," &c. &c., all these published within one month.

execrated as sneaks and cowards. No point of morality was
ever touched upon in these stories, any more than in the lewd
literature provided for the same readers in the lives of Mother
Needham, Sally Salisbury, Mother Wisebourne, Elizabeth Mann,
commonly called the Royal Sovereign, or Mary Parramore. Subsequent productions by Defoe, to be noticed in their place, show
that, as connected with *Applebee's Journal,* he availed himself of
the official privilege of visiting these abandoned and apparently
lost criminals; and that he studied how, if possible, they might
be benefited. True, they appeared inaccessible to the direct
teachings of religion, and the precepts of pure morality; but
facts proved that histories of the lives of criminals like themselves could engage their attention; and, without further
possible degradation, might not the offences related, be shown
to bring misery to the offender? Some moral reflections could
be carefully interspersed in the narrative, and the whole story
lead its readers, imperceptibly perhaps, to the conclusion, that
virtue alone secures happiness; and that, while life remains, it
is never too late to mend.

Besides, multitudes of these hopeless wretches were constantly being expatriated, as the only condition upon which
they were permitted to live. They had before them a voyage
of some months, during which they were kept, for safety, under
the strictest seclusion and discipline. Might not a ray of
hope find its way into their darkened minds, during this
tedious journey, if—allured by a glaring titlepage,—they could
be induced to read of men and women who had been quite as
bad as themselves, yet had in the new world—whither they
were going,—begun to lead honest lives, had ultimately obtained
freedom, and even riches, and some degree of higher pleasures
never enjoyed before? Any convict, thus reconciled to banish-
ment, and prevented from returning to England, would be one
human life saved from the inevitable penalty of human justice;
and, continued longer within reach of that Higher Mercy
that extends to the "uttermost." These were the circumstances, and such, doubtless, among the motives, that induced
Defoe to write books, never intended for the drawing-room
tables of the nineteenth century; but admirably suited to improve the condition of the poor outcasts, with whom he had
been so remarkably brought into contact.

The fourth week of his connection with *Applebee's Journal* he inserted a Letter, written by himself, under the disguise of a female pickpocket and shoplifter, who after conviction had been respited, and transported.   She had succeeded in getting back to England, where she remained undiscovered until, meeting with an old male acquaintance who recognised her, he threatened to give her up to certain death unless she gave him money, and she says, " the Rogue has a Milch Cow of me as long as I live."   She concludes by asking what she ought to do under the circumstances, and signs the communicatiou, " MOLL."   This was undoubtedly the precursor of " Moll Flanders," and shows how early, after his connection with *Applebee,* our author's attention was drawn to the helpless and hopeless condition of those who had once fallen into crime.

During some part of this year, but I have not found the exact date, there was published " The Compleat Art of Painting.   A poem Translated from the French of M. du Fresnoy. By D. F., Gent.   London : Printed for T. Warner, at the Black Boy in Paternoster Row, 1720.   Price one Shilling." The work is certainly by Defoe, though the subject is one of the last upon which he would have been expected to write. Judging from the book itself, I think that Warner, the publisher, required some Manual for the use of young students ; and having consulted Defoe, the latter conceived that by translating Du Fresnoy into English verse, and short sections, the tyro might soon have the whole of it fixed in his memory.   For such purpose this translation is very well adapted ; but like much of our author's poetry it will not bear verbal criticism, and was never intended to be so used.

On the 27th of August, the South Sea Stock had declined, during the preceding month, from 1000 to 800 per cent., when Defoe, whose warnings had been unheeded, inserted an article in *Applebee's Journal,* so remarkable for the great force of its prophetic irony, that I specially notice it in passing.   After stating that two single persons in Camberwell, who had cleared from thirty to forty thousand pounds by Stocks, were so full of anxiety for what might befall them, as to cause Bills to be put up in the church, desiring the prayers of all good Christians, that they might not be brought to want, he says, " I must confess, this is a most religious Application, and may have some secret Reasons for it, which my Information does not furnish me with : And I send it to you, that you may recommend the practice to Sir *John Blount,* Sir *Theo. Janssen,* and to all the Directors of the South Sea Company, and such like People ; or to those of them who are in most Danger of Poverty and Starving." The world generally had no thought then that the depression in Stock was more than temporary ; or, that the *millionnaires* thus singled out, and their coadjutors, would be ere long stript of all their gains, by the unusual process of an *ex post facto* Act of Parliament.

In August and September are several able articles on unsuitable matrimonial engagements,—on the way to secure conjugal happiness, even where there exist differences of opinion between the parties ; and, on the constancy of woman's love. All these foreshadow the work on Religious Courtship. At the same period the Plague began to rage in Marseilles, and the articles written by our author in several of the journals show how much his mind was engaged on that subject.

The financial panic that followed the Bubbles had become universal in October 1720, when Stocks had fallen unreasonably ; persons reputed, shortly before, to be worth hundreds of thousands were daily becoming bankrupts ; South Sea Stock had now fallen from 2000 to 115 ; numerous suicides occurred daily ; public credit was destroyed ; and Parliament was being called upon by multitudes of infuriated victims to do justice upon those who were considered to be the authors of all these calamities. At this juncture, Defoe, and some with whom he acted, thought it desirable to commence a Paper which should be devoted to the discussion of the financial evils under which the nation was suffering, and the best means of restoring public credit. The first number of this Paper appeared on the 5th of October 1720, with the title, " The Director." It was written by Defoe, and published by W. Boreham, every Wednesday and Friday ; but I am unable to say how long it continued, though I think, only until the emergency had passed away, through the interference of Parliament.

CHAPTER XIV.

*Mist's trial and sentence—For new offences he is committed to Newgate—
His illness there—Defoe's kindness to him—Assists in publishing
" Letters selected out of ' Mist's Journal' "—Clamours against the
South Sea Directors and Parliament—" The London Journal" pro-
secuted therefor—Defoe's Son apprehended as Editor and proprietor
of the London Journal—Defoe publishes " Moll Flanders." " Religious
Courtship." " A Journal of the Plague Year." " The Life and
Actions of L. D. Cartouche"—Defoe free from pecuniary embarrass-
ments, makes provision for his family—Obtains a Lease of Kingswood Heath—Publishes " Colonel Jacque."*

1721—22.

DURING the year 1721, Defoe appears to have almost confined himself to the performance of his duties to the
Government ; the prosecution of his journalistic labours, and
the preparation of a series of works not published until the
early part of the following year. It is some proof, however, of
the great value of his time, that according to the records of the
parish of Stoke Newington, he paid a fine of *Ten Pounds*, upon
the 10th of April 1721, to be excused from serving parochial
offices.

The misfortunes which Mr. *Mist* had brought upon himself
are so connected with the Life of Defoe, at this period, that I
must turn back to that Jacobite worthy, whom we left in
prison awaiting his trial for misdemeanour ; pending which,
Defoe had kindly undertaken to translate and revise the
" Foreign Affairs," &c., of his *Journal*. On the 3rd of December 1720, " Nathaniel Mist, the Printer, was tried before
the Lord Chief Justice Pratt, at Guildhall, for having scandalously reflected on his Majesty's Seasonable Interposition in
favour of the Protestants abroad, and was accordingly found
guilty." On the 13th of February 1721, *Mist* was brought
up, and the Court pronounced judgment, as follows, viz., " That
he stand twice in the pillory, at Charing Cross, and the Royal
Exchange ; pay a fine of £50 ; suffer three months' imprisonment in the King's Bench, and give Security for his good

Behaviour for Seven Years." On the occasion of Mr. Mist standing in the pillory, Defoe's *Hymn to the Pillory* was reprinted, and some hawkers were committed to the Workhouse for crying it among the crowd.

In the next number of *Applebee's Journal*, Defoe inserted an admirable article on the duty of public journalists towards the Government, and signed " Solomon Waryman." From inability to pay his fine, and give the required security, Mr. Mist remained in prison, and on the 27th of May two letters appeared in his *Journal*, one reflecting on the King, and the other against the Duke of Marlborough. This was brought before the House of Commons, and Mist being placed at the bar, and persisting in silence as to the names of the writers of such letters, was committed close prisoner to Newgate; his foreman was apprehended for selling the Papers, and several persons were committed to the same prison for hawking them in the streets. In *Applebee's Journal* of the 18th and 25th June, and the 1st of July, Defoe renews his warnings to the press,—deprecates public clamour against offenders,—and urges the clemency of the Government towards them. In addition to these services, he continued his oversight of the " Foreign Affairs" of *Mist's Journal*, and visited him in prison; where he also assisted in making a selection, for separate publication, from the Letters which had previously appeared in the Journal,—writing for him the Dedication, and the greater part of the Preface, to the first volume. It was intended that the publication should consist of two volumes, and be immediately published; but the anxiety of Mist, as to the circumstances to which he was reduced, combined with the unhealthiness of his cell, brought on an illness that endangered his life, and prevented further progress for some time. He was to have been tried on the 9th October; but his illness was then so severe, that, on affidavits, the Court postponed the matter to the next following Sessions. On the 14th of the same month Defoe returned, in *Applebee's Journal*, to the consideration of the responsibilities of Journalists, by publishing an able article signed " Caution," in which he publicly censures some of them, and Mr. *Mist* by name; he did not, however, remit his great kindness to him, as a sick prisoner in Newgate, but continued to visit and comfort him. As soon as health permitted, he assisted him in the preparation of the second volume of Letters selected from the *Journal*. On the 9th of December, when Mr. *Mist* was ultimately brought up for trial, no evidence was offered against him, and he was discharged. There can be little or no doubt, from his own words some years later, that the influence of Defoe with the Government had much to do with this merciful termination of *Mist's* imprisonment. Considering the opposite characters and principles of the two men, the incessant demands upon Defoe's time, and,—that the only tie between them was one that had been equally irksome to both,—it would be difficult to find a brighter example of self-denying, unobtrusive, and truly Christian conduct, than this of our author.

The two volumes above referred to were published on the 9th of January following, and entitled, " A Collection of Miscellany Letters, Selected out of Mist's Weekly Journal. London. Printed by N. Mist in Great Carter Lane, 1722."* A.

In the Preface to the first volume, written in prison, Mr. Mist begins with considering seriously how to make up the deficiencies caused by the expenses of his prosecution, fines, fees, and absence from business; and says that, among other things, nothing appeared so promising as the publication of Select Letters out of his weekly Paper, by subscription. He then describes a visit made to him by Defoe, as follows :—" I remained some Hours in this perplexed Condition, and cannot tell when I should have been extricated out of it, had not a judicious, learned, and merry Friend, (as good Luck would have it,) made me a Seasonable Visit. The Gentleman find-

---

* On the 18th of February 1727, Mr. Mist published two additional volumes, called the *third* and *fourth*, with the same titles. Defoe had nothing to do with them; nor therefore have I, except to say that their existence is scarcely known. The only copy I have seen is in the possession of my friend, W. J. Thoms, Esq.

A. In Vol. 1. Defoe wrote the Dedication; from page iii. to xii. of the Preface; and was author of the Letters numbered XI.; XII.; XVIII.; XX.; XXV.; XXVII.; XXXI.; XXXVII.; XXXVIII.; XLI.; XLVI.; XLVII.; XLVIII.; LI.; LIII.; LIV.; LV.; LVII.; Postscript p. 182; LXI.; LXIII.; LXVI.; LXVIII.; LXXI.; LXXII; LXXIII.; LXXVI.; LXXVIII.; LXXX.; LXXXI.; LXXXII. (p. 241); LXXXVII.

In Vol. 2, Defoe revised the Preface; and wrote the Letter numbered XXXVIII. (page 116)

ing me in a very pensive Posture, reproached my want of
Fortitude very frankly, and was very liberal in Exhortations,
supported by Arguments drawn from History, Philosophy, and
Religion, to bear my Misfortunes patiently." On this Mist
lays open his scheme, and then follows the part written by
Defoe, which consists of a very learned and humorous dissertation on Titlepages, Dedications, and Prefaces in general;
and especially on the course Mr. Mist should adopt in the
present case. The Dedication and Preface to the Second
Volume were only revised by Defoe. As the publication of
Mist's Journal had never been suspended, it will be obvious
that there were other causes for the decline in its circulation
than those he states in the following sentence. "The Concerns and Distractions of my Trial and subsequent Sufferings,
besides the attendant Expenses, disconcerted all my Business,
threw me out of my Concerns with several Booksellers, and
gave an Opportunity to another Paper to creep into the
Houses of my Customers, and paved the way to my most
heavy Misfortune." His expenses, and concerns with Booksellers could have nothing to do with a diminished circulation ;
but he did not like to confess that the real popularity of his
Paper had depended on Defoe's writings therein; nor that
the transference of our author's pen to *Applebee's Journal*,
caused that Paper to " creep into the houses" of Mr. Mist's
customers.

 In June, 1721, while a Committee of the House of Commons was still engaged in investigating the conduct of the
Directors, of several members of the administration, and of
other Members of Parliament, in connection with South Sea
Stock, the clamours of an infuriated people out of doors, for
vengeance on the delinquents, became so violent as to jeopardize the free discussion of the Legislature. The leaders in
this agitation would have hanged all the Directors ; but as that
could not be accomplished, some of the newspapers passed
their rash censures upon the clemency of the House of Commons with respect to the ill-gotten estates of the Directors, and
the Members implicated. Defoe wrote, in support of the proceedings of Parliament, several eloquent articles in *Applebee's
Journal.* He urged justice with mercy towards the guilty ;

and pleaded for compassion·to their wives and children, who in any case would be plunged down, from the highest affluence to comparative poverty, if not to absolute starvation.

One of the greatest Scandals of the times was, that the investigations of the Parliamentary Committee disclosed the existence of Directors of the Directors. It would have been scarcely possible for the South Sea Bubble to have attained the magnitude it reached before bursting, without assistance from some of those to whose care the financial interests of the Nation had been entrusted. The Directors had been directed by men high in the councils of the King; and it was found that James Craggs, Esq., Secretary of State, and John Aislabie, Esq., Chancellor of the Exchequer, had both largely participated in the plunder of the nation. Death, natural or unnatural, immediately released the former from personal consequences; and justice satisfied itself by confiscation of his newly acquired wealth. Mr. Aislabie attempted to defend himself, in several speeches before the House; and unwisely published those speeches in separate pamphlets. To one of these Defoe replied, assuming the publication to be a libel. His Tract is "A Vindication of the Honour and Justice of Parliament, against a most Scandalous Libel, entituled the Speech of John A———, Esq. London. Printed for A. More, near St. Paul's, and sold by the Booksellers of London and Westminster." Mr. Aislabie was stripped of his fraudulent gains, dismissed from his office, expelled the House of Commons, and disqualified from sitting again in that Assembly.

Among the newspapers who most violently cried for blood and spoliation, and censured any merciful proceedings of parliament, was the *London Journal;* and a vote of the House of Commons was passed that the writers of that Paper should be brought to justice. The author of the articles was Thomas Gordon, who being sent for by the Committee, was not to be found; but *Applebee's Journal* of the 17th of June, says, "The Printer of the *London Journal* and others, have been under Examination as we hear, on Account of that Paper; and 'tis reported that their most Secret Authors are thereby discovered."

In consequence of these, and other proceedings against journalists and pamphleteers, Defoe published in *Applebee's*

Journal of the 15th of July an Article commencing, " I hear
a great Discourse in the Town about punishing Libels, occasioned by the late Examination of Authors, Printers, &c., and
this has moved my Curiosity to enquire into an old Question,
which I could never yet get answered, and I doubt never shall,
viz., What a Libel is?" In discussing the question he shows
himself an able jurist, and proposes an amendment of the law ;
but my present object is only to draw attention to a common
sense remark, on the motives of some writers of libels. He
says, " The Indictment is loaded with the usual Adverbs,—
seditiously, maliciously, or traitorously and seditiously, and the
like ;—when perhaps the mistaken unhappy Scribbler has had
no Sedition, or Treason, or Malice in his Head, and the Indictment ought only to have said—greedily, covetously, and
avariciously ;—the Man having had no Design at all, but
merely to get a Penny, and perhaps to buy him Bread."
Shortly after the publication of the above, *Mist's Journal*
ominously remarked, " It is thought by those of the greatest
Judgment and Experience, that the *London Journal* will perish
at the FALL OF THE LEAF." The *Post-Boy* of August 15th
says, " We hear that Mr. Wilkins, the Printer, and Mr. Peele,
the Publisher of the *London Journal,* taken up on Saturday
last, for the Journal of that Day, have been admitted to Bail."
And the *Daily Courant* of the next day announces the following :—" On the 14th instant Benjamin Norton Defoe, was
committed to Newgate, for writing and publishing a Scandalous and Seditious Libel, by way of Introduction to last
Saturday's *London Journal.*"

Thus, in due order of time, events have sufficed to answer
a question that may possibly have occurred to the reader's
mind,—what has the *London Journal* to do with the Life of
Defoe ? Benjamin Norton Defoe was our author's second
son ; and, while the printer and publisher of the *London Journal*
were admitted to Bail, he was committed to Newgate,—as the
author, or responsible editor of the Paper. No farther proof
is needed that he inherited, at least, some of his father's
literary talent ; as it would certainly require an able man to
succeed Thomas Gordon and John Trenchard, who had preceded him in that capacity. He had been injudiciously
writing against the proceedings of Parliament, and on the

opposite side to his father, who had opposed him as warmly as he would have done any other man, in a cause involving not only the constitutional question of the freedom and supremacy of the Legislature; but also, humanity and mercy in the administration of justice. Yet, with such public opposition, the father had mixed warning and caution; and, when he foresaw that a state prosecution would be the inevitable result, had endeavoured, in his Essay on Libel, quoted above, so to state the motives of his son, as might possibly mitigate his punishment.

Defoe was evidently unwilling it should be thought by any one that he was the offender. The next number of *Applebee's Journal* relates all the circumstances of the apprehension and committal, but adds, "the Rumour of its being the well known Daniel Defoe that was committed, is a mistake, he not having, as we hear, been questioned about it." *Read's Journal* of the same date says that Benjamin Norton Defoe "was admitted to Bail before Mr. De la Faye, himself being bound by Recognizance in the sum of £1000, and his two Sureties in the sum of £500 each, for his appearance at the King's Bench Bar on the first Day of next Term." *Applebee's Journal* of the 26th August, contains a paragraph from which,— as well as from subsequent statements, evidently written by Defoe himself,—I am compelled to conclude that Defoe was not on friendly terms with his son; that he was greatly annoyed that his name should have publicly appeared,—and especially at an advertisement, to which he refers as follows:—" The *late* writers of the *London Journal* have published an Advertisement to signify their great Dignity and Quality, *pretending* that the young Scribbler that has lately fallen into the Hands of Justice, is not the writer of *their* Letters, but that they are too great to be named; whereas 'tis eminently known who the Persons are, and they are in particular, Enemies to Religion, as well as to the Government;—Deists and Atheists, with an *Independent Whig* at the Head of them. Also 'tis known, that the young Defoe is but a Stalking Horse and a Tool, to bear the Lash and the Pillory in their stead, for his Wages; that he is the Author of the most Scandalous Part, but is only made Sham *Proprietor* of the whole, to skreen the true Proprietors from Justice; and we hear their Paper sinks upon it every Day."

Of course Defoe's connection with *Applebee* was kept as

secret as possible, and therefore any adverse allusions to B. N. Defoe, might be designed to mislead the public and the readers of the *Journal;* but yet, several successive Numbers show that the subject was continually upon the father's mind, at a time when all the other Journals were silent respecting it. Nothing is recorded in the public prints as to any further proceedings having been taken against B. N. Defoe; and I cannot doubt that out of consideration for his father, the Ministry forbore the preparation of any Indictment, and discharged the son from his recognizances.

The attention of my readers has already been directed to the fact that several of Defoe's works, not yet published, were fore-shadowed in his weekly Essays, or Letters Introductory, published in *Applebee's Journal.* These Essays not only furnish us therefore, with valuable comments on all matters of public interest, but also,—apparently without design by the author,—frequently make us acquainted beforehand with the subjects of some of the larger Works upon which he might be at the time engaged. Thus the ravages of the Plague in the south of France, in 1721, had naturally excited much apprehension in England, and many vivid accounts of its devastations, from our Author's pen, had appeared in the *Daily Post,* and in the *Journals* of *Mist* and *Applebee.* These accounts were supplemented, in the last-mentioned paper, between the 16th of September, and the 18th of November, by no less than five Essays on the Plague, several of which clearly prove that he was at that time composing his celebrated " Journal of the Plague Year," and that he was incurring much labour in order to found it, as far as possible, on actual facts. Another topic of great interest, not only in France, but throughout Europe, in October of the same year, was the trial and execution of Lewis Dominique Cartouche, the greatest Robber in the history of the world, whose gangs, dispersed over France, were said to number more than six hundred men; many of whom continued to murder and plunder in concert several years after the death of their leader. The *Journals* in which Defoe wrote, contain much information as to the exploits and extermination of this formidable organization, and he afterward published two pamphlets on the subject.

When giving an account of the first connectio[n] Defoe and *Applebee's Journal*, I explained the peculi[ar] of Mr. Applebee's printing business involving an i[ntercourse] with the inmates of Newgate; and fully consi[dered] motives and objects of our author in writing several the moral benefit of such convicts as, after being ~~reprieved~~ from the gallows, were about to be transported to the plantations of America for the remainder of their lives. The first of such works was published on the 27th of January 1722, and is entitled, " The Fortunes and Misfortunes of the Famous MOLL FLANDERS, &c., who was born in Newgate, and during a Life of continu'd Variety for Threescore years, besides her childhood, was twelve years a whore, five times a wife (whereof once to her own Brother), Twelve years a Thief, Eight years a transported Felon in Virginia, at last grew Rich, lived Honest, and died a Penitent. Written from her own Memorandums. London : Printed for and sold by W. Chetwood, at Cato's Head, in Russell Street, Covent Garden ; and T. Edlin, at the Prince's Arms, over against Exeter Change, in the Strand.˙ 1721." This title was plainly not designed to attract the pure and delicate to proceed farther with the book ; but to strike the attention of the unfortunate class for whom it was intended. The very titlepage however suggested a glimmering of hope, that they also *might* yet attain Riches, become Honest, and die Penitent. That the book was read with great avidity is evident from the fact that three editions were required during the same year, and two the year following.* The writer felt the difficulty of his task, and confesses it in the Preface where he says, " the best Use is to be made even of the worst Story, and the Moral 'tis hop'd will keep the Reader serious, even where the Story might incline him to be otherwise. To give the History of a Wicked Life repented of, necessarily requires that the wicked Part should be made as wicked as the real History of it will

---

* It is possible that Defoe was indebted for the name of his heroine to the following :—if not, the fortuitous coincidence is at least remarkable. In the *Post-Boy* of the 9th of˙January 1722, and previously, is an Advertisement of Books sold by John Darby, and among them is, " The History of Flanders, with Moll's Map."

bear, to illustrate and give a Beauty to the Penitent part,
which is certainly the best and brightest, if related with equal
Spirit and Life." He says further, " Throughout the infinite
variety of this Book the Fundamental is most strictly adhered
to; there is not a wicked Action in any Part of it, but is first
or last rendered Unhappy and Unfortunate. There is not a
superlative Villain brought upon the Stage, but either he is
brought to an unhappy End, or brought to be a Penitent.
There is not an ill thing mention'd, but it is condemn'd, even
in the Relation, nor a virtuous just Thing, but it carries its
Praise along with it." But the most powerful inducement to
the writing and publishing this book is related in the following
paragraph :—" Her application to a sober Life, and industrious
Management at last in Virginia, with her Transported Spouse,
is a Story fruitful of Instruction to all the unfortunate
Creatures who are oblig'd to seek their Re-establishment abroad;
whether by the Misery of Transportation, or other Disaster ;
letting them know that Diligence and Application have their
due Encouragement, even in the remotest part of the World,
and that no Case can be so low, so despicable, or so empty of
Prospect, but that an unwearied Industry will go a great way
to deliver us from it, will in Time raise the meanest Creature to
appear again in the World, and give him a new Cast for his
Life." Space forbids my entering upon the narrative ;—
which, in addition to its moral reflections, abounds with lively
interest, arising from unlooked for incidents and coincidents,
—is full of rich painting of nature, in the midst whereof
the apparently artless story of the vices and follies of the pretended narrator, continually appears more like the gushing of
a fountain, than, as it really is, the flowing of a polluted
stream.

Having already given to the world two Volumes of admirable unsectarian morality entitled *The Family Instructor*, Defoe now furnished another portion of his great design of
leaving behind him a series of treatises, as guides to domestic,
social, and commercial prosperity and happiness ; which great
design he lived ultimately to complete. The Volume was
published on the 20th of February and is entitled, " Religious
Courtship : Being Historical Discourses, on the Necessity of

Marrying Religious Husbands and Wives only.   As also, of
Husbands and Wives being of the same Opinions in Religion
with one another.   With an Appendix, Of the necessity of
taking none but Religious Servants, and a Proposal for the
better Managing of Servants. London. Printed for E. Matthews, at the Bible, and A. Bettesworth, at the Red Lyon, in
Paternoster Row ; J. Brotherton, and W. Meadows in Cornhill, 1722." This was not a book, like its predecessor, to run
rapidly through several Editions.   As a work of pure and
orthodox morality, its progress was slow, but sure. Seven years
elapsed before a Second Edition was required ; but in 1789,
the twenty-first was published, and they have since been innumerable,—from the respectable octavo, to the coarse paper
publications for cheap distribution.   It is still the most popular work ever published on the subject; and would alone
secure the lasting fame of its author, independently of any
other of his productions.   The framework of the book is skilfully contrived, yet no art whatever is apparent.   The reader
becomes interested in the welfare of a particular family, and is
carried along through the history of its members ; sharing their
happiness, and, as a friend, touched with their cares and
anxieties.   It combines the rare advantages of a continuous
narrative with those of natural and well sustained dialogue, a
form of writing in which Defoe greatly excelled.   Like his
other works on religion and morality, it is based on the Bible
alone, and is equally acceptable to all denominations of orthodox Protestants.   It displays, throughout, the characteristics
of his best stile of writing, and is distinguished as much for its
practical utility as for its ability.   Defoe seems to have anticipated the judgment of posterity as to the value of this work,
when he wrote in the Preface, " The Story represented here is
capable of such, and so many Applications to the Cases of
young People, whose Settlement is always in View, that there
will never be a Time when the Instruction will be useless."

Twenty-four days after the world had received the story of
the coarse lewdness of " Moll Flanders" the felon, our author
presented the sweet domestic influences of " Religious Courtship ;" and now, with a prodigality of genius, unwearied in
itself, and unwilling by sameness to weary others, only twenty-

five days more were allowed to elapse before the magic scene was again changed—this time to the deepest gloom : the De-stroying Angel overshadows a great City, and a cry is heard in the streets, " Bring out your Dead !"

Defoe was about four years old at the time of the great Plague; and therefore, supposing him to have remained in London the whole time, he could have had no personal know-ledge beyond the dim recollections of childhood ; but, as he grew up to maturity, he must have conversed with many who had witnessed all its horrors,—have listened—at a time when the memory is most retentive—to many a thrilling story of its de-vastations,—and have had pointed out to him the localities, not obliterated by the Fire, where its deadly rage was most violent. Such a mind as his, was probably better stored with the real history of the Plague than that of any other man living in 1721, when it again threatened to visit his country, and when the attention of all thinking people was painfully directed to its progress in France.

The articles I have transcribed from *Applebee's Journal* into his recently collected writings, show how intensely he thought upon the subject ;—how anxious he was to avoid a panic on the one hand, and yet to arouse sufficient public alarm, to induce people to make all possible preparation for the preser-vation of themselves and families.   He desired also, at a time when death seemed to be almost at the door, to awaken sinners to thoughts of religion, and a world to come.   One of the Essays from *Applebee's Journal*, is the result of his examination of the Bills of Mortality in 1665, undertaken for the purpose of his Volume ; in which he states, as a firm conviction, that many thousands died of the Plague without being recorded ; and he urges the necessity of an accurate Registration of deaths, not only from Plague, but also from all other diseases, as the only basis of all just calculations upon the subject.   Such were the circumstances, and the objects that induced Defoe to write his most affecting narrative.   It was published on the 17th of March, and is entitled, " A Journal of the Plague Year: Being Observations or Memorials of the most Remarkable Occurrences ; as well Publick as Private, which happened in London during the last Great Visitation in 1665.   Written by a Citizen who continued all the while in London.   Never

made public before.   London.   Printed for E. Nutt at the
Royal Exchange ; J. Roberts in Warwick Lane ; A. Dodd
without Temple Bar ; and J. Graves in St. James's Street.
1722."

Our author knew by experience the importance of bringing
forward some person who was trustworthy, a substantial man,
of good moral and religious character, and allowing him to
relate, the occurrences in which he had taken part, and the
things he had seen with his own eyes.   Hence the fiction of
the worthy Saddler, who says he "lived without Aldgate
about mid-way between Aldgate Church and Whitechapel-
Bars, on the left Hand, or North side of the Street."   It is
now impossible clearly to distinguish what is authentic from
that supplied by the imagination of our Author ; but if we
could separate what is only personal to the narrator, his establishment and family,—from all that relates to the develope-
ment and progress of the disease ; I believe we should find
that the latter is much more an authentic history than has
been credited.

Without a knowledge of the book itself, it would be difficult
to understand, that a subject, so uninviting as the Plague,
could have been treated in a manner interesting to all readers.
But we turn over the titlepage, and without even the formality
of any Introduction or Preface, we meet with a man who tells
us what he knows.   Occasionally he wanders in his story, and
sometimes mentions very trivial things, but they only prevent
monotony, and every little incident helps to increase the conviction that the whole is a reality.   In his "Journal of the
Plague Year," Defoe has carried his peculiar art of circumstantial fidelity to the greatest perfection ; and it is no wonder
that so grave a work should have deceived the celebrated Dr.
Mead, the head of his profession, and at that time directed by
the Government to report on the precautionary means for
preventing the Plague.*   The plain matter-of-fact stile of our

---

* "A Discourse on the Plague: By Richard Mead, Fellow of the College
of Physicians, and of the Royal Society; and Physician to his Majesty. 9th
Edition. London. 1744."   At page 106, after quoting our author's work,
as an authority, he gives the reference, in a foot-note, as follows :—" Vid. a
Journal of the Plague in 1665. by a Citizen. London, 1722."

author in this Journal,—the artful manner in which he has throughout concealed all art under a truthful simplicity,—his well-timed lectures upon the uncertainty of life, and the tone of sincere, but not obtrusive piety, that pervades the narrative, eminently fitted it to be a seasonable and useful book when it first appeared. It cannot now be read without the deepest interest; and it will continue to be read as long as the memory of the Great Plague shall stand on the records of history.

I have already noticed the excitement caused throughout Europe by the depredations of a great organization of robbers, spread over a considerable part of France in the year 1721, and have stated that Defoe, writing on " Foreign Affairs " in several of the *Journals*, had much to say respecting the trial and execution of Cartouche; and, of the subsequent efforts made for the extermination of his gangs. The general interest in what concerned this extraordinary man was so great, that our Author considered a more full account than could be gathered from the newspapers would be acceptable, and therefore on the 27th of April, he published a thick pamphlet, entitled, " The Life and Actions of Lewis Dominique Cartouche: Who was broke Alive upon the Wheel at Paris, Nov. 28, 1721, N. S., Relating at large his remarkable Adventures, desperate Enterprises, and various Escapes. With an Account of his Behaviour under Sentence, and upon the Scaffold; and the manner of his Execution. Translated from the French. London: Printed for J. Roberts, in Warwick Lane, 1722. Price 1s. 6d." Whether this was an actual translation of a French book, or not, I am unable to say; but it is probable that his only authorities were the French News Letters, which he translated for the *Journals*. In that case it would have been more correct had he stated that it was translated *with license*, as I find many things relating to the boyhood of Cartouche, that I think were only imagined by the writer of his Life. I allude particularly to his conversation with the Gypsies in a wood, when he had run away, after committing his first considerable schoolboy theft; his conversations with his father, verbally given in the book, and also that with the stranger, his fellow-worshipper in the Church of the Jesuits, when they discovered each other to be thieves, and instantly embraced.

In relating the execrable conduct of this daring robber and murderer Defoe does not fail to show the fearful terrors of a guilty conscience.   When the portrait of Cartouche had been sent to all the market towns in France, and the Archers were night and day in search of him, it is said, " So many Villanies as Cartouche was concerned in, either as Actor or Contriver, could not remain long unpunished.   He was sensible of it himself, and his midnight Sleeps were continually interrupted by an anxiety of Soul, and gloomy Horror.   He endeavour'd to divert them with other Amusements, but his Pleasures were hourly interrupted by more serious Reflections. He was startled at the least Noise, at the sight of a strange Face, or even at the appearance of an Acquaintance.   He thought his Friends were afraid of him, and would discover him to get rid of him.   Thus it pleased God to anticipate, by his own Justice, the Judgment of Man which was now coming upon him."   The suspension of all business, and the general rejoicing in Paris, when Cartouche was at last taken, are described ; and then follows many particulars of that morbid sympathy manifested in the minds of the educated and superior classes towards extraordinary villains, when justice has overtaken them.   Defoe says, " Some gave him Money, others pitied him, and offer'd to use their Interest to obtain his Pardon : In a Word, every one shew'd an unaccountable Affection for him.   Ladies of the highest Quality went to visit him," and their conversations are related.   After attempting to escape, and endeavouring in vain to destroy himself, he was ultimately brought to confess his crimes, at the place of execution.   He was only twenty-eight years of age at the time of his death.

In 1722, Defoe had begun to experience that his multifarious labours and imaginative genius were mines of wealth.   There is reason to believe, that, out of the large gains that now flowed in upon him, he first silenced the remaining clamours of his old creditors, and then provided for his wife, by a life interest in his property at Stoke Newington.   His eldest daughter, Maria, had married a person of the name of Langley, and we have no means of knowing anything as to her marriage portion ; but may conclude that no marked partiality would be shown, by such a father, to one child more than another.   His second daughter, Hannah, must have been near thirty years of age, and not seeming likely to marry, he endowed her with Stock in the South Sea Company, purchased when it was depressed below its intrinsic value, after the bursting of the Bubbles.*   This disposition of the money was however only intended to continue until the father could find for her a permanent investment.

Defoe had an old and valued friendship, of some twenty years' standing, with the Rev. William Smithies, an Evangelical clergyman, who was Rector of St. Michael's, Mile End, within the Liberties of the Borough of Colchester.   That this gentleman had influence with the Corporation is apparent, from the fact that his Son afterward became Town Clerk of the Borough. This clerical friend negociated, on behalf of Defoe, a Lease for ninety-nine years of an Estate, within his own parish of Mile End, known by the name of Kingswood Heath, the property of the Mayor and Commonalty of the Borough of Colchester. Mr. Chalmers and Mr. Wilson have both referred to this lease, but inasmuch as they have stated the money consideration at only one-half the real amount, and said that Defoe was obliged shortly afterward to assign the property to another person, I give a brief abstract of an original Deed relating thereto, now in my possession.

The Indenture is dated the 29th Sept. 1723, "Between Daniel Deffoe of Stoke Newington in the County of Middlesex Esquire and Hannah Deffoe Daughter," &c., Spinster of the one Part, " and Mary Newton of Ipswich," &c., Widow of the other Part.   It then recites the Lease from the Corporation of Colchester to Defoe, dated the 6th of August 1722, of all the " Lands, Tenements, Pastures, Woods, and Wood Grounds" known by the name of Kingswood Heath, including also several " ffarms," Houses, Buildings, &c. &c., all in the Parish of St. Michael Mile End, also all the Timber or Timber Trees, Pollings, Logg Trees, Staddles, &c., " together with the Pound

---

* While the rage of speculation was going on in 1720, Defoe declared himself perfectly disinterested, not having meddled with any stock or projects. Yet his daughter afterward wrote as follows, to the Company :—"Aug. 30, 1722.   Mr. Lockyer.   Pay to James Ruck the dividend due at Midsummer last upon 706*l*. 13*s*. 4*d*., being all the Stock I then had in the Books of the South Sea Company, and this shall be sufficient ; from yours

HANNAH DE FOE."

there, with all the Estray," &c., including every Right and
Privilege the grantors possessed in such parish. To hold the
same for "ninety and nine Years," "from the ffeast of Saint
Michael the Arch Angell then next ensuing," at and under
"the yearly Rent of one Hundred and Twenty Pounds payable
half yearly," &c. &c. It next recites another Indenture dated
the 1st of Sept. 1722, "Between the said Daniel Deffoe," &c.,
of the one Part, "and the said Hannah Deffoe," &c., of the
other Part. Reciting as last before, and further, that though
the Lease from the Corporation, &c., was made and executed to
the said Daniel Deffoe "in his own Name yet the same was
made for and on the proper Account and Benefitt of her the
said Hannah Deffoe And the money paid as the Consideration
for ffelling the Timber and Granting the Lease was paid to the
Chamberlain of the said Borough with the proper Money of her
the said Hannah Deffoe." It then witnesses that the said Daniel
Deffoe declares that his name was only used in the Lease for
her, and that the "Two sums of Five Hundred Pounds and
ffive Hundred Pounds" paid, &c., "was the proper Money of
her the said Hannah Deffoe," and all the proceedings as if they
had been in her own name. "Now this Indenture witnessed
that, in consideration of Two Hundred Pounds to the said
Daniel Deffoe and Hannah Deffoe," &c. &c., to them, &c., "paid
by the said Mary Newton," &c., the receipt whereof they
acknowledge, they Bargain, Sell, Assign, &c., the Lease and
all the property, &c., demised therein to the said Mary Newton,
&c. To have and to hold the same, &c., "Provided always
that if the said Daniel Deffoe and Hannah Deffoe," &c. &c.,
shall well and truly pay or cause to be paid, &c., the sums of
Two Hundred and Ten Pounds, &c., "at the Dwelling House
of Edmund Raynham scituated in Colchester," &c. &c., "then
these Presents are to be Void," And the said Daniel Deffoe and
Hannah Deffoe declare and promise that they have not done
and will not do anything by which the Indentures or Lease
may, &c., be defeated or made Void, &c. &c., and they covenant
to her peaceable possession, and further that they will pay the
said Sum of Two Hundred and Ten Pounds, &c., and will perform all the covenants of the Lease, &c. In witness thereof,
&c., they have put their Hands and Seals, &c. Signed and
Sealed. " Daniel De Foe." " Hannah Defoe." Witnessed

by William Coe & Edm. Raynham. Endorsed the day and year within written, is a full Receipt for the Two Hundred Pounds Consideration, &c. Signed " Daniel De Foe." " Hannah De Foe." This is witnessed by the same parties. Then follows another Indorsement, dated " November ye 13th, 1727. I doe hereby acknowledge to have had & received of Mr. Dan. Defoe ye Sum of Two Hundred and Twenty Pounds in full of the principall & interest due on this Mortgage and doe hereby assign over all my interest and right to ye within premises, As witness my hand ye day & year above written. Mary Newton. Witnesses Mary Wade, Thomas Newton."

Gathering together the dates of the above transaction, it is plain that the intention of the father was to give his daughter one thousand pounds, so invested as to secure her an independency for life. With this view, the South Sea Stock of 706l. 13s. 4d. was probably purchased early in 1722. The Lease of Kingswood Heath was granted the 6th August, and between that day and the 30th, when Hannah Defoe wrote for the South Sea Dividends, the Stock was sold and the money placed in her father's hand; the declaratory Deed between them, stating that the Lease was for her benefit, dating the next following day. I cannot but notice the promptitude and business character of this act of Defoe, in thus providing at once for any contingency affecting his own life. I find that on the 30th August 1722, South Sea Stock was quoted at 89$\frac{3}{8}$, and therefore the amount realized by Hannah Defoe represented 800l. Stock. The first moiety of five hundred pounds was paid thereout on the 29th of September, and when the remaining five hundred pounds became due at Michaelmas 1723, it would appear that Defoe was short of cash, and, as a most fitting manner of raising the deficiency, they joined in mortgaging the Lease to Mary Newton for 200l. It will be observed, too, that when the mortgage and interest were paid off, the 13th Novr. 1727, Daniel Defoe's name alone is used as the payee, his daughter having been made safe by the Deed of Sept. 1, 1722. The value of the estate of Kingswood Heath improved rapidly, and after the death of her parents, Hannah Defoe lived upon her income in respectable gentility, until her own death, in 1759, when she left her property to a son of her sister Henrietta.

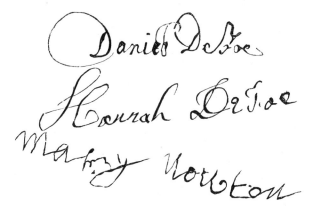

FACSIMILES OF THE THREE SIGNATURES TO A DEED CONCERNING DEFOE'S ESTATE
AT COLCHESTER.

COLCHESTER CASTLE.

Having in " Moll Flanders" pourtrayed the life of a female Convict, with such moral considerations as in his judgment might help to raise up those who had fallen, so low as to be abandoned by all, except those of their own class; Defoe thought fit to prepare a similar representation of the life of a criminal of the male sex. It is the counterpart of its predecessor; and I cannot doubt that he was actuated by the same good motives as before. He had this additional incitement, that the number of convicts who contrived to return from transportation had greatly increased; and it moved his heart to see these poor wretches, on being identified, taken to Newgate, and from thence to the gallows.* There is also reason to believe that he was encouraged to continue his efforts, by the knowledge that " Moll Flanders" had been useful to some of those for whose reading it was specially intended. His present book was published on the 20th of December, and is entitled, " The History and Remarkable Life of the truly Honourable Colonel Jacque, vulgarly call'd Col. Jack; who was Born a Gentleman, put 'Prentice to a Pick-Pocket, was Six and Twenty Years a Thief, and then Kidnapp'd to Virginia. Came back a Merchant; was Five times married to Four Whores; went into the Wars, behav'd bravely, got Preferment; was made Colonel of a Regiment; came over, and fled with the Chevalier; is still abroad compleating a Life of Wonders, and resolves to dye a General. London. Printed and sold by J. Brotherton, at the Royal Exchange; T. Payne, near Stationers' Hall; W. Mears at the Lamb, and A. Dodd, at the Peacock without Temple Bar; W. Chetwood, in Covent Garden; J. Graves in St. James's Street; S. Chapman, in Pall Mall; and J. Stagg, at Westminster Hall. 1722."

It will be observed that we have again a flaring title, to attract the eyes of those with whom the first difficulty is to get them to read at all; a class who have no morals to be injured, but capable of improvement if their attention can be secured. This is the fulcrum Defoe has used, and having fastened the attention by his wonderful power, omits no opportunity of turning it in the direction of honesty, per-

---

* Shortly after Colonel Jacque, (on the 26th of January, 1723), he published an excellent Essay on this subject in *Applebee's Journal*.

severance, and religious principle, ending in success. The preface clearly shows his philanthropic design. In the first paragraph he divides the book into, " the pleasant and delightful Part," and " the useful and instructive Part." He says, " Here's Room for just and copious Observations on the Blessing and Advantages of a sober and well govern'd Education ; and, the Ruin of so many Thousands of Youths of all Kinds, in this Nation, for want of it ; also how much publick Schools and Charities might be improved to prevent the Destruction of so many unhappy Children, as in this Town, are every Year Bred up for the Gallows." And, when speaking of the childhood of his hero, he says, " Though Circumstances form'd him by Necessity to be a Thief, a strange Rectitude of Principles remain'd with him, and made him early abhor the worst Part of his Trade, and at last wholly leave it off. If he had come into the World with the Advantage of Education, and been well instructed how to improve the generous Principles he had in him, what a Man might he not have been !" Turning to those for whose good the book was primarily intended, he remarks, " Every wicked Reader will here be encouraged to a Change, and it will appear that the best and only good End of a wicked and misspent Life is Repentance. That in this, there is Comfort, Peace, and often times Hope ; and, that the Penitent shall be return'd like the Prodigal, *and his latter End be better than his Beginning*."

The Life of Colonel Jack, like its predecessor, is a book that a religious, or even prudent father could not safely place in the hands of his children ; yet is there much in the character of the hero that entitles him to respect. Of unknown, but shameful birth, and incapable by external circumstances of becoming anything but a thief,—there was one single, saving thought, impressed during infancy, and not obliterated during all the vicissitudes of twenty-six years of a life of dishonesty ; —*to remember that he was a Gentleman*. Conscience held this fast, and when people used to admire the features of the homeless and friendless young vagabond, and then pity him and let him go, he says, " I lay'd up all these things in my heart." When he slept in a Glass House, and begged or stole for food, yet if he was sent of an errand, he always " did it punctually and carefully, and made haste again ;" and, if trusted with any-

thing, he " never touch'd it to diminish it."   So, when he was
ultimately Kidnapped away from vicious associates, and sold
as a slave to an American planter, this life-long dream of gentility contributed to its own realization ; first, by his obtaining
his freedom, then becoming Overseer, and afterward a Merchant.   He was of more than ordinary natural ability ; and his
wise conduct, in reforming the habits and developing the capa-
bilities of the Negroes under his management, affords Defoe
an opportunity of correcting the cruel treatment to which
these poor creatures were even then subjected, by men calling
themselves Christians.   Throughout the whole of the book it
is never forgotten that the " Ways of Wisdom" are the only
ways to happiness, and that " All Kinds of Wickedness are
attended with Misery."   Thus when Jack was rising, and in
a transition from the condition of Overseer to that of Planter,
he wanted money, to stock some land that his master had
granted him ; and he sent to England for a sum of about a
hundred pounds, which he had formerly gained as a pick-
pocket, and had placed at interest.   This he ordered to be laid
out in England in such goods as would be useful to his new
plantation.   They were purchased, and all duly shipped, but
the vessel and its cargo were lost as it entered the bay of Virginia.   The money had been dishonestly obtained, and the
goods it produced were buried in the sea, probably in sight of
their anxious and agonised owner.   I cannot conclude this
brief notice of Colonel Jack without expressing the opinion
that nothing ever written by Defoe, or probably any other
novelist, excels, in word-painting, his description, at pages
twenty-three to thirty-three, of Jack's first important exploit
as a thief ;—of the hiding, losing, and recovery of his money—
in the hollow tree,—near the Blind Beggars in Bednal Green ;
and, of the cares and anxieties attending the possession of
wealth.

Notwithstanding the obvious objections of fastidious delicacy
to this book, and paying due respect to the refinement of
modern civilization, I venture to doubt whether more good was
effected, at the time, even by our author's excellent work on
" Religious Courtship," than by " Colonel Jack," remembering
the different classes for whom they were respectively written.
Copies of the early editions are now very rare.

CHAPTER XV.

Defoe publishes " History of the Life of Peter, the Czar of Muscovy ;"
" The Highland Rogue, or Rob Roy ;" " Roxana, or the Fortunate
Mistress ;" " The Great Law of Subordination ;" " A Tour thro' the
whole Island of Great Britain."—Mist again offends Government,
and is severely punished—Crimes of the Cartoucheans—Defoe pub-
lishes " A Narrative of the Proceedings in France for discovering the
Murderers of English Gentlemen near Calais."—John Sheppard and
his Exploits—Defoe visits him in Newgate, and publishes " The History
of the Remarkable Life of John Sheppard ;" also, " A Narrative of
all the Robberies, Escapes, &c., of John Sheppard."—Jonathan Wild,
his Trial and Execution—Defoe publishes " The true Account of the
Life and Actions of Jonathan Wild."

1723—25.

MY readers will have been surprised at the intimate knowledge Defoe possessed as to the history, and especially
the military affairs of Northern Europe. This Memoir has already
noticed his *Wars of Charles XII.*, published in 1716 ; and a continuation, equal in bulk to an additional volume, in 1720. Also
the *Memoirs of a Cavalier,* under Gustavus Adolphus ; and
the two pamphlets relating to *Count Patkul* and *Baron Goertz.*
All these had reference mainly to Swedish history, though
necessarily including much concerning Poland, North Germany,
Denmark, and Russia. I may add, that though written with
as little of partiality as is generally to be found in descriptions
of events that had then recently occurred, yet they all exhibit
a bias in favour of the interests of Sweden. This bias is most
evident in the first mentioned book ; which, taking the King
of Sweden for its hero, may be pronounced anti-Russian in
spirit and execution. I have a remarkable reason for now
adverting to this ; namely, that in the year at which we have
now arrived, a work was published treating almost entirely of
the same great wars and events, from a different point of view,
and yet bearing the same indisputable proof of Defoe's authorship. It is entitled, " An Impartial History of the Life and
Actions of Peter Alexowitz, the present Czar of Muscovy : From

his Birth down to the present Time. Giving an Account of his Travels and Transactions in the several Courts of Europe, with his Attempts and Successes in the Northern and Eastern Parts of the World. In which is intermixed the History of Muscovy. Written by a British Officer in the Service of the Czar. London. Printed for W. Chetwood, at Cato's Head in Russel Street Covent Garden; &c. &c. 1723. Price bound, 5s."

It seems needless to commend a book on such a subject, written by an author so qualified as Defoe. He who could invest the most ordinary events with an undefinable attraction, was equally skilful in describing the great actions of one of the greatest of men. The Czar is of course now the hero, and partiality so far enters in, as to prevent any detailed accounts of the devastating cruelties inflicted by his orders in Livonia, and other conquered territories. Yet that the author cannot be charged with unfairness will be evident from his admitting that the Czar and the King of Poland agreed, without adequate provocation, to make war upon and dismember Sweden, thus becoming responsible for the calamities that followed. He says, " I have nothing to do to enter here into a Disquisition of the Justice of this War, or of the particular Causes moving the Czar to engage in it. That his Czarish Majesty was Agressor, that we do not dispute." " A little Time may contrive, what a great many Years may be employed to Execute. Here in a few Hours they concerted that dreadful War between them and the King of Sweden, which proved at first so fatal to them both, and which in its whole course was fatal to all the Northern part of Europe, destructive to the whole Countries ; and in which first and last above 500,000 People have lost their Lives. Nay, I have heard it affirmed that Sweden alone has by this very War been drained of 300,000 Men, to the irreparable Desolation of that Kingdom, and we shall find abundant Reason to believe that Poland and Muscovy, and the Provinces adjoining, put them altogether, have lost a much greater Number." In another place he says, " Success had now made the King of Sweden famous, I will not say it had made him insolent, because a Historian should write in Temper, even of those Actions, which were not performed in Temper, and treat all Sides with an impartial Respect."

The above will suffice to prove that the book was not written

VOL. I.

in the spirit of a blind partizan of the Czar; yet I find in it numerous quotations from his other Work, the *Wars of Charles XII.*, in adducing which, he calls them "the Swedish Account." The two stories are in fact different; they never contradict each other, yet the former may properly be called the Swedish account, and the latter the Russian account. There is also a singular coincidence in the termination of the two works; namely, that though the *Life of the Czar* professes in the titlepage to extend "from his Birth down to the present Time," (1723,) yet it terminates with his triumphal entry into St. Petersburgh, on the 20th September 1714. The first edition of the *Wars of Charles XII.* ends with that monarch's return from Turkey to Pomerania, which he accomplished "by the swiftest Riding that has ever been heard of," and his entering Straelsund on the 22nd November 1714.

I do not conceive it possible that even Defoe could have produced these two works from the same collected materials; and conclude therefore that he derived his information for the *Wars of Charles XII.* from Swedish sources, and from Russian sources the groundwork for his *Life of the Czar*. Whether any Papers, "By a Scots Gentleman in the Swedish Service," were used by Defoe while preparing the former; or, any Journal or Manuscript, "By a British Officer in the Service of the Czar," while writing the latter, must, however probable, always remain uncertain.

From his correspondence with Scotland, and his great love of what was daring and romantic, Defoe had on several occasions, in *Mercurius Politicus*, and other Journals, noticed the exploits of Rob Roy, the Freebooter of the Western Highlands. On the 5th of October he published a pamphlet respecting him, with the following title :—"The Highland Rogue : or, the Memorable Actions of the celebrated Robert Mac Gregor, commonly call'd Rob Roy. Containing a Genuine Account of his Education, Grandeur, and sudden Misfortune; his commencing Robber, and being elected Captain of a Formidable Gang; his Exploits on the Highway, breaking open Houses, taking Prisoners, commencing Judge, and levying Taxes; his Defence of his manner of Living; his Dispute with a Scotch Parson upon Predestination; his joining with the Earl of Mar

in the Rebellion; his being decoy'd and imprison'd by the
Duke of ———, with the manner of his Escape, &c. Intro-
duced with the Relation of the unequal'd Villainies of the
Clan of the Mac Gregors several years past. The whole im-
partially digested from the Memorandums of an authentick
Scotch MS. Printed for J. Billingsley, under the Royal
Exchange; J. Roberts, in Warwick Lane; A. Dodd, without
Temple Bar; and J. Fox, in Westminster Hall. 1723.
Price 1s."

. In this instance also, our author selected a real person as his
hero; but, as he knew that Rob Roy was not likely to contradict him, he did not hesitate to combine what existed only in
his own imagination, with what is probably true. Yet he
gravely begins his preface by saying,—" It is not, a romantick
Tale that the Reader is here presented with, but a real History: Not the Adventures of a *Robinson Crusoe*, a *Colonel
Jack*, or a *Moll Flanders*; but the Actions of the HIGHLAND
ROGUE; a Man that has been too notorious to pass for a mere
imaginary Person." There is great art in making this lawless
descendant of the Covenanters engage in controversy with a
Minister, who, from his doctrine, was more an Antinomian
than a Predestinarian; and I think that, on the whole, the
freebooter has the best of the argument, especially when he reasons antithetically :—" There can be no Duty where there is
no free Action; and therefore, whether you preach or not,
whether they (the elect) pray or swear, go to Church or a
Bawdy-House, give Alms or pick Pockets, the Case is still the
same."

It is worthy of remark that in order to heighten the interest
of the reader, Defoe asserts this account of Rob Roy to be a
real history, as contradistinguished from " the Adventures of
a Robinson Crusoe." I do not forget that in the preface
to Crusoe he had, for the same purpose, called that book
a history. My object is not to assert or deny the historical character of " Rob Roy," but to notice that, in the
absence of all inducements to the contrary, he here admits,—
I might say, inversely asserts,—that *Robinson Crusoe* is a fiction. If so, it could not have been taken from any Journal or
Manuscript of Selkirk. I think this remark entitled to greater
weight, because, on the 8th of February in the same year,

Defoe advocated in his Paper, the *Daily Post,* a Bill, then before Parliament, for making navigable the River Dun, in the County of York ; and, as to one of the grounds of opposition, " That this Navigation will occasion such an Inundation as will drown no less than 30,000 acres of Land," he replies, " And yet all that is said of *this kind,* is as mere Romance as the Life of *Robinson Crusoe. Vox et præterea nihil.*" By these apparently gratuitous introductions, I think it evident that now, the fame of the work being securely established, he wished the world to know it only as one of imagination.

In the preliminary remarks to the consideration of " Moll Flanders," I have designated the period when it was written " the age of crime ;" and have stated what I believed to be the circumstances, and the motives that impelled Defoe to use his pen so as to inculcate moral principles in the only way that seemed accessible to those who were lost to all goodness, and abandoned by the world. We have seen that he took the worst possible case first, namely, a female convict felon, respited from the gallows, but doomed to slavery ; and he made her a living example that hope remained even for those so deeply degraded. The second of such works showed how a male thief, though not a convict, was able—by holding fast one single thought of good,—to emancipate himself ultimately from evil ; and to become a useful, respectable, and even an honourable member of society. But though thieves might also be lewd, yet the converse does not necessarily follow ; and therefore, a large class of criminals remained, who were not professional thieves, and who would,—from disinclination to see any of their own features in the characters,—refuse to make any personal application of the moral reflections in the two books already published. Yet, that the same necessity existed for some efforts to save women who were lost to virtue, is evident from what I have already stated at to the futility of the whippings, cart- ings, and fines, inflicted at the instance of the " Societies for the Reformation of Manners." This necessity was increased by the obscenity of the lewd literature of the time, in which there was not merely a negation of every moral word or thought, but the grossest vice, exhibited openly ; and encouraged, in printed histories of living characters, whose names and resi-

The Famous ROXANA.

[FRONTISPIECE TO "THE FORTUNATE MISTRESS", 1724.]

dences were stated, and who appeared to glory in the shame of publication.

Under these circumstances Defoe determined to write the history of a lewd, abandoned woman; and, as the heart was the fountain of iniquity, he endeavoured to reach it through the conscience, by moral and religious reflections on the consequences of such a life. This work was published on the 14th of March 1724, and is entitled, "The Fortunate Mistress: Or, a History of the Life and vast Variety of Fortunes of Mademoiselle de Beleau, afterwards call'd The Countess of Wintselsheim, in Germany. Being the Person Known by the Name of the Lady ROXANA, in the Time of King Charles II. London: printed for T. Warner, at the Black Boy in Paternoster Row; W. Meadows, at the Angel in Cornhill; W. Pepper, at the Crown in Maiden Lane, Covent Garden; S. Harding, at the Post House in St. Martin's Lane; and T. Edlin, at the Prince's Arms against Exeter Change, in the Strand. 1724."

In the two preceding works of the same class, Defoe had selected the lives of persons born under the greatest possible disadvantages; and he brought them, through much crime and misery, to a condition of prosperity and comparative happiness. They began ill, but ended well. With the same good object in view, the plan of Roxana is entirely different; and I think it excels both the others in originality of invention, and perfection of delineation. The daughter of a French refugee of fortune,—she was beautiful and accomplished. With a dowry of two thousand pounds, was early married, and became the mother of five children. But she was vain of her beauty, of dress, and of splendour. She was avaricious; and was willing to buy wealth and ease at the price of honour and virtue. Moreover, she was so unnaturally selfish as to abandon all her legitimate children in their infancy; that she might lead a life of luxurious infamy. A long career of vice followed, involving the usual vicissitudes of prosperity and adversity; the former predominating, so far as external circumstances were concerned, but ever accompanied by the torments of a guilty conscience. At length, in the decline of life, the children she had so long deserted, trace her out, by a chain of events as singular as they are delightfully told, establish

their relationship; and this, disclosing the wickedness
of the mother, Roxana, now the proud Countess of Wintselsheim, falls from the lofty position she had attained, and is
plunged into poverty and disgrace for the remainder of her
miserable existence.   There are many incidents in the story,
very distasteful to a pure and virtuous mind, and the book is
even less presentable, according to our modern views of
delicacy, than either of its predecessors; yet no reader
can possibly mistake the lessons designed to be taught,
namely, that prosperous wickedness has a worm at the
root, that turns all its fruits to rottenness; and that sin
ensures its own effectual punishment.   In addition to this
general conclusion, every separate sinful action is made the
subject of reprehension; there are frequent flashes of conscience which make Roxana tremble, and pause in her guilty
courses; and the moral and religious reflections that run
through the work, could not fail to benefit readers who having
fallen themselves, were incapable of being injured by the
relation of Roxana's crimes.   This, it should always be
remembered, was the class for whom Defoe wrote the book.
He was the last man to add fuel to a flame he was endeavouring to extinguish.   With him the prosperity of the wicked
always comes to an end, even in this life.   He did not tell the
story for the sake of amusement; but that he might infuse with
it moral instruction and good principles, as an essential part of
the narrative.   The characters and manners are those of the
time,—his portraits are natural,—and I cannot but hope that
many poor degraded women would be brought, by the perusal,
to think seriously; and through repentance, seek to lead new
and better lives.   Mr. Wilson mentions a tradition that Defoe
was persuaded by his friend Southerne to leave out of the
second edition of Roxana, the whole of the story relating to
her daughter Susannah; but he does not say that he ever saw
any such edition, and admits that most of the subsequent
editions contain the story.   I do not call in question the
existence of the tradition, though I have found no other
reference to it; but I must state that, at a period when the
publication of every book was advertised in some of the
Journals, I never found any notice of a second edition of
Roxana during Defoe's life, nor within a year after his death.

There was an edition in 1735, and others in 1742; 1745; 1755; 1765; 1774, and 1775; many of these vary in matter as well as in title, from the first edition, and also from each other.

In Defoe's "Religious Courtship," it will be remembered that there is an Appendix "Of the Necessity of taking none but Religious Servants, and a Proposal for the better Management of Servants." For want of room, he seems to have been unable to say all that he then thought needful on this part of the subject; and he therefore probably continued, from that time, to collect materials for a distinct Treatise, which was published on the 4th of April, with the following very full title :—"The Great Law of Subordination considered : or, the Insolence and Unsufferable Behaviour of Servants in England duly enquir'd into. Illustrated with a great Variety of Examples, Historical Cases, and Remarkable Stories of the Behaviour of some particular Servants, suited to all the several Arguments made use of, as they go on. In Ten Familiar Letters. Together with a Conclusion, being an earnest and moving Remonstrance to the House-Keepers and Heads of Families in Great Britain, pressing them not to cease using their utmost Interest (especially at this Juncture,) to obtain sufficient Laws for the effectual Regulation of the Manners and Behaviour of their Servants. As also a Proposal, containing such Heads or Constitutions, as wou'd effectually answer this great End, and bring Servants of every Class to a just (and yet not a grievous) Regulation. London : Sold by S. Harding, at the Post-House, in St. Martin's Lane; W. Lewis, in Covent Garden; T. Worrall, at the Judge's Head, against St. Dunstan's Church, Fleet Street; A. Bettesworth, in Pater-Noster-Row; W. Meadows, in Cornhill; and T. Edlin, at the Prince's Arms, against Exeter-Exchange, in the Strand. 1724. Price Three Shillings and Sixpence." In the preface he says, "The unsufferable Behaviour of Servants in this Nation is now (it may be hop'd) come to its Height; their Measure of Insolence, I think, may be said to be quite full. Private Families have struggled long with it; the injur'd Reputation of Masters, Mistresses, Young Ladies, and Gentlemen, which has lain so long at the Mercy of their Servants'

Tongues, has groan'd under it; the Patience of the Heads of Families, under the Rudeness and Insults they have suffer'd, has been enough, and indeed too much provok'd; the poor Husbandman, Artificer, and Manufacturer, have suffer'd sufficiently; in a Word, the Grievance is become National, and calls aloud for a Remedy."

This book is an illustration of the declaration—"There is nothing new under the Sun." Making allowance for the changes of a century and a half, in mere circumstances; the spirit of the book is, in many respects, as applicable to the present time as to the age in which it was written. I refer here particularly to our author's stories of the insolence, the demand for high wages, the love of finery, the wastefulness, and ingratitude of servants. It is frequently remarked that these domestic grievances grow worse; but I am obliged to say that this volume does not prove them to have changed. If Defoe's account of the servants of that period is not exaggerated, it is only fair to admit, that in many things, they have since greatly improved. In some important respects, this work remarkably illustrates what I have already said of the general debauchery of the times, among the lower classes. Defoe stigmatizes drunkenness as "the mother sin," which, he says, spread through society after the Restoration, and produced poverty, lewdness, profane swearing, theft, and murder; so that "the World seems to stand with the bottom upward." Referring to Jonathan Wild, he says, "I have been told, our famous Thief-taker (as they call him,) has a List of seven thousand Newgate-Birds, now in Services in this City, and Parts adjacent, all with Intent to rob the Houses they are in."

After several amusing stories of servants, and others who abused their privileges, under the pretext of English Liberty; he gives a short sketch of the origin of the rights and liberties of Englishmen, and thus introduces his celebrated "Tour through Great Britain," the account of which he was then preparing for the press. "As thus I made myself Master of the History of the ancient State of England, I resolv'd in the next Place, to make myself Master of its present State also; and to this Purpose I travell'd, in three or four several Tours, over the whole Island, critically observing, and carefully informing myself of every thing worth observing in all the Towns and Countries through which I pass'd." He introduces, in the third person, a more specific notice of his qualifications for such a task, in the following modest way :—" I took with me an ancient Gentleman of my Acquaintance, who I found was thoroughly acquainted with almost every Part of England, and who was to me as a walking Library, or a moveable Map of the Countries and Towns through which we pass'd." He adds, " I may in time give you a full account of the Country, which indeed is well worth a Traveller's Pains to see, and a Reader's trouble to look over ; but I have not now time to revise my Journals, and the Minutes which I took of Things every where as I pass'd, which are of a very diverting, as well as instructing variety ; that Part I must refer to another Occasion."

Mr. Wilson says it does not appear that there was ever more than one edition of " The Great Law of Subordination Considered." In a limited sense this may be correct ; but it was republished with an entirely different title, as stated in the List of Defoe's Works prefixed. I think the first title was unfortunately chosen, and failed to sell the book ; besides which, it was a mistake in the author to expect from national legislation, such domestic reforms as could only be effected by moral and religious education. Nevertheless the book abounds with anecdotes, dialogues, and stories of the misdoings of all kinds of servants, related in Defoe's peculiar and charming manner ; and might be read in the present day, by multitudes both of masters and servants, with great advantage.

From the fact that Defoe published very few works during the year 1723, I think the Tours, to which he alludes in the last-mentioned volume, must have been made in that year. The detection of the plot in which Bishop Atterbury was engaged, and the punishment of the conspirators, aroused the loyalty of the people ; treason dared not to show its face in England ; and during the latter half of the year Defoe found his constant presence in London less necessary than at any previous period, since his appointment as Censor of the Journals. It is a new thing to consider our author in the character of an antiquary and topographer of his native country ; but he who had written well on almost all subjects, and was acquainted with the geography of countries least known and most remote, now proved himself well qualified to give " a particular and diverting Account of whatever is curious and worth Observation " in Great Britain. Noticing that books had been already published on the subject, he refers to the constant changes taking place in this busy commercial country, as follows :—" The Fate of Things gives a new Face to Things ; produces Changes in low Life, and innumerable Incidents ; plants and supplants Families ; raises and sinks Towns ; removes Manufactures and Trade ; Great Towns decay, and small Towns rise ; new Towns, new Palaces, and new Seats are Built every Day ; great Rivers and good Harbours dry up, and grow use- less ; again, new Ports are opened ; Brooks are made Rivers ; small Rivers navigable Ports ; and Harbours are made where there were none before, and the like." He then relates at large, what has been already briefly stated from his preceding work, that in England he had made seventeen large circuits or separate journies, and three general Tours through the whole country ; and that besides having lived some time in Scotland, he had travelled critically over great part of it ; " he has viewed the North Part of England, and the South Part of Scotland five several Times over ; all which is hinted here, to let the Readers know what Reason they will have to be satis- fy'd with the Authority of the Relation." No doubt some of these journies had been made, and materials collected, on former occasions, when travelling on government or other business.

The narrative is conveyed in the form of Letters, and is diversified by accounts of local manners and customs, distin- guished families, and anecdotes of historical and otherwise remarkable events ; related in the most simple and engaging manner. The habits, customs, dialects, and characters of the people are pourtrayed, with great force of description, sur- rounded with whatever is interesting in the works of nature or the productions of art. The whole of the volumes are full of a genial and charming spirit, and,—notwithstanding more modern publications of greater pretensions,—will always be read with delight, and referred to with instruction, for their accu- racy as to the state of Great Britain at the period when they were written.

The first volume was published on the 22nd of May, and as it contains a " Diary of the Siege and Blockade of Colchester in the year 1648," there is prefixed, a folding Perspective Map, or Prospect of that Siege. The title is as follows, " A Tour thro' the whole Island of Great Britain, Divided into Circuits or Journies. Giving a Particular and Diverting Account of whatever is·Curious and worth Observation, viz., I. A Description of the Principal Cities and Towns, their Situation, Magnitude, Government, and Commerce. II. The Customs, Manners, Speech, as also the Exercises, Diversions, and Employment of the People. III. The Produce and Improvement of the Lands, the Trade, and Manufactures. IV. The Sea Ports and Fortifications, the Course of Rivers, and the Inland Navigation. V. The Publick Edifices, Seats, and Palaces of the Nobility and Gentry. With Useful Observations upon the Whole. Particularly fitted for the Reading of such as desire to Travel over the Island. By a Gentleman. London : Printed and sold by G. Strahan, in Cornhill. W. Mears, at the Lamb, without Temple Bar. R. Francklin, under Tom's Coffee-house, Covent Garden. S. Chapman, at the Angel in Pall-Mall. R. Stagg, in Westminster Hall, and J. Graves, in St. James's Street. 1724."

The numerous other duties, many of them journalistic, and therefore imperative, devolving on Defoe, caused a delay of a year, and the Second Volume of his Tour was not published until the 8th of June 1725. The title-page is the same as before, but the volume contains a Map of England and Wales by Herman Moll, the Royal Geographer. In the preface, he again directs attention to the rapid changes that are taking place ,in the country, and the following describes an establishment in the metropolis, which, even in those anti-sanitary days, Defoe could not let pass, without a touch of his satire :—" Since the finishing of the last Volume, the South Sea Company have engaged in the Greenland Fishery, and have fitted out a Fleet of twelve great Ships, which they have built new from the Stocks, and have made that great Wet-Dock between Deptford and Redriff, the Centre of all that Commerce, and the Buildings, the Works, and the Management of all that they call their Cookery ; that is, the Boyling their Blubber into Oyl. 'Tis well if they do not make Stink enough, and gain too little,

especially to the neighbouring Places of Deptford and Redriff."
To us, who have always been accustomed to call Lancashire
and Yorkshire *the Manufacturing districts,* the following is remarkable :—" We have now finish'd the whole South of Trent ;
which, being the most populous Part of the Country, and in-
finitely fuller of great Towns, of People, and of Trade, has also
the greatest variety of Incidents in its passing over."

The great time occupied in digesting his materials, and the
causes already adverted to, prevented the publication of the
third Volume, " which completes this Work, and contains a Tour
thro' Scotland, &c.　With a Map of Scotland by Mr. Moll,"
until the 13th of August 1726.　Except the words just quoted,
the title is the same as before.　In the preface to this last
volume, he returns to mention briefly the rapid improvement
and extension of London; and says, that since the second
volume, " there is a little City of Buildings, Streets, and
Squares, added to those mentioned before, at the West End
of Hanover and Cavendish Square."　Defoe made a special
visit to this part of the town while the erections were going
on, and wrote more than one very graphic Essay thereon in
Applebee's Journal.　They will be found among my collection
of his recently discovered Writings.　From the close of the
preface to the last Volume, it seems that our author's " Tour
thro' Great Britain" contains the results " of a Tedious and
very Expensive five years Travel."

On the 15th of June 1727, the work was advertised as being
republished in three volumes complete; but whether it was
then entirely reprinted or not, I am unable to say.*　The
works of Richardson, the novelist, show that he was a careful
student of Defoe ; and he is said to have furnished some additions which appeared in an impression of our author's Tour,
published in 1732.　The many subsequent editions are all in
four volumes duodecimo, and they were successively " added
to," " continued," and adapted to the changes going on in the
country, until the character of the original is lost under the
mutilations and patches.　An edition, dated 1778, is called the
eighth, and the title states, that it was " originally begun by

---

* A small number of copies of the original edition were printed on large
paper, at the price of ten shillings each volume.

the celebrated Daniel Defoe, continued by the late Mr. Richardson, and brought down to the present time, by a Gentleman of
Eminence in the literary world." It is stripped of the finest
passages illustrating the manners of the people ; it has lost the
charm of his simple narrative, and is, in fact, no longer the
work of Defoe. The original edition, as Defoe left it, can
never be out of date, and is of increasing interest and value, as
a perpetual memorial of much that has no longer a visible
existence. Respect for the character of the author, and the
integrity of his work, demands that every edition subsequent
to his death in 1731, be repudiated on his behalf.

In *Mist's Journal* for the 8th of June 1723, there was inserted a libel against the Government, for which he was again
apprehended; and, though liberated on bail, was tried and found
guilty. On the 18th of May 1724, he was brought up to
receive Judgment, at the King's Bench Bar, and was sentenced
to pay a Fine of one hundred pounds, to suffer a year's Imprisonment, and to find Sureties for his good Behaviour during
Life. His noble, but disloyal Jacobite correspondents were
always ready to bring him into trouble; but they had no
power to help him out again, nor inclination to comfort
or compensate him, for the losses he sustained. Mist seems
to have learnt no wisdom by sad experience ; but whenever the
hand of justice was withdrawn, he cast aside the good advice
of his best friend, Defoe; forgot all his promises of future
caution, relapsed, and again brought justice upon himself. His
frequent trials, fines, imprisonments, and consequent absence
from business, had now reduced him to the verge of ruin; and,
he again had recourse to the friend whose advice, if taken,
would have prevented all these calamities. Defoe had long
since broken off the business connection between them, refusing any responsibility without full control; but, he knew
what it was to be ruined by imprisonment for political offences,
and though he had no sympathy for the principles of *Mist*, he
again charitably undertook to render him some temporary
assistance, and to write occasional articles for the *Journal* on
moral and social, but not on political subjects. In one of
these, published the 8th of August 1724, he treats with grave
reprehension, Mandeville's " Fable of the Bees," and a much

more objectionable work arising out of it, by the same author, but which he declines to name. The Essay will be found annexed, but I refer to it here because I cannot avoid the conviction, that it was written under the influence of a secret conscientious misgiving, that some injury to morality, though not intended, might be caused by his last published novel, Roxana. It is remarkable too, that his Essay contains no reference to the authority of Scripture, or even to Religion; but recurring to the subject the following week, he observes, " When men differ in Opinions, some Proposition must be laid down, in which both agree, otherwise the Dispute may never end. For this Reason I will not quote Scripture upon them ; for it seems as if they had harden'd their Hearts against its Authority."

I have already stated that Defoe wrote two pamphlets respecting the murders and robberies committed in France by Cartouche, and his gangs. The former of such pamphlets, containing the Life, Exploits, and Execution of Cartouche, has been already noticed. Before his death, this great robber had confessed the names of a large number of his followers, and the crimes they had committed. The horror produced by these revelations gave such an impulse to the course of justice, that several hundreds of these villains were shortly afterward executed. The confederacy being thus broken up, some of the members became leaders of smaller parties, marauding separately, but sometimes together. On the 21st of September 1723, John Lock, Esq., an English Gentleman, returning from Paris, was robbed and murdered within a few miles of Calais by one of these gangs, and a few minutes afterward three other Englishmen, Edward Seabright, Esq.; Henry Mompesson, Esq. ; John Davies, Esq., and their servants, being on their way to Paris, came to the spot, and were also robbed and murdered by the same miscreants. One of the servants, however, Robert Spindelow, though pierced through with many wounds, and left for dead, afterward recovered. As soon as this man was convalescent, Defoe seems to have had an interview with him, and to have written, as if from his mouth, a full account of this sad affair, which appeared in *Applebee's Journal* of the 2nd November 1723. A further

publication was postponed, until Defoe had collected information as to the crimes of the Cartoucheans, subsequent to the
death of their great leader. On the 17th of August 1724,
he published a thick pamphlet, entitled, " A Narrative of the
Proceedings in France for Discovering and Detecting the
Murderers of the English Gentlemen, Sept. 21, 1723, near
Calais, &c. &c. *Translated from the French*, &c. London.
1724. Price *2s.*" The title was no doubt designed to sell the
book, by giving prominence to what most interested the
English people at the time. It is in fact a continuation of his
previous work, and the first page following the title is headed,
" An Account of the Cartoucheans in France." The relation
of the murders of the English Gentlemen and their servants,
does not commence earlier than page 88 ; and the statement of
Spindelow, the only survivor, so corresponds with that in
Applebee's Journal, that I think Defoe had no reason for
saying it was a translation, except that it might thus appear
better authenticated. On the evidence of Spindelow, two of
the murderers were executed.

Although Cartouche occupies a high place in the annals of
crime in France, a name so stained with the blood of his
fellow-creatures can scarcely be mentioned without execration.
Nothing of this kind attaches to the name of John Sheppard,
whose brief but wonderful career of infamy produced at the
time a degree of public excitement, that might be fitly termed
a popular mania ; whose sad fate has never ceased to be pitied,
even by the virtuous,—and whose acts of ingenuity and daring
courage, have invested his character with as much of admiration, as could be bestowed on so great a criminal. His escape
from the Round-house in St. Giles's, had not been considered
worthy of notice in the public prints, and his escape from the
New Prison was only reverted to, when he attempted unsuc-
cessfully to get out of Newgate. The first time his name appeared in any newspaper, so far as I have been able to find,
was on the 1st of August 1724, when Defoe inserted in
Applebee's Journal the following paragraph :—" Sheppard, the
Notorious House-breaker, who lately escaped from New Prison,
and was retaken by Jonathan Wild, and committed to Newgate, attempted to escape also from that Gaol, a day or two

ago; several Saws and Instruments proper for such a Design being found about his Bed. He is since confined in an Apartment called the Stone Room, kept close, and sufficiently Loaded with Irons to prevent his Designs for the future." Defoe had probably no intercourse with Sheppard until shortly before the escape from the Condemned Hold, on the evening of the 31st of August; an event which seems to have electrified the whole of the Metropolis. I have no doubt that, *as Mr. Applebee,* Defoe visited Sheppard after his condemnation; and seconded the efforts of the reverend Ordinary to impress his mind with a proper sense of religion. I come to this conclusion from the fact that the prisoner seems never to have known Defoe by any other name. Five days after his escape, he wrote a Letter to the Hangman, to which he added as a postscript, " Pray my Service to Mr. Ordinary, and Mr. Applebee." Defoe went immediately to Newgate after the escape, examined the place, enquired into the particulars, and published an account of the transaction in *Applebee's Journal* of the 5th of September.

From this time, to the 16th of November,—when he was executed,—Sheppard and his exploits, were in everybody's thoughts; and the theme of conversation,—in the palace, the drawing-room, the Courts of Law, the Coffee-houses, the Exchange, and the markets;—in the Streets, by the firesides of rich and poor, and in the haunts of the houseless and criminal population. *Applebee's Journal* contains no less than sixteen articles respecting him, and every other Newspaper and Journal, a like proportion. He was recaptured at Finchley on the 10th of September, and the same evening was visited by a Divine and several Gentlemen, to whom he related his escape, and his adventures afterward. I have little doubt that Defoe was one of these, as a full account of the same by him was printed in *Applebee's Journal* of the 12th. This Account is continued, in the most graphic manner, in the Journal of the following week. During these interviews Defoe obtained the information and materials for a pamphlet; but, while it was in the hands of the printers, Sheppard outdid all his former exploits, by his escape from the Castle of Newgate, through six strong Rooms, over the top of the Gaol, and thence to the roof of a house, from which he passed into the street, and obtained his

liberty. The relation of this, in *Applebee's Journal* of the 17th
of October, is much more circumstantial than that of any of
the other Papers, and was evidently written after an examination of the premises.

On the 19th of October, the pamphlet above referred to was
published, entitled, " The History of the remarkable Life of
JOHN SHEPPARD ; containing a Particular Account of his
many Robberies and Escapes, &c. &c. Including his last
Escape from the Castle at Newgate. London. Printed and
Sold by John Applebee, in Blackfryers. 1724. Price one
Shilling." This publication, having been already in the press,
could contain no further reference to the last Escape than the
bare mention thereof. The *Journal* of the following Saturday
published a long sensational Advertisement of the book, which
passed through three editions in as many weeks. The following, from *Applebee's Journal* of October 31st, is important, as
showing, that some person connected with *Applebee* was well
acquainted with Sheppard's handwriting ; that it was one who
had won, equally with the clergyman mentioned, the affectionate esteem of the culprit ; that there had been an arrangement for a further publication, of the nature of a Dying
Speech ; and the postscript proves, that notwithstanding the
apparent cheerfulness of the writer, he had fears that he would
be recaptured, in which case, he still wished the person whom
he called Mr. Applebee, to write an Account that should be
published immediately after his death :—" The following Letter
was brought on Saturday last, (Oct. 24,) about Eleven o'clock,
to Mr. Applebee's House in Black-Fryers, by a Person like an
Ostler ; and is well known to be in the Hand-Writing of John
Sheppard. The Original whereof is now to be seen at Mr.
Applebee's.

" MR. APPLEBEE,
        " This with my Kind Love to you, and pray give
my Kind Love to Mr. Wagstaff ; hoping these lines will find
you in good Health, as I am at present ; but I must own you
are the Loser for want of my Dying Speech ; But to make
up your Loss, if you think this Sheet worth your while, pray
make the best of it. Though they do say that I am taking
among the Smugglers, and put in Dover Castle, yet I hope

I am among Smugglers still. So no more, but your humble Servant,

"JOHN SHEPPARD.

"And I desire you would be the Post Man to my last Lodging.
"So farewell now, I quit the English Shore.
"Newgate Farewell."

Then follows, a Letter to Mr. Austin, the Keeper of New-gate, and a copy of Verses composed and subscribed by Sheppard.

The wretched fugitive, who had displayed so much ingenuity and perseverance in obtaining his liberty, exhibited no prudence in preserving it; and was therefore again apprehended on the 31st of October, reconveyed to his old lodgings in Newgate, and loaded with 300 pounds weight of iron. Defoe gives a very characteristic account of all the details, in *Applebee's Journal* of the 7th of November, concluding,—"On Monday last, several Noblemen and Persons of Distinction went to Newgate to see the famous John Sheppard. We hear that his Majesty has been pleased to send for the two Prints of Shep-pard, shewing the Manner of his being chained to the Floor in the Castle of Newgate, and describing the Manner in which he made his Escape from thence on the 15th of October." The Papers all give accounts of the great numbers of people of rank crowding to see the prisoner; and the *British Journal* says that in the first week of November, the Keepers of Newgate received above two Hundred Pounds as presents. Sir James Thornhill, the King's History Painter, took a full-length draught of him. Hogarth also went and painted his portrait; while Defoe was engaged in committing to writing the substance of a more complete account than that previously published; and which should be brought down to the end of his life.

On the 10th of November, Sheppard was taken to West-minster for legal identification, before he could be executed; and *Applebee's Journal,* of the following Saturday, gives an ad-mirably vivid account, by our author, of the whole proceedings. I cannot resist quoting two or three sentences, which seem to set the peculiarities of Sheppard's natural disposition before the reader; combining a strange admixture of childish sim-plicity, vanity, tender-heartedness, and even religious feeling,

with total inability to resist evil.   Being asked by the Judges,
" how he came to repeat his Crimes after his Escapes, he pleaded
Youth and Ignorance, and withal his Necessities; saying he
was afraid of every Child and Dog that looked at him, as
being closely pursued ; and had no opportunity to obtain his
Bread in an honest Way."   The Judges were incredulous as
to the possibility of his last Escape without treacherous conni-
vance, and held out to him hope of his Majesty's clemency, if
he would confess who assisted him.   " He averred, that he
had not the least Assistance from any Person, but God
Almighty."   He seems indeed to have thought that the ease
with which he could liberate himself, extenuated, if it did not
justify, what he had done.   " He told the Court, that if they
would let his Handcuffs be put on, he, by his Art, would take
them off, before their Faces."

On the above occasion, and also that of his Execution on
Monday the 16th Nov., the crowds of people in the streets of
London were said to have been greater than had ever been
known, and many persons were seriously injured.   The following remarkable circumstance is stated to have occurred at the
place of execution:—" Before Sheppard's death, he sent for
Mr. *Applebee*, a printer, into the Cart, and, in view of several
thousands of People, delivered to him a Pamphlet, entitled,
A Narrative of all his Robberies and Escapes." Read's Journal
says, " At the place of Execution he behaved very gravely,
spoke very little, *gave a Paper to a Friend;* and, after some
small Time allow'd for Devotion, he was turned off."   It must
be admitted that something of the kind took place ; but it can
scarcely be doubted that any person connected with *Read's
Journal* must have personally known Mr. Applebee, and would
have given his name, had he been there.   *Applebee's Journal*
is entirely silent upon the subject, and yet such an occurrence
was certainly a striking advertisement of the work Defoe had
written,—which was actually in print at the time,—and the
whole edition sold off the following day.   He to whom the
Paper was given was the person whom Sheppard knew as Mr.
Applebee, and from what has been already stated, the conclusion seems to be, that this formal delivery of the document,
professedly written by Sheppard, into the hands of its real
author, was a preconcerted arrangement, gratifying to the vanity

of the departing malefactor ; and a compliance, on the part of Defoe, with the request, " I desire you would be the Postman to my last Lodging."

The pamphlet in question is entitled, " A Narrative of all the Robberies, Escapes, &c., of JOHN SHEPPARD : Giving an Exact Description of the manner of his wonderful Escape from the CASTLE in Newgate, and of the Methods he took afterwards for his Security.   Written by himself during his Confinement in the Middle Stone Room, after his being retaken in Drury Lane.   To which is Prefix'd, a true Representation of his Escape from the Condemn'd Hold, curiously engraven on a Copper Plate.   The whole Publish'd at the particular Request of the Prisoner. London : Printed and sold by John Applebee, a little below Bridewell Bridge in Black-Fryers. 1724.   Price Six Pence."   The rapidity with which this book sold is probably unparalleled.   On the 21st of November, only five days after the Execution, the fifth Edition was published, and it reached a seventh Edition on the 12th of December.   It is now exceedingly rare, but the British Museum contains a copy of the third Edition.

Notwithstanding the length of this notice, I cannot quit the above pamphlet, without a few remarks on the natural and simple manner in which the whole story is related.   There is such an air of candour and truthfulness, pervading all the details of the most minute circumstances, as only Defoe could impart to any narrative, whether real or imaginary.   This is especially the case in the description of the last Escape from Newgate ; in relating which, his mind seems to linger with a feeling of gratitude towards the Iron Bar " of about two feet and a half in length, and an inch square," which did him so good service ; and he pronounces it " a most notable Imple- ment."   The relation of this part is told with the same spirit as the ingenious and successful contrivances of Crusoe ; and the attention of the reader is so concentrated, as to lose sight of the Criminal, and to think only of the Man, struggling for liberty and life.   Throughout the story there is perceptible, continuous alternations of mind, between expressions of sincere penitence dictated by conscience ; and the irrepressible vanity of his exploits, which was a predominant feature of his character.   The following illustrates these changes :—" Blueskin has atoned for his Offences. I am now following, being just on the brink of Eternity, much unprepared to appear before the Face of an angry God." Yet the same paragraph closes with criminal indignation and contempt. " Blueskin's Courage dropt him, saying that he would first refresh his Horse, and then follow ; but he designedly delayed till we quite lost the Coach, and hopes of the Booty. In short, he was a worthless Companion, a sorry Thief, and nothing but the cutting of Jonathan Wild's Throat, could have made him so considerable." Again, just before the pious remarks I have quoted, he describes, with great glee, his escape from St. Giles's Round House, where the noise and falling of bricks and tiles he had dislodged, brought a crowd of people together; and he says,—" Before the Beadle and Assistance came up, I had dropped into the Church-Yard, and got over the lower end of the Wall, and came amidst the Crowd who were staring up, some crying,—*There's his Head ! There he goes behind the Chimney, &c.* I was well enough diverted with the Adventure, and went off about my Business." The book concludes appropriately,—"*I beseech the infinite Divine Being of Beings to pardon my numberless and enormous Crimes, and to have mercy on my poor departing Soul.*" Only a deep student of human nature, and of the character of Sheppard in particular, could have ventured instantly to add the following Postscript:—" After I had escaped from the Castle, concluding that Blueskin would have certainly been decreed for Death, I did fully resolve and purpose to have gone and cut down the Gallows the Night before his Execution."

The notices of Sheppard to which I have referred, as having been published in *Applebee's Journal*, will be found in my collection of Defoe's Writings ; as well as two Letters Introductory by him, published in the same paper the 21st and 28th of November 1724, professedly from Betty Blueskin,—niece to Moll Flanders,—declaring her affection for Sheppard.

Turn we away from this poor, sinful, misguided youth, who expiated his crimes with his life, at the early age of twenty-two years; amidst a pitying multitude of countless thousands of people. We are required immediately to notice an in-human monster, such as no preceding or subsequent age could have produced in England ;—a thief-maker, and a thief-taker, who seduced the ignorant and idle,—such as Sheppard and hundreds more,—into crimes of dishonesty ; used them as the instruments of his nefarious trade, and when they had served his turn, or were likely to bring him into danger, procured that their tongues should be for ever silenced, by causing them to be hanged out of his way.   His career of wholesale villany had been long and prosperous, but " a little cloud like a man's hand" had passed over him on the 14th of October, when a knife was plunged into his throat by one of his doomed victims ; and that cloud was beginning to gather blackness on the 10th of November, when Defoe, without mentioning his name, put the following words into the mouth of John Sheppard :—" I have often lamented the Scandalous practice of Thief-Catching, as it is called ; and the publick Manner of offering Rewards for stolen Goods, in defiance of two several Acts of Parliament ; the Thief-Catchers living sumptuously, and keeping public Offices of Intelligence.   These, (who forfeit their Lives every day they breathe, and deserve the Gallows as richly as any of the Thieves,) send us their Representatives to Tyburn once a month : thus, they hang by proxy, while we do it fairly in person."*

It is my intention to say as little as possible of Jonathan Wild, whom I have introduced as above, only because the closing scenes of his wicked Life put in motion the pen of Defoe.   He was arrested on the 15th of February, 1725 ; and, after examination, was committed to Newgate, for taking money to restore goods stolen in his presence, by his own men.   Bail was refused, though applied for on his behalf by Counsel ; and Butler, one of his instruments, under condemnation, received the royal Pardon, in order that he might become an evidence against his old master.   The following will show, that Wild added religious hypocrisy to his other detestable qualities :   In the case for which he was afterward hanged, the prosecutor had paid the sum required for returning the goods of which she had been robbed, and then asked what she must give him for himself, to which he replied, " Good woman ! I desire nothing of you for my part, but your Prayers."   In another similar case, being applied to on Sunday, he said, " I never do

---

* " Narrative, &c., of John Sheppard, &c.," p. 15.

business on the Lord's Day." When he had procured sentence
of death to be passed upon any of his own gang, the maxim
that always fell from his lips was, " Honesty is the best
Policy." It is remarkable that while every event preparatory
to Wild's trial was being duly chronicled in all the other
Journals, *Applebee's* Paper continued silent, excepting a few
lines, until the 8th of May, which was the Saturday preceding
the day appointed for his trial. In that Number it is plain,
that Defoe, as the author of the Journal, had had an interview with the prisoner, and there are printed the christian and
surnames of no less than ten men who had been hanged " for
returning from Transportation;" all " discovered and convicted by Jonathan Wild." Also, of six men and three
women who escaped the gallows from no fault of his, as they
were " also convicted by him for returning from Transportation, but have received Mercy, and been Transported again."
The article adds, " and in our next Week's Journal will be
inserted a List of the Persons Discovered, Apprehended, and
Convicted by the said *Jonathan Wild*, for several Robberies on
the Highway, and also for several Burglaries and Felonies;
together with the Persons' Names they robbed, as taken from
his own Mouth in Newgate."

The object of this wretched Miscreant was doubtless, to
make an impression upon the Court at his trial; by having
copies of the Journal produced and read, to show the great
services he had rendered to his country. Defoe knew better,
and though the Lists were inserted, no word of comment was
added; but it was made clear that the publication was only in
compliance with the wish of a man whose Life was in
jeopardy. The object of Wild is further evident from the fact
that the trial having been fixed for Friday, the 14th, his
Counsel managed that it should not come on until the following day, when *Applebee's Journal* again appeared, with the
promised additional List of Persons whom Wild had sent to
the Gallows. This is a horrible array, of no less than *thirty-
four* for Highway Robberies; and *twenty-two* for House-
breaking, among whom are included Wm. Rigglesden, the
Attorney, Cock-Eyed Jack, Blueskin, and John Sheppard. The
List concludes as follows :—" Note. Several others have been
also Convicted for the like Crimes, but remembering not the

Persons' Names who had been robbed, he omits the Criminals' Names; and likewise several others, whom he has Convicted for Shoplifting, picking of Pockets, &c., of the Female Sex, which are Capital Crimes; the Prosecutors of them not willing to be exposed."

Applebee's Journal of the following week gives a much more brief Account of the trial of Wild than the other Journals; but the number for the 29th May, contains a very graphic account of his unsuccessful attempt to poison himself in prison; and of his Execution on the 24th, when the concourse of people was even greater than that which attended on Jack Sheppard. Defoe says, " In all that innumerable Crowd, there was not one Pitying Eye to be seen, nor one Compassionate Word to be heard; but on the contrary, wherever he came, there was nothing but Hollooing and Huzzas, as if it had been upon a Triumph; nay, so far had he incurred the Resentment of the Populace that they pelted him with Stones, &c., in several Places, one of which, in Holborn, broke his Head to that Degree, that the Blood ran down plentifully; which Barbarity was as unjustifiable as unusual, yet may serve to deter others from treading in his Steps." The Crimes of Wild seem to have inspired every one with such horror and loathing that there was no general desire to know more of the events of his Life. Two pamphlets had been issued in March, by T. Warner, but the sale had not encouraged others. Several small publications appeared after his Execution, but *Applebee's Journal* pronounced them all spurious and incorrect. It was able to do so on Wild's own authority, he having given, exclusively to Defoe, the information and Papers for an accurate account. This pamphlet was published on the 8th of June, and is entitled, " The True, Genuine, and Perfect Account of the Life and Actions of Jonathan Wild; Taken from good Authority, and from his own Writings. Printed and Published by John Applebee, in Black-Fryers. 1725." A second Edition was issued two days afterward, and a third after another interval of two days.

CHAPTER XVI.

Mist discovers Defoe's connection with the Government, and endeavours to assassinate him, but is disarmed and wounded—Defoe publishes "A New Voyage round the World"—" Every-Body's Business is No-Body's Business"—"An Account of the Conduct and Proceedings of the late John Gow, executed for Piracy"—Defoe's quarrel with the " London Journal" about " Robinson Crusoe"—Publishes " The Complete English Tradesman"—Advertisement of a Stolen Pocketbook proves Defoe to be connected with commerce.

1725—26.

IT is necessary that we now return to the 12th of December 1724, when there appeared in *Applebee's Journal,* immediately following the Letter Introductory, a further communication by Defoe, but with the signature of " T. EXPERIENCE," and dated the 25th of November. Subsequent numbers proved that this was the precursor to a series of articles on the nature of Friendship,—its instability, the decay of true friendship, and the prevalence of ingratitude, especially with reference to a recent experience of the writer. All these Papers will be found in my Collection of his Writings, but are referred to here because they relate an important incident in Defoe's Life. I have already noticed the great kindness of Defoe to Mr. Mist, in preventing him, often, from being imprisoned ; and when unable to do that, in visiting, comforting him, procuring his discharge, and attending meantime to his Journal, so that he might not be ruined by his own disloyal principles and perverse conduct. All this I need not recapitulate, but only add, that while the kind disposition of Defoe continued unchanged after their separation; and, throughout four government prosecutions that had fallen upon Mr. Mist, the latter had suddenly turned, from being a false and ungrateful friend, into an open and bitter enemy. In an affair of so much delicacy, the former connection between them, and Defoe's engagement with the government, forbade the mention of names ; but it will be obvious to those who have read of the earlier part of their intercourse, that no other than Mist can possibly be intended. In the course of this series of Articles Defoe says, on the 19th of December, " I know a Person at this Time abused and insulted by one who, without the least Obligation, he had fetched three times out of Prison. Nothing can oblige an ungrateful mind ; I have heard a Person of very good Experience say, he had been five times ill-treated, and in a manner ruined, by the very particular People that he had kept from Starving." Pursuing the subject on the 2nd of January 1725, he ceases to use the previous caution of speaking in the third person, and gives us the following remarkable paragraph :—" My particular Case, as I have said above, *I cannot yet publish ;* but that you may judge a little the Nature of it, and whether I give a right judgment or no, let me tell you your friend's answer does not in the least come near it. My Case concerns Blood and Life, and abundantly makes good that proverbial saying, *Save a Thief from the Gallows, and he will cut your Throat.* Take it at a distance thus : Suppose a man has an Opportunity to save a Gentleman from the utmost Distress, and the immediate Danger of Life,—say it were from Thieves or Enemies, or what you will ;—and suppose that very Person, (I may not call him Gentleman any more) basely using, insulting, and provoking him, and at last drawing his Sword upon his said Benefactor, and using his utmost Endeavour to destroy him ; but his Efforts failing, and being disarmed fairly at his Weapon, you are to suppose then, that his Friend, however provok'd, gave him his Life, embrac'd him, sent for a Surgeon to dress a Wound he had, in his own Defence, been oblig'd to give him ; and after this, shewing him several acts of Friendship and Kindness. Suppose this Man thus a Second time oblig'd, in a degree so Extraordinary, yet on all Occasions, returning Abuses of the worst and grossest Nature ; I say, suppose all this, and you reach a part of my Case, tho' but a Part." So far extend Defoe's own statements, in the only possible direction to which they can point. His first communication thereon, as we have just seen, is dated the 25th November 1724 ; and, notwithstanding all his caution, exhibits irrepressible symptoms of soreness from recent injury. There cannot, I think, be any doubt, that Defoe wrote the leading Article, and other-

To Face y^e Title.   J. Clark sc.

[FRONTISPIECE TO "NEW VOYAGE ROUND THE WORLD".]

wise assisted in *Mist's Journal* of the 24th October 1724, so that
the date of the outrage is fixed within the space of the intervening month.   The connection between these two men had
continued, with interruptions, more than seven years; but
after the 24th Oct., Defoe's hand is never seen again in *Mist's
Journal*. My only remark, at present, upon this strange instance
of ungrateful violence, is that it must have proceeded from
imaginary wrong of a very grievous nature.   I can conceive
no other cause of the outrage than that Mr. Mist had learnt,
in some way, that during all the time Defoe was connected
with his Journal, he was also holding an appointment under
the government, but concealing the fact; and, as Mist was now
under prosecution of the same government, he may have
erroneously conceived that Defoe's censorship was the cause of
his present and past troubles.   I allow that there is no direct
proof of this conjecture; but I also submit that circumstantial
evidence could scarcely be more conclusive.

On the 8th of May, 1725, Defoe published a work, again
proving, not only his great skill in nautical affairs, but containing a marvellous acquaintance with the geography of a part
of the world then little known.   It is entitled "A New
Voyage round the World, by a Course never sailed before.
Being a Voyage undertaken by some Merchants, who afterwards proposed the setting up an East India Company in
Flanders. Illustrated with Copper Plates. London : Printed for
A. Bettesworth, at the Red Lyon in Pater-noster Row; and
W. Mears, at the Lamb, without Temple Bar. 1725." The
title of this work was not wisely chosen. It has no preface, and
though the chief Commander, or captain of the Expedition,
tells his story in the first person, the reader is not made acquainted with his name.   Thus some of the charm of a personal interest in the narrative is lost.   Making allowance for
this drawback, the work is one of the most instructive and best
written of Defoe's imaginary Voyages.   The Vessel was a
Letter of Marque during the war with Spain, but not a Pirate ;
being loaded with a valuable cargo.   The Captain's Commission enabled him to go where he pleased; but his instructions
required him to search out suitable places for colonization and
commerce.   The great object of Defoe seems to have been, to

avoid the dry details of most of the accounts then existing, by
marking out a new course; and thus, combining amusement,
with an accurate geographical account of the Pacific Ocean,
and part of the Continent of South America. These important ends he has admirably accomplished.   When ready to
depart from Manilla the idea occurred, to the commander of
the expedition, of steering away North, and endeavouring to
find a north-eastern passage to England.   He debates the
matter with himself, in a most able manner; considering the
various directions in which the attempt might be made, and
naively says,—as if foreseeing and ridiculing future expeditions
to the polar regions,—" It is true that these Northern Discoveries might be inimitably fine, and most glorious Things to
the British Nation."   Common sense prevails, and he sails
southward, and turns eastward, through then almost unknown
islands of the Pacific Ocean, to South America.   All this part
of the work is filled with the character and productions of the
places at which the ship touched, and the habits and appearance of the people ; and is made intensely interesting by the
charming manner in which the scenes are related.   The most
original and finest part of the book however, is the latter half,
containing, first his own excursion, with a Spanish Gentleman
and attendants, from Baldivia in Chili through the defiles of
the Andes ; and, the subsequent journey of a detachment of
fifty sailors, overland, from the same point, across Chili and
Patagonia; the ships meanwhile sailing from Baldivia round
Cape Horn, and meeting the enterprising Travellers at the
mouth of the River Camarones, on the Atlantic Coast.
Through all this, the genius of the writer lavishes his inexhaustible power of word-painting ; equal, in the exercise of his art,
—whether it be an individual portrait ;—the picture of a
domestic interior, with all its Chilian surroundings ;—the
patient winding, through dark ravines, and up fearful ascents,
of men, and mules, and baggage ;—the lurid midnight light of
volcanoes, in the midst of lofty mountains, and deep vallies ;—
or, the illimitable outspread space, to the east, of desert and
lake, seen, far as the eye can stretch,—from the summit, whence
flow the great Rivers of the Continent.   All this is enlivened
with variety of incident, and with entertaining dialogue, that
completes the charm of the journey.

I make two brief quotations in justification of these en-comiums.   The Captain awoke in the middle of the night, in consequence of the outer door of the house having been opened :—" What are they burning there ? says I to my Patron ! You will see presently, says he ; adding, I hope you will not be surprized ; so he led me out to that Door.   But who can express the Thoughts of a Man's Heart, coming on a sudden into a Place where the whole World seemed to be of a light Fire ?   The Valley was on one Side so exceeding bright, the Eye could scarce bear to look at it ; the sides of the Moun-tains were shining like the Fire itself ; the Flame from the top of the Mountain on the other Side, casting its Light directly upon them, from thence the Reflection into other Parts looked Red and more Terrible ; for the first was white and clear, like the Light of the Sun ; but the other being, as it were, a Reflection of Light, mix'd with some darker Cavities, repre-sented the Fire of a Furnace ; and, in short, it might well be said, here wasno Darkness ; but certainly, at the first View, it gives no Traveller any other Idea than that of being at the very Entrance into Eternal Horror."   The following is a description of the external appearance of a Chiliau Gentleman, in the region of the Andes.   " He was dressed in a Jerkin made of an Otter's Skin, like a Doublet ; a Pair of long Spanish Breeches of Leather, dressed after the Spanish Fashion, Green, and very soft, and which looked very well, but what the skin was I could not guess ; he had over it a Mantle, of a kind of Cotton, dyed in two or three grave Brown Colours, and thrown about him like a Scotsman's Plaid ; he had Shoes of a particular make, tied on like Sandals, flat-heeled, no Stockings, his Breeches hanging down below the Calf of his Leg, and his Shoes lacing up above his Ancles ; he had on a Cap of the Skin· of some small Beast like a Racoon, with a bit of the Tail hanging out, from the Crown of his Head backward ; a long Pole in his Hand, and a Servant, as oddly dress'd as himself, carried his Gun ; he had neither Spado nor Dagger."   In conclusion, I consider that this land expedition, across the continent of South America, is only paralleled, as a work of imagination, by that of Singleton and his companions across the deserts of Africa.   So real was the description, in the whole of this Work, that shortly after its appearance, a Map or Chart was independently published, on which was traced out this new Course of a Voyage round the World; and I have recently, with the aid of the best modern maps, followed the land expedition from the Coast of Chili to that of Patagonia without finding any geographical error.

The want of appreciation of our author's voluminous Work on *The Great Law of the Subordination of Servants*, did not deter him from returning to the subject; but this time, he chose the more accessible form of a pamphlet, which was published on the 25th of June, and is entitled, " Every-Body's Business is No-Body's Business ; or, Private Abuses, Publick Grievances : Exemplified in the Pride, Insolence, and Exorbitant Wages of our Women-Servants, Footmen, &c. With a Proposal for Amendment of the same ; as also for clearing the Streets of those Vermin call'd Shoe-Cleaners, and substituting in their stead many Thousands of Industrious Poor, now ready to Starve. With divers other Hints, of great use to the Publick. Humbly submitted to the Consideration of our Legislature, and the careful perusal of all Masters and Mistresses of Families. By Andrew Moreton, Esq. London. Printed for W. Meadows, in Cornhill; and sold by T. Warner, Paternoster Row ; A. Dodd, without Temple Bar ; and E. Nutt, at the Royal Exchange. 1725." I have, in an earlier part of this Memoir, noticed the fact that all the later Works of Defoe were published without his Name, and have endeavoured to assign reasons for it ; it is less easy to say why at this time, and for some only of his subsequent productions, he assumed the name of Andrew Moreton. I shall consider, in its place, the probable reason ; and now only observe, that the pamphlet before us is the first so published. The subject appears to be of a trifling nature, yet as the evil was one that greatly interfered with domestic comfort, Defoe did not think it beneath his animadversion. He speaks of female servants confederating together to exact increased wages, and to subdivide work,— of their insolence and love of dress, in which they are often mistaken for members of the families in which they live ; never saving anything out of their wages, and too often, when out of place becoming immoral, as the consequence of their vanity and destitute circumstances. He exposes these errors in a strain,

humourous and amusing to masters and mistresses, but with
great severity towards the Servants.   Besides his reforms of
domestic Servants, he would revolutionize the race of Shoe-
Blacks, compelling them to work in mines, wool-combing, and
agricultural labour ; and leaving shoe-cleaning to the old
women in the respective parishes.   For all these purposes, and
also for registry of messengers and porters, he invokes the
action of the legislature.   In showing how rapidly a young
servant maid from the Country becomes initiated into London
ways, he gives the following striking picture of the habits of
the times.   She is prompted, by others of her own class, to
demand higher wages, " and so gives warning from Place to
Place, till she has got them up to the tip-top.   Her Neat's
Leathern Shoes are now transform'd into lac'd ones with high
Heels ; her yarn Stockings are turn'd into fine Worsted ones,
with silk Clocks ; and her high Wooden Pattens are kickt
away for Leathern Clogs ; she must have a Hoop too, as well
as her Mistress ; and her poor, scanty, Linsey Woolsey Petticoat is changed into a good Silk one, four or five Yards wide
at the least : Not to carry the Description farther, in short,
plain Country Joan is now turn'd into a fine London Madam,
can drink Tea, take Snuff, and carry herself as high as the
best."   This book went through four editions in two weeks,
and the author of an answer intitled, *Every Man mind his own
Business, &c.*, complains, that " Mr. Moreton's Essay is read
in every House ; his Doctrines, like Weeds, spread all abroad ;
and every Master and Mistress copy this great Original."   On
the 24th of July, Defoe published a fifth Edition, to which he
added a preface.   He declares, " As my intentions are good,
so have they had the good Fortune to meet with Approbation
from the sober and substantial Part of Mankind.   As for the
vicious and vagabond, their ill-will is my Ambition."

The connection between Defoe and Applebee, and the
special access thus afforded our author to the condemned
criminals, were productive of a thick pamphlet published on
the 11th of June, entitled, " An Account of the Conduct and
Proceedings of the late John Gow, alias Smith, Captain of the
late Pirates, Executed for Murther and Piracy committed on
Board the George Galley, afterwards called the Revenge ; with

a Relation of all the horrid Murthers they committed in Cold Blood. As also of their being taken at the Islands of Orkney, and sent up Prisoners to London. London. Printed and Sold by John Applebee, in Black Fryers. 1725. Price One Shilling." This must be taken as in the main a true history ; but, acquainted as Defoe was with the habits and manners of pirate life, he has infused into it the spirit of his own genius. His description of the contrivances, by which the Pirates were entrapped to their own destruction, is related in his happiest manner, and the whole pamphlet is one of the most characteristic of his minor works.

I must here notice, as shortly as possible, a controversy into which Defoe was drawn by the *London Journal,* on a matter of trifling moment; but which seems to have irritated him considerably. Charles Gildon had, in his pamphlet against Robinson Crusoe, pointed out the inconsistency, that Crusoe was made to " pull off his clothes," swim from the island to the wreck, and then " fill his pockets with biscuit." At that time *four* editions of the first volume of Crusoe had been published, and no reply, that I know of, was made to Gildon ; but in subsequent editions the text was corrected. In some it stands, " I rolled up part of my clothes on my back ;" but in others the only alteration is, the substitution of the word " hands," instead of " pockets." In the *London Journal* of the 4th of September 1725, at which time that Paper is believed to have been written by Bishop Benjamin Hoadley, there was an Article on the dearth of News, and the expediency of resorting to Fiction, however extravagant, to satisfy the craving of the multitude ; and the writer says, that books of Voyages and Travels, filled with monstrous and incredible stories, have become popular, because they satisfied this morbid appetite. He goes on, as follows :—" We may remember that we have been most of us, when Children, wonderfully pleased with the achievements of *Tom Thumb, Jack the Giant-Killer, Don Bellianis of Greece, The Seven Champions of Christendom,* and such like extraordinary Heroes ;. and many of us, in our more advanced Age, are little less delighted with such Books as, *The Life and Adventures of Robinson Crusoe ;* which seems to have had that uncommon Run upon the Town for some Years past, for no other Reason but that it is a *most palpable Lye*, from Beginning to End ; and I doubt not that the famous Passage of his *Swimming to Shore* NAKED, *with his* POCKETS *full of Biscuits*, tho' a most notorious *Blunder* in the Author, has pass'd for a very good Jest, and been received with abundance of Pleasure by many of his Readers."

Although Defoe had very strong reasons for wishing to conceal his personal connection with *Applebee's Journal*, the above seems to have so disturbed him as to obscure his usual prudence ; and in the number for the 18th of September, he begins his weekly Essay with lamenting the loss of a ship called the *Charming Fanny*, on her way from Italy to England, laden with *Brimstone*. After enlarging metaphorically and satirically for some time, he says,—" Give us but one *Charming Fanny*, loaded with Brimstone, and let us Writers touch it with an inflamed Pen, a Pen rightly dipt in *Styx*, and *Phlegethon*, and if we don't set all Europe on Fire, we must have less Skill than we think we have, and less Power of doing Mischief than we hope we have. Do but take our late *London Journal* for a Leader, who with but one Touch of his Pen destroy'd a Lover, and two beautiful Ladies at a Blow, in his very last Paper, and all in Shadow ; but the merriest Thing of all was, that he had but the week before given poor *Robinson Crusoe* the LYE, most courteously and genteely, for writing an Allegorick History of his own Life ; and yet could, the very next Paper, work out a most tragical Story, I do not say *Lye*, of his own Brain, merely to fill up his Paper with, and murther three innocent Creatures that were never alive ; all done most accurately, to convince the Reader that his former Censure was just, according to the Honour of a Journalizing Critick." Our author seemed so ill able to digest the assertion that *Robinson Crusoe* was a Lie, that on the 20th of November following, he returned to the attack against the *London Journal* ; but, as nothing new appeared in the controversy, it is sufficient to say, 1. That he does not notice the blunders of the *London Journal*, in making Crusoe swim naked *from* instead of *to* the ship ; and also, that he thus swam with his pockets full of Biscuit, which Defoe had never stated. Yet this was all that was adduced to prove the Book a " Lie from beginning to End." 2. The *London Journal* made no allusion

to the Work being "an allegorick History" of a real life.
That was what no one could know except from the author
himself.   3. The *London Journal* acknowledges the universal
popularity attained by Crusoe, six years after its first publication.

Defoe seems also to have been highly incensed at a "murdering Rogue," who called his pirate-ship, *Robinson Crusoe.*
" The Pyrates among our Island Colonies, and about New Providence, the Coast of Carolina and Virginia, do not seem to be
diminished.   Other Desperadoes, as bold and daring as Roberts
appear, with stout Ships under them ; and, as if they made
sport of their bloody and villainous Actions, they tell us, one
of their Ships is called *Robinson Crusoe*, and is commanded by
one Robinson, a desperate Pyrate, the most bloody-minded
murdering Rogue they have yet heard of."*

It required no effort of the many-sided talents of Defoe to
put away fancy and imagination, and address himself to the
instruction of persons engaged in Trade.   He had already
written much on the subject in his *Review* and *Mercator ;* but
those Essays were chiefly of a temporary and disconnected
character.   They had acquired him a great reputation with the
Government of his country, and the Mercantile World ; but he
felt that more than this was needed ; and never having forgotten the conviction that seized him in 1694, after his own
early misfortunes in Trade, namely, " *that Providence had other
Work for him to do ;*" he now sat down, at the age of sixty-four,
to the composition of one of his greatest and most useful
Works ; a manual, or *vade-mecum,* for all persons engaged in
Trade, but especially the young.   As no work of his underwent
so many subsequent alterations at the hands of its Author as
this, I must notice the successive appearance of its parts.   It
was first published, in one Volume, on the 11th of September,
1725, with the following long title : " The Complete English
Tradesman, in Familiar Letters ; Directing him in all the
several Parts and Progressions of Trade, viz :—I. His acquainting himself with Business during his Apprenticeship.   II. His
Writing to his Correspondents, and obtaining a general Knowledge of Trade ; as well what he is not, as what he is employ'd

---

* " Applebee's Journal," 28th July, 1722.

in. III. Of Diligence and Application, as the Life of all
Business. IV. Cautions against Over-Trading. V. Of the
ordinary Occasions of a Tradesman's Ruin; such as Expensive
Living—Too early Marrying—Innocent Diversions—Giving and
taking too much Credit—Leaving Business to Servants—Being
above Business—Entering into dangerous Partnerships, &c.
VI. Directions in the several Distresses of a Tradesman, when
he comes to fail. VII. Of Tradesmen Compounding with their
Debtors; and why they are so particularly severe. VIII. Of
Tradesmen ruining one another by Rumour and Scandal. IX.
Of the Customary Frauds of Trade, which even honest Men
allow themselves to Practice. X. Of Credit, and how it is only
supported by Honesty. XI. Directions for Book-Keeping,
punctual Paying Bills, and thereby maintaining Credit. XII.
Of the Dignity and Honour of Trade in England, more than
in other Countries : and how the Trading Families in England
are mingled with the Nobility and Gentry, so as not to be
separated or distinguished. Calculated for the Instruction of
our Inland Tradesmen; and especially of Young Beginners.
London. Printed for Charles Rivington, at the Bible and
Crown in St. Paul's Church-yard. 1725." From the concluding sentence, and also from the fact that the work, and its
continuation, was for several years regularly advertised in almost
all the Journals, I cannot doubt that Mr. Rivington had a
large interest in the copyright; and that the work was a very
lucrative one, both to him and the Author. Mr. Wilson has
inaccurately placed the first appearance of this work in the year
1727; and, after subjecting Defoe to "bodily infirmities," says
that "his pen was probably urged forward by the imperious
demands of necessity." Defoe was afflicted with stone, which
occasionally gave him excruciating pain, but did not at that time
otherwise affect his general health. That he was then in prosperous pecuniary circumstances, I have sufficiently proved. During
the early part of the following year, *The Compleat Tradesman* was
re-issued, the only alteration being that of the date of the title.
This was done to prepare for a Second Edition, published on
the 10th of September, 1726. The titlepage is the same as
before to the end of Section XII., and then proceeds, as follows:—
"The Second Edition, to which is added a Supplement, containing, I. A Warning against Tradesmen Borrowing Money

upon Interest.   II. A Caution against that destructive Practice
of drawing and remitting, as also discounting Promissory Bills,
merely for a supply of Cash.   III. Direction for the Tradesman's
Accounts, with Brief, but plain Examples, and Specimens for
Book-Keeping.   IV. Of Keeping a Duplicate, or Pocket
Ledger in Case of Fire.   London : Printed for Charles Rivington, at the Bible and Crown in St. Paul's Church Yard. 1726."
For the convenience of those who had already the first Edition,
it was advertised that the Supplement might be had alone, price
one Shilling.   The Second Edition is printed in a smaller type,
the preface considerably altered, and the text of the Work
carefully revised by the author.   None of these changes are
referred to in the Volume, or in the Advertisement of its publication ; but the latter declares it to be " the most useful
Work of its kind yet extant."   In the following year this
Edition was also reissued with only an alteration in the date of
the titlepage.

Meanwhile, our Author had prepared a Second Volume,
which was published on the 13th of May, 1727, entitled, " The
Compleat English Tradesman.   Volume II.   In Two Parts.
Part I. Directed chiefly to the more Experienc'd Tradesmen ;
with Cautions and Advices to them after they are thriven, and
suppos'd to be grown rich, viz., I. Against running out of their
Business into needless Projects and dangerous Adventures, no
Tradesman being above Disaster.   II. Against oppressing one
another by Engrossing, Underselling, Combinations in Trade,
&c.   III. Advices, that when he leaves off his business, he
should part Friends with the World ; the great Advantages of
it ; with a Word of the Scandalous Character of Purse-proud
Tradesmen.   IV. Against being litigious and vexatious, and apt
to go to Law for Trifles ; with some Reasons why Tradesmen's
Differences should, if possible, be all ended by Arbitration.
Part II. Being useful Generals in Trade, describing the Principles and Foundation of the Home Trade of Great Britain ;
with large Tables of our Manufactures, Calculations of the Product, Shipping, Carriage of Goods by Land, Importation from
Abroad, Consumption at home, &c.   By all which, the infinite
Number of our Tradesmen are Employ'd, and the General
Wealth of the Nation rais'd and increas'd.   The Whole Calcu-
lated for the Use of all our Inland Tradesmen, as well in the

City as in the Country.   London : Printed for Charles Rivington, at the Bible and Crown in St. Paul's Churchyard. 1727."
The complete work was republished, in two thick volumes, on
the 10th of August, 1728, and again in 1732.

In the preface to the first volume he states in a few modest
words his reason for writing it : " Had I not seen, in a few
years experience, many young Tradesmen miscarry for want of
those very Cautions which are here given, I should have
thought this Work needless, and I am sure had never gone
about to write it ; but as the contrary is manifest, I thought,
and think still, the world wanted either this or something
better."   The book is as well contrived as it is ably written ;
full of counsel and caution, it abounds in lessons of practical
wisdom ; sometimes conveyed in the gravest terms, but at
others in powerful and caustic satire ; and yet, by apt illustrative cases he engages the close attention of the reader, and
never fails to mingle amusement with instruction.   He closes
the preface of the first volume by saying,—" What I have
spoken of, I have endeavoured to do fully and pertinently ; and
I think I may say of the following Sheets,—That they contain
all the directions needful to make the Tradesman thrive ; and if
he pleases to listen to them with a temper of Mind willing to be
directed, he must have some uncommon ill Luck if he mis-
carries."

The second volume is equally valuable as the first, though
not confined to the young Tradesmen. He says, " it is directed
to the Men of Business ; as well to the overgrown, as to the
growing ; the upper Class, as well as the lower ; and it may be
absolutely necessary to both."   He states in the preface that
he has been obliged to leave out a very useful Chapter, addressed to the old as well as the young Tradesman, and
therefore he touches upon it here : " The Subject was against
that dangerous Thing, which the wise Man calls *Striking
Hands with a Stranger* ; by which I mean, and so did Solomon also, the Tradesmen's being bound for one another.
Three Things every Tradesman ought to consider before he is
bound for another.   1. Whether he is able to pay the Debt ;
for he that is bound for a Debt, must expect to pay the
Debt. 2. That when he binds himself for his Friend, he binds
his Wife, Children, and Estate ; and brings them all into the

Hazard.   3. That he binds also, all those innocent Tradesmen who deal with him, and perhaps trust him ; who put their Estates and Families, as it were, into his Hand ; and who, in Justice, ought not to be embark'd in the Risque, or brought to run more Hazards than they are aware of." By such close reasoning as this, he appeals to the understandings and consciences of those whom he instructs ; yet amidst thousands of truths, tersely expressed, for easy recollection, when circumstances require, this volume, like its predecessor, abounds with lively illustrations and amusing anecdotes, preventing the possibility of weariness to the reader.   He concludes the Preface to the second volume by saying, " The whole Design is now perfected ; the World will see no more Volumes upon this Subject ; our Business being not to multiply Books, but to make the Advices compleat, that they may make the Tradesman so.   Farewell !"   There was singular truth in the above remark !   The world has required " no more volumes upon this subject ;" and making allowance for change in habits and manners, the instruction conveyed in " The Complete Tradesman," is now as seasonable, appropriate, and valuable, as when it received the author's valediction.

The *Daily Courant* of March 15th, 1726, advertises for the recovery of a small Pocket Book, *lost* on the 12th, between Blackwell Hall Bag-Gate, and Gerrard's Hall Inn, in Basing Lane ; containing eighteen Notes and Bills on several Persons, all of whose names follow.   I notice this because Defoe's name appears twice in the list.*   The Advertisement con-

		£	s.	d.
* A Note of John Burrows to Edward Mortimer . .		20	0	0
Do. of Daniel Defoe to John Clarke		18	0	0
Do. of George Hotchkis to Pile		20	0	0
Do. of Thomas Webb to Tiley		4	2	0
Do. of Richard Pangbourne to Mills . . .		16	0	0
Do. of Do. Do. to Townsend . .		10	0	0
Do. of Richard Brooks to Thurman		30	0	0
Do. of Thomas Reade to Frampton		20	0	0
A Bill by Stephen Hide on Charrington		8	0	0
Do. by John Motte on Ward		20	0	0
Do. by Daniel Wendow on Watson		20	0	0
Do. by Richard Arundel on Do.		17	10	0
Do. by Joseph Brookes on De Foe		50	0	0

cludes by saying that if they are brought to " Mr. George Willey, at the Blue Boar, in Friday Street; or, to Mr. Timothy Perry in Bucklersbury," half a Guinea Reward will be paid, " *and on Questions asked.*" The *Daily Post* of that day contains the same Advertisement, but in it our author's name is spelt " Daniel Deffoe."

This interesting fact tends to prove that Defoe was, at least occasionally, engaged in commercial transactions, at so late a period of his life. In all probability he purchased Broad Cloths for Merchants residing abroad ; paying for them with his own Bills ; and the lost Pocket Book was that of a West of England cloth manufacturer, or his Factor. The following explanation of the wholesale dealing in cloths, from p. 4 of the preface to our author's " Plan of the English Commerce," seems to throw a full light upon the matter. After stating that the master clothier does not know to what part of the world his goods are ultimately shipped, Defoe says, " He sends them up to London to the Factor, that sells them, whether at *Blackwell Hall,* or in his private Warehouse, and when sold he draws Bills for the Money ; there his circle meets." In the same page he also describes the mode of buying.

	£	s.	d.
A Bill by Ben. Stevens on Partridge	10	0	0
Do. by Do. on Do.	10	15	0
Do. by Richard Points on Will. Points . . .	12	0	0
Do. by Gillam on Osborne	10	0	0
Do. by Zealy on Fawson	8	0	0

CHAPTER XVII.

Remarks on Defoe's love of the Supernatural and Wonderful—" The Political History of the Devil"—" Mere Nature Delineated"—"An Essay upon Literature"—"A General History of Discoveries and Improvements"—Defoe writes " The Protestant Monastery"—Offers the Manuscript to the Journals and is rejected—Probable causes of this ; also for his assuming the name of Andrew Moreton, and ceasing to write for "Applebee's Journal"—Publishes his pamphlet with an explanatory Preface—"A System of Magick"—Spanish preparations against Gibraltar — Defoe publishes " The Evident Approach of a War"—" The Use and Abuse of the Marriage Bed"—" History and Reality of Apparitions"—"A New Family Instructor."

1726—27.

MR. WILSON disparaged Defoe by saying " the course of his studies, aided perhaps by his misfortunes," led him to speculate upon the subject of spirits, and their communication with the visible world. If by the course of his studies is intended his early education, it was doubtless similar to that of other youths, who never thought of writing on such subjects. If the words refer to any later period, his works are doubtless the result of his studies. His misfortunes had nothing to do with the matter. His belief in the existence of supernatural agency, for good or for evil,—as to the influence of such agency in the physical world,—and on the human mind,—was constant, from his youth to old age ; and was unaffected either by prosperity or adversity. Speaking phrenologically, Defoe possessed large perceptive faculties, with much Wit, Ideality, Wonder, Eventuality, and Causality ; all governed by Conscientiousness and Veneration. His convictions, as to the existence and operation of good and evil spirits, were closely connected with his religion ; and when he declares, that " those who have prevailed with themselves to believe there is no Devil, soon come to it, *That there is no God*," he does not intend to utter an abstract dogma,—but speaks of active influences exercised in, and upon, all circumstances of life. A mind like that of Defoe was inclined to seize upon everything wonderful and supernatural ; and to embellish or expand the original account.

But in every such excursion he would carefully abstain from what was contrary to absolute truth, and avoid every appearance of profanity ; what he wrote for amusement would tend to eradicate ignorant delusions ; that which engaged the attention must also be fraught with some instruction ; the story must inculcate the doctrine of a Divine Providence, overruling, on behalf of those who follow its guidance, all the influence of spiritual enemies ; and, must teach its readers to contemplate another world, where the good and the evil are for ever separated.

When Defoe therefore turned his thoughts to the composition of three treatises on supernatural subjects, he simply followed the suggestions of a peculiar natural disposition, which had already manifested itself in many of his previous works. Not to mention here, his accounts of apparitions, or actual perceptions of good and evil spirits, I may advert to those strong impulses of the mind, by which he believed himself directed by a good spirit to do, or not to do, any particular act ; and of which he says, " I am a Witness to many of these Things, as well in my own Life, as in my Observation of others." I have noticed in this Memoir, one turning point in his life ; when, about thirty years of age, he was induced to refuse an offer of employment abroad, that would probably have prevented all his literary productions. An impulse told him that *Providence had other work for him to do !* A similar influence on his future life occurred in 1715, when he was impelled to *Write to the Judge !* From that originated the appointment to which the world is indebted for the Journalistic Writings now first published under his name. In the Preface to " The Family Instructor," written the same year, he states his firm belief that *the Spirit of God directed his hand in the Work.* In the " Life of Duncan Campbell,"—also in his " Vision of the Angelick World,"—and, in " The Friendly Demon,"—he has stated his views on the converse of Spirits with Mankind. If it should be alleged that he was credulous and superstitious, I reply, that the charge, if applicable at all, is not so in a reproachful sense ;—he received the truths of Revelation with the simple faith of a child ;—and his works show, not only that he was " mighty in the Scriptures," but that they were, to him, the ultimate appeal in all controversy, and his refuge in all trials and difficulties. He rejected the cold formality of a religion that referred all things in the government of the Universe to the operation of fixed and general laws. His God was one who could hear him when he cried, and answer him; he wished to be led by the hand of Providence; and, as he believed that his Father had sent forth " Ministering Spirits to minister to those who should be heirs of Salvation," he desired to recognise their beneficent influence. Conversely, to a mind like his, belief in the malevolent influence of evil spirits was a necessary consequence. It cannot be doubted that this belief exerted a most favourable influence upon him; that, with conscious rectitude, it caused him to rise above the malice of men,—reconciled him to many distressing events,—and enabled him to pass through all the vicissitudes of his long and laborious life, confiding in a Power unseen, but ever present, and able to protect and guide him.

His convictions on these matters were not singular, but were entertained by many of his contemporary authors, Beaumont, Aubrey, Glanvil, Hutchinson, and other learned and pious men. The great mass of the people, of all ranks, believed, at that time, not only in the active agency of spirits and apparitions; but also, in witchcraft, astrology, second-sight, soothsaying, fortune-telling, and many other pretended supernatural powers. It was no part of Defoe's belief that man could command or control, at his own will, the agency of good or evil spirits, or apparitions; and he therefore opposed, and ridiculed with his powerful satire, the jugglery of conjurors, and the incantations of those who professed, as magicians and wise men, to exercise such authority. In this respect his writings are calculated to divert, and yet to instruct, by dispelling many superstitions from the minds of the ignorant.

It may be confessed, that in some of the stories related, he has allowed his fancy to carry him a great length; and also, that some of his phenomena do not well accord with what is now known of the philosophy of the human mind; but the greatest demand upon his reader's credulity, is made with such inimitable gravity, and verisimilitude of fact, as to create satisfaction in being so agreeably deceived. In no instance does he suffer his imagination to conduct him so far into the world of spirits as to pass the confines of what might be innocently read and believed, by any Catholic and orthodox Christian. The progress of civilization is gradual, but slow. Education

[FRONTISPIECE TO "THE HISTORY OF THE DEVIL", 1726]

has effected much, since Defoe lived, to enlighten the minds of the humbler classes in all secular and material knowledge ; but the disposition to lift up the veil that conceals the world of spirits, lies deep in the heart of our common nature, and is difficult of access to external culture and improvement. Hence— what are called the occult sciences, " good and bad luck," and numerous other delusions are still believed in ; while witchcraft and ghosts have only given place to " Spiritualism," and other similar evils.   Defoe saw the difficulty of effectually separating the positively good,—because divine part of his subject,—from the merely innocent and instructive;—and both, from the pernicious, because devilish part ; yet he attempted it in the three treatises we have to notice,—and with greater success than any other writer.   The books were intended to be read by the people ; and therefore, while they show much research and learning, it is gene- rally presented in a form easy to be understood.   They contain very little of science, and no attempts to gratify morbid curiosity, by improper speculation as to the secrets of nature.   He could not have selected a subject more likely in itself to be popular ; or one of which it might be said more truly, that depraved ideas among the people urgently needed correction.   Morality was the science of Defoe ; and, knowing the credulity of the ignorant, he wisely gave it a useful, instructive, and religious direction.

The first of these Works was published on the 7th of May 1726, and is entitled, " The Political History of the Devil, as well ancient as modern : In Two Parts.   Part I. Containing a State of the Devil's Circumstances, and the various Turns of his Affairs, from his Expulsion out of Heaven, to the Creation of Man ; with Remarks on the several Mistakes concerning the Reason and Manner of his Fall.   Also his Proceedings with Mankind ever since Adam, to the first planting of the Chris- tian Religion in the World.   Part II. Containing his more private Conduct, down to the present Times : His Government, his Appearances, his Manner of Working, and the Tools he works with.

> " Bad as he is, the Devil may be abus'd,
>   Be falsly charg'd, and causelessly accus'd,
>   When Men, unwilling to be blam'd alone,
>   Shift off those crimes on him which are their own."

London :   Printed for T. Warner, at the Black Boy in Pater- noster Row. 1726."

The following, placed after the titlepage, will suffice to show the nice discernment of propriety in the Author. " It is not the easiest Thing in the Case before me, to determine who has the most Right to a Dedication of this Work. Ancient Usage would have directed a solemn Author to address these Sheets to the great Majesty of Heaven, in congratulation of his glorious Victory over the Devil and his Angels; but I decline that Method as profane. The same Reasons forbid me addressing to Him who conquer'd him on Earth ; and who, when the Devil was so insolent as to assault Him, made him fly like a vanquish'd Rebel, with but the Word, *Get thee behind me.* I had then some Thoughts of inscribing it to Satan himself, but I did not really know how to relish holding a Parley with the Devil, and talking to him in the first Person ; nay, and as it were, making all my Readers to do so too; and besides, as I knew there was so very little in the whole Work that Satan would be pleased with, I was lothe to Compliment him while I was exposing him. These Difficulties presenting, I think the giving my Reasons for the making no Dedication, is Dedication enough."

The second Edition, which is an entire reprint, was published on the 20th of April in the following year. The word " Political" is omitted from the title and the head-lines; and a Preface is substituted in the place of what I have quoted above. In this Preface, he says, " The Subject is singular, and it has been handled after a singular Manner. The wise World has been pleased with it, the merry World has been diverted with it, and the ignorant World has been taught by it; none but the malicious part of the World has been offended at it : Who can wonder, that when the Devil is not pleased, *his Friends should be angry ?* The Author affirms, and has good Vouchers for it, that the whole Tenor of the Work is solemn, calculated to promote serious Religion, and capable of being improv'd in a religious manner. But he does not think that we are bound never to speak of the Devil but with an Air of Terror, as if we were always afraid of him." After reciting some other objections, he concludes by saying, " It is enough to me that the Devil himself is not pleased with my Work, and less with the Design of it; let the Devil and all his fellow Complainers stand on one side, and the honest, well

meaning, charitable World, who approve my Work on the
other, and I'll tell Noses with Satan, if he dares."

I quote the following paragraph by Defoe from *Applebee's
Journal*, of the 18th of December, 1725, as the origin of the
next Work to be considered in chronological order :—" They
write from Hanover, December 11, that there has been presented to his Majesty a young Man about fifteen years of
Age, who was found in the neighbouring Forest of Hamelon ;
where he walked and ran on his Feet and Hands, and climb'd
the Trees like a four-footed animal. Not having the Use of
Speech, it cannot be known how or when he came thither,
where he lived only on Herbs and Moss. They began to
accustom him by Degrees to the usual human Nurriture, and
the King has given Orders to instruct him as much as possible." This was the first account of the celebrated Peter,
the Wild Boy, who was shortly afterward brought to England,
where he lived until February 1785, but never showed signs
of reason, or could be taught to speak. Dean Swift noticed
him in a pamphlet entitled, " It cannot rain but it pours,"
and he was also made the subject of some of Lord
Monboddo's singular speculations. Defoe was one of the first
to give a full account of this singular human phenomenon, in
a thick pamphlet published on the 23rd of July 1726, and
entitled, " Mere Nature Delineated : Or a Body without a
Soul. Being Observations upon the young Forester lately
brought to Town from Germany. With suitable Applications.
Also a brief Dissertation upon the Usefulness and Necessity of
Fools, whether Political or Natural. London : printed for T.
Warner, at the Black Boy, in Paternoster Row, 1726. Price
1s. 6d." Beyond the circumstances in which this Boy was
discovered, and the result of a personal visit to him, Defoe
had no facts upon which to write so large a production as
this pamphlet. There were however abundance of contradictory reports, and many hypotheses as to the boy's origin
and previous life ; and to these Defoe addressed himself, detecting and disproving such as appeared improbable,—admitting
that he was found in the situation and condition described,—
but leaving all else in the same uncertainty as he found it.
He rightly argued, from the severity of the climate, the season

of the year, his want of clothing, shelter, and food, that it was not possible he could long have existed in that state.   But he was not disposed to consider the boy an idiot; because he thought he saw signs of reason, and concluded him capable of instruction.   In this, our author was theorising, and created a difficulty for which he could not account; namely, how the young Forester should be destitute of speech unless he had been so exposed for a considerable time.   Subsequent events disproved the theory, and disposed of the difficulty; the boy was an idiot, and could not be taught anything.   He had, in all probability, just before wandered into the Forest, and when his friends found him so well provided for by King George I., they remained silent, and did not claim him, from a conviction that such a course would be the best both for the boy and themselves.

This is perhaps the most speculative and excursive of Defoe's Works.   He considers the possibility of thinking, without a knowledge of words, expressive of our ideas of sensible objects; and says that this boy " seems to be the very Creature which the learned World has, for many Years past, pretended to wish for, viz., one that being kept entirely from human Society, so as never to have heard any one speak, must therefore either not speak at all; or, if he did form any Speech to himself, then they should know what language Nature would first form for Mankind."   He was at that time preparing his work on the origin of Letters, and he states here the basis of his argument, namely, that " Divine Art dictated Letters originally upon Mount Sinai."   He introduces the character of modern hand-writing, and has a paragraph on the calligraphy of recent English Monarchs.   From the case of this wild boy he draws some reflections on the importance of education, and the difficulty of teaching those who have grown up in entire ignorance.   He moralises on the sad condition of this poor youth, and then proceeds to comment upon the follies and weakness of the times.   In various parts of the book,—but especially in that on Fools,—his sarcasms are severely personal on Dean Swift, and on the Duke of Wharton.   In one place, he calls the former—" the Copper Farthing Author," in allusion to the Dean's pamphlet against Wood's Copper Coinage. Returning to the attack he says,—" he that can Preach and read Prayers in the Morning, write Bawdy in the Afternoon, banter Heaven and Religion and write profanely at Night; and then read Prayers and Preach again the next Morning, and so on in a due Rotation of extremes, is much fitter than I am for turning the Tears of the Unhappy into a Ballad, and making a mock of human Misery." His onslaughts on the eccentric and profligate Duke, are thrice repeated in different forms, one of which, is a long quotation from a pretended Manuscript, entitled—*An Essay upon the extraordinary Accomplishments, and the particular Felicity of those, who have made a Proficiency in the Art of having no meaning.*

Although Defoe had contributed so much to the literature of his country, and would, as a biblical student, feel interested in any inquiry into the early history of letters, we should scarcely have expected him to take the subject into his own hands. As if to show, however, that the whole range of human knowledge was within his grasp, he did so, in a work to which he had already alluded, in the last noticed pamphlet. The title is, " An Essay upon Literature : or, an Enquiry into the Antiquity and Original of Letters ; Proving, That the two Tables, written by the Finger of God in Mount Sinai, was the first Writing in the World ; and that all other Alphabets derive from the Hebrew. With a Short View of the Methods made use of by the Ancients, to supply the want of Letters before, and improve the use of them, after they were known. London. Printed for Thomas Bowles, Printseller, near to the Chapter-House, St. Paul's Churchyard ; John Clark, Bookseller, under the Piazzas, Royal Exchange ; and John Bowles, Printseller, over against Stocks Market. 1726." The subject was one little known to the general public, and of great curiosity to the learned. It involved important consequences ; and, as there then existed few books on the subject, and scarcely any in the English language, much research and deep thought were required. Our author succeeded in producing a work, original in its plan,—excellent in its keeping the leading idea, through the successive parts, before the minds of his readers ; and containing much instruction within a narrow compass. The book exhibits the learning of our author in the dead languages, yet his peculiar talent has made it as entertaining as it is instruc-

tive. Succeeding writers have more amply discussed the subject, but this little volume is well worthy of being reprinted.
It is now amongst the rarest of his works.

Defoe had for some months ceased to be connected with
Applebee's Journal, and probably with all newspapers; so far
as any engagement was concerned. This was probably one of
the reasons why his next work appeared in the serial form of a
monthly publication, which could be proceeded with in the intervals heretofore allotted to the journals. Change of labour
must have been the only relaxation of his mind, during the
composition of his more weighty treatises ; and he had now
reached an age when long-continued habits could not be easily
or safely changed. The "Essay on Literature" had drawn him,
not only into the History of Letters, but also of writing, printing, and the manufacture of Paper, and other materials connected with the existing state of literature. From this point,
his view must have widened out, until the first result was made
public in a thick pamphlet, entitled, "A General History of
Discoveries and Improvements in Useful Arts ; Particularly in
the great Branches of Commerce, Navigation, and Plantation,
in all Parts of the Known World. A work which may Entertain the Curious with the view of their present State ; prompt
the indolent to retrieve those Inventions that are Neglected,
and animate the diligent to advance and perfect what may be
thought wanting. To be continued Monthly. Numb. I. for
October. London. Printed for J. Roberts, at the Oxford
Arms, in Warwick Lane. 1726. Price one Shilling." This
work was continued to Number IV., published in January 1727,
and containing an index to the whole work. It makes no pretension to science or philosophy; but, treating the various
steps in the progress of civilization, as Discoveries and Improvements, respectively, he gives their history from the Flood
down to his own time. The whole forms an octavo volume
full of valuable information, agreeable from its numerous and
apt illustrations, displaying great knowledge of ancient geography and of Trade and Commerce, during the early periods
of the World's History. As very few subjects were ever considered by Defoe without reference to Religion, so this contains many passages from the Bible, quoted in support of his

statements, and there is a sweet and simple truthfulness pervading the book, that makes it very fascinating to the reader.

Writing next on a subject of social and domestic interest, our author reassumed his pseudonym of Andrew Moreton; and the preface to his publication greatly strengthens my conclusion that he had adopted such signature for concealment, *in all matters likely to be noticed by any of the public Journals.* He first used it in June 1725, which was the earliest occasion of its apparent necessity; after his life had been put in jeopardy by the murderous attack of Mr. Mist. I have stated my impression that the assault, and subsequent abuse, of which Defoe complained, was the consequence of Mist having discovered our author's long existing connection with the Government. Although Defoe's complaints of such abuse and ingratitude were published in *Applebee's Journal*, yet, as Mr. Mist's name was not mentioned, it may be fairly concluded that Mr. Applebee was then ignorant, what circumstances were alluded to, or the cause thereof. After the conduct of which Mist had shown himself capable, it is not probable that he would conceal his animosity. His hatred would become more intense after Defoe had disarmed him, and given him his life; and we are told the abuse was continued. I think that Defoe's connection with the Government became generally known to the proprietors of the public papers, through the malignant agency of Mr. Mist, and that this caused the termination of the connection between Defoe and Applebee, on the 12th of March 1726. It is a strange proof of the suddenness of this change, that the *Journal* of that day contains two " Letters Introductory." The former is by a new Author or Editor, who signs the name of " Barnaby Whitelock," and dates from " Will's Coffee-house, March 8." He urges Mr. Applebee to alter the management and writing of his Paper, and reflects upon the quality of past articles. Then immediately follows the " Letter Introductory" of Defoe, which I suppose was in type before the rupture. He continues,—and leaves unfinished,—a series of Articles on the probabilities of Peace and War; but from that date, I find nothing more from his pen in *Applebee's Journal,* excepting a Letter signed " Andrew Moreton," in the Number for the 21st of September 1728. He there complains of another person having appropriated his *Scheme for the Prevention of Street Robberies ;* and the letter appears, by the editorial remarks, to be inserted as only an act of public justice, to one who is treated as a stranger.

The pamphlet occasioning these remarks was published on the 19th of November 1726, and Defoe has added a preface of six pages, for the purpose of explaining, why the work was printed separately, instead of appearing, as he had intended, in the form of a Letter to some Journal. His explanation throws light on the subject we are considering ; though no posthumous clearing up of the matter could have been contemplated by him. The desire to benefit his fellow-creatures was still as strong as ever ; and this tract was written without any view of profit to himself. The preface says, " I hope the Reader will excuse the Vanity of an over officious Old Man, if like Cato, I enquire whether or no before I go hence and be no more, I can yet do anything for the Service of my Country." A tone of depression is cast over the preface, and he says, " it has been the Fate of much better Men than myself, to be despised when living, tho' revered when dead." From the following I conclude that he who would have been gladly offered payment, in the early part of the same year, for anything he had pleased to write, had been recently insulted by the proposal that he should pay, as an Advertisement, for the insertion of this tract in some of the Journals. " Alas! I have but small Health, and little Leisure to turn Author, being now in my 67th year, almost worn out with Age and Sickness. The Old Man cannot trouble you long ; take then in good part his best Intentions, and impute his Defects to Age and Weakness. Assure yourself, gentle Reader, I had not published my Project in this Pamphlet, could I have got it inserted in any of the *Journals, without Feeing the Journalists or Publishers*. I cannot but have the Vanity to think, they might as well have inserted what I sent them, *Gratis*, as many Things I have since seen in their Papers. But I have not only had the Mortification to find what I sent rejected, but to lose my Originals, not having taken Copies of what I wrote. However, to justify my Complaints to the World, I shall, in a proper Place, let them know the Substance of what was rejected, and by whom." The gratuitous offer of his manuscript proves that the hostility was not on Defoe's side; and the rejection, that there was a general feeling against him amongst the Journals. I can conceive of no other way of accounting for this great change than that already given, nor any other reason why Defoe should have assumed the name of Andrew Moreton, for certain literary purposes, at the same time. In the instance before us, I believe the manuscript was rejected, because, notwithstanding the signature of Andrew Moreton, the handwriting was known to be that of Defoe. I have in an earlier part of this Memoir endeavoured impartially to consider his moral conduct, in secretly connecting himself, under government, with the management of Tory Journals; and have concluded that he placed himself, by so doing, in a questionable position; but that, in such position, he greatly served his country,—at a critical period, when such services were necessary,—by promoting the settlement and security of the new dynasty, and by the suppression of Jacobite treason and sedition. He also served the *Journals* with which he so connected himself; by keeping them, as far as possible, from breaking the laws; and, in his own words, " knocking their heads against stone walls." In all this, he had never swerved from the political, moral, or religious principles of his early life; but I am bound in candour to admit, that as the success of his labours depended on his connection with the government being concealed from the proprietors of the Journals; his position, however much they were benefited by it, was a false one, so far as they were concerned; and the *dénouement*, we have been considering, brought him the painful humiliation he has above so feelingly described.

The pamphlet that led to this explanation is entitled, " The Protestant Monastery: or, a Complaint against the Brutality of the present Age. Particularly the Pertness and Insolence of our Youth to aged Persons. With a Caution to People in Years, how they give the Staff out of their own Hands, and leave themselves to the Mercy of others. Concluding with a Proposal for erecting a Protestant Monastery, where Persons of small Fortunes may end their Days in Plenty, Ease and Credit, without burthening their Relations, or accepting Publick Charities. By Andrew Moreton, Esq. Author of Every-Body's Business is No-Body's Business. London:

Printed for W. Meadows, at the Angel in Cornhill; and sold by J. Roberts, in Warwick Lane; E. Nutt, under the Royal Exchange; A. Dodd, without Temple Bar; and N. Blanford at Charing Cross.   1727.   Price Sixpence." Having stated the day of Publication, it will be seen that the title-page was post-dated, or the pamphlet was re-issued.   It is a short but faithful complaint and remonstrance against the too common undutiful conduct of children towards their aged parents; with a confession that the injudicious management of parents, in suffering their sons and daughters to assume, prematurely, the liberty and authority of upgrown persons, is a great cause of the evil.   His remarks and advice on everything connected with the subject are excellent; but there is no authority for Mr. Wilson's statement, that Defoe's own case is concerned in the Pamphlet.   I admit that he had not been on friendly terms with his second son, but Benjamin Norton Defoe was now about forty years of age,—he was engaged upon the *London Journal,* and resided away from his father's home.   They were perhaps still estranged, and had no intercourse with each other; but the father had comfort in his daughters and second wife, at his own Mansion in Stoke-Newington, where he continued to reside, in easy circumstances, at the time when this pamphlet was published.   His sole object in writing it was, that he might appropriately introduce his project for a " Protestant Monastery,"—which was a very valuable suggestion for the comfort of aged persons; and includes many features of the modern establishments denominated *Homes for decayed Gentlewomen,* &c.   The proposal of Defoe was, that the Institution should be independent, and governed by the resident members; each of them contributing four hundred pounds to the capital Stock.

After my preliminary remarks on our author's " History of the Devil," a brief notice will suffice for the second of his supernatural treatises, which, though dated 1727, was published on the 19th of December 1726, and is entitled " A System of Magick; or, a History of the Black Art. Being an Historical Account of Mankind's most early Dealing with the Devil; and how the Acquaintance on both sides first began.

Eberlein del.

J. Vand Gucht Sculp

FRONTISPIECE TO "THE HISTORY OF MAGICK", 1727.

> ' Our Magick, now, commands the Troops of Hell,
> The Devil himself submits to Charm and Spell.
> The Conj'rer, in his Circles and his Rounds
> Just whistles up his Spirits, as Men do Hounds.
> Th' obsequious Devil, obeys the Sorcerer's Skill,
> The Mill turns round the Horse, that first turns round the Mill.'

London: Printed and sold by J. Roberts in Warwick Lane. 1727." It was advertised as being " By the Author of the Political History of the Devil," and is undoubtedly the reciprocal of that work :—the one expatiates on the transactions of the Devil with the visible world ; and the other gives an account of mankind's dealings with the Devil.

In the outset of his preface he guards himself against the supposition that he can sanction juggling, conjuring, and the low arts by which mankind are deluded and cheated. " If by a *System* of this terrible Thing called Magick, my Readers should expect a Body of the Black Art as a Science, a Book of Rules for Instruction in the Practice, or a Magical Grammar for Introduction to Young Beginners, all I can say to such is, that they will be mistaken." He then goes on to denounce the modern practices of Mountebanks and so called Cunning Men, saying, " 'Tis a strange Piece of Art where Fools cheat Fools, and the Blind and Ignorant are imposed upon by the Blind and the Ignorant." He considers that this Itch in the brains of the people, to run after impostors, who defraud them of their money, can only be reached by ridicule and satire ; and, to expose and run down the pretended Magic of the age, is the object of his work ; starting the subject " from its Original, and pursuing it to the end of its Prospect." He says, " Let no Man be disgusted at the good Account we give of the Original and Wisdom of the Magi ; their Magick was truly Science, whereas ours is neither Magick nor Science, but a kind of Devilism ; a practice carried on by Men that would be wicked, if they did not want Wit ; and are no otherwise Harmless, than as they happen to be Fools." This will give an idea of the scope of the volume, which exhibits great research in its historical part,—while its morality and religion are derived from, and accordant with the Scriptures. The turn he has given to the work, namely that the first Magi were wise and honest ;—those of the middle ages madmen and rogues ;—and, the modern practitioners wicked fools, is as

amusing as true.   The stories he has collected together, to
illustrate his subject, are well chosen, and related with admirable humour.   The reader will find some curious discussions
on the corruptions of religious worship, and the origin of
witchcraft and idolatry ; with remarks upon the follies they
have occasioned, and the knavery that produced them.   He
levels all the force of his satire upon the deluders, and deluded
lovers of the Black Art ; and, in his zeal for religion, uses great
severity against the Atheists and Sceptics of his own day.
There is much value in his delineations of the manners of
former times, written in a popular stile, with a useful and
moral purpose ; and the work may always be read with pleasure
and profit.   A Second Edition, with additions, was published
on the 16th of January 1731.

In the recently discovered writings of Defoe will be found
some paragraphs of news relating to the intermarriages between
the Royal Families of France and Spain.   Some of the particulars are very interesting, and all of them pitiable, so far as
the poor little children, who were thus attempted to be vic-
timised for State purposes, are concerned.   All the schemes,
however, of the Regent of France, to unite the two countries
more closely by these Baby marriages, were rendered abortive ;
and, shortly after his death, were productive of a war between
the two countries.   As soon as the young King of France
became old enough to think for himself, he disliked the Infant
Queen provided for him by his uncle, and sent her back to
Madrid ; announcing shortly afterward, his intention to marry
the daughter of Stanislaus late King of Poland.   This greatly
exasperated Spain, and war between them became imminent
about the close of the year 1726.   The Alliance between Germany, France, and England, under the Treaties of Vienna and
Hanover, would draw the latter into the quarrel, and Spain
appeared quite willing to encounter the force of three great
kingdoms.   Madrid was then the asylum of the Dukes of
Ormond and Wharton, as well as most of the leading English
Jacobites ; and, though the British Ambassador had not left
that Capital in the middle of January 1727, a Spanish Camp,
was already formed at St. Roche for the purpose of besieging
Gibraltar.   It was under these circumstances that Defoe again

dipped his pen in politics, and published an able and patriotic
Tract, entitled, " The Evident Approach of a War ; and something of the Necessity of it, in Order to Establish Peace, and
Preserve Trade. *Pax Quæritur Bello.* To which is added, an
Exact Plan and Description of the Bay and City of Gibraltar.
London : Printed and Sold by J. Roberts in Warwick Lane ;
and A. Dodd in the Strand. 1727. Price 1s. 6d." He remarks
on the strange political madness, that those should be most
eager for war, who are least able to carry it on ; and, that it
might be said to the Spaniards, " as the Turks once said to the
Muscovites, that they hardly knew how to make War, and
were not worth making Peace with." He looks at the question also from a commercial point of view ; and, speaking of the
dependance of Spain upon other nations, he says, " Not any of
their Priests have a Cassock, nor the Nuns a Veil, nor the
Gentlemen a Cloak, but what is of foreign Manufacture." He
thinks that Exchange Alley and the Stock-Jobbers are assisting the agitation, for their own advantage ; and, in reply to
the inquiries that were being made everywhere, says, " If they
ask us here, whether it is Peace or War ? we answer, with the
Story in the Gospel,—The Emperor is of Age, *Ask him !*
The King of Spain is of Age, *Ask him !*" On the whole, he
seems incredulous, that Spain could be so infatuated as to embark in a war with the three greatest powers in the world.

There has probably been no practical improvement whatever, as to the ill circumstances too frequently leading to, or
arising out of, the Marriage Union, since the days of Defoe ;
yet, what is called modern refinement, and delicacy of expression, makes it difficult for his biographer to do justice to a
treatise on the subject by him, inculcating the highest
morality, and written with great seriousness and force of argument. Not a word in his book is intended to pander to im-
purity ; but on the contrary, his standard of matrimonial
delicacy of conduct is placed so high, as to be rather aimed at,
than attained. Defoe was a sincere advocate for the state of
matrimony ; and considered that when rightly entered into, it
was the highest condition of human felicity. To reason
against the institution from the numerous unhappy matches,
he says, " is only arguing the Ignorance and Corruption of

Mankind ; which, as they are the Cause, so they are discovered
in the unhappy Consequences.   Did men expect Happiness in
a married Condition, they would begin it and end it after
another manner, and take greater thought before they engaged
in it."   The matter of the work is excellent ; the illustrative
stories and dialogues, entertaining and instructive,—the satire
is free from any admixture of levity,—and the moral so pure
and convincing, that the reader is constrained to do justice to
the piety and benevolence of the author.   But the difficulty
of the biographer is not removed by these admirable qualities ;
—the diction is that of more than a century ago, and many
words were then commonly used that are now rarely heard
among those who call themselves polite ; nor was it possible,
exercising all the caution and delicacy of which he was capable,
that the author could do justice to his subject, without relating
circumstances, from which the viciously disposed might stir up
the impurities already existing in their own minds.   I am of
opinion that while virtuous and pious readers, of both sexes,
who have attained mature years, may read this book with great
profit ; yet the advantage of its *general* circulation among
adults is questionable ; and it is, I think, by no means a book
to be placed in the hands of young unmarried persons of the
present age.

The first publication of this treatise took place on the 30th
of January 1727, when the titlepage commenced, " Conjugal
Lewdness : or Matrimonial Whoredom," &c. &c., but this
being considered offensive to delicacy, the sale was suspended
until the title could be cancelled, and a less objectionable one
substituted.   This done, the work was reissued on the 10th of
June following, entitled, " A Treatise concerning the Use and
Abuse of the Marriage Bed : shewing I. The Nature of Matrimony ; its Sacred Original, and the true Meaning of its
Institution.   II. The gross Abuse of Matrimonial Chastity,
from the Wrong Notions which have possessed the World, degenerating even to Whoredom.   III. The Diabolical Practice
of Attempting to prevent Child-bearing by Physical Preparations.   IV. The fatal Consequences of clandestine or forced
Marriages, thro' the Persuasion, Interest, or Influence of
Parents and Relations, to wed the Person they have no Love
for, but often times an Aversion to. V. Of unequal Matches,

as to Disproportion of Age ; and how such, many ways, occasion a Matrimonial Whoredom.   VI. How married Persons may be guilty of Conjugal Lewdness, and, that a Man may, in effect, make a Whore of his own Wife. Also, many other Particulars of Family Concern.

> ' Loose Thoughts, at first, like subterranean Fires,
> Burn inward, smothering, with unchaste Desires;
> But getting Vent, to Rage and Fury turn,
> Burst in Volcanoes, and like Etna burn ;
> The Heat increases as the Flames aspire,
> And turns the solid Hills to liquid Fire.
> So sensual Flames, when raging in the Soul,
> First vitiate all the Parts, then fire the Whole ;
> Burn up the Bright, the Beauteous, the Sublime,
> And turn our lawful Pleasures into Crime.'

London : Printed for T. Warner, at the Black-Boy in Paternoster-Row.   1727.   Price 5s."

I conclude my notice of the work with an Extract from the Preface, which shows that he had some misgiving as to the propriety of publishing it, and only did so after long and solemn reflection, actuated by purely conscientious motives. " It is almost thirty years since the Author began this Piece. He has all that Time heard, with a just Concern, the Complaints of good Men upon the hateful Subject.   The Grave and the Sober, the Lovers of Virtue and of Religion, have, with Grief, express'd themselves upon the growing Scandal ; and they have often press'd him to finish and bring out this Reproof ; and have join'd with his Opinion of the Justice of it. Sincerely aiming at the Reformation of the Guilty, and despising all unjust Reproaches from a vicious Age, he closes his Days with this Satyr ; which he is so far from seeing Cause to be ashamed of that he hopes he shall not, where he is going to, Account for it.   At least, he can Appeal to that Judge, who he is soon to come before, that as he has done it with an upright Intention, for the good of all Mankind, so he has used his utmost Endeavour to perform it in a Manner the least liable to Reflection ; and, in his Judgment, the most likely to answer the true End of it, viz., the Reformation of the Crime.   And with this Satisfaction, he comfortably prays for its Success."

The third and last of Defoe's Treatises on supernatural

subjects was published on the 18th of March, and is entitled,
" An Essay on the History and Reality of Apparitions. Being
an Account of what they are, and what they are not. As,
also, how we may distinguish between the Apparitions of Good
and Evil Spirits, and how we ought to behave to them. With
a great variety of surprizing and diverting Examples, never
publish'd before.

> ' By Death transported to th' Eternal Shore,
> Souls so removed re-visit us no more :
> Engross'd with Joys of a superior kind,
> They leave the trifling thoughts of Life behind.'

London : Printed and sold by J. Roberts in Warwick Lane.
1727." The subject was a popular one, but the title was not
happily selected, and probably a very large impression had been
printed. A shilling pamphlet on ghosts would have found a
multitude of readers, and perhaps have quickly run through
several Editions ; but the thick and apparently unattractive
volume, price five shillings, seems to have hung on the bookseller's hands. To remedy this, our author assumed again the
name of Andrew Moreton, wrote an entirely new titlepage,
and the work was republished on the 23rd of November 1728.
The sheets are those of the first edition, but the title is much
fuller than before,—" The Secrets of the Invisible World Disclos'd : or, an Universal History of Apparitions, Sacred and
Prophane, Under all Denominations ; whether Angelical, Diabolical, or Human Souls departed. Shewing,—I. Their various
Returns to this World ; with sure Rules to Know, by their
Manner of Appearing, if they are Good or Evil Ones. II.
The Differences of the Apparitions of Ancient and Modern
Times ; and an Enquiry into the Scriptural Doctrine of Spirits.
III. The many Species of Apparitions ; their real Existence,
and Operations by Divine Appointment. IV. The Nature of
seeing Ghosts before, and after, Death ; and how we should
behave towards them. V. The Effects of Fancy, Vapours,
Dreams, Hyppo, and of real or imaginary Appearances. VI.
A Collection of the most Authentic Relations of Apparitions, particularly that surprising One attested by the
learned Dr. Scott. By Andrew Moreton, Esq. Adorn'd
with Cuts.

Frontispiece   *J. V. der Gucht Sculp*

[FRONTISPIECE TO "THE HISTORY OF APPARITIONS" 1727.]

' Spirits in whatsoever Shape they chuse,
Dilated or Condensed, Bright or Obscure,
Can execute their Airy Purposes,
And works of Love or Enmity fulfil.'—*Milton.*

London. Printed for J. Peele, &c. 1728." On the 13th of
February 1729, it was again republished by J. Clarke, A.
Millar, and J. Green, the title remaining the same as in the
second issue.

Defoe had many years before proved his power of giving a
vivid appearance of reality to accounts of Apparitions; and this
Volume contains, among the Cases he has collected together,
instances that his skill had not declined with his increasing
years. He also very clearly states his belief in the converse
" between our Spirits cased up in Flesh, and the Spirits un-
embodied; who inhabit the unknown Mazes of the invisible
World; those Coasts which our Geography cannot describe;
who between Somewhere and Nowhere dwell, none of us know
where, and yet we are sure must have Locality, and for aught
we know, are very near us." He supposes them to be an
intermediate order of beings between angels and men, possessing limited powers, and that they are the immediate agents
in dreams, premonitions, and secret hints, " calling upon Men
to seek for Direction and Counsel from that Hand who alone
can both direct and deliver." He altogether denies, as contrary to the teaching of the Bible, that ghosts and apparitions are the departed souls of those they are said to represent, and says, " Could Souls departed come back to demand
redress of Grievances, and to put Men in Mind of the injustice
done them, I doubt it would make but sad Work among some
Families who now possess large Estates. But much as I think
there is Reason to apprehend the Prayers of the oppressed
Widow and Orphan, I must acknowledge, I see no Reason to
be afraid of their Ghosts." He supports his opinion that good
spirits sometimes assume visible appearances, from what is recorded both in the Old and New Testaments. Whatever may
be thought of his argument, the volume abounds with interesting information; amusing stories alternate with grave and just
reflections, but each in its order, and proper place. If he
makes his readers laugh at some of his old wives' tales and
superstitious dialogues, he is always serious, and reverential

when he touches on scriptural authority, or that part of his
subject bordering on the eternal world.   When he tells apparently incredible stories, he says less of their authenticity than
of the morals they are intended to convey ;—and urges that
there is more to apprehend from within, than from any external supernatural appearance.   " Conscience indeed," he says,
" is itself a frightful Apparition, and is a Ghost to him sleeping
or waking.   Nor is it the least testimony of an invisible
World, that there is such a Drummer in the Soul, that can
beat an Alarm when he pleases, and so loud as no other Noise
can drown it, no Power silence it, no Mirth allay it, no Bribe
corrupt it."   His consideration of the whole subject, brought
him to the conclusion, that, " There's no scorning the Terrors
of a Messenger from the other World, but by a settled Composure of the Soul, founded on the basis of Peace and Innocence, or Peace and Penitence, which is in effect all one.
This is the only Face that a Man can hold up to the Devil ;
and with it he can boldly talk to, and despise him."

The mission of Defoe, as a teacher of the highest morality,
—the Truth as it is in Jesus,—was not yet fully accomplished.
It had become common for young persons of good families to
travel abroad, in France, Spain, and Italy ; and many such
had, through inexperience, and the sensuous glare of high
ritual, become perverted from the Protestant Faith ; or, on the
other hand, from witnessing how little influence such a religion
produced on personal morality, had cast off belief in the Scriptures.   Several eminent clergymen of the Church of England,
and a very large number of Dissenting ministers, and their
congregations, had, within a few years, abandoned the doctrine
of the Divine Trinity, and become Socinians.   Many of these,
and their families, Defoe had long known and esteemed.   The
controversy was still going on ; and he saw with pain the
dangers that beset the path of youth, at the critical moment
when each began to walk alone on the journey of life.   In his
eyes Popery was blind Superstition, decked in fine colours to
entice the unthinking ; and on the other hand, he saw what
to him was a grievous heresy, that exalted mere human reason,
until it would depose the Saviour from his Throne.   It was a
wise thought therefore of our author, but a somewhat difficult

task, to prepare a manual of information on these two subjects of religious controversy. Remembering the eminent success of his two former volumes of family instruction, he concluded to adopt a similar method with his present work; hoping that the greater difficulties would be counterbalanced by the more matured intelligence of those who were to be taught.

The result of his studies is contained in a volume, entitled, " A New Family Instructor; in Familiar Discourses between a Father and his Children, on the most Essential Points of the Christian Religion. In Two Parts. Part I. Containing a Father's Instructions to his Son, upon his going to Travel into Popish Countries; and, to the rest of his Children, on his Son's turning Papist; confirming them in the Protestant Religion, against the Absurdities of Popery. Part II. Instructions against the Three Grand Errors of the Times; viz., 1. Asserting the Divine Authority of the Scriptures; against the Deists. 2. Proofs, that the Messias is already come, &c., against the Atheists and Jews. 3. Asserting the Divinity of Jesus Christ, that he was really the same with the Messias, and that the Messias was to be really God; against our Modern Hereticks. With a Poem upon the Divine Nature of Jesus Christ, in Blank Verse. By the Author of the Family Instructor. London. Printed for T. Warner, at the Black Boy in Paternoster Row. 1727." This work is known to few comparatively, even of those who are familiar with the other volumes. Its controversial character, and also the fact that many other able works have been since written on the same great subjects, have prevented it from attaining popularity.

An Introduction of eighteen pages relates to the historical part of the book, and leads to the first Dialogue, of which there are seven in Part I., and four in Part II. He says he had made it his study for several years, to find out some family whose example might be historically recommended to the world; and where other Parents might have a Pattern laid before them, a rule to walk and act by;—" and from whom, I might take a Light to guide myself, in the great Work of instructing Families, and that Children might have a Standard for their Conduct in Ages to come." He then ingeniously selects a pious Apothecary, in the City of London, who instructs his family in all religious and other duties; and a son

of this good man is, in due time, bound an Apprentice to an
Italian merchant, residing in the same street.   The master is
equally devout, and carries on the good work of Instruction
the Father had begun.   In the course of business the Merchant
sends the youth to Languedoc, where for a time he had the
advantage of Protestant worship; but while he was there, the
Edict of Nantes was revoked, and the horrible cruelties he
witnessed, during the destruction of the Protestant Interest in
France, created in his mind an abhorrence of Popery.   On this
he removed to Leghorn, was successful in business on his own
account, and after some years returned.   He settled himself as
an Italian merchant in London, married, had seven children,
left off business, and lived in good figure and fashion, in or
near the City, till he was very old.   Such, briefly, were the
circumstances that prepared this man, to impart to his children
the Christian and doctrinal instruction forming the body
of the work before us.   The Dialogues contain a great
amount of knowledge gleaned from ecclesiastical history; and
yet the whole is admirably brought within the capacity of
those taught.   Defoe had deeply studied the controversies with
which he had to deal, and was armed with the arguments used
by both parties; but the Bible was his most powerful weapon.
The Word of God had become so familiar to him that he could
cite it freely, on all proper occasions; and few lay writers
have ever shown so much judgment, in biblical quotation, as
Defoe, in the present, and many other of his works.

I cannot forbear noticing the remarkable contrast between
our author's manner of treating the subject discussed in the
former part of the book, from that of the latter.   The following quotations give his own reasons for, and at the same time
illustrate, the contrast to which I allude, viz., that of Banter
and Satire on Popery; but of deep solemnity when discoursing
on the doctrine of the Trinity.   In the preface he says:—"As
to Popery, 'tis treated indeed, with Ridicule and Jest; but
then it is not in a Way of Buffoon and Raillery, but the
Ridicule is form'd upon its own Absurdities, as well in Doctrine as in Practice; and those Practices reduced into Evidence: So that no Injustice is willingly done the Papists,
either as to their Persons or their Principles.   If they have exposed themselves by offering such gross Things to the World, as

to make the very Children laugh at them ; if their Practice is
loaded with innumerable Fripperies ; if a ridiculous Pageantry
glares in our Faces in their most solemn Things ; they must
bear with the World for mobbing them off the Stage ; and if
they are hiss'd at, they must be content, while they do Things
that cannot be otherwise treated." The preface gravely concludes as follows :—" The Arguments upon the weighty Subject
of the Divinity of our Saviour, have been so long, and so
learnedly controverted in the World, that some are apt to say,
there remains nothing to be said upon those Points, that has not
been said before ; but I must take upon me to answer in the
Negative, and refer to the Work within ; where, I believe, some
Arguments are brought for the Affirmative, which however old
the Dispute is, and however learned the Disputants, yet have
never been handled before, at least among us. The Author
says, those Arguments have been convincing, nay, confirming
to himself ; and, he hopes, they may be so to others. At
least, he has done his Endeavour, with Diligence and Sincerity ;
and hopes he may, with a composed Mind, expect a Blessing.
AMEN."

CHAPTER XVIII.

*Defoe publishes " Parochial Tyranny," and "Augusta Triumphans "—
Remarks on the Beggars' Opera—Defoe publishes " A Plan of the
English Commerce"—Baker's account of Defoe's family and residence—
Defoe and Baker commence " The Universal Spectator"—" Second
Thoughts are Best"—As Andrew Moreton he presents copies to the
Lord Mayor, &c., and also to their Majesties—Publishes " Street
Robberies Considered"—" An Humble Proposal to the People of
England for the Encrease of their Trade"—" Reasons for a War in
order to establish Tranquillity and Commerce"—Robert Dodsley, his
first work, " Servitude, a Poem"—Assisted by Defoe—Writes " The
Compleat English Gentleman."*

1727—29.

HAVING occasion to address himself to another public
and civic grievance, which called loudly for redress, our
author published, on the 9th of December 1727, a pamphlet,
entitled, " Parochial Tyranny : or, the Housekeepers Complaint against the insupportable Exactions and partial Assessments of Select Vestries, &c. With a Plain Detection of
many Abuses committed in the Distribution of Publick
Charities. Together with a Practical Proposal for amending
the same; which will not only take off great Part of the
Parish Taxes now subsisting, but ease Parishioners from serving troublesome Offices, or paying exorbitant Fines. By
Andrew Moreton, Esq. London : Printed for W. Meadows,
&c." No date. At the time when Defoe wrote, and for
many years afterward, select vestries were elected for life;
and, being therefore irresponsible, feasting, corruption, and a
long train of local evils abounded. He says, " As the old
Members drop off, none are put in their Places except those
who are willing to pursue the old Practices; so Rogues succeeding Rogues, the same Scene of Villainy is carried on to
the Terror of the Parishioners. If, mistaken in their object,
they happen to choose an honest Man among them, he is compelled to absent himself; for he is placed in a Situation like

the Owl amongst Birds.   He who becomes a Member of a
Select Vestry, like a Man who goes to the Mint, if he go
in honest, is perfectly sure not to come out so." Although
much improvement has been effected in the law and administration of parochial affairs; it remains true, as a general rule,
that in almost every old parish, especially in the metropolis,
there is still a clique of inferior trading busybodies, who
monopolize the local government of the district.

The most important minor production of Defoe, under the
assumed name of Andrew Moreton, was published on the 16th
of March 1728.   It is a thick pamphlet, entitled, " *Augusta
Triumphans* : or, the Way to make London the most flourishing City in the Universe.   I. By establishing an University
where Gentlemen may have Academical Education under the
Eye of their Friends.   II. To prevent much Murder, &c. by
an Hospital for Foundlings.   III. By suppressing pretended
Mad-Houses, where many of the fair Sex are unjustly confined,
while their Husbands keep Mistresses, &c., and many Widows
are lock'd up for the sake of their Jointure.   IV. To save our
Youth from Destruction, by clearing the Streets of impudent
Strumpets, Suppressing Gaming-Tables, and Sunday Debauches.
V. To avoid the expensive Importation of Foreign Musicians,
by forming an Academy of our own.   VI. To save our lower
Class of People from utter Ruin, and render them useful, by
preventing the immoderate use of Geneva : With a frank Ex-
plosion of many other common Abuses, and incontestible Rules
for Amendment.   Concluding with an effectual Method to
prevent Street Robberies ; and a Letter to Col. Robinson, on
Account of the Orphans' Tax.   By Andrew Moreton, Esq.
London : Printed by J. Roberts, &c.   1728."   There was a
second Edition of this work in the following year.   Only a
slight alteration was made in the title, by omitting the reference to " Foreign Musicians," and substituting the words,
" By forming an Academy of Sciences at Christ's Hospital."
The body of the work remained unaltered.
There is something truly affecting in the contemplation of
this true patriot, labouring on in his old age, that he might
leave behind him a legacy of good thoughts to the great City
that gave him birth.   He begins, " A Man who has the Publick

Good in View, ought not in the least to be alarm'd at the tribute of Ridicule which Scoffers constantly pay to projecting Heads : It is the Business of a Writer, who means well, to go directly forward, without regard to Criticism, but to offer his Thoughts as they occur.   I have but a short Time to live, nor would I waste my remaining Thread of Life in Vain, but having often lamented sundry Publick Abuses, and many Schemes having occur'd to my Fancy, which to me carried an Air of Benefit, I was resolv'd to commit them to Paper before my Departure, and leave, at least, a Testimony of my good Will to my Fellow-Creatures." In order rightly to appreciate the foresight and sagacity of our author's proposals, we must cast ourselves backward one hundred and forty years, when none of these beneficent projects had any existence, even in thought, except to himself.   It is now too late to consider the desirableness of his suggestions ; they are no longer projects, but many of them existing Institutions, indispensable to the well-being of the country.   A century after he had urged it in this pamphlet, there rose up the London University. Within a few years after our author's death, an Hospital for Foundlings was incorporated, by royal charter.   His proposal for a Royal Academy of Music has long been an accomplished fact.   He urged the enaction of a law for the protection of women against brutal husbands, and that the offenders, in aggravated cases, should be sent to the House of Correction.   Such a summary law now exists ; but a century was required before the world attained to Defoe's measure of civilization.   In his argument on this point, he nobly and eloquently says : — " Some may think this too low a Topic for me to expatiate upon ; to which I answer, that it is a Charitable and a Christian one ; and therefore, not in the least beneath the Consideration of any Man who had a Woman for his Mother." As a remedy for the evils of private Mad-Houses, he proposed that licensed establishments should be constituted for the cure of those who were really lunatic ;—that such establishments should be " subject to proper Visitation and Inspection ;"—that no person should be sent there "without due Reason, Inquiry, and Authority." This, thank God, is now all effected under the authority of the State, by the agency of the Commissioners in Lunacy and their officers, and by Acts of Parliament. He pro-

posed that shameless women parading themselves in the streets
should be brought to justice on information of any inhabitant;
and, to aid in the suppression of Gaming Tables, he insisted
that gambling debts ought to be void in law.   These repressive
measures have been long adopted and are still in force; but
one equitable suggestion of Defoe's in connection there-
with has been overlooked, namely, that the creditors of a
Bankrupt should be able to recover any sum of money he
may have lost by gambling, from the Gamester who won it.   In
considering "An Effectual Method to prevent Street Robberies," he says, " the Watchmen, for the most Part, being
decrepid, superannuated Wretches, with one Foot in the Grave,
and the other ready to follow; so feeble, that a Puff of Breath
can blow 'em down.   Poor crazy Mortals !   Much fitter for
an Alms-house than a Watch-house.   A city watch'd and
guarded by such Animals, is wretchedly watch'd indeed."   He
adds that the Thieves make a jest of them, and sometimes
compel the watchmen to light them to their Roguery.   He
urges that " the Watch be composed of stout able-bodied Men,
and of those, at least treble the Number now subsisting; that
is to say, a Watchman to every forty Houses, Twenty on one
side of the way, and Twenty on the other."   He recommends
that all these men be armed, and that more public Lamps, and
of better construction, be set up.   I confess that he does not
come up to our modern Gaslights and Police; but he proposed
in 1728 such efficient arrangements as were not generally
adopted within a hundred years afterward.

In the same part of his pamphlet he says, " our Rogues are
grown more wicked than ever, and Vice in all Kinds is so much
wink'd at, that Robbery is accounted a petty Crime.   We take
pains to puff 'em up in their Villany, and Thieves are set out
in so amiable a Light in the *Beggars' Opera*, that it has taught
them to value themselves on their Profession, rather than be
asham'd of it."   These were bold words to publish immediately
after George II. and his Queen had sanctioned the performance with their presence; but they were only a small part of
the truth.   In the beginning of March, the *Beggars' Opera*
was at about the highest point of its first run of popularity, at
the Theatre in Lincoln's Inn Fields.   When the immoral
effects of this drama are referred to, in all the polite literature

of that period, and later times,—the lights are extinguished, so as to hide the details of the scenes enacted, during the same period, outside the walls of the building.   The newspapers, published from day to day, and from week to week, must be examined, in order to appreciate the demoralizing consequences of the performance; and no reader of those Papers can for a moment doubt, that an epidemic of lewdness and dishonesty was so prevalent, in the metropolis, as to jeopardize the administration of the law.   The vice of uncleanness was popular; and robberies so abounded, that in one Newspaper, published on the 2nd of March, mention is made of no less than sixty-three offenders;—and on the 20th of May, nineteen criminals were hanged together at Tyburn.*   The difficulties of the Government will be apparent in the fact that, on the previous day, a Royal Proclamation had been issued, offering one hundred pounds reward for every conviction of robbery, " in addition to all other Rewards already allowed by Law."   The publication, therefore, of Defoe's " Method to prevent Street Robberies," was opportune and necessary.   We shall find that, at a later period in the same year, he extended and remodelled this portion of his present work, so as to constitute a distinct pamphlet.

The Treatises of Defoe, written under the title of " The Complete English Tradesman," had been necessarily restricted to that which was within the power, and for the advantage of the Trader, considered as an individual only; but it will be evident that much remained to be said of Trade in connection with the general interest and prosperity of the nation.   The history, condition, and policy of the commerce of the country, with proposals for its improvement, opened out the subject of another of those treatises on Trade, which no man living was so well able to write.   This he published on the 23rd of March, with the following title, " A Plan of the English Commerce. Being a Compleat Prospect of the Trade of this Nation, as well

---

* On the 24th of March, 1728, Orator Henley's Discourse was on " The Alarms of the Times, from the numerous Robberies, Bankruptcies, Insolvent Debtors, Self-murderers, and other general Complaints."   Yet Dean Swift could write with great asperity against Dr. Herring, afterward Archbishop of Canterbury; because he had preached a sermon in which he spoke of the demoralization caused by the Beggars' Opera.

the Home Trade as the Foreign. In Three Parts. Part I.,
containing a View of the Present Magnitude of the English
Trade, as it respects,—1. The Exportation of our own Growth
and Manufacture. 2. The Importation of Merchant Goods
from abroad. 3. The prodigious Consumption of both at Home.
Part II., Containing an Answer to that great and important
Question now depending, Whether our Trade, and especially our
Manufactures, are in a declining Condition, or No ? Part III.,
containing several Proposals, entirely new, for extending and
improving our Trade, and promoting the Consumption of
our Manufactures, in Countries wherewith we have hitherto
had no Commerce. Humbly offered to the Consideration of
the King and Parliament. London : Printed for Charles
Rivington. 1728." In the second edition, the title was
shortened, and the date is stated to be 1730, but from some
cause unknown, it was not published until the 13th of January
1731. It contains an Appendix of forty pages, on " A View
of the present apparent Encrease of Commerce in all the
Trading Parts of Europe ; but especially in England, as it is
influenced by the late Peace with Spain." The copyright of
this work seems to have been the property of Mr. Rivington,
who published a third edition,—called by mistake the second,—
in 1737. He announces it to be, " By the late ingenious Mr.
Daniel De Foe."*

In the preface, after describing the subdivision of avocations
and pursuits, combined in the full meaning of the word Commerce, from the raw material to the ultimate consumer, he thus
quietly reproves the pretensions of those who meddle with more
than they understand. " When we speak of some Men, who
are the most acquainted in the World of Business, we say they
are Men of a general Knowledge ; and such a Man is an universal Merchant. I have indeed heard such Language talked

---

* In the year 1859, one of the greatest living authorities on Trade and
Commerce, the Right Hon. Lord Overstone, caused 150 copies of a handsome volume on commerce to be privately printed for distribution among his
friends. It was edited by J. R. McCulloch, Esq., the Political Economist,
and is entitled, " A Select Collection of Scarce and Valuable Tracts on Commerce, from the Originals of Evelyn, Defoe, Richardson, Tucker, Temple, and
others. With a Preface, Notes, and Index. London, 1859." Defoe's part
in the volume consists of more than forty pages from the second edition of
his " Plan of the English Commerce."

among the Trading Part of Mankind, but I cannot say that I
ever saw the Man. The Commerce of the World, especially
as it is now carried on, is an unbounded Ocean of Business ;
trackless and unknown, like the Seas that it is managed upon ;
the Merchant is no more to be follow'd in his Adventures, than
a Maze or Labyrinth is to be trac'd out without a Clue. The
Author of this is not quite so arrogant, after a Complaint of
this Nature, as to tell you he shall present you with this universal Plan, for the whole Trade of the World. It is enough,
if he is able to offer a Plan for the Trade of our own Country,
in which it is but too true, there are many that talk of a
general Commerce, to one that understands it." It would be
impossible in this notice to give an adequate conception of
the vast stretch of our author's mind, the soundness of his
judgment, and the force of his reasoning, as exhibited in this
work. His mind seems to grasp, and apply to his purpose, all
parts of the globe, and especially those least generally known
in his time. In suggesting new openings for the Manufactures of his own country, he speaks with the authority of an
intimate personal acquaintance, as to the geography of remotest
nations ; the people, their condition, the productions they could
supply us with, and the nature of the exports that would supply
the wants and promote the happiness of each of them ; and at
the same time add to the industry, the wealth, and the influence of England. The English Merchant was a character
upon whom Defoe delighted to dwell,—he gloried in the national
wealth ; and in those, whose enterprize brought that wealth, in
converging streams from distant lands. He rose in dignity when
the names of successful merchants were enrolled among the
ancient nobility ; and he shared the pride of a people whose trade
placed them in a condition superior to that of all other nations.

I have abstained from stating why I have rejected a multitude of books that have been erroneously attributed to Defoe.
My reason for so doing, after conviction that he was not their
author, has been that the explanations would have occupied
much space, and have added nothing of value to the memoirs
of his life. I must, however, briefly notice an important work
assigned to him by no less authority than Sir Walter Scott,
Walter Wilson, William Hazlitt, Sir G. C. Lewis, and others ;

and placed conspicuously in all Lists of his writings. I allude
to "The Military Memoirs of Captain George Carleton," a
volume published on the 27th of July 1728. It was with
great misgivings that I first began to entertain doubts as to
its paternity; but in order to remove all possible doubt, I read
through it, carefully and critically, several times, until, contrary
to my inclination, the conviction was forced upon me that
Defoe had nothing whatever to do with any part of the work.
I found, however, that the same research which overturned its
genuineness, furnished much internal and other evidence in
favour of its authenticity.   Upon this I was led to a further
investigation, which admitted no other conclusion than that
Captain George Carleton was a real personage, and himself
wrote this true and historical account of his own adventures.*

In the beginning of this volume I observed that we know
little of Defoe's domestic circumstances; and that little, appears
only incidentally, or from others. Mr. Henry Baker, the celebrated natural philosopher, who married one of his daughters,
left behind him some valuable papers, and among them are the
letters that passed between himself and his wife during their
courtship.   To these he prefixed a narrative of their early
acquaintance, which contains some notices of his more celebrated father-in-law, as follows:—"In the year 1724, Mr.
H. Baker engaged in an undertaking which required his
spending some days every week at Newington. Amongst
the first who desired his acquaintance there, was Mr.
Defoe, a gentleman well known by his writings, who had
newly built there a very handsome house, as a retirement

---

* When preparing to write this Memoir, it became evident that I should
have publicly to take the responsibility of rejecting this book. I wrote therefore to my friend James Crossley, Esq., of Manchester, as follows:—" I fear
you will think me rash in rejecting Captain Carleton. I would gladly have
retained him, could I have found any sufficient reason for so doing. I can
find none, external or internal. I think it a true story written by Carleton
himself." I need not say it was satisfactory to find my judgment confirmed
by so able a critic. Mr. Crossley replied, " With respect to Captain Carleton there cannot be a question that Defoe had nothing whatever to do with
it. After carefully going into the point Thirty years ago, I came to the conclusion that he could not possibly have written it, and that it is the genuine
Narrative of a real Man of this World, who is identified in the List of Officers
given by Lord Stanhope in the second edition of his ' War of the Succession
in Spain.'   I have never seen any reason since to alter my view."

from London, and amused his time, either in the cultivation of a large and pleasant Garden, or in the pursuit of
his studies, which he found means of making very profitable.
He was now at least sixty years of age, afflicted with the gout
and stone, but retained all his mental faculties entire.   Mr.
Baker readily accepted his invitation, and was so pleased with
his conversation, that he seldom came to Newington without
paying a visit to Mr. Defoe.   He met usually at the tea-table
his three lovely daughters, who were admired for their beauty,
their education, and their prudent conduct; and if sometimes
Mr. Defoe's disorders made company inconvenient, Mr. Baker
was entertained by them, either singly, or together, and that
commonly in the garden, when the weather was favourable.
Mr. Baker very soon discovered the superior excellencies of
Miss Sophia, the youngest daughter, of whose person and
manners he speaks in strains of the highest eulogium.   He
knew nothing of Mr. Defoe's circumstances; only imagined,
from his very genteel way of living, that he must be able to
give his daughter a decent portion; he did not suppose a large
one.   On speaking to Mr. Defoe, he sanctioned his proposals,
and said, he hoped he should be able to give her a certain sum
specified; but when urged to the point some time afterwards,
his answer was, that formal articles he thought unnecessary;
that he could confide in the honour of Mr. Baker; that when
they talked before, he did not know the true state of his own
affairs; that he found he could not part with any money at
present; but at his death, his daughter's portion would be
more than he had promised; and he offered his own bond as a
guarantee for the payment."   With this, it seems Mr. Baker
was not satisfied, and some altercation took place which produced a coldness between them for some time; but Mr. Baker
constantly visited his dear Sophia.   After things had continued
in this state almost two years, says Mr. Baker, Defoe consented to engage his house at Newington as a security, and
articles were executed accordingly.   Defoe had no ready money
to part with, but gave a bond for 500l. payable after his death.
It bore date, April 5th 1729, and the marriage was celebrated
upon the 30th of the same month.

The coldness alluded to by Mr. Baker must, however, have
passed away some time before the marriage; otherwise he and

Defoe could not have been concerned together in commencing and establishing a new weekly journal, more than six months previously to the marriage.   It is entitled, *The Universal Spectator and Weekly Journal*.   Number I. was written by Defoe, and was published on Saturday, the 12th of October 1728.   This is proved not only by the internal evidence of the article itself, annexed among Defoe's writings, but also by Mr. Baker, as stated below.   It was the last periodical Paper projected by Defoe, and continued to exist, after his son-in-law's retirement, until 1746.

The Hope Collection of Newspapers, in the Bodleian Library, contains a volume of *The Universal Spectator*, from the commencement to April 1735.   It furnishes ample proof of having been Mr. Baker's own copy, and was purchased, in 1828, with the Library of the Reverend William Baker, his grandson, and late Rector of Lyndon, in Rutlandshire.   At the commencement of the volume, Mr. Baker has written the following : " Having for above four Years and a half been the Chief Manager of *The Universal Spectator*, and all my Essays during that time being collected together here, I desire, that after my Death, this Book may be preserved in my Family, since the printing them together may perhaps sometime hereafter be of use. H. BAKER." Below this, Mr. Baker has written a Tabular account stating by whom the Essays were written respectively during his Management ; and he has further, to the same extent, inscribed the names of the writers on the Papers themselves.   Upon Number 1 he has written Defoe's name, and on Number 241, published May 19, 1733, is written, " This is the last I wrote.   By H. Baker."

The terror excited by the insecurity of property, and even of life,—during the continued performance of *The Beggars' Opera*,—induced those who had wealth and influence, in many parishes, seriously to consider the " Scheme to prevent Street Robberies," included by our author in his " Augusta Triumphans." Upon this prospect of practical measures being taken, some literary thief, in the hope of reward, endeavoured to rob him of the whole Scheme, by causing paragraphs to be inserted in the public Journals claiming it, and announcing an intention of laying it before the Parliament for their approval, during the next Session. This impudent proceeding roused the indignation of Defoe, and incited him to address the following Letter to *Applebee's Journal*, in which Paper it was inserted on the 21st September 1728 :—

" Sir,—Nothing is more easy than to discover a Thing already found out. The old Proverb, which says, *One Man beats the Bush, and another catches the Bird,* being verified between me and that anonymous Gentleman, whom the publick Prints have lately complimented with a Discovery to prevent Street Robberies; tho' by-the-by, we have only his vain *Ipse dixit,* and the ostentatious Outcry of Venal News-Writers, in his Behalf.

" But to strip him of his borrow'd Plumes, these are to remind the Publick, that about 6 months ago, in a Treatise, entituled, *Augusta Triumphans : or, the Way to make London the most flourishing City in the Universe,* I have laid down a plain and practicable Scheme, for the total Suppression and Prevention of Street Robberies ; which Scheme is approved of by many Learned and judicious Persons.

" Oh ! but say the Advocates of this Second-hand Schemist, our Project is to be laid before the Parliament ! Does that make his better, or mine worse ? Have not many silly Projects been laid before Parliament e'er now ? Admit it be not the same, as I have but too much Reason to believe it is ; cannot the Members of both Houses read Print as well as Written-hand ? Or does he think they are so prejudiced as to dislike a Thing the worse for being offered without view of Gain ? I trust *Andrew Moreton's* Scheme, generously offered for the Publick Good, will meet with as fair a Reception as that of this Hireling Projector.

" Mine is already published, let him Generously follow my Example, and no doubt if his Scheme be preferred, the Government will reward him. If mine get the better, I ask nothing, the Publick Good is my only View.

" If my Antagonist be Necessitous, where is the Merit: he does it for his own Sake, not the Publick's ? If he be not Necessitous, what a sordid Wretch is he to withhold his Scheme for Lucre, putting it up at Public Sale ? So that, if you don't give him his Price, you shan't have it.

" Some People indeed are so fond of Mysteries, they run down everything that is Plain and Intelligible ; they love Darkness, Whispers, and *Free-Masonry ;* despising whatever comes in the Shape of a Pamphlet, be it never so useful or commendable ; but in Spite of Prejudice, Truth is the Standard, by which I hope all honest and impartial Men will judge me.

" Though I must Confess I am not a little Piqued to be jockied out of my Labours, when Thanks are all I ask, and that is a poor Project indeed which is not worth Thank ye.

" But not to be behind Hand with my Gentleman in the Clouds, who would have the Parliament buy his Pig in a Poke, and build up his Fortune at my Expense ; I determine next Sessions to present Copies of my aforesaid Book to divers Honourable Worthy Members of both Houses, unto whom I have the Honour to be known, and then we shall see whose Scheme shall have the Precedence.

" In the mean Time, I beg of you to hand my Protest to the World, and am,

" Sir, your very humble Servant,
" ANDREW MORETON."

" Clapton, Sept. 17."

From the warmth of expression used by our author, and the reference in his Letter to " Venal News-Writers," and a " Hireling Projector," I cannot avoid the suspicion that this flagrant attempt, to defraud him of the credit of his Scheme, was connected with the Press ; and attributable to the circumstances already related, under which he had become separated from the Journals more than two years previously.   But however that may have been, the ancient spirit of the literary gladiator was roused to immediate action, of which the above Letter was only the precursor.   He instantly recast his Scheme, and extended it into a distinct pamphlet, which he entitled, " Second Thoughts are best : or, a Further Improvement of a late Scheme to prevent Street Robberies.   In which our Streets will be so strongly guarded, and so gloriously illuminated, that any Part of London will be as safe and pleasant at Midnight as at Noonday ; and Burglary totally impracticable.   With some Thoughts for suppressing Robberies in all the publick Roads of England, &c.   Humbly offered for the Good of his Country, submitted to the consideration of the Parliament, and Dedicated to his Sacred Majesty King George II. By Andrew Moreton, Esq. London: Printed for W. Meadows, at the Angel in Cornhill; and sold by J. Roberts in Warwick Lane. 1728. Price Sixpence."

Part of Defoe's policy was, to withhold the general publication of his pamphlet, after a few copies had been printed;— and, on the 5th of October, *Read's Journal* announces that there had been presented, " A Proposal humbly offered to the Rt. Hon. the Lord Mayor, Court of Aldermen, and Recorder of the City of London; as also to his Majesty's Justices of the Peace for the County of Middlesex, and City and Liberty of Westminster, for Preventing Street Robberies." The same *Journal* of the following week says,—" On Sunday last (6th), Andrew Moreton, Esq., presented to their Majesties at Windsor, his Scheme for preventing Street Robberies." He then embodied in his pamphlet the substance of his Letter to *Applebee's Journal,* and also an account of the presentation to their Majesties, and many Members of both Houses of Parliament; after which, on the 12th of October, it was issued to the public, and advertised in the *London Journal,* and other Papers. Immediate and voluntary action was taken on the publication of this seasonable pamphlet, as appears from the following paragraph in one of the *Journals* of the 19th of October:— " Many of the Gentry and principal Inhabitants of the Villages about London are going to associate, to concert Measures for suppressing of Robbers, and we hear some further Rewards will be offered for apprehending them than those already order'd by Law." As to the " Hireling Projector" and his rival Scheme, I find no further mention of either of them; and believe that the vigorous, but expensive onslaught by Defoe, had effectually put an end to both.*

---

* The following Advertisement in *Read's Journal,* October 26, shows that the name of "Andrew Moreton, Esq.," was known to be only a pseudonym of Daniel Defoe:—

" This Day is published, Villany Exploded: or, the Mystery of Iniquity laid open: In a Faithful Relation of all the Street Robberies, committed by the Notorious Gang now in Newgate; discovering all their private as well as publick Transactions, Intrigues and Villanies. With a Copy of Articles which they Swear to keep, the Songs which they Sing, and the Places they resort to: Also, Directions how they may be avoided, and taken. With

The "Scheme for preventing Street Robberies," and its extension in "Second Thoughts are Best," relate almost entirely to what may be termed public and organised arrangements; some of which would even require the sanction of the Legislature before they could be enforced. Defoe was not the man to leave half his work undone; and knowing that much could be effected by properly directed private and individual efforts, he addressed himself to that part of the subject, and on the 12th of November 1728, published a thick pamphlet, entitled, "Street Robberies Considered. The reason of their being so frequent, with probable Means to prevent 'em. To which is added, Three short Treatises:— I. A Warning for Travellers; with Rules to know a Highwayman, and Instructions how to behave upon the Occasion. II. Observations on Housebreakers. How to prevent a Tenement from being broke open. With a Word of Advice concerning Servants. III. A Caveat for Shopkeepers: with a Description of Shoplifts, how to know 'em, and how to prevent 'em; also a Caution of Delivering Goods: with the Relation of Several Cheats practised lately upon the Publick. Written by a Converted Thief. To which is prefix'd some Memoirs of his Life. *Set a Thief to catch a Thief.* London. Printed for J. Roberts in Warwick Lane. Price 1s." No Date. After so much said respecting the preceding productions of our author on this subject, little need be added on this, the character of which is explained by its copious title. The suggestions it contains were calculated for the times, and suited to encourage a state of preparation against any attack of thieves, and such a calm resolution and self-reliance,—at the needful moment,—as would frequently be found to disconcert and frustrate the intentions of marauding villains. The opportunities of Defoe during the years of his connection with *Applebee's Journal,* had enabled him to assume in this pamphlet the disguise of a " converted thief;" and he had largely experienced the advantage of conveying instruction and amusement under the form of autobiographical narrative. The Government was at length so fully convinced of the per-

---

several Diverting Stories; and remarks, on 'Squire Moreton's, alias D——l Def—e's Scheme. Taken from the mouths of Levee, Vaux, Featherby, and Burnham. By the Author of Dalton's Narrative. Printed for T. Read, and sold by the Booksellers of London and Westminster, 1728. Price 1s."

nicious consequences of such performances as *The Beggars'
Opera*, that in December 1728, when a Sequel thereto was in
rehearsal, at the Theatre in Lincoln's Inn Fields, it was immediately suppressed without any public performance.

Mr. Mist had been compelled,—in consequence of his disloyalty,—to save his life by self-banishment. The circumstances
have at present nothing to do with the Life of Defoe, farther
than that the *Journal* was changed from *Mist's* to *Fog's*, and was
continued, on the same principles as before, but with much
greater caution. The second complete edition of " The Compleat English Tradesman," in two volumes, had been published
on the 10th of August 1728 ; and, as I entertain no doubt that
the copyright of the work was the property of Mr. Rivington,
the publisher, Defoe had probably no motive of pecuniary gain
in recommending its circulation. He could not but be gratified that the work had been extensively sold, and eminently
useful ; and, to promote that usefulness still farther, he made
it the subject of the only Essay I have found written by him
in *Fog's Journal ;* and the last communication I have found
from him in any public *Journal.* It was published in the
Number for January 11th, 1729, and besides avoiding any
signature, he only alludes to himself as the *late* author of the
Compleat Tradesman. He first speaks of three great Essen-
tials of a Nation's Good :—Religion, Loyalty, and Trade, and
then avails himself of the close of the old year, and the
beginning of the new, to press, upon all Merchants and Tradesmen, the duty and advantages of making up their Books and
accounts, that they may know how they stand ; after which
they may cheerfully enjoy the pleasures of the Christmas
Season. He assigns as a reason for not further enlarging on
the topic, that this has been already well done in *The Compleat
Tradesman,* to which he refers his Readers. The article was
calculated to be useful ; and the recommendation of the Book
could not, I think, have been more delicately effected.

When Defoe wrote the above, he was engaged in preparing
a pamphlet, which may be considered as a further Supplement
to his *Compleat Tradesman ;* but occasioned by the threatening
prospect of a war. It was published on the 15th of March,

and is entitled, " An Humble Proposal to the People of
England, for the Encrease of their Trade, and Encouragement
of their Manufactures ; whether the present Uncertainty of
Affairs issues in Peace or War.   By the Author of the Compleat Tradesman.   London : Printed for Charles Rivington, at
the Bible and Crown in St. Paul's Church-yard, 1729.   Price
One Shilling."   In the preface, he refers to the recent revival
of an old quarrel, whether Trade has declined, or not declined.
He affirms that the good of Trade is little or nothing concerned
in the quarrel, and it is hardly worth while to set the parties
right.   " Nor do they," he says, " seem to desire to be set
right, but rather to want an Occasion to keep up a Strife,
which perhaps serves some other of their wicked Purposes,
better than Peace would do ; and indeed, those who seek to
Quarrel, who can reconcile ?"   He declines, therefore, to
meddle with that question, his object being to show how Trade
may be increased by greater industry and enterprise, and he concludes, " The following Sheets are as one Alarm more given to
the lethargick Age, if possible, to open their Eyes to their own
Prosperity ; the Author sums up his Introduction to it in this
short, positive Assertion, which he is ready to make good, viz.,
That if the Trade of England is not in a flourishing and
thriving Condition, the Fault and only Occasion of it is all our
own, and is wholly in our own Power to amend, whenever we
please."   In a similar strain, he proceeds with the " Proposal "
he has to make, thus :—" As by my Title I profess to be
addressing myself to English Men, I think I need not tell
them that *they live by* TRADE : That their Commerce has rais'd
them from what *they were,* to what *they are ;* and may, if cul-
tivated and improv'd, raise them yet farther to what *they never
were ;* and this, in few Words, is an Index of my present
Work."   This will suffice to show the tone of authority in
which he addresses " the People of England " on the subject
of Trade.   Perhaps he did not intend dictation to be evident
to the reader, but it doubtless arose from an instinctive
consciousness of his own superior knowledge ;—and was
fully justified by his age, his wisdom, and experience.   This
Tract also proves that the energy and clearness of his mind
remained ; and that he determined to use to the last the
great talents with which he was entrusted, in promoting the

prosperity, and with it the material power and glory of his country.

The above pamphlet was immediately followed by one that I believe to have been his last political effort, though it has reference also to Commerce. It is entitled, " Reasons for a War, in Order to Establish the Tranquillity and Commerce of Europe. *Pax Quæritur Bello.* London : Printed for A. Dodd, and R. Walker, without Temple Bar; E. Nutt and F. Smith, at the Royal Exchange; and sold by the Booksellers and Pamphlet Shops, Mercuries and Hawkers, of London and Westminster. 1729. Price Sixpence." He still shows the unabated activity of his patriotism; and, as to public opinion, he says, " In few Words, as we had it once aptly expressed in King William's Time, on a like Occasion, *the Pulse of the Nation beats high for a War.*" He shows the injury done to Trade by the protracted uncertainty of diplomatic proceedings, and concludes, that a short and sharp War, followed by Peace, would be preferable to the lasting necessity, for years, of being always prepared.

With the single exception of the " Memoirs of Captain George Carleton," no book has given me so much concern, on the ground of Authorship, as " Madagascar: or, Robert Drury's Journal, during Fifteen Years Captivity on that Island," &c. &c. This volume was first published on the 24th May 1729, and is, in many respects, one of the most interesting accounts that appeared, between the date of *Robinson Crusoe,* and the death of Defoe. Madagascar was a centre, around which much of our Author's genius, in fictitious writing, turns; and, although surrounded by savage human beings, the isolation of the English boy Drury is perfect. Many parts of the book, on Religion, and the Original of Government, are avowedly the work of an editor; and there are occasional turns of humour resembling Defoe, but the language rarely does so. It is certain, that there was a Robert Drury,—that he had been a captive as stated,—that he wrote a large account of his adventures,—that he was seen, questioned, and could give any information required,—after the publication of this Book. In the latter part of his life Defoe had many imitators.

I think one of them very ably edited Drury's Manuscript. Possibly Defoe may have read it, and inserted some sentences; but, as I am in doubt, even of that, I cannot place the book in the List of his works.

I must here make a brief excursion in order to explain Defoe's connection with the work next requiring notice. Robert Dodsley, who afterward became an eminent bookseller, and author of *The Economy of Human Life*, &c., was born at Mansfield, Notts, in the year 1703; and it is stated, ran away from his apprenticeship to London, where he became a footman. While in that capacity, he composed, in 1729, a short poem called " Servitude;" and being at a loss how to proceed further, he ventured to show it to a person,—probably a bookseller,—who upon reading it over, " told me," he says, " he wonder'd I had not taken notice of a late Pamphlet, entitled, *Every Body's Business is no Body's Business*, done by one, who writes himself *Andrew Moreton*, Esq. I told him I had never seen it; and, upon his answering it would be worth my while, I bought the Book." The above is almost conclusive that Dodsley's first adviser knew Andrew Moreton to be only an assumed name; and I have recently shown that it had been publicly stated in print, a year previously, that Daniel Defoe was the writer who used that signature. By means which cannot now be ascertained, the young footman obtained access to Defoe, and sought his advice and assistance. Our author was now in his sixty-ninth year, and in the early part of September had been " exceedingly ill;" but he was always ready to do good, and finding merit in the author and his work, he not only revised the poem, but also,—seeing it would not fill a sheet,—he wrote a preface and introduction of fourteen pages, and then kindly added, as a postscript, six pages of quiet banter on his own popular tract, *Every Body's Business is no Body's Business*, in order to give his humble *protégé* the reflex benefit of such popularity. It is probable that he also assisted in the publication of the pamphlet, which appeared on the 20th of September 1729, and is entitled, " Servitude: a Poem. To which is prefix'd, an Introduction, humbly Submitted to the Consideration of all Noblemen, Gentlemen, and Ladies, who keep many Servants. Also a Postscript, Occasion'd by a late

Trifling Pamphlet, entituled, *Every Body's Business is no Body's.*

'———— *Feci e Servo ut esses Libertus mihi,*
Propterea quid serviebas liberaliter :
————————————————*Gaudeo,*
Si tibi quid feci aut facio, quod placeat Domine.'—TER.

Written by a Footman. In Behalf of Good Servants, and to excite the Bad to their Duty. London: Printed for T. Worrall, at the Judge's Head, over against St. Dunstan's Church in Fleet Street. Price 6d." The whole forms a pamphlet of thirty-two pages, of which, as already stated, the prose part, written by Defoe, occupies twenty. As the poem relates chiefly to the duties of Servants, under the several heads of, Servitude; Honesty; Carefulness; Obedience; Diligence; Submission to rebukes; Neatness; Receiving and Delivering Messages; and Discretion; so Defoe has, in the Introduction, used the same heads in remarking on the duties of Masters as well as Servants. I make but one quotation to show how much of practical wisdom he could press into so apparently trifling a production. " It is certain there is nothing procures a more faithful Service from a grateful Temper, than the Liberality of a Master. Rewards are not given to good and faithful Servants, but paid. Nor ought that Time to be accounted lost, which is spent in the Service of a noble Benefactor; for such a one will never fail to reward Merit, even beyond its Desert. A generous Man, that loves his Servant well, is as a God unto him ;—both gives him Blessings, and protects him from Dangers. As on the other hand, a diligent and discreet Servant is one of the best Friends that a Man can be blest with, for he will do whatsoever Service a Friend can, and may not only be commanded to do it, but there is also less Hazard of losing him than the other. But the Misfortune is, we are look'd upon as incapable of performing any Service of a higher Nature than waiting at Table, carrying a Message, or the like ; we are not thought fit to be entrusted with Secrets, to be employ'd in any Business of Importance ; nor in short, to transact any Thing which requires Thought or Conduct. And in this View it is not probable we should ever possess any Place in a Gentleman's Esteem, beyond that of his Dog, or his Horse." In a similar manner, under each head of the pamphlet, our author inculcates the relative obligations of kindness, order, confidence, forbearance, and affection, between the heads of families and their domestic Servants.

At the time when Defoe thus lent his beneficent hand to the friendless footman, he was preparing another work for publication; but, from causes which I shall have presently to consider, only one sheet of it appears to have been set in type, as a printer's proof. The following letter to his printer, " Mr. J. Watts, in Wild Court," relates to this work, and is of great importance, as fixing a date beyond which nothing further appears to have been done in the matter :— .

" S^r,—I am to ask yor Pardon for keeping the Enclosed so long, Mr. Baker having told me yor Resolution of taking it in hand, and working it off. But I have been exceedingly Ill. I have Revised it again and contracted it very much, and hope to bring it wi^{thin} the Bulk you desire, or as near it as possible. But this, and some needful alterations will oblige you to much Trouble in the first Sheet, and perhaps almost as bad as setting it over again, which cannot be avoided. I will endeavour to send the Rest of the Copy so well corrected as to give you very little Trouble. I here return the first Sheet, and as much Copy as will make near 3 Sheets more. You shall have all the remainder so as not to let you stand still at all.

" I am, Sir,

" Your Most Humble Servant,

" De Foe."

"Sept. 10th, 1729."

The work was to have been entitled, " The Compleat English Gentleman : containing Useful Observations on, The General Neglect of the Education of English Gentlemen, with the Reason and Remedies. The Apparent Differences between a Well-Born and a Well-Bred Gentleman. Instructions how Gentlemen may Recover a Deficiency of their Latin, and be Men of Learning, Tho' without the Pedantry of Schools." The manuscript and proof appear to have been withdrawn from the hands of the printer, and to have remained in the possession of Defoe's descendants, the family of Baker, for more than a hundred years ;

after which it became the property of Dawson Turner, Esq.; and, in 1859, was purchased by James Crossley, Esq. I had then an opportunity of examining the work, and taking an abstract of its contents, as follows :—

" Part I. Chapter 1. Of the Gentleman born, in the common Acceptation of the Word, as the Gentry amongst us are pleased to understand it. 2. Some Examples from History, and from good Information, of the want of Care taken in the Education of Princes, and Children of the Nobility in former Times, as well in this Nation as in foreign Countries, and how fatal the Effects of it has been in their future Conduct ; with some few Examples of the contrary also. 3. Examples of the different Education of Princes, and Persons of Rank from the beginning of the XVIth Century, viz., from the Reign of Henry the VIIIth inclusive. With Observations down to the present Time ; on the Happiness of these Reigns in general, where the Princes have been educated in Principles of Honour and Virtue ; and something of the contrary. 4. Of Royal Education. 5. (The title is erased). 6. Of the G———; of Himself, his Family, and Fortune. Part II. Chap. 1. Of the *Fund* for Encrease of our Nobility and Gentry in England; being the Beginning of those we call Bred Gentlemen : with some Account of Difference. 2. (There is no heading). 3. Of the general Ignorance of the English Gentry, and the true Cause of it, in the Manner of their Introduction into Life. 4. Of what may be the unhappy Cause of the general Defect in the Education of our Gentry ; with a rational Proposal for preventing those consequences."

The corrections to the proof of the printed sheet, seemed to be in a different handwriting from the Manuscript itself. The latter contains many notes and emendations. Parts are written in short-hand ; and the abbreviations of words are very numerous. Mr. Crossley would do great service to all lovers of pure English Literature, if he could be persuaded to publish this valuable work of Defoe.

CHAPTER XIX.

Retrospect of Defoe's life and circumstances from 1715 *to* 1729—*Proved to have been in affluence during his later years, and at death—An un-explained trouble induces him to assign his property to his son, and to quit his home—His affecting letter to Baker—Probable nature of the trouble that thus afflicted him—Publishes " An Effectual Scheme for Preventing Street-Robberies"—Death of Defoe—Correction as to the day of his death—Remarks of public journals—Sale of his library—Administration of his effects—Conclusion.*

1729—31.

WE are drawing toward the close of our author's life ; and it may be well to take a retrospective glance, so that we may estimate the condition of his worldly circumstances at the period we have now reached,—towards the close of 1729. During many of his latter years nothing has been mentioned by himself, relative to any of the pecuniary embarrassments that attended him throughout the reigns of King William and Queen Anne ; though then, his distress, from merciless creditors, was a frequent theme of complaint. His government duties, from the end of 1715, had required him to be mostly in London, rendering any safe seclusion from old creditors impracticable ; had such seclusion even been necessary. There cannot, I think, be any doubt that he had been able to effect such arrangements as satisfied all legal demands, and put an end to the unhappy consequences of his early misfortunes. His labours, from 1719 to 1729, were, in extent, more like those of ten ordinary writers, than the achievements of a single intellect ; and his gains must have been in some measure, proportionate. His government appointment from 1715, to at least 1726, being for literary services,—requiring great tact and judgment, and involving much caution and responsibility,—would alone be rewarded with a salary probably more than adequate to the maintenance of his household. We have seen him at one time writing for, and managing, a monthly periodical, a weekly Journal, a tri-weekly Post, and a daily Paper. A very moderate estimate of his income, as a *Journalist* alone, between 1716 and 1726, would suffice to place him in affluence. If to these we add, only from 1719 to 1729, the profits arising out of nearly sixty published works, comprising twenty-seven octavo volumes, and the remainder pamphlets,—many of which works were eminently successful,—it is impossible to imagine that a man without any extravagant habits, who is said to have spent this part of his life, " either in the cultivation of a large and pleasant garden, or in the pursuit of his studies, which he found means of making very profitable," could be in any danger of pecuniary calamity.

This point is of so much importance to the consideration of the remainder of his life, that I turn from the argument of probabilities, to the statement of facts : which, though not numerous, are I think conclusive. We have seen that in 1721, he paid a fine of ten pounds, rather than serve some office in the parish of Stoke Newington ; proving that his time was then so valuable, that exemption from a few hours weekly devotion to parochial affairs, which many would have looked upon as a pleasant relaxation, was by him cheaply purchased at that price. Defoe was living at Stoke Newington in 1709, and continued to do so. We do not know the exact date when he erected a house for himself, but Mr. Baker's statement, that, " In the year 1724, he had newly built there a very handsome house, as a retirement from London," is sufficient for the purpose. The house is mentioned in Robinson's History of Stoke Newington ; and must have been a commodious mansion, standing in about four acres of ground.* Mr. Baker also speaks of Defoe's " very genteel way of living," at that time ; and that " his three lovely daughters were admired for their beauty, their education, and their prudent conduct." We have also seen that in 1722, he made provision at Colchester for the pecuniary independence of the eldest of his unmarried daughters, and that in November 1727, he paid off a mortgage of 220l. there, making 1020l. altogether, so that she might possess it free from incumbrance. If we may believe the statements of his literary opponents,—who could have no motive in asserting an untruth

---

* It is said that Dr. Price lived some years in this house, as the domestic chaplain of a subsequent owner. In recent times it was occupied and owned by William Frend, Esq., M.A., of the Rock Life Office. About two years ago, it was entirely pulled down.

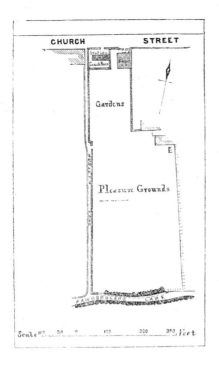

DEFOE'S HOUSE,

WITH THE PLAN OF HIS GROUNDS, AT STOKE NEWINGTON.

on such a point,—he also kept his coach.* He had settled his
affairs, and when Mr. Baker proposed to marry his daughter
Sophia, he said he could not part with money at that time, but
that at his death her portion would be more than he had promised
to give her.   From these negociations with Mr. Baker it also
appears, that he had another estate in Essex; which, with that at
Newington, he had secured for the future benefit of his family.

In order to bring the whole subject of pecuniary circumstances together, I must anticipate what belongs thereto during
the short remainder of his life, and immediately subsequent to
his death. It appears, that being under some real or supposed
necessity of personal concealment, Defoe made a temporary
transfer of all his property to his son, and he complains,—in a
letter which we shall have more fully to consider presently,—
that while that son is thus " living in a profusion of Plenty," he
has been so inhuman as to refuse to provide for his mother
and two sisters, though " bound under Hand and Seal, besides
the most sacred promises" to do so.   It is sufficient for our
present purpose to say that this is proof of affluence misapplied ;
not, in any sense, of poverty.   To the same effect, in such
Letter, is his injunction to his son-in-law, Mr. Baker, " Stand
by them when I am gone, and let them not be wronged, while
he is able to do them right.   I hope they will want no help
but that of Comfort and Counsel."   This can only mean that
he had made ample provision for his wife, and daughters, after
his death ; and that, whatever cruelty this unnatural son might
now be able to inflict on them, yet that after his own decease,
it was possible they might want nothing but " comfort and
counsel" in the recovery of the estates.   The sequel proved
that his anticipation was correct.   His widow, Susannah, continued to reside at Stoke Newington, and both his still
unmarried daughters were afterward in independent circumstances.   Whether Mr. Baker's assistance was required or not,
in the recovery of the property, is immaterial to our present
consideration ; it is enough that the property existed at the
time of Defoe's death, that his family inherited it ; and, that it
was a competency for all who had any natural claims upon

---

* He certainly erected Coach House and Stables, with his Mansion, as
will be seen by the illustration.

him. The last words Defoe is known to have uttered to any member of his family, make it probable that he had secured a further portion for his daughter Sophia. He tells her husband, Mr. Baker,—apparently in answer to an inquiry,—" I have not the Policy of Assurance; I suppose my Wife, or Hannah, may have it." I respectfully submit, therefore, that everything written by Mr. Wilson and Mr. Hazlitt, as to poverty, and merciless creditors, having assailed Defoe towards the end of his life; and, as to his having been thrown into prison, and dying insolvent,—is erroneous. Not merely unsupported by a single fact, but contrary to all the evidence we have.

It is true, however, that the end of his life was full of calamities, mental and physical, too heartrending to be contemplated without deep sympathy, by any human being. For many years previously to 1729, he had suffered from those dreadful maladies, the gout and stone. Incidentally the torment they produced is alluded to in several of the essays from *Applebee's Journal.* These diseases were engendered, or at least aggravated, by sedentary habits, and close application to study; he was consequently subjected to frequent and increasingly acute paroxysms of illness during many years. So early as 1724, Mr. Baker says, " Sometimes Mr. Defoe's disorders made company inconvenient." I have on several occasions remarked, that though, in his later works, he was evidently preparing for and expecting death; yet his great mental powers seemed to have lost none of their force. And that when approaching his seventieth year, his reasoning was clear, his fancy playful and exuberant, and his satire keen, as they had been at any time previously. Yet he was now to undergo a shock, in which his shattered bodily frame was unable to sustain the wounded spirit; all his wonted courage, resistance, and reaction failed him ;—and, under the weight of the stroke, he left his comfortable home and loving family, and wandered into the world—a heart-broken fugitive—to the day of his death.

The only direct account we have of these painful circumstances, though other Letters on both sides are referred to, is contained in one long communication, from himself to his son-in-law Mr. Baker. We must also lament, that when Mr. Baker preserved that important letter, for future generations, he did not record, with it, some explanation of events seemingly so mysterious. None of the biographers of Defoe have attempted to penetrate the obscurity; and their few conjectures are, as we have seen, unfounded, and inconsistent.

I have already noticed, that Defoe's Letter of Sept. 10th, 1729, to his printer, describes the state in which his unpublished work, " The Compleat Gentleman," then was. I now recal attention to the concluding words of that note,—" You shall have all the remainder, so as not to let you stand still at all." He even sent him, with the first sheet revised, " as much copy as will make near three sheets more;" yet, as I have remarked, the printer must have been stopped immediately thereafter, no more copy forwarded, and that already sent withdrawn. The work is now in the same state as on the day when its author wrote as above; and I think it may be fairly concluded, from this, and other facts, that the great calamity, under which he abandoned all that was dear to him, occurred immediately after that date. I would further remark that there are three important points to be borne in mind, while studying this matter; *first*, he received a blow " from a wicked, perjur'd, and contemptible enemy;"—*second*, that fearing further consequences, he sought concealment; having first legally conveyed his property, during the remainder of his own life only, to his son, for the benefit of Mrs. Defoe and two unmarried daughters;—*third*, that the son converted the property to his own use, and by this unnatural conduct gave his aged, infirm, unhappy father, an additional wound that proved mortal. I now come to the Letter in question, which may truly be pronounced one of the most painfully affecting in the English language:—

" DEAR MR. BAKER,
" I have yo' very kind and affecc'onate Letter of the 1st: But not come to my hand till ye 10th; where it had been delay'd I kno' not. As your kind Manner, and Kinder Thought, from wch it flows, (for I take all you say to be as I always believed you to be, sincere and Nathaniel like, without Guile,) was a particular Satisfacc'on to me; so the stop of a Letter, however it happened, depriv'd me of that Cordial too many Days, considering how much I stood in need of it, to support a Mind sinking under the Weight of Afflicc'on too heavy for my Strength, and looking on myself as Abandon'd of

every Comfort, every Friend, and every Relative, except such
only as are able to give me no Assistance.

"I was sorry you should say at ye Beginning of your Letter,
you were debarred seeing me.   Depend upon my Sincerity for
this, I am far from debarring you.   On ye contrary, it would
be a greater Comfort to me than any I now enjoy, that I
could have yor agreeable Visits wth Safety, and could see both
you and my dear Sophia, could it be without giving her y^e
Grief of seeing her Father *in tenebris,* and under ye Load of insupportable Sorrows.   I am sorry I must open my Griefs so
far as to tell her, it is not ye Blow I rec^d from a wicked, perjur'd, and contemptible Enemy, that has broken in upon my
Spirit; wch as she well knows, has carryed me on thro' greater
Disasters than these.   But it has been the injustice, unkindness, and, I must say, inhuman dealing of my own Son, w^{ch}
has both ruin'd my Family, and, in a Word, has broken my
Heart; and as I am at this Time under a weight of very heavy
Illness, wch I think will be a Fever, I take this Occasion to
vent my Grief in ye Breasts who I know will make a prudent
use of it, and tell you, that nothing but this has conquered or
could conquer me.   *Et tu! Brute.*   I depended upon him, I
trusted him, I gave up my two dear unprovided Children into
his Hands; but he has no Compassion, but suffers them and
their poor, dying Mother to beg their Bread at his Door, and
to crave, as if it were an Alms, what he is bound under Hand
and Seal, besides the most sacred promises, to supply them
with; himself, at ye same Time, living in a profusion of
Plenty.   It is too much for me.   Excuse my Infirmity, I can
say no more; my Heart is too full.   I only ask one Thing of
you as a dying request.   Stand by them when I am gone, and
let them not be wrong'd, while he is able to do them right.
Stand by them as a Brother; and if you have anything within
you owing to my Memory, who have bestow'd on you the best
Gift I had to give, let y^m not be injured and trampled on by
false Pretences, and unnatural Reflections.   I hope they will
want no help but that of Comfort and Council; but that they
will indeed want, being too easie to be manag'd by Words and
Promises.

"It adds to my Grief that it is so difficult to me to see you.
I am at a distance from Lond^n in Kent; nor have I a Lodg-

ing in London, nor have I been at that Place in the Old
Bailey, since I wrote you I was removed from it.   At present
I am weak, having had some fits of a Fever that have left me
low.   But those Things much more.

"I have not seen Son or Daughter, Wife or Child, many
Weeks, and kno' not which Way to see them.   They dare not
come by Water, and by Land there is no Coach, and I kno'
not what to do.

"It is not possible for me to come to Enfield, unless you
could find a retired Lodging for me, where I might not be
known, and might have the Comfort of seeing you both now
and then ; Upon such a circumstance, I could gladly give the
days to Solitude, to have the Comfort of half an Hour now
and then, with you both, for two or three Weeks.   But just
to come and look at you, and retire immediately, 'tis a Burden
too heavy. The Parting will be a Price beyond the Enjoyment.

"I would say, (I hope) with Comfort, that 'tis yet well.   I
am so near my Journey's end, and am hastening to the Place
where yᵉ Weary are at Rest, and where the Wicked cease to
trouble ; be it that the Passage is rough, and the Day stormy,
by what Way soever He please to bring me to the End of it, I
desire to finish Life with this temper of Soul in all Cases : *Te
Deum Laudamus.*

"I congratulate you on yᵉ Occasion of yoʳ happy advance
in yʳ Employment.   May all you do be prosperous, and all
you meet with pleasant ; and may you both escape the torments and troubles of uneasie Life.   May you Sail yᵉ dangerous Voyage of Life with *a forcing Wind,* and make the
Port of Heaven *without a Storm.*

"It adds to my Grief that I must never see the pledge of
your mutual Love, my little Grandson.   Give him my Blessing, and may he be to you both your Joy in Youth, and Your
Comfort in Age, and never add a Sigh to your Sorrow.   But,
alas ! that is not to be expected.   Kiss my dear Sophy once
more for me ; and if I must see her no more, tell her this is
from a Father that loved her above all his Comforts, to his
last Breath.

"Yoʳ unhappy,

"D. F.

"About two Miles from Greenwich, Kent,
   "*Tuesday, Augˢᵗ* 12, 1730.

" P.S.—I wrote you a Letter some Months ago, in answer
to one from you, about selling ye House; but you never sig-
nified to me whether you received it.   I have not the Policy
of Assurance; I suppose my Wife, or Hannah, may have it.
                                    " *Idem.*   D. F."

Having, as I trust, set at rest the question of Defoe's pecuniary circumstances, during his later years; and shown that
neither poverty nor debt existed, or had anything to do with
the deplorable condition in which he closed his life, I desire
now to consider the nature of his trouble; and the cause,—so
far as a key may be found in the words, " a wicked, perjur'd,
and contemptible Enemy."   Before doing so, however, I must
remark, that there is not a word in the above letter to his son-
in-law, as to any debt, creditor, law-suit, writ, or obligation;
nor does he require any pecuniary aid, even for his own personal expenditure.   After tracking our author through all that
can be ascertained of his history; it is as difficult to conceive
that he could have an enemy,—unconnected with politics,—
as it would be to understand, that an enemy, properly designated as above, could hold the same political principles as
himself.   A political or other antagonist described in such
terms, must have had the power, as well as the inclination, to
injure the man he hated.   Defoe had been many years in the
confidence of the Whig government of his country; and possibly still held in 1729 the lucrative appointment conferred
upon him in 1715.   Assuming the existence of a political and
powerful enemy, it is pertinent to inquire next, how, and in
what manner, a " blow " could be struck that would be most
injurious, and most sensibly felt?   Any communication to the
Government, accompanied by apparent proof, that Defoe had
been, or was, disloyal to the House of Hanover, would be
effectual; equally so might be any evidence that while he was
in the pay of the government, he had been connected with
the management of *Journals* opposed to the government;—
unless such evidence could be disproved, or satisfactorily explained.   An attack on either of these points would, if successful, not only deprive him of his appointment, but expose
him to the severest resentment of the Ministry.

I must now turn back to the government Letters written

by Defoe in 1718, to Mr. de la Faye.* It will be found there, that on the retirement of Lord Townshend from the office of Secretary of State, and the accession of Lord Stanhope, *within two years* after Defoe's appointment of secret Censor of Journals, he felt it necessary, for his own safety, to put in writing a full account of his appointment, his duties, and the manner of performance. The second and longest of those Letters contains a prophetical foreboding of some future trouble, such as had now befallen him;—he says,—" I beg leave to observe, Sir, one Thing more to his Lordship in my own behalf, and without which, indeed, I may one Time or other, run the hazard of fatal Misconstructions. I am, Sir, for this service posted among Papists, Jacobites, and enraged High Tories—a Generation who, I profess, my very Soul abhors ; I am obliged to hear traitorous Expressions, and outrageous Words against his Majesty's person and government, and his most faithful Servants, and smile at it all, as if I approved it." He recommends himself, therefore, to Lord Stanhope's protection, adding, " or I may be undone the sooner, by how much the more faithfully I execute the Commands I am under." If such a recommendation of himself was needful after the changes of only two years, how much more exposed to danger might the writer be after all the political changes of the following ten or eleven years !

About the time when Defoe wrote as above, the youthful but profligate Lord Wharton, and a knot of his associates, began to frequent Mist's printing office, and to write sedition and treason for his *Journal.* The proprietor of the Paper, as disloyal as any of them, was a willing tool, except when the terrors of the law compelled him to listen to Defoe's prudent advice. During Defoe's connection with *Mist's Journal,* many papers in his hand-writing—" rallying the Whigs,"—must have come into the possession of Mr. Mist ; along with his annotations and alterations, made upon the disloyal manuscripts of contributors. As a gentleman, and also as wishing to avoid suspicion of his connection with the government, Defoe doubtless behaved courteously, to men whose treasonable principles his very soul abhorred; and they might possess private letters

---

* See Defoe's six recently discovered Letters in the Introduction.

from him suggesting alterations in their essays written for the *Journal.*

After Defoe had finally abandoned Mist to his fate,—pillories, fines, and imprisonments followed each other in rapid and repeated succession; during all which, the fascination of the Duke of Wharton's talents and title continued unabated, though the miserable and reckless Journalist frequently suffered for the writings of his noble but now exiled patron. At length, in the beginning of 1728, to save himself from a traitor's doom, Mr. Mist escaped to France; and for a considerable time afterward resided with the Duke,—sharing his declining fortune, and his extravagance, as he had long shared his disloyalty,—until poverty ultimately separated them.

The Editor of *Read's Journal,* on the 20th Jan., 1728, calls Mist " The Calumniator General of Great Britain," and says, " This Vendor of Scandal and Sedition, for fear of being overloaded with the Reward due to his Merit, took the opportunity this Morning of slinking away in a Mist."   Yet the *Journal* was kept on, for treasonable purposes, by Mist's servant, J. Wolfe, until September following, when he also fled to France, and the *Journal* became Fog's.   The Duke of Wharton wrote, in France, the last articles in Mist's Journal.

On the 27th July 1728, the Journal says, " 'Tis wrote from Rouen, That upon the late turn of Affairs in England, his Grace the Duke of Wharton has set up a School in that city; and hath taken Mr. Bingley, formerly a Prisoner in Newgate, to be his Usher : at the same Place Mr. Mist, lately Printer of this Paper, drives a Hackney Coach.   And, tis said, that all three are in a fair Way of getting a decent Livelihood."   This was gravely intended by the Duke, as an advertisement.   He had commenced a school near Rouen, and Mr. Mist drove to and from the city.

I must now remind my readers that about the end of the year 1724, an attempt was made to assassinate Defoe by a man whom he had much befriended, and fetched three times out of prison.   Defoe was obliged, in his own defence, to wound his assailant; but ran immediately for a surgeon to attend him.   Such noble forbearance extorted from the miscreant, at the moment, expressions of regret and of gratitude to the man who thus generously gave him his life; yet Defoe is

obliged to complain that this perjured wretch strove afterward
to do him all possible injury.   The description of the benefits
he had formerly conferred on that man are applicable to no
one but Mr. Mist; and the only conceivable cause of the murderous attack, was, that Mist had discovered Defoe's connection
with the Government, while also in the management of his
Journal. Defoe's complaint, and my conclusion thereupon, are
both confirmed by the fact that shortly afterward, Defoe's
journalistic labours abruptly terminated, in so painful a manner
to himself, that he speaks of being " baffled and disheartened
by Journalists," and being refused, by all the Journals, the insertion of a communication, entirely unconnected with politics,
and that would previously have been gladly received and paid
for.   I attribute this change to Mist having communicated to
them his discovery; with all the malignity of which he was capable.

The attempt at assassination having only recoiled upon Mr.
Mist; and the second blow, aimed through the owners of the
Journals, having inflicted upon Defoe more annoyance than
actual injury; it is natural to suppose Mr. Mist's revenge was
still unsatisfied, and that, when he had joined the Duke of
Wharton in France, these events would become topics of discourse between them.   In such a case, what could be more
likely than that two such characters should devise means of
striking a more deadly blow at the object of their political
and private resentment?   Or,—if they possessed manuscript
documents, obnoxious to the English government, but containing Defoe's editorial hand-writing,—what would appear more
feasible than that his ruin might be effected by placing such
papers in the hands of Mr. Walpole, the British Ambassador
in Paris, with whom it is known that the Duke of Wharton
obtained a long interview, shortly after Mr. Mist's arrival in
France?   I admit that what took place then can only be conjectured; but it is of the utmost importance that the biographer
of Defoe should omit nothing that might possibly shed a ray
of light upon the darkness surrounding the close of his life.
If then any such documents as I have supposed were furnished,
as proofs that Defoe had been as disloyal as Mr. Mist, or the
Duke and his associates,—in fact had been one of the con-
fraternity,—and yet, so far from being obliged to fly from
justice, had imposed upon the Ministry under the pre-

tence of being a Whig, and had actually been employed and
paid as such by the government for many years; if, I say, so
grave a charge was brought against our author, it is worthy
of consideration how, notwithstanding the falsity and malignity
of the accusation, he would be immediately able to clear himself, seeing that his service under the government had been
necessarily of a secret nature, and the truth, as to particulars,
known but to very few persons.   His Letters, written in 1718,
furnish us with the names of six such persons; but the
political changes of more than ten years would make it difficult to prove his complete innocence of the charges that might
be brought against him.

The Lord Chief Justice Parker, through whose influence
Defoe obtained his appointment, had been, as Earl of
Macclesfield, removed from office in 1725, for official corruption.   Lord Townshend, in whose Secretaryship he was appointed, had retired in 1718.   Lord Stanhope, who succeeded
as Secretary of State, and was made acquainted by Defoe in
writing, with all the particulars, had died in 1721.   The Earl
of Sunderland, who was Defoe's friend, and knew the circumstances, had retired from office in consequence of being implicated in South Sea Transactions.   Mr. De la Faye, to
whom the Letters of 1718 were written, when he was in the
Secretary of State's Office, was now in the Household of
George II., and might be difficult of access, or unable to
interfere; and Mr. Buckley, who then instructed Defoe, might
now be dead.

I do not doubt he would have succeeded in clearing himself, and indeed he says to Mr. Baker, in the letter we are
now considering, " my Spirit has carried me on thro' greater
Disasters."   Nor can I doubt that the blow he received was
something of the nature I have indicated.   Or, that the
" wicked, perjur'd, and contemptible Enemy" who caused it
was Nathaniel Mist.   I think that Defoe must have received
an intimation of the nature of such a charge ; and, fearing
that he might be deprived of his personal liberty, and end
his almost exhausted life in a gaol, before he should be
able to justify himself; he first did what he thought necessary
to secure the comfort of his wife and daughters, and then,
leaving his home, sought for safety in concealment.

His mental sufferings,—during his subsequent wanderings from place to place,—are to be measured, not by the real gravity of his circumstances, but by the aspect in which those circumstances appeared to his own mind; and therefore, if on a calm consideration of his letter to Mr. Baker, it should seem that his case was not so bad as he thought, we shall but withdraw some part of our interest from apparent shadows, in order to concentrate our sympathising pity on him, to whose agonized spirit they were terrible realities. His noble intellect may yet have remained clear on ordinary subjects; but I much fear that, the combined influence of his advanced years,—of a long life of intense mental activity,—the excruciating pain of chronic disease,—the superadded distraction of a fever at the time of his writing,—the blow received through his wicked enemy,—and the further consequences he apprehended therefrom,—and lastly, the unkindness of his own son, had all contributed to unsettle his reasoning faculties, and take away his judgment, while they left his imagination wild and free, to heighten the billows that were going over him. In his own words, he was " *in tenebris*," and near his journey's end; there was only one ray of light in his horizon, but that enabled him to say,—" 'Tis yet well : be it that the Passage is rough, and the Day stormy, by what Way soever He please to bring me to the End of it, I desire to finish Life with this temper of Soul in all Cases : *Te Deum Laudamus.*"

I think it very possible that he had no sufficient grounds to apprehend that his personal liberty was in any jeopardy. When in his Letter he tells Mr. Baker that his mind is sinking, and looks on himself " as abandoned of every Comfort, every Friend, and every Relative," &c., he was clearly incapable of seeing that it was he who had abandoned those blessings, and not they him. However unkind was the conduct of his Son, the failure of the unhappy father's mind is apparent when he says that such conduct " has both ruined my Family, and in a Word, broken my Heart;" and yet in the same paragraph, hopes that after his death, which he expected would be immediate, " they will want no help, but that of Comfort and Council." I might add many other instances of mental delusion from this strangely pathetic effusion of a broken heart; one only must suffice, in which he speaks of his " two dear

VOL. I.

unprovided Children and their poor dying Mother," having
to beg their bread at his son's door. He truly believed what
he wrote, and his anguish was great accordingly. Had there
been in him any desire to deceive or exaggerate, he would not
have used these words to the husband of his youngest
daughter, Sophia, who was then nearly thirty years old.
Hannah and Henrietta, though middle-aged women, were two
children in the eyes of their aged and distracted father,—who
seems to have forgotten the ample provision he had made,
years before, for the independence of the elder; and, as a just
and impartial parent, doubtless also for the younger. Nor
does there seem any real ground for speaking of his wife as
" their poor dying Mother," when in the same letter he had
informed Mr. Baker that the only reason why she had not
visited him in his retirement, was that she " dare not come by
Water, and by Land there is no Coach." I cannot leave the
subject without saying that these marks of decay, in so great a
mind, have not been seen and described without much pain to
the writer; and, for the sake of our common humanity, I trust
there are few who could read and well consider this last known
letter of Defoe without feelings of deep emotion and sorrow.

On first thought we should doubtless expect that now the
authorship of Defoe was ended. In this we should err. The
force of long continued habit, the loneliness of his condition,
and the consciousness that his mind was sinking while he
brooded over his accumulated troubles, roused him to some
exertion by which his thoughts might be diverted. To write
had become a necessity, and we may conclude that he finally
laid down his pen only when his hand became paralyzed by
Death. The world is indebted to Mr. Crossley for the discovery of what, in all probability, was our author's last work.*
It is entitled " An Effectual Scheme for the immediate preventing of Street Robberies, and Suppressing all other Disorders of the Night; with a brief History of the Night-
Houses, and an Appendix relating to those Sons of Hell called
Incendiaries. Humbly Inscribed to the Right Honourable
the Lord Mayor of the City of London. London. Printed for

---

* *Vide* " Notes and Queries," First Series, III. 195.

J. Wilford, at the Three Flower de Luces, behind the Chapter
House in St. Paul's Church Yard. 1731. Price 1s." After
noticing Defoe's previous scheme for Preventing Street Robberies, Mr. Crossley goes on to mention this Tract, which he
says, " has never yet been noticed or attributed to him by any
one. It is far more curious and valuable than *Second Thoughts
are Best*, and is perfectly distinct from that tract. It gives
a history, and the only one I ever met with, written in
all Defoe's graphic manner, of the London Police, and the
various modes of Street Robbery in the Metropolis from
the time of Charles II., to 1731, and concludes by suggestions of effectual means of prevention. It is evidently the
work of one who lived in London during the whole of the
period."

Probably the change of thought, while writing the above
work, produced a beneficial effect, in calming the agitation of
his mind, and at least diminishing his unfounded apprehensions
as to his personal safety. It is certain that between August
1730, and the following spring he returned to London, and to
the parish of St. Giles's, Cripplegate, wherein he was born.
There, at a lodging in Ropemaker's Alley, Moorfields, he
peacefully died of a lethargy on the evening of Monday the
26th of April, in the year 1731, and in the seventy-first year
of his age. He was buried from thence, in Tindall's Burying
Ground, now better known as Bunhill Fields.

It must not be supposed that the retreat in which Defoe
breathed his last was some mean, obscure corner, the abode
only of poverty. Moor-fields was then an open country, as its
name* imports ; and Rope-maker's Alley perhaps the most
agreeable place of residence within the limits of the City. The
following Advertisement from the *Daily Courant* of May
16, 1710, is sufficient proof :—" In Rope-Maker's Alley, in
Little Moor-fields, is a very sweet and large House to be lett.
The Drawing Room and Parlour well Wainscotted to the Top.
A good Wash-house and Chamber over it in case of Sickness,
or other Occasions. With a very large Garden Wall'd in and
well Planted, the Walks well Gravell'd ; the House stands alone
by itself, in the midst of pleasant Gardens. 'Tis fit for a
Gentleman of a considerable Family, or any that wants a

large House for a Boarding School, or such Occasion. Inquire
of Mr. Hudson in the said Alley."

The day of Defoe's death has been variously and erroneously
stated. The Parish Register of St. Giles's correctly gives the
26th April, and the Register of the Burial Ground corresponds.
In addition, I have examined the records of the event in *nineteen* periodical publications, fifteen appearing at intervals from
daily to weekly ;—three monthly, and one quarterly. It is
remarkable that the last,—the " Historical Register," which
must have derived all its News from the current Papers, is the
only *one* stating it to have been on April 24th. Of the remainder, *eight* fix the 26th of April as the day ; and *ten* rather
corroborate this than otherwise ; using the words, " A few days
ago :" or, " about the end of the month." I conclude therefore
that the date in the Historical Register was a misprint.

Nearly all the Newspapers and Magazines, noticed his
eminence as an Author ; and the fame of his numerous and
varied writings. The *Grub Street Journal*, then newly established,—and one of the ablest Weekly Papers,—calls him, in its
issue for April the 29th,—" The Great Author deceas'd ;" and
the editor says feelingly,—" It is no small comfort to me, that
my *Brother* died in a good old age,—in a place made famous
by the decease of several of our Members ; having kept himself
out of the dangerous Alleys of those High-flying *Rope-Makers*,
who would fain have sent him long ago to his long Home, by
the Shortest Way with the Dissenters. The Members were so
much afflicted at the News of the Death of that ancient Orna-
ment of our Society, *Mr.* DANIEL DE FOE, that they were
incapable of attending to the Papers which were to be read to
them. Upon which our President adjourned the consideration
of them to the next Meeting." *The Daily Journal* of April 29th,
says, " A few Days ago dy'd Mr. Daniel Defoe, Sen., a person
well known for his numerous and various writings. He had a
great Natural Genius ; and understood very well the Trade and
Interest of this Kingdom. His knowledge of Men, especially
those in high Life, (with whom he was formerly very conversant), had weaken'd his Attachment to any political Party ;
but in the Main, he was in the interest of Civil and Religious
Liberty ; in behalf of which he appear'd on several remarkable
Occasions." Perhaps it was from a high sense of propriety

that Mr. Baker's Journal, *The Universal Spectator*, is the only
·Paper I have found, out of all shades of political opinions, that
contains no word in praise of his deceased father-in-law.
I searched for this Paper, in the hope that its authority would
place the day of Defoe's death beyond dispute; but found only
the simple announcement, on May 1st, " A few Days ago died
Daniel Defoe, Sen, a Person well known for his numerous
writings." Thus had our Author been spared to live down,
by his integrity, consistency, and purity of life, not only the
animosities engendered during a party warfare of forty years;
but also, all the effects of Mr. Mist's first wicked success,
when four years previously, every avenue of the periodical press
had been suddenly closed against Defoe's name and writings.
All was now so changed that even Boyer, whom he had often
corrected for untruthfulness and constant habit of profane
swearing, was constrained to admit, in the next number of his
" Political State," that Defoe " had a good natural Genius, and
he was generally looked on as a Man who thoroughly understood the theory of Trade, and the true interest of this Nation."
Boyer could not, however, part from his deceased antagonist
without a sneer, and therefore adds, " but he never had the
good fortune to be much taken notice of by any Minister of
State, so that he got but little by his knowledge." I have
quoted these last words, as the only attempt at disparagement
I have been able to discover, among the numerous contemporary
notices of Defoe's death and character. How totally they are
contrary to truth my readers are competent to say; and, that
a bitter literary opponent should be driven, after thirty years'
strife, to the utterance of a remark so puerile, is perhaps the
highest testimony to the character of him against whose memory
it was directed. Of such men as Boyer, Defoe was wont to
say, " I count their Censure Fame."

In noticing some of Defoe's later Works we have seen that
he was preparing calmly to meet death; not with indifference,
but with Christian Faith. He was never ashamed to profess
his religion publicly before all men; and I do not remember
any work of his, whether it be newspaper, novel, treatise,
history, or pamphlet, without some reference to scripture,
morality, or religion. With him God's revealed Word entered

into politics, voyages and travels, fiction, trade and commerce, and all domestic, National, and private affairs. But though death appeared to occupy more of his thoughts as it approached nearer; the subject had long been familiar to him, as one of deep personal consideration. At the time when he had achieved his greatest literary success, and the World was proclaiming him famous, he sat down and wrote *Serious Reflections of Robinson Crusoe, with his Vision of the Angelic World.* At a still earlier period, 1705, it required, in him, no effort of Christian Courage to print in his newspaper the following reflections ; " I believe nothing would contribute more to make us good Christians, than to be able to look upon all Things, Causes, and Persons here, with the same Eyes as we do when we are looking into Eternity. Death sets all in a clear Light; and when a Man is, as it were, in the very Boat, pushing off from the Shore of the World, his last views of it, being abstracted from interests, hopes, or wishes, and influenced by a near view of the future state,—must be clear, unbiassed, and impartial."* Amidst the incessant activity that resulted in his being the most voluminous, as well as one of the greatest and best of English Authors, he lived a life of Faith in Christ, and knew that, to die would be gain.

There is reason to believe that no serious family difficulties occurred in the settlement of Defoe's worldly affairs ; but rather that,—the disposition he had made of his property during life, rendering any last Will and Testament unnecessary,—the widow and two daughters at once entered upon and enjoyed the competency he had provided for them. I have found no reference to the house being vacated, or the furniture being disposed of, but about six months after his death his Library, or the greater part of it, was sold to Mr. Olive Payne, the bookseller in Round Court, in the Strand, who published a Catalogue of his Books, and those of the Rev. Philip Farewell, D.D. I have searched in vain for this Catalogue, and fear that a copy does not exist.† The Advertisement calls our

---

* Review, II. 201.
† See a long advertisement of the Catalogue in *The Daily Advertiser*, 13 Nov. 1731.

author, " the Ingenious Daniel De Foe, Gent., lately deceas'd;"
and speaks of the Library as " containing a curious Collection
of Books relating to the History and Antiquities of divers
Nations, particularly England, Scotland, and Ireland." Further
on, the description says, " N.B. Manuscripts. Also several
hundred Curious, Scarce Tracts on Parliamentary Affairs,
Politicks, Husbandry, Trade, Voyages, Natural History,
Mines, Minerals, &c.   Several Curious Prints, Medals, &c."
The Books are stated to be " in very good condition, mostly
well-bound, Gilt and Lettered."   The lowest price was marked
in each book,—they were to be sold on the 15th of November,
and afterward, until all disposed of.   Eight booksellers'
shops, &c., are specified, where Catalogues were to be had
gratis.

Defoe's widow did not long survive her husband, but died
in December of the following year.   The register of the
Bunhill Fields burial ground contains the following entry:
1732. Decr. 19. Mrs. Defow, Stoke Newington." Most probably they were both interred in the same grave.

I regret being compelled again to advert to the error of his
later biographers, as to Defoe's pecuniary circumstances; but
as a posthumous case has been adduced of what they considered specific proof, I have no alternative.*   Several preliminary assertions are made to lead up to the point; as, that
" the events that befel him during the last year or two of his
life could have produced no other result than his dying insolvent," and that " He who had nothing to leave had no
occasion for a will.   Accordingly there is none to be found in
Doctors' Commons." These two statements are answered by the
facts I have already given :—he had, before those events, secured
his estates for the benefit of his family, and a will was therefore unnecessary.   The demands and education of a numerous
family, are next said to have quickly absorbed the profits of
his later publications.   But the education of all his children
must have been completed, and half their number had themselves become heads of families, before their father's publica-

---

* Wilson's " Life of Defoe," iii. 611.   Hazlitt's " Life of Defoe," p. cxxx.

tions began to be considerably profitable. His biographers
next take a burthen of debt forty years old, and hang it in
their own words, " as a mill-stone about his neck, and plunge
him *at last* in irrecoverable poverty." I have already shown
that all we know of the latter part of his life is incompatible
with any such statement. The culmination of error is as
follows.—" The books in Doctors' Commons inform us that, in
September 1733, letters of administration, on his goods and
chattels, were granted to Mary Brooks, widow, a creditrix,
after summoning in official form the next of kin to appear."

It is not my duty to account for the conduct of Defoe's
family. Much that relates to the end of his life will remain
for ever unknown. I have already remarked upon Mr.
Baker's silence, and think it was designed. A desire to do no
injustice restrains me from more specific allusion to several
points, in which both he and Mr. Benjamin Norton Defoe
seem to have come short of their duty to a dying father, and
in their respect for his memory after death. His estate was
already divided among his children, subject to the maintenance
of his widow; and, in the absence of any Will, there could be
no testamentary provision for payment of his funeral expenses,
or any small sum owing at the time of his death for lodgings.
For the same reason, there would be no common residuary
fund, available for such purpose. I am aware that this involves a reflection upon his children, and I would gladly have
avoided it; but the fact is undeniable, that while those children received fortunes gained by their father's genius and
exertions, a trifling debt,—which his lethargic death compelled
him to leave unpaid,—was still owing, two years and a half
afterward. He was buried from the place of his seclusion;
and would necessarily leave behind him trunks, or other recep-
tacles, containing books, papers, wearing apparel, and personal
appendages. Upon these the occupier of the house would have
a lien, for whatever was due as rent; and, after waiting a reasonable time, and failing to procure payment in any other manner,
would be empowered, by letters of administration, to dispose of
them for her own benefit. This is my explanation of the matter,
and I trust Mrs. Brooks was paid in full; but if not, no reflection rests upon the memory of Defoe, nor can he be said
to have died at last in poverty, who gave his children ample

means of discharging any such obligation that might be so left by him unpaid.

Thus have I completed my task of re-writing the Life of one who combines in himself the remarkable qualities of being the most voluminous and versatile of English authors,— Daniel Defoe. A man whose large intellect gave to the world a library of his own writings:—consisting of poetry, satire, irony, humour, and pathos; of treatises and pamphlets on peace and war, party conflicts in Church and State, and on civil and religious liberty; of trade and commerce, at home and abroad, its freedom and extension; of morals and instruction, as applicable to children, to the relations of the sexes, in courtship, and in marriage; to the duties and obligations of servants and masters, tradesmen, merchants, and gentlemen; of works on municipal and social institutions, including hospitals, colleges, asylums, and police; of romances, more intensely real and natural than those of any other author; of history, and of real and imaginary voyages and travels, including the geography, and the natural and artificial productions of every part of the globe; of books on the marvellous and supernatural, comprising, dæmons, apparitions, dreams, and magic. In every department of this vast range of literary labour, he was an able writer,—in many he excelled all who had preceded him,—and in some, is still,—and will probably ever remain,—unequalled. Throughout these ubiquitous manifestations of his genius, we have found in him, inflexibility of purpose, indomitable courage, and unwearied perseverance, combined with devoted loyalty to the constitutional government of his country, and an earnest faith in the revelation of God. From infancy he had known the Bible; and to the end of life it continued to be with him the supreme test of all human action. His conviction of a constantly watchful and overruling Providence was so strong as to verge on superstition. In an age of political and religious strife he took a prominent part; but he lived and died a true Protestant and a Catholic Christian.

During half a century after his decease, his undying works became known to all nations; but the memory of their author was almost forgotten. Within the present age, Scott, Talford,

Coleridge, Lamb, Whately, and many other great writers, have paid tribute to his extraordinary genius, and have eloquently expatiated on the beauties of his various works. It would too much extend this volume to quote their eulogies, or to correct in further detail the errors now first brought to light.

In conclusion,—I have avoided, as far as convenient, any beaten track, and have endeavoured to relate, in plain language, but as briefly as possible, the results of my own researches; availing myself of the labours of others, only when continuity of narrative required. For similar reasons I think it undesirable here, to trace downward what is known as to the direct and collateral descendants of Defoe. The only light his posterity possess, to attract the attention of the world, is that reflected from their illustrious ancestor. Even that, however, ought to insure regard, from a great country that has yet paid so little public honour to the memory of one of the noblest of her sons.

INDEX

TO

THE LIFE OF DEFOE.

END OF VOL. I.